Modern
REAL ESTATE
Practice in New York
for Salespersons

11th EDITION

Sam Irlander

Dearborn™
Real Estate Education

This publication is designed to provide accurate and authoritative information in regard to the subject matter covered. It is sold with the understanding that the publisher is not engaged in rendering legal, accounting, or other professional advice. If legal advice or other expert assistance is required, the services of a competent professional should be sought.

President: Dr. Andrew Temte
Chief Learning Officer: Dr. Tim Smaby
Vice President, Real Estate Education: Asha Alsobrooks
Development Editor: Evonna Burr

MODERN REAL ESTATE PRACTICE IN NEW YORK FOR SALESPERSONS 11TH EDITION
© 2011 Kaplan, Inc.
Published by DF Institute, Inc., d/b/a Dearborn Real Estate Education
332 Front St. S., Suite 501
La Crosse, WI 54601
www.dearborn.com

Printed in the United States of America
Fourth printing with corrections 2013
ISBN: 978-1-4277-3141-8 / 1-4277-3141-1
PPN: 1510-5221

Contents

Preface

Welcome to the real estate business. Whether your plans ultimately land you in the residential or commercial real estate arenas, you have chosen an industry and practice that is filled with excitement. With almost 40 years of active commercial real estate transactional experience, no two days have ever been the same for me. I know that will be the case for you.

As you begin the journey toward learning the subjects required to obtain a real estate license in New York, you may encounter moments where you feel as if you've entered a foreign country surrounded by individuals speaking a foreign language. Don't be discouraged. This textbook was specifically developed to speak to the student in an organized, clear, and accessible manner.

The 11th edition of *Modern Real Estate Practice in New York for Salespersons* is derived from experience and knowledge. It covers all the required topics outlined in the 75-hour Real Estate Salesperson Prelicense Course syllabus established by the New York Department of State (DOS). I have written updates to existing material, and I have authored new chapters that specifically address the additional curriculum mandated by the DOS. This includes, but is not limited to, the following topics: property insurance, condominiums and cooperatives, commercial and investment properties, income tax issues, mortgage brokerage, and property management.

To access learning objectives, key terms, chapter outlines, and other instructor materials created for students, please go to *www.mrepny. com* and enter the following Student Access Code: **63112.**

With this new edition, we will continue to feature this publication at a Web site dedicated exclusively to *Modern Real Estate Practice in New York for Salespersons* and *Modern Real Estate Practice in New York for Brokers*, as well as all their ancillary products. At *www.mrepny.com*, both students and instructors will have access to a robust assortment of study and teaching tools, including the instructor's manual. Instructors are encouraged to contact their sales representative to obtain access to the PIN-protected instructor's manual that accompanies this textbook.

The author would also like to recommend that students and instructors contact the Real Estate Educators Association at *www.reea.org*. The association offers workshops, publications, and conferences, and has a chapter in New York State.

Like previous editions, this one is dedicated to the hundreds of thousands of real estate students and instructors whose enthusiastic acceptance has made this the best-selling real estate textbook in the Empire State. Once again, many valuable suggestions for the new edition have come from those who use the book.

Those suggestions have always played a great part in the evolution of the text. For this 11th edition, we paid particular attention to your classroom needs and the state's revised syllabus. We also made every effort to make this textbook learning-friendly, using classroom-tested features such as highlighted key terms and concepts and margin notes. Web addresses have also been updated and new Web sites added.

The author wishes to thank those who participated in the preparation of the 11th edition (as well as previous editions) of *Modern Real Estate Practice in New York for Salespersons*, including the following:

- Roberta Bangs, Real Estate Associate Broker, Director of Training and Compliance Manager, Pearl River Office Better Homes and Gardens – Rand Realty
- Eileen Klempner, Director of Professional Development, Orange County Association of REALTORS®
- Diane Levine, Esquire, Office Brokerage Manager, Sotheby's International Realty, Inc.
- Uri Shamir, Licensed Real Estate Broker, Professor, Real Estate Educator and Sales Training Motivator

The publisher also wishes to acknowledge the contributions of Frank P. Langone of The Real Estate Training Center, who has offered his insight and knowledge on the development of this text.

Their combined criticisms and comments have made this the best edition yet.

Previous editions over the years owe a great debt of thanks to the following: Anthony Aguelire, RETC of Greater New York; John Alberts; Newt Alderman; David M. Alexander, Greater Rochester Association of REALTORS®; Joseph Amello, New York Department of State; Georgianne Bailey, New York State Association of REALTORS®; Ronald Baroody; Gail Bates, New York Department of State; Professor Kenneth Beckerink; Abraham Berkowitz; Rose Bernstein; Michael K. Brady, IFA, RAM, State University of New York; Antonio F. Brown; Rhonda Brown, Esq.; Robin Carlson, MS Ed, Manfred Real Estate Learning Center, Inc.; Thomas Carozza; John Cyr; Demetrios Cortisides; Charles E. Davis; Beverly L. Deikler, Esq.; Barry Deickler; Judith J. Deickler, GRI; William R. Deickler, William R. Deickler Contracting, Inc.; Ruth De Roo; Paul Desseault; Thomas E. DeCelle; Anthony J. DiChiara, GRI, ME, MS, Niagara University; Joseph DiIanni; Liz Duncan, National Association of REALTORS®; Jonathon Easterling; Arthur Elfenbein, New York University Real Estate Institute; Marie Esposito; Cindy Faire; Professor Patrick J. Falci, St. John's University; Jim Foley; Alexander M. Frame, Real Estate Education Center; Donald Friedman; Richard Fuchs; Thomas Galvin; Neil Garfinkel, Esquire, Abrams Garfinkel Margolis Bergson LLP; Harold Geringer; Harry Goldberg; Christine di Grande Jones; Gaye Green; Paul Henderson; David Henehan; Benjamin Henszey; Barry Hersh, Clinical Associate Professor, New York University, SCPS Real Estate Institute; Gerry Hoffman; Michael J. Jesmer, Syracuse Real Estate, Inc.; Harold Kahn; Peter A. Karl III, SUNY Institute of Technology; Leon Katzen, Esq.; Ezra Katzen; John Keaton; Walter Kerut; Eli Kimels; Eileen Klempner, Orange County Association of REALTORS®; Sandra Kleps, Greater Rochester Association of REALTORS®; Garrett Lacara; William Lang, Jr.; Norman Lank; George Lasch; William Lester; Richard Levin, Greater Rochester Association of REALTORS®; Irving Levine; Richard Levine, New York Real Estate Institute; William Lippman, Esq.; James Loeb; Jeff Lubar, National Association of REALTORS®; Mary Manfred, Real Estate Learning Center, Inc.; John Mataraza; Bill

Mattle; Robert Mendohlson; Stephen Mendolla; P. Gilbert Mercurio, Westchester County Board of REALTORS®; Robert Michaels; Don Milton, Greater Rochester Association of REALTORS®; Mary Ann Monteleone, Long Island Board of REALTORS®; Mary Anne Moore, New York Department of State; Nicholas Morabito; Mark Morano, New York State Association of REALTORS®; Professor Karen Morris, Esq.; James Myers, Esq.; Joseph M. O'Donnell; Amy Penzabene, New York Department of State; Hung Pham; John Piper, Greater Rochester Association of REALTORS®; William Plunkett, New York Real Estate Institute; Barbara Portman; Selwyn Price; James V. Pugliese, CRB, GRI, Coldwell Banker Prime Properties; Edween Reagh; Larry Rockefeller; Willard Roff, New York Department of State; Louis Ryen; Rolando Santiago; Ernest Schade; Karen Schafer; Rita Scharg; Alvin Schwartz; Norman Schwartz; Professor Uri Shamir, Queens College; Sally Smith; John Sobeck; Richard J. Sobelsohn, The Sobelsohn School; Marcia Spada; D.J. Sperano, Fingerlakes Community College/Corning Community College; Eileen Spinola, Real Estate Board of New York; Robert Stack, American Real Estate School; Charles M. Staro, New York State Association of REALTORS®; William Stavola, New York Department of State; Micheal Stucchio; Anna Y. Tam, American Real Estate School; Eileen Taus, Westchester Board of REALTORS®; Dominic Telesco; Thomas Thomassian; Wendy A. Tilton, New York University; James R. Trevitt, Broome County Board of REALTORS®; Dorothy Tymon; John Tyo; Rex Vail; Christine Van Benschoten; Karen Van DeViver, Greater Rochester Association of REALTORS®; George M. Vaughn, GRI, CRB, CRS, LTG; Thomas R. Viola, State Division of Housing and Community Renewal; John A. Viteritti, New York University and Long Island University; Michael Wallender, counsel to the New York State Association of REALTORS®; Thomas Wills III; Jane A. Willson, Expo Services, Ltd.; Chris W. Wittstruck, Esq.; Jeff Wolk; John A. Yoegel, PhD, DREI, John Yoegel Seminars; and Babette Yuhas, Greater Syracuse Board of REALTORS®.

■ FROM THE AUTHOR

In particular, I would be remiss if I did not thank Asha Alsobrooks, Trude Irons, and Evonna Burr, whose faith in me afforded this opportunity to take my life's experience and knowledge and incorporate them into this textbook. A special thanks must go to Lori Walters for introducing me to Dearborn Real Estate Education and for being that special person and shining light. To all of you, I offer my sincere "thank you!"

Special thanks must go to Joseph Amello (Retired) and Jodi DeLollo of the DOS, as well as to Steven Spinola, Former Education Chair of the New York State Board of Real Estate and president of the Real Estate Board of New York. I am thankful and privileged to have been included in the updating of the new state requirements and to be a part of your board. Finally, I must thank my wife, Janet, and my two sons, Max and Ian, for putting up with me during this writing period. You guys have the patience of saints.

In closing, may the real estate business bring you the same joy, excitement, and success that I have been blessed with for the past 39 years.

Sam Irlander
Parker Madison Partners, Inc
501 Fifth Avenue
New York, NY 10017
 212-973-9688
sirlander@recompartners.com

■ ABOUT THE AUTHOR

Sam Irlander has been a licensed transactional commercial broker in New York for more than 39 years. He maintains licenses in many states and has taught real estate since 1981 at various institutions, including the following: The New School, New York University, Baruch College, The Real Estate Board of New York, The Long Island Board of REALTORS®, and Hunter College. Effective fall 1995, Sam was appointed adjunct assistant professor of real estate at New York University. He serves as chairman of the commercial division real estate program at Baruch College's Newman Institute and has just been appointed the first director of the Bernard H. Mendik Education Center at the Real Estate Board of New York (REBNY). His duties as director will include assisting REBNY as it integrates state requirements into its education programs in meaningful and challenging ways. He will also continue to teach many of these courses.

He is court-certified as an expert witness in real estate and has chaired arbitration hearings for alternative dispute resolution cases. In his career in commercial brokerage, he has represented most of the entertainment industry, including Twentieth Century Fox Film Corp., New World Entertainment, Warner Chappell Publishing, Sony, Warner Brothers, and others.

CHAPTER 1

License Law

■ KEY TERMS

administrative discipline
agency disclosure forms
apartment information
  vendor
apartment-sharing agent
appraisers
Article 12-A
Article 78 procedure
associate broker
blind ads
change of association
change of broker
commingling
continuing education

denial, suspension, or
  revocation of license
Department of State
  (DOS)
distance learning
dual licensure
escrow
exemption
home inspectors
irrevocable consent
kickbacks
listing agreement
misdemeanor
mortgage bankers

mortgage brokers
net listing
pocket card
real estate broker
real estate salesperson
reciprocity
record of association
revocation
sponsoring broker
suspension
termination of association
  notice
violations

■ PURPOSE OF REAL ESTATE LICENSE LAWS

In 1922, New York State passed laws that regulated the real estate industry. The primary purpose of these laws was to provide consumer protection and to protect the welfare, health, and safety of the general public and prevent economic loss resulting from the dishonest practices of others in expectation of a fee or other valuable consideration.

FIGURE   1.1

Important State Laws to Remember

REAL PROPERTY LAW ARTICLE 12A – COVERS BROKER'S LICENSE LAW

Section:

440 – Definitions

440-a – License required for real estate brokers and salespersons

441 – Application for license

441-a – License and pocket card

441-b – License fees

441-c – Revocation and suspension of licenses

441-d – Salesperson license suspended by revocation of employer's license

441-e – Denial of license; complaints; notice of hearing

441-f – Certiorari to review action of department

442 – Splitting commissions

442-a – Compensation of salesperson; restrictions

442-b – Discontinuance or change of salesperson's association; report

442-c – Violations by salesperson; broker's responsibility

442-d – Actions for commission; license prerequisite

442-e – Violations

442-f – Saving clause

442-g – Nonresident licensees

442-h – Rules of the Secretary of State

442-i –State Real Estate Board

442-j – Effect of invalid provision

442-k – Power and duties of the State Real Estate Board

442-l – After-the-fact referral fees

443 – Disclosure regarding real estate agency relationships

443-a – Disclosure obligations

Sections 175.1–175.27 – Rules for the guidance of real estate brokers and salespersons

Section 176.1 – Rules relating to approval of courses of study in real estate

Sections 176.2–176.21 – Requirements for qualification of an approved entity to offer real estate courses for initial licensing as broker or salesperson

Sections 177.1–177.19 – Continuing education

The **New York Department of State (DOS)**, Division of Licensing Services, has the power to issue licenses and enforce the real estate license law. The law is enforced through fines, reprimands, and the **denial, suspension, or revocation of licenses**. The Department currently licenses more than 155,000 brokers and salespersons.

State Board of Real Estate

The Division of Licensing Services shares regulatory duties with New York's State Board of Real Estate, which has 15 members. At least five are real estate brokers; the remainder are members of the public, and the secretary of state serves as chairperson. *The board has the power to promulgate rules and regulations in some legal areas and also examines applicants, approves real estate schools, and helps enforce the real estate laws.*

Violation of the license law is a misdemeanor punishable by up to a year in jail and a fine of up to $1,000. A misdemeanor is a criminal offense or infraction of criminal laws that is punishable by fine and/or imprisonment, but other than in a penitentiary.

The New York Real Property Law, **Article 12-A**, which went into effect in 1922, is the main source of law for real estate licenses in New York. Copies of the law and regulations may be obtained by writing to the following:

New York Department of State
Division of Licensing Services
A.E. Smith Office Building
80 South Swan Street, 10th floor
Albany, NY 12210

The Division of Licensing Services maintains a consumer assistance phone line in Albany at 518-474-4429, and a Web page at *www.dos.state.ny.us/licensing/*. The e-mail address is *licensing@dos.state.ny.us*. New York State's TTY phone number is 800-662-1220.

Who Must Be Licensed?

Real estate licensing is required for any person who

1. performs a real estate act,
2. for another, and
3. for or in anticipation of compensation or other valuable consideration (unless otherwise specifically exempt from state license laws).

Broker A **real estate broker** can be defined as any person, firm, partnership, or corporation that for a fee (or the expectation of a fee) performs for another any of the following 11 services:

1. Negotiates any form of real estate transaction
2. Lists or attempts to list real property for sale
3. Negotiates a loan secured by a mortgage (other than a residential mortgage loan [one- to four-family dwelling], as defined in Section 590 of the New York Banking Law)
4. Negotiates a lease
5. Collects rents for more than one client
6. Sells a lot or parcel of land by auction
7. Negotiates the sale of a parcel of subdivided land
8. Exchanges real property
9. Relocates commercial or residential tenants
10. Engages in the sale of condominiums and cooperatives
11. Sells a business that has more than half its value in real estate

In addition to holding a real estate brokerage license, soliciting, processing, placing, and/or negotiating mortgage loans on one- to four-family dwellings for a fee requires registration with the state banking department as a mortgage broker.

Salesperson   A **real estate salesperson** is one who assists a broker in the performance of any of the aforementioned 11 services performed by the broker. Brokers are authorized to operate their own real estate business, but salespersons may work only in the name of and under the direct supervision of a sponsoring broker. *The salesperson may never accept a commission or other compensation of any kind from anyone except the supervising/principal broker.*

Associate broker   An **associate broker** is an individual who is qualified to be a broker but has chosen to work as a salesperson under the sponsorship and supervision of another broker. The associate broker must meet all the qualifications for a broker's license and pass the broker's examination, but is licensed to transact business in the name of the **sponsoring broker**, exactly as a salesperson would. In New York, associate brokers may also hold a broker's license in their own name. When a broker or associate broker holds more than one license, this is commonly called **dual licensure**.

Note: In New York, an individual bearing a broker status may only work within the association of another broker in the following manner:

- As an officer or director of a real estate brokerage corporation, the individual must be registered and classified as a broker with the Department of State, Division of Licensing Services. (class 31 license)
- As a general partner of either a general partnership or limited partnership, the individual must be registered and classified as a broker with the Department of State, Division of Licensing Services. (class 33 license)

It should be noted that salespersons and associate brokers may never hold

- officer positions (or have officer titles in a corporation) or
- positions as a general partner in either a general partnership or limited partnership.

Licensing of legal entities such as corporations and partnerships will be covered later in this chapter.

Exceptions   The provisions of the license law requiring licensure do not apply to the following:

- Public officers while they are performing their official duties
- Persons acting under order of a court (executors, guardians, referees, receivers, administrators)
- Attorneys licensed in New York (Note: Attorneys who set up a brokerage business with associated salespersons under their sponsorship and supervision must obtain a broker's license but need not take the prelicense courses or state examination.)
- A resident manager employed by only one owner to manage or maintain rental property when the leasing of units or the collection of rents is part of the manager's regular duties
- Certain authorized tenant organizations and not-for-profit corporations enforcing the housing code of the City of New York

FIGURE 1.2	Salesperson	Broker
Requirements for Licensing in New York	At least 18	At least 20
	No felony or misdemeanor*	No felony or misdemeanor*
	Permanent resident of United States	Permanent resident of United States
	Sponsoring broker	Two full years' experience or three years' equivalent experience*
	75-hour course (must pass end-of-course exam)	120 hours' study (must pass end-of-course exam)
	Pass state exam ($15)	Pass state exam ($15)
	$50 (two years) license fee	$150 (two years) license fee

* For example, lying on an application is considered a misdemeanor (some exceptions possible).

REALTOR®   The term REALTOR® has nothing to do with state licensing. It refers to a member of a private trade organization, the National Association of REALTORS®. Use of the logo (which is registered) is reserved only for members of the National Association of REALTORS®.

■ QUALIFICATIONS FOR LICENSURE

A licensed salesperson must

■ be 18 or older;
■ be honest and trustworthy;
■ never have been convicted of a felony or misdemeanor (some exceptions are made for an executive pardon, a certificate of good conduct from a parole board, or a certificate of relief from disabilities; however, regardless of these exceptions, it is at the sole discretion of the DOS whether or not they will issue a real estate license to a previously convicted felon);
■ be either a citizen or a lawful permanent resident of the United States;
■ have a fair and basic understanding of the English language;
■ successfully complete a 75-hour prelicensing course that has been approved by the Department of State;
■ pass the state's licensing examination;
■ pay the required license fee; and
■ have a sponsoring broker before obtaining the license.

Figure 1.2 shows the requirements for salesperson's and broker's licenses.

A licensed broker must meet the same requirements, except that

■ the minimum age is 20;
■ the required courses of study total at least 120 hours of approved real estate courses as mandated by the secretary of state;
■ a sponsoring broker is not needed; and
■ the prospective broker must submit proof of two full years' experience as a licensed salesperson within the employ and supervision of one or more licensed real estate brokers *or* three years' equivalent experience in the

general real estate business. The applicant can establish and satisfy the experience requirement by affidavit sworn under the penalty of perjury. The experience requirement is based on a point system, which will be discussed later in this chapter.

Associate brokers must meet all the same requirements as that of any other broker; however, they must submit an application signed by the sponsoring employing broker.

With respect to brokers, the DOS issues licenses in several different classes:

- *Class 30* is for the applicant planning to work as an associate broker. Although fully qualified as a broker, the associate chooses to work within another broker's firm. As with a salesperson's application, the associate broker's application is signed by a sponsoring broker. Should the associate broker ever wish to operate independently, no further study or examination would be necessary. Application would simply be made to the DOS for a license in the new class.
- *Class 31* is issued to the officer of a corporation who conducts a brokerage business under a corporate name. (Salespersons and associate brokers may not be principals or own voting stock in a licensed brokerage corporation.) For new corporations, the application must include the filing receipt, which indicates that the corporation has been duly formed.
- *Class 33* is for the broker who intends to do business under the name of a partnership. A copy of the county clerk's certificate of partnership must accompany the application.
- *Class 35* is for individual brokers who will do business in their name only, such as "John Smith" or "Jane Brown, licensed real estate broker."
- *Class 37* signifies licensure as a trade-name broker, who will own the business as a sole proprietorship. The local county clerk, after ascertaining that no one else uses the requested trade name, will issue a d/b/a (doing business as) certificate that must accompany the license application, for example, "Juan Sanchez, d/b/a House Calls Realty."
- *Class 49*, *limited liability company* or *limited liability partnership broker*, is for the member or manager of a brokerage operating under one of these types of organizations. For a new limited liability company, a copy of the articles of organization or a filing receipt must be filed with the application.

Brokers who intend to use anything other than their own name for the firm must submit the proposed name for approval to the DOS, which will check, among other things, whether the name is identical with or misleadingly similar to one already in use for a brokerage. *It is prudent to postpone ordering stationery, advertising, business cards, or a Web page domain until the name has been cleared.*

Education Requirements

The DOS certifies certain educational institutions to offer two qualifying education courses. One qualifying course covers the necessary 75 hours' instruction for a salesperson's license; the second 45-hour qualifying course completes the 120-hour prelicensing requirement for a broker. The courses must be taken in order. Topics to be covered and the time devoted to each are set by law. Successful completion of each course requires at least 67½ hours' (or 90 percent of a 75-hour course) attendance and the passing of a final examination. As of July 1, 2008, the education requirement for prelicensing applicants can be satisfied in the following manner:

Salesperson:

■ By attending 75 hours of state-approved classroom instruction
■ Or by completing 75 clocked hours of state-approved course content via **distance learning**, which consists of classes completed online

Note: Paragraphs b and c of Section 441, Subdivision J, have been changed as follows:

■ Paragraph b has been changed to permit computer-based and distance learning; before the change in law, computer-based and distance learning (as it applies to prelicensing courses) was prohibited.
■ Previously, prelicensing courses were recognized by DOS for life. Under the new paragraph c, they will only be good for eight (8) years from date of completion (see the next paragraph for the paragraph c change).

Paragraph c change   Previously, salesperson prelicensing courses were recognized by DOS for life. Under the new law, salesperson prelicensing courses will only be valid for eight years from date of completion. This eight-year course time limit also includes the *30-hour remedial course* for licensees who completed 45 hours of salesperson prelicense education before the change in the law but had not taken the broker's prelicense course prior to July 1, 2008. In that event, such a licensee would have to sit for the 30-hour remedial course to otherwise qualify for a broker's license. A student who takes the 30-hour remedial course can receive continuing education credit for taking the course; however, the course will *not* satisfy the change in law requiring that all nonexempt students take the required three hours of Fair Housing every license cycle. Therefore, the new 75-hour salesperson course and the 30-hour remedial qualifying course can only be used within eight years from the date of completion.

This specifically means the following:

■ In order to receive credit for the course and completion of same, any broker applicant who has otherwise successfully completed the 75-hour salesperson course will have to apply for a broker license within eight years from completion of the salesperson requirements.
■ The applicant who fails to do so will have to repeat the 75-hour prelicense course before enrolling in the broker prelicense course.

The only exception to the aforementioned is if the applicant for a broker's license has completed the 45-hour salesperson prelicense course before July 1, 2008, and subsequently completed the 30-hour remedial course. The 30-hour remedial course would expire eight years from the completion date.

■ LICENSE EXAMINATIONS

State license examinations are open to any interested person, whether before or after completion of a 75-hour prelicense course. All exam centers require online reservations with prepayment of a $15 fee. This applies to both broker and salesperson licensing exams.

Test Centers

Each test taker must register online for the exam location and date of choice by visiting the DOS Web site at *www.dos.state.ny.us/licensing/eaccessny.html.* Applicants should check the Web site for specific locations, dates, and complete information:

Albany (Alfred E. Smith Building), 80 South Swan Street

Binghamton (State Office Building), 44 Hawley Street, 15th Floor

Buffalo (State Office Building), 65 Court Street, Hearing Room, Part 5

Franklin Square (VFW Hall), 68 Lincoln Road, Basement

Hauppauge (Perry B. Duryea Jr. State Office Building), 250 Veterans Memorial Hwy Basement

New York City (State Office Building), 123 William Street, 19th Floor

Newburgh (Federal Building, Orange Ulster BOCES), 471 Broadway, 2nd Floor

Plattsburgh (Clinton Community College), Lake Shore Drive, Route 9 South

Rochester (Finger Lakes DDSO), 620 Westfall Road, NYS Testing Sign (DDSO is on the left; do not enter through the main lobby.)

Syracuse (American Postal Workers Union), 407 East Taft Road (Use back door.)

Utica (State Office Building), 207 Genesee Street, 1st Floor, Room 107

Watertown (State Office Building), 317 Washington Street, 11th Floor

Applicants who require special testing accommodations should not apply online but should contact DOS for assistance instead.

Examinees should arrive 30 to 45 minutes before the scheduled examination time or up to an hour ahead at the New York City exam center. Each should bring a government-issued signature photo ID and two no. 2 pencils. An identifying thumbprint will be taken. Scrap paper is furnished and must be turned in before the applicant leaves the room. Calculators must be noiseless and handheld, with no printout or alphabetic keyboard. Cell phones, PDAs, and other electronic devices must be turned off.

The examinations consist of multiple-choice questions such as those in this textbook. One hour is allowed for the salesperson's test and two and one-half hours are allowed for the broker's test. A passing grade is 70 percent, and a successful examination is good for a license application anytime during the next two years. For those who fail, unlimited retakes are allowed, with a $15 fee for each.

Test results are available online and also mailed to applicants. The application for the salesperson license should be completed online after passing the exam. A salesperson license will be issued after acceptance by the sponsoring broker, provided all information is completed correctly and all requirements for licensure are satisfied.

■ LICENSING PROCEDURE

The salesperson's license application (see Figure 1.3) is provided by the school where the 75-hour course was successfully completed and is signed by the broker who will supervise the new licensee and be responsible for the licensee's activities. It is accompanied by a $50 license fee and proof that the applicant has passed the state licensing exam. The applicant can accomplish this by applying online at *www.dos.state.ny.us/licensing/eaccessny.html.*

The broker's application includes details of all past transactions during the apprenticeship period as a salesperson, with information about transactions during the required two years' full-time activity as a licensed salesperson or during three years' equivalent experience in general real estate.

The applicant for an associate broker's license not only lists past transactions but also includes the signature of the principal broker with whose firm the new associate broker will be working.

Both applications include a child support statement, certifying whether applicants have any obligation to pay child support and, if so, whether they are four months or more in arrears. The child support statement section must be completed by all applicants. This is regardless of the fact that the applicant may not have children. Failure to complete the section will result in the application being returned by DOS.

Fees

The DOS charges the following application fees:

- Broker, original license and renewal: $150
- Associate broker, original license and renewal: $150
- Salesperson, original license and renewal: $50
- Branch office, original and renewal: $150
- License examination: $15

Note: Fees are subject to change; therefore, the applicant is urged to check with the DOS at the time of application.

Issuing the License

Each license is good for two years from the date of issuance. Each licensee is issued a license and a **pocket card** from the Department of Motor Vehicles.

A salesperson's principal broker keeps the salesperson's license; the pocket card must be carried by the salesperson at all times. The DOS only requires that the sponsoring broker license be prominently displayed in the place of business; the associate broker's and the salesperson's licenses may be displayed as well, if the broker wishes. The display of these licenses is optional. Should the broker choose to display associate broker and salesperson licenses, the broker should take measures to create a distinct separation between brokers' licenses and salespersons' licenses at the area of display.

The provision under Section 441-a, Subsection 6, has been modified, so that as of July 1, 2008, the DOS requires (with the assistance of the Department of Motor Vehicles) that each pocket card contain a photo of the licensee. The pocket card must be shown on demand. In the event the licensee loses a pocket card or the card is damaged or destroyed, a duplicate card will be issued upon request, proof, and submission of loss of same. At this time, a fee of $10 must accompany the request.

To receive a license in the state of New York, an individual must do the following:

- Successfully complete the required education
  — Salesperson: 75 hours (must pass end-of-course final exam)
  — Broker: 120 hours (must pass end-of-course final exam)
- Pass a state exam (salesperson and broker applicants)
- Submit a fully completed application that includes
  — self-employed/legal entity filing (broker only) or
  — broker signature of association (associate broker or salesperson)
- Pay the required licensing fee

Licensing Corporations, Partnerships, and Other Legal Entities

A license issued to a corporation entitles a designated officer to act as a broker, but that person also must secure a license personally. One officer may act as the real estate broker under the corporate or business license. Every other officer or partner who wishes to act as a broker must secure another license, which will expire on the same day as the corporate or business license. An officer or partner of a licensed corporation or other legal entity may not be licensed as a real estate salesperson or associate broker.

FIGURE 1.3

Real Estate Salesperson Application

UNIQUE ID NUMBER (for office use only)	EFF. DATE	FEE $50	NYS Department of State Division of Licensing Services P.O. Box 22001 Albany, NY 12201-2001

Real Estate Salesperson Application

Read the Instruction Sheet for details before completing this application form. You must answer each question and TYPE or PRINT responses in ink.

APPLICANT'S LAST NAME   FIRST NAME   M.I.   SUFFIX

HOME ADDRESS - NUMBER AND STREET (PHYSICAL ADDRESS REQUIRED, P.O. BOX MAY BE ADDED TO ENSURE DELIVERY)   APT/UNIT

CITY   STATE   ZIP+4   COUNTY

DAYTIME TELEPHONE NUMBER   SOCIAL SECURITY NUMBER (SEE PRIVACY NOTIFICATION)
(   )

E-MAIL ADDRESS (THIS ADDRESS WILL BE APPLICANT'S USER ID FOR ON-LINE ACCOUNT) HAS THIS E-MAIL ADDRESS CHANGED SINCE TAKING EXAMINATION?   ☐ YES   ☐ NO

BUSINESS NAME (EXACTLY AS IT APPEARS ON THE BROKER'S LICENSE)   OFFICE LICENSE/UNIQUE ID NUMBER (BEGINS WITH 1099, 1039 OR 39)

BUSINESS ADDRESS WHERE APPLICANT WILL BE PERMANENTLY STATIONED - NUMBER AND STREET
☐ LOCATION IS PRINCIPAL OFFICE
☐ LOCATION IS BRANCH OFFICE

CITY   STATE   ZIP+4   COUNTY

1   Background Data

                                                                          YES   **NO**

1. What is your date of birth? _____

2. Have you ever applied for or been issued a real estate broker's or salesperson's license in this state?   ____   ____
   ➜ **IF "YES,"** in what year? _____   Under what name? _____
   LICENSE/UNIQUE ID NUMBER (if applicable) _____

3. Have you ever been convicted in this state or elsewhere of any criminal offense that is a misdemeanor or a felony?   ____   ____
   ➜ **IF "YES,"** you must submit with this application a written explanation giving the place, court jurisdiction, nature of the offense sentence and/or other disposition. You must submit a copy of the accusatory instrument (*e.g.,* indictment, criminal information or complaint) and a Certificate of Disposition. If you possess or have receive a Certificate of Relief from Disabilities, Certificate of Good Conduct or Executive Pardon, you must submit a copy with this application.

4. Are there any criminal charges (misdemeanor or felonies) pending against you in any court in this state or elsewhere?   ____   ____
   ➜ **IF "YES,"** you must submit a copy of the accusatory instrument (*e.g.,* indictment, criminal information or complaint.)

5. Has any license or permit issued to you or a company in which you are or were a principal in New York State or elsewhere ever been revoked, suspended or denied?   ____   ____
   ➜ **IF "YES,"** you must provide all relevant documents, including the agency determination, (if any).

```
(For Office Use Only – Revenue Unit)
```

DOS-0022 (Rev. 6/08)   PAGE 1 OF 3

Real Estate Salesperson Application (continued)

Real Estate Salesperson Application

2   Certification of Satisfactory Completion

_____
(Name of School)

Real Estate Salesperson Course (Code) # S-_____

This certifies that _____ has satisfactorily completed a 75-hour salesperson qualifying
(Name of Student)

course in real estate approved by the Secretary of State in accordance with the provisions of Chapter 868 of the Laws of 1977;

that attendance of the student was in compliance with the law and that a passing grade was achieved on the final examination.

The course was completed on _____ .

Authorized Signature

X_____   *Date* _____

(School Seal)

---

3   Child Support Statement — *You must complete this section. If you do not complete it, your application will be returned.*

"X" A or B, below

I, the undersigned, do hereby certify that *(You must "X" A or B, below)*:

A. [   ] **I am not under obligation to pay child support**.   (SKIP "B" and go directly to **Applicant Affirmation**).

B. [   ] I am under obligation to pay child support (You must "X" any of the four statements below that are true and apply to you):

    [   ] I do *not* owe four or more months of child support payments.

    [   ] I am making child support payments by income execution or court approved payment plan or by a plan agreed to by the parties.

    [   ] My child support obligation is the subject of a pending court proceeding.

    [   ] I receive public assistance or supplemental social security income.

---

4   Applicant Affirmation — I affirm, under the penalties of perjury, that the statements made in this application are true and correct. I further affirm that I have read and understand the provisions of Article 12-A of the Real Property Law and the rules and regulations promulgated thereunder.

_____
Applicant Print Name

X _____   *Date* _____
   Applicant's Signature

F I G U R E   1.3

Real Estate Salesperson Application (continued)

Real Estate Salesperson Application

5   DMV Consent Section — IMPORTANT Information Regarding Your Photo ID

The Department of State produces photo ID cards in cooperation with the NYS Department of Motor Vehicles (DMV). If you have a current NYS Driver License or Non-Driver ID card, please provide your 9-digit DMV ID Number in the space provided below. Then read the informed consent and sign this form. If you do not have a current NYS photo Driver License or Non-Driver ID card, please have your photo taken at any nearby DMV office BEFORE you complete this application. For more details, refer to our enclosed notice, "Request for Photo ID."

INFORMED CONSENT

I authorize the NYS Department of State and the NYS Department of Motor Vehicles (DMV) to produce an ID card bearing my DMV photo. I understand that DMV will send this card to the address I maintain with the Department of State. I also understand that the Department of State and DMV will use my DMV photo to produce all my subsequent ID Cards for as long as I maintain my license/registration with the Department of State.

DMV ID # _____/_____/_____ - _____/_____/_____ - _____/_____/_____

X _____   _____
   Applicant's Signature   *Date Signed*

6   Association Statement — I am sponsoring this application in accordance with the Real Property Law, §441.1(d).

Broker License/Unique ID number _____

Broker Print Name _____

Broker Signature _____   Date _____

**Please remember to include with this application any required
explanations and statements along with your application fee
(checks should be made payable to NYS Department of State).**

It is important that you and/or your broker update any changes to your
business address through your online account so you can continue to receive
renewal notices and any other notifications pertinent to your license.

■ MAINTAINING A LICENSE

Various license laws and regulations affect a licensee's business practices.

Change of Business Address, Status, or Name

All principal brokers who are changing either the principal office or a branch office address must notify the DOS online within five days of the change. The broker must pay for the address change for all current licensees at that address before the system will accept the change. The charge per affected license is $10. Once the changes and payment are made and accepted by the system, a new license will be mailed to each licensee at the new business address.

Those desiring a license status change (such as from associate broker to broker), change of employment, or name change must submit notice of change and the appropriate fee online.

Commissions

No individual may legally accept a commission or other compensation for performing any of the activities regulated by the license law, unless that person

- holds a valid New York real estate license at the time the activity is performed and
- maintains the license from the start of a transaction up to the point that all compensation is received.

Salespersons may not accept a commission from anyone other than their supervising broker (except from a former broker for fees already earned but not paid when the salesperson was associated with that broker).

Brokers may not receive compensation from more than one party to a transaction without the full knowledge and consent of all parties involved (dual compensation). Brokers may share commissions only with their own salespersons and associate brokers or with other licensed brokers.

The law against sharing a commission with any unlicensed person effectively prohibits **kickbacks** (return of a portion of the commission) to either buyers or sellers (with some exceptions). It should be noted that, generally speaking, the difference between a kickback and a referral fee can be best described as follows:

- A kickback occurs when
    - compensation is passed to another without the full disclosure and informed consent of all interested parties to the transaction.
- A referral fee occurs when
    - all interested parties to a transaction and/or the party being referred have agreed to be referred, and
    - the party being referred has been given full disclosure and has granted informed consent to the receipt of a referral fee.

An example of a referral fee is when a real estate licensee refers a client to another real estate licensee with the intention that the referring party receive a referral fee from the broker who receives the referral.

A kickback is illegal and will subject the licensee to disciplinary action. A referral fee, given the appropriate procedures, falls within the law. It is important to note that for licensees all referral fees are treated as compensation. As such, all compensation must go directly to and through the broker. Licensees within the employ of a broker may never collect compensation of any kind directly from anyone other than their sponsoring broker.

Disclosure of Interest

Licensees may neither buy nor acquire an interest in property listed with them for their own account without first making their true position known to the owners involved. Similarly, licensees may not act as brokers or salespersons in the sale of property in which they have an interest without revealing the interest to all parties to the transaction. When self-dealing, the licensee must be on alert for the potential creation of a dual agency. This topic will be covered in greater detail in Chapter 2.

Offers to Purchase

All offers to purchase property must be presented promptly to the owner of the property.

■ TERMINATION OR CHANGES IN ASSOCIATION

When a salesperson or associate broker terminates an association with a broker, the supervising broker must file a **termination of association notice** with the DOS. License terminations and changes of associations are to be made online. A termination must be filed by the existing broker before the new broker's performing a change of association. When a **change of association** or **change of broker** occurs, the former broker returns the license to the salesperson and at the same time files a termination of association with the DOS. Each function requires a $10 fee, which must be paid by credit card at the time of termination or change. Each broker will need the unique identification number of the licensee who is being terminated or changed. Principal brokers must be logged into their personal online real estate account in order to perform these transactions.

A salesperson whose license has expired and who wishes to affiliate with and renew under a different broker must establish a new **record of association**. The new broker must file the change of association before the renewal. A termination by the prior broker is not required in this situation.

After the new broker notifies the DOS and pays the fee, the salesperson then makes the necessary changes on the license by crossing out the former information and in its place adds in the number, name, and address of the new broker. The salesperson makes the same changes on the pocket card. The new broker retains the license, and the salesperson retains the pocket card.

Revocation or suspension of a principal broker's license automatically causes the licenses of those associated with the broker to be suspended, until they associate with a different broker.

Real estate salespersons who terminate their association with a broker must turn over to the broker any and all listing information (and buyer representation agreements) obtained during the association. This is required whether the information was originally given to the salesperson by the broker or acquired by the salesperson during the association. Retention of listing information by a licensee following voluntary or involuntary termination of a licensee is a licensing offense. Listings are the property of the broker. In addition, licensees should also be careful to observe any covenant(s) and/or restriction(s) that may be contained in their employment contracts or independent contractor agreements (as the case may be). Generally speaking, it is advised that an amicable "exit agreement" be executed between a licensee and the previous employing broker at termination of association. This exit agreement will protect the rights of the parties to that agreement. To coin a phrase: "Good contracts make for good friends."

■ RENEWAL AND CONTINUING EDUCATION

Real estate licenses must be renewed every two years. A licensee who does not renew within two years of expiration must retake the licensing examination. Renewals must be done online at *www.dos.state.ny.us/licensing/eaccessny.html*.

Continuing Education

To renew a license, a licensee must complete 22½ hours of **continuing education** every two years.

As of July 1, 2008, Section 441 of the Real Property Law (RPL) has been amended to require that the 22½ hours of continuing education contain at least three hours on fair housing and/or discrimination in the sale or rental of real property.

Continuing education can be accomplished (1) by attendance within a classroom environment with no end-of-class exam required, or (2) by clocking 22½ hours of prescribed and approved course material via distance learning, or (3) by a combination of classroom attendance and distance learning totaling 22½ hours of approved continuing education.

The hours may be accumulated in modules as short as three-hour courses, and distance learning is available through the Internet or on CD-ROM. A list of approved continuing education courses can be obtained by calling 518-486-3803 or by e-mailing *licensing@dos.state.ny.us*. A list of approved schools is available on the DOS Web site.

Previously, active licensed brokers who had been continuously licensed and active as full-time salespersons and/or brokers for the preceding 15 years and attorneys licensed to practice in the state of New York were exempt from the continuing education requirement. This exemption section will not change for any individual who achieved **exemption** status before July 1, 2008.

After July 1, 2008, this continuing education exemption will no longer be granted to brokers who fulfill the 15-year requirement after that date. No exemption will be granted to any licensee who was not already exempt before July 1, 2008.

In order to qualify for the exemption from continuing education after July 1, 2008, a licensee must

1. have a broker's license,
2. have been licensed for 15 years continuously *before July 1, 2008,* and
3. have held an exemption prior to the change in law.

Those grandfathered with this exemption under the old laws are advised to be timely in renewing their licenses. If the license is allowed to lapse, the licensee will lose the exemption forever and be required to complete continuing education every two years following the lapse.

■ BROKERAGE MANAGEMENT IN ACCORDANCE WITH LICENSE LAWS

Brokers must follow various laws and regulations as they operate their brokerage businesses.

Place of Business

Every New York real estate broker must maintain a principal place of business within the state (with the rare exception of some nonresident brokers).

Business name and sign Any business name used by a New York real estate broker must first be approved by the DOS.

- Signage that is posted outdoors must be posted conspicuously on the outside of the building and be readable from the sidewalk.
- Signage that is posted indoors (as in an office building, for instance) must have the broker's name and the words "Licensed Real Estate Broker" posted in the space that lists the names of the building's occupants. The words "Licensed Real Estate Broker" may be abbreviated to "Lic. R. E. Broker."

Branch offices A broker may maintain a branch office or offices, and a separate license must be maintained for each. Section 441-a, Subsection 3, of the Real Property Law has been amended so that as of July 1, 2008, each branch office must be under the direct supervision of the broker to whom the license to operate a branch office was issued. This would also include the following:

- A representative broker of a corporation (also known as a corporate broker/class 31 license)
- A representative broker or manager of a limited liability company (class 49)
- A representative broker of a general or limited partnership (class 33)

The principal broker must pay expenses for the branch office and supervise it closely. Except as otherwise provided under Section 175.20, Subsection (b), salespersons and associate brokers may never manage and operate branch offices. Section 175.20, Subsection (b) specifically provides that

- every branch office be under the direct supervision of the broker to whom the license is issued (this includes a representative broker of a corporation or partnership holding such license); and
- a salesperson licensed for a period of not less than two years and who has successfully completed a course of study in real estate approved by the secretary of state be permitted to operate such a branch office *only under the direct supervision of the broker* (Section 175.21), provided that the names of such salesperson and supervising broker have been filed and recorded in the division of licenses of the DOS.

Maintaining Documents

Every real estate broker must maintain a file of all **agency disclosure forms**, listings, offers, closing statements, and certain other documents for a period of no less than three years. (Most brokers keep all records indefinitely as a matter of good business practice.)

Delivery of Documents

A real estate broker must immediately deliver to all parties signing the document duplicate originals of any document relating to a real estate transaction prepared by the broker or one of the broker's salespeople. Failure to do so may subject the licensee to disciplinary action by the DOS.

Care and Handling of Funds

A real estate broker must not **commingle** money or other properties belonging to others with the broker's own funds. Brokers who hold money belonging to others in their possession must maintain a separate, federally insured New York bank account (the name of the titled account must include the words **escrow** or trust account) to be used exclusively for the deposit of these monies and must deposit them immediately. Within a reasonable time, the broker must render an account of the funds to the client and remit any funds collected to the proper party. Interest earned, if any, does not belong to the broker. The broker's responsibility in this role also includes maintaining information on the institution where escrowed funds have been deposited (including the branch name and address holding the account), recording the account number(s) needed to identify which account is housing the funds, and, if the account is to be interest bearing, noting to whom the benefit of the interest will inure. Any cash deposit of more than $10,000 must be reported to the Internal Revenue Service (IRS).

Obligations to Other Parties and Other Brokers

The license law expressly prohibits a broker from interfering with or trying to frustrate other parties' existing contracts. In addition, license law also prohibits the aggravation of another licensee's agency relationship(s).

No broker may accept the services of any other broker's associates without that broker's knowledge, and brokers may not pay another broker's associates directly without that broker's knowledge.

Brokers are prohibited from negotiating the sale, lease, or exchange of any property directly with an owner who has an existing written contract that grants exclusive authority to another broker. This means that brokers may not interfere with another broker's exclusive **listing agreement**. A listing agreement is the broker's employment agreement. (This subject will be covered in greater detail in Chapters 2 and 3).

■ OTHER LICENSES OR REGISTRATIONS INVOLVING REAL ESTATE

An **apartment information vendor's** license is available to anyone older than 18 who is trustworthy and able to maintain a $5,000 interest-bearing escrow account. The license is renewable annually for a $400 fee. Apartment information vendors engage in the business of furnishing information concerning the location and availability of residential rental property, including apartments. They must provide prospective tenants a contract or receipt with specific information regarding the services they offer. They also must display a sign in all offices bearing the same information, post their license in all offices, and notify the DOS of any changes in name or address. A buyer or a renter is not required to engage the services of a real estate broker, so the services of apartment information vendors allow buyers and renters to facilitate a sale or rental without the assistance of a real estate licensee.

An **apartment-sharing agent** finds roommates and arranges for sharing of homes. The one-year license costs $400, and the agent must maintain a trust account of $2,500.

Certification or licensing of **appraisers** is not required for all appraisal work but is necessary for most appraisals related to mortgage loans. New York State licenses and certifies appraisers at different levels, depending on the applicants' experience, education, and examinations.

Mortgage Banking Companies

Mortgage bankers are not thrift institutions (a financial institution designed to hold personal savings accounts while simultaneously promoting home purchasing; the term is currently used to describe savings banks and savings and loan associations) and do not offer either checking or savings accounts. Because they do not use depositors' money, they are subject to considerably less regulation than thrift institutions. They make or extend real estate loans that may later be sold to investors (with the mortgage company receiving a fee if it continues servicing the loans). Mortgage bankers originate a large percentage of all home loans. Mortgage bankers must file a $50,000 surety bond with the superintendent of banks or establish a trust fund in the same amount that can be used to reimburse customers, if it is determined that the mortgage banker has charged improper fees. They are not mortgage brokers.

Mortgage Brokers

Mortgage brokers *are registered* with the State Banking Department to bring borrowers and lenders together. They normally charge a fee, often of the borrower, for their services. The superintendent of banks may require a mortgage broker to obtain a surety bond or establish a trust fund in the amount of $25,000.

Any person who negotiates or seeks to negotiate a mortgage loan other than a mortgage loan on residential property in the state of New York is required to be licensed as a real estate broker or as a salesperson associated with a real estate broker. This license is issued by the DOS. However, in any transaction involving a mortgage loan on residential property (defined as four or fewer units contained within a building intended for dwelling purposes), registration with the New York State Banking Department is required.

Home Inspectors

New York State has required licensing for **home inspectors** since January 2006. License requirements resemble those for real estate salespersons: required hours of study, examinations, and supervised apprenticeship. Real estate salespersons and brokers who refer buyers to home inspectors must make sure that those they suggest are licensed. Lists of licensees are available at the DOS Web site.

Home inspectors are required to complete continuing education for every cycle of licensing. The requirements differ from those of real estate licensees in the following ways:

■ An applicant whose license expires on/or before December 2008 will be required to complete 6 hours of DOS-prescribed approved continuing education (prior to completion of their application renewing the license).
■ An applicant whose license expires after December 2008 will be required to complete 24 hours of DOS-prescribed approved continuing education (prior to completion of their application renewing the license).

Disclosure Required for Uncapped Wells

Chapter 163, amended Section 242 of the Real Property Law, requires a seller of real property to disclose to a buyer, before entering into a contract for purchase and sale, the existence of any "uncapped natural gas wells" that are known by the seller to exist on the property in question. The law is intended to protect buyers from the significant expenses that may occur after closing when natural gas wells must be capped.

Reciprocity versus Mutual Recognition of Licensure

Reciprocity Reciprocal agreements are reached through and between states that are willing to recognize each others' license laws as well as the requirements needed to achieve licensing within their jurisdictions.

All states devise their statutory laws somewhat differently, but a majority of the requirements for achieving licensing are the same throughout the United States.

As a result, state A can reach a **reciprocity** agreement with state B that recognizes licenses attained in either state as valid in the other. When this type of agreement between states exists, in order to achieve a license within another state after having received a license in one, no additional education or testing is required. At this time, New York has reciprocal agreements with ten states (see Figure 1.5); however, certain requirements must be fulfilled, as discussed in the section "Licensing Nonresidents."

Mutual recognition   Mutual recognition applies to states that are not willing to enter into reciprocal agreements with other states but are willing to recognize previous education completed by a licensee from another state and previous experience achieved while licensed in another state.

These states may require applicants to achieve additional education if their home state has reduced hourly requirements for licensing; these applicants will probably have to take the state-law portion of the state licensing exam.

Licensing Nonresidents

Nonresidents of New York may be licensed as New York real estate brokers or salespersons by conforming to all the provisions of the license law, except maintaining a place of business within the state. Some New Jersey brokers, for example, hold licenses in both states.

The department will recognize the license issued to a real estate broker or salesperson by another state if the laws of the home state of the licensee permit licenses to be issued to New York licensees without requiring that state's licensing examination be taken. (See Figure 1.5.) If a particular state's laws do not include these provisions, the nonresident applicant must pass the licensing examination.

Every nonresident applicant must file an **irrevocable consent** form (see Figure 1.4), which makes it easier for the nonresident to be sued in the state of New York. A nonresident licensee, by virtue of the irrevocable consent form, agrees to receive service of legal process within the state of New York. The form is designed to allow for the suing of a nonresident within the state of New York without the claimant having to serve the nonresident in the nonresident's state of residence.

■ ADVERTISEMENTS

Advertising must not be misleading in any way. All real estate advertisements must contain the name of the broker's firm and must clearly indicate that the party who placed the ad is a real estate broker. Any ad that does not identify that the advertiser is a real estate broker is termed a **blind ad**. Blind ads that contain only a telephone number are prohibited.

On Web sites as well as in print ads, a salesperson's name may not be displayed more prominently than the broker's or firm's name. Any Internet ad must contain a link to the firm's Web site. The broker must supervise a salesperson's Web site.

FIGURE 1.4

Irrevocable Consent Form

- This form is to be used by a corporate applicant if the applicant is a foreign corporation.
- Nonresident individuals and partnerships must use the form on the other side of this sheet.
- This form must be signed by either the president, vice president, secretary or treasurer of the foreign corporation.

STATE OF NEW YORK
DEPARTMENT OF STATE
Division of Licensing Services

Uniform Irrevocable Consent and Designation
Foreign Corporation

This irrevocable consent and designation is made by _____ ,

(Name of Corporation)

a corporation incorporated under the laws of the State of _____ on the _____ day of

_____ 20 _____ , with its principal office at _____ .

_____ hereby irrevocably submits to the

(Name of Corporation)

jurisdiction of the courts of the State of New York and, further, hereby irrevocably designates the Secretary of State of the State of New York as its agent upon whom may be served any summons, subpoena or other process naming the corporation in any action or special proceeding commenced in the State of New York.

By this consent and designation, the corporation agrees that service of process upon the Secretary of State shall be, in all respects, as valid and binding as if personal service had been made upon the corporation within the State of New York.

IN WITNESS HEREOF, this consent and designation is signed by an authorized officer this _____ day of

_____ 20 _____ .

_____

(Name of Corporation)

By: _____

(Signature)

Name: _____

Title: _____

State of _____

County of _____

On this _____ day of _____ 20 ___ before me personally came _____

_____ to me known, and who, being duly sworn,

did depose and say that (he)(she) resides in _____ and that (he)(she) is the

(State)

_____ of the corporation described in and which executed the above instrument,

(Title)

and that, by order of the board of directors of the corporation, (he)(she) has executed the above document for and on behalf of the corporation by signing (his)(her) name thereto.

_____

Notary Public

DOS-17 (Rev. 3/08)

FIGURE 1.4

Irrevocable Consent Form (continued)

- This form is to be used by nonresident individuals and nonresident partnerships.
- Foreign corporations must use the form on the other side of this sheet.
- This form must be signed by all the partners of the foreign partnership.

STATE OF NEW YORK
DEPARTMENT OF STATE
Division of Licensing Services

Uniform Irrevocable Consent and Designation
Individual and Partnership

(I)(we) _____ ,
(Name of Individual or Partners)

doing business under the name_____ ,
hereby irrevocably submit(s) to the jurisdiction of the courts of the State of New York, and, further, hereby irrevocably designate(s) the Secretary of State of the State of New York as (my)(our) agent upon whom may be served any summons, subpoena or other process naming (me)(the partnership or any partner) in any action or special proceeding commenced in the State of New York.

By this consent and designation, (I)(we) agree that service of process upon the Secretary of State shall be, in all respects, as valid and binding as if personal service had been made upon (me)(the partnership and each of the partners) within the State of New York.

IN WITNESS HEREOF, this consent and designation is signed by (me) (us) this _____
day of _____ 20 _____ .

Signed: _____

Address: _____

Signed: _____

Address: _____

Signed: _____

Address: _____

State of _____

County of _____

On this _____ day of _____, 20 _____ before me personally came _____
_____ to me known and known to me to be the person(s) who (is) (are) named in and who executed the foregoing instrument, and (he)(she)(they) duly acknowledged that (he)(she)(they) executed the same.

_____
Notary Public

DOS-17 (Rev. 3/08)

FIGURE 1.5

Real Estate Reciprocity

Arkansas	Broker only—two years' current licensure (business and residence must be in Arkansas).
Colorado	Broker and associate broker—current licensure (business and residence address must be in Colorado). Colorado associate brokers must submit a salesperson application fee along with their certification and irrevocable consent form.
Connecticut	Broker and salesperson—current licensure only (business and residence must be in Connecticut).
Georgia	Broker and salesperson—current licensure only (business and residence must be in Georgia). Must have obtained their license by passing Georgia exam.
Massachusetts	Broker only—two years' current licensure (business and residence must be in Massachusetts).
Mississippi	Broker and salesperson—current licensure only (business and residence must be in Mississippi). Must have obtained their license by passing Mississippi exam.
Nebraska	Broker and salesperson—current licensure only (business and residence must be in Nebraska).
Oklahoma	Broker and salesperson—two years' current licensure (business and residence must be in Oklahoma).
Pennsylvania	Broker and salesperson—current licensure only (business and residence must be in Pennsylvania).
West Virginia	Broker and salesperson—current licensure only (business and residence must be in West Virginia).

All need current certification (dated within six months) from the real estate commission where the license was obtained, completed application, irrevocable consent form, and the appropriate fee.

Applicants seeking a reciprocal real estate salesperson's license must be sponsored by a broker holding a current New York State broker's license.

All advertisements that state that a *property is in the vicinity of a geographic area or territorial subdivision* must include as part of the advertisement the name of the geographic area or territorial subdivision in which the property actually is located.

For Sale Signs

A broker must obtain an owner's prior consent to place a For Sale sign on the owner's property. Neglecting to do so is considered an infraction of license law and will subject the licensee to disciplinary action by the DOS.

■ SUSPENSION AND REVOCATION OF LICENSES

The DOS may hear complaints and/or initiate investigations into any alleged **violations** of the license law or its rules and regulations. Those found guilty of untrustworthiness or incompetence may have their license temporarily suspended (**suspension**) or permanently cancelled (**revocation**) or may be fined or reprimanded (**administrative discipline**). Untrustworthiness or incompetence will include any of the following acts:

- Making any substantial misrepresentation (defined as a false statement or the concealment of a material fact, done in order to induce someone to take a certain action, whether done maliciously, ignorantly, or carelessly)
- Making any false promise likely to influence, persuade, or induce
- Making a false statement or misrepresentation through agents, salespersons, advertising, or otherwise
- Accepting, if a salesperson, a commission or valuable consideration for any real estate service from any person except the licensed broker with whom the salesperson is associated
- Acting for or receiving compensation from more than one party in a transaction without the knowledge and consent of all parties involved (it is always recommended that consent be achieved in writing)
- Failing within a reasonable amount of time to account for or remit any monies belonging to others that come into a licensee's possession
- Failing to immediately deliver duplicate or original documents to an interested party in a transaction
- Failing to make the appropriate property defect disclosure(s) when these defects are known to the licensee
- Being untrustworthy or incompetent to act as a real estate licensee
- Paying a commission or valuable consideration to any person for services performed in violation of the law
- Obtaining a license falsely or fraudulently or making a material misstatement in the license application
- Negotiating with an owner or a landlord with knowledge that the owner or landlord has an exclusive written contract with another broker
- Aggravating the agency relationship of another
- Offering a property for sale or lease without the authorization of the owner
- Accepting the services of any salesperson who is associated with another broker
- Giving legal opinions or performing title examinations
- Entering into a **net listing** contract (when a seller authorizes a broker to procure a specified amount of money for the property and allows the broker to keep any money above the specified amount obtained from the sale)
- Discriminating because of race, creed, color, national origin, age, sex, disability, sexual orientation, or marital status in the sale, rental, or advertisement of housing or commercial space
- Failing to provide definitions of exclusive-right-to-sell and exclusive-agency listings when the listing involves the sale or rental of three or fewer family dwellings (Section 175.24). Section 175.24 does not apply to cooperatives and condominiums.
- Engaging in improper, fraudulent, or dishonest dealing
- Committing any other violation of license law

Investigation of Complaint and Hearing

If the DOS feels that a complaint warrants further investigation, it will send an investigator to interview the alleged violator about the charge. In most cases, that involve a complaint against a licensee within the employ of a broker, the interview will begin with the sponsoring broker of record. This interview's purpose is to determine whether the broker has been supervising his staff appropriately (as required under Section 175.21 of the Real Property Law). In some cases, the investigation is preceded by a formal letter of complaint from the department. If the investigation results in sufficient evidence, the department will conduct a hearing. Individuals accused of violation of the law may defend themselves or be represented by an attorney. The department investigates roughly 2,500 complaints annually, with about 1,000 resulting in disciplinary action.

Penalties

Offenders who have received any sum of money as commission, compensation, or profit in connection with a license law violation may be held liable for up to four times that amount in damages in addition to having their license suspended or revoked. If a license is revoked, one year must pass before a new license application can be made.

The DOS also may impose a fine not to exceed $1,000 per violation. Violation of the license law also constitutes a **misdemeanor**, and a licensee may be tried in criminal court in addition to the DOS hearing. Criminal actions can be prosecuted by the attorney general of the state of New York. A misdemeanor is punishable by a fine of not more than $1,000 and/or imprisonment for not more than one year. The DOS does not have the power to imprison license law violators.

Appeal

The action of the DOS is subject to review. Any determination in granting or renewing a license, revoking or suspending a license, or imposing a fine or reprimand may be appealed to the secretary of state. Judicial appeal is made through an **Article 78 procedure**, an appeal to the New York State Supreme Court. An Article 78 proceeding is the appeal process available to any private individual when a public body of government renders an adverse decision against him or her. A private individual might decide to institute an Article 78 proceeding to secure relief/grievance from overcharges applicable to real property assessments or when seeking compensation from condemnation of a private party's property.

Revocation of Broker's License

Revocation of a broker's license automatically suspends the licenses of all salespersons and associate brokers affiliated with that broker until they find another supervising broker and their licenses are reissued.

When a salesperson is accused of violating the license law, the supervising broker is also held accountable if the broker knew or should have known of the violation or, having found out about the problem, retained any fees or commissions arising from the transaction. The broker in this situation is said to have "vicarious liability." As depicted previously, *vicarious liability* can be defined as responsibility for the wrongful acts of another. This subject will be covered in Chapter 2.

■ UNLICENSED REAL ESTATE ASSISTANTS

In today's real estate market, many real estate agents find that using unlicensed assistants is very useful. These assistants can do a fair amount of paperwork and legwork, leaving the agents free to use their time finding clients and negotiating transactions. However, unlicensed assistants may not perform any real estate activities for which a license is required. According to the DOS, an unlicensed assistant may safely engage in the following activities:

- Answer the phone, forward calls, and take messages
- Arrange appointments for the licensee
- Follow up on loan commitments after a contract has been negotiated and generally secure status reports on the loan progress
- Assemble documents for closing
- Write ads for the approval of the broker and place approved classified advertising
- Type contract forms for the approval of the broker
- Compute commission checks
- Place signs on or remove them from properties
- Order items of repair as directed by the broker
- Prepare flyers and promotional information for approval by the broker
- Schedule appointments for licensees to show listed property
- Gather information for a comparative market analysis
- Gather information for an appraisal
- Monitor licenses and personnel files
- Perform secretarial and clerical duties such as typing letters and filing

An unlicensed assistant may not list or sell property, prospect for listings, show property, hold open houses alone, or answer buyer's questions about property. In addition, there have been instances in which some brokers use an individual referred to in the marketplace as a "shower" to open doors for customer viewing appointments. Generally, the shower is not a licensed individual, and as such, is committing a licensing infraction. To avoid this infraction of license law, brokers are advised to properly license any individuals performing this or any other duty requiring a license.

■ DOS DETERMINATIONS

In recent years, the DOS has acted in cases such as the following:

- Associate broker failed to provide the required written disclosure of agency (as explained in Chapter 3); the DOS fined him $500. The principal broker also was fined and penalized.
- Salesperson lied on her license renewal application and said she had completed continuing education requirements. An audit turned up the false statement. The DOS revoked her license.

- Salesperson did not lie on license renewal but frankly stated he had failed to complete the continuing education courses required. The DOS suspended his license until he provided proof he completed the courses.
- Broker's license was suspended because he failed to pay child support, not to be reinstated until family court confirmed he was current with his payments.
- Broker had misappropriated rental income he was collecting on behalf of a landlord, and when ordered to make restitution, paid with bad checks. The DOS revoked his license and indicated it could not be reinstated until the full sum was repaid to the landlord, including interest.

■ SUMMARY

In New York, licensees must be permanent residents of the United States, must never have been convicted of a felony or misdemeanor, and must pass state examinations before licensure. A salesperson must have completed a prescribed 75-hour qualifying course, be at least 18 years old, and be sponsored by a licensed broker. A broker must be at least 20 years old, with an additional 45 hours of approved study (120 hours total) and two full years' experience as a licensed salesperson. Some exceptions to these requirements are possible.

The real estate license, which covers a two-year period, costs $50 for a salesperson and $150 for a broker. An associate broker's license designates a fully qualified broker who chooses to remain in a salesperson capacity under a supervising broker. Those exempt from licensing requirements include New York state attorneys, public officials while performing their public duties, and persons acting under court order. A license is not required of a resident manager employed by only one owner to collect rents. Certain tenant organizations in New York City may also perform real estate services without being licensed.

Every broker must have a principal place of business within the state, post a sign readable from the sidewalk or in the lobby of an office building, obtain a separate license for each branch office, and display the principal broker's license prominently. Brokers who handle other people's money must maintain a separate escrow account for those funds. The broker must immediately deliver duplicate originals of all documents to the persons signing them and must keep a file of all documents relating to real estate transactions for at least three years.

Commissions may be collected only by the supervising broker and may be shared only with other brokers and the broker's own associated salespersons and associate brokers. Advertisements must contain the name of the broker's firm.

Laws, rules, and regulations governing licensees are administered by the New York DOS, which may, after hearings, suspend or revoke licenses. Violations of these laws, rules, and regulations are also misdemeanors.

CHAPTER 1 QUIZ

1. A neighbor has no real estate license and canvasses homeowners by phone to determine whether they are interested in selling their homes. A licensee gives the neighbor $25 for every lead she turns up. Does this violate license law?

   a. No, because the gift is not more than $25.
   b. No, because the neighbor does not actually list or sell property.
   c. Yes, because the licensee is paying compensation for services that require licensure.
   d. Yes, because the neighbor is using a home telephone with no broker's sign outside her house.

2. Real estate license laws were instituted to

   a. raise revenue through license fees.
   b. limit the number of brokers and salespersons.
   c. match the federal government's requirements.
   d. protect the public while maintaining high standards for those issued a license.

3. In New York, real estate licenses are issued by the

   a. Real Estate Commission.
   b. Board of REALTORS®.
   c. Department of State.
   d. Department of Education.

4. Which of the following acts require that a New York resident hold a valid real estate license?

   a. Giving a cousin advice about pricing her home for the market
   b. Writing a lease for a tenant in a building he owns
   c. Accepting a TV from a grateful neighbor for whom she arranged a home equity loan
   d. Selling the house of his dead aunt while settling her estate

5. In order to satisfy the education requirements for a real estate salesperson's license, how many hours of education must an applicant take?

   a. 45 hours
   b. 60 hours
   c. 75 hours
   d. 90 hours

6. A duly licensed salesperson may accept bonus compensation from

   a. a grateful seller.
   b. a grateful buyer.
   c. another salesperson.
   d. none of these.

7. A fully qualified broker who chooses to act as a salesperson under the employ of another broker's sponsorship is licensed as a(n)

   a. adjunct salesperson.
   b. sales associate.
   c. associate broker.
   d. principal broker.

8. To obtain a broker's license, you must reach the age of

   a. 18.
   b. 19.
   c. 20.
   d. 21.

9. In order to satisfy the education requirements for a broker license, an applicant must have first completed a total of how many hours of prescribed study?

   a. 45
   b. 75
   c. 90
   d. 120

10. Which of the following is required for an applicant to show in order to be eligible for a broker's license in New York State?

    a. Completion of 50 hours in real estate courses
    b. Age of at least 18
    c. Completion of two years' experience as a licensed salesperson
    d. Membership in the New York State Association of REALTORS®

11. Real estate licenses in New York State are good for

    a. one year.
    b. two years.
    c. three years.
    d. four years.

12. Nonresident brokers seeking a New York license must

    a. post a bond of $5,000.
    b. be a citizen of the United States.
    c. find a New York attorney or another broker to act as a sponsor.
    d. file an irrevocable consent to service form allowing them to be sued in New York State.

13. In the office of a broker, which of the following must be displayed?

    a. All brokers' licenses
    b. All licenses
    c. No licenses
    d. Only salespersons' licenses

14. A salesperson told the telephone company to print the following ad under "Real Estate" in the Yellow Pages: Licensed Salesperson, Residential Property a Specialty, 473-4973. In order to have placed an appropriate ad, she should have included her

    a. area code.
    b. broker's name.
    c. office address.
    d. home phone number.

15. A real estate license is temporarily suspended or permanently cancelled if a licensee is found to be untrustworthy or

    a. incompetent.
    b. malicious.
    c. irresponsible.
    d. unproductive.

16. The Department of State has revoked the license of a real estate licensee for fraud. Which is *TRUE*?

    a. The licensee has the right to appeal the revocation through an article 78 proceeding.
    b. His salespersons may continue in business for 90 days because they were not found guilty.
    c. The licensee may continue his business for 90 days if he posts a bond with the DOS.
    d. The licensee may have his license reinstated if he signs an irrevocable consent form.

17. If a principal broker loses her license, her associated salespersons must immediately

    a. appoint one of their number to serve as supervisor.
    b. stop listing and selling until they have associated with another broker.
    c. obtain brokers' licenses.
    d. request that the DOS reassign them.

18. All of the following would be required of a real estate salesperson *EXCEPT*

    a. to be licensed by the state.
    b. to be at least 18 years old.
    c. to already have experience in real estate.
    d. to be supervised by a sponsoring broker.

19. A homeowner lists his house with broker A. The homeowner offers a bonus commission of $500 to the agent who brings a good buyer before December. A salesperson who is associated with the cooperating firm of broker B, effects the sale on November 1. The salesperson may collect that bonus from

    a. the homeowner and from no other.
    b. broker B and from no other.
    c. broker A and from no other.
    d. no one.

20. A real estate broker must keep all documents for the DOS pertaining to a real estate transaction on file for a period of no less than

a. two years.
b. three years.
c. seven years.
d. indefinitely.

21. The term *commingling* pertains to

a. mixing the broker's funds with escrow deposits.
b. soliciting the services of another broker's salespersons.
c. failing to deliver duplicate originals of contracts.
d. promoting business at social gatherings.

22. Which of the following cash deposits must a real estate broker report to the IRS?

a. $5,000
b. $15,000
c. $10,000
d. $7,500

23. An apartment information vendor's license is available to individuals who are able to

a. pass the licensing exam.
b. file a $10,000 surety bond.
c. obtain a sponsoring broker.
d. maintain a $5,000 interest-bearing escrow account.

24. After December 2008, the continuing education requirement for license renewal of home inspectors in New York will

a. disappear.
b. require fewer hours.
c. require more hours.
d. become identical to the requirement for brokers.

CHAPTER 2

The Law of Agency

■ KEY TERMS

accountability

agency

agency coupled with an interest

agent

attorney-in-fact

brokerage

buyer's broker

Clayton Act

client

commercial transaction

commission

confidentiality

cooperating agent

customer

disclosure

dual agency

estoppel

express agency

Federal Trade Commission (FTC)

fiduciary

fiduciary duties

fiduciary relationship

first substantive contact

fraud

general agent

group boycott

implied agency

informed consent

latent defects

law of agency

listing agreement

loyalty

market allocation

meeting of the minds

misrepresentation

multiple listing service

obedience

power of attorney

price-fixing

principal

procuring cause of sale

puffing

ratification

ready, willing, and able buyer

reasonable care

residential transaction

restraint of trade

seller's agent

self-dealing

Sherman Act

special agent

subagent

tie-in arrangements

undisclosed dual agency

undivided loyalty

universal agent

■ OVERVIEW OF AGENCY DISCUSSION

In this chapter, the basic **law of agency** is covered, with emphasis on the duties of agents to their clients and standards for dealing with their customers. Chapter 3 discusses the various types of possible agency relationships and the need for brokers to develop policies for disclosure of representation.

■ WHAT IS AN AGENT?

Real estate brokers and salespersons are commonly referred to as agents. Legally, however, the term refers to strictly defined legal relationships. In the case of real estate, it is a relationship between licensees and buyers, sellers, landlords, or tenants. In the law of agency (the body of law that governs these relationships), the following terms have specific definitions:

- **Agent**—an individual who is employed or authorized (and consents) to transact business on behalf of another, usually for a fee. In the real estate business, the broker firm acts as the agent of the
  — seller,
  — buyer,
  — landlord, or
  — tenant.
- **Principal**—the individual who hires and delegates to the agent the responsibility of representing the principal's interests.
- **Agency**—the fiduciary relationship that is created between the principal and the agent.
- **Fiduciary**—term describing the role that the agent takes on when the agency relationship is created, a relationship based on the highest form of trust and confidence. The agent is empowered (within the limitations of the agency appointment) to transact business on behalf of the principal.
- **Client**—a term that may be used to describe the principal.
- **Customer**—the third party with whom the agent deals on behalf of the agent's principal. The customer is owed "fair and honest dealing" by an agent transacting business on behalf of a principal, but the relationship between the agent and the customer is not a fiduciary one.

There is a distinction between the duties owed by the agent to a client and the treatment owed to a customer. The principal, or *client*, is the one to whom the agent gives advice and counsel, and whose interest must be put above the interests of all other parties to a transaction, including the interests of the agent.

The agent is entrusted with certain *confidential information* and has *fiduciary responsibilities* (discussed in greater detail later) to the principal. In contrast, the customer is entitled only to factual information and honest dealings as a consumer but does not receive advice and counsel or confidential information about the principal. The agent works <u>for</u> the principal and *with* the customer.

Types of Agents

Through the creation of the agency relationship, the scope of authority granted an agent will determine which of the three types of agent categories that relationship falls under. The three categories of agent relationships may be classified as follows:

1. Universal agent
2. General agent
3. Special agent

A **universal agent** has the authority to represent the principal in *all matters concerning all transactions that can be delegated*. Universal agents can enter into any contract on behalf of the principal. However, under the New York State General Obligations law, the aforementioned may not occur without a prior *written notarized power of attorney*. They can act for the principal in the broadest scope and range of areas. This type of agency cannot happen without this written document known as a **power of attorney**. A guardian or an individual who looks after a mentally incompetent party is an example of a universal agent. That appointed party (appointed by the courts via a written decree that replaces the written power of attorney) tends to all the needs and cares of the noncompetent party.

A **general agent** is empowered to represent the principal in *all matters concerning one transaction*. The general agent is granted authority to only transact a *specific range of matters*. As in the case of a universal agent, the general agent may bind the principal to any contract within the scope of the agent's authority. This type of authority also can be created by a power of attorney. A property manager is usually an example of a general agent, performing various duties on behalf of the property owner/principal. These duties consist of rent collection, bill paying, accounting/bookkeeping functions, and maintenance of the property. As you can see, the property manager acts on numerous levels for the principal. However, unlike with the universal agent who bears the broadest scope of authority to transact on all matters concerning all transactions, the scope of authority granted to a general agent is limited to that assignment only.

A **special agent** is authorized to represent the principal in *one specific transaction or business activity under detailed instructions*. Under this agent category, the scope of authority granted the agent by the principal is extremely limited. For example, think of a principal and a real estate broker entering into a listing agreement (an employment agreement that engages a licensee). The role established for a real estate broker through the listing agreement is usually that of a special agent. If hired by a seller, the broker's duty is limited only to finding a ready, willing, and able buyer for the property. If hired by the buyer, the broker's duty is limited to finding a suitable property for the buyer. As a special agent, the broker is not authorized to bind the principal to any contract.

An **agency coupled with an interest** is a relationship in which the agent has some interest in the property being sold. Such an agency *cannot be revoked by the principal, nor can it be terminated on the principal's death*. For example, a broker might supply the financing for a condominium development, provided the developer agrees to give the broker the exclusive right to sell the completed condo units. Because this agent has a special interest in the transaction, the developer may not revoke the listing agreement after the broker provides the financing.

■ CREATION OF AGENCY

An agency relationship can be created by either an oral or a written agreement between the principal and the agent. It can also be implied from words or conduct. Of course, to ensure that all parties have a clear understanding of the agency relationship, it is in everyone's best interest to create an agency relationship with a written agreement.

Following are the two ways or methods by which agency relationships can be created:

1. Express agency
2. Implied agency

Express Agency

The most common way of creating an agency relationship is through an *express agreement*, an agreement that is *expressed in words, either spoken or written.*

A written agreement that creates an **express agency** relationship between a seller and a real estate broker is called a **listing agreement**. Think of the listing agreement as you would an "employment contract." A listing agreement employs and authorizes the broker to find a buyer or a tenant for the owner's property.

An agency relationship also can be created between a buyer or a tenant. This is achieved by the use of a document called a *buyer broker agreement*, an *agreement to procure*, or a *buyer agency agreement*. This buyer agency agreement describes the activities and responsibilities the principal expects from the broker in finding the appropriate property for purchase or lease.

Implied Agency

An agency also could be created with an *implied agreement*. This occurs when *both the principal and the agent act as if an agency exists*, even though they have not expressly entered into an agreement. Providing services that are accepted by the principal can create an **implied agency** relationship. For instance, brokers advise a seller on a fair listing price, give helpful hints on how the seller can make the house more marketable, show the property to several buyers, and continually refer to themselves as the **seller's agent**. The seller sets the listing price according to the broker's advice, makes the recommended repairs to the house, and agrees to numerous showings. In this case, there may be an implied agency relationship.

The dangers of this type of relationship arise when a seller's agent offers advice to the buyer/customer. The seller's agent may unknowingly be creating what is called an illegal **undisclosed dual agency**. This subject will be covered in greater detail later within this chapter.

Note that it is not always the seller's agent who creates the impression of an agency relationship. At times, the buyer customer may treat the seller's agent in a manner that gives the impression that an agency relationship has been created.

In this event, the seller agent should immediately correct the buyer customer's impression. This will avoid the risk of creating an undisclosed dual agency.

When someone claims to be an agent but there is no agreement, the principal may establish an agency by one of two implied agency subcategories: **ratification** and **estoppel** (defined as when a party is prevented by the party's own acts from taking a different position because it would cause detriment to another party).

Ratification can be defined as an after-the-fact or retroactive acceptance of the relationship or previous agreement that may not have existed before. Ratification occurs when one party continues to accept what was bargained for after the parties realize that a mistake or misrepresentation occurred. For example, B is purchasing furniture from A, who has made representations as to the condition of the furniture. B pays for and takes control of the furniture but feels that the condition was not as represented. Instead of returning immediately to A and demanding return of his money, B uses the furniture. Therefore, B has ratified the agreement.

Estoppel can be defined as accepting the benefits of the previously unauthorized act. This occurs when an individual does not stop another from performing services on her behalf even though the agents had no prior authority.

As you can see, ratification and estoppel can create ostensible relationships, which are generally found to be false and misleading. The reason for this is simply that there has been no clarity or disclosure as to the relationship of the parties. A licensee must always make relationships clear to all parties in a transaction (Section 175.7).

Failure to disclose one's relationship at **first substantive contact** will subject the licensee to disciplinary action by the DOS. *First substantive contact* can be defined as follows:

- The point at which a licensee exchanges or expresses information regarding a property to an interested party (other than information provided in advertising)
- The point at which an interested party begins to discuss or detail personal financial or other information concerning the party's interest or ability to conclude a transaction

At the time these events occur, the licensee must disclose to a buyer, seller, landlord, or tenant (as the case may be) the nature of the licensee's relationship within the transaction.

The legal requirement for written agency disclosure (discussed in Chapter 3) reduces the chances for misunderstanding in a **residential transaction**. A *residential transaction* can be defined as any transaction involving the sale or rental of a building that contains four or fewer units intended for dwelling purposes. (Any transaction involving the sale or rental of a building that contains greater than four units would be considered a **commercial transaction**.)

Although the written agency disclosure forms for cooperative and condominium units in buildings that contain greater than four units are now required under state law, licensees are still obligated to make known their relationship to the parties within a transaction (Section 175.7).

However, members of the general public tend not to understand the complexities of the law of agency. Buyers easily can assume that when they contact a broker to show them property, the broker becomes "their agent." *Under the law, it is a person's actions, not just words, that control the creation of an agency relationship.*

Compensation   It is commonly assumed that a licensee is the agent of the one who pays the compensation. However, this is not true. *The source of compensation does not determine agency*; the agent does not necessarily represent the person who pays the commission. Creation of the agency relationship by the respective parties (as detailed previously) becomes the sole determining factor as to employment and necessary duties therewith. In fact, agency can exist even if no fee is involved (a *gratuitous agency*). Buyers, sellers, and brokers can make any agreement they choose about compensating the broker, regardless of which one is the agent's principal. For example, the seller could agree to pay a commission to a broker who is the buyer's agent. Written agency agreements should always state how the agent is to be compensated. The agent is reminded that Section 175.7 also covers compensation. Under Section 175.7, an agent may never receive compensation from more than one party to that transaction without the full knowledge and written consent of all interested parties to the transaction.

■ AGENCY AND BROKERAGE

The business of bringing buyers and sellers or landlords and tenants together in the marketplace in order to conclude a real estate transaction is known as **brokerage.**

The principal who employs the broker may be

- a seller,
- a prospective buyer,
- an owner who wishes to lease property, or
- someone seeking property to rent.

The broker acts as the *agent* of the principal, who usually compensates the broker with a **commission** or fee for having successfully performed the service for which the broker was employed. As you already have learned, the principal is also known as the *client.*

Importance of Agency Law to Licensees

Agency law has become an increasingly vital topic for all real estate agents. While most legal principles of agency law have remained unchanged for decades, the practical application of those laws to real estate agents has dramatically changed the face of the real estate business in recent years. Various real estate boards and organizations promulgate a code of ethics that their members must adhere to. They offer educational seminars to create greater awareness of the duties and responsibilities that licensees owe to others.

Whom does the agent represent? In the early 1980s, the Federal Trade Commission found that the public was confused about whom a real estate agent was working for. When buyers who bought property listed by a different firm were asked whom they thought the selling agent was working for, more than 70 percent said they believed the selling agent was working for them. The reality was that in the vast majority of these transactions, the agent was legally bound to represent and work for the best interests of the seller.

Many states began drafting legislation that would require agents to disclose whom they represent to all the parties involved. In 1991, New York enacted a disclosure law that, in the opinion of many, was a model for the nation. (Agency disclosure is discussed in Chapter 3.)

Seller as Principal

If a seller contracts with a broker to market the seller's real estate,

- the broker becomes an *agent of the seller;*
- the seller is the *principal,* or the broker's *client;*
- a buyer who contacts the broker to review properties listed with the broker's firm is the broker's customer; and
- though obligated to deal honestly with all parties to a transaction and to comply with all aspects of the license law, the broker is strictly *accountable only to the principal—in this case the seller.*

The listing contract for residential properties usually authorizes the broker to use licensees employed by the broker as well as the services of other cooperating brokers in marketing the seller's real estate. In the creation of an agency relationship, the broker is generally appointed as the sole agent transacting on the principal's behalf. Therefore, any salesperson of that broker or brokerage is considered an agent of the managing broker, and as a result, also becomes a **subagent** of any principal who is using the firm's services. In addition, it should be noted that any **cooperating agent** (the broker from another company who finds the buyer) may be acting as

- a *subagent* of the seller,
- an agent for the listing broker (broker's agent), or
- an agent for the buyer.

Buyer as Principal

The practice of buyers hiring brokers to find the desired real estate is becoming more common. In this situation, the broker and the buyer usually draw up an agreement that details the nature of the property desired, the amount of the broker's compensation, and how it is to be paid. This arrangement can also be created orally. (See the sample buyer agency agreement in Chapter 3.) The buyer becomes the *principal,* or the broker's *client.* In this case, the broker, as agent, is the **buyer's broker** and is strictly accountable to the buyer. The seller becomes the *customer* or the third party to the transaction.

The same relationships apply when a prospective tenant hires a broker to locate property for rent.

Broker as Principal

A broker is licensed to act as the principal's agent and thus can collect a commission for performing assigned duties. A salesperson or associate broker, on the other hand, has no authority to make contracts or receive compensation directly from a principal.

All of a salesperson's activities must be performed

- in the name of the supervising broker and
- under the direct control and supervision of the employing broker.

Brokers are fully responsible for the real estate actions of all salespersons licensed under them. *The broker is the salesperson's principal.*

The salesperson functions as an *agent* of the broker and a *subagent* of the principal (the buyer or the seller). Thus, both the broker and the broker's salespersons and associate brokers have a fiduciary relationship with the principal.

Basic Agency Relationships

Before we discuss the fiduciary responsibilities owed to principals by their agents, it is important to take a quick look at the types of agency relationships that may exist in a given transaction. The first agency relationship is between the seller and the listing broker. The broker agrees to perform diligently to find a ready, willing, and able buyer. The seller is the principal; the broker is the agent.

The broker typically employs licensed salespersons to assist in the disposition of the broker's duties. The licensed salesperson or associate broker helps the broker to list and market property. The salespersons are the agents of the broker and the subagents of the seller. Both the listing broker and the affiliated salespersons owe their fiduciary duties to the seller (unless otherwise agreed).

The listing broker and cooperating brokers from other firms that share listing information will begin to market the listed property. As they do so, they work with various prospective buyers. Cooperating brokers and salespersons who choose to represent the seller owe their fiduciary duties to the seller, not the buyer. They fall under the category of subagents. However, some cooperating brokers may be working under a buyer-broker agency agreement (which need not be in writing) and represent the buyer. They owe their fiduciary duties to the buyer, not the seller. Others may work not as subagents but simply as cooperating brokers.

Compensation from more than one party in a transaction   As discussed earlier, compensation has nothing to do with whom a licensee owes their allegiance to. Fact situations may arise in which a broker may encounter the need or opportunity to receive compensation from both parties in a transaction. As discussed in Chapter 1, in accordance with penalties indicated in the license law, an agent may not collect compensation from two parties within the same transaction unless the following two events have occurred:

1. The agent has provided to all the interested parties to that transaction full disclosure of the joint compensation.

2. The agent has received the informed consent to proceed from all the interested parties to the transaction.

Dual agency   Dual agency is defined as representing both parties within the same real estate transaction. The broker has two clients in the same transaction.

As is the case in any situation in which the parties demand loyalty and partiality, it is rarely possible for the broker to offer **undivided loyalty** to two or more principals in the same transaction. Thus, real estate license laws prohibit a broker from representing and/or collecting compensation from both parties to a transaction without their prior knowledge and written consent.

More difficult to handle is the situation in which a seller's broker, for example, emotionally adopts a buyer and unconsciously begins to work for the buyer's best interest, so that an unintended, undisclosed, and therefore illegal dual agency results.

A common complaint against agents is that of **undisclosed dual agency.** This relationship occurs when an agent acts in the best interests of one party to a transaction while legally representing the other party.

An example might be when a buyer's agent sells a close relative's property to a client without the **informed consent** of that client.

Another example might be when an agent and customers meet in an open house environment and warm up to each other. The customers may have no interest in the property covered by the open house but may request that the agent show them other properties. Although the agent conducting the open house may not intend to create a buyer/agent relationship, one may simply arise out of implication by the agent accepting the assignment. *In an open house, it is safe to conclude that the licensee conducting the open house is always an agent of the seller and cannot offer buyer representation on the premises without the permission of the seller client.* In order to avoid this situation, the agent is advised to make the relationship clear before commencing any working relationship with the customer. Section 175.7 requires that real estate brokers always make it clear for which party they are acting.

Self-dealing   Problems can also occur when a broker lists property, then decides to buy it and collect the agreed-on commission. This is called **self-dealing.** At that point, those brokers represent themselves but continue to act as the sellers' agents as well. Agents in this position are advised to give up the listing, collect no commission, and just represent themselves as buyers.

Self-dealing also occurs when licensees employed by a broker attempt to acquire or dispose of real property for their own account. Most employment contracts between licensees and their employing brokers prohibit any self-dealing unless it is accomplished in the name of the brokerage with whom the licensee is registered.

For example, a salesperson wishes to place this advertisement in the classified section of the newspaper: "House for sale by owner. Contact Ian at 555-5555."

Although license law does not prohibit licensees from selling their own property, it does establish procedures for how this should be done.

As it stands, the ad the salesperson wants to place is considered a blind ad, which is not permitted. A blind ad is defined as any ad that does not identify the advertiser as a licensee. (See Chapter 1.)

A situation like this one falls under the restrictions of the self-dealing section of an employment contract, and the responsibility falls to broker-employers to exert their authority over the activities of salespersons or associate brokers in such cases.

■ FIDUCIARY RESPONSIBILITIES

Brokers have the right to reject agency contracts that in their judgment violate the law, ethics, or high standards of their office. After a brokerage relationship has been established, however, brokers owe the principal a host of duties, including the exercise of care, skill, and integrity in carrying out lawful instructions.

In particular, each agency relationship requires that the agent provide the principal with six primary **fiduciary duties,** which can be memorized as CC-LOAD (see Figure 2.1):

1. Care
2. Confidentiality
3. Loyalty
4. Obedience
5. Accounting
6. Disclosure

An agent's **fiduciary relationship** with the principal is a relationship of the highest form of trust and confidence. (Other types of fiduciaries include trustees, executors, guardians, managing agents, banks, and attorneys.) If the principal cannot count on the agent to act in the principal's best interest, the agency relationship is meaningless.

Care

Brokers must exercise **reasonable care** while transacting business entrusted to them by a principal. In the eyes of the law, the individual licensee is considered an

FIGURE 2.1

Agent's Responsibilities

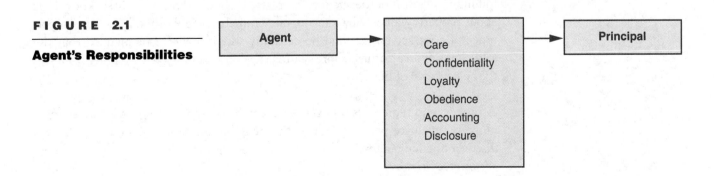

expert. Therefore, real estate brokers are expected to have special skills and expertise in the real estate field. The definition of *care* includes a licensee's obligation to exercise diligence on behalf of the client. Brokers must be knowledgeable about real property laws, land-use issues, financing, transfer of title, and the like.

Brokers should be skilled in the following areas:

- Valuing property (to determine a reasonable listing price and a reasonable purchase price)
- Clarifying the principal's needs
- Discovering pertinent facts about the neighborhood, the property, and the parties to the transaction and disclosing this information to the principal
- Filling in and explaining in simple terms the purpose and effect of the contract forms involved (the listing agreement or buyer agency agreement and the purchase contract), while never engaging in the practice of law (unauthorized practice of law can result in license revocation as well as other civil penalties)
- Recommending that the principal seek expert advisers (such as attorneys, accountants, or inspectors) when appropriate
- Making best efforts to sell or find the property
- Explaining different financing options available from local lenders
- Negotiating offers and counteroffers
- Meeting deadlines

If a broker represents the seller, care and skill include helping the seller arrive at an appropriate and realistic listing price; discovering facts that affect the seller and disclosing them; properly presenting the contracts that the seller signs; making reasonable efforts to market the property, such as advertising and holding open houses; and helping the seller evaluate the terms and conditions of offers to purchase.

For example, suppose a broker sells a home a few days after the listing agreement is signed. While the seller is initially pleased with the quick sale, she later realizes that the broker set the listing price too low. The seller also discovers that plans for a nearby shopping center were approved a few months ago. When the shopping center is completed in eight months, her property will be worth even more. The broker, who claimed to be an expert on her neighborhood, had no idea about the new shopping center. There were also several clauses in the sales contract that the seller didn't understand. When she asked the broker about them, he shrugged off her concern. Now she realizes that the clauses were important and were not to her advantage. If she had understood their effect, she would have consulted an attorney. The broker breached his duty to exercise reasonable care and skill when fulfilling the terms of the agency contract. He should have had a basic knowledge about property values, new developments in the neighborhood, and the importance of contract terms. And he certainly should have recommended that the seller consult an attorney before signing the contract or make the contract subject to the approval of her attorney.

A broker who represents a buyer is expected to help that buyer locate suitable property; evaluate property values, the neighborhood, and property conditions; discover financing alternatives; and handle offers and counteroffers with the buyer's interest in mind.

For example, the buyer's broker might discover that the seller is facing foreclosure if the property is not sold promptly but doesn't relay that information to the buyers. If the buyers had known, they might have bought the property for less than the amount they offered. The broker violated fiduciary duty to the buyer.

The broker is liable to the principal for any loss resulting from the broker's negligence or carelessness.

Confidentiality

An agent may not disclose any confidential information learned from or about the principal. For example, if the agent is representing the seller, information about the principal's financial condition may not be disclosed to potential buyers, including the fact that the principal will accept a price lower than the listing price. The same rule applies to any confidential facts that might harm the principal's bargaining position, such as the fact that the seller must quickly move out of the area. Similarly, a buyer's broker would not reveal the buyer's readiness to pay more if necessary.

Confidential information may never be revealed, even if it would mean a larger commission or a quicker closing date for the agent. Even after the agency relationship has terminated—for instance, after the sale has closed—confidential information should be kept confidential.

A broker may not maintain **confidentiality**, however, if the information is something the broker is obligated to disclose because of the duty to deal honestly with a customer. For example, if the seller's broker knows about a hazardous condition on the property or that the roof leaks or the plumbing needs repairs, such information must be disclosed to the buyer.

The agent should exercise extreme care to avoid violating the responsibility of confidentiality when communicating or dealing with other agents. For example, a common occurrence in the real estate industry is dealing with cooperating agents (particularly those not employed by the listing broker). Cooperating agents may ask whether the listing price is negotiable. Listing agents should *never* imply or reply that the price is negotiable because their principal would then likely never achieve an amount equal to or greater than the listed price. The listing agent would be guilty of violating the fiduciary responsibility of confidentiality. This would lead to disciplinary action against the licensee.

Loyalty

The duty of **loyalty** dictates that an agent must always place the principal's interests above those of all other persons, including the agent's own interests. The seller's agent, for example, must try to obtain the highest possible price, the buyer's agent to obtain the lowest. The agent must never take advantage of a chance to profit at the principal's expense.

For example, an offer with a lower purchase price may be in the seller's best interest because of the financing terms, closing date, or other concessions. The agent must exert maximum effort to negotiate such an offer, even though it may mean a smaller commission.

Even when agents find themselves working for no compensation, they must have the interests of their principals in mind before considering themselves.

Obedience

The fiduciary relationship obligates the broker to obey the legal and reasonable instructions of the principal.

This duty of **obedience** is not absolute, however. The broker may not obey any instructions that are unlawful or unethical. For example, the broker may not follow instructions to make the property unavailable to members of a minority group or to conceal a defect in the property, such as a leaking roof.

Brokers who know or have reason to suspect that a client will ask them to do something unlawful or unethical should either refuse to accept the listing or terminate an existing listing.

Accounting

Brokers must be able to report the status of all funds belonging to others that are entrusted to their possession. Real estate license laws require that brokers give duplicate originals of all documents to all parties affected by such documents and keep copies of them on file for *three years*. In addition, brokers must immediately deposit all funds entrusted to them in special accounts with titles that must include the words *trust* or *escrow*. It is illegal for brokers to commingle (mix) such monies with business operating funds or personal funds or to retain any interest such monies earn. This duty to account to the principal is also called **accountability**.

Disclosure

It is the broker's duty to pass on to the principal all facts or information the broker obtains that might affect the principal's decisions. The duty of **disclosure** is sometimes known as the *duty of notice*. It includes not only useful information the broker knows but also relevant information or *material facts* that the agent should have known. (A material fact is any fact that affects the value of the property and is important to a person making a decision.) Under the theory of law known as "presumption of knowledge," this applies to anything "the broker should have known."

In the course of a transaction, principals must make critical decisions. Agents must supply their clients with all the material facts so that the principals may make informed choices.

The broker must volunteer pertinent information, whether or not the client knows enough to ask for it. For example, a broker has presented an offer to her principal, the seller. The offer involves seller financing (the buyer will make a small down payment, and the seller will finance the difference between the down payment and the purchase price). The broker knows that the buyer has a history of defaulting on his obligations. Even though the seller does not ask the broker about the buyer's credit history, the broker must express a concern and perhaps recommend that the seller require the buyer to obtain a preapproved mortgage. In many cases, a broker may be held liable for damages for failure to disclose material facts.

Some types of information considered imperative to disclose include the following:

- *The relationship between an agent and other parties to the transaction.* For instance, if the agent is representing the seller and the buyer is a relative of the agent, the agent must disclose that fact to the seller. Other relationships that must be disclosed include those with close friends and close business associates.
- *Whether agents are acting for themselves (self-dealing).* New York forbids brokers and salespersons to buy or sell property in which they have a personal interest without informing the seller or purchaser of that interest. It is prudent to make such a disclosure in writing as part of the purchase contract before it is signed. If a buyer's broker has a similar type of relationship with the property seller, that relationship must be fully disclosed to the buyer.
- *The existence of other offers.* All offers should be *immediately* submitted to the principal until the sale is closed. The seller's agent must remember that it is up to the principal to reject or accept an offer; it is not the agent's job to evaluate the offers and submit only the most favorable. Failing to submit all offers immediately is a violation of license law. This requirement applies even to properties that are in contract and waiting to close.
- *The status or form of the earnest money deposit.* The seller's agent always must inform the principal if the earnest money is in the form of a promissory note or a postdated check. If the broker fails to do so and the seller cannot collect on the note or check, the broker may be liable to the seller for the amount of the deposit.
- *The buyer's financial condition.* If the seller's broker knows of any negative information about the buyer, the broker must inform the seller at once. The buyer's broker, however, must keep the buyer's financial condition confidential, unless to do so would breach the agent's duty to treat the seller honestly.
- *The value of the property.* One reason that sellers use real estate brokers to market their properties and buyers use brokers to help them purchase properties is that brokers have expertise in the area of property values. Brokers must always give their true opinions of a property's value and should never inflate that value to obtain a listing or complete a sale. Brokers would be wise to disclose the sales prices of comparable properties, including those the brokers should know about if they had studied the marketplace. The buyer's broker should suggest the lowest price the buyer should pay based on comparable values and how long a property has been listed or why the seller is selling.
- *Any commission split.* The listing broker should disclose to the seller any fee-sharing arrangement with a cooperating broker. This means that the listing broker must describe to the seller the general company policy regarding cooperating with subagents, cooperating agents, and buyer's agents. This usually occurs at the time the listing agreement is entered into.

- *Contract provisions.* Brokers must explain to their client the important provisions of any contract the client is going to sign. If the client requires anything more than a simple explanation, the broker must advise the client to seek competent legal advice.
- *Property deficiencies.* A broker representing a buyer must disclose the deficiencies of a property as well as contract or financing issues that are not to the buyer's benefit.

Breach of Fiduciary Duties

If agents breach their fiduciary duties, they may be subject to a variety of penalties. Some of these penalties can be imposed regardless of whether the agent's breach of duties caused the principal any actual harm. Penalties for breaching fiduciary duties may include the following:

- Loss of the commission
- Loss of the agent's license or other disciplinary action by the state
- Adverse judgment in a civil suit (defined as a lawsuit where violations of civil law have allegedly occurred)
- Rescission (voiding) of the transaction by court order

Scope of Authority

While agents must fulfill their fiduciary responsibilities, they must also act within the scope of their authority. Real estate agents, who are almost always special agents, have only the authority granted to them by their listing or buyer broker agreements. For example, the listing broker is authorized to find a ready, willing, and able buyer but generally has no authority to sign contracts for the seller, initial changes to an offer, receive the purchase price on behalf of the seller, or permit early occupancy.

The authority granted to a listing broker should be stated expressly in the listing agreement. In a typical listing contract, the seller specifically authorizes the broker to place a sign on the property, advertise, show property, cooperate with other brokers, and accept earnest money deposits.

Usually, the broker is not given the right to sign contracts, although in exceptional cases, the broker may be appointed as **attorney-in-fact** under a separately granted power of attorney. (One need not be an attorney to be appointed an attorney-in-fact.)

A buyer's broker is generally given the authority to seek out appropriate property. The broker is not usually given the right to sign a purchase contract on behalf of the buyer.

Agent's Responsibilities to Other Parties in the Transaction

Even though an agent's primary responsibility is to the principal, the agent also has obligations to third parties. The duties to the third party or customer include

- fair and honest dealing;

- disclosure of material facts that the licensee knows or should know that affect the desirability or value of the property (or the buyer's ability to complete the transaction) and that are not easily discoverable by the customer; and
- accounting for all monies belonging to others and trusted in the licensee's possession.

Opinion versus fact   Whatever the specific topic, brokers, salespeople, and other staff members must be careful about the statements they make to third parties. They must be sure that the customer understands whether the statement is an *opinion* or a *fact*. Statements of opinion are only permissible as long as they are offered as opinions and without any *intention to deceive*. When rendering an opinion, the agent should ensure that the customer does not solely rely on this opinion in the purchase of the property.

For instance, a broker is showing a house to buyers and says, "This house has the best view in the neighborhood." This statement is obviously a statement of opinion, and because the buyers can look out the window and judge the view for themselves, the statement is not intended to deceive.

Statements that exaggerate a property's benefits are called **puffing**. If the broker in the previous example said, "This house has the best view in the whole county— no, the whole state!" her statement would be considered puffing. It is an obvious exaggeration. Puffing is considered a sales tactic and is legal. However, real estate agents must be careful to make sure that their puffing is not accepted by buyers as fact. For instance, telling a prospective buyer that a home "will appreciate at least 50 percent in the next five years" may be an exaggeration, but it is also a misleading statement that a buyer might easily accept as a fact. Licensees must be sure that none of their statements can be interpreted as *fraudulent*. **Fraud** is the *intentional misrepresentation of a material fact in such a way as to harm or take advantage of another person*.

Misrepresentations   One of the most common complaints against real estate agents is that of **misrepresentation**. Misrepresentations violate the broker's obligation of honest dealing. Most complaints come from buyers.

To successfully sue a real estate agent for misrepresentation, the plaintiff (the one bringing the suit) must be able to prove that

- the broker made a misstatement (oral or written) to the buyer or failed to disclose a material fact to the buyer that should have been disclosed;
- the broker either knew or should have known that the statement was not accurate or that the information should have been disclosed;
- the buyer reasonably relied on such statement; and
- the buyer was damaged as a result of that reliance.

Misrepresentation can be an *affirmative* (intentional) statement, such as "A new roof was put on this house three years ago," when the broker knows that the roof is 12 years old. It can also be a failure to disclose a latent defect (discussed previously). For instance, if the broker knows the basement regularly floods but does not disclose that fact to the buyer, the broker is guilty of misrepresentation.

The misstatement does not have to be intentional to be misrepresentation. Real estate agents can be liable for misrepresentation if they knew or *should have known* a statement was false.

Brokers around the country have been held liable for misrepresentations in the following types of cases:

- *Termite infestation.* The broker, acting for the seller, plastered over termite damage.
- *Free of liens and encumbrances.* The broker mistakenly told the buyer that the seller owned the property free and clear of all encumbrances.
- *Filled land.* The broker made an unauthorized statement to the buyer that the property was not a "filled lot." (The house later sank when the fill settled.)
- *Easements.* When a buyer asked a broker about easements on a property, the broker said not to worry. Three months later, the city used the easement to lay water pipes.
- *Zoning.* The broker misrepresented the property's zoning.

If a contract to purchase real estate is obtained as a result of misstatements made by a broker or salesperson, the contract may be disaffirmed or renounced by the purchaser. In such a case, the broker will lose a commission. If either party suffers loss because of misrepresentations, the broker can be held liable for damages.

For the buyer's broker, a hidden defect requiring disclosure to the seller would be the buyer's financial inability or unwillingness to complete the purchase. Take, for example, a buyer who filed for bankruptcy two years ago. The buyer, through a broker, intends to submit an offer to purchase that would be contingent on the buyer obtaining financing. Because a buyer's broker who knows of a bankruptcy is required to disclose that fact to the seller, the buyer's broker would not be guilty, in this case, of violating the fiduciary responsibility of confidentiality. Bankruptcy would generally affect any buyer's ability to obtain future financing, so it becomes a material fact concerning the buyer's ability to perform and conclude a transaction, and as such it requires disclosure. In the reverse, if no financing contingency was required for the sale to take place, no disclosure would be required on the part of the buyer or the buyer's broker.

Environmental concerns   Disclosure of environmental health hazards, which can render properties unsalable, also may be required. Frequently, the buyer or the buyer's mortgage lender will request inspections or tests to determine the presence or level of risk. Licensees are urged to obtain advice from state and local authorities responsible for environmental regulation whenever toxic-waste dumping, contaminated soil or water, nearby chemical or nuclear facilities, or health hazards such as radon, mold, asbestos, or lead paint may be present.

Latent defects   Brokers and salespersons should be aware that some courts have ruled that a seller is responsible for revealing to a buyer any material (important) latent defects relating to the property. A **latent** (or hidden) **defect** is one that is not discoverable by ordinary, reasonable inspection; that is, it is simply not visible to the human eye without further inspection. Regardless of whether the agent represents the buyer or the seller, the broker likewise is responsible for disclosing known hidden defects to the buyer. Buyers have been able either to rescind the sales contract or to receive damages when latent defects are not revealed. Examples of such hidden defects include a leaking underground oil storage tank, a buried drain tile that causes water to accumulate, and a driveway built partly on adjoining property.

New York courts are continuing to rule on the duties of real estate agents toward their customers. While the traditional principle of caveat emptor (let the buyer beware) is still the law, it has been modified in certain circumstances to require both the seller and the broker to disclose known material facts. Today, with new seller property condition disclosure requirements, one can almost say "let the seller beware." To protect themselves from liability in this area, brokers should ask the seller for all the pertinent facts about the physical condition of the property. Brokers do not have to complete a detailed physical inspection; asking the seller for all pertinent facts should be sufficient. Although sellers may be understandably reluctant to discuss such facts, brokers can assure sellers that such disclosure will protect sellers from potential liability, protect brokers from potential liability, and enable brokers to market property in the most effective way possible.

Today, most listing agreements contain clauses intended to protect brokers against a seller's lack of property condition disclosure. Sellers, in most cases, will be asked to warrant and represent to listing brokers that they have disclosed all material facts known to them at the time they entered into the listing agreement. This clause may even include an indemnity (hold harmless) section that provides protection to brokers against any liability that arises or results from a seller's lack of disclosure to a broker.

According to the Department of State, Division of Licensing Services, it is not the broker's duty to verify all of the seller's representations, unless the broker uses such representations in marketing the property. However, if the broker knows *or has reason to know* that the seller has indeed made a misrepresentation or failed to disclose material facts, the broker is required to make a full disclosure. Remember the following:

- A broker acts as an agent.
- An agent is one who transacts on behalf of others; therefore, it is safe to deduce that an agent is a direct extension of the principal and, as such, may be held equally responsible for lack of making property condition or other material disclosures that would affect the price of the property.

New York State requires sellers to furnish prospective buyers with a 48-item Property Condition Disclosure Statement, which is discussed in Chapter 3.

Stigmatized properties   In a New York Supreme Court Appellate Division case, *Stambovsky v. Ackley* (the haunted house case), a seller was held responsible for failing to disclose that a house was haunted. The court did rule that the broker was not at fault.

To clear up the problem of stigmatized properties, a 1995 amendment to the New York State Real Property Law (Section 443-a) provides that an owner, occupant, or agent need *not* disclose the fact that the property is or is suspected to be the site of a homicide, suicide, other death, or any other felony.

In addition, the fact that the property was ever owned or occupied by someone who had or was suspected to have the HIV infection or AIDS or any disease highly unlikely to be transmitted through occupancy of a dwelling also need not be disclosed.

Megan's Law   New York courts have held that brokers have no obligation to search the state records on which convicted pedophiles must register their addresses. A buyer's broker should, however, advise clients that the registry is available for public inspection.

To gain information about the possibility that crimes have been committed on a property, prospective purchasers may submit a written inquiry; and the sellers or the seller's agent may choose whether or not to respond to the inquiry.

■ THE BROKER'S COMPENSATION

The broker's compensation is specified in the listing agreement, management agreement, or other contract with the principal and is subject to negotiation between the parties. Compensation is usually computed as a percentage of the total amount of money involved, but it could be a flat fee or any other consideration.

Compensation usually is considered to be earned when the broker has accomplished the work for which the broker was hired after a seller accepts an offer from a ready, willing, and able buyer. A **ready, willing, and able buyer** is one who is *prepared to buy on the seller's terms, is financially capable, and is ready to take positive steps to complete the transaction.*

Many listing agreements contain a preclusive agreement (an "as, if, and when" clause) providing that the broker will not collect the commission unless and until the sale has actually closed. Brokers, however, are usually entitled to a commission if the transaction is not completed for any of the following reasons:

- The owners change their mind and refuse to sell (with no preclusive agreement as previously mentioned) when a licensee presents a full-price offer with no contingencies.
- The owners commit fraud with respect to the transaction.
- The owners are unable to deliver possession within a reasonable time.
- The owners insist on terms not in the listing (for example, the right to restrict the use of the property). The owners and the buyers agree to cancel the transaction.

In other words, *a broker generally is due a commission if a sale is not consummated because of the seller's default.* In rare situations, the commission may still be due even when it is the buyer who defaults.

Generally, three events entitle brokers to compensation under the law:

1. They must be the holder of a valid license at all times during the transaction and collection.
2. They were either employed under a listing or other employment agreement or were authorized to perform the services in question.
3. They were the procuring cause.

Note: In every transaction, items 2 and 3 above go hand in hand. In other words, the one who is either authorized or employed always ends up being the procuring cause.

Brokers are entitled to a fee if they are the **procuring cause of sale**; produce a ready, willing, and able buyer; or bring about a meeting of the minds. If several brokers disagree as to which one brought about a sale, the one with the best claim to be the procuring cause is that broker who brought the parties into agreement, as evidenced by the sales contract. A **meeting of the minds** is said to have taken place when the parties are in agreement on price, down payment, financing method, and other essential terms.

New York's Real Property Law makes it illegal for a broker to share a commission with unlicensed people. This regulation forbids any form of gift or compensation, such as giving a television to a friend for providing a valuable lead or paying finder's fees and portions of the commission.

Compensation by both parties is permissible if there is full knowledge and written consent of both parties.

Salesperson's Compensation

A salesperson's compensation is set by agreement between the broker and the salesperson. A broker may pay a salary to a salesperson or, more commonly, a share of the commissions from transactions originated by a salesperson (the commission "split"). *The salesperson may never accept compensation directly from any buyer or seller, and may not accept compensation from any broker (see paragraph directly below), except the one broker with whom he or she is associated* (Article 175.B).

A salesperson may, however, accept compensation from a former broker for fees earned while associated with that broker.

■ TERMINATION OF AGENCY

An agency may be terminated by the following:
- Death or incompetence of either party
- Destruction or condemnation of the property
- Expiration of the terms
- Mutual agreement
- Renunciation by agent
- Revocation by principal
- Bankruptcy
- Completion of the purpose

Because the agency relationship involves so many responsibilities, it is important to know how agencies are created and how they are terminated. An agency relationship may be terminated at any time (except when coupled with an interest) for any of the following reasons:

- Death or incompetence of either party (Although death will terminate an agency, it does not necessarily terminate a contract of sale or listing agreement that was entered into during life by the deceased party.)
- Destruction or condemnation of the property
- Expiration of the terms of the agency
- Mutual agreement to terminate the agency
- Renunciation by the agent or revocation by the principal (In New York, the principal acting in good faith always has the power to cancel a listing at any time. The principal may, however, be required to reimburse the broker for expenses if the principal cancels before the agency's expiration. Damages could be awarded to the agent if the principal acted in bad faith.)

- Bankruptcy of either party
- Completion or fulfillment of the purpose for which the agency was created

The question of when an agency relationship ends can be important. For example, suppose agent John listed and sold Margaret's property. Three weeks after closing, Margaret shows up at one of John's open houses. Is Margaret still John's client? Probably not, but John must clarify this with Margaret. Because it is often difficult to treat a former client as a customer, some firms will obtain a written dual agency consent agreement from both parties or enter into a buyer agency relationship with the former client.

The broker may not disclose to a new client any information obtained in confidence from a former client during the agency relationship. Even though the agency relationship may have terminated, the duty of confidentiality has not.

ANTITRUST

Each brokerage is free to set its own fee schedules and to negotiate different charges with individual clients. Any agreement between two different firms to set standard rates, however, is a serious violation of antitrust laws. Additionally, any agreement between two or more companies to boycott some other company is a violation. The subject of boycotting has taken on greater importance recently with the emergence of discount brokerages. Discount brokerage firms offer "unbundled" services in return for low fees. In some cases, the only service offered may be entering the client's property into the local **multiple listing service** (MLS).

Real estate licensees must refrain from any discussion of fees except when two firms are cooperating on the sale of a multiple-listed property. Merely remaining in the room while prohibited discussions are going on has been considered evidence of guilt in the past. Antitrust violations can have drastic consequences.

ANTITRUST LAWS

The real estate industry is subject to federal and state antitrust laws.

Antitrust can be defined as any business activity that would otherwise result in

- a monopoly and/or
- a restraint of trade, and
- that would be deemed a harmful act or
- that would act as an impedance against free enterprise and competition.

Four distinct acts violate antitrust laws:

1. Price-fixing
2. Group boycotts
3. Market-allocation agreements
4. Tie-in arrangements

We will examine each of the four violations shortly, but first let's look at the history of these laws.

History of Antitrust Laws

In 1890, the **Sherman Act** was enacted into law. Previous to the enactment of the law, a variety of business monopolies began to develop. This required government to react to this dilemma. In 1914, the **Federal Trade Commission (FTC)** was created by Congress with powers that included

- overseeing business practices,
- the ability to declare that certain trade practices were deemed unfair, and
- enforcing compliance with the Sherman and Clayton Acts.

Similarly, in 1914, the **Clayton Act** was created. Its purpose was to supplement the Sherman Act (which lacked the teeth for enforcement); the act itself covered the same general purpose of the Sherman Act. The Sherman and Clayton acts prohibit the four activities detailed in the following paragraphs.

Price-Fixing

Illegal **price-fixing** occurs when competing brokers get together to set commission rates, rather than letting competition in the open market establish those rates. This is deemed by the federal authorities to be a *conspiracy to price fix*.

A conspiracy is defined as *two or more persons or parties acting in a manner that would otherwise negatively impact the ability of others to compete within a marketplace*.

Each real estate company, of course, is free to set its own fee schedule and to negotiate various rates with individual buyers or sellers if it wishes. The violations occur *when competing firms agree to act together*, in what the U.S. Justice Department calls **restraint of trade**.

It's not that simple, though. Real estate companies—and agents—have been prosecuted under the Sherman Antitrust Act for what appeared to be innocent discussions with agents from other firms. A licensee should walk away immediately, even from what might seem like the most trivial conversation about rates with someone from another brokerage. (The only exception might be a conversation about a particular property the two firms have cooperated in selling.)

For example, broker Max and broker Ian are owners of two competing real estate firms. As friendly competitors, they meet for dinner. Ian asks Max, "What are you guys getting these days for commission rates on sale transactions?"

The resulting conversation would be considered conspiracy to *price fix*.

Group Boycott

In the past, discussions about the negative qualities of a third company have been interpreted as a **group boycott**—a conspiracy to boycott that firm and drive it out of business. Licensees must learn which topics must be avoided when engaging in conversation with agents from other companies.

For example, broker Mark and broker Eileen are owners of two competing real estate firms. They are also friendly competitors. One night over a casual dinner,

Mark brings to Eileen's attention that ABC Realty, a real estate brokerage firm, has just come to town. Mark suggests to Eileen, "Let's not do business with ABC Realty. Maybe they'll just go away."

This would be considered a conspiracy to *group boycott*.

Market Allocation

Market allocation might occur when competing firms agree to split up an area and refrain from doing business in one another's territories.

For example, as in the group boycott example above, broker Maggie and broker Isabel, owners of two friendly competing real estate firms, are meeting for coffee. Isabel suggests to Maggie, "You have always done business primarily on the east side of town, while I have always done business on the west side of town. Why don't we draw an imaginary line down the center of town, and I won't do business in your area if you don't do business in my area."

This would be a *market-allocation agreement*.

Tie-in Arrangement

A **tie-in arrangement** normally occurs when a selling party conditions the sale of an item. The condition might require the buyer (as a prerequisite to the purchase of that item) to purchase another unrelated item or the seller will refuse the sale of the original item to the buyer.

For example, a buyer approaches a seller to purchase the seller's property. As a condition of sale, the seller requires the buyer to obtain title insurance *only from the seller's title company or mortgage company* or the seller will not sell the property to the buyer.

That would be considered a *tie-in arrangement*.

Penalties for violating antitrust laws   Penalties for violating antitrust laws exist for individuals and business entities.

Violation of the Sherman and Clayton acts for *individuals* bears one or both of the following penalties:

1. Fines of up to $350,000
2. Felony prison sentencing of up to three years

The Department of Justice may impose other fines, and the FTC, which has no penal sanctions, has powers of enforcement as they relate to the Sherman and Clayton acts.

Violation of the Sherman and Clayton acts for *business entities* bears one or both of the following penalties:

1. Fines of up to $10,000,000
2. Other fines imposed by the Department of Justice

It should be noted that the great disparity in fines between business entities and individuals is meant to compensate for the fact that a business entity cannot serve a prison sentence; therefore, heavy fines are assessed to deter a repeat offense.

■ SUMMARY

The law of agency covers the legal relationship between real estate brokers and salespersons and the sellers, buyers, landlords, and tenants who hire them to assist in real estate transactions. The person who hires an agent is known as the principal, or client. The relationship between them is known as a fiduciary one, a relationship of trust and confidence. Third parties with whom the agent deals are simply customers. The client is owed specific fiduciary duties. The customer is owed only honest dealing.

A universal agent may represent the client in all matters. A general agent such as a property manager is entrusted with a specific range of matters. Most real estate brokers act as special agents and are authorized to represent the client in one specific matter.

An agency can be created by an express agreement, oral or written, or by the action of the parties. An agent does not necessarily represent the party that pays the compensation. Dual agency, in which the broker represents both parties, is a difficult situation, but legally possible if both parties give written consent to the situation.

The agent's fiduciary duties to the principal include reasonable care, confidentiality (except when it would mean dishonesty to the customer), loyalty, and obedience to lawful instructions, accounting, and disclosure. Agents need not disclose the existence of "stigmas" on the property, but like the seller, they are responsible for disclosing latent, or hidden, defects.

The broker's compensation may be in the form of a percentage of the sales price, a fixed fee, or an hourly wage. By law, it is considered earned when the broker presents a ready, willing, and able buyer. However, the broker and principal/client can always modify this and determine that the brokerage commission shall not be deemed earned until further action, for example, a contract signing or closing has occurred.

An agency can be terminated by the death, bankruptcy, or incompetence of either party; destruction of property; expiration of the term of the agency agreement; renunciation by the agent or revocation by the principal; or completion of the purpose for which the agency was created. The duty of confidentiality, however, lasts after the agency has ended.

However, when a listing agreement is executed, the relationship between broker and buyer or seller is contractual and the language of the contract controls. For example, if a seller signs an exclusive right-to-sell agreement and the seller dies during the term, the listing agreement does not terminate.

Antitrust laws prohibit competing brokers from discussing or publishing commission rates charged to clients. Brokers also must refrain from negative discussions about other brokers to avoid the appearance of a group boycott.

In conclusion, it is important that all representation agreements and agency disclosures be in writing.

CHAPTER 2 QUIZ

1. Which of the following *BEST* describes the relationship between broker and seller under a listing agreement?
   a. Special agency
   b. General agency
   c. Ostensible agency
   d. Universal agency

2. A broker hired by an owner to sell a parcel of real estate *MUST* comply with
   a. all instructions of the owner.
   b. the law of agency.
   c. the principle of estoppel.
   d. all instructions of the buyer.

3. A buyer's broker is told by the buyer that he had filed for bankruptcy the year before. The buyer's broker
   a. should discuss with the buyer her duty to reveal the bankruptcy to the MLS.
   b. is required to disclose this material fact to the seller.
   c. may politely refuse to provide any information to the seller that would violate her duty of confidentiality to the buyer.
   d. has no responsibility to the seller because she is the buyer's agent.

4. A listing may be terminated when either broker or principal
   a. gets married.
   b. goes bankrupt.
   c. overfinances other property.
   d. becomes terminally ill.

5. When retained by the buyer, the broker owes a prospective seller
   a. obedience to lawful instructions.
   b. confidentiality about the seller's financial situation.
   c. fair and honest dealing.
   d. undivided loyalty.

6. Which of the following *BEST* describes a licensee representing both parties in the same transaction?
   a. Fraud
   b. Puffing
   c. Dual agency
   d. General agency

7. A seller who wishes to cancel a listing agreement in New York
   a. must cite a legally acceptable reason.
   b. may not cancel without the agent's consent.
   c. may be held liable for damages by the broker.
   d. may not sell the property for six months afterward.

8. A broker is able to collect a commission from both the seller and the buyer only when
   a. the broker holds a state license.
   b. the buyer and the seller are related.
   c. both parties have been provided with full disclosure and have given the broker their informed consent.
   d. both parties have attorneys.

9. A house was purchased in 1950 for $4,500. The seller knows properties have appreciated and asks the broker to try to sell it for $100,000. The broker knows the value could be more than $200,000. The broker should
   a. take the listing as offered and sell it quickly.
   b. purchase the house himself for the full $100,000, including in the contract that he is a licensed broker.
   c. buy the house through his aunt, who has a different last name.
   d. tell the seller that the house is worth much more.

10. An example of a latent defect would be a
    a. large crack in the dining room ceiling.
    b. roof with warped shingles.
    c. used-car lot next door.
    d. malfunctioning septic tank.

11. Commissions usually are earned when
    a. the buyer makes a purchase offer.
    b. the seller accepts the buyer's offer without conditions.
    c. a new mortgage has been promised by the lender.
    d. the title to the property is searched.

12. Even if a proposed transaction does not go through, the broker sometimes may collect a commission if the
    a. buyer turns out to be financially unable.
    b. seller refuses to do repairs required by the lender.
    c. seller commits willful default and backs out.
    d. lender does not appraise the house for the sales price.

13. A meeting of the minds occurs when the
    a. seller signs a listing agreement.
    b. buyer is introduced to the seller.
    c. buyer and seller agree on the price and terms of the sale.
    d. final closing (settlement) of the transaction takes place.

14. A property owner signed a 120-day listing with Greater Realty. After 60 days, the owner decided not to sell. He told Greater Realty he no longer wanted the agency to market his house. When is the agency of Greater Realty terminated?
    a. On the 121st day
    b. After a reasonable time
    c. On the 61st day
    d. When the listing expires

15. A seller's broker must disclose to a prospective buyer that the
    a. heating system does not work well.
    b. last owner was murdered there.
    c. seller has AIDS.
    d. house is haunted.

16. In the spirit of cooperation, a broker approached two other community brokers and recommended that they set standard fee schedules and commission rates. This recommendation is
    a. legal if other community brokers are allowed to participate in the agreement.
    b. legal if the agreement is in writing.
    c. illegal if salespersons working for the brokers are not consulted.
    d. illegal under any circumstances.

17. To successfully sue a broker for misrepresentation, the buyer must be able to prove that
    a. the buyer asked the broker to verify the misstatement.
    b. the misstatement is in writing.
    c. the buyer was damaged from relying on the truth of the statement.
    d. the seller knew of the statement.

18. A seller's willingness to accept a buyer's offer for a lot only if the buyer will purchase homeowners' insurance from the seller's insurance brokerage is an example of
    a. a tie-in arrangement.
    b. a market allocation agreement.
    c. price-fixing.
    d. a restraint of trade.

19. A broker does not think the seller will seriously consider an offer he received for 20 percent less than the listing price. The broker
    a. should discourage the potential buyer from making the offer.
    b. should encourage the potential buyer to increase the offer.
    c. should wait until he receives more realistic offers and present all offers together.
    d. is required to submit the offer to the seller.

20. An acronym to help remember the fiduciary duties of a broker is
    a. CC-MOAP.
    b. CC-LOAD.
    c. CL-DOAL.
    d. PP-COLA.

CHAPTER

3

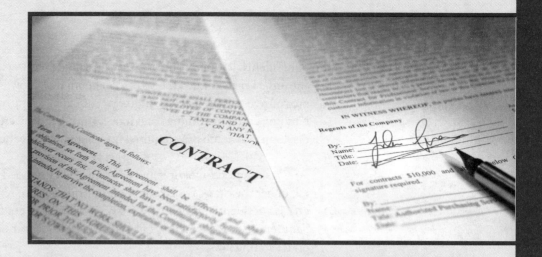

Agency and Real Estate Brokerage

■ KEY TERMS

advance consent to dual agency

advance consent to dual agency with designated sales associate

agency disclosure forms

Bedbug Disclosure Law

broker's agent

commercial transaction

dual agency

exclusive-agency listing

exclusive right to represent

exclusive-right-to-sell listing

first substantive contact

listing broker

open listing

Article 14 – Property Condition Disclosure Act

residential transaction

selling broker

subagency

undisclosed dual agency

vicarious liability

■ NEW YORK AGENCY DISCLOSURE REQUIREMENTS

New York's Real Property Law (RPL), Section 443 requires that brokers and salespersons give prospective sellers and buyers (or landlords and tenants), upon first substantive contact, a disclosure statement that describes the roles of sellers' agents, buyers' agents, listing brokers' agents, and dual agents. (See Figures 3.1 and 3.2.) Buyers or sellers are asked to sign an acknowledgment certifying that they have read the disclosure form and understand the role of the particular agent in the transaction. The written disclosure is intended, among other things, to warn members of the public not to reveal to the other party's agent any information they would prefer to keep confidential.

RPL 443-1f applies to residential transactions involving four or fewer units intended for dwelling purposes.

A **residential transaction** is defined as *any transaction involving the sale or lease of four or fewer units intended for dwelling purposes*. However, it *does not include* unimproved real property. Before January 1, 2011, cooperative or condominium units in a building containing more than four dwelling units were exempt from providing the disclosures that are now required under the new Agency Disclosure Law.

Any transaction involving five or more units intended for dwelling purposes would fall under the category of a **commercial transaction**, regardless of whether the property is a residential property. It is important not to confuse the definition of *residential transaction* (as explained above) with the definition of *residential* as a category under zoning laws.

New Agency Disclosure Law

On August 31, 2010, New York State Governor David Paterson signed into law amendments to the state's real estate agency disclosure law. The new law went into effect January 1, 2011.

The purpose of this law was to increase transparency of the real estate process and offer increased protections for consumers and real estate brokers. In addition, this law was also intended to facilitate residential real estate transactions. By doing so, the law works to alleviate any further confusion by the public concerning which party is represented by a real estate broker.

The amendments to Section 443 greatly impact real estate brokers by requiring that **agency disclosure forms** be completed for all residential transactions. In addition, the law also contains a provision permitting consumers to now give their **advance consent to dual agency** representation (this subject will be covered in greater detail later in this chapter). The advance consent to a dual agency is where the party agrees in advance to allow the agent to act in a dual agent capacity.

It is important to note that in addition to the advanced consent to a dual agency, the broker is obligated to provide a later disclosure *when the dual agency relationship has been actually created*. Failure to provide this follow-up disclosure would be treated as a violation of the broker's fiduciary duties of

- full disclosure, and
- providing reasonable care to the consumer.

Furthermore, the aforementioned would be a direct demonstration of the broker's untrustworthiness in the transaction; a violation pursuant to Section 441-c of the Real Property Law.

Before this law took effect, verbal consent for agency disclosure was acceptable for multifamily buildings over four units. Cooperative and condominium properties that contained greater than four units were also excluded/exempted from having to provide these disclosure forms to the respective interested parties to the transaction. The new law specifically states that a written agency disclosure form must be used on all residential transactions. Under the new law, the exclusion/exemption for these properties has been eliminated.

The amendments have created a section on the agency disclosure form where consumers can now give advanced consent to being represented by two agents from the same real estate broker in the same transaction. This is referred to as **advance consent to dual agency with designated sales associate.**

These amendments will ensure that brokers and consumers are legally protected by requiring written disclosure in all residential transactions. The advanced consent provision benefits all parties to the transaction. For example, licensees who show numerous listings to potential buyers would not need to have separate agency disclosure forms prior to showing each listing. This is an important distinction, particularly for New York City licensees. These licensees frequently represent or assist buyers and, as a result, may show numerous availabilities before a transaction occurs. The advance consent provision of the law now reflects the realities of the broad state marketplace and better serves to facilitate the transaction.

Signed Acknowledgments

A listing agent should obtain the seller's signed acknowledgment before entering a listing agreement for a residential transaction. Likewise, a buyer's agent should obtain the buyer's signed acknowledgment before entering an agreement to represent the buyer. In 2006, the New York legislature passed a bill replacing the agency disclosure form with separate forms for sales and lease transactions and defining allowable dual agency. The law took effect January 1, 2007, and revisions went into effect on January 1, 2008.

A seller's agent *must* provide the disclosure and obtain the acknowledgment from all prospective buyers or their buyer agents at the time of the **first substantive contact.** First substantive contact with a buyer occurs when the buyer walks into the agent's office and begins discussing the buyer's real estate needs or financial situation, or when the buyer meets the agent at the advertised listed property with the intent to inspect the property for purchase. Disclosure should be made to the buyer *prior to* entering the property being shown.

Similarly, buyers' agents must provide the disclosure to the seller or the seller's agent at the time of first substantive contact. That might occur when the seller begins explaining the reasons for selling or simply greets an agent who is showing someone through the property. A copy of the required disclosure is shown in Figure 3.1. A similar form is used for landlord-tenant agency disclosures (see Figure 3.2).

Section 175.23a of the rules for guidance of real estate brokers and salespersons promulgated by the New York secretary of state (titled "Records of transactions to be maintained") requires each licensed broker to keep and/or maintain transaction records obtained in the course of a broker's business—with copies of the signed agency disclosure forms—for no less than three years from conclusion of business.

FIGURE 3.1

Agency Disclosure Form for Buyer and Seller

New York State
DEPARTMENT OF STATE
Division of Licensing Services
P.O. Box 22001
Albany, NY 12201-2001

Customer Service: (518) 474-4429
www.dos.state.ny.us

New York State Disclosure Form for Buyer and Seller

THIS IS NOT A CONTRACT

New York State law requires real estate licensees who are acting as agents of buyers or sellers of property to advise the potential buyers or sellers with whom they work of the nature of their agency relationship and the rights and obligations it creates. This disclosure will help you to make informed choices about your relationship with the real estate broker and its sales agents.

Throughout the transaction you may receive more than one disclosure form. The law may require each agent assisting in the transaction to present you with this disclosure form. A real estate agent is a person qualified to advise about real estate.

If you need legal, tax or other advice, consult with a professional in that field.

Disclosure Regarding Real Estate Agency Relationships

Seller's Agent

A seller's agent is an agent who is engaged by a seller to represent the seller's interests. The seller's agent does this by securing a buyer for the seller's home at a price and on terms acceptable to the seller. A seller's agent has, without limitation, the following fiduciary duties to the seller: reasonable care, undivided loyalty, confidentiality, full disclosure, obedience and duty to account. A seller's agent does not represent the interests of the buyer. The obligations of a seller's agent are also subject to any specific provisions set forth in an agreement between the agent and the seller. In dealings with the buyer, a seller's agent should (a) exercise reasonable skill and care in performance of the agent's duties; (b) deal honestly, fairly and in good faith; and (c) disclose all facts known to the agent materially affecting the value or desirability of property, except as otherwise provided by law.

Buyer's Agent

A buyer's agent is an agent who is engaged by a buyer to represent the buyer's interests. The buyer's agent does this by negotiating the purchase of a home at a price and

on terms acceptable to the buyer. A buyer's agent has, without limitation, the following fiduciary duties to the buyer: reasonable care, undivided loyalty, confidentiality, full disclosure, obedience and duty to account. A buyer's agent does not represent the interest of the seller. The obligations of a buyer's agent are also subject to any specific provisions set forth in an agreement between the agent and the buyer. In dealings with the seller, a buyer's agent should (a) exercise reasonable skill and care in performance of the agent's duties; (b) deal honestly, fairly and in good faith; and (c) disclose all facts known to the agent materially affecting the buyer's ability and/or willingness to perform a contract to acquire seller's property that are not inconsistent with the agent's fiduciary duties to the buyer.

Broker's Agents

A broker's agent is an agent that cooperates or is engaged by a listing agent or a buyer's agent (but does not work for the same firm as the listing agent or buyer's agent) to assist the listing agent or buyer's agent in locating a property to sell or buy, respectively, for the listing agent's seller or the buyer agent's buyer. The broker's agent does not have a direct relationship with the buyer or seller and the buyer or seller can not provide instructions or direction directly to the broker's agent. The buyer and the seller therefore do not have vicarious liability for the acts of the broker's agent. The listing agent or buyer's agent do provide direction and instruction to the broker's agent and therefore the listing agent or buyer's agent will have liability for the acts of the broker's agent.

Dual Agent

A real estate broker may represent both the buyer and seller if both the buyer and seller give their informed consent in writing. In such a dual agency situation, the agent will not be able to provide the full range of fiduciary duties to the buyer and seller. The obligations of an agent are also subject to any specific provisions set forth in an agreement between the agent, and the buyer and seller. An agent acting as a dual agent must explain carefully to

F I G U R E 3.1

Agency Disclosure Form for Buyer and Seller (continued)

both the buyer and seller that the agent is acting for the other party as well. The agent should also explain the possible effects of dual representation, including that by consenting to the dual agency relationship the buyer and seller are giving up their right to undivided loyalty. A buyer or seller should carefully consider the possible consequences of a dual agency relationship before agreeing to such representation. A seller or buyer may provide advance informed consent to dual agency by indicating the same on this form.

Dual Agent with Designated Sales Agents

If the buyer and seller provide their informed consent in writing, the principals and the real estate broker who represents both parties as a dual agent may designate a sales agent to represent the buyer and another sales agent to represent the seller to negotiate the purchase and sale of real estate. A sales agent works under the supervision

of the real estate broker. With the informed consent of the buyer and the seller in writing, the designated sales agent for the buyer will function as the buyer's agent representing the interests of and advocating on behalf of the buyer and the designated sales agent for the seller will function as the seller's agent representing the interests of and advocating on behalf of the seller in the negotiations between the buyer and seller. A designated sales agent cannot provide the full range of fiduciary duties to the buyer or seller. The designated sales agent must explain that like the dual agent under whose supervision they function, they cannot provide undivided loyalty. A buyer or seller should carefully consider the possible consequences of a dual agency relationship with designated sales agents before agreeing to such representation. A seller or buyer may provide advance informed consent to dual agency with designated sales agents by indicating the same on this form.

This form was provided to me by _____ (print name of licensee) of _____ (print name of company, firm or brokerage), a licensed real estate broker acting in the interest of the:

    (____) Seller as a (check relationship below)   (____) Buyer as a (check relationship below)

        (____) Seller's agent   (____) Buyer's agent

        (____) Broker's agent   (____) Broker's agent

                        (____) Dual agent

                        (____) Dual agent with designated sales agent

For advance informed consent to either dual agency or dual agency with designated sales agents complete section below:

        (____) Advance informed consent dual agency

        (____) Advance informed consent to dual agency with designated sales agents

If dual agent with designated sales agents is indicated above: _____ is appointed to

represent the buyer; and _____ is appointed to represent the seller in this transaction.

(I) (We) _____ acknowledge receipt of a copy of this disclosure

form: signature of {   } Buyer(s) and/or {   } Seller(s):

_____   _____

_____   _____

Date: _____   Date: _____

DOS-1736-a (Rev. 11/10)

FIGURE 3.2

Agency Disclosure Form for Landlord and Tenant

New York State
DEPARTMENT OF STATE
Division of Licensing Services
P.O. Box 22001
Albany, NY 12201-2001

Customer Service: (518) 474-4429
www.dos.state.ny.us

New York State Disclosure Form for Landlord and Tenant

THIS IS NOT A CONTRACT

New York State law requires real estate licensees who are acting as agents of landlords and tenants of real property to advise the potential landlords and tenants with whom they work of the nature of their agency relationship and the rights and obligations it creates. This disclosure will help you to make informed choices about your relationship with the real estate broker and its sales agents.

Throughout the transaction you may receive more than one disclosure form. The law may require each agent assisting in the transaction to present you with this disclosure form. A real estate agent is a person qualified to advise about real estate.

If you need legal, tax or other advice, consult with a professional in that field.

Disclosure Regarding Real Estate Agency Relationships

Landlord's Agent

A landlord's agent is an agent who is engaged by a landlord to represent the landlord's interest. The landlord's agent does this by securing a tenant for the landlord's apartment or house at a rent and on terms acceptable to the landlord. A landlord's agent has, without limitation, the following fiduciary duties to the landlord: reasonable care, undivided loyalty, confidentiality, full disclosure, obedience and duty to account. A landlord's agent does not represent the interests of the tenant. The obligations of a landlord's agent are also subject to any specific provisions set forth in an agreement between the agent and the landlord. In dealings with the tenant, a landlord's agent should (a) exercise reasonable skill and care in performance of the agent's duties; (b) deal honestly, fairly and in good faith; and (c) disclose all facts known to the agent materially affecting the value or desirability of property, except as otherwise provided by law.

Tenant's Agent

A tenant's agent is an agent who is engaged by a tenant to represent the tenant's interest. The tenant's agent does this by negotiating the rental or lease of an apartment or house at a rent and on terms acceptable to the tenant. A tenant's agent has, without limitation, the following fiduciary duties to the tenant: reasonable care, undivided loyalty, confidentiality, full disclosure, obedience and duty to account. A tenant's agent does not represent the interest of the landlord. The obligations of a tenant's agent are also subject to any specific provisions set forth in an agreement between the agent and the tenant. In dealings with the landlord, a tenant's agent should (a) exercise reasonable skill and care in performance of the agent's duties; (b) deal honestly, fairly and in good faith; and (c) disclose all facts known to the agent materially affecting the tenant's ability and/or willingness to perform a contract to rent or lease landlord's property that are not consistent with the agent's fiduciary duties to the tenant.

Broker's Agents

A broker's agent is an agent that cooperates or is engaged by a listing agent or a tenant's agent (but does not work for the same firm as the listing agent or tenant's agent) to assist the listing agent or tenant's agent in locating a property to rent or lease for the listing agent's landlord or the tenant agent's tenant. The broker's agent does not have a direct relationship with the tenant or landlord and the tenant or landlord can not provide instructions or direction directly to the broker's agent. The tenant and the landlord therefore do not have vicarious liability for the acts of the broker's agent. The listing agent or tenant's agent do provide direction and instruction to the broker's agent and therefore the listing agent or tenant's agent will have liability for the acts of the broker's agent.

Dual Agent

A real estate broker may represent both the tenant and the landlord if both the tenant and landlord give their in-

Agency Disclosure Form for Landlord and Tenant (continued)

formed consent in writing. In such a dual agency situation, the agent will not be able to provide the full range of fiduciary duties to the landlord and the tenant. The obligations of an agent are also subject to any specific provisions set forth in an agreement between the agent, and the tenant and landlord. An agent acting as a dual agent must explain carefully to both the landlord and tenant that the agent is acting for the other party as well. The agent should also explain the possible effects of dual representation, including that by consenting to the dual agency relationship the landlord and tenant are giving up their right to undivided loyalty. A landlord and tenant should carefully consider the possible consequences of a dual agency relationship before agreeing to such representation. A landlord or tenant may provide advance informed consent to dual agency by indicating the same on this form.

Dual Agent with Designated Sales Agents

If the tenant and the landlord provide their informed consent in writing, the principals and the real estate broker who represents both parties as a dual agent may designate a sales agent to represent the tenant and another sales agent to represent the landlord. A sales agent works under the supervision of the real estate broker. With the informed consent in writing of the tenant and the landlord, the designated sales agent for the tenant will function as the tenant's agent representing the interests of and advocating on behalf of the tenant and the designated sales agent for the landlord will function as the landlord's agent representing the interests of and advocating on behalf of the landlord in the negotiations between the tenant and the landlord. A designated sales agent cannot provide the full range of fiduciary duties to the landlord or tenant. The designated sales agent must explain that like the dual agent under whose supervision they function, they cannot provide undivided loyalty. A landlord or tenant should carefully consider the possible consequences of a dual agency relationship with designated sales agents before agreeing to such representation. A landlord or tenant may provide advance informed consent to dual agency with designated sales agents by indicating the same on this form.

This form was provided to me by _____ (print name of licensee) of _____

(print name of company, firm or brokerage), a licensed real estate broker acting in the interest of the:

    (____) Landlord as a (check relationship below)   (____) Tenant as a (check relationship below)

        (____) Landlord's agent   (____) Tenant's agent

        (____) Broker's agent   (____) Broker's agent

                  (____) Dual agent

                  (____) Dual agent with designated sales agent

For advance informed consent to either dual agency or dual agency with designated sales agents complete section below:

        (____) Advance informed consent dual agency

        (____) Advance informed consent to dual agency with designated sales agents

If dual agent with designated sales agents is indicated above: _____ is appointed to

represent the tenant; and _____ is appointed to represent the seller in this transaction.

(I) (We) _____ acknowledge receipt of a copy of this disclosure

form: signature of {   } Landlord(s) and/or {   } Tenant(s):

_____   _____

_____   _____

Date: _____   Date: _____

DOS-1735-a (Rev. 12/10)

RPL 443-3f states that should any buyer or seller refuse to sign the forms, the agent may make a written oath or affirmation that the disclosure form was provided to that party (see Figure 3.3). This statement can be kept in the broker's file in place of the signed acknowledgment. As is the case for all records of transactions held by the broker, they should be maintained for a minimum of three years following conclusion of the transaction (Section 175.23). It should be noted that the aforementioned disclosure form does not apply to commercial transactions.

RPL 443 ("Disclosure regarding real estate agency relationship form") also provides for brokers' agents. A **broker's agent** is a cooperating broker who is an agent of the listing broker but not strictly a subagent of the seller. A broker's agent has fiduciary duties to the seller, but the seller is not liable for acts of the broker's agent unless the seller specifically authorizes those acts. This is intended to eliminate a principal's "vicarious liability" for acts of subagents within a transaction. This liability usually arises from the acts of others. (Although this concept came directly from the Department of State, it remains to be seen whether this limited liability will be upheld by the courts.)

A second disclosure requirement is found in the Department of State (DOS) Regulation 175.7, which states, "A real estate broker shall make it clear for which party he is acting and he shall not receive compensation from more than one party except with the full knowledge and consent of all parties." This requirement applies to all types of transactions, not just residential.

The requirement regarding compensation from more than one party is not strictly limited to compensation related to the sale itself; *it applies to any compensation that is in any way related to the transaction.* Thus, a selling agent who accepts compensation for arranging the buyer's loan (mortgage broker's commission) must disclose this to the parties, in addition to sharing in the commission split (if any) for the sale.

FIGURE 3.3

Disclosure Affirmation

DECLARATION PURSUANT TO SECTION 443 (3) (F) OF THE REAL PROPERTY LAW

_____ (name), being duly sworn, deposes and says:

1. I am the principal broker/associate broker/licensed salesperson affiliated with _____ (name of agency).

2. I make this Affidavit in compliance with Section 443 (3) (F) of the New York State Real Property Law.

3. On the _____ day of _____ , 20____ , I presented to _____ (name of buyer or seller) the disclosure forms required pursuant to Section 443 of the Real Property Law. The form of the Disclosure Form as presented is attached to this statement.

4. The above named buyer/seller refused to execute an acknowledgment of the receipt of this disclosure form despite my request that it be executed.

5. A copy of this statement and additional copies of the Disclosure Form are being mailed to the person(s) named in paragraph 3, contemporaneously with the execution of this Affidavit.

_____

(Name)

Signing an agency disclosure form (which does not apply to commercial transactions) does not in and of itself create an agency relationship but also does not relieve the agent from other requirements under the law of agency. It is not a contract between agent and client. This form is intended to give full disclosure by a licensee to the appropriate party receiving the disclosure and to create awareness for the benefit of the general public. Merely having a prospective buyer sign the acknowledgment that a disclosure form stated that the broker was acting as a buyer's agent does not make it so. The relationship should be established through a separate written buyer-agency agreement, similar to the listing agreement used by sellers' agents.

■ AGENCY ALTERNATIVES

An agent is someone who represents a principal in a transaction. The agent owes the principal the duties of *reasonable care, confidentiality, loyalty, obedience, accounting,* and *disclosure of any facts* that might affect the principal's decisions. Agency relationships between a broker and a seller are usually created through a contractual agreement, for example, a written *listing agreement*, in which a broker agrees to act as the agent of a seller. Agency relationships between a broker and a buyer are usually created through *buyer-broker agency agreements*. In either case, whether one enters into a listing agreement with a seller or a buyer-broker agreement with a buyer, both agreements will create the agency relationship. Both agreements can be thought of as "employment contracts."

Real estate brokers frequently enlist the help of other brokers to market their listed properties. In many places throughout the state of New York, a common example of this sort of collaboration is a *multiple listing service* (MLS) for residential properties. By using the MLS as a marketing vehicle, participating brokers agree to work together to achieve a sale. As a result, commissions are generally shared between the **listing broker** and the **selling broker** (the one who finds the buyer). Under certain circumstances, this arrangement *may* create a relationship referred to as **subagency**.

Subagency means that

- the selling broker is acting as a subagent of the seller, or
- the selling broker may be acting as the *broker's agent*.

Note: When a property is listed within the MLS, it will generally (unless otherwise posted) represent an "invitation to a subagency relationship." This means that a selling broker who accepts the offer of subagency through the MLS has fiduciary responsibilities that will be owed to the seller of the property. As in any invitation that one receives in life, acceptance is not mandatory; however, declaration and disclosure of the selling broker's relationship should be made at *first substantive contact*. However, several MLS contracts offer "cooperation" to various types of agents, not just subagents. Licensees should always be familiar with the agreements they will be using when practicing their trade.

For example, selling broker Mary Anne contacts a listing agent from the MLS. Mary Anne introduces herself as the buyer's broker, or as the exclusive agent on behalf of the buyer. That introduction is a rejection of the invitation to the subagency relationship offered through the MLS; not *all* MLS postings are invitations to subagency. Mary Anne is clearly stating that she will continue acting exclusively on behalf of her principal, a buyer, and will not take on the role of seller's agent, acting on behalf of the property's seller.

■ SUBAGENCY

When a broker accepts a listing from a seller, the agency relationship is clear:

- ■ The broker becomes the seller's agent.
- ■ By extension, any salespersons who work for the broker become subagents of the seller because they are agents of the broker.

The situation is less clear, however, in the case of another broker who procures a buyer for the property. Is the other broker acting as a subagent of the seller, an agent of the buyer, or an agent of the listing broker?

In the past, listed properties (particularly those offered through a multiple listing service) were offered on a "blanket unilateral offer of subagency." As a result of this arrangement, the party (someone not in the employ of the seller's listing broker) procuring the buyer would act as a subagent of the seller. As a subagent of the seller, this party owed fiduciary responsibilities to the seller and would not act as the buyer's agent. This arrangement created vicarious liability (responsibility for the actions of another) to the seller. Today, although this form of agency relationship still exists, it is not as common as in the past. There are alternative agency relationships that eliminate a seller's vicarious liability.

Brokerage without Subagency

As a principal, the seller is liable for actions not only of the listing agent but also of subagents. This potentially enormous liability—for human rights violations, among other problems—is the reason that some sellers do not want to offer any form of subagency relationship.

A seller who does not wish to offer subagency to MLS members but still wants to gain exposure through an MLS can direct that the listing agent may split the commission with another broker who produces the buyer, without the other broker acting as the seller's subagent. The seller agrees to pay the selling broker part of the commission but does not risk being held liable for any statements or actions on the part of the selling broker. With more and more buyers being represented by their own brokers these days, this simple offer of cooperation and commission sharing solves problems that used to arise about how the buyer's broker was to be paid.

Please note that although New York City does not have a formalized MLS, the attorney general's office has ruled (by letter) that if the selling agent is from a different brokerage company than the listing agent, the selling agent is a buyer's agent and not a subagent of the seller or selling agent.

Disclosure of Subagency

Buyers who use the services of a seller's broker to find a property often believe the broker is working on their behalf when, in fact, the broker has a fiduciary duty to act in the best interest of the seller.

For example, Jameson is looking for a house. She contacts Mendez, a broker, who shows her many houses over the course of several weeks. Jameson tells Mendez the kind of house she is looking for and gives him information about her ability to buy and her time frame for buying. By the time Jameson finds a house she is interested in, she feels very comfortable with Mendez and begins to think of Mendez as her real estate agent. In fact, Mendez is a subagent of the seller. Jameson makes an offer on the house, telling Mendez that she is willing to pay up to $8,000 more than her initial offer. Mendez has a duty to relay this information to the seller, who immediately counteroffers with a higher selling price. Because she wrongly believed Mendez to be acting on her behalf, Jameson will end up paying more for the house than she otherwise might have.

The written Agency Disclosure Statement shown in Figure 3.1, which Jameson should have received at the outset, should have warned her that Mendez, however helpful, was working for the seller and could not keep her information confidential.

■ DUAL AGENCY

In New York, within specific parameters, dual agency is a legal form of agency relationship. In a **dual agency**, the broker represents both buyer and seller in the same transaction. Because the buyer and seller have competing goals, dual agency represents an inherent conflict of interest for the broker. It is often impossible for a dual agent to fully satisfy the fiduciary requirements of confidentiality and full disclosure with respect to both parties in a transaction. Consequently, dual agency by its nature may involve something less than full representation of each client and must be undertaken with care. In a dual agency relationship, the parties give up their right to full disclosure and undivided loyalty from the dual agent.

Disclosure of any information concerning either party to the transaction becomes a violation of that party's fiduciary relationship with the agent that acts in a dual capacity. This is a very dangerous relationship for the agent because any comment can be construed by either party to the transaction as favoritism of one party over the other.

In 1997, Florida became the first state to outlaw dual agency relationships.

Informed Consent

Dual agency is legal; however, it is legal only with

- the full disclosure by the agent to all interested parties to the transaction, and
- the receipt by the agent of the informed consent of all interested parties to the transaction.

Before January 1, 2011, the aforementioned had to occur before the creation of the agency. Currently, under the new amendment to Section 443, advance consent to this type of arrangement is now permissible.

The advanced informed consent can now be secured simply by checking off the appropriate box on a *written disclosure form document* and signed by all the interested parties. This document should indicate that the parties consent to the dual agency and understand that

- the agent may not provide undivided loyalty to either party;
- the parties' confidential information regarding pricing strategy will be protected, as well as any other information agreed to by the parties;
- the agent may be paid fees as specified, by either one or both parties;
- dual agency does involve potential conflicts of interest because one principal may feel compromised unfairly or one might be favored over the other;
- if either principal is uncomfortable with the dual agency process, that principal should not proceed; and
- the parties should have obtained their attorneys' advice before proceeding in a dual agency situation.

There is no blanket consent to dual agency. Each agreement must apply only to specific parties.

When dual agency exists but is not fully disclosed or consented to by the parties, the broker faces serious consequences. These include loss of license or other disciplinary action, loss of commission on the sale, and liability for damages if the sale is rescinded. Because of these risks, brokers must be constantly aware of the potential for *undisclosed dual agency* situations.

Undisclosed Dual Agency

A broker does not have to embark intentionally on a dual agency situation to suffer the consequences of undisclosed dual agency. In fact, **undisclosed dual agency** *is often unintentional*. Although the buyer and the seller may specifically request that a broker act as a dual agent, a dual agency situation may arise without the broker's realizing it. Examples of such situations include in-house sales and sales by cooperating brokers who are acting as buyers' agents.

In-house sales   Whenever a broker takes a listing, the broker is the agent, and all salespeople who work for the broker are agents of the broker and therefore subagents of the seller. This is true for all salespeople in all offices of the brokerage. Any time that a salesperson or broker acts as a buyer's agent (either explicitly or implicitly) with respect to any of the firm's own listings, dual agency exists, and appropriate steps must be taken to avoid liability.

Company policy   The possibility of dual agency should be discussed with clients at the time the agency agreement (listing or buyer's broker) is entered. Clients should be informed of the possibility of in-house sales and of the policy of the broker's office regarding such sales. Many real estate firms incorporate additional clauses relating to these situations within their agency agreements.

For example, a buyer's broker agreement may contain a provision that states, "When a buyer is brought to a listing that is handled by the same brokerage firm representing that buyer, in this event, the agent represents the seller and not the buyer." The agent is advised to exercise special care and to be clear about the agent's relationships in these types of situations. This is not intended to suggest that a dual agency is unlawful but to make clear that company policy may require the agent to work in this fashion. In either case, the agent should be cognizant of all applicable laws directing this subject.

■ SINGLE AGENCY

In a single agency, the broker represents only one of the parties in a transaction, either the buyer or the seller, but not both. The party represented by the broker is the *broker's principal or client*, and other parties or their agents are treated as customers by the broker. If the broker's client is the seller, the broker deals with buyers or their agents as customers only. If the buyer is the broker's client, sellers are treated as customers.

A single agency broker may choose to represent only sellers (seller agency) or only buyers (buyer agency), but also may choose to represent either, one at a time. This can lead to potential conflicts. A buyer-client (principal) might be interested in a property listed by a seller client (also a principal). When such situations arise, the single agency broker could formally terminate the agency relationship with the buyer. If this occurs, the broker also should inform the seller of the previous agency relationship with the buyer, although the broker may not disclose confidential information that was obtained during the time the buyer was a client. The broker may not, for example, disclose to the seller that the buyers are willing to pay x number of dollars for a property they really like because this is information the broker learned while representing those buyers. This situation would require careful handling.

Handling In-House Sales

A substantial part of many brokerage businesses consists of *sales of in-house listings* (listings generated by the same broker or the broker's licensees). As agents of the broker and subagents of the seller, all salespersons in the brokerage have an obligation to use their best efforts to find a buyer for properties that are listed with the brokerage. In-house sales also avoid the need to split the commission with another brokerage.

For example, Jane lists her home for sale with ABC Realty, and she also asks ABC to help her find a new home. She decides to make an offer on Fred's property, which is also listed with ABC. Because ABC is the agent of both Jane and Fred (as sellers), this situation gives rise to a dual agency. ABC cannot act as the selling broker in Jane's purchase from Fred without the informed consent of both parties. The same dilemma might arise even if Jane had no previous contact with ABC. She might have specifically hired one of its associates to act as her buyer's broker and then asked to see Fred's house. ABC would again be in the position of acting as agent for both buyer and seller.

Designated Agency

The DOS has approved a technique by which the in-house dual agency problem can be handled when a firm's buyer-client expresses interest in property that same company has listed. The secretary of state has stated that

you (the managing broker) can designate one of your agents to represent the buyer and another to represent the seller. If designated sales agents are appointed, the firm continues as a dual agent representing both the buyer and seller in the same trans-action. The designated sales agents, however, will, by virtue of the new agreement with the buyer and seller, function as single agents giving undivided loyalty to their respective clients.

Previously under Section 443, informed consent (by both parties) to dual agency and then informed consent to the designated agent arrangement had to be obtained (in each and every case) before the creation of same. Under the new amendment to Section 443, advance consent to this type of arrangement is now permissible.

Handling Cooperative Sales

Cooperation among brokers is common practice in the real estate industry. When a property is sold through a broker who is not the listing broker, it is important to clarify the agency relationships among all the people involved. Cooperating or selling brokers (or their salespeople) must inform the listing agent whether they are acting as a subagent of the seller, as an agent of the buyer, or simply as a broker's agent with no agency relationship with either buyer or seller. The relationship would affect the amount of information a listing agent would share about the seller's motivation or financial situation.

■ AGENCY FORMS

Most agency relationships of any type are created by written agreement between the agent and the principal. In the case of real estate agency, the relationship between the seller and the listing agent is defined by the *listing agreement*. The relationship between the buyer and the agent is defined by the *buyer broker agency agreement. Although it is prudent to have these agreements in writing, these relationships can also be created orally.*

In all commercial leasing transactions, it is not unusual for a broker to represent a tenant as a client. All the same requirements for disclosure, loyalty, and confidentiality apply to a tenant agency.

Listing Agreements

In New York, a licensee may enter into three authorized relationships:

1. Exclusive-right-to-sell listing
2. Exclusive-agency listing
3. Open listing

These relationships are created via listing agreements. The primary difference among these types of listings relates to the conditions under which the broker

Three Authorized Relationships in New York
- Exclusive-right-to-sell
- Exclusive-agency
- Open listing

will have earned a commission. Their similarities and differences are illustrated in Figure 3.4.

Exclusive-right-to-sell listing   The **exclusive-right-to-sell listing** provides the greatest protection for the broker. The broker under this arrangement has earned a commission if the property is sold during the listing term, regardless of who procures the buyer.

Exclusive-agency listing   An **exclusive-agency listing** entitles the broker to a commission if the property is sold during the listing term, unless the seller acting alone is the one who procures the buyer. In this relationship, unlike the exclusive-right-to-sell relationship, the seller reserves the right to conduct their own sale without compensating the exclusive agent. If the seller procures the buyer without involving any broker, no commission is due. In such cases, you may see two advertisements for the same property: one by the exclusive agent and one by the seller himself or herself.

Ultimately, the seller is acting in direct competition with the appointed agent to see who will produce the sale faster. Although this is the seller's right, it may not always be in the best interest of both agent and principal.

Open listing   The **open listing** is the least restrictive of the three types. In an open listing, the seller may employ any number of brokers and need pay a commission only to that broker who successfully produces a ready, willing, and able buyer. In essence, the seller will only pay a fee to the party that *effects a sale* and to no other. A seller who personally sells the property without the aid of any of the brokers is not obligated to pay any of them a commission. A listing contract generally creates an open listing unless the wording specifically provides otherwise. It should be noted that most open listings are not reflected in writing; however, special circumstances might call for the terms of the open listing to be memorialized.

While the open listing may seem the most favorable to the seller, it usually means that no one agent is motivated to spend a great deal of time or advertising money on the property, because no compensation will be due if someone else sells it first. Remember, brokers are businesspeople, too.

When a broker represents a landlord in procuring tenants for a property, the most common agreement is the *exclusive right to lease*, which is similar to the exclusive right to sell. The broker earns a commission if the property is leased during the term of the agreement, regardless of who procures the tenant.

F I G U R E   3.4

Types of Listing Agreements

Exclusive-right-to-sell	Exclusive-agency	Open listing
One broker	One broker	Multiple brokers
Broker entitled to a commission, regardless of who sells the house	Broker paid only if procuring cause	Only selling broker paid
	Seller retains right to sell without obligation	Seller retains right to sell without obligation

Exclusive right to lease   In this type of arrangement, a property owner engages one broker to act as the owner's exclusive leasing agent. As this arrangement directly resembles the exclusive-right-to-sell listing agreement, the only difference is that the subject property is being leased and not sold. This relationship is common in large commercial and residential projects. Regardless of which party procures the tenant/lessee, the exclusive leasing agent is paid a fee. With respect to disclosures under this relationship, Regulation 175.7 states clearly that brokers must always make it clear as to which party they represent in the transaction.

Net listing   With a net listing, the broker is free to offer the property for sale at any price. If the property is sold, the broker pays the seller only a certain net amount previously agreed on and keeps anything above that. *This type of listing is illegal in New York.* It lends itself to fraud and is seldom in the seller's best interest. It also violates fiduciary responsibilities owed to a principal by the agent. Today, very few states in the union allow this type of relationship to exist.

Multiple listing   Not a type of listing, a multiple listing service (MLS) is organized within a geographic area by a group of brokers who agree to distribute and share listing information.

The multiple-listing agreement, while not actually a separate form of listing, is in effect an exclusive-right-to-sell or exclusive-agency agreement with an additional authority to distribute the listing to other brokers who belong to the MLS. The obligations among member brokers of a multiple-listing organization vary widely. Most provide that on sale of the property the commission will be divided between the listing broker and the selling broker. Terms for division of the commission vary by individual arrangement among brokers.

Under most multiple-listing contracts, the broker who secures the listing is not only authorized but obligated to turn the listing over to the MLS within a definite period so that it can be distributed to other member brokers.

The Internet and multiple listing   Many brokers/brokerages showcase their listings on their own Web pages. Larger groups of listings are found on local, regional, and statewide multiple-listing Internet sites. Meanwhile, *Realtor.com* and other sites compete for the largest number of nationwide listings. In addition, several sites offer exposure to for-sale-by-owner (FSBO) properties.

As a result, most homebuyers today use the Internet to browse the market, particularly at the start of their searches. In the end, however, most sales are eventually made face to face through the services of a real estate broker. It is important to note that, for any property listed on the broker's Web site, when a sale occurs, the broker should immediately remove the listing from the for-sale section of the site. Failure to do so will subject the licensee to disciplinary action by the DOS.

Termination of listings   A listing, like any agency relationship, may be ended for any of the following reasons:

- Performance of the object (sale of the property)
- Expiration of the time period stated in the agreement
- Abandonment by a broker who spends no time on the listing

- Revocation by the owner (although the owner may be liable for the broker's expenses)
- Cancellation by the broker or by mutual consent
- Bankruptcy, death, or insanity of either party (unless contractual)
- Destruction of the property
- A change in property use by outside forces (such as a change in zoning)

All listings should specify a definite period during which the broker is to be employed. *The use of automatic extensions of time in exclusive listings is illegal in New York.*

For example, a listing agreement calls for the following terms: "For 180 days, after which, the agreement shall continue on a month-to-month basis until either party cancels the agreement with one week's notice."

This would be considered an automatic extension and is unlawful. All listing agreements must have a beginning date and an ending date. This does not mean that one cannot extend an agreement with a client; however, any extension should be arranged for with the client *prior to expiration of the listing agreement's original term.*

Information needed for listing agreements   When taking a listing, the broker must obtain as much information as possible on the parcel of real estate. This ensures that all possible contingencies can be anticipated, particularly when the listing will be shared in a multiple-listing arrangement. Some of the information accompanies the actual listing contract; some is furnished to prospective buyers on separate information sheets. The information includes the following (where appropriate):

- Names and addresses of owners
- Adequate description of the property
- Size of lot (frontage and depth; if irregular, square footage)
- Number and size of rooms and total square footage
- Construction and age of the building
- Information relative to the neighborhood (schools, transportation)
- Current taxes
- Amount of existing financing
- Utilities and average payments
- Appliances to be included in the transaction
- Date of occupancy or possession
- Possibility of seller financing
- Zoning classification (especially important for vacant land)
- Detailed list of exactly what personal property and which fixtures will or will not be included in the sales price

The listing agent should verify that the person offering the property for sale is the actual owner of the property. In New York City, ownership records can be found on the Department of Finance Web site under ACRIS, *www.nyc.gov/html/dof/html/jump/acris.shtml.* ACRIS stands for Automated City Register Information Service. The agent should also search the public records.

In addition, the agent should search the public records for information on zoning, lot size, and yearly taxes. The true tax figure must be used, disregarding any present veteran's, aged, disabled, senior apartment, Gold Star parent, STaR, or religious exemption, or any addition for unpaid water bills. However, when providing a customer with current property tax information, the licensee is cautioned to also provide full disclosure to the customer that the property tax in question will *only* remain at that amount within the year of sale and that the likelihood (as a result of the sale) is that the property tax will be higher in the following tax year(s). If the licensee has failed to be clear on this issue and the customer purchases the property relying solely on information regarding the lower property tax amount, future litigation and/or a complaint filed against the licensee with the DOS might result.

Seller disclosures   For one- to four-family dwellings, each buyer, before any binding contract of sale is signed, is entitled to receive a Property Condition Disclosure Statement from the seller. (See Figure 3.5.)

In New York State, every seller of residential real property is required to complete and sign a property condition disclosure statement. This requirement falls under subdivision two of **Article 14—Property Condition Disclosure Act**. Furthermore, the original disclosure form or a copy must be delivered to the buyer or the buyer's agent. Delivery of the disclosure document must occur prior to the signing by the buyer of a binding contract of sale for the property in question. At that point, under the Act, it is required that a copy of the property condition disclosure statement containing the signatures of both seller and buyer be attached to the real estate purchase contract.

The law does not prevent the parties to a contract of sale from entering into agreements with respect to the physical condition of the property to be sold. This includes, but is not limited to, agreements for the sale of real property "as is."

The property condition disclosure statement starts with "1. How long have you owned the property?" and proceeds through questions about the property's environment, structure, and mechanical conditions, to "48. The property is located in the following school district_____." Any buyer who does not receive the statement is entitled to a $500 credit toward purchase. Whether or not the seller provides the disclosure form has no effect on the seller's liability for undisclosed defects. A seller's agent should inform the client about the property disclosure form and provide a blank copy, but should offer no assistance in filling it out or any legal advice about ignoring it. The requirement and a listing of the penalties associated with the failure to provide the seller disclosure are contained in article 14 of the Real Property Law.

New York State requires that a functioning carbon monoxide detector and smoke alarm be installed in every one- or two-family house, co-op, or condo offered for sale. All sellers and landlords of housing built before 1978 must disclose the presence of known lead-based paint or lead-related hazards to prospective buyers/renters, both at the time of listing and later before the closing/renting. (See Figures 3.6, 3.7, 3.8, 3.9.) Another requirement for landlords is the installation of window guards if children under ten years of age will be living in the apartment. (See Figure 3.10.)

The disclosure would be included with the sample listing contract shown in Figure 3.12. Sellers and landlords must also provide a HUD/EPA booklet on the subject. Failure to comply with lead-paint disclosure requirements bears a penalty of $11,000 per occurrence.

Environmental hazards   When property is listed, questions should be raised about the possible presence of environmental hazards. The real estate broker must not assume expertise in these matters. It is enough to be alert for situations that might raise a red flag and to recommend, where it seems indicated, that the seller consult a licensed engineer. In some situations, an environmental audit may be indicated. As always, troublesome questions can be taken to an attorney. Environmental hazards are increasingly important, not only because buyers may suffer damage to their health but also because in some cases purchasers have been held responsible for cleanup costs tied to existing problems.

Rental income-producing property   In the sale of multifamily dwellings and other income-producing properties, the seller should be ready to present a reconstructed statement of income and expenses, preferably prepared by an accountant. A rent roll should show the name of each tenant, amount of rent, expiration date of each lease, and amount of security deposits. The listing agent should verify zoning and the legality of existing use. The seller should be informed of the need for a certificate of occupancy at transfer. Arranging with tenants to show the property at reasonable times also is important.

Truth-in-Heating Law   New York's Truth-in-Heating Law requires the seller to furnish, on written request, two past years' heating and cooling bills to any prospective buyer of a one- or two-family home. Sellers also must furnish a statement of the extent and type of insulation they have installed, together with any information they may have about insulation installed by previous owners.

Bedbug Disclosure Law   Due to the recent bedbug infestations throughout the nation, as of September 2010, New York City has amended its administrative code to include a new **Bedbug Disclosure Law**, Section 27-2018.1: "Notice of Bedbug Infestation History."

Section 27-2018.1 specifically requires the owner or the owner's managing agent to furnish a prospective tenant with a form (Notice Form) that provides any bedbug infestation history for the previous year. This information is directly associated with the rental unit in question. This disclosure is also intended to include any infestation history concerning the building where the rental unit is situated. The state Division of Housing and Community Renewal (DHCR) has created a notice form (see Figure 3.11). This form must be given to any tenant signing a lease after August 31, 2010.

In the event that a property owner or the owner's managing agent fails to provide this form, a tenant may file a written complaint with the DHCR at *www.dhcr. state.ny.us/Forms/* and the DHCR will order the property owner to provide the tenant with the form.

Property Condition Disclosure Statement

NYS Department of State
Division of Licensing Services
P.O. Box 22001
Albany, NY 12201-2001
(518) 474-4429
www.dos.state.ny.us

Property Condition Disclosure Statement

Name of Seller or Sellers: _____

Property Address: _____

_____

General Instructions:

The Property Condition Disclosure Act requires the seller of residential real property to cause this disclosure statement or a copy thereof to be delivered to a buyer or buyer's agent prior to the signing by the buyer of a binding contract of sale.

Purpose of Statement:

This is a statement of certain conditions and information concerning the property known to the seller. This Disclosure Statement is not a warranty of any kind by the seller or by any agent representing the seller in this transaction. It is not a substitute for any inspections or tests and the buyer is encouraged to obtain his or her own independent professional inspections and environmental tests and also is encouraged to check public records pertaining to the property.

A knowingly false or incomplete statement by the seller on this form may subject the seller to claims by the buyer prior to or after the transfer of title. In the event a seller fails to perform the duty prescribed in this article to deliver a Disclosure Statement prior to the signing by the buyer of a binding contract of sale, the buyer shall receive upon the transfer of title a credit of $500 against the agreed upon purchase price of the residential real property.

"Residential real property" means real property improved by a one to four family dwelling used or occupied, or intended to be used or occupied, wholly or partly, as the home or residence of one or more persons, but shall not refer to (a) unimproved real property upon which such dwellings are to be constructed or (b) condominium units or cooperative apartments or (c) property on a homeowners' association that is not owned in fee simple by the seller.

Instructions to the Seller:

a. Answer all questions based upon your actual knowledge.
b. Attach additional pages with your signature if additional space is required.
c. Complete this form yourself.
d. If some items do not apply to your property, check "NA" (Non-applicable). If you do not know the answer check "Unkn" (Unknown).

Seller's Statement:

The seller makes the following representations to the buyer based upon the seller's actual knowledge at the time of signing this document. The seller authorizes his or her agent, if any, to provide a copy of this statement to a prospective buyer of the residential real property. The following are representations made by the seller and are not the representations of the seller's agent.

GENERAL INFORMATION

1. How long have you owned the property? . . . .   _____

2. How long have you occupied the property? . . . .   _____

3. What is the age of the structure or structures? . . . .   _____
   Note to buyer – If the structure was built before 1978 you are encouraged to investigate for the presence of lead based paint..

4. Does anybody other than yourself have a lease, easement or any other right to use or occupy any part of your property other than those stated in documents available in the public record, such as rights to use a road or path or cut trees or crops? . . . .   ☐ Yes ☐ No ☐ Unkn ☐ NA

5. Does anybody else claim to own any part of your property? *If Yes, explain below* . . . .   ☐ Yes ☐ No ☐ Unkn ☐ NA

_____

F I G U R E   3.5

Property Condition Disclosure Statement (continued)

Property Condition Disclosure Statement

6. Has anyone denied you access to the property or made a formal legal claim challenging your
    title to the property? *If Yes, explain below* . . . . ☐ Yes ☐ No ☐ Unkn ☐ NA
    _____
    _____

7. Are there any features of the property shared in common with adjoining landowners or a
    homeowner's association, such as walls, fences or driveways? *If Yes, describe below* . . . . . ☐ Yes ☐ No ☐ Unkn ☐ NA
    _____
    _____

8. Are there any electric or gas utility surcharges for line extensions, special assessments or
    homeowner or other association fees that apply to the property? *If Yes, explain below* . . . . . ☐ Yes ☐ No ☐ Unkn ☐ NA
    _____
    _____

9. Are there certificates of occupancy related to the property? *If No, explain below* . . . . ☐ Yes ☐ No ☐ Unkn ☐ NA
    _____
    _____

ENVIRONMENTAL

Note to Seller:

In this section, you will be asked questions regarding petroleum products and hazardous or toxic substances that you know to have been spilled, leaked or otherwise been released on the property or from the property onto any other property. Petroleum products may include, but are not limited to, gasoline, diesel fuel, home heating fuel, and lubricants. Hazardous or toxic substances are products that could pose short or long-term danger to personal health or the environment if they are not properly disposed of, applied or stored. These include, but are not limited to, fertilizers, pesticides and insecticides, paint including paint thinner, varnish remover and wood preservatives, treated wood, construction materials such as asphalt and roofing materials, antifreeze and other automotive products, batteries, cleaning solvents including septic tank cleaners, household cleaners and pool chemicals and products containing mercury and lead.

Note to Buyer:

If contamination of this property from petroleum products and/or hazardous or toxic substances is a concern to you, you are urged to consider soil and groundwater testing of this property.

10. Is any or all of the property located in a designated floodplain? *If Yes, explain below* . . . . . ☐ Yes ☐ No ☐ Unkn ☐ NA
    _____
    _____

11. Is any or all of the property located in a designated wetland? *If Yes, explain below* . . . . . . ☐ Yes ☐ No ☐ Unkn ☐ NA
    _____
    _____

12. Is the property located in an agricultural district? *If Yes, explain below* . . . . ☐ Yes ☐ No ☐ Unkn ☐ NA
    _____
    _____

13. Was the property ever the site of a landfill? *If Yes, explain below* . . . . ☐ Yes ☐ No ☐ Unkn ☐ NA
    _____
    _____

FIGURE 3.5

Property Condition Disclosure Statement (continued)

Property Condition Disclosure Statement

14. Are there or have there ever been fuel storage tanks above or below the ground on the property? .... ☐ Yes ☐ No ☐ Unkn ☐ NA
    - If Yes, are they currently in use? .... ☐ Yes ☐ No ☐ Unkn ☐ NA
    - Location(s) _____

    _____
    - Are they leaking or have they ever leaked? *If Yes, explain below* .... ☐ Yes ☐ No ☐ Unkn ☐ NA
    _____
    _____

15. Is there asbestos in the structure? *If Yes, state location or locations below* .... ☐ Yes ☐ No ☐ Unkn ☐ NA
    _____
    _____

16. Is lead plumbing present? *If Yes, state location or locations below* .... ☐ Yes ☐ No ☐ Unkn ☐ NA
    _____
    _____

17. Has a radon test been done? *If Yes, attach a copy of the report* .... ☐ Yes ☐ No ☐ Unkn ☐ NA

18. Has motor fuel, motor oil, home heating fuel, lubricating oil or any other petroleum product, methane gas, or any hazardous or toxic substance spilled, leaked or otherwise been released on the property or from the property onto any other property? *If Yes, describe below* ..... ☐ Yes ☐ No ☐ Unkn ☐ NA
    _____
    _____

19. Has the property been tested for the presence of motor fuel, motor oil, home heating fuel, lubricating oil, or any other petroleum product, methane gas, or any hazardous or toxic substance? *If Yes, attach report(s)* .... ☐ Yes ☐ No ☐ Unkn ☐ NA
    _____
    _____

STRUCTURAL

20. Is there any rot or water damage to the structure or structures? *If Yes, explain below* ..... ☐ Yes ☐ No ☐ Unkn ☐ NA
    _____
    _____

21. Is there any fire or smoke damage to the structure or structures? *If Yes, explain below* .... ☐ Yes ☐ No ☐ Unkn ☐ NA
    _____
    _____

22. Is there any termite, insect, rodent or pest infestation or damage? *If Yes, explain below* ... ☐ Yes ☐ No ☐ Unkn ☐ NA
    _____
    _____

23. Has the property been tested for termite, insect, rodent or pest infestation or damage? .... ☐ Yes ☐ No ☐ Unkn ☐ NA
    If Yes, please attach report(s)

24. What is the type of roof/roof covering (slate, asphalt, other)? .... _____
    - Any known material defects? .... _____
    - How old is the roof? .... _____

F I G U R E   3.5

Property Condition Disclosure Statement (continued)

Property Condition Disclosure Statement

- Is there a transferable warrantee on the roof in effect now? *If Yes, explain below* . . . . .   ☐ Yes ☐ No ☐ Unkn ☐ NA

_____

_____

25. Are there any know material defects in any of the following structural systems: footings, beams, girders, lintels, columns or partitions? *If Yes, explain below* . . . .   ☐ Yes ☐ No ☐ Unkn ☐ NA

_____

_____

MECHANICAL SYSTEMS AND SERVICES

26. What is the water source? *(Circle all that apply)* . . . .   well,   private,   municipal, other: _____

- If municipal, is it metered? . . . .   ☐ Yes ☐ No ☐ Unkn ☐ NA

27. Has the water quality and/or flow rate been tested? *If Yes, describe below* . . . .   ☐ Yes ☐ No ☐ Unkn ☐ NA

_____

_____

28. What is the type of sewage system? *(Circle all that apply)* . . . .   public sewer,   private sewer, septic,   cesspool

- If septic or cesspool, age? . . . .   _____
- Date last pumped? . . . .   _____
- Frequency of pumping? . . . .   _____
- Any known material defects? *If Yes, explain below* . . . .   ☐ Yes ☐ No ☐ Unkn ☐ NA

_____

_____

29. Who is your electrical service provider? . . . .   _____
- What is the amperage? . . . .   _____
- Does it have circuit breakers or fuses? . . . .   _____
- Private or public poles? . . . .   _____
- Any known material defects? *If yes, explain below* . . . .   ☐ Yes ☐ No ☐ Unkn ☐ NA

_____

_____

30. Are there any flooding, drainage or grading problems that resulted in standing water on any portion of the property? *If Yes, state locations and explain below* . . . .   ☐ Yes ☐ No ☐ Unkn ☐ NA

_____

_____

31. Does the basement have seepage that results in standing water? *If Yes, explain below* . . . .   ☐ Yes ☐ No ☐ Unkn ☐ NA

_____

_____

Are there any known material defects in any of the following? *If Yes, explain below. Use additional sheets if necessary* . . . .

32. Plumbing system? . . . .   ☐ Yes ☐ No ☐ Unkn ☐ NA

33. Security system? . . . .   ☐ Yes ☐ No ☐ Unkn ☐ NA

34. Carbon monoxide detector? . . . .   ☐ Yes ☐ No ☐ Unkn ☐ NA

FIGURE 3.5

Property Condition Disclosure Statement (continued)

Property Condition Disclosure Statement

35. Smoke detector? . . . . ☐ Yes ☐ No ☐ Unkn ☐ NA

36. Fire sprinkler system? . . . . ☐ Yes ☐ No ☐ Unkn ☐ NA

37. Sump pump? . . . . ☐ Yes ☐ No ☐ Unkn ☐ NA

38. Foundation/slab? . . . . ☐ Yes ☐ No ☐ Unkn ☐ NA

39. Interior walls/ceilings? . . . . ☐ Yes ☐ No ☐ Unkn ☐ NA

40. Exterior walls or siding? . . . . ☐ Yes ☐ No ☐ Unkn ☐ NA

41. Floors? . . . . ☐ Yes ☐ No ☐ Unkn ☐ NA

42. Chimney/fireplace or stove? . . . . ☐ Yes ☐ No ☐ Unkn ☐ NA

43. Patio/deck? . . . . ☐ Yes ☐ No ☐ Unkn ☐ NA

44. Driveway? . . . . ☐ Yes ☐ No ☐ Unkn ☐ NA

45. Air conditioner? . . . . ☐ Yes ☐ No ☐ Unkn ☐ NA

46. Heating system? . . . . ☐ Yes ☐ No ☐ Unkn ☐ NA

47. Hot water heater? . . . . ☐ Yes ☐ No ☐ Unkn ☐ NA

_____

_____

_____

_____

48. The property is located in the following school district _____ ☐ Unkn

Note: Buyer is encouraged to check public records concerning the property (e.g. tax records and wetland and floodplain maps).

The seller should use this area to further explain any item above. If necessary, attach additional pages and indicate here the number of additional pages attached.

_____

_____

_____

_____

_____

_____

_____

_____

Property Condition Disclosure Statement (continued)

Property Condition Disclosure Statement

Seller's Certification:

Seller certifies that the information in this Property Condition Disclosure Statement is true and complete to the seller's actual knowledge as of the date signed by the seller. If a seller of residential real property acquires knowledge which renders materially inaccurate a Property Condition Disclosure Statement provided previously, the seller shall deliver a revised Property Condition Disclosure Statement to the buyer as soon as practicable. In no event, however, shall a seller be required to provide a revised Property Condition Disclosure Statement after the transfer of title from the seller to the buyer or occupancy by the buyer, whichever is earlier.

Seller's Signature

X _____   *Date* _____

Seller's Signature

X _____   *Date* _____

Buyer's Acknowledgment:

Buyer acknowledges receipt of a copy of this statement and buyer understands that this information is a statement of certain conditions and information concerning the property known to the seller. It is not a warranty of any kind by the seller or seller's agent and is not a substitute for any home, pest, radon or other inspections or testing of the property or inspection of the public records.

Buyer's Signature

X _____   *Date* _____

Buyer's Signature

X _____   *Date* _____

F I G U R E   3.6

Disclosure of Lead-Based Paint and Lead-Based Hazards

LEAD-BASED PAINT OR LEAD-BASED PAINT HAZARD ADDENDUM

It is a condition of this contract that, until midnight of _____ , Buyer shall have the right to obtain a risk assessment or inspection of the Property for the presence of lead-based paint and/or lead-based paint hazards* at Buyer's expense. This contingency will terminate at that time unless Buyer or Buyer's agent delivers to the Seller or Seller's agent a written inspection and/or risk assessment report listing the specific existing deficiencies and corrections needed, if any. If any corrections are necessary, Seller shall have the option of (i) completing them, (ii) providing for their completion, or (iii) refusing to complete them. If Seller elects not to complete or provide for completion of the corrections, then Buyer shall have the option of (iv) accepting the Property in its present condition, or (v) terminating this contract, in which case all earnest monies shall be refunded to Buyer. Buyer may waive the right to obtain a risk assessment or inspection of the Property for the presence of lead-based paint and/or lead based paint hazards at any time without cause.

*Intact lead-based paint that is in good condition is not necessarily a hazard. See EPA pamphlet "Protect Your Family From Lead in Your Home" for more information.

Disclosure of Information on Lead-Based Paint and Lead-Based Paint Hazards

Lead Warning Statement

Every Buyer of any interest in residential real property on which a residential dwelling was built prior to 1978 is notified that such property may present exposure to lead from lead-based paint that may place young children at risk of developing lead poisoning. Lead poisoning in young children may produce permanent neurological damage, including learning disabilities, reduced intelligence quotient, behavioral problems, and impaired memory. Lead poisoning also poses a particular risk to pregnant women. The Seller of any interest in residential real property is required to provide the Buyer with any information on lead-based paint hazards from risk assessments or inspections in the Seller's possession and notify the Buyer of any known lead-based paint hazards. A risk assessment or inspection for possible lead-based paint hazards is recommended prior to purchase.

Seller's Disclosure (initial)

_____ (a) Presence of lead-based paint and/or lead-based paint hazards (check one below):

❏ Known lead-based paint and/or lead-based paint hazards are present in the housing (explain).

_____

_____

❏ Seller has no knowledge of lead-based paint and/or lead-based paint hazards in the housing.

_____ (b) Records and reports available to the Seller (check one below):

❏ Seller has provided the Buyer with all available records and reports pertaining to lead-based paint and/or lead-based paint hazards in the housing (list documents below).

_____

_____

❏ Seller has no reports or records pertaining to lead-based paint and/or lead-based paint hazards in the housing.

Buyer's Acknowledgment (initial)

_____ (c) Buyer has received copies of all information listed above.

_____ (d) Buyer has received the pamphlet *Protect Your Family from Lead in Your Home.*

_____ (e) Buyer has (check one below):

❏ Received a 10-day opportunity (or mutually agreed upon period) to conduct a risk assessment or inspection for the presence of lead-based paint and/or lead-based paint hazards; or

❏ Waived the opportunity to conduct a risk assessment or inspection for the presence of lead-based paint and/or lead-based paint hazards.

Agent's Acknowledgment (initial)

_____ (f) Agent has informed the Seller of the Seller's obligations under 42 U.S.C. 4582(d) and is aware of his/her responsibility to ensure compliance.

Certification of Accuracy

The following parties have reviewed the information above and certify, to the best of their knowledge, that the information provided by the signatory is true and accurate.

Buyer: _____ (SEAL) Date _____

Buyer: _____ (SEAL) Date _____

Agent: _____ Date _____

Seller: _____ (SEAL) Date _____

Seller: _____ (SEAL) Date _____

Agent: _____ Date _____

F I G U R E   3.7

Disclosure of Information on Lead-Based Paint and/or Lead-Based Hazards (Leasing)

Disclosure of Information on Lead-Based Paint and/or Lead-Based Paint Hazards

Lead Warning Statement

Housing built before 1978 may contain lead-based paint. Lead from paint, paint chips, and dust can pose health hazards if not managed properly. Lead exposure is especially harmful to young children and pregnant women. Before renting pre-1978 housing, lessors must disclose the presence of known lead-based paint and/or lead-based paint hazards in the dwelling. Lessees must also receive a federally approved pamphlet on lead poisoning prevention.

Lessor's Disclosure.

(a) Presence of lead-based paint and/or lead-based paint hazards (Check (i) or (ii) below):

(i)_____ Known lead-based paint and/or lead-based paint hazards are present in the housing (explain).

_____

(ii)_____ Lessor has no knowledge of lead-based paint and/or lead-based paint hazards in the housing.

(b) Records and reports available to lessor (Check (i) or (ii) below):

(i)_____ Lessor has provided the Lessee with all available records and reports pertaining to lead-based paint and/or lead-based paint hazards in the housing (list documents below).

_____

(ii)_____ Lessor has no reports or records pertaining to lead-based paint and/or lead-based paint hazards in the housing.

Lessee's Acknowledgment (initial)

(c)_____ Lessee has received copies of all information listed above.

(d)_____ Lessee has received the pamphlet *Protect Your Family from Lead In Your Home.*

Agent's Acknowledgment (initial)

(e)_____ Agent has informed the lessor of the lessor's obligations under 42 U.S.C. 4852d and is aware of his/her responsibility to ensure compliance.

Certification of Accuracy

The following parties have reviewed the information above and certify, to the best of their knowledge, that the information they have provided is true and accurate.

_____	_____	_____	_____
Lessor	Date	Lessor	Date
_____	_____	_____	_____
Lessee	Date	Lessee	Date
_____	_____	_____	_____
Agent	Date	Agent	Date

FIGURE 3.8

New York City Lead Paint Notice

 (03/07)

NEW YORK CITY LEAD PAINT NOTICE
[To be Attached to the Lease of the Apartment]
LEASE/COMMENCEMENT OF OCCUPANCY NOTICE FOR PREVENTION OF LEAD-
BASED PAINT HAZARDS—INQUIRY REGARDING CHILD

You are required by law to inform the owner if a child under six years of age resides or will reside in the dwelling unit (apartment) for which you are signing this lease/commencing occupancy. If such a child resides or will reside in the unit, the owner of the building is required to perform an annual visual inspection of the unit to determine the presence of lead-based paint hazards. **IT IS IMPORTANT THAT YOU RETURN THIS FORM TO THE OWNER OR MANAGING AGENT OF YOUR BUILDING TO PROTECT THE HEALTH OF YOUR CHILD.** If you do not respond to this notice, the owner is required to attempt to inspect your apartment to determine if a child under six years of age resides there.

If a child under six years of age does not reside in the unit now, but does come to live in it at any time during the year, you must inform the owner in writing immediately. If a child under six years of age resides in the unit, you should also inform the owner immediately at the address below if you notice any peeling paint or deteriorated subsurfaces in the unit during the year.

Please complete this form and return one copy to the owner or his or her agent or representative when you sign the lease/commence occupancy of the unit. Keep one copy of this form for your records. You should also receive a copy of a pamphlet developed by the New York City Department of Health and Mental Hygiene explaining about lead-based paint hazards when you sign your lease/commence occupancy.

CHECK ONE: ☒ A child under six years of age resides in the unit

☐ A child under six years of age does not reside in the unit.

_____(Occupant signature)

Print occupant's name, address and apartment number_____
_____

(NOT APPLICABLE TO RENEWAL LEASE) Certification by owner: I certify that I have complied with the provisions of §27-2056.8 of Article 14 of the Housing Maintenance Code and the rules promulgated thereunder relating to duties to be performed in vacant units, and that I have provided a copy of the New York City Department of Health and Mental Hygiene pamphlet concerning lead-based paint hazards to the occupant.

_____(Owner signature)

RETURN THIS FORM TO_____
_____

OCCUPANT: KEEP ONE COPY FOR YOUR RECORDS
OWNER COPY/OCCUPANT COPY

Annual Notice to Tenant or Occupant in Buildings with Three or More Apartments

To: Tenant

From: Landlord

Date:

ANNUAL NOTICE

PROTECT YOUR CHILD FROM LEAD POISONING AND WINDOW FALLS

New York City law requires that tenants living in buildings with 3 or more apartments complete this form and return it to their landlord before February 15, each year. If you do not return this form, your landlord is required to visit your apartment to determine if children live in your apartment.

Peeling Lead Paint	Window Guards
By law, your landlord is required to inspect your apartment for peeling paint and other lead paint hazards at least once a year if a child under 6 years of age (5 years or younger) lives with you.	By law, your landlord is required to install window guards in all your windows if a child under 11 years of age (10 years or younger) lives with you, OR if you request them (even if no children live with you).
▪ You must notify your landlord in writing if a child under 6 comes to live with you during the year. ▪ If a child under 6 lives with you, your landlord must inspect your apartment and provide you with the results of these paint inspections. ▪ *Always report peeling paint to your landlord. Call 311 if your landlord does not respond.* ▪ Your landlord must use safe work practices to repair all peeling paint and other lead paint hazards.	▪ ONLY windows that open to fire escapes, and one window in each first floor apartment when there is a fire escape on the outside of the building, are legally exempt from this requirement. ▪ It is against the law for you to interfere with installation, or remove window guards where they are required. Air conditioners in windows must be permanently installed. ▪ Window guards must be installed so there is no space greater than 4½ inches above or below the guard, on the side of the guard, or between the bars.
These requirements apply to buildings with 3 or more apartments built before 1960. They also apply to buildings built between 1960 and 1978 if the landlord knows that lead paint is present.	These requirements apply to all buildings with 3 or more apartments, regardless of when they were built.

Fill out and detach the bottom part of this form and return it to your landlord.

✁ ---

Please check all boxes that apply:

☐ A child under 6 years of age (5 years or younger) lives in my apartment.

☐ A child under 11 years of age (10 years or younger) lives in my apartment and:
  ☐ Window guards are installed in all windows as required.
  ☐ Window guards need repair.
  ☐ Window guards are NOT installed in all windows as required.

☐ No child under 11 years of age (10 years or younger) live in my apartment:
  ☐ I want window guards installed anyway.
  ☐ I have window guards, but they need repair.

Last Name	*First Name*		*Middle Initial*
Street Address	*Apt.#*	*City* *State*	*Zip Code*
Signature		*Date*	*Telephone Number*

Deadline for return: February 15

Return form to: Name and address of landlord or managing agent. Call **311** for more information on preventing window falls and lead poisoning.

DOHMH-approved: October 01, 2006

F I G U R E   3.10

Window Guard Rider Form

APPENDIX A

THE CITY OF NEW YORK
DEPARTMENT OF HEALTH
AND MENTAL HYGIENE

Michael R. Bloomberg   Thomas R. Frieden, MD, MPH
Mayor   *Commissioner*

WINDOW GUARDS REQUIRED
Lease Notice to Tenant

You are required by law to have window guards installed in all windows
if a child 10 years of age or younger lives in your apartment.

Your landlord is required by law to install window guards in your apartment:
if a child 10 years of age or younger lives in your apartment,
OR
if you ask him to install window guards at any time (you need not give a reason).

It is a violation of law to refuse, interfere with installation, or remove window guards where required.

CHECK ONE

☒ CHILDREN 10 YEARS OF AGE OR
YOUNGER LIVE IN MY APARTMENT

☐ NO CHILDREN 10 YEARS OF AGE OR
YOUNGER LIVE IN MY APARTMENT

☐ I WANT WINDOW GUARDS EVEN THOUGH
I HAVE NO CHILDREN 10 YEARS OF AGE
OR YOUNGER

SAMPLE

_____
Tenant (Print)

_____
Tenant's Signature: Date

_____
Tenant's Address   Apt No.

RETURN THIS FORM TO:

_____
Owner/Manager

_____
Owner/Manager's Address

For Further Information Call:
Window Falls Prevention (212) 676-2162

WF-013 *(Rev. 11/02)*

FIGURE 3.11

Bedbug Disclosure Form (Notice Form)

NOTICE TO TENANT
DISCLOSURE OF BEDBUG INFESTATION HISTORY

Pursuant to the NYC Housing Maintenance Code, an owner/managing agent of residential rental property shall furnish to each tenant signing a vacancy lease a notice that sets forth the property's bedbug infestation history.

Name of tenant(s):

Subject Premises:

Apt. #:

Date of vacancy lease:

BEDBUG INFESTATION HISTORY
(Only boxes checked apply)

[ ] There is no history of any bedbug infestation within the past year in the building or in any apartment.

[ ] During the past year the building had a bedbug infestation history that has been the subject of eradication measures. The location of the infestation was on the _____ floor(s).

[ ] During the past year the building had a bedbug infestation history on the _____ floor(s) and it has not been the subject of eradication measures.

[ ] During the past year the apartment had a bedbug infestation history and eradication measures were employed.

[ ] During the past year the apartment had a bedbug infestation history and eradication measures were not employed.

[ ] Other: _____ .

Signature of Tenant(s): _____ Dated: _____

Signature of Owner/Agent: _____ Dated: _____

DBB-N (DHCR 10/10)

At this time, there is no requirement on the part of real estate licensees (other than managing agents) to assist or complete the Notice Form or Complaint Form. It is strongly recommended that a real estate licensee avoid providing any guidance as to the completion of these forms. The licensee should always refer parties to their respective legal counsel for assistance. A real estate licensee who offers guidance that could otherwise be construed as advice on this section of law runs the risk of violating the prohibition concerning the unauthorized practice of law (*Duncan v. Hill*).

Other government requirements   If the U.S. Department of Housing and Urban Development (HUD) has determined that the property is in a flood-prone area, a buyer may need to obtain flood insurance before placing certain kinds of mortgages. The listing agent can anticipate this by consulting a flood area map at the time of listing. Maps may be ordered from the Federal Emergency Management Agency, Flood Map Distribution Center, 6930 (A-F) San Tomas Road, Baltimore, MD 21227-6227, or by calling toll-free 800-333-1363. The Web site is *www.fema.gov.*

Some municipalities may have restrictive ordinances regarding aquifer protection zones, wetlands protection, or steep slopes. Listing agents should keep current with all potential restrictions on use of land.

The New York regulatory scheme   In January 2003, the New York attorney general adopted rule changes that amended the state regulations regarding investment advisors.

Financial planners wear many different hats and include such parties as

- money managers,
- real estate agents,
- accountants,
- insurance agents, and
- financial advisors.

Investment advisors are defined as parties who engage in the business of rendering advice to a member of the general public concerning the buying selling or holding of securities.

The new rules include but are not limited to the following:

- Filing requirements and registration with the state for any investment advisor with six or more clients
- Mandatory compliance by advisors and representative agents with all examination requirements, including passing the Uniform Investment Advisor Law exam (series 65) or the Uniform Combined State Law exam (series 66) and the General Securities Advisor Law exam (series 7)
- Required filing of financial information with the attorney general's office
- Requirements to make and maintain records for a period of not less than five years

New York State requirements   The New York Real Property Law requires that the broker have attached to or printed on the reverse side of an exclusive agreement for a one- to three-family dwelling, a separately signed statement to the following effect:

> *An exclusive-right-to-sell listing means that if you, the property owner, find a buyer for your house or if another broker finds a buyer, you must pay the agreed-on commission to the present broker.*
>
> *An exclusive-agency listing means that if you, the property owner, find a buyer, you will not have to pay a commission to the broker. However, if another broker finds a buyer, you will owe a commission to both the selling broker and your present broker.*

If an exclusive listing of residential property is obtained by a broker who is a member of an MLS, the listing agreement must allow the seller to choose whether all negotiated offers to purchase will be submitted through the listing broker or through the selling broker. The DOS has made it clear that a buyer's broker has a right to be present. The aforementioned does not apply to cooperatives and condominiums.

Sample listing agreement   The individual specifics of a listing may vary from area to area. Following is a section-by-section analysis of a sample agreement; the items in the list below refer to the specific provisions of the contract, identified by the circled numbers in Figure 3.12.

1. *Exclusive right to sell.* The title specifies that this document is an "exclusive right to sell" the property.
2. *Date.* The date of the listing contract is the date it is executed (signed); this may not always be the date the contract becomes effective.
3. *Names.* The names of all persons having an interest in the property should be specified.
4. *Broker or firm.* The name of the broker or firm entering into the listing must be clearly stated in the agreement, along with the property address.
5. *Contract.* This section establishes the document as a bilateral contract and states the promises by both parties that create and bind the agreement.
6. *Termination of agreement.* Both the exact time and the date should be stated to avoid misunderstandings.
7. *Listing price.* Many brokers prefer not to refer to this as the asking price.
8. *Commission rate.* This important paragraph establishes the broker's rate of commission. Each brokerage firm is free to set its own fee schedule and to negotiate commission rates if it wishes to. The paragraph also makes an offer of cooperation to other members of the MLS and states whether the seller will allow the listing agent to offer part of the commission to a buyer's broker.
9. *Extension clause.* This section, permitted in New York, protects the broker if, after the listing expires, the owner sells the property to someone with whom the original broker had dealt during the listing period. This extension clause does not apply if the owner has relisted the property with another agent.
10. *Negotiation.* The owner agrees to refer all inquiries to the agent and chooses to have any offers submitted by either the listing agent or the selling agent, who may belong to a different firm.

F I G U R E   3.12

Listing Agreement

(1) EXCLUSIVE RIGHT TO SELL AGREEMENT

THIS AGREEMENT is effective **(2)** _____,19___, and confirms that _____ **(3)** has (have) appointed
_____ **(4)** to act as Agent for the sale of property known as _____, New York.

(5) In return for the Agent's agreement to use Agent's best efforts to sell the above property, the Owner(s) agree(s) to grant the Agent the exclusive right to sell this property under the following terms and conditions:

PERIOD OF AGREEMENT

1.   This agreement shall be effective from the above date and shall expire at midnight on _____ **(6)** _____, 19__.

PRICE AT WHICH PROPERTY WILL BE OFFERED AND AUTHORITY

2.   The property will be offered for sale at a list price of _____ **(7)** and shall be sold, subject to negotiation, at such price and upon such terms to which Owner(s) may agree. The word Owner refers to each and ALL parties who have ownership interest in the property and the undersigned represent(s) they are the sole and exclusive owners and are fully authorized to enter into this agreement.

(8) COMMISSION TO BE PAID TO AGENT

3.   The Agent shall be entitled to and Owner shall pay to Agent one commission of _____ of the selling price. Both the Owner(s) and the Agent acknowledge that the above commission rate was not suggested nor influenced by anyone other than the parties to this Agreement. Owner(s) hereby authorizes Agent to make an offer of cooperation to any other licensed real estate broker with whom Agent wishes to cooperate. Any commission due for a sale brought about by a Sub-Agent (another broker who is authorized by Agent to assist in the sale of Owner(s) property) or to an authorized Buyer(s) Agent shall be paid by the Agent from the commission received by the Agent pursuant to this Paragraph.

       The commission offered by Agent to Sub-Agents shall be _____ of the gross selling price. The commission offered by Agent to Buyer(s) Agents shall be _____ of the gross selling price.

       In the event that Owner(s) authorizes Agent to compensate a Buyer('s) Agent, Owner(s) acknowledges Owner's(s') understanding that such Buyer's Agent is not representing Owner(s) as Sub-Agent and that the Buyer's Agent will be representing only the interests of the prospective purchaser.

(9) OWNER(S) OBLIGATIONS AFTER THE EXPIRATION OF THIS AGREEMENT

4.   Owner(s) understands and agrees to pay the commission referred to in paragraph 3, if this property is sold or transferred or is the subject of a contract of sale within _____ months after the expiration date of this agreement involving a person with whom the Agent or a Cooperating Broker or the Owner(s) negotiated or to whom the property is offered, quoted or shown during the period of this listing agreement. Owner(s) will not, however, be obligated to pay such commission if Owner(s) enters into a valid Exclusive Listing Agreement with another New York State licensed real estate broker after the expiration of this agreement.

(10) WHO MAY NEGOTIATE FOR OWNER(S)

5.   Owner(s) agree(s) to direct all inquiries to the Agent. Owner(s) elect(s) to have all offers submitted through Agent __ or Cooperating Agent __.

(11) SUBMISSION OF LISTING TO MULTIPLE LISTING SERVICE

6.   Both Owner(s) and Agent agree that the Agent immediately is to submit this listing agreement to the Westchester Multiple Listing Service, Inc. ("WMLS"), for dissemination to its Participants. No provision of this agreement is intended to nor shall be understood to establish or imply any contractual relationship between the Owner(s) and WMLS nor has WMLS in any way participated in any of the terms of this agreement, including the commission to be paid. Owner(s) acknowledge(s) that the Agent's ability to submit this listing to WMLS or to maintain such listing amongst those included in any compilation of listing information made available by WMLS, is subject to Agent's continued status as a member in good standing of the Westchester County Board of REALTORS, Inc., and Agent's status as a Participant in good standing of WMLS.

(12) FAIR HOUSING

7.   Agent and Owner agree to comply fully with local, state and federal fair housing laws against discrimination on the basis of race, color, religion, sex, national origin, handicap, age, marital status and/or familial status, children or other prohibited factors.

Listing Agreement (continued)

(13) AUTHORIZATION FOR "FOR SALE" SIGN AND OTHER SERVICES

8.   Agent __ is (__ is not) authorized to place a "For Sale" sign on the property. Owner acknowledges that Agent has fully explained to Owner(s) the services and marketing activities which Agent has agreed to provide.

(14) REQUIREMENTS FOR PUBLICATION IN WMLS COMPILATION

9.   This listing agreement is not acceptable for publication by WMLS unless and until the Owner(s) has duly signed this agreement and an acknowledgement reflecting receipt of the definitions of "Exclusive Right to Sell" and "Exclusive Agency" required by the New York State Department of State - Division of Licensing Services.

(15) RENTAL OF PROPERTY

10.   Should the Owner(s) desire to rent the property during the period of this agreement, Agent is hereby granted the sole and exclusive right to rent the property, exclusive "FOR RENT" sign privilege and the Owner(s) agrees to pay Agent a rental commission of _____. The applicable commission for the lease term is due and will be paid __ upon the execution of the lease __ upon the date of occupancy. The commission for each and any subsequent renewal thereof, is due and will be paid upon the commencement of each renewal term.

(16) TERMINATION

11.   Owner(s) understands that if Owner(s) terminates the Agent's authority prior to the expiration of its term, Agent shall retain its contract rights (including but not limited to recovery of its commission, advertising expenses and/or any other damages) incurred by reason of an early termination of this agreement.

(17) ADDITIONAL POINTS

12.   Additional Points of Agreement, if any:_____
_____

(18) IN-HOUSE SALES

13.   If the Broker has an agency relationship with the buyer ["buyer's broker"] and that buyer expresses interest in property owned by a seller who also has an agency relationship with the Broker ["seller's broker"], a conflict has arisen.

The Broker shall immediately advise both the buyer client and the seller client of the pertinent facts including the fact that a dual agency situation has arisen, and that the **following options are available:**

[a] **The Broker and buyer could dissolve their Agency relationship.** The buyer may then seek to retain another broker, and/or an attorney, or may represent (her)himself. This would release the buyer from any Broker employment contract which was entered into with the Broker.   Broker may continue to act as agent for the seller.

[b] **The Broker and the seller could dissolve their Agency relationship.** The seller may then seek to retain another broker, and/or an attorney, or may represent (her)himself. This would release the seller from any listing agreement which was entered into with Broker. The Broker may continue to act as Agent for the buyer.

[c] **With fully informed consent, the buyer and seller may elect to continue with the brokerage firm serving as a consensual dual agent, which is the exception to the general rule that agents serve one principal. As a dual agent, the firm and its licensee agents have a duty of fairness to both principals. By mutual agreement the buyer and seller may identify who will negotiate for each principal. For example: [a] the licensee who signed the buyer as a principal of the brokerage firm may negotiate on behalf of the buyer principal and [b] the licensee who signed the seller as a principal of the firm may negotiate on behalf of the seller principal.**

In either case, the brokerage commission will be paid by the seller in accordance with the listing agreement with the seller, unless different arrangements have been negotiated.

As a dual agent, the firm and its agents cannot furnish undivided loyalty to either party.

As a dual agent, the firm and its licensee agents have a duty not to disclose confidential information given by one principal to the other principal, such as the price one is willing to pay or accept. Such information may already be known to the firm and its agents. If the information is of such a nature that the agent cannot fairly give advice without disclosing it, the agent cannot properly continue to act as an agent.

The buyer, seller and broker shall memorialize the option of their mutual choice by executing a statutory disclosure notice. If there is no mutual agreement, the proposed transaction between buyer and seller shall not be pursued.

Listing Agreement (continued)

(19) ALL MODIFICATIONS TO BE MADE IN WRITING

14.   Owner(s) and Agent agree that no change, amendment, modification or termination of this agreement shall be binding on any party unless the same shall be in writing and signed by the parties.

_____   _____   (AGENT) _____
(OWNER)   (DATE)

_____   _____   By: _____
(OWNER)   (DATE)   (Authorized Representative)   (DATE)

Owner's Mailing Address:_____   Agent's Address: _____

_____   _____

Owner's Telephone: _____   Agent's Telephone: _____

(20) DEFINITIONS

In accordance with the requirements of the New York State Department of State the undersigned Owner(s) does (do) hereby acknowledge receipt of the following:

1.   Explanation of "Exclusive Right to Sell" listing;
2.   Explanation of "Exclusive Agency" listing;
3.   A list of Participants of Westchester Multiple Listing Service, Inc.

EXPLANATION OF EXCLUSIVE RIGHT TO SELL: (As worded verbatim by the Department of State)

An "exclusive right to sell" listing means that if you, the owner of the property find a buyer for your house, or if another broker finds a buyer, you must pay the agreed commission to the present broker.

EXPLANATION OF EXCLUSIVE AGENCY: (As worded verbatim by the Department of State)

An "exclusive agency" listing means that if you, the owner of the property find a buyer, you will not have to pay a commission to the broker. However, if another broker finds a buyer, you will owe a commission to both the selling broker and your present broker.

(21) "THE FAIR HOUSING ACT"

The Civil Rights Act of 1968 known as the Federal Fair Housing Law makes illegal any discrimination based on race, color, religion, sex or national origin in connection with the sale or rental of housing. The 1988 amendment to this Act (The Fair Housing Amendments Act of 1988) expands the coverage of this law to handicapped persons and families with children. Agent and Owner agree to comply fully with State and local statutes and Federal Fair Housing laws.

Article X of the REALTOR Code of Ethics states:
"REALTORS shall not deny equal professional services to any person for reasons of race, color, religion, sex, handicap, familial status or national origin. REALTORS shall not be parties to any plan or agreement to discriminate against a person or persons on the basis of race, color, religion, sex, handicap, familial status or national origin."

(22) _____
                                                        Owner

_____
                                                        Owner

11. *Multiple listing service.* The agent will circulate information on the listing to all members of the MLS immediately. In some other areas, the listing office may have one, two, or three days of "office exclusive" before the listing is submitted to the MLS.

12. *Fair housing.* Both parties agree to comply with local, state, and federal fair housing laws.

13. *For Sale sign.* The agent may not place a sign on the property without authorization.

14. *Requirements.* The owner(s) must sign this agreement before it is acceptable for publication.

15. *Rental.* If the owner wishes to rent the property during the life of the agreement, the agent has sole and exclusive right to act as the rental agent. The owner will pay the agent a commission for this service.

16. *Termination.* The agent is entitled to payment for advertising expenses, damages, and commission if the owner terminates the agreement before it expires.

17. *Additional points.* Anything not illegal may be agreed on by seller and agent. For example, an understanding that "no commission will be due if seller's brother purchases within 30 days" would go here.

18. *In-house sales.* A broker must notify the seller and the buyer that a dual agency situation exists and that both the seller and buyer can dissolve their agency agreement with the broker or with informed consent continue with the broker serving as a consensual dual agent.

19. *Signatures.* The contract should be signed by all owners. The sales associate signs on behalf of the broker or firm; the contract is not made with the individual salesperson.

20. *Definitions.* The seller must receive an explanation of types of listings.

21. *Civil rights legislation.* This clause serves to alert the owner that both federal and state legislation protect against discrimination.

22. *Owner's acknowledgment.* The seller acknowledges notification of listing definitions.

■ BUYER AGENCY

In a buyer-broker agency relationship, the broker represents the buyer as a client, rather than treating the buyer as merely a customer. Buyer agency allows the broker to provide services to buyers that might otherwise be inappropriate, such as help negotiating the terms of the contract to the buyer's best advantage. The buyers who specifically retain their own agents would be subject to **vicarious liability** for the acts of their agents, just as sellers are for theirs. As previously discussed, vicarious liability means being responsible for the acts of another.

Working Relationships with Buyers

Buyers as customers   Not every buyer wants to be represented by an agent. In fact, no law exists that would require a buyer or a seller to engage the services of a real estate licensee. Some buyers like working with several different brokers. Some buyers, especially experienced buyers, are happy with the services provided by a seller's agent: help in finding a suitable property, information about property values, help in preparing and presenting their offer, and aid in securing financing. All these services can be provided to a customer by an agent representing a seller.

Buyers as clients Other buyers, however, want more than customer services. They need and want advice, something the seller's broker cannot provide them. These are the buyers who will benefit most from buyer agency.

Sellers' agents are cautioned not to assist buyers in any way that might be construed as creation of an agency relationship by implication. This can ultimately create an undisclosed dual agency. (See Chapter 2 for more on this subject.)

Compensating Buyer Agents

An agency relationship does not depend on the source of the agent's compensation. Buyer agents may be compensated by

- the buyer,
- the seller, or
- both, but only with full disclosure to all interested parties to the transaction and with the informed consent of all interested parties to the transaction.

Naturally, the way in which fees are to be paid should be stated in writing and clearly understood well in advance to avoid potential conflict between the buyer and the broker.

Seller-paid fee The seller might agree to pay the buyer's broker fee, particularly during negotiations with a buyer who may be short of cash. The payment of fees does not determine whom an agent represents. As long as the agency relationship is clear and explicit, it does not matter legally whether the buyer or the seller pays the fee.

The seller may pay the buyer's broker fee through a commission split or by crediting the buyer a specific amount out of the sales proceeds at closing. The most common method is *the commission split*, where the listing broker has written authorization to split the commission with the buyer's broker. Remember, regardless of which party is charged with compensating the broker, agents only represent the party that hired them and no other.

Buyer-paid fee Buyer's agent compensation also can be paid directly by the buyer. This arrangement has the advantage of avoiding any appearance that the buyer's agent is acting as a subagent of the seller and also gives the buyer's agent greater control over getting paid. The compensation may take the form of an hourly rate, a flat fee, or a percentage commission:

- *Hourly rate.* Under an hourly rate arrangement, the broker actually is acting as a consultant. The hourly fee is payable whether or not the buyer actually purchases a property.
- *Percentage fee.* A percentage fee is based on the sales price of the home the buyer purchases or any valuable consideration exchanged and/or received. The primary benefit of this arrangement is that real estate agents and their clients are accustomed to a percentage arrangement. The obvious

disadvantage is that the broker may have a conflict of interest, because the higher the price, the higher the fee.

- ■ *Flat fee.* Under this arrangement, the buyer's broker is paid a flat fee if the buyer purchases a house located through the broker. The amount of the fee is based on the broker's estimate of the work and skills involved.

Some buyer's agent agreements provide that the buyer is obligated to pay the fee but will receive a credit for any amount the seller agrees to pay. Thus, the buyer would not pay the buyer's broker fee in a typical MLS sale, where the buyer's broker will get a split of the listing broker's commission. However, the buyer would be obligated to pay the fee if the seller had not listed the property or offered any commission to a selling broker.

As always, if the agent is paid by both parties, both must understand the arrangement and give their written consent.

Buyer-Agency Agreements

Agreements between buyers and buyers' agents are sometimes referred to as *buyer listings, buyer representation agreements*, or *buyer-broker agency agreements*. Like a listing agreement, a buyer-agency agreement is also an employment contract. In this case, however, the broker is employed as the buyer's agent. The purpose of the agreement is to find and procure a suitable property. An agency agreement gives the buyer a degree of representation that is possible only in a fiduciary relationship.

Types of buyer-agency agreements   Following are the three basic types of buyer-agency agreements:

1. *Exclusive buyer-agency agreement.* The buyer is legally bound to compensate the agent whenever purchasing a property of the type described in the contract. The broker is entitled to payment regardless of who located the property. Even if the buyer finds the property independently, the agent is entitled to payment. The broker has an **exclusive right to represent** the buyer. (See Figure 3.13.)
2. *Exclusive-agency buyer-agency agreement.* The broker is entitled to payment only upon locating property that the buyer ultimately purchases. The buyer is free to find a suitable property without being obligated to pay the agent.
3. *Open buyer-agency agreement.* This agreement permits the buyer to enter into similar agreements with an unlimited number of brokers. The buyer is obligated to compensate only the broker who locates the property ultimately purchased by the buyer.

A broker also may wish to represent a buyer with respect to a single property only. In this arrangement, the buyer agrees to pay the broker a fee if the buyer purchases a specific property. The broker does not reveal the exact location of the property until the agreement is signed.

In any buyer-agency agreement, the buyer's broker should clarify the types of services to be offered to the buyer-client (in addition to the traditional services

FIGURE 3.13

Exclusive-Right-to-Represent Agreement

BUYER AGENCY AGREEMENT
Exclusive Right-to-Represent

BROKER EXCLUSIVE RIGHT TO REPRESENT AGREEMENT. COMMISSIONS OR FEES FOR REAL ESTATE SERVICES TO BE PROVIDED HEREUNDER ARE NEGOTIABLE BETWEEN BROKER AND BUYER. IT IS UNDERSTOOD THAT THE GREATER ROCHESTER ASSOCIATION OF REALTORS®, INC. ("GRAR") AND THE GENESEE REGION REAL ESTATE INFORMATION SERVICE, INC. ("GENRIS") IS NOT A PARTY TO THIS BUYER AGENCY AGREEMENT.

1.   APPOINTMENT OF BROKER:
The BUYER/TENANT _____ (hereinafter called the "BUYER") retains and appoints as Buyer's Broker (hereinafter called the "BROKER") _____(firm) represented by _____ (agent) as Buyer's exclusive agent to locate and/or negotiate for the purchase or lease of real property of the general nature shown below. Buyer acknowledges that Broker may be an agent for an owner in the sale or lease of property in which Buyer expresses an interest, whereupon Broker shall promptly notify Buyer of such conflict of interest and available options. **An "exclusive right to represent" agreement means that if you, the Buyer, find a property to purchase or lease, or if another Broker finds you a property, you must pay the agreed compensation to the present Broker.**

2.   PURPOSE OF AGENCY:
Buyer desires to purchase/lease real property (which may include items of personal property) described as follows:
Type: ☐ Residential   ☐ Commercial   ☐ Residential Investment   ☐ Industrial   ☐ Vacant Land   ☐ Other _____

_____.

3.   BROKER'S REPRESENTATIONS AND SERVICES: Broker represents that Broker is duly licensed under the laws of the State of New York as a real estate broker. Broker will assist Buyer in locating property, negotiating any offer by Buyer to purchase or lease such property, and presenting Buyer's offer to the owner of property or to such owner's agent.

4.   BUYER'S OBLIGATIONS: During the term of this Agreement, Buyer agrees:
    a. To work exclusively with Broker and not with other owners, real estate brokers, or salespersons with respect to viewing properties and to refer to Broker all inquiries in any form from any other real estate broker, salesperson, prospective seller or any other source;
    b. To conduct in good faith all negotiations for property exclusively through Broker; and
    c. To provide to Broker upon request (i) the general nature, location, requirements and preferred terms and conditions, which Buyer is seeking in connection with the acquisition of desired property; and (ii) relevant personal and financial information to assure Buyer's ability to obtain financing.

5.   TERM OF AGENCY: Broker's authority to act as Buyer's exclusive agent under this Agreement shall begin _____ and shall end at midnight on _____ or upon closing of a property purchased under this Agreement and payment of Broker's compensation. However, if Buyer purchases or leases a property within _____ days after this Agreement ends (the "Effective Period") that was shown to the Buyer by Broker, or by anyone else during the life of this Agreement, Buyer will pay Broker the same compensation agreed to in Section 6 below. Buyer will not owe any compensation to Broker if such purchase or lease occurs during the life of another written Buyer Agency Agreement Buyer enters into after this Agreement ends but before the expiration of the Effective Period.

6.   COMPENSATION OF BROKER.   In consideration of the services performed by Broker under the terms of this Agreement, Buyer agrees to pay Broker the following fee(s): (Initial all applicable sections.)

_____ **a. Transaction Fee:** Buyer shall pay Broker a Transaction Fee which is the greater of $ _____ or _____ % of the gross purchase or lease price (and renewals, if applicable) of any property purchased or leased by Buyer. This Transaction Fee shall be due and payable upon closing of the Purchase and Sale Contract or Lease providing, however, if such Contract or Lease fails to close due to default by the Buyer, this Transaction Fee shall become immediately due and payable to Broker. Broker shall use commercially reasonable efforts to obtain payment of the Transaction Fee from the seller or lessor of the property, but Buyer shall have the obligation to pay Broker the Transaction Fee set forth in this Agreement if Broker cannot obtain payment of such fee from the seller or lessor of the property.

_____ **b. Hourly Fee:** Buyer shall pay Broker at the rate of $ _____ per hour for all services performed by Broker under the terms of this Agreement, to be billed monthly and to be paid within five (5) days after Buyer receives a bill for such services from Broker. This Hourly Fee shall be credited against the Transaction Fee, if any, described above and shall be kept by Broker whether or not a Transaction Fee is earned.

_____ **c. Non-Refundable Retainer:** Buyer shall pay Broker a Non-Refundable Retainer of $ _____ to be paid to Broker herewith whether or not Buyer purchases or leases any property. This Retainer shall be credited against the Transaction Fee, if any, described above whether or not a Transaction Fee is earned or against the Hourly Fee, if any, described above and shall be kept by Broker.

_____ **d. Other:** _____

_____.

Exclusive-Right-to-Represent Agreement (continued)

7.   OTHER POTENTIAL BUYERS: Buyer understands that other potential buyers have entered or may enter into similar agency contracts with Broker which may involve the purchase or lease, through Broker, of the same or similar property or properties as Buyer is attempting to purchase or lease. Buyer consents to Broker's representation of such other buyers to the extent permitted by law.

8.   NONDISCRIMINATION: Broker and Buyer agree that all actions carried out under this Agreement shall be in full compliance with local, state and federal fair housing laws against discrimination on the basis of race, creed, color, religion, national origin, sex, familial status, marital status, age or disabilities.

9.   EARLY CONTRACT TERMINATION: In the event this Agreement is terminated by Buyer prior to the time specified in Section 5 for any reason other than Broker's fault, Buyer will be liable for and will pay all damages and expenses incurred by Broker, including without limit any compensation due Broker in Section 6 above.

10.   RESPONSIBILITY OF BUYER(S) UNDER THIS CONTRACT: All Buyers to be named on a purchase and sale contract must sign this contract. If more than one person signs this contract as Buyer, each person is fully responsible for keeping the promises made by the Buyer.

11.   RENEWAL AND MODIFICATION OF CONTRACT: Buyer may extend the life of this Agreement by signing a Renewal Agreement. All changes or modifications to the provisions of this Agreement must be made in writing and signed by Buyer(s) and Broker.

12.   PROFESSIONAL COUNSEL: Broker hereby recommends that Buyer seek legal, tax, property financing, property inspection, appraisal, environmental engineering and other professional advice (if appropriate) relating to any proposed transaction. Buyer agrees that Buyer will not rely on Broker for such professional advice nor rely on Broker for payment of such services.

13.   ATTORNEY'S FEES: In any action, proceeding or arbitration arising out of this Agreement, the prevailing party shall be entitled to reasonable attorney's fees and costs.

14.   OTHER: _____

_____ .

15. ENTIRE AGREEMENT AND ASSIGNABILITY: This Agreement constitutes the complete Agreement between Broker and Buyer relating to the exclusive agency of Broker for Buyer. No modification of any terms of this Agreement shall be valid or binding unless such modification is in writing and signed by Buyer and Broker. This Agreement is not assignable without written approval of Buyer and Broker.

In consideration of the above, Buyer and Broker accept this Agreement and agree to its terms and conditions.

BUYER _____   BROKER _____

BUYER _____   BY _____

DATE _____   DATE _____

rendered by real estate licensees to buyers as customers). These could include such tasks as the following:

- Structuring of the transaction
- Investment analysis
- Assistance in development
- Assistance in financing
- Negotiating the sale

Naturally, a buyer's broker must advise the buyer to seek professional legal, tax, or other experts should the need arise.

As with a listing agreement, the time and date of termination should be specified to prevent later conflicts. If the broker wants to be reimbursed for a sale that takes place on a certain property after the buyer-agency agreement terminates, the broker should insert an extension clause like that found in most listing agreements. Of course, buyer-agency agreements can be terminated by mutual consent.

Sometimes a buyer wants to purchase a property listed by the buyer's broker. In this case, unless the buyer's broker is divested from the buyer-broker relationship, the buyer's broker would be put in the position of acting as a dual agent. Another type of conflict might arise if the broker were showing more than one buyer-client the same property. The buyer-agency agreement should anticipate these types of conflicts. For instance, some agreements provide that the broker will represent the buyer in all cases except in-house listings. Many agreements include an acknowledgment by the buyer that the broker may represent more than one buyer and that if more than one buyer is interested in the same property, it will not be considered a conflict of interest.

■ SUMMARY

New York requires brokers and salespersons to provide a written disclosure of agency at first substantive contact with prospective buyers or sellers. The disclosure is repeated when a purchase contract is signed by the parties. Licensees may state that they are acting as agent for the seller, landlord, buyer, tenant, or a broker.

When a broker becomes agent for a seller or buyer, the broker's salespersons become subagents of that same principal. Cooperating brokers from other firms may operate as subagents of the listing agent, as agents for their own buyers, or as subagents for the seller. The party paying the commission does not determine the principal.

In some situations, agents find themselves working for both parties. Dual agency is legally possible, though difficult. It requires written consent from both buyer and seller. However, under the new amendment to Section 443, advance consent to this type of arrangement is now permissible.

The DOS allows a system of designated brokers to represent both parties for in-house sales. As in the case of a dual agency, under the new amendment, advance consent to this type of arrangement is also permissible.

Listing agreements take three forms. An exclusive-right-to-sell listing promises the broker a commission if the property is sold during the listing period. An exclusive-agency listing promises a commission if the broker sells the property; if the owners sell on their own, no commission is due. An open listing simply promises a commission to whatever broker produces the buyer. Net listings, which promise the broker anything above a certain sales price, are illegal in New York. Multiple listing is a form of shared marketing among broker members who can find buyers for each others' listings.

Agencies are created by listing agreements or buyer-agency agreements. They can be terminated in several ways, including death, bankruptcy, or insanity of either party (if contractual). The seller always has the right to withdraw a listing but may be liable for the broker's expenses.

The buyer of any one- to four-family dwelling is entitled to a written disclosure of property condition statement from the seller. The buyer who does not receive one is entitled to a $500 credit, which does not, however, relieve the seller of any liability for undisclosed defects.

CHAPTER 3 QUIZ

1. A salesperson agreed to meet a buyer at a home listed by the salesperson's broker. When must the salesperson provide the buyer with an agency disclosure?
   a. In advance of the first in-person meeting
   b. Before entering the property
   c. After showing the property
   d. When the buyer expresses interest in making an offer

2. A listing contract will terminate as the result of *performance of the object*. This means that the
   a. property has been destroyed.
   b. seller and broker agree to cancel.
   c. owner has decided not to sell.
   d. property has been sold.

3. The agency disclosure form must be presented, explained, and signed
   a. when the customer makes an offer.
   b. when the seller accepts an offer.
   c. at the first substantive contact.
   d. when the seller and buyer first meet.

4. When communicating the present property tax information on a listed property, the listing broker should disclose
   a. the current seller's three-year payment history.
   b. the procedure that can be followed to protest property valuation.
   c. how the assessed valuation and tax rate are determined.
   d. that the tax amount is valid only for the year of the sale.

5. In a single agency agreement in which a broker represents a seller, the
   a. buyer is the client.
   b. seller is the client.
   c. seller is the customer.
   d. buyer is a subagent.

6. Which listing agreement provides the broker with the greatest incentive to successfully market the property?
   a. Open listing
   b. Exclusive-agency listing
   c. Net listing
   d. Exclusive-right-to-sell listing

7. Upon first contact, cooperating brokers must inform the listing agent whether they are acting as agents or subagents of other parties. This would be due to the fact that these relationships impact the listing agent's
   a. motivation in presenting the property.
   b. responsibilities to the seller.
   c. potential commission.
   d. disclosure of information.

8. When a broker takes a listing, all salespeople who work for the broker are considered
   a. subagents for the broker and the seller.
   b. agents for the broker and subagents for the seller.
   c. dual agents for the seller and the buyer.
   d. not designated until they enter into an agreement.

9. In which listing agreement would sellers have the ability to reserve the right to conduct their own sale without compensating the exclusive agent?
   a. Exclusive right-to-sell listing
   b. Exclusive-agency listing
   c. Multiple listing
   d. Net listing

10. A broker who lists a property on the broker's Web site should remove the listing from the for-sale section of the site
    a. when the listing appears on an MLS.
    b. 90 days after it appears.
    c. when an offer is made.
    d. after a sale occurs.

11. Which of the following *BEST* describes a residential transaction?

    a. Sale or lease of a property containing ten units or more
    b. Located in a residential zone
    c. Transaction involving the sale or lease of four or fewer units intended for dwelling
    d. Involving a sales price of $1 million or less

12. In a dual agency relationship, the parties give up their right to

    a. undivided loyalty.
    b. obedience.
    c. care.
    d. accounting.

13. A broker represents a homebuyer as a buyer's agent. The broker wants to show the buyer a property that a seller has listed with him. If the broker shows the buyer the property, he

    a. will have done nothing wrong.
    b. is violating license law.
    c. should first get the informed, written consent of both buyer and seller to act as a dual agent.
    d. must first notify the secretary of state that he intends to represent both buyer and seller.

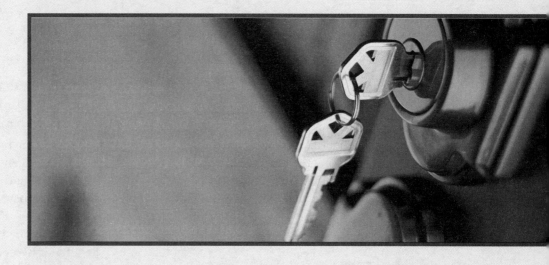

CHAPTER

4

Estates and Interests

■ KEY TERMS

act of waste
agricultural real estate
air rights
beneficiaries
bundle of legal rights
chattels
commercial real estate
common elements
condominium
condop
convey
conveyance
cooperative
co-ownership
corporation
curtesy
devise
dower
emblements
escheat
estate for years
estate in land
fee simple
fixture
freehold estates

general partnership
grant
homestead
illiquidity
improvement
industrial real estate
interest
joint tenancy
joint venture
land
leasehold estates
life estate
limited liability company
limited partnership
littoral rights
mixed-use real estate
parcel
partition
partnership
passive income
personal property
real estate
real property
remainder interest
remainderman

residential real estate
reversionary interest
right of survivorship
riparian rights
S corporation
severalty
sole proprietorship
special-purpose real
    estate
subsurface rights
surface rights
syndicate
tenancy by the entirety
tenant
tenant in common
title
trade fixture
trust
trustee
trustor
undivided interest
unities of time, title,
    interest, and
    possession

■ REAL ESTATE TRANSACTIONS

Rights of ownership include the following:

- ■ Possession
- ■ Control of property
- ■ Enjoyment
- ■ Exclusion
- ■ Disposition

Real property is fixed in nature. Unlike investment vehicles such as stocks and bonds that are considered liquid investments (easily converted to cash), real property investment is considered to be a nonliquid or illiquidity investment. **Illiquidity** refers to the difficulty in selling an asset for full value on short notice (lack of assets that can be quickly converted to cash).

The purchase or rental of real estate is quite different from dealings in personal property such as automobiles, groceries, or televisions. Even the simplest of real estate transactions brings into play a body of complex laws.

Real property has often been described as a **bundle of legal rights**. A person who purchases real estate is actually buying the rights previously held by the seller. These *rights of ownership* include the right to *possession*; the right to *control the property* within the framework of the law; the right of *enjoyment* (to use the property in any legal manner); the right of *exclusion* (to keep others from entering or occupying the property); and the right of *disposition* (to be able to sell or otherwise transfer the property). (See Figure 4.1.) Included within these ownership rights are further rights: to **devise** (leave by will), mortgage, encumber, cultivate, explore, lease, license, dedicate, give away, abandon, share, trade, or exchange the property.

■ LAND, REAL ESTATE, AND REAL PROPERTY

The words *land, real estate,* and *real property* often are used to describe the same thing. There are, however, important differences.

FIGURE 4.1

The Bundle of Legal Rights

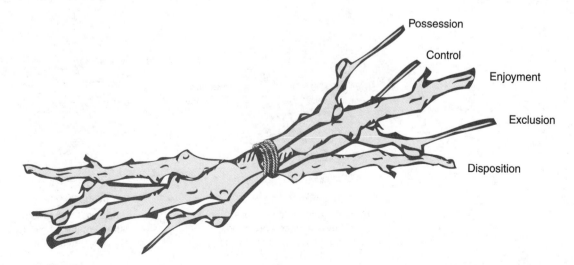

Possession
Control
Enjoyment
Exclusion
Disposition

Land

The term **land** or fee (*fee* is a term used to describe an estate in land; *estate* is the degree, quantity, nature, and extent of interest that a person possesses in real and personal property) refers to more than just the surface of the earth; it includes things permanently attached to the land by nature only, such as trees and water. Land or fee ownership also includes minerals and substances below the earth's surface together with the air above up to infinity.

Thus *land* is defined as the *earth's surface extending downward to the center of the earth and upward to infinity, including things permanently attached by nature only*. (See Figure 4.2.)

A specific tract of land is commonly called a **parcel**, which has specific boundaries.

Real Estate

The term **real estate** is broader than the term *land* and includes all permanent **improvements**—buildings on the land as well as streets, utilities, sewers, and other *man-made additions* to the property.

Real estate is defined as the *earth's surface extending downward to the center of the earth and upward into space, including all things permanently attached to it by nature and by people*. (See Figure 4.2.)

Real Property

The term **real property** is broader still and includes the *bundle of legal rights of ownership*.

Thus, *real property* is defined as the *earth's surface extending downward to the center of the earth and upward into space, including all things permanently attached to it by*

Land and Real Estate

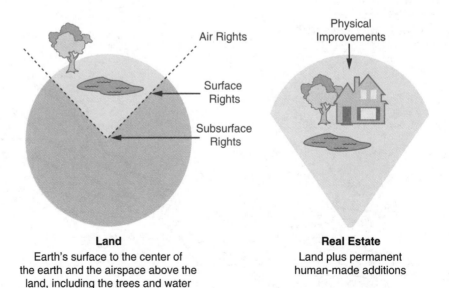

Land
Earth's surface to the center of the earth and the airspace above the land, including the trees and water

Real Estate
Land plus permanent human-made additions

nature and by people, as well as the interests, benefits, and rights included in ownership. (See Figure 4.3.)

In everyday usage, the term *real estate* or *realty* is incorrectly used for *real property*.

Subsurface rights, the rights to the natural resources lying below the earth's surface, may be owned separately.

A landowner, for example, may sell or lease to an oil company the rights to any oil and gas found in the land. Much of the farmland in southwestern New York is subject to oil and gas leases. Mineral rights also may be leased or sold separately.

The rights to use the airspace above the land may also be sold or leased independently of the land itself. Such **air rights** are an increasingly important part of real estate, particularly in large cities, where air rights over railroads have been purchased to construct office buildings such as the Met-Life Building in New York City. For the construction of such a building, the developer must purchase not only the air rights above the land but also numerous small portions of the actual land to construct the building's foundation supports. In certain cities within New York, these air rights have become even more important. For example, in Manhattan, vacant land is almost nonexistent; so where land rights are available, they are extremely expensive, which affects the cost and feasibility of new development projects. As a result, redevelopment of existing properties usually includes the acquisition of additional air rights as an alternative when possible.

Until the development of airplanes, air rights were considered to be unlimited. Today, however, the courts permit reasonable interference with these rights by aircraft, as long as the owner's right to use and occupy the land is not interfered with. Governments and airport authorities often purchase air rights next to an airport to provide glide patterns for aircraft.

The rights in one parcel of real property could, therefore, be owned by many people:

- An owner of the **surface rights**
- An owner of subsurface mineral rights

F I G U R E   4.3

Real Property

The Bundle
of Rights

Real Property
Real estate plus
"bundle of legal rights"

FIGURE 4.4

Riparian Rights

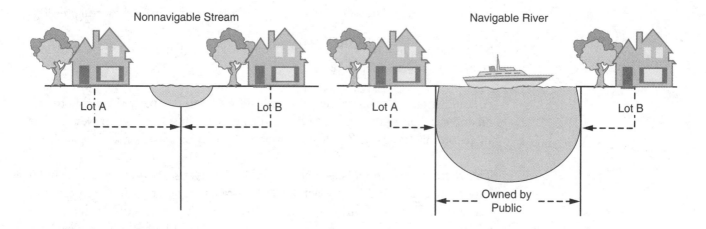

An owner of subsurface gas and oil rights
- An owner of the air rights

Riparian rights are the owner's rights in land bordering a river or stream. In New York, persons owning land bordering nonnavigable streams own the property to the midpoint of the stream. Those whose land borders navigable streams own the property to the high-water mark (the limit of the rise of medium tides); the riverbed belongs to the state. (See Figure 4.4.)

Closely related to riparian rights are the **littoral rights** of owners whose land borders large lakes, bays, and oceans. They may enjoy unrestricted use of the water but own the land only up to the high-water mark. (See Figure 4.5.) All land below this point is owned by the government.

Riparian and littoral rights may not be sold separately or kept when the land is sold. Where land adjoins streams, an owner is entitled to all *accretions*, which are increases resulting from the deposit of soil by the action of the water or wind. An

FIGURE 4.5

Littoral Rights

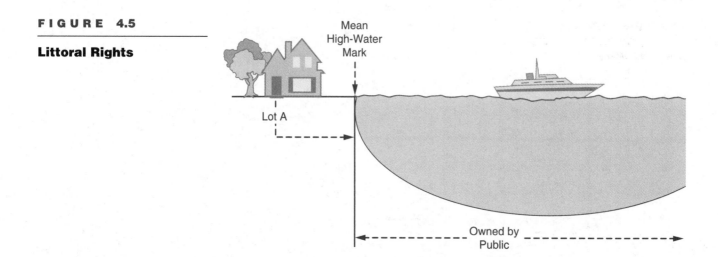

FIGURE 4.6

Real Versus Personal Property

Real Estate		Personal Property	
Land and anything permanently attached to it		Movable items not attached to real estate; items severed from real estate	

Fixture		Trade Fixture	
Item of personal property converted to real estate by attaching it to the real estate with the intention that it become permanently a part thereof		Item of personal property attached to real estate that is owned by a tenant and is used in a business; legally removable by tenant	

owner also may lose land through gradual erosion or through *avulsion*, because of a change in the channel of a stream.

■ REAL PROPERTY VERSUS PERSONAL PROPERTY

Nearly everything that can be owned may be classified as either real or personal property.

Personal property is all property that does not fit the definition of real estate. Personal property is *movable*, or mobile. Items of personal property, also referred to as **chattels**, include possessions such as refrigerators, drapes, clothing, money, bonds, and bank accounts. (See Figure 4.6.)

It should be noted that cooperative ownership is considered to be personal property ownership. A cooperative transaction includes the purchase and sale of stock within a corporation that owns the real property containing the unit represented by the purchased shares of stock. This subject will be covered further in this chapter and in greater detail in Chapter 24.

It is possible to change an item of real estate to personal property. A growing tree is real estate, but if the owner cuts down the tree and thereby severs it from the earth, it becomes personal property. The process is known as *severance*.

The reverse situation is also possible. Personal property can be changed to real estate. If an owner buys cement, stones, and sand and constructs a concrete walk, materials that were originally personal property are changed into real estate because they have become permanent improvements on the land.

Trees and crops are generally fall into two classes: (1) trees, perennial bushes, and grasses that do not require yearly cultivation are considered real estate, and (2) annual crops of wheat, corn, vegetables, and fruit, known as **emblements**, are generally considered personal property. A mobile home is usually considered personal property unless it is permanently attached to the land by a foundation.

Fixtures

An article of personal property that has been permanently attached to land or a building is known as a **fixture** and becomes part of the real estate. Examples of fixtures are furnaces, elevator equipment, kitchen cabinets, light fixtures, and sinks. Almost any item that has been added as a *permanent part* of a building is considered a fixture.

Legal tests of a fixture When it comes to the purchase of a home, fixtures often become the subject of lawsuits, and licensees are advised to counsel their principal concerning these matters. Specifically, a licensee should advise the seller that any fixture(s) that the seller intends on removing from the property be listed and specified in the contract for purchase and sale.

For example, a seller forgets to exclude an expensive chandelier from a contract of purchase and sale. This exclusion may result in a lawsuit to determine whether the item was personal property or a fixture.

In the resulting lawsuit, the courts will apply one or all of four basic tests to determine whether an article is a fixture (and therefore a part of the real estate) or removable personal property. These tests are based on (1) the adaptation of the article to the real estate, (2) the method of annexation (attachment) of the item, (3) the intention and relationship of the parties, and (4) the existence of an agreement.

Although these tests seem simple, court decisions do not always agree on whether something is a fixture. Annexation alone is not a final test. The front door key, for example, is not attached, but it is clearly a fixture that belongs with the house.

The distinction between personal and real property is of great importance in the sale of real estate. When a contract for the sale of property is being negotiated, buyers and sellers must be guided by clear written agreements about what "goes with" the real estate being sold.

Trade fixtures An article owned by a tenant and attached to a rented space for use in conducting a business is a **trade fixture**. Examples of trade fixtures are bowling alley equipment, store shelves, and restaurant equipment. Agricultural fixtures such as chicken coops and toolsheds also are included in this definition. (See Figure 4.6.)

Trade fixtures remain the personal property of the tenant and may be removed on or before the last day the property is rented. However, the tenant must restore the property to its original condition, repairing holes left by bolts, for example. Trade fixtures not removed become the property of the landlord.

Four Legal Tests of a Fixture

1. The adaptation of the article to the real estate
2. The method of annexation of the item
3. The intention and relationship of the parties
4. The existence of an agreement

Uses of Real Estate

Real estate brokers deal with many different types of real property. (See Figure 4.7.) Real estate generally can be classified in the following categories:

- **Residential**—all property used for housing, from acreage to small city lots, both single-family and multifamily, in urban, suburban, and rural areas
- **Commercial**—business property, including offices, shopping malls, theaters, hotels, and parking facilities
- **Industrial**—warehouses, factories, land in industrial districts, and research facilities (Industrial property is sometimes referred to as *manufacturing property* in New York City.)
- **Mixed-use**—any lawful combination of the other five basic categories of real property permitted by local zoning
- **Agricultural**—farms, timberland, pastureland, and orchards
- **Special purpose**—religious institutions, schools, cemeteries, hospitals, and government-held lands

■ ESTATES (OWNERSHIP) IN LAND

A buyer's choice of ownership type will affect the buyer's legal right to sell in the future without the consent of others and also the right to leave the property to chosen heirs. The real estate practitioner needs to understand various forms of ownership so that buyers, sellers, tenants, and landlords can be alerted to the need for legal input to avoid future problems.

The amount and kind of **interest** (ownership) that a person has in real property is an **estate in land**. Estates in land are either freehold estates or leasehold estates (those involving rentals).

Freehold estates exist indefinitely, for a lifetime, or forever. In essence, a freehold estate represents ownership in property. A good memory device for freehold estates is the following: "One is *free to hold* the property until such time that one wishes to dispose of same."

The ability to hold a property indefinitely can only occur when one owns the property.

The freehold estates recognized in New York are (1) fee simple, (2) qualified (determinable) fee, (3) fee on condition, and (4) life estates.

FIGURE 4.7

Uses of Real Property

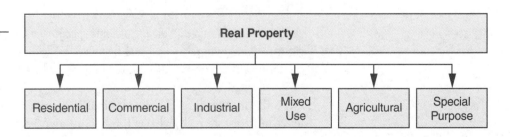

The first three of these estates continue for an indefinite period and can be inherited after the owner's death. A life estate ends at the death of the person on whose life it is based.

Leasehold estates are estates for a specific period of time. They are classified as personal property as follows:

■ **Estate for years**. Commonly established by a lease, written or (if for a period of less than one year) oral. An estate for years gives the tenant possession of the property for a fixed time.

■ *Periodic estate, estate at will, estate at sufferance*. These leasehold estates are covered at length in Chapter 7. Each lasts for an indefinite length of time.

Fee Simple Estate

An estate in **fee simple** is the *most complete type of ownership in real estate*. A fee simple estate is one in which the owner is entitled to all rights in the property. There is no time limit—it is said to run forever. On the death of its owner, the estate passes to the owner's heirs. The terms *fee, fee simple*, and *fee simple absolute* are basically the same. New York law provides that a **grant** (sale or gift) of real property automatically **conveys** (transfers) fee simple ownership unless the terms of the grant show a clear intention to convey a lesser estate.

Qualified Fee Estate

Sometimes a gift or sale provides that the real property must be used for a specific purpose. The deed that transfers the property might state that Smith gives the land "to the Jones Foundation so long as it is used for a wildlife preserve." If the Jones Foundation later builds a corporate headquarters on the land, ownership will *automatically* revert to Smith (or Smith's heirs); the Jones Foundation owned only a *qualified fee*.

Fee on Condition

A *fee on condition* is slightly different. The deed transferring ownership to the Jones Foundation might have been worded so that if the land were ever used for any purpose except a wildlife preserve, the land would *not automatically* revert back to Smith. Smith or Smith's heirs would, however, have the right to file suit in court to recover the property.

Real estate brokers and salespersons need to familiarize themselves with qualified fee and fee on condition to alert sellers and buyers to the need for legal counsel if such a situation is encountered.

Life Estates

A **life estate** is *limited to the life of some specific person*. The owner does not have the right to pass ownership to heirs because the life estate ends with the death of the owner or a third party. Life estates may be ordinary or *pur autre vie*.

An ordinary life estate lasts as long as the owner, the life tenant, is alive. A may leave a life estate to B, who will have full ownership for life. B does not, however, have the right to leave the property to anyone at death. A has already established who will become the next owner.

A life estate *pur autre vie* (for another life) lasts as long as a particular third party, named by the original owner, is alive. Mrs. A might, for example, leave her home to son B, to be owned by B "as long as my brother, Felix, is alive and living in the home." B (or B's heirs) would be complete owner of the property, but only until Felix's death.

Remainder and reversion   The person who sets up the life estate provides for the future ownership of the property. After the death of the life tenant, the property may revert to the original owner or pass to someone else. (See Figure 4.8.) This also applies to qualified fee and fee on condition.

- **Remainder interest.** Mr. A may leave the family homestead to the second Mrs. A for her lifetime with the provision that it pass, at her death, to the son of his first marriage, A Jr. During Mrs. A's lifetime, A Jr. owns a *remainder interest* and is known as a **remainderman**.
- **Reversionary interest.** Mr. A may give his home to poor relative B for B's lifetime with the provision that at B's death ownership reverts (returns) to A (or, if A has died, to A's heirs). During B's lifetime Mr. A owns a reversionary interest.

A life tenant's interest in real property is true ownership. The life tenant may not, however, permanently injure the land or property, an act known in legal terms as an **act of waste.** A life tenant is entitled to all income and profits arising from the property. A life interest could theoretically be sold, leased, mortgaged, or given away, but it always will terminate (end) on the death of the person against whose life the estate is measured.

Not Used in New York State

A husband's interest in the real estate of his deceased wife is called **curtesy. Dower** is the interest that a wife has in the real estate of her deceased husband. New York law no longer recognizes dower and curtesy.

In a community property state (California is a conspicuous example), property acquired during the marriage is presumed to belong equally to husband and wife,

FIGURE   4.8

Life Estate

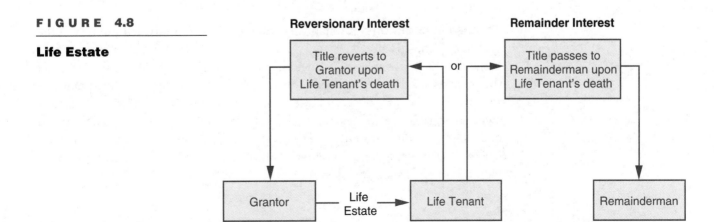

with the exception of gifts and inheritances. New York is not a community property state and recognizes no special community property rights in real estate.

In some states, the estate known as **homestead** gives the owner special rights in property used as a family home. New York does not have any special right of homestead.

■ FORMS OF OWNERSHIP

A fee simple estate in land may be held (1) in **severalty**, where **title** (ownership) is held by one owner; (2) in **co-ownership**, where title is held by two or more persons; or (3) in **trust**, where title is held by a third person for the benefit of another.

The form by which property is owned is important to the real estate broker for two reasons: (1) *the form of ownership existing when a property is sold determines who must sign the various documents involved* (listing contract, acceptance of offer to purchase, sales contract, and deed); and (2) *the purchasers must determine in what form they wish to take title*. When questions about these forms are raised, the real estate broker should recommend that the parties seek legal advice.

The word **tenant**, when used with various forms of ownership, does not refer to someone who is renting the property; instead, it means the owner.

Severalty

Severalty is the ownership of property by one person only. Ownership is severed or separated from any form of co-ownership and is also referred to as *sole ownership*. When the owner dies, the property passes to the owner's heirs or as otherwise provided by the owner's will.

Concurrent or Co-Ownership

When title to one parcel of real estate is owned by two or more persons or organizations, those parties are said to be concurrent owners or *co-owners*. New York recognizes the following forms of ownership: (1) tenancy in common, (2) joint tenancy, and (3) tenancy by the entirety (a special type of joint tenancy).

Tenancy in common   A tenant in common owns an **undivided interest** in the property. Although an owner may have, say, a one-half or one-third interest in a property, it is impossible to distinguish physically which specific half or third of the property is owned. The deed creating a tenancy in common may or may not state the fractional interest held by each co-owner. If no fractions are stated, each owns an equal share. For example, if five people hold title, each would own an undivided one-fifth interest. On the death of a co-owner, the deceased's interest would pass to heirs or devisees named in the owner's will (and the tenancy in common would continue). (See Figure 4.9.)

FIGURE 4.9

Tenancy in Common

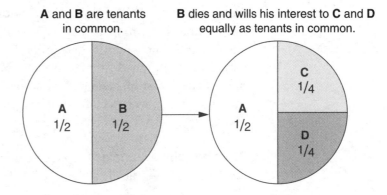

A second important characteristic of a tenancy in common is that *each owner* may sell, convey, mortgage, or transfer that interest *without the consent* of the other co-owners.

In New York, a **conveyance** (sale or gift) to persons not married to each other automatically creates a tenancy in common unless otherwise stated in the deed. Property inherited by two or more persons is owned by them as tenants in common unless the will states otherwise.

When an unmarried couple buys a home together, they have a decision to make. If one dies, should that person's share go to heirs named in a will or, if there is no will, to what the state calls *natural heirs*: spouse, parents, siblings, children? If so, they will take title as tenants in common. If, however, they would like the surviving partner to become complete owner automatically, their deed should make it clear they are taking title as joint tenants. Licensees should never render legal advice as to how the property vesting rights should be held.

FIGURE 4.10

Joint Tenancy with Right of Survivorship

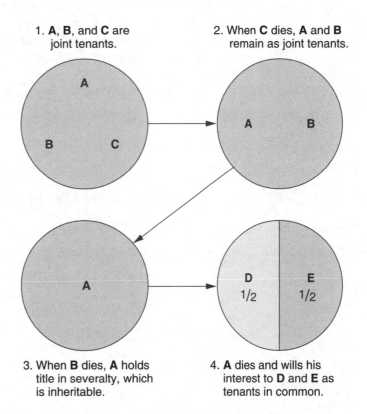

Joint tenancy with the right of survivorship   With joint tenancy, the property is owned by a group made up of two or more persons. The death of one of the joint tenants simply means there is one fewer person in the group. The remaining joint tenants automatically receive the share owned by the deceased tenant, by **right of survivorship**, no matter what that person's will might have ordered. Only the last survivor, who becomes sole owner, may dispose of the property by will to that person's heirs. (See Figure 4.10.)

Creating joint tenancies   To create a joint tenancy in New York, language in the deed must specifically state that title is taken in that form of ownership.

The following four **unities** are required to create a joint tenancy:

1. Unity of *time*—All joint tenants acquire their interest at the same time.
2. Unity of *title*—All joint tenants acquire their interest by the same deed.
3. Unity of *interest*—All joint tenants hold equal ownership interests.
4. Unity of *possession*—All joint tenants hold an undivided interest in the entire property.

> **Four Unities Required to Create a Joint Tenancy**
> 1. Time
> 2. Title
> 3. Interest
> 4. Possession

Terminating joint tenancies   Joint tenants are free to convey (sell or give away) their share of ownership, but the person who receives it cannot be a joint tenant with the other owners. In Figure 4.11, Lee can sell her interest (ownership) to Wilbur. Sims and Tobey remain joint tenants and would automatically inherit from each other, but Wilbur is a tenant in common with them. If Wilbur dies, his share will go to his own heirs.

During life, joint tenants with the right of survivorship may sell or (without the consent of any other joint tenant) transfer their interest in the real property to anyone they choose.

Any subsequent owner resulting from a sale or transfer of a joint tenant automatically becomes a *tenant in common* with any remaining joint tenants. (This is assuming that there were more than two joint tenancies at the time of original acquisition by the joint tenants.)

Upon death of a joint tenant, the decedent/joint tenant's share is shared equally with any remaining joint tenants.

FIGURE   4.11

Combination of Tenancies

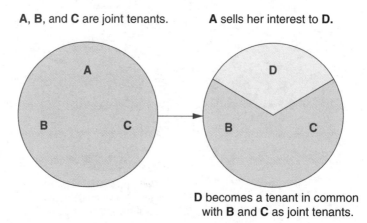

A, B, and C are joint tenants.

A sells her interest to D.

D becomes a tenant in common with B and C as joint tenants.

Termination of co-ownership by partition suit   Tenants in common or joint tenants may file in court a suit to **partition** the land. The right of partition is a legal way to end co-ownership when the parties do not agree. If the court determines that the land cannot be physically divided (acreage, for example), it will order the real estate sold and the proceeds divided among the co-owners. Such a forced sale, however, may not yield full market value.

Tenancy by the entirety   A **tenancy by the entirety** is a *special joint tenancy between husband and wife*. (It is used in New York, but not in all states.) The owners must be husband and wife when they receive the property. They have rights of survivorship, but there is no right to partition.

In New York, a conveyance to a married couple automatically creates in them a tenancy by the entirety unless the deed specifies otherwise. Divorce breaks a tenancy by the entirety, and the ex-spouses immediately become tenants in common.

■ TRUSTS

Property owners may provide for their own financial care and/or that of others by establishing trusts. Trusts of these types are normally established for a variety of purposes. Examples of why trusts are created would include but not be limited to reasons such as:

■ transfer of wealth to the next generation, and/or
■ tax considerations.

Such trusts may be created by agreement during a property owner's lifetime (inter vivos or living trust) or established by will after the owner's death (testamentary trust).

There are three parties to a trust: the trustor, the trustee, and the beneficiary or beneficiaries. The individual creating a trust, the **trustor**, makes an agreement conveying assets to the **trustee** with the understanding that the trustee will assume certain duties. These duties include the care and investment of the trust assets to produce income. After payment of operating expenses and trustee's fees, this income is paid to or used for the benefit of one or more **beneficiaries**. These trusts may continue for the beneficiaries' lifetimes or until the beneficiaries reach certain ages.

■ OWNERSHIP OF REAL ESTATE BY BUSINESS ORGANIZATIONS

Ownership by a business organization makes it possible for many people to hold an interest in the same parcel of real estate. Investors may be organized in various ways to finance a real estate project. Sometimes, real estate is owned by the organization itself, sometimes directly by the investors. Business organizations may be categorized as partnerships, corporations, syndicates, or limited liability companies. The purchase or sale of real estate by any business organization involves complex legal questions, and legal counsel is required.

All of the following types of business organizations contrast with **sole proprietorship**, a business owned by one individual.

Partnerships

An association of two or more people to carry on a business as co-owners and share in the business's profits and losses is a **partnership**. Partnerships are classified as general and limited.

In a **general partnership**, all partners participate to some extent in the operation and management of the business and may be held personally liable for business losses and obligations. General partners have unlimited personal liability for all losses that exceed the partnership's assets. Each of the general partners to the partnership share joint and several liability with the others.

A **limited partnership** includes general partners as well as limited (popularly known as "silent") partners. The business is run by the general partner or partners. The limited partners may not participate in day-to-day management activities of the partnership and can be held liable for the business's losses *only to the extent of each partner's investment*. The limited partnership is a popular method of organizing investors in a real estate project. If a general partner dies, the partnership is dissolved, unless the partnership agreement provides otherwise or allows for a substitution of another general partner.

Corporations

When formed, a corporation starts out as a C corporation. A **corporation** is an artificial person or legal entity created under the laws of the state from which it receives its charter. Because the corporation is a legal person, it also receives its own IRS employer identification number (EIN). The EIN is similar to an individual taxpayer's Social Security number.

Real estate ownership by a corporation is an *ownership in severalty*. Due to their perpetual existence, corporations may not be owners of real property with individuals as joint tenants with the right of survivorship, but may be tenants in common with others.

A corporation is managed and operated by its *board of directors*, which is elected by the shareholders. As a legal entity, a corporation exists indefinitely (in perpetuity). The death of one of the shareholders, officers, or directors does not affect title to property owned by the corporation.

Individuals participate, or invest, in a corporation by purchasing stock. Because stock is *personal property*, shareholders do not have a direct ownership interest in real estate owned by a corporation. Each shareholder's liability for the corporation's losses usually is limited to the amount of the shareholder's investment.

A C corporation

■ has no limitations on how many classes of stock it may issue;
■ has no limitations on how many shareholders may be holders of stock; and
■ is taxed twice:
  — once on the profits to the corporation and
  — once on the dividends distributed to the individual shareholders.

A simplified form of corporation, the **S corporation**, is allowed only a limited number of shareholders. Profits are passed directly to shareholders so that they are taxed only once. As previously mentioned, all corporations are formed and start out as C corporations. Formation of an S corporation is achieved by filing an "election to create an S corporation" with the IRS and the state. Only if the election is accepted by the necessary taxing authorities can the S corporation be considered formed. Under current tax laws, the election must be made within the first 150 days of the formation of the corporation. Failure to do so within the prescribed time period will make the entity a C corporation.

An S corporation

■ is taxed once at an individual level (and not on a corporate level as C corporations are);
■ may only have one class of stock;
■ may not have more than 100 shareholders;
■ may only have domestic citizens and no foreigners as shareholders;
■ may not have more than 20 percent of the corporation's income derived through passive activities; and
■ must report profits and losses of shareholders to the IRS through the S corporation's issuance of a K-1 to each shareholder as applicable.

Limited Liability Company

The **limited liability company** (LLC) is a hybrid entity that combines the freedom to manage the company offered by partnerships with the limited liability for all the owners and income tax advantages offered by corporations. LLCs do not have shareholders. The term *shareholder* is substituted with the term member. An LLC affords its members the advantage of corporate protections that are not available in partnerships. The owners pay taxes on earnings and profits received from the limited liability company.

Syndicates

A **syndicate** is *a joining together of two or more people or firms to carry out one or more business projects*. It may be organized into a number of ownership forms, including co-ownership (tenancy in common, joint tenancy), partnership, trust, limited liability company, or corporation.

A **joint venture** is an organization of two or more people or firms to carry out a *single project*. A joint venture lasts for a limited time and is not intended to establish a permanent relationship. It should be noted that a joint venture is *not a legal entity* but an arrangement between two or more parties wishing to venture together. Although the venture may lead to future business between the joint venture parties, it may be limited to the one-time transaction for which the venture was created.

The real estate practitioner who organizes or sells a real estate venture involving investors who expect to benefit without active participation should be alert for special registration or licensing required by the state department of law for syndication activity.

■ COOPERATIVE, CONDOMINIUM, AND CONDOP OWNERSHIP

In this century, apartment dwellers have turned to arrangements under which they own their living space. Cooperative ownership was the first to develop; condominium ownership appeared later (covered in greater detail in Chapter 24).

Cooperative Ownership

Under the usual cooperative (co-op) arrangement, title to land and building is held by a *corporation*. Purchasers of these units (shareholders) resemble tenants because by buying stock in the corporation, they receive proprietary leases to their apartments. The proprietary lease then becomes their occupancy agreement for the unit in question. As shareholders of the corporation that owns the underlying land and improvements to the land, they exercise control over the administration of the building through an elected board of directors. The board of directors takes on the role of fiduciary to the shareholders. Barring any violation of antidiscrimination laws, directors usually may approve or disapprove of prospective purchasers of the apartment leases. At this time, cooperative boards are not required to provide reasons for rejecting a prospective purchaser of the shares to a co-op apartment.

Under federal tax laws, cooperatives are deemed non-for-profit organizations. Because of this tax status, they were previously restricted from receiving in excess of 20 percent of their annual operating budget from any passive activity derived from

■ rents received on cooperative-owned property, such as commercial spaces, garages, vending machine receipts, and retail rents; and
■ interest payments on invested capital.

This IRS rule was commonly known as the 80/20 rule. "Eighty" denotes the active income portion (80 percent) of the cooperative. These funds are received by the cooperative in the form of monthly maintenance from its shareholders. The 20 percent portion reflects the passive income that may be derived from other "passive" activities.

As of December 2007, this rule has been repealed. This subject is discussed in further detail in Chapter 24. (One response to the former 80/20 rule has been the rise of a new hybrid of cooperatives and condominiums called *condops*. Condops will be discussed further following condominiums.)

Shareholder/tenants contribute monthly fees to cover

- maintenance costs;
- assessments of any kind or nature administered by the board of directors;
- the corporation's property taxes; and
- the underlying mortgage/debt servicing on the building. This mortgage/debt service is above and beyond the financing obtained by any shareholder covering the shareholder's individual living unit.

The corporation, however, is financially vulnerable. If other tenants cannot pay their monthly charges, the cooperative is required to cover those costs until either of the following occurs:

- The shares of the owner/occupant in arrears are foreclosed on through the cooperative's right to institute a foreclosure proceeding on those shares. This proceeding will result in the loss of the unit occupant's ownership in the shares as well as cancelling of the proprietary lease covering the unit.
- Prior to the aforementioned foreclosure proceeding, shareholders who are in arrears of maintenance redeem their stature as shareholders in good standing by paying all delinquent maintenance, late fees, and/or other penalties called for under the proprietary lease.

It is for these reasons that cooperatives have the right to approve new shareholders. Cooperative ownership is found in and around New York City more than in other parts of the state. It should be noted that, generally speaking, cooperatives are created by conversion from rental to cooperative ownership rather than by design as new construction.

Although the stock in a cooperative is considered personal property, a real estate license is needed for the sale of cooperatives. In addition, the IRS allows the owners of cooperative apartments to treat the units as if they were real estate for income tax purposes.

Condominium Ownership

The owners of each **condominium** apartment hold a fee simple title to their own dwelling unit and also to a percentage of the other parts of the building and land, known as the **common elements**.

The condominium form of ownership is often used for apartment buildings. These may range from freestanding highrise buildings to town house arrangements. Common elements include such items as the land, walls, hallways, elevators, stairways, and roof. Lawns and recreational facilities such as swimming pools, clubhouses, and golf courses also may be considered common elements.

In addition, condominium ownership has become more popular for commercial property or office buildings. The word *condominium* could apply even to a group of single detached houses whose ownership was organized in this fashion.

As with single-family and multifamily housing, the owner of a condominium unit receives a separate tax bill and may mortgage the individual living unit. Default in the payment of taxes or a mortgage loan by one unit owner may result in a foreclosure sale of that owner's unit but will not affect the ownership of the other unit owners.

Operation and administration In New York State, a condominium property is customarily administered by an association of unit owners or a board of managers elected by the unit owners. It may manage the property on its own or engage a professional property manager. Owners pay monthly charges for maintenance expenses.

Town house ownership is a hybrid form. Town house occupants own the land directly beneath their unit and the living unit, including roof and basement, in fee simple. Sometimes a small lawn or patio is individually owned as well. Single houses on extra-small lots, in what is known as *cluster housing*, sometimes use this form of ownership. A town house owner becomes a member of a homeowners' association, which owns the common elements.

Time-sharing is a variation of condominium ownership in which the buyer receives the right to use a living unit (commonly referred to as interval ownership), usually in a resort area, for a specific portion of a year. The buyer might own an undivided one-twelfth interest together with a right to use the facility for one month of the year.

Condop

The term **condop** refers to another hybrid form of real property ownership. This type of ownership uses two forms of ownership concepts:

1. Condominium
2. Cooperative

Although both condominium and cooperative ownership are merged to form a hybrid referred to as a condop, the property is truly organized (per the corporation's organizational bylaws) as a condominium. This hybrid emerged as developers attempted to eliminate any concerns resulting from the former 80/20 rule (discussed previously).

In a condop, the builder/developer seeks retention of any commercial spaces within the project. This normally will include office space, retail space, professional space, and/or garage space.

The developer's interests are only in the retention of the commercial spaces. The purpose of this retention is focused on income-producing potential. Regardless of how a property is set up organizationally, the developer's primary intent is always to sell off the living units to buyers. Once this has been accomplished, the result is as follows:

- Two or more *condominium* ownership interests are created in the land by
  — the developer who retains the commercial spaces and
  — the condominium association on behalf of the residential units of the property.
- Each owner receives a deed for their fee simple ownership interest in the property.

This type of ownership arrangement is commonly found in new construction and long-term leaseholds. Developers of new condominium construction will normally seek to sell off to others their full interest in the property. This is achieved through individual unit sales. However, as indicated above, when a property is organized as a condop, the developer generally wants to retain ownership interest in certain portions of the property that will generate income.

Previously, under the old 80/20 tax law covering co-ops and condos, by segregating the living units from the commercial portions of the property into two (or more) separate ownership interests, the developer was able to eliminate the potential of the cooperative exceeding the 20 percent passive income rule. Furthermore, the tax advantage created within a condop is that the unit shareholder receives an added income tax deduction that a condominium owner is not eligible for. This deduction comes to the condop owner in the form of an interest deduction on the underlying mortgage to the property. As previously discussed, the owner of shares in a cooperative will pay monthly maintenance. This monthly payment includes all costs that the condominium/cooperative needs to operate the property. One of the elements contained in maintenance payments includes the debt service on the property's underlying mortgage. Because condominiums (with few exceptions) do not have underlying mortgages, this deduction is unavailable in this type of ownership. Over and above the income-producing potential to the developer, this type of organizational structure creates the additional marketing tool of the living units.

The key qualities of the condop structure are as follows:

- Land is organized in condominium form.
- Each condominium owner operates separately from the other.
- The part of the property (generally the lower part) that holds the commercial spaces is retained by the developer, while the living units (generally the upper part) are controlled by the condominium/cooperative homeowners.
- The developer sets up the home ownership interests in the form of cooperative structure; however, because land ownership was set up as condominium, the section containing the living units bears similarity to that of a cooperative with condominium bylaws.
- The developer creates this hybrid form of ownership to also take advantage of certain tax benefits that are available within cooperative ownership and not in condominium ownership.
- The primary difference between a cooperative and a condominium (outside of the fact that the owner only owns shares within the cooperative corporation that owns the property) is the fact that cooperatives have an underlying mortgage on the property, which is over and above each unit holder's unit financing.
- Condominiums (generally with few exceptions) do not have any underlying mortgages. This is a major contributor to the value difference between condominiums and cooperatives.
- Generally, the lack of an underlying mortgage makes condominium ownership more expensive than purchasing a cooperative unit; however, there are exceptions to this.

■ OTHER WAYS TITLE IS TRANSFERRED

When a person dies leaving no will and no relatives who qualify as natural heirs, the deceased's real estate becomes the property of the state of New York, through the process known as **escheat**. Land is rarely acquired through long use without the owner's consent in a complex legal process known as *adverse possession*.

■ SUMMARY

Land includes not only the earth's surface but also the mineral deposits under the earth and the air above it. The term *real estate* further includes man-made improvements attached to the land. Real property includes real estate plus the bundle of legal rights associated with its ownership.

The same parcel of real estate may be owned and controlled by different parties, one owning surface rights, another owning air rights, and yet another owning the subsurface rights.

Ownership of land also includes the right to use the water on or adjacent to it. Riparian rights give the owner of land next to water that cannot be navigated by boat ownership to the middle of the stream. A river that can be navigated belongs to the landowner only up to the high-water mark; the riverbed belongs to the state. Littoral rights are held by owners of land bordering large lakes and oceans and include use of the water and ownership of the land up to the high-water mark.

All property that does not fit the definition of real estate is classified as personal property, also known as chattels. When articles of personal property are permanently attached to land, they may become fixtures and part of the real estate. Personal property installed by a tenant for a business purpose, however, is classified as a trade fixture, remains personal property, and may be removed.

Real property can be classified according to its general use as residential, commercial, industrial, agricultural, or special purpose.

An estate is the amount and kind of interest a person holds in land. Freehold estates are estates of indefinite length. Leasehold estates involve the right to use the property for a specified length of time without owning it. They concern landlords and tenants.

Estates that can be inherited include fee simple, fee on condition, and qualified fee estates. Life estates can be granted for the life of the new owner or for the life of some third party (pur autre vie). At the end of the life estate, ownership can go back to the original owner (reverter) or pass to a designated third party (remainder).

Sole ownership or ownership in severalty indicates that title is held by one person or entity.

Under tenancy in common, individual owners may own an unequal share, may sell their own interest, and have the right to leave the share to any designated beneficiaries. When two or more persons not married to each other hold title to real estate, they own it as tenants in common, unless their deed specifically states otherwise.

Joint tenancy involves two or more owners with the right of survivorship. Upon the death of one owner, that person's share passes to the remaining co-owners. The intention to establish joint tenancy with right of survivorship must be stated clearly in the deed, and four unities must exist. Both tenants in common and joint tenants have the right to force a sale by partition.

Tenancy by the entirety is a special joint tenancy for property acquired by husband and wife. Unless their deed specifically states that they wish to own the property in another way, they will own it by the entirety. Neither can force a sale by partition. Divorce changes their ownership to tenancy in common.

Real estate ownership also may be held in trust. Title to the property is conveyed by the trustor to a trustee, who administers it for the benefit of a beneficiary.

Various types of business organizations may own real estate. A corporation is a legal entity and holds title to real estate in severalty. A partnership or limited liability company may own real estate in its own name. A syndicate is an association of two or more persons or firms who join together for the purpose of making investments. Many syndicates are joint ventures organized for only a single project.

With cooperative ownership, title to the property is held by a corporation that pays taxes, principal, and interest on the building's mortgage and operating expenses. The purchaser of an apartment receives shares in the corporation and a long-term lease to the living unit and pays monthly charges to cover a share of expenses.

Under condominium ownership, each occupant/owner holds fee simple title to a living unit plus a share of the common elements. Each owner receives an individual tax bill and may mortgage the unit. Expenses for operating the building are collected by a condominium owners' association through monthly assessments. In town house ownership, each occupant usually owns the land directly below the unit, and a homeowners' association may own the common elements.

CHAPTER 4 QUIZ

1. A specific tract of land is known as a
   a. devise.
   b. parcel.
   c. chattel.
   d. littoral.

2. The definition of land includes
   a. sewers, roads, and streets.
   b. buildings permanently attached.
   c. the right of enjoyment.
   d. the airspace above the surface.

3. Real property is often called a *bundle of legal rights*. Among these is the right of
   a. navigation.
   b. exclusion.
   c. avulsion.
   d. emblement.

4. A farm owner in Steuben County may find that an oil company wants to lease his
   a. littoral rights.
   b. subsurface rights.
   c. air rights.
   d. riparian rights.

5. Man-made, permanent additions to land are called
   a. chattels.
   b. parcels.
   c. improvements.
   d. trade fixtures.

6. When a building is to be constructed next to land owned by another, the builder may be able to purchase the neighboring landowner's
   a. riparian rights.
   b. surface rights.
   c. unused development rights.
   d. zoning rights.

7. An owner of land along the Mohawk River has certain
   a. riparian rights.
   b. subsurface rights.
   c. air rights.
   d. littoral rights.

8. If an individual were to sell her farm, which of the following will *NOT* be a part of the real estate?
   a. Fences
   b. Permanent buildings
   c. Farm equipment
   d. Growing trees

9. Three sisters own a farm as tenants in common. One of them needs cash for a start-up business, but the other two refuse to sell the farm. Can the sister who needs cash find legal remedy for liquidating her portion of the land?
   a. No, real estate owned by tenants in common cannot be divided.
   b. No, under tenancy in common, all owners must agree to all transactions.
   c. Yes, her lawyer can determine her fair share, and she can sell that land.
   d. Yes, she can file a suit to partition the land to end the co-ownership.

10. When a beautician opened her hair salon, she installed three shampoo basins, four large plate-glass mirrors, and custom workstation counters. Just before the expiration of the lease, she has the right to remove
    a. everything but the shampoo basins because they are attached to the plumbing.
    b. only the mirrors, and then only if holes in the walls are repaired.
    c. the basins, mirrors, and workstation counters.
    d. nothing, because all of the items became fixtures when they were attached.

11. A couple are building a deck off their kitchen. A dealer has just unloaded a truckload of lumber onto their driveway. At this point, the lumber is considered
    a. chattel.
    b. real estate.
    c. a fixture.
    d. a trade fixture.

12. When the homeowners' deck is completed, the lumber will be considered

   a. chattel.
   b. real estate.
   c. a parcel.
   d. a trade fixture.

13. The six basic categories of real property are residential, commercial, industrial, agricultural, special purpose, and

   a. marine.
   b. government-held.
   c. multifamily.
   d. mixed use.

14. Special-purpose real estate includes

   a. apartment houses.
   b. houses of worship.
   c. factories.
   d. shopping malls.

15. Property that is part of the commercial market includes

   a. office buildings for lease.
   b. apartments for rent.
   c. churches.
   d. factories.

16. The simplest form of ownership recognized by law is a(n)

   a. life estate.
   b. leasehold estate.
   c. fee simple estate.
   d. estate at will.

17. A woman inherited her cousin's house, but it is hers only as long as her cousin's dog is alive and well and living in the house. When the dog dies, the house is to go to her cousin's son. The cousin's son is a

   a. beneficiary.
   b. remainderman.
   c. life tenant.
   d. limited partner.

18. A married couple owned a small apartment house by the entirety. The wife had a will leaving half of her estate to her husband and half to her daughter. After the wife was killed in an automobile accident, her daughter owned how much of the apartment house?

   a. None
   b. One-quarter
   c. One-third
   d. One-half

19. Ownership of real property by one person is called ownership in

   a. trust.
   b. severalty.
   c. entirety.
   d. condominium.

20. A house was purchased by two brothers. One paid one-third of the cost, and the other paid the balance. The seller's deed conveyed the property in both of their names without further explanation. The two brothers are

   a. joint tenants, with the one brother owning one-third.
   b. tenants in common.
   c. tenants in severalty.
   d. general partners in a joint venture.

21. If property is held by two or more owners as tenants in common, on the death of one owner, the ownership of the deceased's share will pass to the

   a. remaining owner or owners.
   b. heirs or whoever is designated under the deceased owner's will.
   c. surviving owner and/or the survivor's heirs.
   d. deceased owner's surviving spouse.

22. In New York, a deed conveying property to a married couple, such as to "Mr. A and Mrs. A, husband and wife," creates a

   a. joint tenancy.
   b. tenancy by the entirety.
   c. tenancy in common.
   d. periodic tenancy.

23. Which statement applies equally to joint tenants and tenants by the entireties?

    a. There is no right to file a partition suit.

    b. The deed must state the type of tenancy desired.

    c. There may be more than two owners.

    d. The survivor becomes complete owner.

24. An artificial person created by legal means is known as a

    a. trust.

    b. corporation.

    c. limited partnership.

    d. joint tenancy.

25. A syndicate formed to carry out a single business project for a limited time is commonly known as a

    a. joint venture.

    b. corporation.

    c. limited partnership.

    d. joint tenancy.

26. People who purchase stock in order to live in cooperatives

    a. must also purchase their own apartments.

    b. must inherit their apartments.

    c. must pay rent on their apartments to the condominium board.

    d. receive proprietary leases for their apartments.

27. The members of the board of directors can control who occupies the cooperative because

    a. the cooperative board has the right to approve or disapprove prospective purchasers.

    b. the board owns the apartment leases outright.

    c. cooperatives are exempt from antidiscrimination laws.

    d. cooperatives are deemed not-for-profit organizations.

28. The former IRS 80/20 rule concerns

    a. board requirements for explaining the rejection of prospective share purchasers.

    b. caps on annual increases in monthly maintenance fees paid by shareholders.

    c. acceptable limits on the passive income of cooperatives.

    d. the number of apartments that can be owned by a single investor.

29. The condop form of property ownership developed from the

    a. difficulty in transferring ownership in the condominium form of ownership.

    b. pressure on cooperative boards to loosen ownership requirements.

    c. developers' interest in retaining commercial spaces.

    d. demand among low-income families for affordable housing.

30. Unlike a C corporation, an S corporation has

    a. only foreigners as shareholders.

    b. no limitations on how many classes of stock it issues.

    c. limitations on the number of shareholders.

    d. no tax liability.

CHAPTER 5

Liens and Easements

■ KEY TERMS

adverse possession
affidavit of entitlement to commission
appurtenant
cloud on the title
corporation franchise tax
deed restrictions
dominant estate
easement
easement appurtenant
easement by condemnation
easement by grant
easement by implication
easement by necessity

easement by prescription
easement for light and air
easement in gross
encroachment
encumbrance
estate taxes
general liens
involuntary lien
judgment
license
lien
lis pendens
mechanic's lien
mortgage lien

nonpossessory rights
notice of pending legal action
party wall
possessory rights
priority
right-of-way
satisfaction
servient estate
specific liens
subordination agreements
tacking
tax liens
voluntary lien

■ ENCUMBRANCES

An **encumbrance** is a right or interest in a property held by a party who is not the owner of the property. Encumbrances fall into two categories:

1. *Liens*—financial claims against the property
2. *Usage encumbrances*—restrictions, easements, and encroachments

■ LIENS

A financial claim or charge against real estate that provides security for a debt or obligation of the property owner is a **lien**. If the claim is not paid, the lienholder, or creditor, may ask a court to order the real estate sold to pay off the debt, a process known as *foreclosure of the lien*.

A lien may be voluntary or involuntary. A **voluntary lien** is created by the owner's action, such as placing a mortgage loan. An **involuntary lien** is created by law. A real estate tax lien, for example, is an involuntary lien; it is placed on the property without any action by the property owner.

Liens may also be classified as either general or specific. As illustrated in Figure 5.1, **general liens** usually affect all the property of a debtor, both real and personal. They include judgments, estate and inheritance taxes, debts of a deceased person, corporation franchise taxes, and federal and state income taxes.

Specific liens, on the other hand, are secured by a specific parcel of real estate and affect only that particular property. As illustrated in Figure 5.2, these include mechanics' liens, mortgages, real estate taxes, special assessments, liens for certain public utilities, vendors' liens, vendees' liens, and surety bail bond liens.

- *Real estate taxes* (discussed further in Chapters 13 and 20) always have the first recorded claim against the property. They supersede all prior recorded liens to the property.
- This is representative of the claim recording process and establishes the position of the lien's priority in relation to other prior or later recorded liens. The oldest recorded lien always has priority over subsequent liens; however, real estate taxes always supersede and have priority over all other recorded liens. Priority is established by date and time of recording. This subject will be discussed later in this chapter.
- *Judgments* are court orders to pay a debt, such as an unpaid bill. They become liens against all real property owned by an individual in that county when they are docketed (filed) in the county clerk's office. They also may be filed in other counties in New York State and against personal property.

FIGURE 5.1

General Liens

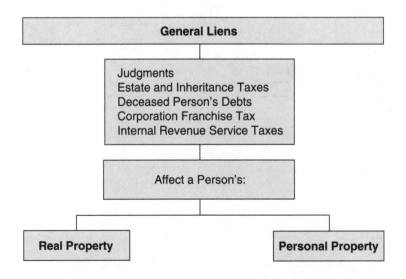

FIGURE 5.2

Specific Liens

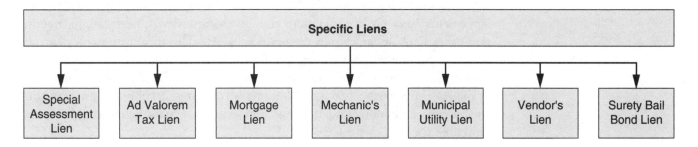

- *Mechanics' liens* are placed against a specific property by workers or suppliers who have not been paid for labor or materials used in construction, improvement, or repairs of that property.

■ EFFECTS OF LIENS ON TITLE

If the buyer agreed, an owner could sell a parcel of real estate even though it was encumbered by a lien. The lien, however, remains with the property because liens and other encumbrances *run with the land*; that is, they will bind successive owners.

Liens attach to property, not to the property owner. Although a purchaser who buys real estate subject to a lien may not be personally responsible for payment of the debt, the property is still encumbered, and the creditor could take court action to foreclose the lien.

Priority of Liens

Tax liens   Real estate taxes and special assessments (**tax liens**) generally take **priority** over all other liens. If the property goes through a court-ordered sale to satisfy unpaid debts or obligations, outstanding real estate taxes and special assessments will be paid from the proceeds first. The remainder will be used to pay other outstanding liens in the order of their priority. For example, if the courts ordered a parcel of land sold to satisfy a judgment lien entered in the public record on February 7, 2007, subject to a first mortgage lien recorded January 22, 1997, and to this year's as-yet-unpaid real estate taxes, the proceeds of the sale would be distributed in the following order:

1. To the taxing bodies for this year's real estate taxes
2. To the mortgage lender for the entire amount of the mortgage loan outstanding as of the date of the sale (if proceeds remain after payments of taxes)
3. To the creditor named in the judgment lien (if any proceeds remain after paying the first two items)
4. To the foreclosed-on landowner (if any proceeds remain after paying the first three items plus costs of foreclosure)

Liens other than general taxes and special assessments take priority from the date of recording in the public records of the county where the property is located. (See Figure 5.3.)

Subordination agreements Subordination agreements are voluntary written agreements between lienholders to change the priority of mortgage, judgment, and other liens under certain circumstances. In addition, it is notable that all leases within income-generating properties will also contain a subordination clause (see the example of a clause that follows); this clause places the interests of the leaseholder as secondary to that of any past, present, or future financing on the property and/or any underlying ground lease (by which the leaseholder leases land from the land owner).

■ **FOR EXAMPLE** "This lease is subject and subordinate to all ground or underlying leases and to all mortgages which may now or hereafter affect such leases or the real property of which the demised premises are a part, and to all renewals, modifications, consolidations, replacements, and extensions of any such underlying leases and mortgages."

■ LIENS OTHER THAN REAL ESTATE TAXES

Aside from real estate tax and special assessment liens, the following types of liens may be charged against real property either by the owner (voluntarily) or by an outside party (involuntarily).

Mortgage Liens

A mortgage lien is a voluntary lien on real estate given to a lender by a borrower as security for the repayment of a loan. It becomes a lien on real property when

- the mortgage funds are disbursed,
- the mortgage document is signed by the borrower (mortgagor),
- same is delivered to the mortgagee (lender), and
- the mortgage is recorded.

FIGURE 5.3

Priority of Liens

First Priority

Real estate taxes/special assessments

Next priority
according to
order of filing
in public record

Property   1024 First St.
                  Anytown USA

10-14-04 First Mortgage lien...
USA---Federal Savings & Loan
2-17-05--Mechanic's lien filed
J.W. Adams Construction
3-1-06--Second Mortgage lien--
American Finance Company

The lender files or records the mortgage in the office of the county clerk or register of the county where the property is located. Mortgage lenders generally require a *first mortgage lien*; this means that (aside from taxes) no other liens against the property will take priority over the mortgage lien. Second mortgages and home equity loans do not, of course, have first priority. When the debt is fully paid, the lien is removed from the property by filing a **satisfaction** of mortgage certificate signed by the lender. In addition, a lien can be removed by recording a document called a "release of lien." For this to occur, the party holding the lien (lienor) must execute the release document in favor of the liened party (lienee).

Mechanics' Liens

A **mechanic's lien** covers a situation in which an owner has not paid for work done on the property or the general contractor has been paid but has not paid subcontractors or suppliers of materials. A claim for a mechanic's lien must be placed within four months of the completion of the work on a single dwelling, while on other types of transactions, liens must be placed within eight months. A mechanic's lien expires in one year but may be renewed. Court action is not required; the lien is simply recorded in the public records.

An example of a lien that falls into the eight-month filing deadline category would be a *broker's lien*. New York's lien law allows certain broker claims for leasing commissions to be filed as written above. On the theory that the negotiation of a long-term lease constitutes an improvement of commercial property, a broker may enter a lien in the public records for unpaid commissions. Such a lien may be filed only

- if the property is to be used for other than residential purposes,
- if the lease is for three years or longer, and
- if the broker was working under a written commission agreement or listing agreement.

The lien must be filed within eight months of the date when the commission became due. This includes entitlement of commissions that are paid over a short or long period of time through installments. Each installment when due gives the broker the right to file the lien on the unpaid installment within eight months from the installment's due date.

Similarly, real property law allows a broker to file an **affidavit of entitlement to commission** for negotiation of a contract for the purchase or lease of any real property. Such an affidavit, although entered in the public records, *does not become a lien* against the property. A broker who leases a commercial or industrial property, however, may file a lien for commissions due.

In 2006, the New York Legislature passed the Commission Escrow Act. This bill was expected to aid residential real estate brokers in collecting their commission on a residential sale. On August 5, 2008, the governor signed into law an amendment to Section 294-b.

The amendment provides that an affidavit of entitlement filed by the broker before a closing would require the seller to deposit the broker's commission in escrow with the county recording officer. In order for this to occur, the listing agreement would have to include a recital of language covering this provision and ultimately allowing the broker to do this. The funds would continue to remain in escrow with the county recording officer until the rights of the interested parties were determined by

- a judge,
- alternative dispute resolution, or
- settlement between the seller and the broker.

The filing would have to occur before the delivery of the deed.

The amendment became law on January 1, 2009. The law is complicated and one should always consult a legal counsel before effectuating a filing based on this new amendment.

Release of liens   When a lien has been paid or has otherwise been considered satisfied, the party that benefited from the lien is required to remove the lien. This is achieved through recording of a document referred to *as a release of lien or satisfaction of lien.*

Judgments   A judgment is a decree issued by a court. A decree that provides for money to be awarded to the creditor is called a *money judgment.* A judgment differs from a mortgage in that a specific parcel of real estate was never given as security for the debt.

A judgment becomes a *general involuntary lien on all real property* in the county owned by the debtor when it is docketed (filed, recorded) with the county clerk. Transcripts of the lien also may be docketed in any other county in New York against the debtor's other real property.

A judgment is a lien against real property for ten years and can be renewed for ten more.

A judgment takes priority from the date the judgment is docketed in the county clerk's office. In order to satisfy a judgment creditor, judgments can be enforced through the sale of the debtor's real or personal property by a sheriff. Although this may be a complicated and costly legal proceeding, it affords the creditor with collection options on the judgment. If the sale yields enough to satisfy the debt after any liens with priority have first been satisfied, the sheriff's report of sale will show that the sale yielded sufficient money to satisfy the debt and the record will be cleared of the judgment.

A judgment also can be satisfied, of course, by the debtor's payment of the debt in full. Debtors who pay such a debt and fail to record a satisfaction piece—a document that states that the debt has been paid in full—are often surprised to find the judgment still on their credit records years later.

Currently in New York, a judgment lien bears statutory interest rates of 9 percent per annum on the monetary judgment amount. The interest is calculated as simple interest. This rate of post-judgment interest is set by the civil procedural law titled the Civil Practice Law and Rules (CPLR). CPLR Section 5004 not only fixes the post-judgment rate of interest at 9 percent per year, but CPLR Section 5003 further states that interest must run from the date of entry of the judgment.

Lis pendens   Considerable time may elapse between the filing of a lawsuit and the rendering of a judgment or other decree. When any suit is filed that affects title to a parcel of real estate (such as an action for specific performance), a **lis pendens** (or **notice of pending legal action**) is immediately recorded to give notice to interested parties, such as prospective purchasers and lenders, that there is a **cloud on the title.**

Other Liens

Federal **estate taxes** and state *inheritance taxes* (as well as the debts of deceased persons) are *general involuntary liens* that encumber a deceased person's real and personal property. These are normally paid or cleared in surrogate court proceedings.

A *vendor's lien* is a *seller's claim* in cases where the seller did not receive the full agreed-on purchase price.

A *vendee's lien* is a *buyer's claim* against a seller's property in cases where the seller failed to deliver title. This may occur when property is purchased under an installment contract (contract for deed, land contract), and the seller fails to deliver title after all other terms of the contract have been satisfied.

Municipalities that furnish water or services, such as refuse collection, are given the right to a lien on the property of an owner who refuses to pay bills.

A real estate owner who must stand trial for a crime may choose to put up real estate instead of cash as surety for bail (or other family members may pledge their real estate). The execution and recording of such a *surety bail bond* creates a lien enforceable by the state if the accused person does not appear in court.

New York levies a **corporation franchise tax** on corporations as a condition of allowing them to do business in the state. Such a tax is a lien on all property, real and personal, owned by the corporation. New York City also imposes a tax on corporations doing business in the city, which becomes a lien on the corporation's property.

An *environmental lien* may be levied by the federal government for costs and damages incurred in removal or remedial action under the Comprehensive Environmental Response, Compensation, and Liability Act (CERCLA), the environmental cleanup act. The lien attaches only to the property subject to the cleanup.

An *Internal Revenue Service (IRS) tax lien* results from failure to pay any portion of federal income or withholding taxes. It is a lien on all the taxpayer's real and personal property.

Other liens include those for unpaid condominium common charges in favor of the board of managers or condominium association; liens for unpaid maintenance or other charges in favor of a cooperative corporation; and liens for New York

State income and transfer taxes and some Uniform Commercial Code (UCC) filings.

DEED RESTRICTIONS

Private agreements that affect the use of land are **deed restrictions** *and covenants.* They usually are placed by the owner when the property is sold, and they may be included in the deed. *Deed restrictions* typically are imposed by a developer to maintain specific standards in a subdivision or to require that a property be used for a specific purpose. For example, property owners in a subdivision may not be allowed to park recreational vehicles in the street.

EASEMENTS

A right acquired by one party to use the land of another party for a special purpose is an **easement**. Easements commonly are created by written agreement between the parties. The principal type of easements are either **appurtenant** or in gross.

Easement Appurtenant

Four Types of Easements

1. Appurtenant
2. In gross
3. By necessity
4. By prescription

The permanent right to use another's land for the benefit of a neighboring parcel is an **easement appurtenant**. For example, *A* and *B* own properties in a lake resort community, but only *A*'s property borders the lake. *A* may grant *B* an easement across *A*'s property to give *B* access to the lake. (See Figure 5.4.) An easement appurtenant *runs with the land* (is permanent), so that if *B* sells the property to *C*, *C* acquires the same right-of-way over *A*'s land. If *A* sells to *D*, *B* still owns the easement. Easements appurtenant involve two adjoining parcels of land. The public often refers to such an easement as a **right-of-way**.

The property that benefits is called the **dominant estate**; the one that is used is the **servient estate**. In the example above, *B*'s property, which can use the neighbor's land, is the dominant estate; *A*'s property, which must allow the use, is the servient estate.

An easement appurtenant is ended if the two adjoining parcels are merged into one, owned by a single owner. It also may be terminated if the owner of the dominant estate (tenement) releases or abandons the easement. In some cases, an easement was only meant to last for a specific length of time and automatically expires.

Easement in Gross

A mere right to use the land of another is an **easement in gross**. Such an easement does not involve any adjoining estate. Common examples are the right to run high-tension, telephone, or cable TV lines. In Figure 5.4, utility lines run by right of an easement along the boundary line between the lots.

FIGURE 5.4

Easements

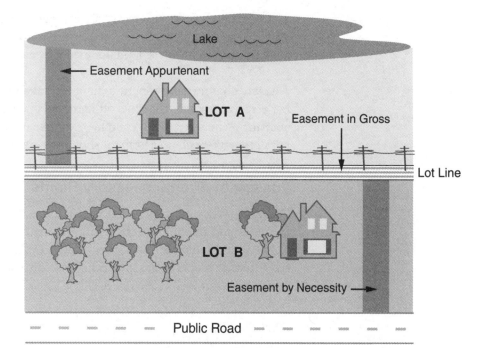

The owner of Lot A has an easement by necessity across Lot B to gain access to his property from the public road. Lot A is dominant and Lot B is servient. The owner of Lot B has an easement appurtenant across Lot A so that Lot B's owner may reach the lake. Lot B is dominant and Lot A is servient. The utility company has an easement in gross across both parcels of land for its electric power lines.

Easement by Necessity

In certain cases, the only access to a parcel is through another's property; that is, entry to one's property is landlocked by the property of another. In these situations, the owners may acquire an **easement by necessity** to reach their land. An easement by necessity would be terminated if the need for it no longer existed.

An easement by necessity is distinguished from an **easement by implication** in that the former easement arises only when "strictly necessary," whereas the latter can arrive when "reasonably necessary." An easement by implication is an easement created by the actions of the parties involved.

Easement by Prescription

Under specific circumstances, one may acquire the permanent right to *use* another's property by doing so for a period (in New York) of ten years, creating an **easement by prescription**. **Tacking** allows consecutive owners to accumulate the ten years' usage. (A similar process, *adverse possession*, sometimes allows the user to acquire actual *ownership*.) Through *tacking*, a party who did not use the property for the entire required period may still claim an easement by prescription. The parties must have been *successors in interest*, such as an ancestor and heir, a landlord and tenant, or a seller and buyer.

Less common types of easements are **easement by grant** (one created deliberately, usually through a deed, by the landowner) and **easement by condemnation** (the government's right to use land, for example, as a sidewalk).

An owner has no natural right to light and air and cannot complain when a neighbor erects a structure that cuts off light and air. To eliminate this possibility, some abutting owners attempt to purchase an **easement for light and air** over a neighbor's property. Such an easement should be granted in writing.

Possessory/Nonpossessory Rights

Possessory rights or possessory occupation is the act of property occupation and indicates and implies certain rights inherent to the occupant. **Nonpossessory rights** would indicate that a person does not occupy the property nor has any rights to that property. Easements fall into the category of nonpossessory rights or interests within land owned by another.

Party Walls

A **party wall** is shared by two buildings and constructed on the boundary line between two owners' lots. The owners own their own side of the party wall and an easement right in the other half. A party wall may not be demolished without the consent of both owners. The owners are responsible for maintaining their half.

Encroachments

When a building, fence, or driveway extends illegally beyond the land of its owner and covers some land of an adjoining owner or a street, an **encroachment** arises. Encroachments usually are disclosed by either a physical inspection of the property or a survey. A survey shows the location of all improvements on a property and whether any improvements extend over the lot lines. If a building encroaches on neighboring land, the neighbor may be able to recover damages or secure removal of the portion of the building that encroaches. Encroachments of ten years may give rise to ownership by **adverse possession** (a method by which title to real property is acquired if possessed but not owned for a statutorily prescribed period of time under certain conditions) or an easement by prescription.

On July 8, 2008, the governor signed an amendment into law modifying the state's controversial law covering adverse possession. Although most of the current law remains in place, the governor eliminated some of the ways that seemed absurd to lawmakers that, by way of case law, had previously supported a claim made by another. As a result of this amendment, the existence of de minimus nonstructural encroachments was deemed permissive and nonadverse. This would include but is not limited to the following:

- Fences
- Hedges
- Shrubbery
- Plantings
- Sheds and nonstructural walls
- Lawn mowing/similar maintenance performed on the property of an adjoining neighbor

■ LICENSES

Not classified as an encumbrance because it is not a permanent right, a privilege to enter the land or to use something of another for a specific purpose is known as a **license**. Examples of license include permission to park in a neighbor's driveway or to erect a billboard. The permission given by a license may be withdrawn. The primary feature of a license is that the license is terminable at the will of the licensor (the issuer of the license).

For example, think of the license agreement that applies when you are loading software on your computer. Unless you accept the terms of the software license agreement, you will not be allowed to load the software on your computer. The license is also terminable at the will of the software maker.

A driver's license is another example. The license is not granted permanently but may be revoked by the state at will.

■ SUMMARY

Encumbrances against real estate may be in the form of liens, deed restrictions, easements, and encroachments.

Liens are financial claims against the real and personal property of a debtor. Liens are either general, covering all real and personal property of a debtor/owner, or specific, covering only the one parcel of real estate described in the mortgage, tax bill, building or repair contract, or other document. Liens can be enforced by court-ordered foreclosure; that is, the sale of the property can be used to satisfy unpaid debt(s).

With the exception of real estate tax liens, which come first, the priority of liens is generally determined by the order in which they are placed in the public records.

Mortgage liens are given to lenders to provide security for mortgage loans. Mechanics' liens protect general contractors, subcontractors, and material suppliers whose work adds value to real estate.

A judgment is a court decree obtained by a creditor, usually for a monetary award from a debtor. When docketed (filed), it becomes a lien on all the debtor's real property in the county where it was docketed, and it may be similarly docketed in any other county in New York. Lis pendens, or notice of pending legal action, is a recorded notice that a lawsuit is awaiting trial in court and may result in a judgment.

Federal estate taxes and state inheritance taxes are general liens against a deceased owner's property. A vendor's lien is a seller's claim against a purchaser who has not paid the entire purchase price, and a vendee's lien is a purchaser's claim against a seller under an installment contract who has not conveyed title.

Deed restrictions are placed on land by sellers who wish to control future uses of the property.

An easement is a permanent right one has to use land owned by another. Easements appurtenant involve two neighboring tracts. The tract benefited is known as the dominant estate; the tract subject to the easement is called the servient estate. An easement in gross is a right such as that granted to utility companies to maintain poles, wires, and pipelines.

An encroachment is the physical intrusion of some improvement on another's land. A license is temporary permission to enter another's property for a specific purpose.

CHAPTER 5 QUIZ

1. Which of the following is considered a lien on real estate?
   a. An easement running with the land
   b. An unpaid mortgage loan
   c. A public footpath
   d. A license to erect a billboard

2. A contractor was hired to build a room addition to a home. The contractor completed the work several weeks ago but still has not been paid. In this situation, the contractor is entitled to file and record a mechanic's lien. Which of the following BEST describes the category of the contractor's mechanic's lien?
   a. General lien
   b. Specific lien
   c. Limited lien
   d. Voluntary lien

3. Which lien usually would be given highest priority?
   a. A mortgage dated last year
   b. Unpaid real estate tax
   c. A mechanic's lien for work started before the mortgage was made
   d. An IRS judgment lien recorded yesterday

4. A contractor remains unpaid for roofing a ranch home. How long does he have in order to file a valid and enforceable mechanic's lien?
   a. Four months
   b. Eight months
   c. One year
   d. Ten years

5. Unless an action of foreclosure on a contractor's mechanic's lien commences, his mechanic's lien will remain against the property for at LEAST
   a. four months.
   b. eight months.
   c. one year.
   d. ten years.

6. A homeowner's neighbor plans to file a suit against the homeowner because of a boundary dispute. When the neighbor learns that the homeowner's property is for sale, which action will the neighbor and her attorney take to protect her interest?
   a. Record a Lis pendens
   b. Record an easement by Prescription
   c. Record an Affidavit of entitlement
   d. Record a Satisfaction piece

7. When a patient failed to pay for his orthopedic surgery, the doctor obtained a money judgment, which, upon docketing, becomes a lien against the patient's
   a. vacant land.
   b. home.
   c. tiffany chandelier.
   d. real and personal property, including all of the above.

8. When the patient pays off his doctor's judgment, he should have the doctor
   a. record a satisfaction certificate.
   b. put a lis pendens on the apartment house.
   c. notify their mortgagee.
   d. grant an easement appurtenant.

9. A buyer entered into a contract for purchase and sale with a seller on a parcel of real estate. If the seller does not close on the contract as called for, which of the following devices could she use to assert her position?
   a. Mortgage lien
   b. Vendee's lien
   c. Lis pendens
   d. Vendor's lien

10. A buyer purchases a summer cottage that has an unpaid mechanic's lien recorded against it. The lien was previously placed by the workman who was not paid by the former owner for constructing a dock. The lien
    a. is void.
    b. remains as a claim against the property.
    c. is the former owner's responsibility only.
    d. is considered satisfied.

11. A telephone company runs its poles and wires with the rights granted by an easement

   a. by necessity.
   b. appurtenant.
   c. by prescription.
   d. in gross.

12. The farmer who allowed promoters to run the Woodstock rock festival on his land most likely granted them a(n)

   a. easement by necessity.
   b. dominant estate.
   c. voluntary lien.
   d. license.

13. To establish an easement by prescription in New York, a person must use another's property openly and notoriously for an uninterrupted period of

   a. 5 years.
   b. 10 years.
   c. 15 years.
   d. 20 years.

14. A landowner's neighbor regularly uses the landowner's driveway to reach his garage on his property. The neighbor has an easement over the landowner's driveway. Which of the following would apply to the landowner's property?

   a. The landowner's property is the dominant estate.
   b. The landowner's property is an estate.
   c. The landowner's property is a leasehold.
   d. The landowner's property is the servient estate.

15. A shared driveway agreement will probably take the form of a(n)

   a. voluntary lien.
   b. easement appurtenant.
   c. affidavit of entitlement.
   d. certificate of satisfaction.

16. A party wall is one that normally

   a. straddles a boundary line.
   b. faces a main road.
   c. is located only on a servient estate.
   d. is owned by one party.

17. A buyer purchases a vacation cottage. The previous owner had an easement appurtenant for access to the lake across a neighbor's land. If the buyer wants to reach the lake, she must

   a. renegotiate with the neighbor.
   b. apply to a court for an easement by necessity.
   c. pay a token rental to the neighbor.
   d. simply go ahead and use the crossing.

18. The lien with first claim against any parcel of real estate in New York State is

   a. unpaid property tax.
   b. a mechanic's lien.
   c. a first mortgage.
   d. the IRS's.

19. An owner of a condominium apartment in Manhattan also owns a cabin on three acres in the Catskills, where she keeps a boat, and a house in Florida. If one of her creditors sues her in Manhattan and obtains a judgment, that judgment may be recorded as a lien against the

   a. Manhattan apartment only.
   b. apartment and cabin.
   c. apartment, cabin, and boat.
   d. apartment, cabin, boat, and Florida house.

20. Deed restrictions are usually created by a

   a. subdivider.
   b. zoning.
   c. neighborhood association.
   d. government agency.

21. The right to cross the land of another in order to obtain access to one's property is an example of an easement

   a. in gross.
   b. by prescription.
   c. by necessity.
   d. in common.

CHAPTER 6

Real Estate Instruments: Deeds

■ KEY TERMS

accession	delivery and acceptance	monuments
alluvion	description	plat of subdivision
attorney-in-fact	devise	point (place) of beginning
avulsion	doctrine of laches	probate
bargain and sale deed	executor	public grant
bargain and sale deed with covenant	executor's deed	quitclaim deed
	executrix	rectangular survey system
benchmarks	full covenant and warranty deed	referee's deed
Bureau of Land Management		seisin
	grantee	special warranty deed
consideration	grantor	survey
conveyance	intestate	testate
covenants	land patents	testator
datum	legal description	title
dedication	metes-and-bounds description	warranty deed
dedication by deed		
deed		

In England during the Middle Ages, when few people were literate, transfer of title occurred in the following manner: The seller took the buyer into the field in question, and they walked the boundaries together ("beating the bounds"). Then the seller reached down, took up a clod of earth to represent the whole field, and handed it to the buyer. At the moment when the buyer seized the clod, he became owner of the land. Today, a document is used instead of a clod of earth, but title still transfers at the moment of delivery and acceptance, and the owner is still said to be *seized* of the property. The Middle English word **seisin** still denotes ownership and control.

■ LEGAL DESCRIPTIONS

One of the essential elements of a valid deed is an adequate **description** of the *land* being conveyed. (The deed does not usually describe buildings on the land.) A **legal description** is *an exact way of describing real estate in as complete of a manner that will be accepted in a court of law.*

Legal descriptions never should be changed or combined without information from a competent authority such as a surveyor or title attorney. Street address and property tax account number, although helpful for quick reference to what is being described, are not usually acceptable as legal descriptions.

Land can be described by the following three methods:

1. Metes and bounds
2. Government survey
3. Reference to a plat (map) filed in the county clerk's office in the county where the land is located, a tax map, or a prior recorded instrument

In New York, a legal description may combine different descriptive methods. Also used is reference to a previously recorded deed or mortgage.

Metes and Bounds

A **metes-and-bounds description** uses the boundaries and measurements of the land in question. A metes-and-bounds description is defined as description by "distance and direction."

It starts at a definite point called the **point (place) of beginning** (POB) and proceeds clockwise around the boundaries of the tract by reference to measurements and directions. A metes-and-bounds description always ends at the point where it began (the POB).

In a metes-and-bounds description, **monuments** are fixed objects used to establish boundaries. In the past, natural objects such as stones and large trees were commonly used as monuments. Today, man-made markers are more common because natural objects may change or be removed. An example of a metes-and-bounds description of a parcel of land (shown in Figure 6.1) follows:

> *A tract of land located in the City of Elmira, County of Chemung, State of New York, described as follows: Beginning at the intersection of the east line of Jones Road and the south line of Skull Drive; thence east along the south line of Skull Drive 200 feet; thence south 15 degrees east 216.5 feet, more or less, to the center thread of Red Skull Creek; thence northwesterly along the center line of said creek to its intersection with the east line of Jones Road; thence north 105 feet, more or less, along the east line of Jones Road to the place of beginning.*

Metes-and-bounds descriptions are used everywhere, from rural undeveloped areas to Manhattan, with street intersections used as monuments. They are most common in the original 13 states.

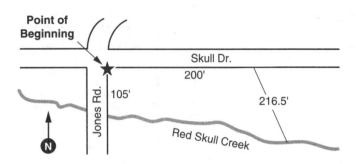

Rectangular (Government) Survey System

The **rectangular survey system,** sometimes called the *government survey method,* was established by Congress in 1785 as a standard method for describing western lands acquired by the government. It is seldom used in New York or any of the other 13 original states.

The rectangular survey system is based on sets of intersecting lines: principal meridians and base lines. *Principal meridians* are north and south lines; *base lines* run east and west. They are located by reference to degrees of longitude and latitude.

Townships   Using these meridians and base lines, land is surveyed into six-mile-square *townships,* each with identifying reference numbers. Each township contains 36 square miles. Each square mile constitutes a section. There are 36 sections within a township. Sections will be discussed next.

Sections   A township is divided into 36 numbered sections. Sections are numbered 1 through 36, as shown in Figure 6.2. Section 1 is always in the northeast, or upper right-hand, corner. *Section 36 is always located in the southeast corner of a township. Each section of land contains 640 acres.*

Section 16 was originally set aside as a *school section.* A school could be centrally located there, and income from the sale or rental of the rest of the section could be used to support the school.

As illustrated in Figure 6.3, each section may be divided into smaller parcels for reference purposes. The southeast quarter is a 160-acre tract; this would be

		N			
6	5	4	3	2	1
7	8	9	10	11	12
18	17	16	15	14	13
19	20	21	22	23	24
30	29	28	27	26	25
31	32	33	34	35	36

W   E

S

FIGURE 6.3

A Section

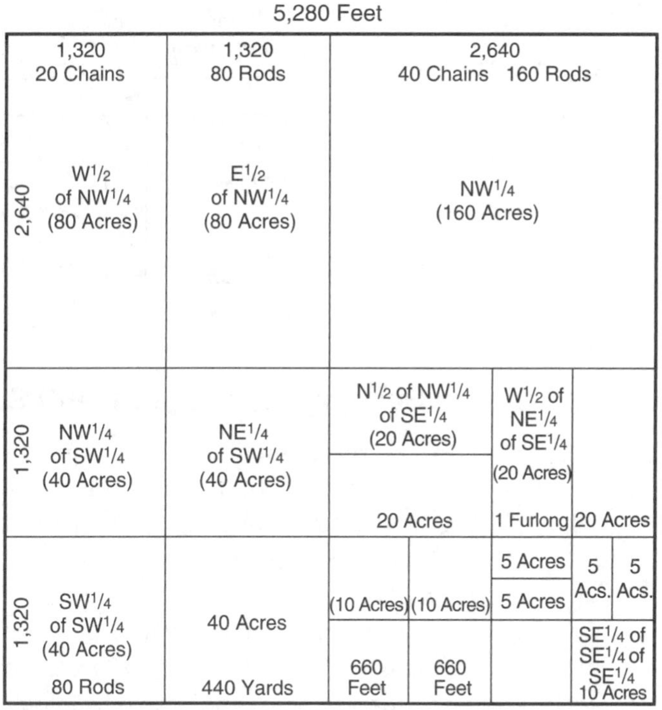

5,280 Feet		
1,320 20 Chains	1,320 80 Rods	2,640 40 Chains 160 Rods

abbreviated as SE¼. Quarter sections can be divided into quarters or halves and further divided by quarters. The SE¼ of SE¼ of SE¼ of Section 1 would be a ten-acre square in the lower right-hand corner of Section 1.

Calculating the amount of acres contained in the legal description of a parcel of land is illustrated here.

In this example (SE¼ of SE¼ of SE¼), apply the following formula:

Formula: 640 divided by 4 divided by 4 divided by 4
Calculation: Step 1: 640 acres ÷ 4 = 160 acres
Step 2: 160 acres ÷ 4 = 40 acres
Step 3: 40 acres ÷ 4 = 10 acres

Recorded Plat of Subdivision

The third method of land description is by *lot and map number* referring to a *plat of subdivision* filed with the clerk of the county where the land is located. The recorded plat of subdivision method is also known as the *block and lot method or filed map.*

It should be noted that every approved subdivision in the state of New York has been recorded in the county clerk's office where the property is situated. For this reason, these subdivision plat maps can be referred to because they provide a legal description of the land parcels.

The first step in subdividing land is the preparation of a *plat (map)* by a licensed surveyor or engineer, as illustrated in Figure 6.4. On this plat, the land is divided into blocks and lots, and streets or access roads for public use are indicated. Lots are assigned numbers or letters. Lot sizes and street details are indicated. The map shown in Figure 6.4 also includes metes-and-bounds descriptions. When properly signed and approved, the subdivision plat may be recorded in the county in which the land is located. Prior to the approval and recording of a plat map of subdivision, the subdivider is prohibited from conducting sales of any subdivided parcels.

In describing a lot from a recorded subdivision plat, the lot number, name or number of the subdivision plat, and name of the county and state are used. For example:

> THAT TRACT OR PARCEL OF LAND, *situated in the Town of Brighton, County of Monroe, and State of New York, known and designated as Lot No. 8 of the Fertile Acres Tract. Said Lot is situated on Dearing Lane and is of the dimensions shown on a map of Fertile Acres filed in the Monroe County Clerk's Office in Liber 125 of Maps at page 95.*

The word *liber* is Latin for *book*. Sometimes a *reel* number is used, referring to a specific reel of microfilm records.

Preparation and Use of a Survey

A licensed surveyor is trained and authorized to locate a given parcel of land. A survey sets forth the legal description. A survey map shows the location and

FIGURE 6.4

Subdivision Plat Map

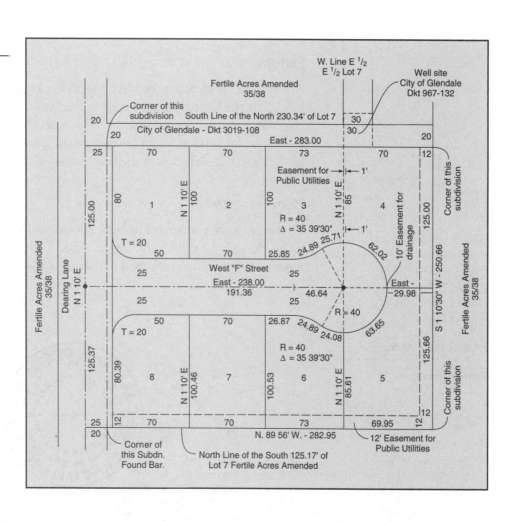

dimensions of the parcel and the location, size, and shape of buildings on the lot. Surveys may be required for conveying (transferring title to) a portion of a given tract of land, placing a mortgage loan, showing the location of new construction, locating roads and highways, and determining legal descriptions.

A survey will also uncover any encroachments encumbering the subject property. For example, a neighbor builds a fence on what appears to be the property line separating two parcels of property, but a survey can determine whether the fence is encroaching on the property of the party that installed the fence or is in fact encroaching on the neighbor's property. In the event that the fence encroaches on the neighbor's side of the property, if not corrected within the statutory period of time, the neighbor whose property was encroached upon may lose that portion of their property. A lack of assertion of one's rights may lead to a loss of those same rights via a lawsuit called a suit to quiet title. This section of law pertinent to the claim may include what is known as the **doctrine of laches**.

■ MEASURING ELEVATIONS

Air Lots

The owner of a parcel of land may subdivide the air above the land into *air lots*. This type of description is found in titles to tall buildings located on air rights or to condominium units. For these types of descriptions, the elevation of the land must be determined.

Datum

A *point, line, or surface from which elevations are measured or indicated* is a **datum**, defined by the United States Geodetic Survey as mean sea level at New York harbor. Many large cities have established a local official datum. In preparing a subdivision plat for condominium use, a surveyor describes each condominium unit by reference to the elevation of the floors and ceilings above the city datum.

Benchmarks

To aid surveyors, permanent reference points called **benchmarks** have been established throughout the United States. (See Figure 6.5.) GPS (global positioning system) devices can also be used to measure elevation.

FIGURE 6.5

Benchmark

▪ DEEDS

A **deed** is a *written instrument by which an owner of real estate intentionally conveys right, title, or interest in a parcel of real estate. In essence, a deed is used to convey real property from one person to another. Personal property, on the other hand, is conveyed by bill of sale.* Sometimes, a deed transfers only a part of the owner's interest.

All deeds must be in writing, in accordance with the requirements of the statute of frauds. The statute of frauds is a legal concept providing that, to be enforceable, all deeds for the partial or full transfer of an interest in real property must always be in writing. Therefore, oral agreements concerning transfers of real property are unenforceable. The owner, who grants (sells or gives the land) is referred to as the **grantor**, and the new owner (who receives the title) is called the **grantee**. A deed is always *executed* (signed) by the grantor (or other authorized person).

Occasionally, in mortgage assumptions and condominium transfers, it also is signed by the grantee.

Requirements for a Valid Conveyance

The requirements for a valid **conveyance** by deed are

- a *grantor* having the legal capacity to execute (sign) the deed;
- a *grantee* named with reasonable certainty so that he or she can be easily identified;
- a *recital of consideration;*
- a *granting clause* (words of conveyance);
- a *habendum clause* (to define the type of estate being conveyed);
- designation of any limitations on the conveyance of a full fee simple estate;
- an *adequate description* (a legal description) of the property conveyed;
- *exceptions and reservations* affecting the title;
- the *signature of the grantor, and (if the deed is to be recorded) acknowledgment;* and
- *delivery* of the deed and *acceptance* by the grantee to pass title.

Grantor In New York, in order to have legal capacity, a person must be a competent party (of sound mind and have reached the age of 18) to effect a valid conveyance. This requirement for competent parties is one of the essential elements of a valid and enforceable contract. A contract executed by an incompetent party such as a minor is *voidable* by the courts; that is, it may be set aside in a lawsuit conducted on behalf of the incompetent party, or in this instance, the minor. A minor may also void (or rescind) a contract upon reaching the age of 18. However, a minor who is married may convey property used as a home as if the minor had reached the age of 18.

Grantee To be valid, a deed must name a grantee in such a way that he or she is readily identifiable. In New York, both grantee and grantor must be identified by address if the deed is to be recorded. In order to receive a grant of real property, a grantee, unlike the aforementioned grantor, need not be a competent party.

Requirements for a Valid Deed

- Legally capable grantor
- Identifiable grantee
- Recital of consideration
- Granting clause
- Habendum clause
- Description of any limitations on conveyances
- Legal description
- Exceptions and reservations
- Grantor's signature and acknowledgment
- Delivery and acceptance

Consideration   To be valid, all deeds must contain a clause acknowledging the grantor's receipt of consideration. **Consideration** is something of value given in an exchange for the transfer of the real property. Where a purchase price is not involved, "love and affection" may be sufficient consideration, though often it is customary to recite a *nominal* consideration such as "$10.00 and other good and valuable consideration." In New York, the full dollar amount of consideration is seldom stated in the deed, except when the instrument is signed by a fiduciary such as an executor or trustee, by an attorney-in-fact pursuant to a power of attorney, or by a referee when the property is bought at a foreclosure auction. In addition, consideration can also be in the form of a promise. For example, a seller's promise to sell and a buyer's promise to buy are together considered to be a form of consideration.

Granting clause (words of conveyance)   A deed must contain words in the *granting clause* that state the grantor's intention to transfer (convey) ownership of the property.

If more than one grantee is involved, the granting clause should cover the creation of their specific rights in the property. The clause might state, for example, that the grantees will take title as joint tenants or tenants in common. This is especially important because specific wording is necessary to create a joint tenancy. Joint tenancy or tenancy in common describes just a few of the available vesting options by which an owner or owners may hold property. In New York, if the vesting option is not stated, a tenancy in common is normally presumed.

Deeds that convey the entire fee simple interest of the grantor usually contain wording such as "to Mary Smith and to her heirs and assigns forever." A deed creating a life estate would convey property "to Mary Smith for the duration of her natural life."

Habendum clause   To define or explain the ownership to be enjoyed by the grantee, a *habendum clause* follows the granting clause. The habendum clause begins with the words "to have and to hold." Its provisions must agree with those set down in the granting clause.

Exceptions and reservations   Grantors may reserve some right in the land for their own use (an easement, for instance). A grantor also may place certain restrictions on a grantee's use of the property. A developer, for example, can restrict the number of houses that may be built on a one-acre lot in a subdivision. Such restrictions may be stated in the deed or contained in a previously recorded document (such as the subdivider's master deed) that is expressly mentioned in the deed.

Description of real estate   For a deed to be valid, it must contain an adequate legal description of the real estate conveyed. Land is considered adequately described if a competent surveyor can locate the property from the description used. For example, a sufficient description of condominium property must include (1) a description of the land on which the building and improvements are located; (2) a designation of the unit conveyed as listed in the declaration, filed in accordance with the New York Condominium Act; and (3) a description of the common interest or the percentage of the common interest that is conveyed with the unit.

Signature of grantor   A deed must be signed by *all grantors*. The grantee, the person receiving the property, need not sign. New York permits a grantor's signature to be executed by an **attorney-in-fact**, a person who has been given power of attorney to sign for the grantor. Anyone can be appointed as an attorney-in-fact. One need not be an attorney to be appointed to this position in a transaction.

Usually, the power of attorney must be recorded in the county where the property is located. Because the power of attorney ends on the death of the person granting the authority, evidence must be submitted that the grantor is alive at the time the attorney-in-fact signs the deed. This is typically done with a phone call placed during the closing.

An *acknowledgment* is a declaration made by a person who is signing a document before an authorized public officer. Although an acknowledgment is usually made before a *notary public*, it can also be taken by a judge, justice of the peace, or other qualified person. This is a commonly confused subject. As previously stated, the party executing the document—and not the notary public—is the party that acknowledges. The signing party must prove to the other party to the agreement (required by law with certain documents, such as a deed) that the signing party is in fact the party executing the document. A notary public acts as a "witness for hire" to certify that this has occurred. Usually, before acting as the witness, a notary will require the acknowledging party to show some form of picture identification. Only after the identification has been presented does the notary sign and seal the document.

To summarize:

- The signing party acknowledges being, in fact, the party signing the document.
- The notary public acts as the legal witness to the acknowledging party's signature.

An acknowledgment is not required to make a deed valid, but in New York all deeds, mortgages, and similar documents must be acknowledged before they can be recorded (entered in the public records). In some cases, they can be signed before a witness, who would then swear to the validity of the signature before an authorized public official. It should be noted that unless the party(s) are in New York when they sign the document, nonresidents of the United States (foreigners or aliens) may not use a notary public to notarize a document intended for recording in New York; it must be acknowledged by the U.S. consulate.

From a purely practical point of view, a deed that is not acknowledged is not satisfactory, and although the deed may still be considered legally valid, future problems might arise. To help ensure good title, a grantee should always require acknowledgment of the grantor's signature on a deed so that it may be recorded.

Delivery and acceptance   Before a transfer of title by deed can take effect, there must be an actual delivery of the deed by the grantor and acceptance by the grantee. *Title is said to pass when a deed is delivered and subsequently accepted.* (*Title is the right to the entire bundle of rights inherent in real property ownership.*) Since title will not pass until the deed is delivered by the grantor, delivery represents a crucial part of any real property transaction.

Execution of Corporate Deeds

A validly created corporation (in accordance with state law) can hold title to both real and personal property. It may also convey real estate only after a resolution passed by its *board of directors*. If all or a substantial portion of a corporation's real estate is being conveyed, the holders of at least two-thirds of the stock also must approve.

Rules pertaining to religious corporations and not-for-profit corporations vary widely and may require a court order authorizing the conveyance. Because the legal requirements must be followed explicitly, an attorney should be consulted for all corporate conveyances.

Types of Deeds

The forms of deeds used in New York are as follows:

- Full covenant and warranty deed
- Bargain and sale deed with covenant against grantor's acts
- Bargain and sale deed without covenant against grantor's acts
- Quitclaim deed
- Executor's deed
- Referee's deed

> **Common Forms of Deeds**
> - Full covenant and warranty deed
> - Bargain and sale deed with covenant against grantor's acts
> - Bargain and sale deed without covenant against grantor's acts
> - Quitclaim deed
> - Executor's deed
> - Referee's deed

The term *covenant* can be best described as "a promise or an agreement." The term *warranty* can be best described as a "guaranty." Therefore, a full covenant and warranty deed can be described as a deed that contains promises and guarantees.

Warranty deeds   For a purchaser of real estate, a full covenant and warranty deed provides the *greatest protection* of any deed (shown in Figure 6.6). In it, the grantor makes certain covenants (promises) and warranties (guarantees), which are legal promises that the grantee will have unchallenged ownership. The basic warranties are as follows:

- *Covenant of seisin (ownership).* The grantor warrants that he or she is the owner of the property and has the right to convey it.
- *Covenant against encumbrances.* The grantor warrants that the property is free from any liens or encumbrances, except those specifically stated in the deed.
- *Covenant of quiet enjoyment.* The grantor guarantees that the grantee's title is good against anyone who challenges the grantee's ownership.
- *Covenant of further assurance.* The grantor promises to obtain and deliver any instrument needed to make the title good.
- *Covenant of warranty forever.* The grantor promises that if at any time in the future the title fails, he or she will be liable.

FIGURE 6.6

Full Covenant and Warranty Deed

Standard N.Y. B.T.U. Form 8003 — 8-73 — Warranty Deed With Full Covenants — Individual or Corporation. (single sheet)   35-3100-021
Form 31-21

THIS INDENTURE, made the   day of   , nineteen hundred and
BETWEEN

party of the first part, and

party of the second part,

WITNESSETH, that the party of the first part, in consideration of Ten Dollars and other valuable consideration paid by the party of the second part, does hereby grant and release unto the party of the second part, the heirs or successors and assigns of the party of the second part forever,

ALL that certain plot, piece or parcel of land, with the buildings and improvements thereon erected, situate, lying and being in the

TOGETHER with all right, title and interest, if any, of the party of the first part of, in and to any streets and roads abutting the above-described premises to the center lines thereof; TOGETHER with the appurtenances and all the estate and rights of the party of the first part in and to said premises; TO HAVE AND TO HOLD the premises herein granted unto the party of the second part, the heirs or successors and assigns of the party of the second part forever.

AND the party of the first part, in compliance with Section 13 of the Lien Law, covenants that the party of the first part will receive the consideration for this conveyance and will hold the right to receive such consideration as a trust fund to be applied first for the purpose of paying the costs of the improvement and will apply the same first to the payment of the cost of the improvement before using any part of the total of the same for any other purpose.

AND the party of the first part covenants as follows: that said party of the first part is seized of the said premises in fee simple, and has good right to convey the same; that the party of the second part shall quietly enjoy the said premises; that the said premises are free from incumbrances, except as aforesaid; that the party of the first part will execute or procure any further necessary assurance of the title to said premises; and that said party of the first part will forever warrant the title to said premises.

The word "party" shall be construed as if it read "parties" whenever the sense of this indenture so requires.

IN WITNESS WHEREOF, the party of the first part has duly executed this deed the day and year first above written.

IN PRESENCE OF:

Forms may be purchased from Julius Blumberg, Inc., New York, NY 10013, or any of its dealers. Reproduction prohibited.

These covenants in a **warranty deed** are not limited to matters that occurred during the time the grantor owned the property; they extend back to all previous owners. The grantee is entitled to money damages if any of the warranties are ever breached.

In New York, the seller need not deliver a full covenant and warranty deed unless the purchase agreement requires it. In many upstate areas, the warranty deed is the one used most commonly. In other areas, a bargain and sale deed with covenant is more usual. However, a full covenant and warranty deed contains the strongest language in the form of protection for a buyer.

Bargain and sale deed with covenant against grantor's acts (special warranty deed) With these deeds, the grantors imply that they have title to the property and add only one covenant, which states that they have done nothing to encumber the property while it was in their possession. This deed is used in most sale transactions and by fiduciaries (executors and trustees). The grantors are willing to warrant about the time they owned the property but not about previous owners.

This **bargain and sale deed with covenant** (against grantor's acts) is normally used in real estate transactions in the New York City area; the buyer may look to title insurance for protection in the event of future title problems. In most other states, this deed is known as a **special warranty deed**.

Bargain and sale deed without covenant A bargain and sale deed without covenant contains no warranties. It does, however, *imply* that the grantor holds title to the property. The grantee has little legal recourse if defects later appear in the title. The bargain and sale deed without covenant is also commonly used in New York City, as well as in foreclosure and tax sales and as a *referee's deed*; however, this type of deed would generally not be acceptable to an institutional lender.

Quitclaim deeds A quitclaim deed provides the grantee with the least protection. It carries no covenant or warranties and conveys only whatever interest the grantor may have. If the grantor has no interest in the property, the grantee will acquire nothing and will have no claim against the grantor. A quitclaim deed can convey title as effectively as a warranty deed if the grantor has good title, but it provides no guarantees.

A quitclaim deed commonly is used for simple transfers within a family and for property transferred during divorce settlements. A quitclaim deed also can be used to clear a cloud on a title when persons who may or may not have some claim to property are asked to "sign off." A quitclaim deed can best be described as "a deed of release" of any claim that one may have or have had to a property.

Executor's and referee's deeds An executor's deed is a bargain and sale deed with covenant; a **referee's deed** contains no covenants or warranties, although it does *imply* seisin (ownership). The *full consideration* (sales price) usually is stated in these cases so that it is a matter of public record.

DEDICATION BY DEED

The developer who turns over the road in a new subdivision to the local government does so by the process known as **dedication** or **dedication by deed**. A quitclaim deed is often used for the process.

Items that are the subject of dedication may include the following:

■ Roads
■ Sidewalks
■ Public areas within a development

The purpose of dedication is to transfer certain areas within a new subdivision or development to a municipality. The subdivider or developer performs the act of dedication to alleviate the financial burden of street cleaning, street paving, trash removal/sanitation services, and maintenance of public areas providing ingress and egress to the subdivision/development.

In some cases involving zoning, the dedication of areas within a development for the exclusive use by the general public entitles the dedicating party to additional *bulk* incentive zoning. (*Bulk* is defined as the total size of a project in zoning terms.)

Land patents document the transfer of land ownership from the federal government to individuals. The **Bureau of Land Management** (BLM) is a governmental agency that is part of the U.S. Department of the Interior. Its purpose is to administer public lands owned by the federal government.

A **public grant** is a transfer of land by a government body to a private individual.

NATURAL PROCESSES

Landowners are entitled to any additional soil (**alluvion**) added to their property by lakes, rivers, or streams. The right of ownership to such new land is called **accession**. Land lost by erosion or the sudden tearing away of land by earthquake or tidal waves is lost to the landowner by the process of **avulsion**.

CONVEYANCE AFTER DEATH

A will differs from a deed in that it outlines the desires of what should happen with the decedent's property upon the death of the person signing the will (the *testator*). Transfer is either

■ by operation of law (due to the manner by which the property was held, for example, a joint tenancy with the right of survivorship (nonwillable) by which the surviving joint tenant(s) are automatically entitled to the decedent's share of the property); or
■ by executor's deed.

Probate or administration is the process by which the property of a deceased person is distributed, under the supervision of the surrogate court in the county where the decedent (the person who died) lived.

If the decedent left a will (died **testate**), he or she (the **testator** or *testatrix*) may have named an **executor** or **executrix** to carry out the provisions of the will. If not, during the process of probate, the court appoints an administrator. Heirs who receive real estate through a will are known as *devisees*. To transfer real property through a will is to **devise** it.

When a person dies **intestate** (without leaving a will), property goes by intestate succession to what the law calls *natural heirs*—surviving spouse, children, and relatives. The statute of descent and distribution lists those persons who are in a close enough degree of kinship to be considered natural heirs. Where neither a will nor natural heirs can be found, the property passes to the state of New York through the process known as escheat, whereby the state acts as your last remaining heir by default.

■ SUMMARY

Documents affecting interests in real estate must contain a legal description that accurately identifies the property involved. Land is described by (1) metes and bounds, (2) rectangular (government) survey, and (3) recorded plat of subdivision.

In a metes-and-bounds description, the actual location of monuments is an important consideration. The description always must enclose a tract of land; the boundary line must end at the point at which it started.

The rectangular survey system is not used in New York. It involves surveys based on principal meridians. Land is surveyed into squares 36 miles in area called *townships*. Townships are divided into 36 sections of one square mile each. Each square mile contains 640 acres.

Land can be subdivided into lots by means of a recorded plat of subdivision. An approved map giving the size, location, and designation of lots and specifying the location and size of streets is filed in the county clerk's or recorder's office of the county where the land is located.

A survey is the usual method of certifying the legal description of a parcel of land. Surveys often are required when a mortgage or new construction is involved.

Air lots, condominium descriptions, and other measurements of vertical elevations may be computed from the U.S. Geodetic Survey datum, which is mean sea level in New York harbor. Most large cities have established local datums. The elevations from these datums are further supplemented by reference points called benchmarks.

The voluntary transfer of an owner's title is made by a deed, executed (signed) by the owner as grantor to the purchaser or donee as grantee.

Among the most common requirements for a valid deed are a grantor with legal capacity to contract; a readily identifiable grantee; a granting clause; a legal description of the property; a recital of consideration, exceptions, and reservations on the title; and the signature of the grantor. In addition, the deed should be acknowledged before a notary public or other officer to provide evidence that the signature is genuine and to allow recording. Title to the property passes when the grantor delivers a deed to the grantee who accepts it.

A general warranty deed provides the greatest protection of any deed by binding the grantor to certain covenants or warranties. A bargain and sale deed with covenant warrants only that the real estate has not been encumbered by the grantor. A bargain and sale deed without covenant carries with it no warranties but implies that the grantor holds title to the property. A quitclaim deed carries no warranties whatsoever and conveys only whatever interest, if any, the grantor may or may not possess in the property.

CHAPTER 6 QUIZ

1. When a couple bought a farm from the wife's parents, they received only a quitclaim deed. This was MOST likely because
   a. that's the type often used for in-family transactions.
   b. the husband will own the farm only during his wife's lifetime.
   c. the couple owns as tenants by the entirety.
   d. a mortgage was involved.

2. The land of a new homeowner in the Buffalo subdivision known as Vista Ridge probably bears a legal description based on
   a. the rectangular survey.
   b. metes and bounds.
   c. his surveyor's report.
   d. the street address.

3. When someone dies leaving no will and no natural heirs, the deceased's property goes to
   a. local charities.
   b. the federal government.
   c. the state of New York.
   d. an escrow fund.

4. Someone who dies without leaving a will is said to have died
   a. devised.
   b. conveyed.
   c. probated.
   d. intestate.

5. The LEAST acceptable legal method for identifying property is
   a. the rectangular survey.
   b. lot and block.
   c. the street address.
   d. metes and bounds.

6. It is essential that every deed be signed by the
   a. grantor.
   b. grantee.
   c. grantor and grantee.
   d. devisee.

7. Title to property transfers at the moment a deed is
   a. signed.
   b. acknowledged.
   c. delivered and accepted.
   d. recorded.

8. Consideration in a deed refers to
   a. gentle handling of the document.
   b. something of value given by each party.
   c. the habendum clause.
   d. the payment of transfer tax stamps.

9. A declaration before a notary or other official providing evidence that a signature is genuine is an
   a. affidavit.
   b. acknowledgment.
   c. affirmation.
   d. estoppel.

10. A notary's acknowledgment of the signature on a deed is necessary
    a. for the deed to be valid.
    b. for the deed to be recorded.
    c. before transfer tax can be paid.
    d. to give constructive notice of the transfer.

11. A seller signs a deed to a buyer as grantee, has it acknowledged, and receives payment from her. The seller arranges to meet the buyer the next morning at the courthouse to give the deed to her. The buyer will own the property
    a. immediately because she has paid for it.
    b. the next morning when she receives the deed.
    c. when she records the deed.
    d. as soon as she signs the deed the next morning.

12. According to the plat map in Figure 6.7, which lot has the most frontage on Manassas Lane?

    a. Lot 10, Block B

    b. Lot 11, Block B

    c. Lot 8, Block A

    d. Lot 7, Block A

13. According to the plat map in Figure 6.7, on the plat, how many lots have easements?

    a. One

    b. Two

    c. Three

    d. Four

FIGURE 6.7

Plat Map of Braddock Estates

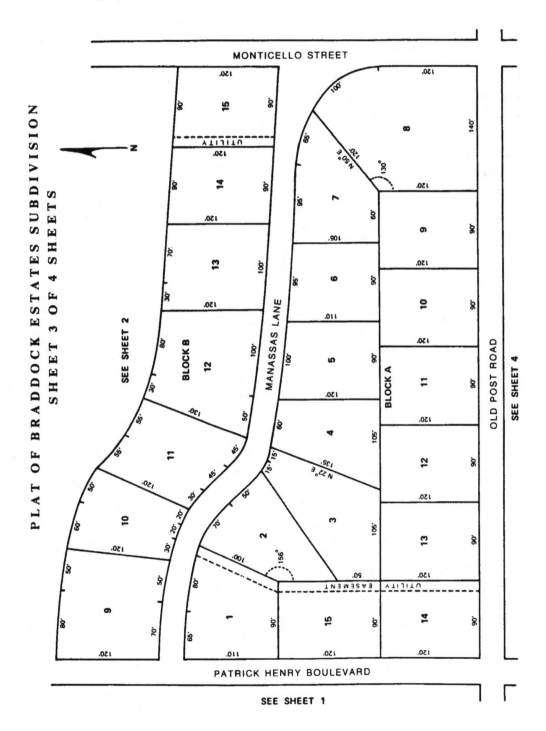

14. The grantee receives greatest protection with what type of deed?

    a. Quitclaim
    b. Warranty
    c. Bargain and sale with covenant
    d. Executor's

15. A bargain and sale deed with covenant against grantor's acts is commonly used

    a. by executors.
    b. upstate.
    c. in divorce settlements.
    d. to clear cloud from a title.

16. The developer of Spring Lake subdivision turned property over to the local government for road and sidewalks through the process called

    a. alluvion.
    b. condemnation.
    c. dedication.
    d. escheat.

17. An example of land lost through avulsion is

    a. conveyance.
    b. easement appurtenant.
    c. tax delinquency.
    d. erosion.

18. Which element of a real estate transaction is seldom included in the deed?

    a. Full dollar amount
    b. Address of the grantee
    c. Legal description of the real estate
    d. Signature of the grantor

CHAPTER

7

Real Estate Instruments: Leases

■ KEY TERMS

actual eviction	lease	periodic estate
assignment	leasehold estate	periodic lease
constructive eviction	lessee	proprietary lease
estate for years	lessor	quiet enjoyment
graduated lease	month-to-month tenancy	security deposit
gross lease	net lease	statute of frauds
ground lease	New York General	sublease
holdover tenant	Obligations Law	suit for possession
implied warranty of	novation	tenancy at sufferance
habitability	option to renew	tenancy at will
index lease	percentage lease	triple-net lease

■ LEASING REAL ESTATE

A **lease** is a contract between an owner of real estate (known as the **lessor**) and a tenant (the **lessee**) that transfers the right to possession and use of the owner's property, usually for a specified period of time. Due to the time restriction of possession of the property, a lease falls under the category of a *nonfreehold estate*. As you learned in Chapter 4, a nonfreehold estate is one in which the tenant is not free to hold the property for an indefinite period of time, whereas a freehold estate constitutes ownership in a property. Therefore, one can conclude that all leases fall within the nonfreehold estate category. A lease agreement establishes the length of time the contract for possession of the demised premises is to run, the amount to be paid by the lessee for the right to use the property, and the rights and obligations of the parties.

The landlord grants the tenant the right to occupy the premises and use them only for purposes stated in the lease. In return, the landlord retains the right to receive payment for the use of the premises as well as a *reversionary right* to retake possession after the lease term has expired.

To prevent misunderstandings, the New York State **statute of frauds** requires the following for a lease to be enforceable:

- A lease for a term of more than one year must be in writing.
- All agreements involving the conveyance of a partial or whole interest in real property must be in writing.

In addition, leases should be signed by both lessor and lessee. Under the statute of frauds, a lease for one year or less need not be in writing to be legally enforceable.

■ LEASEHOLD ESTATES

A tenant's right to occupy realty is called a **leasehold estate**. Just as there are several types of freehold (ownership) estates, there are various leasehold estates. The four most important are the (1) estate for years; (2) periodic estate, or estate from period to period; (3) tenancy at will; and (4) tenancy at sufferance. (See Table 7.1.) All are recognized in New York.

Estate for Years

A leasehold estate that continues for a definite period of time, whether for years, months, weeks, or even days, is called an **estate for years**. It always has a specific starting and ending time. When that time expires, the lessee is required to leave. No notice is required to end the lease when the time is up. A lease for years may be terminated ahead of time by mutual consent, but otherwise neither party may terminate without showing that the other has breached the lease agreement.

An estate for years need not last for years or even for one year. The main point is that it begins and ends at a specific time.

Periodic Estate

Periodic estates, sometimes called *estates from period to period*, continue for an indefinite length of time without a specific expiration date. They may run for a certain amount of time: month to month, week to week, or year to year. The

TABLE 7.1	Type of estate	Distinguishing characteristics
Leasehold Estates	Estate for years	For definite period of time
	Periodic estate	Automatically renews
	Tenancy at will	For indefinite period of time
	Tenancy at sufferance	Without landlord's consent

agreement is automatically renewed for similar succeeding periods until one of the parties gives notice to terminate.

A **month-to-month tenancy** is created when a tenant takes possession with no definite termination date and pays rent on a monthly basis.

Four Types of Leasehold Estates

1. Estate for years
2. Periodic estate
3. Tenancy at will
4. Tenancy at sufferance

A New York tenant who remains in possession of leased premises after expiration of the lease is known as a **holdover tenant**. (Another name for a holdover tenant could be a tenancy at sufferance, discussed below.) If the landlord accepts rent, a tenancy from month to month is created. Or, if the lease term is longer than one month, the landlord may commence proceedings to remove a tenant who has held over. The legal process to remove the tenant in possession is referred to as a "holdover proceeding."

To *terminate* a periodic estate, either the landlord or the tenant must give *proper notice*. To end a month-to-month tenancy, New York State requires one month's written notice; New York City requires 30 days' notice. Notice must be given at least one day before a date on which rent is due. If rent is due on September 1, the landlord who wants the tenant to vacate by October 1 must give notice no later than August 31.

Tenancy at Will

An estate that gives the tenant the right to possess with the consent of the landlord and for no definite time is a **tenancy at will**. It might occur when property has been put on the market and the landlord gives the present tenant (who has no lease) permission to remain until the indefinite time when the sale is closed. The term is indefinite, but the tenancy may be terminated by giving proper notice. Unlike other tenancies, an estate at will is automatically terminated by the death of either landlord or tenant.

Tenancy at Sufferance

A **tenancy at sufferance** arises when tenants continue, after their rights have expired, to occupy the premises *without the consent of the landlord*. Examples of estates at sufferance might be when a tenant *fails to leave* at the expiration of the lease or when a mortgagor refuses to leave after a foreclosure sale. Many New York commercial leases contain clauses stating that tenants may be charged up to double rent for the period they are in possession as a tenant at sufferance or holdover tenant. Although these clauses may not necessarily be enforceable, they are usually intended to deter tenants from holding over after their leases have expired.

■ TYPICAL LEASE PROVISIONS

The lease may be written, oral, or implied, depending on the circumstances. A lease that is for a term greater than one year must be in written form to be enforceable (statute of frauds). New York State requires a *plain English* format for residential leases. The requirements for a valid lease are essentially the same as those for any other real estate contract. In New York, the eight essentials of a valid lease include the following:

1. *Capacity to contract.* The parties must be competent parties.
2. *A demising clause.* The lessor agrees to let and the lessee to take the premises.
3. *Description of the premises.* A description of the leased premises should be clearly stated. If the lease covers unimproved land, the legal description of the real estate should be used. If the lease is for part of a building, such as office space or an apartment, the space itself should be clearly described.
4. *A clear statement of the term* (duration) of the lease must be provided.
5. *Specification of the rent and how it is to be paid.* In New York, unless the lease states otherwise, rent is considered due in arrears rather than in advance. In addition, in commercial leases, rent is always expressed in annual terms payable in equal monthly installments. Stating monthly rents only, may subject the contract to be interpreted by the courts as a month-to-month lease.
6. *The lease must be in writing* if it is to be for more than one year.
7. *Signatures.* A lease should be signed by both parties.
8. *Delivery.* The lease must be delivered by landlord to tenant, with duplicate originals for each.

Use of Premises

A lessor may restrict a lessee's use of premises through provisions included in the lease. This is most important in leases for stores or commercial space. A lease may provide, for example, that the leased premises are to be used *only* as a real estate office. In the absence of such limitations, a lessee may use the premises for any lawful purpose.

In a commercial lease, when a tenant is considering the subleasing or assignment of the lease to another, the use clause is of particular importance. If the use clause restricts the use of the premises to "a real estate office only," although one may have the right to sublease or assign with the landlord's prior written consent, the landlord could withhold consent for the sublease if the new tenant would not be in compliance with the use clause.

Disabled tenants are entitled to make any reasonable alterations that are necessary to accommodate their disabilities. These tenants must pay for the alterations, and landlords may require that a tenant restore the premises to their former state at the end of the lease term. To ensure that restoration will occur at the end of the lease term, the landlord is permitted to require the disabled party to either post a bond or pay additional rent security deposit.

Term of Lease

The term of a lease is the period for which it will run, and it should be set out precisely. The date of the beginning of the term and the date of its ending should be stated, together with a statement of the total period of the lease; for example, "for a term of five years beginning June 1, 2004, and ending May 31, 2009." In addition, any options to extend the lease should be in writing.

Unlike regulated residential leases (governed under state rent control or rent stabilization laws) where an owner of a rent regulated unit must automatically offer the resident of that unit a one- or two-year renewal, commercial tenants have no statutory rights of renewal. The landlord of that property is under no legal obligation to extend or renew the commercial lease.

An **option to renew** is a lease provision giving the tenant the right to extend the lease for an additional period of time on set terms.

If the lease has no specific ending date, it is a **periodic lease**. Generally these leases are month-to-month. A periodic lease (also known as a periodic tenancy or period estate) is automatically renewed each time the tenant pays rent to the landlord.

Security Deposits

Many leases require that a tenant provide a **security deposit** to guarantee payment of rent or safeguard against a tenant's destruction of the premises. Where trade fixtures are to be installed, the landlord may want an extra deposit to ensure that the property will be restored to its original state when they are removed.

Under the **New York General Obligations Law**, landlords must hold all security deposits in trust and *must not commingle* them with their own funds because *such deposits continue to belong to the tenants who have advanced them*. If the building contains six or more units, the landlord must notify tenants in writing where security funds are being held in a New York interest-bearing bank account and must turn over to the tenants all but 1 percent of any interest earned. This amount is retained by the landlord in the form of "an administrative charge" and is intended to offset the monthly banking fees attributable to maintaining a rent security account. A tenant may choose to receive interest annually or at the end of the lease. Any provisions in a lease requiring a tenant to waive any provisions of this law are void. The rules also apply to mobile home parks.

A landlord who conveys rental property must turn over any security deposits to the new owners within five days of the deed's delivery. The landlord also must notify tenants by registered or certified mail that their deposits have been turned over and must include the new owners' name and address. The new owners are responsible for eventual return of the security deposits to the extent received from the grantor. However, if the building contains six or more dwelling units, the new owners are responsible for all security deposits, even if they never received them.

Under New York's Emergency Tenant Protection Act (ETPA), certain apartments are rent-stabilized in New York City and some other locations throughout the state. For a rent-stabilized apartment, no more than one month's rent may be charged for security deposit.

■ LEGAL PRINCIPLES OF LEASES

New York provides that under certain conditions a lease can be recorded. Memoranda of leases that exceed three years in duration also may be recorded. The recording places the world on notice regarding the long-term rights of the tenant. Commercial leases are sometimes recorded. In either case, in New York, leases with a term of greater than three years are eligible for recording. Any term that is less than three years will not be accepted by the county clerk for recording. It should be noted that for a variety of reasons, most landlords would not allow a lease to be recorded. One reason might be that the landlord does not want the terms of the lease to be public knowledge.

When a written nonresidential lease is for more than three years, a lien for a commission may be placed on the premises if the brokerage services were performed pursuant to a written contract. As previously discussed in the chapter covering liens, this is called a broker's lien. Unlike mechanics' liens that must be filed within four months of completion of the work, brokers have up to eight months to assert their liens.

Lead Paint Notification

For any residence constructed *before 1978*, federal law requires that before signing a lease, the tenant must be given a booklet about lead-paint hazards and any information the landlord has about lead hazards on the premises. The requirement does not apply to rentals for terms of fewer than 100 days, studio apartments, zero-bedroom lofts, housing exclusively intended for the elderly, and premises already determined to be lead-free by a certified inspector.

Details about the booklet and enforcement of the requirement may be found in Chapter 18.

Improvements

The tenant may make improvements to the demised premises *only* with the landlord's prior permission, but any such alterations generally become the property of the landlord; they become fixtures. A tenant may, however, be given the right to install trade fixtures. It is customary to provide that such trade fixtures may be removed by the tenant before the lease expires, provided the tenant restores the premises to their original condition. The alteration clause of a lease generally contains the details on requirement of restoration by a tenant at the end of the lease term.

Maintenance of Premises

Every residential New York lease, oral or written, is considered to contain an **implied warranty** (*and covenant*) **of habitability**. The landlord guarantees that the leased property is fit for human habitation and that the tenant will not be subjected to any conditions that could endanger life, health, or safety. The tenant is entitled to what is known as **quiet enjoyment**, undisturbed occupancy. This is often a confused subject. Quiet enjoyment does not apply to peace and quiet. So long as a tenant abides by the lease terms and conditions, this clause applies to the occupant/tenant's right to remain undisturbed by others.

The landlord is required to maintain dwelling units in a habitable condition and to make any necessary repairs to common elements such as hallways, stairs, or elevators. The tenant does not have to make any repairs (unless otherwise provided in the lease) but must return the premises in the same condition they were received with allowances for ordinary wear and tear. This should not be confused with a restoration requirement. Usually, at the end of the lease term, the tenant is required to deliver the demised premises "in a broom-swept condition."

Assignment and Subleasing

The tenant may assign or sublease if the lease terms do not prohibit it. A tenant who transfers the entire remaining term of a lease assigns the lease. One who transfers less than all of the term but retains some of the rights and obligations, such as the right of reentry, subleases. (See Figure 7.1.) The original tenant's interest in the real estate is known as a *sandwich lease*. It is referred to as a sandwich lease because the original prime tenant/sublandlord is said to be sandwiched between the landlord/owner of the property and the subtenant. In most cases, the **sublease** or **assignment** of a lease does not relieve the original tenant of the obligation to make rental payments unless the landlord agrees to waive such liability. Waiver can be achieved via an agreement of **novation**. *Novation* can be defined as either

- a substitution of an old party for a new party or
- a substitution of an old agreement for a new agreement.

Without novation, a sublandlord or an assignor can be held liable and accountable for all remaining unperformed financial and legal aspects of the lease.

This would normally occur when a subtenant or assignee (as the case may be) defaults under any of the terms contained within the master lease. A typical example of a default would be failure to make the appropriate rent payments.

If the building contains four or more residential units and the landlord unreasonably withholds consent to assignment, the lease may not be assigned, but the tenant is released from the lease with 30 days' notice. If the landlord unreasonably withholds consent to a request to sublet, the tenant may nevertheless sublet the unit.

FIGURE   7.1

Assignment Versus Subletting

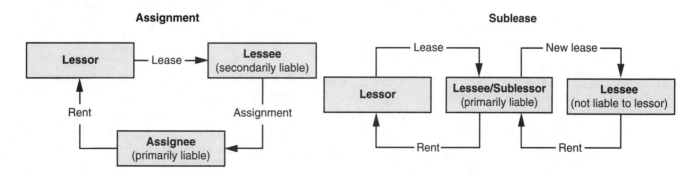

New York's Real Property Law sets guidelines for a detailed written request from the tenant; the landlord's right to ask for additional information within 10 days; and the landlord's written response, including the reasons for any denial, within 30 days. The landlord's failure to respond within the statutory allowed period is legally deemed to be consent to the subletting.

Special regulations apply to the subletting of residential rent-stabilized apartments (rent stabilization is discussed in more detail below): For a furnished sublet, the original tenant may charge the subtenant as much as 10 percent more than the original rent figure; the landlord may in turn collect an additional 5 percent from the original tenant. Any amount collected over these legal amounts can result in forfeiture of tenant's rights to the unit. In addition, the courts *may* conclude that any overage charged constituted "rent gouging" on the part of the original tenant. The original tenant must establish that the apartment is the tenant's primary residence and will be reoccupied. A rent-stabilized apartment may not be sublet for more than half of any four-year period. The original tenant, not the subtenant, is entitled to the right of a renewal lease and any right to purchase should a co-op conversion occur (see Chapter 24).

Apartment Sharing

In New York, a lease may not restrict occupancy of an apartment to the named tenant and that tenant's immediate family. (Landlords may, however, limit the total number of occupants to comply with health laws on overcrowding.) The apartment may be shared with one additional occupant and that occupant's dependent children. If the lease names more than one tenant and one of them moves out, that tenant may be replaced with another occupant and that person's dependent children. At least one of the original tenants named in the lease or that person's spouse must continue to occupy the shared apartment as a primary residence.

The "overtenant" or share tenant must inform the landlord of the name of any occupant within 30 days after the occupant moves into an apartment.

Renewals

Sometimes a lease contains a clause stating that it will be *automatically renewed unless* the tenant gives *notice* of intent not to renew. No such clause is valid in New York, unless the landlord reminds the tenant about the automatic renewal provision 15 to 30 days before the tenant's notice would be due.

The occupant of a rent-stabilized apartment is entitled to a one- or two-year renewal (see Chapter 22). Stabilization laws require a landlord of rent regulated units to offer an existing tenant a renewal. As previously stated, either a one- or two-year lease must be offered no less than 150 days prior to the present lease expiration.

Many leases contain an *option* that grants the lessee (the tenant) the privilege of *renewing* the lease but requires that the lessee give *notice* on or before a specific date of intention to exercise the option. Some leases grant to the lessee the option to purchase the leased premises; the provisions for the option to purchase vary widely. Any option should contain all the essential elements of an offer to purchase.

Termination of Lease

A written lease for a definite period expires at the end of that time period; no separate notice is required to terminate. Oral and written leases that do not specify a definite expiration date (such as a month-to-month or year-to-year tenancy or a tenancy at will) may be terminated by giving proper written notice.

The tenant who signs a lease for senior housing has the right to cancel within three days of signing.

When the conditions of a lease are breached, a landlord may terminate the lease and evict the tenant. This action must be handled through a court proceeding. The landlord who wishes to be rid of a tenant is not allowed to use threats of violence, change locks, discontinue essential services like water or heat, or seize the tenant's possessions.

It is possible for the parties to mutually agree to cancel the lease. The tenant may offer to surrender the lease, and acceptance by the landlord will result in termination. A tenant who abandons leased property, however, remains liable for the rent. The terms of the specific lease will usually dictate whether the landlord is obligated to try to re-rent the space. This is known as *mitigation*.

When the property is sold, *the lease does not terminate*. If a landlord conveys leased real estate, the new owner takes the property subject to the rights of the tenant. The lease *survives* the sale and continues as it was, except in the case of a foreclosure proceeding when the subject is a commercial property. In that situation, the lease or leases are always subordinated to any mortgage or underlying ground lease. This language is found in the subordination clause section of the lease. It simply means that the rights of a lender or landowner (in a ground lease) supersede the rights of the leaseholder. As a result, if rents are deemed by the foreclosing party to be below market, the lease can be terminated by that party. In these types of transactions, the only protection a commercial tenant has from this unfortunate event is to request at or before lease signing a *subordination/nondisturbance agreement* from either the lender to the property or the fee (land) owner via the landlord.

If a tenant dies, the lease remains in effect; the deceased lessee's estate is bound by the terms of the lease. New York State provides, however, that the estate may assign the lease or sublet, subject to the landlord's consent. If consent is unreasonably withheld, the lease is terminated. When the death occurs within a rent-stabilized unit, the law allows the decedent's estate to remain within the premises up to the expiration of the lease term. This is to provide a reasonable time for the estate to wrap up the affairs of the decedent; however, during this period, the estate is not excused from paying rent.

A lease may be terminated by any tenant aged 62 or older who has been accepted in an adult care facility, residential health facility, or housing unit receiving subsidies for housing senior citizens or who is moving to a relative's home for health care. The landlord is entitled to 30 days' notice and a copy of a document of admission to the new facility. A lease may also be cancelled by a tenant who is called up for active military service.

Breach of Lease

When a tenant breaches any lease provision, the landlord may sue for a judgment to cover past-due rent, damages to the premises, or other defaults. Likewise, when a landlord breaches any lease provision, the tenant is entitled to remedies. The landlord's nonperformance of some obligation under a nonresidential lease, short of eviction, does not, however, affect the tenant's obligation to pay rent.

In New York, grounds for which the landlord can institute proceedings include nonpayment of rent, illegal use of the premises, remaining in possession after expiration of the lease without permission, and bankruptcy or insolvency of the tenant.

Suit for possession—actual eviction   When a tenant breaches a lease or improperly retains possession, the landlord may regain possession through a **suit for possession** or summary proceeding to recover possession of real estate. This process is known as **actual eviction**. The landlord must serve *notice* on the tenant before commencing the suit. In New York, only a three-day notice must be given before filing a suit for possession based on a default in payment of rent. When a court issues a judgment for possession, the tenants must leave peaceably, or the landlord can have the judgment enforced by a sheriff, constable, or marshal, who will *forcibly remove* the tenants and their possessions.

Tenants' remedies—constructive eviction   If a landlord breaches any clause of a lease agreement, the tenant has the right to sue, claiming a judgment for damages against the landlord. If an action or omission on the landlord's part results in the leased premises becoming uninhabitable for the purpose intended in the lease, the tenant may have the right to abandon the premises. This action, called **constructive eviction**, terminates the lease if the tenant can prove that the premises have become unusable because of the landlord's neglect. To claim constructive eviction, the tenant must actually move from the premises while the uninhabitable condition exists.

For example, a lease requires that the landlord furnish steam heat; because of the landlord's failure to repair a defective heating plant, the heat is not provided. If this results in the leased premises becoming uninhabitable, the tenant may abandon them. Some leases provide that if the failure to furnish heat is accidental and not the landlord's fault, it is not grounds for constructive eviction.

■ PRO-TENANT LEGISLATION

In New York State, a landlord may not legally retaliate because a tenant joins a tenants' organization. If the landlord fails to furnish heat as stipulated in the lease, tenants in New York may pay a utility company directly and deduct the sum from rent due. In New York City at least one-third of the tenants of a multiple-unit dwelling, acting together, may start a special court proceeding to use their rent money to remedy conditions dangerous to life, health, or safety. Retaliatory evictions are illegal.

■ TYPES OF LEASES

Three primary types of leases are outlined in Table 7.2.

Gross Lease

In a **gross lease**, the tenant pays a *fixed rental* and the landlord pays all taxes, insurance, mortgage payments, repairs, and the like (usually called *operating expenses and debt service*). This type of lease is most often used for residential rentals.

Net Lease

The **net lease** provides that in addition to the rent the *tenant pays some or all of the operating expenses*. The monthly rental paid is net income (profit) for the landlord. Leases for commercial or industrial buildings, ground leases, and long-term leases are often net leases. With a **triple-net lease**, the tenant pays taxes, insurance, and all other expenses except debt service (mortgage payments). It should be noted that although *triple-net lease* is a slang term, it is an accepted expression in real estate terminology.

Percentage Lease

Three Types of Leases

1. Gross lease
2. Net lease
3. Percentage lease

Either a gross lease or a net lease may be a **percentage lease**, normally used for retail business locations. It is commonly used in shopping malls, shopping centers, and high-profile retail locations such as Fifth Avenue and Madison Avenue in New York City.

The percentage lease provides for a minimum fixed rental fee plus a percentage of the tenant's business income that exceeds a stated minimum. (The stated minimum is commonly referred to as *natural breakeven*.) For example, a lease might provide for a minimum monthly rental of $1,200, with the further agreement that the tenant pay an additional amount each month equivalent to 5 percent of all gross sales in excess of $30,000. The percentage charged in such leases varies widely with the nature of the business.

TABLE 7.2

Types of Leases

Type of lease	Legal effect	Landlord pays
Gross lease residential (also small commercial)	Basic rent	Property charges (taxes, repairs, insurance, etc.)
Net lease commercial/industrial	Basic rent plus most or all property charges	Few or no property charges, mortgage (if any)
Percentage lease commercial/industrial	Basic rent plus percent of gross sales (may pay some or all property costs)	Any agreed property charges

Other Lease Types

Several types of leases allow for increases in the rent during the lease period. Two of the more common ones are the **graduated lease**, which provides for increases in rent at set future dates, and the **index lease**, which allows rent to be increased or decreased periodically based on changes in the government cost-of-living index.

Proprietary leases   The owner of a cooperative apartment who buys shares in the corporation that owns the building does not specifically own the apartment. Instead, the owner receives a **proprietary lease** to the living unit. It is the proprietary lease that acts as the shareholder's occupancy agreement.

Ground leases   When a landowner leases land to a tenant who agrees to erect a *building on it*, the lease is referred to as a **ground lease** (a long-term lease made on unimproved land generally for the purposes of constructing an improvement). It is usually for a long enough term to make it worth the tenant's while to invest in the building. These leases are generally *net leases* that require the lessee to pay rent as well as real estate taxes, insurance, upkeep, and repairs. Net ground leases often run for terms of just under 50 years. This is to avoid interpretation by tax laws that the agreement constitutes a transfer. Longer terms are accomplished by options to extend. Although these leases are considered personal property, leaseholders may have some of the rights and obligations of real property owners.

Oil and gas leases   When oil companies lease land to explore for oil and gas, a special agreement must be negotiated. Usually, the landowner receives a cash payment for executing the lease. If no well is drilled within the period stated, the lease expires.

If oil and/or gas is found, the landowner usually receives a fraction of its value as a royalty. In this case, the lease will continue for as long as oil or gas is obtained in significant quantities. Oil and gas leases are common across the southern tier and in the western part of the state of New York. An oil or gas lease constitutes a cloud on title, and a buyer may refuse to purchase unless he or she has specifically agreed to take title subject to such a lease.

■ SUMMARY

A lease grants someone the right to use the property of another for a certain period in return for consideration.

A leasehold estate that runs for a specific length of time creates an estate for years, whereas one that runs for an indefinite period creates a periodic tenancy (year to year, month to month) or a tenancy at will. A leasehold estate is generally classified as personal property.

The requirements of a valid lease include the capacity to contract, a demising clause, description of premises, statement of terms, rent, and signatures. The state statute of frauds requires that any lease for more than a year be in writing. Most leases also include clauses relating to rights and obligations of the landlord and tenant: the use of the premises, subletting, judgments, maintenance of the premises, and termination of the lease period.

In New York, an oral lease is valid if it is for a period of one year or less. A lease for three years or more, if properly acknowledged, may be entered in the public records. State law requires that the owner of six or more residential units hold security deposits in an interest-bearing New York bank account with all interest less a 1 percent fee due the tenant. State law gives the tenant in any building with four or more residential units the right to sublet, subject to the landlord's consent, which may not be unreasonably withheld.

Leases may be terminated by the expiration of the lease period, mutual agreement of the parties, or a breach of the lease by either landlord or tenant. Neither the death of the tenant nor the landlord's sale of the rental property terminates a lease.

On a tenant's default on any of the lease provisions, a landlord may sue for a money judgment or for actual eviction where a tenant has improperly retained possession of the premises. If the premises have become uninhabitable (whether or not due to the landlord's negligence), the tenant may refuse to pay rent until the problem is remedied.

Basic types of leases include net leases, gross leases, and percentage leases, classified according to the method used in determining the rental rate of the property.

CHAPTER 7 QUIZ

1. A lease is considered
   a. a freehold estate.
   b. a nonfreehold estate.
   c. a reversionary interest.
   d. real property.

2. Tracy agrees to rent her upstairs apartment to Beverly for the next six months. Beverly has a(n)
   a. estate for years.
   b. periodic estate.
   c. tenancy at will.
   d. tenancy at sufferance.

3. A landlord agrees to rent his upstairs apartment to a tenant from month to month. To end the arrangement, the landlord must
   a. file a court suit to recover possession.
   b. give at least 60 days' notice from the day the rent is due.
   c. give at least one month's notice from a day before the rent is due.
   d. simply refuse to accept the next month's rent on the day it is due.

4. A tenant's lease has expired. The tenant has neither left nor negotiated a renewal lease, and the landlord has said she does not want the tenant to remain. The tenancy is called a(n)
   a. estate for years.
   b. periodic estate.
   c. tenancy at will.
   d. tenancy at sufferance.

5. A property owner sells her six-unit apartment building in Queens to a buyer. Now
   a. the buyer may give all the tenants 30 days' notice.
   b. tenants should collect their security deposits from the seller.
   c. the buyer must renegotiate all leases with the tenants.
   d. the seller must turn over security deposits to the buyer.

6. The legal process to remove a tenant who remains in possession of leased premises after expiration of the lease is known as a(n)
   a. sufferance case.
   b. holdover proceeding.
   c. order of eviction.
   d. legal removal.

7. An automatic renewal clause in a lease
   a. is not allowed on rent-stabilized apartments.
   b. is granted to every tenant in a building with four or more units.
   c. is illegal in New York State.
   d. requires notice from the landlord calling the tenants' attention to the clause.

8. A renter's apartment lease agreement states that it will expire on April 30, 2011. When must her landlord give notice that her tenancy is to terminate?
   a. January 31, 2011
   b. February 28, 2011
   c. April 1, 2011
   d. No notice required

9. If a tenant falls three months behind in rent payments, a landlord may
   a. turn down the heat.
   b. move out the tenant's possessions, storing them carefully.
   c. start a court suit for possession.
   d. do all of these.

10. In Question 9, the landlord who turns down the heat has terminated the lease through
    a. the demising clause.
    b. constructive eviction.
    c. payment in arrears.
    d. assigning the lease.

11. With a triple-net lease, the tenant pays rent
    a. only.
    b. plus a share of business profits.
    c. plus any increase in property taxes.
    d. plus all operating expenses for the property.

12. A ground lease is usually
    a. terminable with 30 days' notice.
    b. based on percentages.
    c. long term.
    d. a gross lease.

13. The landlord must furnish a lead-paint information booklet
    a. within 100 days after the lease is signed.
    b. if the building is intended exclusively for those older than 55.
    c. only if the building contains six or more units.
    d. for buildings constructed before 1978.

14. A woman manufactures knitwear in a small rented building. In addition to monthly rent, she pays heat, electric, and property taxes on the building. She probably has a
    a. net lease.
    b. periodic lease.
    c. percentage lease.
    d. security lease.

15. In New York, a tenant usually may sublet an apartment if the
    a. new tenant is paying a premium over the rent.
    b. lease does not prohibit it.
    c. lease is for three years or more.
    d. original tenant has a written lease.

16. A homeowner says to his friend, "I'll let you rent my attic apartment for $500 a month until the first of the year." The friend agrees. The agreement
    a. constitutes a binding lease.
    b. is invalid because it is not in writing.
    c. binds the landlord only.
    d. will be enforceable only if it is recorded.

17. A gross lease is MOST likely to be used for rental of
    a. an apartment.
    b. a factory building.
    c. land under a post office.
    d. a farm.

18. If a tenant dies, the lease
    a. is automatically terminated.
    b. remains in effect.
    c. must be sublet by the estate.
    d. reverts to the state.

CHAPTER 8

Real Estate Instruments: Contracts

■ KEY TERMS

agreement in writing and signed
American Bar Association
"as is"
assignment
attorney review clause
bilateral contract
breach of contract
competent parties
consideration
contingencies
contract
counteroffer
earnest money deposit
equitable title
escape clause
executed contract

executory contract
express contract
forbearance
implied contract
laches
land contract
legality of object
liquidated damages
memorandum of sale
mortgage contingency clause
New York State Lawyers' Fund for Client Protection
novation
offer and acceptance
option

parol evidence rule
real estate sales contract
release
rescission
rider
right of first refusal
specific performance
statute of frauds
statute of limitations
"time is of the essence"
unenforceable contract
Uniform Commercial Code
unilateral contract
valid contract
voidable contract
void contract

■ CONTRACT LAW

A **contract** is a *voluntary agreement between legally competent parties to perform or refrain from performing some legal act, supported by legal consideration.*

Depending on the situation and the nature or language of the agreement, a contract may be

- express or implied;
- unilateral or bilateral;
- executory or executed; and
- valid, void, voidable, or unenforceable.

Express and Implied Contracts

In an **express contract**, the parties state the terms and show their intentions in words. An express contract may be either oral or written. A listing agreement is an express contract between seller and broker that names the broker as fiduciary representative (agent) of a seller.

As you learned in a previous chapter, the statute of frauds requires that any contract for the purchase and sale of a parcel of real property, in whole or in part, must always be in writing to be enforceable. As a result, the majority of real estate contracts fall into the category of express contracts.

In an **implied contract**, the agreement of the parties is demonstrated by their acts and conduct. The patron who orders a meal in a restaurant has implied a promise to pay for the food. Similarly, the act of entering a metered taxicab implies that the rider will pay the driver the amount indicated on the taxi's meter upon reaching the destination.

Bilateral and Unilateral Contracts

Contracts also may be classified as either bilateral or unilateral. In a **bilateral contract**, both parties promise to perform under and as required by the contract; one promise is given in exchange for another. A real estate sales contract is a bilateral contract. The seller promises to sell a parcel of real estate to the buyer, who promises to buy via a payment of a certain sum of money. "I will do this, and you will do that." "OK."

A **unilateral contract**, on the other hand, is a one-sided agreement whereby one party makes a promise to be kept only if a second party does something. The second party is not legally obligated to act or perform; however, if the second party does comply, the first party must keep the promise. An option is a real estate example of a unilateral contract. "I will sell you the property for $150,000 within two years if you wish." ("I will do this if you do that.") Only the owner is bound by an option; the other party is free either to buy or not to buy.

An *open listing* is another example of a unilateral contract. In this situation, the sellers extend an offer of compensation to the broker procuring a sale on their property; however, the broker is under no obligation to deliver a sale or accept the terms of the listing.

Executed and Executory

A contract may be classified as either executed or executory. An **executed contract** is one in which both parties have fulfilled their promises and performed the contract. An **executory contract** exists when something remains to be done. A real estate sales contract is executory before final settlement; after the closing it is executed.

A mortgage would be another example of an executory contract. Although the mortgage is signed by the borrower, it remains executory until such time as all payments have been made by the borrower to the lender.

Validity of Contracts

A contract can be described as valid, void, voidable, or unenforceable (see Table 8.1), depending on the circumstances.

A **valid contract** complies with all the essential elements required for a contract to be binding and enforceable on both parties; these elements are discussed in the next section and later in the chapter.

A **void contract** is one that has no legal effect because it does not meet the essential elements of a contract. One of those essential elements is that a contract be for a legal purpose; thus a contract to commit a crime, or to pay interest higher than allowed by usury law, would be void.

A **voidable contract** is one that seems on the surface to be valid but may be voided, or disaffirmed, by one of the parties. For example, a contract entered into with a minor usually is voidable; a minor generally is permitted to disaffirm a real estate contract within a reasonable time after reaching legal age. A voidable contract is considered by the courts to be valid if the party that could disaffirm the agreement does not do so within a reasonable period of time.

An **unenforceable contract** also seems on the surface to be valid; however, neither party can successfully sue the other to force performance. For example, if one party tries to enforce an otherwise valid contract after the statute of limitations has expired, the contract is unenforceable. Unenforceable contracts are said to be "valid as between the parties" because if both desire to go through with it, they can do so.

T A B L E   8.1

Legal Effects of Contract

Type of contract	Legal effect	Example
Valid	Binding and enforceable on both parties	Agreement complying with essentials of a valid contract
Void	No legal effect	Contract for an illegal purpose
Voidable	Valid, but may be disaffirmed by one party	Contract with a minor
Unenforceable	Valid between the parties, but neither may force performance	Certain oral agreements

Elements Essential to a Valid Contract

The five essentials of a valid contract are as follows:

1. **Competent parties**. To enter into a binding contract in New York, a person must be at least 18 years old and of sound mind. A married person younger than 18 is considered an adult for the purposes of buying a principal residence. In New York, the consent of a parent or guardian is required for a minor to get married.
2. **Offer and acceptance**. This requirement, also called *mutual assent*, means there must be a clear meeting of the minds. The contract must express all the agreed-on terms and must be clearly understood by the parties.
3. **Consideration**. The agreement must be based on good and valuable consideration. Consideration is what the parties promise in the agreement to give to or receive from each other. Consideration may consist of money, exchange of value, or mutual promises. The promises might consist of a pledge to perform some act or of **forbearance**, a promise to refrain from doing something. The price or amount must be stated definitely and payable in exchange for the deed or right received.
4. **Legality of object**. To be valid and enforceable, a contract must not involve a purpose that is illegal or against public policy.
5. **Agreement in writing and signed**. New York's **statute of frauds** requires that certain types of contracts be in writing. These include all contracts for the sale of real estate and for leasing real property for more than one year.

The **parol evidence rule** states that the written contract takes precedence over oral agreements or promises. A promise that is not in the written contract may not be legally binding.

Undue influence and duress   Contracts signed by a person under duress or undue influence are voidable (may be canceled) by such person or by a court. Extreme care should be taken when one or more of the parties to a contract is elderly, sick, in great distress, or under the influence of drugs or alcohol. To be valid, every contract must be signed as the free and voluntary act of each party.

Performance of Contract

A contract may call for a specific time by which the agreed-on acts must be completely performed. In addition, some contracts provide that **"time is of the essence."** This means that the contract must be performed within the time limit specified. Any party who has not performed on time is deemed to have breached the contract. This powerful phrase is a two-edged sword, and brokers should leave its use to attorneys.

When a contract does not specify a date for performance, the acts it requires should be performed within a reasonable time, depending on the situation. A real estate contract usually names a date and place for closing. If that date comes and goes without settlement, the contract is still valid, and either party has the right to a reasonable postponement. Either party may later make time of the essence; again, that action should be taken only with a lawyer's advice.

Assignment and Novation

Often after a contract has been signed, one party wants to withdraw without actually ending the agreement. This may be accomplished through either assignment or novation.

It should be noted that standard residential contracts of sale do not have an assignment clause. Furthermore, when the contract is silent on the subject of assignment, it is not allowed. In either case, assignment can occur with the consent of the seller.

Assignment refers to a transfer of all of one's rights and/or duties under a contract. Generally, rights may be assigned to a third party unless the agreement forbids such an assignment. Most contracts include a clause that either permits or forbids assignment.

A contract also may be performed by **novation**, or the substitution of a *new* contract for an existing agreement. Novation may also involve the substitution of a new party for an old party. The new agreement may retain the same parties or substitute a new party for either (*novation of the parties*). A real estate example might be the assumption of a present mortgage by the new owner of a property, with the lender releasing the original borrower and substituting the new one.

Discharge of Contract

A contract may be completely performed, with all terms carried out, or it may be breached (broken) if one of the parties defaults. Various other methods by which a contract may be discharged (ended) are as follows:

- *Partial performance* of the terms along with a written acceptance by the person for whom acts have not been done or to whom money has not been paid
- *Substantial performance*, in which one party has performed most of the contract but does not complete all details exactly as the contract requires, which may be sufficient to force payment with certain adjustments for any damages suffered by the other party
- *Impossibility of performance*, in which an act required by the contract cannot be legally accomplished
- *Mutual agreement* of the parties to cancel
- *Operation of law*, as in the voiding of a contract by a minor, as a result of fraud, owing to the expiration of the statute of limitations, or because of alteration of a contract without written consent of all parties involved

Default—Breach of Contract

A **breach of contract** is a violation of any of the terms or conditions of a contract without legal excuse. A default can be defined as the failure to perform on the terms of the contract by either party to that contract. For example, a seller enters into a contract with a buyer for the purchase and sale of a home and later refuses to sell.

With a real estate sales contract, if a seller defaults, the buyer has a combination of three alternatives:

1. The buyer may *rescind, or cancel, the contract* and recover the earnest money deposit.
2. The buyer may file a court suit, known as an action for **specific performance**, to force the seller to perform the contract (*that is, sell the property*).
3. The buyer may *sue the seller for compensatory damages*.

If the *buyer defaults*, the seller may pursue one of the following four courses of action:

1. The seller may *declare the contract forfeited*. The right to forfeit usually is provided in the terms of the contract, and the seller usually is entitled to retain the earnest money and all payments received from the buyer.
2. The seller may *rescind the contract*; that is, the seller may cancel, or terminate, the contract as though it had never been made.
3. The seller may *sue for specific performance*. This may require that the seller offer a valid deed to the buyer to show that the seller is ready to meet the contract terms.
4. The seller may *sue for compensatory damages*.

Aside from the aforementioned seller remedies, standard residential purchase and sales contracts provide specifically for liquidated damages. Normally, the buyer will lose the earnest money deposit.

Statute of limitations   New York allows a specific time limit of *six years* during which parties to a contract may bring legal suit to enforce their rights. Any party who does not take steps to enforce these rights within this **statute of limitations** may lose them. The six-year period applies to contracts, foreclosures, mortgages, and cases of fraud. Lawsuits to recover real property have a ten-year statute of limitations in New York.

The principle or doctrine of **laches** bears similarity to that of the statute of limitations. Laches is an undue delay or failure to assert a claim or right that can result in the loss of that claim or right. A colloquial way of describing them would be, "Use them or lose them."

■ CONTRACTS USED IN THE REAL ESTATE BUSINESS

The written agreements most commonly used by brokers and salespersons are independent contractor agreements, listing agreements, buyer's broker agreements, real estate sales contracts, option agreements, contracts for deed, and leases.

Broker's Authority to Prepare Documents

The New York Department of State (DOS) specifically states that the real estate broker's license does not confer the right to draft legal documents or give legal advice. However, a decision by the New York Appellate Court has stated that a broker has a right to complete a simple contract. No court decisions have yet been made as to what constitutes a "simple" contract.

The preparation of legal documents by a broker may result in the loss of commissions, loss of license, or other penalties or damages. In upstate areas, many brokers fill in the blanks on forms or simple sales contracts; in the New York City area, the seller's attorney usually prepares the sales contract.

The *Duncan and Hill* decision recommended that New York State brokers and salespersons who prepare purchase and sales contracts protect themselves against charges of unauthorized practice of law by making the contracts subject to (effective only after) approval by attorneys for both the buyer and seller. An attorney then may ask for changes to protect the client's interest; any such changes constitute a counteroffer and need not be accepted by the other party. Offer, acceptance, and binding effect are discussed below.

On the subject of real estate licensees writing purchase contracts, the attorney general of the New York State has concluded that a broker may use a contract form that has been approved by a recognized bar association in conjunction with a recognized REALTORS® association, provided that

■ the form requires only that the broker fill in nonlegal provisions, such as the names of the parties, date and location of the closing, description of the property, and sales price; and
■ the document clearly and prominently indicates on its face that it is a legally binding document and recommends that the parties seek advice from their attorneys before signing.

The attorney general's opinion also states that brokers may not add provisions to standard fill-in-the-blanks contracts unless they make the entire contract subject to the review and approval of each party's attorney.

Contract forms *Printed forms* are used for many contracts because many transactions are similar in nature. The use of printed forms raises three problems: (1) what information should be used to *fill in the blanks*; (2) what printed matter is not applicable to a particular sale and can be *ruled out* by drawing lines through the unwanted words; and (3) what clauses or agreements (called *riders*) are to be added. All changes and additions usually are initialed by both parties. Additional agreements should be drawn up by attorneys, not brokers.

Because New York does not mandate a standard form of sales contract, sales contracts differ from place to place within the state. In simple residential one- to four-family transactions in upstate New York, preprinted forms are commonly used. These forms are usually created by bar associations and boards of REALTORS®. These forms require the party preparing the contract to simply fill in the blanks that apply to the specific transaction. Any unique issues to the transaction are then covered in riders that are attached to the sales contract. If prepared by a real estate licensee, these riders should only be preprinted forms that have previously been approved by the principal and/or the principal's attorney. Remember, a licensee may never engage in the unauthorized practice of law (*Duncan and Hill* decision). When these forms are used, they must contain a boldface heading that instructs the parties to consult with their attorneys before signing.

In transactions occurring in downstate New York, it is not uncommon for sellers' attorneys to prepare their version of the sales contract/riders. At this time, the listing agent will normally prepare a "memorandum of sale" or a "deal sheet." This document will spell out the negotiated terms that have been agreed to by the respective parties to the transaction. Due to the complicated nature of these transactions and the different issues of concern that arise, each sales contract tends to be unique to that transaction.

Listing Agreements

Listing agreements are contracts that establish the rights of the broker as agent and of the buyer or seller as principal. They are considered the employment contract between the principal and the agent in a real estate transaction. Explanations of the types of listing agreements are presented in Chapter 3.

Sales Contracts

A **real estate sales contract** sets forth all details of the agreement between a buyer and a seller for the purchase and sale of a parcel of real estate or shares of stock and a proprietary lease appurtenant thereto and related to a cooperative unit. (Cooperatives are discussed later in this chapter.) Depending on the locality, this agreement may be known as an *offer to purchase, a contract of purchase and sale, an earnest money agreement, a binder and deposit receipt,* or other variations of these titles. New York does not mandate any specific form of listing or sales contract. An example of a real estate contract form used by some brokers appears as Figure 8.1.

For simple transactions, real estate brokers are allowed to fill in the blanks on this contract, which was published by a REALTORS® organization after consultation with the local bar association. Among other provisions, it provides for input by buyer's and seller's attorneys if desired.

The contract of sale is the most basic document in the sale of real estate because it sets out in detail the agreement between the buyer and the seller and establishes their legal rights and obligations. *The contract, in effect, dictates the contents of the deed* and is a blueprint for closing the sale.

Offer and acceptance   One of the essential elements of a valid contract of sale is a meeting of the minds, whereby the buyer and seller agree on the terms of the sale. This usually is accomplished through the process of offer and acceptance.

A broker lists an owner's real estate for sale at the price and conditions set by the owner. A party who wants to purchase the property at those terms or some other terms is found. Upstate, an offer to purchase is drawn up, signed by the prospective buyer, and presented by the broker to the seller. This is an *offer*. If the seller agrees to the offer *exactly as it was made* and signs the contract, the offer has been *accepted*, and the contract is *valid*. The broker then must advise the buyer of the seller's acceptance, obtain lawyers' approval if the contract calls for it, and deliver a duplicate original of the contract to each party.

FIGURE 8.1

Purchase and Sale Contract for Residential Property

PURCHASE AND SALE CONTRACT
FOR RESIDENTIAL PROPERTY

Plain English Form published by and for the exclusive use of the Greater Rochester Association of REALTORS®, Inc., the Monroe County Bar Association, and those County Bar Associations that have approved its use.
COMMISSIONS OR FEES FOR THE REAL ESTATE SERVICES TO BE PROVIDED ARE NEGOTIABLE BETWEEN REALTOR® AND CLIENT.
When Signed, This Document Becomes A Binding Contract. Buyer and Seller Should Consult Their Own Attorney.

TO: _____ ("Seller") FROM: _____ ("Buyer")

OFFER TO PURCHASE

Buyer offers to purchase the property described below from Seller on the following terms:

1. Property Description; Seller's Power and Authority.
Property known as_____
in the County of _____ ☐ Town ☐ City ☐ Village of _____, State of New York,
Zip _____ also known as Tax No. _____ including all buildings and
any other improvements and all rights which the Seller has in or with the property. Approximate Lot Size: _____.
Description of buildings on property: _____
Seller represents to Buyer that: (i) Seller owns the property and has the power and authority to sell it, (ii) Seller is not in bankruptcy, and (iii) Seller has sufficient funds (including the proceeds from this sale) to close this transaction and pay Seller's closing expenses.

2. Other Items Included in Purchase. Any of the following items and all related equipment and accessories for such items now in or on the property are included in this purchase and sale, which Seller represents are owned by Seller: All awnings, carbon monoxide detectors, central vacuum system, curtain and traverse rods, electric garage door opener and remote control devices, exhaust fans, fences, fireplace screens and enclosures, flowers, garbage disposal, heating systems, hoods, humidifier, intercom equipment, lighting fixtures, mail box, plumbing systems, septic and private water systems, satellite dishes, screens, security systems and security codes, sheds, shrubs, smoke detectors, storm doors, storm windows, sump pumps, swimming pool, TV antennae, trees, underground pet containment fencing with transmitter and collar(s), wall-to-wall carpeting and runners, water softeners, window boxes, window blinds and shades, and the following, if built-in: air conditioning (except window units), basketball apparatus, cabinets, dishwashers, microwave ovens, mirrors, outdoor playsets, ovens, shelving, stoves, and trash compactors. Buyer agrees to accept these items in their present condition. Other items to be included in the purchase and sale are: _____
_____.
Items excluded are: _____.
Seller represents that Seller has good title to all of the above items to be transferred to Buyer and will deliver a Bill of Sale for the above items at closing.
☐ Seller shall cause any heating, plumbing, air conditioning, electrical systems and included appliances to be in working order at the time of closing, except for _____. The prior sentence shall not be construed as a warranty or guarantee after closing.

3. Seller's Property Condition Disclosure Statement (check one).
☐ (a) Seller has provided Buyer with the attached Seller's Property Condition Disclosure Statement.
☐ (b) Seller has *not* provided Buyer with Seller's Property Condition Disclosure Statement, and Seller shall credit Buyer $500.00 at closing in lieu of such Statement.
☐ (c) Is not applicable.

4. Price & Payment. The purchase price is _____ Dollars
$_____. Buyer shall receive credit at closing for any deposit made hereunder. The balance of the purchase price shall be paid as follows: (Check and complete applicable provisions.)
☐ (a) Seller agrees to pay at closing: ☐ ____% of the purchase price or ☐ $_____ toward lender approved costs and prepaid items.
☐ (b) Official bank draft or certified check at closing.
☐ (c) Mortgage Assumption pursuant to the terms and conditions of the Mortgage Assumption Addendum.
☐ (d) Seller Financing pursuant to the terms and conditions of the Seller Financing Addendum.

5. Contingencies. Buyer makes this offer subject to the following contingencies. If any of these contingencies are not satisfied by the dates specified (collectively, the "Contingency Deadline Dates"), then either Buyer or Seller may cancel this contract ("Contract") by written notice to the other, provided that the applicable contingency has not otherwise been satisfied after the applicable Contingency Deadline Date and prior to any date on which this Contract is cancelled. (Check and complete applicable provisions.)

Purchase and Sale Contract for Residential Property

_____
Seller's Initials

_____
Buyer's Initials

F I G U R E   8.1

Purchase and Sale Contract for Residential Property (continued)

☐ (a) **Mortgage Contingency.** This offer is subject to Buyer obtaining and accepting a _____
mortgage loan commitment in an amount not to exceed $_____ at an interest rate not to exceed
_____%, for a term of _____ years. Buyer shall immediately apply for this loan and shall have until
_____, 20____ to obtain and accept a written mortgage commitment. The conditions of any such mortgage
commitment shall not be deemed contingencies of this Contract but shall be the sole responsibility of Buyer. If the mortgage
commitment requires repairs, replacements, or improvements, Seller shall furnish the requisite materials and have the work done
before closing, at Seller's expense. However, if the cost of doing so exceeds $_____, Seller shall not be
obligated to furnish such materials and have such work done, and Buyer will be allowed either to receive a credit at closing for
the above amount and incur any necessary expenses to comply with the mortgage commitment requirements, or to cancel this
Contract by written notice to Seller, and any deposit shall be returned to Buyer. Acceptance of a written mortgage commitment
by Buyer shall be deemed a waiver and satisfaction of this contingency.

☐ (b) **Sale and Transfer of Title Contingency.** This offer is subject to the sale and transfer of title of Buyer's existing property
pursuant to the terms and conditions of the Sale and Transfer of Title Contingency Addendum.

☐ (c) **Attorney Approval Contingency.** This Contract is subject to the written approval of attorneys for Buyer and Seller within
_____ calendar days, *excluding Sundays and public holidays*, from date of acceptance (the Approval Period). If either attorney
(i) does not provide written approval within the Approval Period or (ii) makes written objection to or conditionally approves
(collectively, the Objections) the Contract within the Approval Period and the Objection is not cured by written approval by both
attorneys and all of the parties within the Approval Period, then (A) either Buyer or Seller may cancel this Contract by written
notice to the other and any deposit shall be returned to the Buyer or (B) the approving attorney may notify the other party (with a
copy to any attorney listed below) in writing that no approval has been received and that the noticed party has five (5) calendar
days, *inclusive of Sundays and public holidays*, from receipt of the notice (Grace Period) to provide written attorney approval or
disapproval of the Contract. The approving attorney shall provide to the noticed party (with a copy to any attorney listed below) a
copy of the approving attorney's approval letter, whether conditional or not, along with the written notice of the Grace Period. If
written attorney approval or disapproval is not provided to the approving attorney within the Grace Period, then this Attorney
Approval contingency shall be deemed waived by the noticed party and any conditions in the approving attorney's approval letter
shall be deemed accepted by the noticed party.

☐ (d) **Waiver of Attorney Approval Contingency.** This offer is not subject to the Buyer's attorney approval.

☐ (e) **Property Inspection Contingency.** This offer is subject to inspection(s) of the property pursuant to the terms and conditions
of the Property Inspection Addendum.

☐ (f) **Other Contingency(s).** _____
_____.

6. Pre-Closing Inspection. Buyer shall have the right to inspect the property within 48 hours before the time of closing, and Seller
agrees that all utilities shall be on at that time. Seller shall continue to maintain the property in the condition existing as of acceptance
including, but not limited to, utility service continuation, lawn and landscaping care, and snow plowing, subject to reasonable use, wear,
tear and natural deterioration between the date hereof and the closing.

7. Closing Date and Place. Closing shall take place at the _____ County Clerk's Office or the offices
of Buyer's lender on or before _____, 20_____.

8. Possession of Property.

☐ (a) Buyer shall have possession of the property upon closing, in broom-clean condition, with all keys to the property delivered to
Buyer at closing.

☐ (b) Seller shall have the right to retain possession for ____ calendar days after closing at the cost of $_____ per day inclusive of
real property taxes, plus utilities, continuation of lawn, landscaping, pool, and snow maintenance, and refuse collection. At
closing, a key to the property shall be delivered to Buyer. At delivery of possession to Buyer, the property shall be in broom-
clean condition and the remaining keys to the property shall be delivered to Buyer.

☐ (c) Buyer shall have right of early possession for ____ calendar days prior to closing at the cost of $_____ per day inclusive of
real property taxes, plus utilities, continuation of lawn, landscaping, pool, and snow maintenance, and refuse collection. At
possession, the property shall be in broom-clean condition and a key to the property shall be delivered to Buyer; the remaining
keys shall be delivered to Buyer at closing.

In the event of retained possession or early possession, the parties shall enter into a written possession agreement, the form of which
shall be the Monroe County Bar Association's recommended form. The agreement shall require a security deposit of $_____.

9. Representations Pertaining to the Home Equity Theft Prevention Act ("HETPA") (check at least one).

☐ (a) **Buyer.** Buyer represents to Seller as of the date of acceptance that Buyer is acquiring the property to use the property as
Buyer's primary residence and that Buyer will occupy the property as Buyer's primary residence.

OR

☐ (b) **Seller.** To Seller's actual knowledge, Seller represents to Buyer as of the date of acceptance that there is no active lis pendens
filed against the property to foreclose a mortgage pursuant to Article 13 of the New York Real Property Actions and Proceedings
Law, the property is not on an active property tax lien sale list, and Seller is not two (2) months or more behind in Seller's
mortgage payments with respect to the property.

***WARNING: THIS CONTRACT FORM CANNOT BE USED IF THIS TRANSACTION IS COVERED BY THE HOME EQUITY THEFT
PREVENTION ACT (Section 265-a of New York Real Property Law).***

Seller's Initials _____   Buyer's Initials _____

Purchase and Sale Contract for Residential Property (continued)

10. Title and Related Documents. Seller shall deliver at Seller's expense:

A. At least 15 calendar days prior to the closing date, to Buyer or Buyer's attorney, (i) a draft of the proposed deed, (ii) abstract of title, fully guaranteed tax and U.S. Court searches, all dated or re-dated after the date of acceptance, with a local tax certificate for Village or City taxes, if any (all of which shall be continued to and including the day of closing at Seller's expense), and (iii) an instrument survey map dated after the date of acceptance, certified and prepared to meet the standards of the Monroe County Bar Association and Buyer's mortgage lender; and

B. At the closing, to Buyer, a properly signed and notarized, (i) Warranty Deed with lien covenant (or Executor's, Administrator's or Trustee's Deed, if Seller holds title as such), (ii) carbon monoxide detector and smoke alarm affidavits, (iii) documents required by law, (iv) documents required by Buyer's lender, provided there is no cost or liability to Seller, and (v) assignment of leases and transfer of security deposits, if any.

11. Marketability of Title. Seller shall convey good marketable title to the property in fee simple, free and clear of all liens and encumbrances. However, Buyer agrees to accept title to the property subject to: (a) restrictive covenants of record common to the tract or subdivision of which the property is a part, provided these covenants have not been violated or the time for objection to any violation has expired, (b) public utility easements within 10 feet of lot lines which do not interfere with any existing improvements on the property or with any improvements that Buyer may construct in compliance with all present restrictive covenants of record and zoning and building codes, and (c) except for waterfront properties, fences encroaching one foot or less onto the property, provided the fence placement does not impair access to the property from a right of way or cause the property to be in violation of any restrictive covenant, easement, or agreement of record or of any building, zoning or subdivision code.

12. Objections to Title. If Buyer raises a valid written objection to Seller's title which indicates that title to the property is unmarketable, then Seller may cancel this Contract upon written notice to Buyer, and the deposit shall be returned to Buyer. However, if Seller: (a) is able to cure the objection on or before the closing or (b) is able to insure the title objection and Buyer is willing to accept insurable title, then this Contract shall continue, subject to the Seller curing the title objection and/or providing insurable title at Seller's expense. If Seller fails to cure the title objection on or before the closing, or if Buyer is unwilling to accept insurable title, Buyer may cancel this Contract upon written notice to Seller and the deposit shall be returned to Buyer.

13. Transfer Tax, Recording Costs, Mortgage Tax and Closing Adjustments. Seller will pay the real property transfer tax and special additional mortgage recording tax, if applicable. If the purchase price is $1,000,000.00 or more, then the additional transfer tax identified in Section 1402-a of the Tax Law shall be paid by the ☐ Seller ☐ Buyer (check one). Buyer will pay for recording the deed and mortgage, mortgage tax and mortgage assumption charges, if any. Excluding delinquent items, interest and penalties, the following will be prorated and adjusted between Seller and Buyer as of the closing date: taxes, other assessments and municipal charges computed on a fiscal year basis; rent; common charges or assessments; fuel oil; propane; water, pure water and sewer charges. FHA mortgage insurance shall be adjusted in accordance with the FHA formulae.

14. Certificate of Occupancy. If applicable laws require, Seller shall apply for a Certificate of Occupancy for the property no less than ten calendar days after acceptance and furnish it before closing. However, if the cost of obtaining the Certificate of Occupancy exceeds $_____, Seller shall not be obligated to provide the Certificate of Occupancy, and Buyer will be allowed either to receive a credit at closing for the above amount, or to cancel this Contract by written notice to Seller, and any deposit shall be returned to Buyer.

15. Zoning/Building Code Compliance.

A. Zoning Code Compliance. Seller represents to Buyer that the property is zoned for use as a _____ and that the property is in compliance with applicable zoning codes and ordinances.

B. Building Code Compliance. (check only (i) or (ii) below):

☐ (i) Seller shall not provide any certificates of compliance or any other evidence that the improvements which are a part of the property comply with building codes and ordinances.

☐ (ii) Seller shall provide a certificate of compliance or other comparable proof of compliance with building codes and ordinances from the applicable municipality for the following improvements checked, but for no others (check all that apply): [ ] basement living area, [ ] building addition, [ ] converted 3rd floor living area, [ ] deck, [ ] fence, [ ] gazebo, [ ] hot tub, [ ] playset, [ ] pond/fountain, [ ] pool, [ ] shed/outbuilding, [ ] wood stove/freestanding fireplace, [ ] other: (list)_____

_____.

However, if the cost of obtaining the certificates or other comparable proof of compliance for the improvements checked above exceeds $_____ in the aggregate, Seller shall not be obligated to provide such certificates or other proof of compliance and the Buyer will be allowed either to receive a credit at closing in the above amount or to cancel this Contract by written notice to Seller, and any deposit shall be returned to Buyer.

16. Risk of Loss. Risk of loss or damage to the property by fire or other casualty until transfer of title shall be assumed by the Seller. If damage to the property by fire or such other casualty occurs prior to transfer, Buyer may cancel this Contract without any further liability to Seller and Buyer's deposit is to be returned. If Buyer does not cancel but elects to close, then Seller shall transfer to Buyer any insurance proceeds, or Seller's claim to insurance proceeds payable for such damage.

17. Condition of Property. Buyer agrees to purchase the property and any items included in the purchase **AS IS** except as provided in paragraph 2, subject to reasonable use, wear, tear, and natural deterioration between now and closing. However, this paragraph shall not relieve Seller from furnishing a Certificate of Occupancy as called for in Paragraph 14 and/or certificate(s) of compliance as called for in Paragraph 15, if applicable.

18. Services. Seller represents the property is serviced by: ☐ Electric, ☐ Fuel Oil, ☐ Gas (Natural), ☐ Propane, ☐ Public Sewers, ☐ Public Water, ☐ Septic System, ☐ Well, ☐ Other _____.

Seller's Initials   Buyer's Initials

FIGURE 8.1

Purchase and Sale Contract for Residential Property (continued)

19. Deposit to Listing Broker. Buyer ☐ has deposited ☐ will deposit within two calendar days of acceptance $_____ in the form of a _____ with _____ (Escrow Agent) at _____ _____(Bank), which deposit is to become part of the purchase price or returned if not accepted or if this Contract thereafter fails to close for any reason not the fault of the Buyer. If Buyer fails to complete Buyer's part of this Contract, Seller is allowed to retain the deposit to be applied to Seller's damages and may pursue other legal rights Seller has against the Buyer, including but not limited to a lawsuit for any real estate brokerage commission paid by the Seller.

20. Real Estate Broker.
☐ (a) The parties agree that _____ brought about this purchase and sale.
☐ (b) It is understood and agreed by Buyer and Seller that no broker brought about this purchase and sale.

21. Life of Offer. This offer shall expire on _____, 20_____, at _____ .m.

22. Responsibility of Persons Under This Contract; Non-Assignability. If more than one person signs this Contract as Buyer, each person and any party who takes over that person's legal position will be responsible for keeping the promises made by Buyer in this Contract. If more than one person signs this Contract as Seller, each person or any party who takes over that person's legal position, will be fully responsible for keeping the promises made by Seller. However, this Contract is personal to the parties and may not be assigned by either without the other's consent.

23. Entire Contract. This Contract when signed by both Buyer and Seller will be the record of the complete agreement between the Buyer and Seller concerning the purchase and sale of the property. No oral agreements or promises will be binding. Seller's representations in this Contract shall not survive after closing.

24. Notices. Notices under this Contract shall be in writing and deemed delivered upon receipt. Delivery of notices under this Contract shall be made by personal delivery, overnight courier, first class mail, or by fax, provided that the original of the faxed notice shall also be mailed by first class prepaid mail within one calendar day, excluding Saturdays, Sundays and public holidays, following the date of the fax transmission.

If delivery is made by personal delivery, the notice(s) delivered shall be deemed received on the date delivered. If delivery is made by overnight courier or first class mail, the notice(s) delivered shall be deemed received one calendar day, excluding Saturdays, Sundays and public holidays, following the date upon which the notice(s) are deposited with the overnight courier service with delivery charges prepaid or charged to sender's account or with the postal service with required postage affixed. If delivery is made by fax, the notice(s) transmitted shall be deemed received on the date the sender receives confirmation from the recipient's equipment that the entire transmission has been received, provided the required mailing is completed.

Any notices relating to this Contract may be given by the attorneys for the parties.

25. Addenda. The following Addenda are incorporated into and attached to and made a part of this Contract:

☐ Agricultural/Farming Disclosure	☐ Mediation	☐ Seller Financing
☐ All Parties Agreement (FHA/VA)	☐ Mortgage Assumption	☐ Services (Septic & Water)
☐ Electric Availability	☐ Personal Property	☐ Uncapped Natural Gas Well Disclosure
☐ Home Warranty	☐ Property Inspection	☐ Utility Surcharge
☐ Lead Compliance	☐ Sale & Transfer of Title Contingency	☐ Wayne County Disclosure Notice
☐ Other: _____ .		

Dated: _____   BUYER _____

Witness: _____   BUYER _____

☐ ACCEPTANCE OF OFFER BY SELLER   ☐ COUNTER OFFER BY SELLER
Seller accepts the offer and agrees to sell on the terms and conditions set forth.
☐ Waiver of Seller's attorney approval. This offer is not subject to Seller's attorney approval.

Dated: _____   SELLER _____

Witness: _____   SELLER _____

Seller's Initials

Buyer's Initials

F I G U R E 8.1

Purchase and Sale Contract for Residential Property (continued)

_____ **ADMINISTRATIVE INFORMATION** _____

Property Address: _____ MLS# _____

Seller: _____ **Buyer:** _____

Address: _____ Address: _____

_____ Zip: _____ _____ Zip: _____

E-Mail: _____ E-Mail: _____

Phone: (H) _____(W) _____ Phone: (H) _____(W) _____

Attorney: _____ **Attorney:** _____

Address: _____ Address: _____

_____ Zip: _____ _____ Zip: _____

E-Mail: _____ E-Mail: _____

Phone: _____ Fax: _____ Phone: _____ Fax: _____

Listing Broker: _____ **Selling Broker:** _____

Address: _____ Address: _____

_____ Zip: _____ _____ Zip: _____

Phone: _____ Fax: _____ Phone: _____ Fax: _____

Listing Agent: _____ **Selling Agent:** _____

Phone: _____ Fax: _____ Phone: _____ Fax: _____

Cell: _____ Cell: _____

E-Mail: _____ E-Mail: _____

ID#: _____ ID#: _____

_____   _____
Seller's Initials   Buyer's Initials

In other areas of the state, the broker prepares a precontract agreement, known as a *binder,* which may or may not be legally enforceable but usually contains many of the essential terms that will later be included in a contract. It also may acknowledge receipt of an earnest money deposit. Purchase offers often are handled by attorneys. The five steps involved in preparing a fully executed, binding purchase and sales contract are as follows:

1. The attorneys prepare and negotiate the contract of sale.
2. The seller's attorney sends the buyer's attorney a draft contract, which the buyer can agree to or modify by suggesting acceptable changes through the buyer's attorney.
3. After negotiation, the buyer's attorney sends the contract negotiated by the buyer with the down payment (considered an offer at this point) to the seller through the seller's attorney for acceptance.
4. The offer is considered accepted when and after it is signed by the seller and delivered to the office of the buyer's attorney.
5. At this point, it is binding on both parties.

In a few localities, notably in and around New York City, brokers prepare a non-binding **memorandum of sale**, data sheet, or terms sheet. This sheet of information states the essential terms of the agreement. The parties agree to have a formal and complete contract of sale drawn up by an attorney. Throughout the state, a preliminary memorandum might be used in any situation in which the details of the transaction are too complex for a standard sales contract form.

Any attempt by the seller to change the terms proposed by the buyer ("Okay, except that . . .") creates a **counteroffer**. Any counteroffer essentially cancels the original offer. The buyer is no longer bound by the original offer because the seller has, in effect, rejected it. The buyer may accept the seller's counteroffer or reject it or, if desired, make another counteroffer. Any change in the last offer made results in a counteroffer until one party finally agrees completely with the other party's last offer and both parties sign the final contract.

A contract is not considered valid until the person making the offer has been *notified of the other party's acceptance.* Therefore, any offer may be pulled or rescinded by the offeror (the giver of the offer) prior to acceptance by the offeree (the recipient of the offer) and communication of the acceptance.

Equitable title   A buyer who signs a contract to purchase real estate does not receive title to the land; only delivery of a deed can actually convey title. However, after the contract is signed, the buyer has a contract right known as **equitable title**. In New York, a buyer under a land contract (also known as a *contract for deed* or an *installment sales contract*) also acquires equitable title.

In the case of a land contract, the buyer would always be wise to record the land contract. This protects the buyer against the subject property being pledged in the future as collateral to another lender by the seller. If the parties decide not to go through with the purchase and sale, they usually enter into a written **release**, freeing each other from any obligation under the contract.

Destruction of premises New York State has adopted the Uniform Vendor and Purchaser Risk Act, which provides that the seller (vendor) bear any loss, most commonly from a fire, that occurs before the title passes or the buyer (vendee) takes possession.

Earnest money deposits It is customary, but not essential, for a purchaser to provide a cash deposit when making an offer to purchase real estate. This cash deposit, commonly referred to as an **earnest money deposit**, *a down payment, initial equity, or contract deposit, gives evidence of the buyer's intention to carry out the terms of the contract.* It is often held by the party holding the escrow involved in the sale (upstate) or the seller's attorney (New York City area). The state requires that each sales contract name and identify the party holding the deposit and the bank where it is to be held. If the offer is not accepted, the earnest money deposit is returned immediately to the would-be buyer.

The deposit generally should be sufficient to discourage the buyer from defaulting, compensate the seller for taking the property off the market, and cover any expenses the seller might incur if the buyer defaults. However, a purchase offer with no earnest money is valid. Most contracts provide that the deposit and interest earned on it, if any, become the seller's property if the buyer defaults. The seller might also claim further damages.

Earnest money must be held by a broker or lawyer in a special *trust,* or *escrow, bank account.* This money may not be commingled, or mixed, with a broker's personal funds. A broker may not use such funds for personal use; this illegal act is known as *conversion* (a legal term for stealing).

A broker need not open a special escrow account for each earnest money deposit received. One account into which all such funds are deposited is sufficient. A broker should maintain full, complete, and accurate records of all earnest money deposits.

If a contracted sale fails to close, the real estate broker who is holding a deposit in escrow should not turn over the money to either party without written agreement or release from both buyer and seller or their attorneys. In the event of a prolonged disagreement, the money can be placed in the custody of a court pending final settlement.

Parts of a sales contract In New York, the six essentials of a valid contract for the sale of real property are as follows:

1. Contract in writing
2. Competent parties
3. Agreement to buy and sell
4. Adequate description of the property
5. Consideration (price and terms of payment)
6. Signatures of the parties (The signature of a witness is not essential for a valid contract.)

Important, although not essential, for a valid contract are provisions covering

- the grantor's agreement to convey (should specify type of deed) and
- the place and time of closing.

Also included in most sales contracts are the following:

- Encumbrances to which the deed will be made subject
- Earnest money deposit
- Mortgage financing the buyer plans to obtain and other contingencies
- Possession by the buyer
- Title evidence
- Prorations and adjustments
- Destruction of the premises before closing
- Default by either party
- Prior deed
- Prior title insurance policy
- Survey
- Certificate of occupancy
- Personal data (names, addresses, telephone numbers, marital status, Social Security numbers, etc.)
- Tax bills
- Miscellaneous provisions

In addition to the transaction items listed, at the point of contract preparation, the following information will be pertinent to and included in the sales contract:

- **Date.** This section will reflect the date of contract preparation.
- **Identification of the parties.** This section names the interested parties to the transaction (i.e., the buyer and the seller).
- **Legal description.** This section provides a legal description of the subject property (the section, lot and block number; see Chapter 6 for legal descriptions).
- **Personal property provision.** This section addresses any personal property to be transferred or not transferred with the real property.
- **Consideration.** This section is one of the required essential elements (previously discussed in this chapter) for a contract to be valid and enforceable. The exchange of value is stated within this section of the contract; it will normally state the purchase price.
- **Terms of payment.** This section addresses the manner by which payment is to be made and will also include any earnest money deposit due at contract signing.
- **"Subject to" provision.** Generally, this section will spell out any contingencies requisite for the transaction to proceed (i.e., lender financing).
- **Type of deed.** This section sets forth the type of deed to be conveyed by the seller to the buyer (see Chapter 6).
- **Closing time and place.** This section will provide the date and time that the closing is expected to take place. The words "on or about" or "time is of the essence" distinguish the expected date, time of closing, and responsibility of the parties to close.
- **Broker clause.** This section will list the names of any brokers involved in the transaction and a statement as to the party responsible for remuneration of fees (normally paid by the seller).

■ **Apportionments.** This section covers the responsibilities of the parties for any charges or income due either party on the day of closing. These items are always set forth within the closing statement. The closing statement is normally prepared (prior to the closing) by the closing/escrow agent.

■ **Lien law.** This section states that New York lien law establishes that, where particular funds are to be received by owners, contractors, and subcontractors in connection with any improvements of real property, those individuals or entities become statutory trustees to the holding of statutory trust assets.

■ **Condition of property.** This section covers the basis for condition of the property to be delivered to the buyer at closing/transfer of title (i.e., property to be delivered in "as is condition").

■ **Merger clause.** This section covers the avoidance of any precontract discussions and negotiations from surviving the written contract and agreement. In order to be effective, it also stipulates that any amendment, waiver, or change to the agreement must be in writing and executed by the interested parties to the contract.

■ **Loan contingency clause.** This section outlines the buyer's prerequisite requirement to obtain financing as paramount to the completion and closing of the transaction. In the event financing cannot be legitimately accomplished, the buyer would be entitled to void the contract and a refund of the earnest money deposit.

■ **Possession.** This section addresses the point at which the buyer will receive physical possession of the purchased property (i.e., on the day of closing, at some determinable date after the date of closing, or that the buyer receives earlier possession prior to the closing).

■ **Down payment.** This section addresses the buyer's initial investment/monetary responsibility under the contract.

■ **No survival.** This section applies to events following the execution/closing of the contract. Where no survival of terms is applicable, the contract and responsibilities of the parties cease at execution/closing and transfer of title.

When prepared, the sales contract will provide for the agreed-on amount of earnest money deposit to be made by the buyer. Although there is no prescribed statutory deposit amount, by custom, the buyer normally is required to deposit 10 percent of the purchase price to whichever party is acting as the escrow/closing agent to the transaction. In most cases, the seller's attorney holds the earnest money deposit in escrow while simultaneously acting as the closing agent. Advantages to having an attorney holding the earnest money deposit would be

■ appropriate determination concerning the disposition of escrowed funds when an escrow disbursement dispute arises between the buyer and the seller, and

■ elimination of conflicts of interest that may arise concerning brokerage commission disputes.

In addition, it would not be uncommon in simple residential transactions in upstate New York to find that the listing agent is also acting as the escrow/closing agent.

Miscellaneous provisions   In recent years, increasing awareness of consumers' rights has increased the number of disclosures that must be made to a buyer before that person is bound by a purchase contract. Among these in New York are disclosure of agency relationships and disclosures relating to possible problems with lead paint, agricultural districts, and electric service.

When the purchaser intends to secure a Federal Housing Administration (FHA) or a Department of Veterans Affairs (VA) loan, an accompanying **rider** provides that the contract may be voided if the property is appraised by the lending institution for less than the sales price. The FHA requires that before signing a purchase contract, its borrowers acknowledge receipt of a notice that the FHA's appraiser is concerned mainly with overall value and not with detailed condition. The notice states that the FHA recommends (but does not require) that the buyer retain a home inspector. Sometimes provisions are added stipulating that seller or buyer will furnish satisfactory reports on such items as termite or insect infestation or the quality of a private water supply.

In some transfers, a certificate of occupancy must be obtained from a municipality; the contract should make it clear whose responsibility this will be.

With regard to personal property or appliances being transferred with the real estate, the buyer usually agrees to accept them in their present condition, **"as is."** The term as is does not relieve a seller from defects to the property or required disclosures of material facts that affect the value of the property when known to the seller. In the past, the term caveat emptor (Latin for "let the buyer beware") served as a warning to the buyer. Today's seller disclosure laws, when and where applicable, have shifted the responsibility more in the direction of the seller.

The purchaser may want the right to reinspect the property shortly before settlement.

Contingencies are events that excuse performance of either party to the contract. Among the more common are the buyer's need to secure a specific loan, the purchaser's right to a satisfactory licensed home inspector's report, an environmental report on the property within a specified time period, approval of the contract by a family member or the purchaser's attorney within a short period of time, and the buyer's need to sell a present home before buying the next one. If the stated event does not occur, the party is excused from performing, and the contract is voided.

For example, an **attorney review clause** is needed when the buyer and the seller choose to have an attorney study the contract. If consulted, the attorney must complete the contract review within the agreed-on time. The contract will be legally binding at the end of this period unless an attorney for the buyer or the seller disapproves it.

A **mortgage contingency clause** is a common provision that allows the buyer a certain period to obtain a commitment for financing at a specified interest rate for a certain amount of money. It usually lasts for 30 to 60 days, depending on the average time needed to obtain a loan commitment.

For example, the clause might read that the contract is contingent on the buyer obtaining approval for a 30-year mortgage for $100,000 at no more than 8 percent interest within 45 days. For additional protection, the buyer might specify the type of loan he or she prefers (i.e., fixed or variable).

A mortgage contingency rider provides critical protection to the buyer. It allows the buyer to void the purchase contract without penalty in those cases in which the buyer is unable to obtain financing on the terms specified in the contract after making a reasonable or good-faith effort to do so within the time provided. Because this type of clause favors the buyer, some real estate agents suggest that the buyer obtain prequalification from a lender, which gives the seller a degree of confidence that the buyer will not use the clause to void the contract unless some extraordinary circumstance arises.

Where the buyer has another home that must be sold first, the seller may insist on an **escape clause**, or *kickout*. Such a provision allows the seller to look for another offer, with the original purchaser retaining the right, if challenged, either to firm up the first sales contract (dropping the contingency) or to void the contract. If the first buyer chose to drop out, the seller would then be free to accept the other offer.

Liquidated damages are an amount of money, agreed to in advance by buyer and seller, that will serve as total compensation if one party does not live up to the contract. If a sales contract specifies that the earnest money deposit will serve as liquidated damages, the seller will be entitled to only the deposit if the buyer refuses to perform for no good reason. The seller who agrees to accept the deposit as liquidated damages may not sue later for any further damages.

Plain-language requirement (Sullivan Law)   New York law requires that certain written agreements for the sale or lease of residential property be written in a clear and coherent manner with words that are common in everyday usage. The copy also must be appropriately divided and captioned in its various sections. The plain-language requirement does not apply to agreements involving amounts over $50,000. Figure 8.1 is an example of a plain-English contract.

Lead-based paint hazard disclosure   A buyer who purchases almost any residential property built before 1978 must be furnished with a booklet discussing lead-based paint hazards and disclosing any the seller is aware of. Any purchase contract involving the sale of pre-1978 residential property must allow the buyer ten days in which to investigate potential lead-based paint hazards, before the contract becomes binding. However, buyers and sellers may agree to shorten or waive this period (this agreement must be included in the purchase contract itself).

Cooperative Apartment Contracts

Because a cooperative apartment is owned by a corporation, the buyer of a co-op apartment does not receive a deed to real estate. Instead, he or she buys shares in the corporation and receives a proprietary lease to a unit in the building. These shares are personal property rather than real property. They can usually be financed, but through a loan under the **Uniform Commercial Code (UCC)** rather than a mortgage. The IRS, however, treats the owner's interest on the loan as it does mortgages. To summarize:

- In a transaction involving the sale of real property, a mortgage is the financing instrument used.
- In a transaction involving the sale of personal property, a UCC financing instrument is utilized.

When the shares of stock in a cooperative are considered "sold shares," the cooperative board of directors that manages the cooperative building always has the right to approve or disapprove of prospective tenants (owners). The co-op board is not obligated by law to provide a reason for declining a prospective owner. This is with the proviso that its decisions are not based on discrimination against any classes protected by fair housing laws.

The board may charge the seller a flip tax at the time of sale. A flip tax is the percentage amount paid by the selling shareholder to the cooperative at close of title. Flip taxes are income-generating mechanisms for the cooperative. It most cases, they are added to any reserve fund that the cooperative maintains. Reserve funds are used for major capital improvements, compliance with local or governmental laws, lowering outstanding principal balances on the underlying mortgage of the cooperative, or covering operating deficits. Cooperatives will be discussed in further detail in Chapter 23.

Condominium Sales

The buyer of a condominium receives fee simple title to the unit "from the plaster in" and also a percentage of ownership of the common elements. Special contracts are used for condominium sales. In some cases, the condominium association must release its right of first refusal before the condo may be sold to an outsider. In the event the condominium association exercises its **right of first refusal**, in most cases, the condominium must match the price and terms of the existing sales contract.

Chapter 23 contains details on initial sale and resale of condominiums and cooperatives, which are more complex, involving submission of offering plans (the black book), financial plans, marketing statements, and other documents subject to approval by the state's attorney general.

Option Agreements

An **option** is a *contract by which an optionor (owner) gives an optionee (prospective purchaser or lessee) the right to buy or lease the owner's property at a fixed price within a stated time.* The optionee pays a fee (the agreed-on consideration) for this right and has no other obligation. The optionee is free to decide within the specified time to either buy or lease the property or allow the option to expire. The owner is bound to sell if requested; the optionee is not bound to buy. An option is often used by a tenant, who may then choose either to buy or to remain as a tenant. Options must contain all the terms required for a valid contract of sale. In essence, it is a one-way street for the party receiving the option.

Land Contracts

A real estate sale can be made under a **land contract**, sometimes called a *contract for deed* or *an installment contract*. Under a typical land contract, the seller, also known as the *vendor*, retains ownership, while the buyer, known as the vendee, moves in and has an equitable interest in the property. Each land contract is different, but in a common form the buyer agrees to give the seller a down payment and pay regular installments of principal and interest over a number of years. The buyer also agrees to pay real estate taxes, insurance premiums, repairs, and upkeep on the property. Although the buyer obtains possession when the contract is signed by both parties, *the seller is not obligated to execute (sign) and deliver a deed to the buyer until the terms of the contract have been satisfied.* For this and other reasons, the vendee/buyer is advised to record the contract. Depending on the agreement, execution and delivery of the deed might occur when the buyer can obtain a regular mortgage loan and pay off the balance due on the contract.

Real estate is occasionally sold with the new buyer's assuming an existing land contract from the original buyer/vendee. Generally, the seller/vendor must approve the new purchaser.

Land contracts require extensive legal input from lawyers experienced in real estate matters. The broker who negotiates a land contract should consult attorneys for both parties at every step and refrain from specifying any detailed terms in the agreement.

Land contracts are used as financing instruments because by receiving installments over a prescribed period of time (stated within the land contract), the seller acts as the lender.

Land contracts or installment sales contracts bear resemblance to a "layaway plan" in a retail store:

- In a layaway plan, the seller of the item retains ownership of the item until all installments under the layaway plan have been paid.
- In a land contract or installment sales contract, although the buyer receives possession of the property as well as equitable title, the seller holds the deed until all installments have been paid.

Local Forms

To gain familiarity with the forms used in a local area, the student should go to brokers or real estate companies and ask for copies of the sales contract, listing agreement, and other forms they use. More general forms also can be obtained at a title or abstract company and some banks and savings and loan associations, or they may be purchased at local office supply and stationery stores.

Rescission

With contracts for the purchase of some types of personal property, the buyer has three days in which to reconsider and rescind (cancel) the contract. No such right of **rescission** applies to contracts for the purchase of real estate (with certain exceptions, for example, when lead-based paint laws apply).

Sales contract Another form and example of rescission exists when borrowers change their minds about a mortgage loan. In this case, a borrower has three days in which to cancel the transaction if the mortgage was for the refinancing of presently owned and owner-occupied property. No right of rescission, however, applies to mortgage loans used for the purchase of real estate.

Contract Procedures

At this point, if all goes well in the transaction, the contract will be signed. In almost every sales contract, the buyer is the first one to sign. The contract signing normally includes the tendering of an earnest money deposit by the buyer. The purpose behind this practice is that

- the earnest money deposit acts as a good-faith gesture of the willingness of the buyer to conclude the transaction, and
- it also acts as a means for liquidating potential damages in the event of the buyer's default.

After careful review by the attorney for the seller, if the contract information and terms are in order, the contract is usually countersigned by the seller.

In some cases, contract signing occurs by mail. In other cases, it would not be uncommon for a formal sit-down contract signing to occur.

New York State Lawyers' Fund for Client Protection

The New York State Lawyers' Fund for Client Protection was created in 1982. Its mission and purpose is

- the protection of legal consumers from the dishonest conduct in the practice of law,
- the preservation of the integrity of the bar,
- the safeguarding of the good name of lawyers for their honesty in handling of client money, and
- the promotion of the general public's confidence in the administering of the justice system in the state of New York.

The **American Bar Association (ABA)** is the national representative of the legal profession. Its purpose is to serve the general public as well as the legal profession through the promotion of justice, professionalism, and most of all, respect for the law. The ABA provides

- accreditation for law schools,
- continuing legal education (CLE),
- information about the law,
- programs that assist lawyers and judges in their work, and
- a variety of initiatives intended to improve the legal system for the general public.

■ SUMMARY

A contract is defined as an agreement made by competent parties with adequate consideration, to take or to refrain from some lawful action.

Contracts may be classified according to whether the parties' intentions are expressed or implied by their actions. They also may be classified as bilateral, when both parties have obligated themselves to act, or unilateral, when one party is obligated to perform only if the other party does. In addition, contracts may be classified according to their legal enforceability as valid, void, voidable, or unenforceable.

An executed contract is one that has been fully performed. An executory contract is one in which some act remains to be performed.

The essentials of a valid contract are (1) competent parties, (2) offer and acceptance, (3) consideration, (4) legality of object, and (5) agreement in writing and signatures of the parties.

In many types of contracts, either party may transfer rights and obligations by assignment of the contract or by novation (substitution of a new contract).

A party who has suffered a loss because of the other party's default may sue for damages to cover the loss. A party who insists on completing the transaction may ask for specific performance of the terms of the contract; a court may order the other party to comply with the agreement.

A real estate sales contract binds a buyer and a seller to a definite transaction as described in the contract. The buyer is bound to purchase the property for the amount stated in the agreement. The seller is bound to deliver title, free from liens and encumbrances (except for those allowed by the contract).

The *Duncan and Hill* court decision cautioned real estate brokers to make any sales contracts they draw up subject to approval by the parties' attorneys. The DOS expects licensees to limit their assistance in drawing up sales contracts to filling in the blanks on forms approved by local bar associations. Any unusual or complicated provisions must be drawn up by attorneys.

Under an option agreement, the optionee purchases from the optioner, for a limited time period, the exclusive right to purchase or lease the optioner's property. A land contract, or installment contract, is an agreement under which a buyer purchases a seller's real estate on time. The buyer takes possession of and responsibility for the property but does not receive the deed immediately.

CHAPTER 8 QUIZ

1. A homeowner told her buyers, when they first looked at her house, that she intended to remove her grandmother's antique chandelier. It was not mentioned in the contract. Now they are suing her. A judge is likely to say that
   a. the homeowner's oral announcement was enough; she could take the chandelier.
   b. the chandelier should remain because of the rule of parol evidence.
   c. because the chandelier wasn't mentioned in the written contract, it remained personal property.
   d. there was no legal way the homeowner could have retained the chandelier.

2. If someone drives into a filling station and tops off the gas tank, he is obligated to pay for the fuel through what kind of contract?
   a. Express
   b. Implied
   c. Oral
   d. Voidable

3. A contract is said to be *bilateral* if
   a. one of the parties is a minor.
   b. the contract has yet to be fully performed.
   c. only one party to the agreement is bound to act.
   d. all parties to the contract are bound to act.

4. A contract for the sale of real estate that does NOT state the consideration to be paid for the property would be
   a. implied.
   b. executory.
   c. void.
   d. enforceable.

5. During the period after a real estate sales contract is signed but before title actually passes, the status of the contract is
   a. voidable.
   b. executory.
   c. unilateral.
   d. implied.

6. A 17-year-old signs a contract to buy a home for himself. The contract is
   a. voidable.
   b. optional.
   c. executed.
   d. unilateral.

7. A buyer signed an offer to purchase a property for $10,000 less than the asking price and deposited $5,000 with the broker. The owner cannot be reached to tell him of the signed document. At this point, the document is a(n)
   a. voidable contract.
   b. offer.
   c. executory agreement.
   d. implied contract.

8. In some parts of New York, brokers record the essential terms of a real estate sales contract in a document called a(n)
   a. promissory note.
   b. title agreement.
   c. earnest money agreement.
   d. memorandum of sale.

9. Under the statute of frauds, any contract for the sale of real estate must be
   a. drawn up by a lawyer.
   b. on a preprinted form.
   c. in writing.
   d. accompanied by an earnest money deposit.

10. How many days must a buyer who purchases a home built before 1978 be given to investigate potential lead-based paint hazards before the contract becomes binding?
    a. 10
    b. 15
    c. 20
    d. 30

11. The *Duncan and Hill* decision recommended that New York State brokers and salespersons protect themselves against
    a. charges of unauthorized practice of law.
    b. potentially fraudulent earnest money checks.
    c. situations in which clients can claim influence and duress.
    d. sellers who declare contacts forfeited without cause.

12. If a real estate sales contract does *NOT* state that time is of the essence and the stipulated date of transfer comes and goes without a closing, the contract is then
    a. binding for only 30 more days.
    b. novated.
    c. still valid.
    d. automatically void.

13. When a purchaser plans to use an FHA or VA loan, a rider on the sales contract states that the contract may be voided if the property
    a. does not meet local safety codes.
    b. requires more than $10,000 in repairs.
    c. contains lead paint or asbestos.
    d. is not appraised for at least the sales price.

14. A suit for specific performance of a real estate contract asks for
    a. money damages.
    b. a new contract.
    c. a deficiency judgment.
    d. a forced sale or purchase.

15. A buyer has decided not to purchase the seller's house. The seller's compensation for the buyer's failure to live up to the contract is referred to as
    a. forfeiture.
    b. liquidated damages.
    c. cancellation funds.
    d. rescission money.

16. A buyer wants to purchase a home from a seller, but the buyer must sell her own home. The seller has not received any other offers, so she is willing to accept the buyer's offer but wants the contract to include a clause that lets her out of the agreement if another buyer comes forward. The contingency the seller needs is referred to as a(n)
    a. assignment.
    b. escape clause.
    c. refusal rider.
    d. seller-choice provision.

17. A couple offer in writing to purchase a house for $140,000, drapes included, with the offer to expire Saturday at noon. The sellers reply in writing on Thursday, accepting $140,000 but excluding the drapes. On Friday, while the buyers are considering this counteroffer, the sellers decide to accept the original offer, drapes included, and state that in writing. At this point, the buyers
    a. must buy and have a right to insist on the drapes.
    b. are not bound to buy and can forget the whole thing.
    c. must buy but are not entitled to the drapes.
    d. must buy and can deduct the value of the drapes from the $140,000.

18. What is the name for the cash deposit offered when making an offer to purchase real estate?
    a. Earnest money deposit
    b. Liquidation funds
    c. Owner's equity
    d. Evidence of intention

19. The sales contract says the buyer will purchase only if his wife flies to New York and approves the sale by the following Saturday. His wife's approval is a
    a. contingency.
    b. reservation.
    c. warranty.
    d. consideration.

20. Selling a home "as is" does NOT relieve a seller from defects to the property that affect the value when
   a. known to the seller.
   b. repairs will exceed $10,000.
   c. hazardous materials are found.
   d. the home was built before 1978.

21. After a real estate contract has been signed, the buyer might withdraw legally and transfer contractual rights to a third party through
   a. assumption.
   b. alternation.
   c. assignment.
   d. ascension.

22. An option to purchase binds
   a. the buyer only.
   b. the seller only.
   c. neither buyer nor seller.
   d. both buyer and seller.

23. Failure to fulfill one's obligations under a contract is called a
   a. novation.
   b. default.
   c. delinquency.
   d. defect.

24. The purchaser of real estate under an installment contract
   a. generally pays no interest charge.
   b. receives title immediately.
   c. is not required to pay property taxes for the duration of the contract.
   d. is called a *vendee*.

25. Consumers have the right to change their mind and rescind the transaction within three days after a
   a. land contract.
   b. firm purchase contract.
   c. refinance mortgage.
   d. lease option.

CHAPTER 9

Title and Closing Costs

■ KEY TERMS

abstract of title
accrued items
actual notice
adjustments
affidavit
attorney's opinion of title
caveat emptor
chain of title
closing statement
coinsurance clause
constructive notice
credit

debit
escrow
evidence of title
homeowners' insurance
  policy
inflation
liability insurance
marketable title
mortgage reduction
  certificate
prepaid item
prorations

public records
Real Estate Settlement
  Procedures Act
  (RESPA)
reconciliation
replacement cost
suit to quiet title
survey
title insurance policy
Torrens system
Uniform Settlement
  Statement

■ PUBLIC RECORDS AND RECORDING

Turnover in property can occur for a variety of reasons. One of the leading reasons would be a concern about present or future **inflation**. Inflation is the gradual reduction of the purchasing power of the dollar, usually related directly to the increases in the money supply by the federal government.

Before purchasing a parcel of real estate, the prospective buyer wants to be sure that the seller can convey good title to the property. The present owner of the real estate undoubtedly purchased from a previous owner, so the same question has been asked many times in the past.

Recording Acts

Parties interested in real estate may record, or file, documents affecting real estate in the *public records* to give notice to the world of their interest.

Public records are maintained by the recorder of deeds, registrar, county clerk, county treasurer, city clerk and collector, and clerks of various courts of record. Records involving taxes, special assessments, ordinances, and zoning and building also are open for anyone's inspection. Prior to recording systems, the Torrens system was a form of property registration.

Necessity for Recording

A deed or mortgage may not be effective as far as later purchasers are concerned unless it has been recorded. The public records should reveal the condition of the title, and a purchaser should be able to rely on a search of the records.

In New York, to give subsequent purchasers constructive notice of a person's interest, all deeds, mortgages, or other written instruments affecting an interest in real estate must be recorded in the county clerk's office of the county where the real estate is located. All documents must be properly acknowledged and show proof of payment of the real estate transfer tax on deeds or the mortgage tax on mortgages before the documents will be accepted for recording.

Effective January 31, 2011, New York City Register Customer Service and Tax Map Customer Service is only available at the Manhattan Business Center location. Bronx, Brooklyn, and Queens City Register Offices only provide document drop-off, pickup and research.

Effective March 1, 2011, payments by check are only accepted at the Manhattan City Register office. Credit card and cash payments are only accepted at the Manhattan Business Center. The Office of the City Register, in the Finance Division of Land Records, keeps real property and other legal records for Manhattan, the Bronx, Brooklyn, and Queens. The Richmond County clerk serves this function in Staten Island.

A deed will not be accepted for recording in counties outside the city of New York unless it is accompanied by a *real property transfer report*, which will be used by the New York State Board of Equalization and Assessment. A real estate transfer tax (Form TP584) **affidavit** (sworn statement) also must be filed. In New York City, a deed may not be recorded unless it is accompanied by a *multiple dwelling registration statement* or an affidavit that no statement is due, an affidavit stating that the property contains a smoke alarm, and a New York City Real Property Transfer Tax Form. In addition, all transfer forms for New York City must be prepared online using the Automated City Register Information System (ACRIS). New York City will not accept any property transfer forms that are not prepared on the ACRIS system.

The county clerk's office maintains general indexes of instruments recorded in that office. Documents are also recorded in the Office of the New York City Register in borough offices in Manhattan (New York County), Brooklyn (Kings County), the Bronx (Bronx County), and Jamaica (Queens County).

Notice

Through the legal maxim of **caveat emptor** ("let the buyer beware"), the courts hold prospective real estate buyers or mortgagees (lenders) responsible for inspecting the property and searching the public records to find out the interests of other parties. **Constructive notice** assumes that the information is available, so the buyer or lender could have learned it.

Constructive notice, or what a person can find out, is distinguished from **actual notice**, or what the person *actually knows*. An individual who has searched the public records and inspected the property has actual notice of the information learned.

Unrecorded liens   A special search may be needed for unrecorded liens. Estate taxes and franchise taxes are placed against all real estate owned either by a decedent at the time of death or by a corporation at the time the franchise tax became a lien; these liens also are not recorded.

Recording sales contracts   Occasionally, it is desirable to record a real property sales contract. Any document to be recorded must be acknowledged. If neither the buyer nor the seller can be reached for an acknowledgment, a witness to their signatures appearing before a notary will be sufficient.

Chain of Title

The **chain of title** shows the record of ownership of the property over time, indicating who has owned the property in previous years going back to its original owner. An **abstract of title** is a condensed history of all the instruments affecting a particular parcel of land.

In New York, chains of title frequently date back to a grant from the king of England or a grant to a Dutch patroon.

Through the chain of title, the sequence of owners can be traced from its origin to its present owner. When this cannot be done, there is a *gap or a break* in the chain. In such cases, ownership usually must be established by a court action called a **suit to quiet title**, or an Article 15 proceeding. This usually will result in the lifting of a "cloud on the title," which may be accomplished through the court's issuance of a quitclaim deed or judicial deed.

■ EVIDENCE OF TITLE

When dealing with an owner of real estate, a purchaser or lender requires satisfactory proof that the seller or borrower is the owner and has good title to the property. This documentary proof is called **evidence of title**.

Generally four forms of title evidence are used: (1) abstract of title and lawyer's opinion, (2) title insurance policy, (3) Torrens certificate, and (4) certificate of title. A deed is not proof of title. It proves the grantee received the property but not that the grantor had good title to it. The only effective proof is one of the evidences of title, based on an adequate search of public records.

Abstract of Title and Lawyer's Opinion

An abstract of title is a brief history of the instruments appearing in the county record that affect title to the parcel in question. The abstractor lists and summarizes each instrument in order, along with information about taxes, judgments, special assessments, and the like. *However, an abstractor does not pass judgment on or guarantee the condition of the title.* Where the abstract will be used for proof of title, the seller's attorney usually orders the abstract continued to cover the current date. It is then submitted to the buyer's attorney, who *examines the entire document.* The attorney must evaluate all the material and prepare a written report for the purchaser. This report is called an **attorney's opinion of title**. (Abstracts with attorneys' opinions of title are not customary in New York City.)

The abstract illustrated in Figure 9.1 shows that on June 3, 1947, Ida Hughey mortgaged her property at 47 Rowley Street to Rochester Savings Bank for $5,000. The rubber stamp on the record shows that the mortgage was paid off in 1958. The mortgage document evidently carried two legal descriptions: one by plat of subdivision and the other by metes and bounds.

In 1952, Hughey granted a five-year lease on the property to Michael and Mildred Franco, who recorded the document. The next year, the Francos bought the property. This particular abstract later goes on to report a driveway easement the Francos negotiated with their neighbors to the north and then traces the property through several later owners with mortgages placed and paid off along the way.

Mortgage lenders prefer that the seller's title be proved by the use of title insurance, which is required in all commercial transactions and is required by the secondary market for residential loans that are to be resold.

Title Insurance

A **title insurance policy** protects the policyholder against loss if a defect in the owner's title is challenged by anyone at any time. The policy is paid for only once and is in force for the whole period of ownership.

When a seller, a buyer, or a lender applies for a policy, the title company examines the title records. If it is satisfied, the title company agrees to insure against certain undiscovered defects, usually those that may be found in the public records and

FIGURE 9.1

Portion of an Abstract

A B S T R A C T   O F   T I T L E

- T O -

#47   W e s t   s i d e   R o w l e y   S t r e e t ,   b e i n g

P a r t   o f   L o t s   #27   a n d   28   o f   t h e

B r o o k s   T r a c t   (N . P a r t)   i n   t h e

C i t y   o f   R o c h e s t e r

Maps: Liber 2 of Maps, page 120 and 138 .
Liber 3 of Maps, page 45
1935 Hopkins Atlas, Vol. 1, Plate 4

1   Ida May Hughey   Mortgage to secure $5000.00
Dated   June 3, 1947
same day
Rochester Savings Bank   same day at 12:30 P. M.
47 Main Street, West   Liber 1800 of Mortgages, page 344
Rochester, New York

Conveys land in the City of Rochester, being on the

west side of Rowley Street in said City and being part of lots

Nos. 27 and 28 in the Brooks Tract as shown on a map of said

Tract made by M. D. Rowley, surveyor, May 15, 1869 and filed

in Monroe County Clerk's Office and counded and described as

follows:

Beginning at a point in the west line of Rowely

Street 15 feet northerly from the southeast corner of said

lot #27; thence northerly on the west line of Rowley Street,

forth (40) feet; thence westerly on a line parallel with the

south line of said lot #27, 121 feet; thence southerly on a

line parallel with the west line of Rowley Street, 40 feet;

thence easterly 121 feet to the place of beginning.

F I G U R E   9.1

Portion of an Abstract (continued)

Being the same premises conveyed to the mortgagor
by Liber 2258 of Deeds, page 178.

Subject to any restrictions and public utility
easements of record.

- -

2   Ida May Hughey, Landlord   Lease

         -To-   Dated   May 23, 1952
                                      Ack.   same day
Michael Franco   Rec.   August 4, 1952
Mildred Franco, his wife,
Tenants, 17 Glendale Park,   Liber 2769 of Deeds, page 290
Rochester, N.Y., (Second
parties not certified)

First party leases to second parties premises described as #47 Rowley Street, Rochester, New York, being a
12 room house for a term of 5 years commencing July 16, 1952
and ending July 15, 1957 on certain terms and conditions set
forth herein.

Second parties shall have the right of renewal on
the same terms and conditions as herein for an additional
period of 5 years provided that written notice of intention to
renew is served upon Landlord or her assigns at least 30 days
prior to end of initial term hereof.

- -

3   Ida May Hughey,   Warranty Deed

         -To-   Dated Oct. 30, 1953
                                      Ack. Same day
Michele Franco, Mildred   Rec. Same day at 10:50 A.M.
Franco, his wife, as
tenants by the entirety,   Liber 2861 of Deeds, page 411
#47 Rowley St., Rochester,
N.Y. (Second parties not
certified).

Conveys same as #1.

Subject to all covenants, easements and restrictions

such items as forged documents, documents of incompetent grantors, incorrect marital statements, and improperly delivered deeds. Exactly which defects the company will insure against depends on the type of policy; the New York State Insurance Department sets standards. The policy amount is the purchase price in the case of an owner's policy and the loan amount in the case of the lender's policy.

On completing the examination, the title company usually issues a report of title or a commitment to issue a title policy. An owner's policy usually has coverage against unrecorded documents, unrecorded defects of which the policyholder has knowledge, rights of parties in possession, and facts discoverable by survey. The insurance company agrees to defend the title at its own expense and to reimburse the policyholder up to the amount of the policy for damages sustained by reason of any defect not excepted. Title companies in New York must offer a homeowner the right to purchase insurance covering possible increase in future market value.

Title companies issue various forms of policies, the most common of which are the *owner's* title insurance policy (a *fee policy*) and the *mortgagee* or *lender* title insurance policy. An owner's policy protects owners and their heirs or devisees. The mortgagee policy protects the lender's interests.

The Torrens System

The **Torrens system** is a legal registration system used to verify ownership and encumbrances. Registration in the Torrens system provides evidence of title without the need for an additional search of the public records. At any time, the Torrens certificate in the registrar's office reveals the owner of the land and all mortgages, judgments, and similar liens. It does not reveal federal or state taxes and some other items. The Torrens system is no longer used in New York.

Certificate of Title

With an older system, which still may be used for transfers where no lending institution is involved, a *certificate of title prepared by an attorney* is used, and no abstract is prepared. The attorney examines the public records and issues a certificate of title that expresses the attorney's opinion of the title's status. However, it is not a title insurance policy and does not carry the full protection of such a policy. The person who sustains damages by relying on it may look to the lawyer for satisfaction.

Marketable Title

Under the terms of the usual real estate sales contract, the seller is required to deliver marketable or insurable title to the buyer at the closing. Generally, a **marketable title** is one that is free from significant defects (other than those specified in the sales contract), will not expose the purchasers to lawsuits that threaten their quiet enjoyment of the property, and would be accepted by a reasonably well-informed and prudent person. Proper evidence of title is proof that the title is in fact marketable. The title need not be perfect to be considered marketable.

A buyer cannot be forced to accept a conveyance that is materially different from the one bargained for in the sales contract; he or she cannot be forced to buy a problem. Questions of marketable title must be raised by a purchaser (or the purchaser's attorney) before acceptance of the deed. If a buyer accepts a deed with unmarketable title, the only available legal recourse is to sue the seller under the covenants or warranty (if any) contained in the deed.

■ CLOSING THE TRANSACTION

Although salespeople usually are not burdened with the technicalities of closing, they must clearly understand what takes place. A real estate licensee should be able to assist in preclosing arrangements and advise the parties in estimating expenses and the approximate amounts the buyer will need and the seller will receive at the closing.

Generally, the closing of a real estate transaction involves a gathering of interested parties at which the promises made in the *real estate sales contract are kept*, or *executed*; that is, a deed is delivered in exchange for the purchase price. In many sales transactions, two closings actually take place at this time: (1) the closing of the buyer's loan and the disbursement of mortgage funds in exchange for the note and mortgage and (2) the closing of the sale.

As discussed in Chapter 8, a sales contract is the blueprint for the completion of a real estate transaction. The buyer must be sure that the seller is delivering good title and that the property is in the promised condition. This involves inspecting the title evidence; the deed the seller will give; any documents representing the removal of undesired liens and encumbrances; and any survey, physical and/or environmental inspection, termite report, or leases (if there are tenants on the premises). The seller must be sure that the buyer has obtained financing and has the funds to complete the purchase. Both parties should inspect the closing statement to ensure that all monies involved in the transaction have been properly accounted for. In New York State, the parties usually are represented by attorneys.

When everything is in order, the exchange is made and all pertinent documents then are recorded.

Where Closings Are Held and Who Attends

Closings may be held at a number of locations, including the offices of the title company, the lending institution, the office of one of the parties' attorneys, the broker's office, the office of the county clerk (or other local recording official), or an escrow company. Those attending a closing may include any of the following interested parties: buyer, seller, real estate agents, attorneys for the seller and/or the buyer, representatives for the lending institutions involved, and representatives of the title insurance company.

Broker's Role at Closing

Depending on the locality, the broker's role at a closing can vary from conducting the proceedings to not even being present. A broker's job is essentially over when there has been a meeting of the minds. At that point, according to New York State customs, attorneys take over. Even so, a broker's service generally continues after the contract is signed in advising the parties in practical matters, aiding the buyer with a mortgage application, and making sure all details are taken care of so that the closing can proceed smoothly. In this capacity, the broker might make arrangements for such items as appraisals, termite inspections, and repairs or might suggest sources of these services to the parties. An agent can arrange for and accompany the last-minute walk-through of the property just before closing (also known as a *final walk-through*), which most buyers now request.

Lender's Interest in Closing

When a buyer is obtaining a new loan, the lender wants to protect its security interest in the property to make sure that the buyer is getting good, marketable title and that tax and insurance payments are maintained, so that there will be no liens with greater priority than the mortgage lien and the insurance will be paid up if the property is damaged or destroyed.

For this reason, the lender frequently requires the following items: (1) a title insurance policy; (2) a fire and hazard insurance policy with receipt for the premium; (3) additional information such as a survey, a termite or other inspection report, or a certificate of occupancy (for newly constructed buildings, multiple dwellings, and in areas in and around New York City, all buildings); (4) representation by its own attorney at the closing; and (5) establishment of a reserve, or escrow, account for tax and insurance payments. (In New York State, lenders are required to pay interest on escrow accounts for owner-occupied properties.)

Homeowners' Insurance

Where mortgaging is involved, the buyer must bring to the closing proof of insurance on the property and, occasionally, proof of flood insurance. The insurance policy or binder usually names the lender as lienholder, additionally insured, and co-payee in case of loss under the policy.

Although it is possible for a homeowner to obtain individual policies for each type of risk, most residential property owners take out insurance in the form of a packaged **homeowners' insurance policy**. These standardized policies insure holders against the destruction of their property by fire or windstorm, injury to others that occurs on the property, and theft of any personal property on the premises that is owned by the insureds or members of their family.

The homeowners' policy also includes **liability insurance** for personal injuries to others resulting from the insured's acts or negligence, voluntary medical payments and funeral expenses for accidents sustained by guests or resident employees on the property of the owner, and physical damage to the property of others caused by the insured.

Characteristics of homeowners' packages   There are four major forms of homeowners' policies. The *basic* form, known as *HO-1*, provides property coverage against fire or lightning, glass breakage, windstorm or hail, explosion, riot or civil commotion, damage by aircraft, damage from vehicles, damage from smoke, vandalism and malicious mischief, theft, and loss of property removed from the premises when endangered by fire or other perils.

Increased coverage is provided under a *broad* form, known as *HO-2*, that also covers falling objects; weight of ice, snow, or sleet; collapse of the building or any part of it; bursting, cracking, burning, or bulging of a steam or water heating system or of appliances used to heat water; accidental discharge, leakage, or overflow of water or steam from within a plumbing, heating, or air-conditioning system; freezing of plumbing, heating and air-conditioning systems, and domestic appliances; and injury to electrical appliances, devices, fixtures, and wiring from short circuits or other accidentally generated currents.

Further coverage is provided by *comprehensive* forms *HO-3*, the most popular form, and *HO-5*. These policies cover all possible perils except flood, earthquake, war, and nuclear attack. Other policies include *HO-4*, a form designed specifically for apartment renters, and *HO-6*, a broad-form policy for condominium owners. Apartment and condominium policies generally provide fire and windstorm, theft, and public liability coverage for injuries or losses sustained within the unit but usually do not extend to cover losses or damages to the structure. The structure is insured by either the landlord or the condominium owners' association.

Claims

Most homeowners' insurance policies contain a **coinsurance clause**. This provision typically requires that the insured maintain fire insurance on the property equal to at least 80 percent of the **replacement cost** of the dwelling (not including the price of the land). Replacement cost is generally calculated by taking the replacement cost (new) of an item or items minus any accrued depreciation. With such a policy, the owner may make a claim for the cost of the repair or replacement of the damaged property without deduction.

In any event, *the total settlement may not exceed the face value of the policy*. Because of coinsurance clauses, it is important that homeowners review their policies regularly to be certain that the coverage is equal to at least 80 percent of the current replacement cost of their homes. Some policies carry automatic increases in coverage to adjust for inflation.

Federal Flood Insurance Program

Property owners in certain areas must obtain flood damage insurance before they can obtain federally related mortgages. Federally related loans include those made by banks, savings and loan associations, or other lenders whose deposits are insured by federal agencies (Federal Deposit Insurance Corporation [FDIC] or Federal Savings and Loan Insurance Corporation [FSLIC]); those insured by the FHA or guaranteed by the VA; mortgages administered by the U.S. Department of Housing and Urban Development; and loans intended to be sold by the lender to Fannie Mae, Ginnie Mae, or Freddie Mac. An owner may be able to avoid purchasing flood insurance by furnishing a survey showing that the lowest part of the building is above the 100-year flood mark. Information on national flood insurance is available from 800-358-9616, online at www.fema.gov, or by writing to the Federal Emergency Management Agency at Box 1038, Jessup, MD 20794.

RESPA Requirements

The federal **Real Estate Settlement Procedures Act (RESPA)** ensures that the buyer in a *residential* real estate transaction has knowledge of all settlement costs. *RESPA requirements apply when the purchase is financed by a federally related mortgage loan.*

RESPA regulations apply to transactions involving new first mortgage loans, refinance loans, second mortgages, home equity loans, and lines of credit. When a transaction is covered by RESPA, the following requirements must be met:

- *Special information booklet.* Lenders must give a copy of the HUD booklet Settlement Costs and You to every person from whom they receive or for whom they prepare a loan application.
- *Good-faith estimate of settlement costs.* At the time of the loan application or within three business days, the lender must provide the borrower with a good-faith estimate of the settlement costs the borrower is likely to incur. A lender who requires use of a particular attorney or title company to conduct the closing must state whether it has any business relationship with that firm and must estimate the charges for this service.
- *Uniform Settlement Statement (Form HUD-1).* Loan closing information must be prepared on a special HUD form, the **Uniform Settlement Statement,** designed to detail all financial particulars of a transaction. (See Figure 9.2.) The completed statement must itemize all charges imposed by the lender. Unless local custom is for the settlement statement to be prepared at closing, items paid before the closing must be clearly marked as such on the statement and are omitted from the totals. On the borrower's request, the closing agent must permit the borrower to inspect the settlement statement, to the extent that the figures are available, one business day before the closing. Lenders must retain these statements for two years after the date of closing, unless the loan (and its servicing) is sold or otherwise disposed of.
- *Prohibition against kickbacks.* RESPA explicitly prohibits the payment of kickbacks, or unearned fees—for example, when an insurance agency pays a kickback to a lender for referring one of the lender's recent customers to the agency. This prohibition does not include fee splitting between cooperating brokers or members of multiple listing services, brokerage referral arrangements, or the division of a commission between brokers and their salespeople. (RESPA is administered by HUD.)

FIGURE 9.2

RESPA Uniform Settlement Statement

OMB Approval No. 2502-0265

A. Settlement Statement (HUD-1)

B. Type of Loan

1. ☐ FHA 2. ☐ RHS 3. ☐ Conv. Unins.	6. File Number:	7. Loan Number:	8. Mortgage Insurance Case Number:	
4. ☐ VA 5. ☐ Conv. Ins.				

C. Note: This form is furnished to give you a statement of actual settlement costs. Amounts paid to and by the settlement agent are shown. Items marked "(p.o.c.)" were paid outside the closing; they are shown here for informational purposes and are not included in the totals.

D. Name & Address of Borrower:	E. Name & Address of Seller:	F. Name & Address of Lender:
G. Property Location:	H. Settlement Agent:	I. Settlement Date:
	Place of Settlement:	

J. Summary of Borrower's Transaction		K. Summary of Seller's Transaction	
100. Gross Amount Due from Borrower		**400. Gross Amount Due to Seller**	
101. Contract sales price		401. Contract sales price	
102. Personal property		402. Personal property	
103. Settlement charges to borrower (line 1400)		403.	
104.		404.	
105.		405.	
Adjustment for items paid by seller in advance		**Adjustments for items paid by seller in advance**	
106. City/town taxes to		406. City/town taxes to	
107. County taxes to		407. County taxes to	
108. Assessments to		408. Assessments to	
109.		409.	
110.		410.	
111.		411.	
112.		412.	
120. Gross Amount Due from Borrower		**420. Gross Amount Due to Seller**	
200. Amounts Paid by or in Behalf of Borrower		**500. Reductions In Amount Due to Seller**	
201. Deposit or earnest money		501. Excess deposit (see instructions)	
202. Principal amount of new loan(s)		502. Settlement charges to seller (line 1400)	
203. Existing loan(s) taken subject to		503. Existing loan(s) taken subject to	
204.		504. Payoff of first mortgage loan	
205.		505. Payoff of second mortgage loan	
206.		506.	
207.		507.	
208.		508.	
209.		509.	
Adjustments for items unpaid by seller		**Adjustments for items unpaid by seller**	
210. City/town taxes to		510. City/town taxes to	
211. County taxes to		511. County taxes to	
212. Assessments to		512. Assessments to	
213.		513.	
214.		514.	
215.		515.	
216.		516.	
217.		517.	
218.		518.	
219.		519.	
220. Total Paid by/for Seller		**520. Total Reduction Amount Due Seller**	
300. Cash at Settlement from/to Borrower		**600. Cash at Settlement to/from Seller**	
301. Gross amount due from borrower (line 120)		601. Gross amount due to seller (line 420)	
302. Less amounts paid by/for borrower (line 220)	( )	602. Less reductions in amount due seller (line 520)	( )
303. Cash ☐ From ☐ To Borrower		**603. Cash** ☐ To ☐ From Seller	

The Public Reporting Burden for this collection of information is estimated at 35 minutes per response for collecting, reviewing, and reporting the data. This agency may not collect this information, and you are not required to complete this form, unless it displays a currently valid OMB control number. No confidentiality is assured; this disclosure is mandatory. This is designed to provide the parties to a RESPA covered transaction with information during the settlement process.

F I G U R E 9.2

RESPA Uniform Settlement Statement (continued)

L. Settlement Charges		
700. Total Real Estate Broker Fees	Paid From Borrower's Funds at Settlement	Paid From Seller's Funds at Settlement
Division of commission (line 700) as follows:		
701. $ to		
702. $ to		
703. Commission paid at settlement		
704.		
800. Items Payable in Connection with Loan		
801. Our origination charge $ (from GFE #1)		
802. Your credit or charge (points) for the specific interest rate chosen $ (from GFE #2)		
803. Your adjusted origination charges (from GFE A)		
804. Appraisal fee to (from GFE #3)		
805. Credit report to (from GFE #3)		
806. Tax service to (from GFE #3)		
807. Flood certification (from GFE #3)		
808.		
900. Items Required by Lender to Be Paid in Advance		
901. Daily interest charges from to @ $ /day (from GFE #10)		
902. Mortgage insurance premium for months to (from GFE #3)		
903. Homeowner's insurance for years to (from GFE #11)		
904.		
1000. Reserves Deposited with Lender		
1001. Initial deposit for your escrow account (from GFE #9)		
1002. Homeowner's insurance months @ $ per month $		
1003. Mortgage insurance months @ $ per month $		
1004. Property taxes months @ $ per month $		
1005. months @ $ per month $		
1006. months @ $ per month $		
1007. Aggregate Adjustment –$		
1100. Title Charges		
1101. Title services and lender's title insurance (from GFE #4)		
1102. Settlement or closing fee $		
1103. Owner's title insurance (from GFE #5)		
1104. Lender's title insurance $		
1105. Lender's title policy limit $		
1106. Owner's title policy limit $		
1107. Agent's portion of the total title insurance premium $		
1108. Underwriter's portion of the total title insurance premium $		
1200. Government Recording and Transfer Charges		
1201. Government recording charges (from GFE #7)		
1202. Deed $ Mortgage $ Releases $		
1203. Transfer taxes (from GFE #8)		
1204. City/County tax/stamps Deed $ Mortgage $		
1205. State tax/stamps Deed $ Mortgage $		
1206.		
1300. Additional Settlement Charges		
1301. Required services that you can shop for (from GFE #6)		
1302. $		
1303. $		
1304.		
1305.		
1400. Total Settlement Charges (enter on lines 103, Section J and 502, Section K)		

FIGURE 9.2

RESPA Uniform Settlement Statement (continued)

Comparison of Good Faith Estimate (GFE) and HUD-1 Charges		Good Faith Estimate	HUD-1
Charges That Cannot Increase	**HUD-1 Line Number**		
Our origination charge	# 801		
Your credit or charge (points) for the specific interest rate chosen	# 802		
Your adjusted origination charges	# 803		
Transfer taxes	#1203		

Charges That in Total Cannot Increase More Than 10%		Good Faith Estimate	HUD-1
Government recording charges	# 1201		
	#		
	#		
	#		
	#		
	#		
	#		
	#		
	Total		
	Increase between GFE and HUD-1 Charges	$ or	%

Charges That Can Change		Good Faith Estimate	HUD-1
Initial deposit for your escrow account	#1001		
Daily interest charges	# 901 $ /day		
Homeowner's insurance	# 903		
	#		
	#		
	#		

Loan Terms

Your initial loan amount is	$
Your loan term is	years
Your initial interest rate is	%
Your initial monthly amount owed for principal, interest, and and any mortgage insurance is	$ _____ includes ☐ Principal ☐ Interest ☐ Mortgage Insurance
Can your interest rate rise?	☐ No. ☐ Yes, it can rise to a maximum of ___%. The first change will be on _____ and can change again every _____ after _____ . Every change date, your interest rate can increase or decrease by ___%. Over the life of the loan, your interest rate is guaranteed to never be **lower** than ___ % or **higher** than ___ %.
Even if you make payments on time, can your loan balance rise?	☐ No. ☐ Yes, it can rise to a maximum of $ _____ .
Even if you make payments on time, can your monthly amount owed for principal, interest, and mortgage insurance rise?	☐ No. ☐ Yes, the first increase can be on _____ and the monthly amount owed can rise to $ _____ . The maximum it can ever rise to is $ _____ .
Does your loan have a prepayment penalty?	☐ No. ☐ Yes, your maximum prepayment penalty is $ _____ .
Does your loan have a balloon payment?	☐ No. ☐ Yes, you have a balloon payment of $ _____ due in ____ years on _____ .
Total monthly amount owed including escrow account payments	☐ You do not have a monthly escrow payment for items, such as property taxes and homeowner's insurance. You must pay these items directly yourself. ☐ You have an additional monthly escrow payment of $ _____ that results in a total initial monthly amount owed of $ _____ . This includes principal, interest, any mortgage insurance and any items checked below: ☐ Property taxes ☐ Homeowner's insurance ☐ Flood insurance ☐ _____ ☐ _____ ☐ _____

Note: If you have any questions about the Settlement Charges and Loan Terms listed on this form, please contact your lender.

THE TITLE PROCEDURE

On the date when the sale is actually completed, that is, the date of delivery of the deed, the buyer has a title commitment or an abstract that was issued several days or weeks before the closing. For this reason, the title or abstract company is usually required to make a second search of the public records. A last-minute search is often made at the moment of closing.

The title company will ask the sellers to sign an *affidavit of title*. This is a sworn statement in which the sellers assure the title company that since the date of the title examination there have been no judgments, bankruptcies, or divorces involving the sellers; no repairs or improvements that have not been paid for; and that they are in possession of the premises. Through this affidavit, the title company obtains the right to sue the sellers if their statements in the affidavit prove incorrect.

Checking the Premises

The buyer should inspect the property to determine the interests of any parties in possession. A *survey* is frequently required so that the purchaser will know the location, size, and legal description of the property. The survey's result will uncover any encumbrances to the property, such as overhanging tree limbs, fences, inappropriate property lines, or any other physical encumbrance to the property.

The buyer also should make a last-minute inspection before closing to check that the house remains in the condition originally presented and that the seller is leaving any personal property stipulated in the sales contract. This inspection right is often set forth in a clause in the purchase and sale agreement. At closing, the seller will sign an affidavit stating that there is at least one functioning smoke alarm and a carbon monoxide detector on the premises.

Homeseller's Tax Exclusion

The IRS (and New York State) allow a homeseller's exclusion from capital gains tax of up to $250,000 ($500,000 for a married couple filing jointly) if the home has been owned and occupied as a principal residence for at least "an aggregate" of 24 months during the five years before the sale. If the house sells for less than that amount, at closing the seller can sign a statement that the transaction qualifies for the exclusion, and no report of the sale is due to the IRS. Under certain circumstances, including job transfer, health problems, and death in the family, a prorated portion of the exclusion can be used for a sale after less than two years of occupancy and ownership. This subject is covered further in Chapter 20.

Releasing Existing Liens

When the purchaser pays cash or obtains a new mortgage to purchase the property, the seller's existing mortgage usually is paid in full and released in the public record. The release is called a *satisfaction of mortgage*. To know the exact amount required to pay the existing mortgage, the seller secures a current *payoff statement* from the mortgagee. The same procedure is followed for any other liens that must be released before the buyer takes title.

A buyer who is assuming the seller's existing mortgage loan needs to know the exact balance of the loan as of the closing date. The buyer receives a **mortgage reduction certificate** (sometimes called an *estoppel certificate*) from the lender, stating the exact balance due and the last interest payment made.

■ CLOSING IN ESCROW

In the western United States, most transactions are closed in escrow, but the system is seldom used in New York. In New York, closing is on contract and not on escrow.

In an **escrow** closing, a third party coordinates the closing activities. The escrow agent may be an attorney, a title company, a trust company, an escrow company, or the escrow department of a lending institution. Buyer and seller deposit all pertinent documents, money, and other items with the escrow agent. When all conditions of the escrow agreement have been met, the agent pays the purchase price to the seller and records the deed and mortgage (if a new mortgage has been executed by the purchaser). Buyer and seller may never meet.

■ PREPARATION OF CLOSING STATEMENTS

A typical real estate sales transaction involves numerous expenses for both parties in addition to the purchase price. There are a number of property expenses that the seller will have paid in advance or that the buyer will pay in the future. The financial responsibility for these items must be *prorated* (adjusted or divided) between the buyer and the seller. In closing a transaction, it is customary to account for all these items by preparing a written statement to determine how much money the buyer needs to come up with on the day of the closing and how much the seller will walk away with after the broker's commission and all other seller expenses are paid. There are many different formats of closing, or settlement, statements, but all are designed to achieve the same results.

Closing statements in New York are prepared by the buyer's and the seller's attorneys or bank representatives. The broker should, however, be able to give the seller an estimate of sale costs. In addition, the buyer must be prepared with the proper amount of money to complete the purchase (in the form of a certified check), and again the broker should be able to assist by making a reasonably accurate estimate. A broker is not prohibited from acting as an escrow and/or closing agent.

How the Closing Statement Works

The completion of a **closing statement** involves an accounting of the parties' debits and credits. A **debit** is a charge, an amount that the party being debited owes and must pay at the closing. A **credit** is an amount entered in a person's favor: an amount that the party already has paid, an amount for which the party must be reimbursed, or an amount the buyer promises to pay in the form of a loan.

For a clearer understanding of this subject, it can help to think of debits and credits as you would your personal checkbook. When you receive money and deposit it at your banking institution, the bank will *credit* your account. When you write a check to a person or business and the check is presented to your bank for payment, your bank will *debit* your account.

When completing a closing statement or when calculating prorations, the first step is always to determine

- who the paying party is and
- who the receiving party is.

In this way, the preparer can credit and debit the appropriate party.

To determine the amount the buyer needs at the closing, the buyer's debits are totaled. Any expenses and prorated amounts for items prepaid by the seller are added to the purchase price. Then the buyer's credits are totaled. These would include the earnest money (already paid), the balance of the loan the buyer is obtaining or assuming, and the seller's share of any prorated items that the buyer will pay in the future. Finally, the total of the buyer's credits is subtracted from the total amount the buyer owes (debits) to arrive at the actual amount of cash the buyer must bring on the day of closing. Usually, the buyer brings a bank cashier's check or a certified personal check. In addition, the buyer should also bring a few personal checks to cover incidental charges applicable to the day of the closing. These charges may represent the difference between estimated and actual charges that are due on the day of closing of title.

A similar procedure is followed to determine how much money the seller actually will receive. The seller's debits and credits are totaled separately. The credits include the purchase price plus the buyer's share of any prorated items that the seller has prepaid. The seller's debits include expenses, the seller's share of prorated items to be paid later by the buyer, and the balance of any mortgage loan or other lien that the seller is paying off. Finally, the total of the seller's charges is subtracted from the total credits to arrive at the amount the seller will receive at closing. The closing statement represents a **reconciliation** of each party's financial obligations. The closing statement can be seen as the historic memorandum regarding the parties, property, and the day of closing.

Expenses

In addition to the sales price, taxes, interest, and the like, a number of other expenses and charges, including the following items, may be involved in a real estate transaction.

Broker's commission The broker's commission is customarily paid by the seller when the broker is the seller's agent and in a majority of real estate transactions. When the buyer has employed the broker, either party may pay the commission, according to agreement.

Attorney's fees If either party's attorney will be paid from the closing proceeds, that party will be charged with the expense in the closing statement.

Recording expenses   Charges for recording documents vary from one county to another. A county might charge $5.50 for recording a document plus $3.00 per page. Thus, a single-page deed would cost $8.50 to record, while the charge for a four-page mortgage would be $17.50.

The seller usually pays recording charges (filing fees) needed to clear all defects and furnish the purchaser with clear title. Items usually charged to the seller include the recording of satisfaction of mortgages, quitclaim deeds, affidavits, and satisfaction of mechanic's lien claims. Items usually charged to the purchaser include recording the deed and any new mortgage.

Transfer tax   Any New York State conveyance is taxed at a rate of $2 per $500 or fraction thereof of the consideration paid minus the amount of any mortgage being assumed. *(Those who inspect old deeds to estimate sales prices should know that before 1983 the rate was $0.55 per $500.)* The transfer tax must be paid (customarily by the seller) when the deed is recorded. City or county taxes also may be due. Shares in a cooperative are taxed at the same rate.

For example, New York City levies an additional transfer tax of 1 percent on sales of less than $500,000 on one- to three-family dwellings. Other transfers require payment of a higher city tax. The tax is paid by the grantor when the deed is recorded.

In addition, New York State charges a *mansion tax* in the following situations:

■   A buyer that completes the purchase of a dwelling unit in a structure containing up to three dwelling units where the purchase price is $1 million or more is subject to a mansion tax of 1 percent. (The mansion tax can be found under Section 1402-a of the state tax law.)

■   Coverage of the mansion tax extends to an individual condominium or cooperative unit sold for $1 million or more.

■   In order for the tax to be applicable to the real property in question, the property must be used as a personal residence.

Although the genesis of instituting the tax in the late 1980s was designed to tax the wealthy, the cost of today's average residence has placed a tremendous tax burden on the average home-seeker. This dilemma is particularly apparent in Manhattan, where the average dwelling unit is at or over the $1 million threshold.

Personal property transferred with the real estate (drapes, for example) is covered by a bill of sale and is not subject to transfer tax but to state sales tax, unless it is included in the sale of the real estate without additional consideration.

State mortgage tax   New York State imposes a tax of $0.75 for each $100 or fraction thereof for every mortgage recorded within the state, and in many counties there is an additional $0.25 for each $100 or fraction thereof. The first $10,000 of a mortgage for any one- or two-family residence is taxed lower, at a rate of $0.50 for each $100. If the mortgage covers property improved by a structure with six or fewer cooking units, the mortgagee must pay a portion of the mortgage tax—$0.25 for each $100 or fraction thereof. Private lenders do not pay the $0.25 portion; lending institutions do. When a land contract is recorded, mortgage tax is due on the amount borrowed. Local mortgage taxes also may be imposed. In counties that levy additional tax, none is due on the first $10,000 of the loan for a one- or two-family residence.

Title expenses   The responsibility for title expenses varies according to the contract, which usually follows local custom. If the buyer's attorney inspects the evidence or if the buyer purchases title insurance policies, the buyer is charged for these expenses. In some situations, the title or abstract company makes two searches of the public records: the first shows the status of the seller's title on the date of the sales contract or at some time before closing, and the second continues through the date on which the purchaser's deed is recorded. In some areas, the seller pays for the initial search and the purchaser pays for the redate charge. (There often is no redate charge if the closing occurs within six months of the initial search.) In other areas, it is customary that the buyer pay for the full search.

Loan fees   When the purchaser is securing a mortgage to finance the purchase, the lender (mortgage company) usually charges a service charge known as *points* or an *origination fee*. One point represents 1 percent of the borrowed amount. The fee may consist of any combination of points. The fee is a flat charge and is usually paid by the purchaser at the time the transaction is closed. The buyer also may be charged an assumption fee for assuming the seller's financing and, in some cases, may pay discount points. As discussed in Chapter 10, the seller also may be charged discount points.

Tax reserves/impounds and insurance reserves (escrows)   A *reserve or impound* is a sum of money set aside to be used later for a particular purpose. The mortgage lender usually requires that the borrower establish and maintain a reserve so that there will be sufficient funds to pay property taxes and renew hazard insurance when these items become due. To set up the reserve, the borrower makes a lump-sum payment or equal monthly installment payments to the lender when the mortgage money is paid out, usually at the time of closing (or after closing, as the case may be). After that, the borrower pays into the escrow account an amount equal to one month's portion of the estimated general tax and insurance premium as part of the monthly PITI (principal, interest, property taxes, and insurance) payment to the mortgage company.

Additional fees   An FHA borrower owes a lump sum for prepayment of the mortgage insurance premium if it is not being financed as part of the loan. A VA mortgagor pays a fee directly to the VA at closing. If a conventional loan carries private mortgage insurance, the buyer prepays one year's insurance premium at closing.

Appraisal fees   When the buyer applies for a mortgage loan, the lender will usually require that an appraisal be performed. The purpose of the appraisal is to establish the value of the property as it relates to the loan amount and determine if justification for extending the loan exists. This is a process that the buyer pays for.

Survey fees A purchaser who obtains new mortgage financing customarily pays the survey fees. In some cases, the sales contract may require that the seller furnish a **survey**. This process always occurs when financing is provided by a lender. The survey is used to establish the existence of any encumbrances on the property.

Prorations

Most closings involve the dividing of financial responsibility between the buyer and seller for items such as loan interest on an assumed mortgage, taxes, rents, fuel oil, and utility bills. These allowances are called **prorations**, or **adjustments**. Prorations are necessary to ensure that expenses are divided fairly between the seller and the buyer. For example, when the coming year's property taxes have been paid in advance, the seller is entitled to partial reimbursement at the closing. If the buyer assumes the seller's existing mortgage, the seller usually owes the buyer a credit for accrued interest through the date of closing.

Accrued items, or *payments in arrears*, are owed by the seller but eventually will be paid by the buyer. The seller, therefore, gives the buyer credit for these items at closing. Because interest usually is paid in *arrears* (the opposite of in *advance*), each payment covers interest for the preceding month. At a midmonth closing, the seller who has not made the current month's payment would owe six weeks' back interest on a mortgage.

Prepaid items, or *payments in advance*, are items to be prorated (such as taxes or fuel oil left in the tank) that have been paid for by the seller but not fully earned (not fully used up). They are, therefore, credits to the seller. The buyer reimburses the seller for any advance paid items, less the charges the seller has accrued prior to the date of closing; the buyer is only paying for the unused portion of the item in question.

General rules for prorating The rules or customs governing the computation of prorations for the closing of a real estate sale vary:

■ In New York, it is generally provided that *the buyer owns the property on the closing date*. In practice, however, either the buyer or the seller may be charged with that day's expenses.
■ Mortgage interest, real estate taxes, water bills, and similar expenses are computed in some areas by using *360 days in a year and 30 days in a month*. That is commonly referred to as the 360/30-day rule. In this method of proration, each month of the year is said to have 30 days. In other areas, prorations are computed using the actual number of days in the calendar year and month of closing. That is commonly referred to as the 365-day rule. When a contract in New York is silent as to which method of proration is to be used, custom dictates the use of the 360/30-day rule.
■ *Special assessments* for municipal improvements such as sewers, water mains, or streets are usually paid in annual installments over several years. Sellers are sometimes required to pay off special assessments entirely. In other cases, buyers may agree to assume future installments.
■ *Rents* are usually adjusted on the basis of the actual number of days in the month of closing. The buyer often will agree in the contract or by a separate

letter to collect any uncollected rents for the current month and remit a share to the seller.

■ *Security deposits* generally are transferred by the seller to the buyer; the tenant must be notified of the transfer of deposit.

Accounting for Credits and Charges

Items accounted for in the closing statement fall into two general categories: (1) prorations or other amounts due to either the buyer or seller (credit to) and paid for by the other party (debit to) and (2) expenses or items paid by the seller or buyer (debit only). Since expenses act as a one-time charge to the party in question, they are *never* credits to either party.

Items credited to buyer
(*debited to seller*)

1. Buyer's earnest money*
2. Unpaid principal balance of outstanding mortgage being assumed by buyer*
3. Interest on existing assumed mortgage not yet paid (accrued)
4. Portion of current rent collected in advance
5. Purchase-money mortgage
6. Unpaid water bills

Items credited to seller
(*debited to buyer*)

1. Sales price*
2. Fuel oil on hand, usually figured at current market price
3. Insurance and tax reserve (if any) when mortgage is being assumed by buyer
4. Refund to seller of prepaid water charge or similar expenses
5. Portion of general real estate tax paid in advance

Items with an asterisk (*) are not prorated; they are entered in full as listed. The *buyer's earnest money*, while credited to the buyer, *is never debited to the seller*. The buyer receives a credit because the buyer has already paid that amount toward the purchase price. Under the usual sales contract, the money is held in escrow by the broker or attorney until the settlement, when it will be included as part of the total amount due the seller. The money remains in the escrow account until the seller receives the funds at either closing or upon the buyer's default. If the seller is paying off an existing loan and the buyer is obtaining a new one, these two items are accounted for with a debit only to the seller for the amount of the payoff and a credit only to the buyer for the amount of the new loan.

Accounting for expenses   Expenses paid out of the closing proceeds are usually debited only to the party making the payment.

For example, as a helpful guide, the seller's closing costs may consist of some or all of the following items:

■ Prorations for any
   — unpaid property taxes or
   — advance rent received for the month of closing (as applicable)
■ Unpaid mortgage or other liens
■ Document preparation fees
■ All appropriate state and city transfer taxes (as applicable)
■ Seller's legal fees
■ Brokerage commissions

The buyer's closing costs may consist of some or all of the following items:

- Down payment deficiency after crediting the earnest money deposit and all loans
- Advance mortgage interest
- Loan discount points
- Loan origination fees
- Appraisal fee
- Assumption fee on any assumed mortgage
- Mortgage insurance premiums (as applicable)
- Lender reserve requirements for property taxes and property insurance premiums
- Title insurance premiums
- Buyer's attorney fees
- Lender's attorney fees
- Mortgage recording fees
- Deed recording fees
- Survey fees
- Pest and other inspection fees
- Seller personal property purchase costs
- Prorations for any
  - seller prepaid property taxes or
  - property/flood insurance premiums when seller's policy is assumed

■ THE ARITHMETIC OF PRORATION

The three basic methods of calculating prorations are as follows:

1. The yearly charge is divided by a 360-day year or 12 months of 30 days each.
2. The monthly charge *is divided by the actual number of days in the month of closing* to determine the amount.

Calculating prorations using the 360/30-day method

Step 1. To calculate the amount charged versus the amount to be received, first determine if the item of proration is

- a monthly charge or
- an annual charge.

Step 2. Divide the charge by the appropriate period to arrive at a daily rate:

- 360 days for items charged or calculated annually and/or
- 30 days for items charged or calculated monthly.

Step 3. Establish the appropriate number of days to prorate.

Step 4. Multiply the appropriate number of days by the daily rate in step two to arrive at the proration amount.

Step 5. Make appropriate debits and credits:

- Debit the party who is charged with the payment of the item in question.
- Credit the other party who is receiving payment on the item in question.

3. The yearly charge *is divided by 365* to determine the daily charge. Then, the actual number of days in the proration period is determined, and this number is multiplied by the daily charge. The same steps illustrated in steps 1–5 apply to this method of proration. However, step 2 would be changed to reflect the use of 365 days in a year and the actual number of days in the month.

In some cases, when a sale is closed on the 15th of the month, the half-month charge is computed simply by dividing the monthly charge by two.

Depending on which computation method is used, the final proration figure will vary slightly.

■ SAMPLE CLOSING STATEMENTS

The closing statement lists sales price, earnest money deposit, and all adjustments and prorations between buyer and seller. Figure 9.3 shows a buyer's closing statement, and Figure 9.4 shows a seller's closing statement for the same transaction. The property is being purchased for $89,500, with $49,500 down and the seller taking back a mortgage for $40,000. Closing takes place on August 12.

Prorations

The buyer is taking over a house on which taxes have been paid, in one case until the end of the year. The buyer, therefore, will reimburse the seller for the time in which the buyer will be living in a tax-paid house. Specifically, the seller has paid city and school taxes of $1,176.35 for the tax year that started July 1 and will receive a large portion of that back as a credit from the buyer. County taxes of $309.06 were paid January 1 for the year ahead, so the buyer will also credit the seller for the four months and 18 days remaining in the year, an adjustment of $118.52.

The buyer owes the seller (total seller's credits) the purchase price plus unearned taxes, for a total of $90,657.68. Toward this sum, the buyer receives credit for an earnest money deposit of $500 in a broker's escrow account. (The seller's attorney and the broker will take this sum into consideration later when the commission is paid.) The buyer also receives credit for the $40,000 bond and mortgage given to the seller at closing. The buyer, therefore, gives the seller cash (or a certified check) for the remaining sum, $50,157.68.

The upper half of the closing statement accounts for the transaction between buyer and seller; the lower part details each one's individual expenses. The buyer pays to record the deed and mortgage, part of the mortgage tax, and the buyer's attorney's fee.

FIGURE 9.3

Buyer's Closing Statement

SELLER'S CREDITS

Sale Price _____ $ 89,500.00

ADJUSTMENT OF TAXES

School Tax 7/1   to 6/30   Amount $ 1176.35 Adj. 10 mos. 18 days $ 1,039.16

City/School Tax 7/1/   to 6/30/   Amount $_____ Adj. _____ mos. _____ days $_____

County Tax 19____   Amount $ 309.06   Adj. 4 mos. 18 days $ 118.52

Village Tax 6/1/   to 5/31/   Amount $_____ Adj. _____ mos. _____ days $_____

City Tax Embellishments   Amount $_____ Adj. _____ mos. _____ days $_____

Total Seller's Credits $ 90,657.68

PURCHASER'S CREDITS

Deposit with ____ Nothnagle ____ $ 500.00

(Assumed) (New) Mortgage with Seller $480.07 p/m $ 40,000.00

beg. 9-12 , 12% int., 15 yrs. $_____

                                          $_____

                                          $_____

                                          $_____

                                          $_____

                                          $_____

                                          $_____

Total Purchaser's Credits $ 40,500.00

Cash (Recd) (Paid) at Closing $ 50,157.68

EXPENSES OF PURCHASER		EXPENSES OF SELLER	
Mortgage Tax	$ 275.00	Title Search Fee	$_____
Recording Mortgage	$ 11.00	Transfer Tax on Deed	$_____
Recording Deed	$ 12.00	Filing of Gains Tax Affidavit	$_____
		Discharge Recording Fee	$_____
ESCROWS:		Mortgage Tax	$_____
____ mos. insurance	$_____	Surveyor's Fees	$_____
____ mos. school tax	$_____	Points	$_____
____ mos. county tax	$_____	Mortgage Payoff	$_____
____ mos. village tax	$_____	Real Estate Commission	$_____
PMI FHA Insurance	$_____	Water Escrow	$_____
Total:	$_____		$_____
Bank Attorney Fee	$_____		$_____
Points	$_____		$_____
Title Insurance	$_____		$_____
Interest	$_____		$_____
	$_____	Legal Fee	$_____
	$_____	Total	$_____
	$_____		
Legal Fee	$ 500.00	Cash Received:	$
Total	$ 798.00	Less Seller's Expenses:	$
		Net Proceeds:	$

Cash paid to Seller: $ 50,157.68

Plus Purchaser's Expenses: $ 798.00

Total Disbursed: $ 50,955.68

FIGURE 9.4

Seller's Closing Statement

SELLER'S CREDITS

Sale Price _____ $ 89,500.00

ADJUSTMENT OF TAXES

School Tax 7/1   to 6/30   Amount $ 1176.35   Adj. 10 mos. 18 days $ 1,039.16

City/School Tax 7/1/   to 6/30/   Amount $_____ Adj. _____ mos. _____ days $ _____

County Tax 19____   Amount $ 309.06   Adj. 4 mos. 18 days $ 118.52

Village Tax 6/1/   to 5/31/   Amount $_____ Adj. _____ mos. _____ days $ _____

City Tax Embellishments   Amount $_____ Adj. _____ mos. _____ days $ _____

Total Seller's Credits $ 90,657.68

PURCHASER'S CREDITS

Deposit with __Nothnagle__ _____ $ 500.00

(Assumed) (New) Mortgage with __seller__ ___ $ 40,000.00

12% interest, 15 years, payments $ _____

$ 480.07, beginning 9/12 $ _____

$ _____

$ _____

$ _____

$ _____

$ _____

Total Purchaser's Credits $ 40,500.00

Cash (Rec'd) (Paid) at Closing $ 50,157.68

EXPENSES OF PURCHASER		EXPENSES OF SELLER	
Mortgage Tax	$_____	Title Search Fee	$ 220.00
Recording Mortgage	$_____	Transfer Tax on Deed	$ 358.00
Recording Deed	$_____	Filing of Gains Tax Affidavit	$ 1.00
		Discharge Recording Fee	$_____
ESCROWS:		Mortgage Tax	$ 100.00
____ mos. insurance $ _____		Surveyor's Fees	$_____
____ mos. school tax $ _____		Points	$_____
____ mos. county tax $ _____		Mortgage Payoff	$_____
____ mos. village tax $ _____		Real Estate Commission	$ 4870.00
PMI/FHA Insurance $ _____		Water Escrow	$_____
Total: $_____		school tax	$ 1,182.14
		Federal express	$ 14.00
Bank Attorney Fee	$_____		$_____
Points	$_____		$_____
Title Insurance	$_____	Legal Fee	$ 550.00
Interest	$_____	Total	$ 7,295.14
	$_____		
	$_____	Cash Received:	$ 50,157.68
	$_____	Less Seller's Expenses:	$ 7,295.14
Legal Fee	$_____	Net Proceeds:	$ 42,862.54
Total	$_____		

Cash paid to Seller: $

Plus Purchaser's Expenses: $

Total Disbursed: $

The seller's expenses include last-minute payment of the school tax (plus a small late-payment penalty), for which the seller is largely reimbursed. Also paid by the seller is the required lender's share of the mortgage tax (seller/lender happens to be a corporation). The seller pays the real estate commission, legal costs of proving title, transfer tax, and incidental out-of-pocket expenses incurred by the seller's attorney, who also deducts a fee and turns over the net proceeds to the seller.

■ SUMMARY

The public records give constructive notice to the world of different parties' interests in real estate. Possession of real estate gives notice of possible rights of the person in possession. Actual notice refers to whatever one actually knows; constructive notice is what one could find out by investigating.

Title evidence shows whether a seller is conveying marketable title, one so free from defects that the buyer can be assured title will not be challenged. Four forms of title evidence may be used throughout the United States: (1) abstract of title and lawyer's opinion, (2) owner's title insurance policy, (3) Torrens certificate, and (4) certificate of title. A deed proves that a previous grantor transferred interest but does not prove the grantor actually had any interest in the property.

At closing, a buyer may be required to show hazard insurance coverage to a lender. A standard homeowners' insurance policy covers fire, theft, and liability and may be extended to cover less common risks. Insurance covering only personal property is available to those in apartments and condominiums. For some property located in floodplains, flood insurance is needed to obtain a federally related mortgage loan. Many homeowners' policies contain a coinsurance clause requiring that the policyholder insure for at least 80 percent of the replacement cost of the house. Otherwise, the policyholder may not be reimbursed for full repair costs in case of loss.

The federal RESPA requires disclosure of all settlement costs when a residential real estate purchase is financed by a federally related loan. RESPA requires that lenders use a Uniform Settlement Statement.

The actual amount paid by the buyer at closing is computed by preparing a closing statement. This lists the sales price, earnest money deposit, and all adjustments and prorations between buyer and seller.

CHAPTER 9 QUIZ

1. A title insurance policy is in force for the whole period of ownership and is paid for

    a. once.
    b. twice a year, along with property taxes.
    c. once a year.
    d. through monthly mortgage payments.

2. An instrument affecting title to a parcel of real estate gives constructive notice to the world when filed with the

    a. county clerk.
    b. city clerk.
    c. secretary of state.
    d. title company.

3. An interested buyer checked the public records. She found that the seller was the grantee in the last recorded deed and that no mortgage was on record against the property. She may assume that

    a. all taxes are paid and no judgments are outstanding.
    b. the seller has good title.
    c. the seller did not mortgage the property.
    d. no one else is occupying the property.

4. An abstractor inspects the county records for documents affecting title and then

    a. writes a brief history of the title.
    b. insures the condition of the title.
    c. personally inspects the property.
    d. issues a certificate of title.

5. If the broker holds the buyer's earnest money in a separate trust account, when does the seller usually receive it?

    a. At the time the offer is accepted
    b. After approval by the buyer's and seller's attorneys
    c. When the buyer receives a firm mortgage commitment
    d. When the property is actually transferred

6. Last year, Maureen gave a house in Watertown, valued at $110,000, to her son. He assumed an existing $30,000 mortgage on the property. Transfer tax due on the gift was

    a. $220.
    b. $320.
    c. $440.
    d. $0.

7. A daughter needs to know how much her parents paid for the Elmira house they bought from a builder in 1954. She finds tax stamps on their old deed totaling $22.55. She can conclude that they paid roughly

    a. $6,000.
    b. $20,500.
    c. $22,550.
    d. $60,000.

8. Last summer, a homeowner sold his house in Schenectady for $160,000. The new owners assumed his existing mortgage in the amount of $76,578. State transfer tax on the sale came to approximately

    a. $91.85.
    b. $176.00.
    c. $334.00.
    d. $640.00.

9. A Manhattan resident purchases farmland in Clinton County as an investment. The deed she receives should

    a. not be recorded.
    b. be recorded in Manhattan.
    c. be recorded in Clinton County.
    d. be recorded in both the borough of Manhattan and Clinton County.

10. The principle of caveat emptor states that if the purchaser buys a faulty title, responsibility for the problem lies with the

    a. buyer.
    b. seller.
    c. broker.
    d. abstractor.

11. Which is *NOT* acceptable proof of title?

    a. Torrens certificate
    b. Title insurance policy
    c. Abstract with lawyer's opinion
    d. Deed signed by the last seller

12. The booklet *Settlement Costs and You* must be distributed by

    a. escrow companies.
    b. real estate brokers.
    c. property insurers.
    d. mortgage lenders.

13. When recording a deed in New York City, an affidavit must be provided to show that the house has

    a. hazard insurance.
    b. title insurance.
    c. a working smoke alarm.
    d. insulation.

14. Which is *NOT* among a lender's main interests at closing?

    a. That the buyer is getting good, marketable title
    b. That tax payments will be maintained
    c. That insurance payments will be maintained
    d. That property value will keep pace with inflation

15. The terms *basic, broad,* and *comprehensive* describe types of

    a. title insurance.
    b. mortgage documents.
    c. homeowners' insurance.
    d. attorney's services.

16. What percentage of the replacement cost of a home should be covered by fire insurance?

    a. 50 percent
    b. 80 percent
    c. 100 percent
    d. 120 percent

17. The requirement to have flood insurance is related to the property's location and

    a. the percentage of the buyer's down payment.
    b. federal participation in the mortgage loan.
    c. the dollar value of the mortgage loan.
    d. the type of homeowners' insurance the buyer obtains.

18. The RESPA Uniform Settlement Statement must be used for

    a. every real estate closing.
    b. transactions financed by FHA and VA only.
    c. residential transactions financed by federally related loans.
    d. all transactions involving commercial property.

19. A mortgage reduction certificate is issued by a(n)

    a. lending institution.
    b. attorney.
    c. abstract company.
    d. grantor.

20. Earnest money left on deposit with the broker or the lawyer is a

    a. credit to the seller.
    b. credit to the buyer.
    c. debit to the seller.
    d. debit to the buyer.

21. The buyers are assuming an old mortgage loan that had a principal balance of $27,496 as of June 1. Interest is at 12 percent, payable in arrears. The June payment has not been made, and closing is on June 15. Which is *TRUE* as to the interest adjustment?

    a. Credit buyer $274.96; debit seller $274.95
    b. Credit buyer $412.44; debit seller $412.44
    c. Credit seller $137.48; debit buyer $137.48
    d. No adjustment necessary

22. The calendar year's taxes amount to $1,800 and were paid ahead on January 1. If closing is set for June 15, which is *TRUE?*

    a. Credit seller $825; debit buyer $975
    b. Credit seller $1,800; debit buyer $825
    c. Credit buyer $975; debit seller $975
    d. Credit seller $975; debit buyer $975

23. Which item is usually *NOT* adjusted between buyer and seller?
    a. Recording charges
    b. Property taxes
    c. Rents
    d. Interest on assumed mortgage

24. The seller collected June rent of $800 from the tenant in the upstairs apartment. At the closing on June 15,
    a. credit buyer $400; debit seller $400.
    b. credit buyer $400; credit seller $400.
    c. debit buyer $400; credit seller $400.
    d. credit buyer $800; no debit to seller.

25. Which phrase *BEST* describes the role of the closing statement?
    a. Documentation of borrower's responsibilities
    b. Projection of payments due to lender
    c. Reconciliation of each party's financial obligations
    d. Seller's disclosures of property conditions

26. A buyer is purchasing a home from a seller with a $300,000 mortgage from a federally insured deposit institution. A survey must be completed as part of the transaction. What party *MOST* likely required the survey?
    a. The buyer's lender
    b. The buyer's attorney
    c. The seller's attorney
    d. County assessor

27. RESPA expressly prohibits the payment of kickbacks, which are
    a. mortgage discounts.
    b. tax rebates.
    c. split commissions.
    d. unearned fees.

28. A monthly PITI payment is composed of money for
    a. price, income, term, and interest.
    b. payables, investment, time, and insurance.
    c. points, interest, title insurance, and inflation.
    d. principal, interest, property taxes, and insurance.

29. New York State's mortgage tax on one- or two-family residences is
    a. a single flat rate.
    b. based on the size of the mortgage loan.
    c. based on the location of the property.
    d. based on characteristics of the lender.

30. In which situation would a payoff statement be requested before a closing?
    a. The seller is providing financing for the buyer.
    b. The buyer is assuming the seller's mortgage.
    c. The buyer is not assuming the seller's mortgage, and the seller's mortgage will be paid off at closing.
    d. The seller is purchasing a more expensive property and is refinancing the current mortgage for that purchase.

CHAPTER

Mortgages

■ KEY TERMS

acceleration clause

adjustable-rate mortgage (ARM)

alienation clause

amortized loans

annual percentage rate (APR)

balloon payment

biweekly mortgages

bond

buydown

debtor in possession

default

deficiency judgment

down payment

equity

estoppel certificate

foreclosure

fully amortized loan

grace period

hypothecation

interest

lien theory

loan servicing

loan-to-value ratio

mortgage

mortgage bankers

mortgage brokers

mortgagee

mortgagor

negative amortization

note

PITI

points

prepayment premium (penalty)

primary mortgage market

principal

private mortgage insurance (PMI)

recourse loan

reduction certificate

satisfaction of mortgage

Sonny Mae (SONYMA)

straight loan

subject to a mortgage

term

term loan

title theory

usury

■ MORTGAGE DEFINED

A **mortgage** is a pledge of property (collateral) given by a borrower as security for a loan. Some states recognize the lender as the owner of mortgaged land. These states are called **title theory** states. Connecticut, for example, is a title theory state. In either case, security/collateral instruments are based upon the theory of **hypothecation**. The borrower pledges the property without giving up ownership or possession of the property.

New York, however, interprets a mortgage purely as a lien on real property and is called a **lien theory** state. That is to say, the borrower owns and possesses the property, while the lender holds a lien on the property. In a lien theory state, any financing transaction where real property is involved will be a two-party, two-instrument transaction:

■ Two parties: mortgagor/borrower and mortgagee/lender
■ Two instruments: note/bond and mortgage

These subjects will be discussed next.

If a mortgagor (borrower) defaults, the lender can foreclose on the lien (generally through a court action), offer the property for sale, and apply the funds received from the sale to reduce or pay off the debt.

Loan Instruments

When property is to be mortgaged, the owner must execute, or sign, two separate instruments (sometimes combined into one form):

1. A **note** or **bond**, which is a personal promise to repay a loan. It acts as evidence of the borrowing as well as the promise to repay the debt. The promissory note signed by a borrower (known as the *maker* or *payer*) states the amount of the debt, the time and method of payment, and the rate of interest.

    In essence, when executed by a borrower, a note obligates that individual to repay the loan predicated on the terms of the borrowing. Notes are accepted by the courts (or through some other dispute resolution process such as arbitration) as *prima facie* (face value) evidence if signed by a borrower. For this reason, promissory notes need not be witnessed to be enforceable. In some cases, promissory notes are used as negotiable instruments.

    Figure 10.1 is an example of a note commonly used in some areas of New York State.

2. A mortgage, which is a pledge of property given as collateral by a borrower as security for a loan. The mortgage creates a lien on the property covered by the mortgage as security for the debt. The **mortgagor** (the borrower) is the one who does the mortgaging, pledging real estate as security for a loan. The **mortgagee** (the lender) accepts, takes and holds the mortgage, and gives money in exchange. Remember, lenders do not give mortgages, they receive them as collateral in exchange for currency.

FIGURE 10.1

Note

NOTE

........April 12......., 20 ..00........   ....Albany......, ...New York.....
                                                 [City]   [State]

........222 Kelly Avenue, Albany, New York 12203........
[Property Address]

1. BORROWER'S PROMISE TO PAY

In return for a loan that I have received, I promise to pay U.S. $...79,000.00........ (this amount is called "principal"), plus interest, to the order of the Lender. The Lender is ...First City Savings and Loan........ .....Association of Albany, New York........ I understand that the Lender may transfer this Note. The Lender or anyone who takes this Note by transfer and who is entitled to receive payments under this Note is called the "Note Holder."

2. INTEREST

Interest will be charged on unpaid principal until the full amount of principal has been paid. I will pay interest at a yearly rate of ....9.5....%.

The interest rate required by this Section 2 is the rate I will pay both before and after any default described in Section 6(B) of this Note.

3. PAYMENTS

(A) Time and Place of Payments

I will pay principal and interest by making payments every month.

I will make my monthly payments on the ....1st........ day of each month beginning on ....May 1........, 20 ..00........ I will make these payments every month until I have paid all of the principal and interest and any other charges described below that I may owe under this Note. My monthly payments will be applied to interest before principal. If, on ....April 1, 2030........, I still owe amounts under this Note, I will pay those amounts in full on that date, which is called the "maturity date."

I will make my monthly payments at ....130 North LaSalle Street, Albany, New York........ .... or at a different place if required by the Note Holder.

(B) Amount of Monthly Payments

My monthly payment will be in the amount of U.S. $...664.29........

4. BORROWER'S RIGHT TO PREPAY

I have the right to make payments of principal at any time before they are due. A payment of principal only is known as a "prepayment." When I make a prepayment, I will tell the Note Holder in writing that I am doing so.

I may make a full prepayment or partial prepayments without paying any prepayment charge. The Note Holder will use all of my prepayments to reduce the amount of principal that I owe under this Note. If I make a partial prepayment, there will be no changes in the due date or in the amount of my monthly payment unless the Note Holder agrees in writing to those changes.

5. LOAN CHARGES

If a law, which applies to this loan and which sets maximum loan charges, is finally interpreted so that the interest or other loan charges collected or to be collected in connection with this loan exceed the permitted limits, then: (i) any such loan charge shall be reduced by the amount necessary to reduce the charge to the permitted limit; and (ii) any sums already collected from me which exceeded permitted limits will be refunded to me. The Note Holder may choose to make this refund by reducing the principal I owe under this Note or by making a direct payment to me. If a refund reduces principal, the reduction will be treated as a partial prepayment.

6. BORROWER'S FAILURE TO PAY AS REQUIRED

(A) Late Charge for Overdue Payments

If the Note Holder has not received the full amount of any monthly payment by the end of ....fifteen........ calendar days after the date it is due, I will pay a late charge to the Note Holder. The amount of the charge will be ....5..% of my overdue payment of principal and interest. I will pay this late charge promptly but only once on each late payment.

(B) Default

If I do not pay the full amount of each monthly payment on the date it is due, I will be in default.

(C) Notice of Default

If I am in default, the Note Holder may send me a written notice telling me that if I do not pay the overdue amount by a certain date, the Note Holder may require me to pay immediately the full amount of principal which has not been paid and all the interest that I owe on that amount. That date must be at least 30 days after the date on which the notice is delivered or mailed to me.

(D) No Waiver By Note Holder

Even if, at a time when I am in default, the Note Holder does not require me to pay immediately in full as described above, the Note Holder will still have the right to do so if I am in default at a later time.

(E) Payment of Note Holder's Costs and Expenses

If the Note Holder has required me to pay immediately in full as described above, the Note Holder will have the right to be paid back by me for all of its costs and expenses in enforcing this Note to the extent not prohibited by applicable law. Those expenses include, for example, reasonable attorneys' fees.

7. GIVING OF NOTICES

Unless applicable law requires a different method, any notice that must be given to me under this Note will be given by delivering it or by mailing it by first class mail to me at the Property Address above or at a different address if I give the Note Holder a notice of my different address.

Any notice that must be given to the Note Holder under this Note will be given by mailing it by first class mail to the Note Holder at the address stated in Section 3(A) above or at a different address if I am given a notice of that different address.

MULTISTATE FIXED RATE NOTE—Single Family—**FNMA/FHLMC UNIFORM INSTRUMENT**   Form 3200 12/83

To help in keeping the terms straight, it is useful to note the *OR and EE rule:*

- Words that end in *OR* are the OWNERS or GIVERS of what is being given.
- Words that end in *EE* are the RECEIVERS of whatever is being given.

The mortgage document will always state the terms of the note and clearly establish that the land is security for the debt. It identifies the lender as well as the borrower and includes an accurate legal description of the property. It should be signed by all owners of the property. It also sets forth the obligations of the borrower and the rights of the lender.

In some areas of the country, and in certain situations such as title theory states, lenders prefer to use an instrument known as a *trust deed*, or *deed of trust*, rather than a mortgage. In these states, it is a three-party, two-instrument transaction.

The parties to these trust deed transactions consist of

- the trustor/borrower;
- the beneficiary/lender; and
- the trustee/third neutral party that holds the title.

The third party holds the title for the benefit of the borrower if the loan is repaid under the terms and conditions of the borrowing and for the benefit of the beneficiary/lender in the unfortunate event of a borrower default.

A trust deed conveys the real estate as security for the loan to a third party, called the trustee. Appointment of a trustee in title theory states is required. Because a borrower signs the deed and conveys it to the benefit of the lending party, the lender may not hold the naked title. It is for this reason that a third neutral party is appointed and charged with holding the deed in trust.

As previously mentioned, a trustee will hold a deed for two basic events:

1. In case of default, the lender with a trust deed can gain possession of the property more promptly and more simply than can a lender who forecloses on a mortgage.
2. In the event the loan is repaid in full under the terms and conditions of the borrowing, the trustee will reconvey the property back to the borrower via an instrument known as a reconveyance deed.

Duties of the Mortgagor

The borrower's obligations usually include the following:

- Paying the debt as promised in the note
- Paying all real estate taxes on the property
- Maintaining adequate hazard insurance to protect the lender if the property is destroyed or damaged
- Obtaining the lender's authorization before making any major alterations
- Maintaining the property in good repair at all times

Failure to meet any of these obligations can result in a borrower's **default**. When this happens, the mortgage usually provides a **grace period** (30 days, for example) during which the borrower can meet the obligation and cure the default. If the borrower does not do so, the lender has the right to foreclose the mortgage and collect on the note. The most frequent cause of default is the borrower's failure to pay monthly installments.

Most mortgages contain a *late-payment clause*. For one- to six-family owner-occupied residences, New York allows a late-payment penalty 15 days after payment is due. An individual may charge a 2 percent penalty; a lending institution may charge 4 percent on government-backed mortgages and 5 percent on conventional loans.

Provisions for Default

A mortgage may include an **acceleration clause** to assist the lender in a foreclosure. If a borrower defaults, the lender has the right to accelerate the debt—to declare the entire debt due and owing immediately.

Other clauses in a mortgage enable the lender to take care of the property in the event of the borrower's negligence or default. If the borrower does not pay taxes or insurance premiums or make necessary repairs on the property, for example, the lender may step in and do so to protect its security. Any money advanced by the lender to cure such defaults is either added to the unpaid debt or declared immediately due and owing from the borrower.

Foreclosure

When a borrower defaults in making payments or in fulfilling any of the obligations set forth in the mortgage, the lender can enforce its rights through a **foreclosure**, with the property sold at public auction. Foreclosure is an action that occurs in a court proceeding. The action brought forth and instituted by the lender is both in "equity and possession."

There are two general types of foreclosure proceedings—judicial and strict foreclosure. Strict foreclosure, in which the lender may regain title to the property, is rarely used. Judicial foreclosure is the procedure followed in most cases. On a borrower's default, the lender may declare the whole debt immediately due and payable and ask the court to order a public sale, which is advertised. The real estate is sold to the highest bidder. The borrower has the right to redeem the property *until the moment of sale* by producing full payment, including back interest and costs incurred in the foreclosure proceedings. In New York, the defaulting borrower does not have the right to redeem the property after the foreclosure sale. The buyer at a foreclosure sale receives a deed signed by a court-appointed referee. The buyer receives the property free of the mortgage and all junior liens but subject to any prior liens. (Any unpaid property taxes must be paid out of the proceeds of the sale.)

Deed in lieu of foreclosure   An alternative to foreclosure is for the lender to accept a deed in lieu of foreclosure from the borrower. This is sometimes known as a *friendly foreclosure* because it is by agreement rather than by civil action. The major disadvantage is that the mortgagee takes the real estate subject to all junior liens, whereas foreclosure eliminates all such liens. In addition, the Internal Revenue Service (IRS) considers the amount of debt that was forgiven as taxable income to the borrower, which is why **debtors in possession** seek a workout with their lender whenever possible. At this time, the law on this subject is being questioned.

Deficiency judgment   If a foreclosure sale does not produce sufficient cash to pay the loan balance in full after deducting expenses and unpaid interest, the mortgagee may be entitled to seek a personal judgment against the signer of the note for the unpaid balance. Such a judgment is called a **deficiency judgment**. It may be obtained against the original borrower and any later owners of the property who assumed the debt by written agreement. If, on the other hand, there are any surplus proceeds from the foreclosure sale after the debt is paid off and expenses and subordinate liens are deducted, they are paid to the borrower. When this clause is contained in a mortgage, the loan is said to be a **recourse loan**. This is where the borrower personally guarantees payment of the note.

The lender in this case has the property and the borrower to look to for repayment.

Sale of Property That Is Mortgaged

Anyone who purchases real estate and takes over the mortgage presently on it may take the property *subject to* the mortgage or may *assume* the seller's mortgage and *agree to pay* the debt. This technical distinction becomes important if the buyer later defaults and the mortgage is foreclosed.

When property is sold **subject to a mortgage**, the purchasers do not assume the note and mortgage and are not personally obligated to the lender to pay the debt in full. The original borrower/seller remains contingently liable to repay the balance of the loan. The new owners have bought the real estate knowing that they should make the loan payments or risk losing the property through a foreclosure sale. If a foreclosure sale did not pay off the entire debt, however, the new owners would not be personally liable for the shortfall.

In contrast, when the new owners not only purchase the property subject to the mortgage but assume and agree to pay the debt (sign the note or bond), they become personally responsible. If the mortgage is foreclosed and the court sale does not bring enough to pay the debt in full, a deficiency judgment against both the assumer and the original borrower can be obtained for the unpaid balance. When a mortgage is assumed, the original borrower is advised to obtain a novation from the lender, thereby releasing the original borrower from any further obligation under the note. Without novation, the original borrower/seller remains contingently liable.

The divorcing spouse who signs off ownership of a house is still personally responsible for any mortgage, although no longer a part owner. Only the lender can release a borrower from liability.

When a mortgage is being assumed or paid off early, the borrower requires a statement from the mortgagee detailing the amount currently due. This **reduction certificate** is often referred to as an **estoppel certificate**.

Alienation clause/resale clause/due-on-sale clause   Real estate lenders frequently wish to prevent future purchasers of property from assuming the existing loans. For this reason most lenders include an **alienation clause** (also known as a *resale clause* or *due-on-sale clause*) in the note. An alienation clause provides that on the sale of the property, the lender has the choice of either declaring the entire debt immediately due or permitting the buyer to assume the loan. Think of this clause as "alienating" the rest of the world from benefiting from the loan without the lender's permission.

In New York State, any mortgage is assumable unless the document contains a specific alienation clause.

Assignment of the mortgage   Sometimes the holder of the bond and mortgage wants to raise immediate cash by selling it, usually at a discount, to an investor. (The sale of notes and mortgages occurs within secondary market operations.) The bond or mortgage may be sold (assigned) to a third party, or assignee; it is a negotiable instrument. In order to be assigned, the note and mortgage must contain an assignment clause. An estoppel certificate signed by the borrower will verify the amount owed and interest rate.

Recording of the Mortgage

The mortgage document must be recorded in the recorder's office of the county in which the real estate is located. This gives notice to the world of the borrower's obligations and establishes the lien's priority over future mortgages or other liens.

First and second mortgages   Mortgages and other liens normally have priority in the order in which they have been recorded. A mortgage on land that has no prior mortgage lien on it is a first mortgage or a senior loan. When the owner of this land later places another mortgage for additional funds, the new mortgage becomes a second mortgage, or junior lien, when recorded. In recent years, the term *home equity loan* or *line of credit* is used for what is really a second mortgage.

The first mortgage has first claim to the value of the land pledged as security. The priority of mortgage liens may be changed by the execution of a *subordination agreement* if the first lender agrees to yield first place to the second lender.

Satisfaction of the Mortgage Lien

When all payments have been made and the note is paid in full, the mortgagor wants the public record to show that the debt has been paid and the lien satisfied. The lender is required to execute a release of mortgage, or satisfaction of mortgage.

This **satisfaction of mortgage** should be recorded in the public records to show that the mortgage lien has been removed from the property. According to New York law, financial institutions must file a satisfaction of mortgage within 45 days of a request to do so and provide a copy to the mortgagor. Penalties can be imposed for noncompliance, and after a 90-day period the mortgagor may file an affidavit with the recording officer that shows the lien has been satisfied.

Common Mortgage Terms

Among the most basic words needed to discuss mortgages efficiently are *down payment, loan-to-value ratio, equity, interest, servicing,* and *principal.*

The buyer of a $100,000 home who has only $10,000 to give a seller as a **down payment** or initial investment will have to borrow the rest with a mortgage loan. If $90,000 is being borrowed on property worth $100,000, the loan is said to have a 90 percent **loan-to-value (LTV) ratio** (amount borrowed divided by the property's value).

It is important to note at this time that a lender will loan money at the lesser of either the purchase price of the property or the appraised value, *whichever is less.*

Loan servicing is provided by the institution that collects and credits payments, issues monthly or annual reports on the status of the loan to the borrower, and handles contact with the borrower on behalf of that lender or another lender. Loan servicing bears similarity to a managing agent's management of real property on behalf of self or for another person.

After the transaction has closed, the buyers will have $10,000 **equity** in the home, *equity* being defined as the amount the owner would receive if the property were sold and all liens against it paid off. In a few years, if the loan has been paid down to $89,000 and the property's value has increased to $110,000, the owner's equity would amount to $21,000 ($110,000 value, minus $89,000 **principal** still owed).

Interest is a charge made by a lender for the use of money. Payment of interest can be best described as paying "rent" for the use of another's money while owed. Interest rates charged by lending institutions vary as changes occur in the availability of money to lend.

■ TYPES OF MORTGAGES

Mortgages may be conventional or nonconventional. These loans when granted are sponsored by a government agency, such as the Federal Housing Administration (FHA) or the Department of Veterans Affairs (VA). However, for many different types of mortgages, the source of the financing is the same.

Primary Sources of Real Estate Financing

Funds used to finance the purchase of real estate come from a variety of sources that make up the **primary mortgage market**—lenders who supply funds directly to real estate borrowers. The primary mortgage market is where loans are originated. Some lenders then keep the loans in their own portfolios, whereas others later sell them to other investors in the *secondary mortgage market* (discussed more fully in Chapter 11).

Today most mortgage borrowers begin by browsing mortgage providers on the Internet, using Web sites like *www.lendingtree.com* and *www.eloan.com.*

Institutional lenders   Most of the loans made to finance real estate purchases are obtained from financial institutions designed to hold individuals' savings. Institutional lenders include savings associations (thrifts), commercial banks, and savings banks.

Credit unions   Credit unions are cooperative organizations whose members place money in savings accounts. In the past, most made only short-term consumer and home-improvement loans, but in recent years they have been branching out into mortgage loans for their own members.

Insurance companies   Amassing large sums of money from the premiums paid by policyholders, insurance companies invest much of it in real estate loans, most often large, long-term loans on commercial and industrial properties. They also purchase large blocks of FHA-insured and VA-guaranteed loans on the secondary mortgage market.

Mortgage banking companies   Mortgage bankers are not thrift institutions and offer neither checking nor savings accounts. They are licensed by the New York Banking Department. Mortgage bankers make real estate loans that later may be sold to investors (with the mortgage company receiving a fee if it continues to service the loans). Mortgage bankers originate a large percentage of all home loans. They are not mortgage *brokers*. Mortgage bankers must have a net worth of at least $250,000 and an existing line of credit of at least $1 million from a credit facility approved by the superintendent of banks. They must file a $50,000 surety bond with the superintendent of banks or establish a trust fund in the same amount that can be used to reimburse customers if it is determined that the mortgage banker has charged improper fees.

Mortgage brokers   Residential mortgage brokers act as third-party intermediaries between lenders and borrowers, bringing lenders and borrowers together for a fee. They are registered with the state banking department. They charge a fee, often of the borrower, for their services. The superintendent of banks may require that a mortgage broker obtain a surety bond or establish a trust fund in the amount of $25,000. They must prove a certain amount of experience in mortgage financing when they register. Mortgage bankers and mortgage brokers are discussed in Chapter 12.

The State of New York Mortgage Agency   Sonny Mae (SONYMA) provides lower-interest loans for specific purposes in specific locations. Loans with low down payments are made through local lending institutions to first-time homebuyers. Income and home price limits vary from one region to another but are usually in the moderate category. In designated target areas, higher income limits apply, and the purchaser need not be a first-time buyer. The program varies from time to time; information is available by mail from SONYMA, 260 Madison Avenue, New York, NY 10016, or by phone at 800-382-HOME (4663). The Web site is *www.nyhomes.org/index.htm*.

Rural Development   Formerly the Farmer's Home Administration, this federal agency under the Department of Agriculture provides credit to rural residents. Loan programs fall into two categories: (1) guaranteed loans made and serviced by a private lender and guaranteed by the agency; and (2) insured loans that are made and serviced directly by the agency. For low-income homebuyers in rural areas, mortgage interest may be subsidized to as low as 1 percent for the insured product. There is no down payment or PMI requirement for either product. Only modest residences are eligible. The address of a local office and further information is available from Rural Development, New York State Office in Syracuse at 315-477-6457. Information is also available on the Internet at *www.rurdev.usda. gov/ny*.

Low down payments   For years homebuyers have received help in obtaining low-down-payment mortgage loans through insurance and guarantees from the FHA, the VA, and SONYMA. In addition, **private mortgage insurance (PMI)** companies offer programs to help those who need high LTV ratios on conventional (non-government-backed) loans. The various types of loans are discussed in more detail in Chapter 11.

Under current federal tax laws, first-time homebuyers of any age are allowed to withdraw up to $10,000 from an IRA to be used within 120 days as down payment on a home, without the usual 10 percent penalty for early withdrawal before age 59½. The money is, as always, still subject to income tax in the year taken and used, and none of the $10,000 can be used toward the tax.

Types of Amortization

Most mortgage loans are **amortized loans**. With amortized loans, equal periodic payments of interest and principal are made, so that when the loan matures, the entire principal balance of the loan is zero. Payments over a term of 15 to 30 years are set high enough to include not only interest due but also a portion of the principal owed. At the end of the term, the full amount of the principal will have been paid off. The process is known as *amortization of the debt*.

Most amortized mortgage loans are paid in monthly installments. These payments may be computed based on different mortgage plans.

The most common plan requires that the mortgagor pay the same amount in each payment period, usually each month. The lender credits each payment first to the interest due and then applies the rest to reduce the amount borrowed (the principal). Each month, as the principal is reduced, less interest is due, so more of the payment can be used to whittle down the debt. At the end of the **term**, that is, the originally scheduled number of years, the entire debt has been paid off. This is known as a **fully amortized loan**. It should be noted that as is the case in all loans of 20 to 30 years in length, for approximately the first 7 years, most of the loan payments go toward interest. The payment breakdown might resemble this:

- Approximately 95 percent of the payment toward interest satisfaction
- Approximately 5 percent of the payment going toward principal reduction

A mortgagor may choose a straight payment plan that calls for payments of interest only, with the principal to be paid in full at the end of the loan term. This is known as a **straight loan** or **term loan**. Such plans are generally used for short-term home improvement loans or construction loans rather than for residential first mortgage loans. However, in this type of payment, no principal reduction occurs through payments; therefore, the final payment results in a **balloon payment** in which the full amount of principal balance is due at time of maturity.

A combination of the two plans already mentioned is a partially amortized loan. Monthly payments may include enough to pay down the debt for a specific number of years. At the end of that period the entire remaining principal is due in a balloon payment. In many cases, rather than the borrower making the balloon payment, the borrower may roll it over into a new loan.

An **adjustable-rate mortgage (ARM)** shifts the risk or reward of changing interest rates from the lender to the borrower. As rates rise and fall, changes are made in the monthly payment or, occasionally, in the remaining principal.

In recent years, some hybrid mortgages have offered combinations of fixed and adjustable rates in ways that may fit certain borrowers' financial situations and future plans. Some mortgage plans remain at a fixed interest rate for the first three, five, or even seven years, with rates adjusted after that. This type of loan generally will experience **negative amortization**. Negative amortization occurs when the payment under the loan is not enough to cover the interest due for that period. When this occurs, the deficient amount is added to the remaining unpaid principal balance. The result is a higher principal balance amount. Negative amortization will only occur if the borrower continues to make the same payment. If the borrower makes the new higher monthly payment, negative amortization will not occur. At the adjustment period, borrowers under this plan often wonder why, if interest rates have fallen, they are paying a larger payment than previously; the reason is that the lower rate is applied to this higher principal balance amount.

Biweekly mortgages involve payments every two weeks instead of monthly. Some borrowers wrongly interpret this to mean "twice a month" and feel some magic is involved in the faster repayment of principal. A biweekly schedule, however, can occasionally involve three payments in one month. With 26 half-payments, it produces the equivalent of 13 monthly payments a year. The extra payment is used entirely to reduce the principal debt faster than originally scheduled, so that a 30-year fixed-rate loan can be paid off in about 23 years. Most biweekly loans involve automatic payment from the borrower's checking or savings account. (With adjustable-rate loans, extra principal payments reduce the monthly payment at the time of next adjustment, but they do not affect the term of the loan.)

Borrowers are sometimes offered biweekly payment plans by outside companies. The original traditional mortgage remains in place, but the firm collects 26 biweekly payments a year. It makes the borrower's usual monthly payments, then forwards the extra payment annually to reduce principal. A charge is made for the service. Borrowers who have the discipline, however, can make extra prepayments on their own in separate checks clearly marked "to be applied entirely to principal" and achieve the same results without paying for the service.

Interest

A lender charges a certain percentage of the principal as interest each year the debt is outstanding. The amount of interest due on any payment date is calculated by figuring total yearly interest based on the unpaid balance and dividing that figure by the number of payments made each year.

On an amortized loan of $100,000 for 30 years at an annual interest rate of 8½ percent, the amount due after the first month's payment has been made can be calculated as follows:

1. $100,000 × 8.5% = $8,500 annual interest
2. $8,500 ÷ 12 = $708.33 first month's interest
3. $768.92 monthly payment to amortize the loan in 30 years
4. $708.33 first month's interest due
5. $60.59 left to reduce principal first month
6. $100,000 original principal at start of month
7. – $60.59 principal reduction
8. $99,939.41 principal due at end of first month

The following month, because less is now owed, not quite so much interest will be due, and the principal can be reduced by a slightly larger amount.

Table 10.1 shows an *amortization schedule* for the first eight months of this 360-payment loan.

Interest is usually due at the end of each payment period (payment in arrears, as opposed to payment in advance) because a borrower must have had use of the borrowed funds prior to owing interest on that money. For example, a mortgage payment that is made on February 1, 2011, would represent payment for the previous month of January. The principal and interest on a 30-year mortgage is shown in Figure 10.2. Amortization formulas are complicated. Most real estate practitioners carry special calculators with built-in tables.

TABLE 10.1

Amortization Schedule

Loan amortization schedule				Simple interest loan	
			Principal		$100,000.00
			Monthly payment		$768.92
			Annual interest rate		8.500
			Term in months		360
Payment	**Old balance**	**Interest payment**	**Principal payment**	**Total payment**	**New balance**
1	$100,000.00	$708.33	$60.59	$768.92	$99,939.41
2	99,939.41	707.90	61.02	768.92	99,878.39
3	99,878.39	707.47	61.45	768.92	99,816.94
4	99,816.94	707.04	61.88	768.92	99,755.06
5	99,755.06	706.60	62.32	768.92	99,692.74
6	99,692.74	706.16	62.76	768.92	99,629.98
7	99,629.98	705.71	63.21	768.92	99,566.77
8	99,566.77	705.26	63.66	768.92	99,503.11

FIGURE   10.2

Level-Payment Amortized Plan

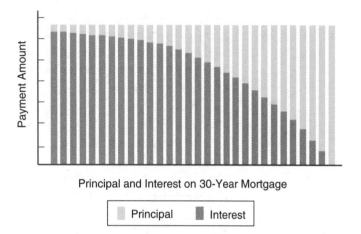

Principal and Interest on 30-Year Mortgage

☐ Principal   ■ Interest

Usury   The maximum rate of interest that may be charged on mortgage loans is set by state law. Charging interest in excess of this rate is called **usury**. New York has a *floating usury rate*. The maximum rate that may be charged is adjusted up or down at specific intervals by the New York State Banking Board.

Loans in the amount of $2.5 million or more and loans made to corporations are generally exempt from usury laws, except for New York's criminal usury limit of 25 percent on loans up to $2.5 million. Lending institutions are also exempt up to the criminal usury limit. *Other individuals making mortgage loans, except sellers, however, are still bound by the New York usury limit.*

Such an individual might be an employer making a mortgage loan to an employee or a real estate broker lending the buyer money to help with a sale (which the broker should not do without the consent of the seller). In those cases, the person making the loan should check with the state banking department to make sure the interest charged is within current limits.

Points   When a new mortgage is placed, the lending institution may ask for a lump-sum payment of extra prepaid interest in the form of up-front **points**. Each point or discount point represents 1 percent of the new loan amount. On an $80,000 loan, each point would be $800; a charge of two points would total $1,600. Payment of points is a one-time affair, usually at the time of closing but occasionally at mortgage application or issuance of a mortgage commitment by the lender. Points may be paid by either the buyer or the seller, depending on the terms of the sales contract.

As a general rule, each discount point paid on a 25- to 30-year loan translates to approximately ⅛ of 1 percent of the rate on the yield to the lender. For example, a loan at 10 percent without any points paid at closing of the loan, and a loan at 9½ percent with four discount points paid at closing represent the same loan:

    4 points = ⁴⁄₈, or 0.5%
    9.5% + 0.5% = 10% yield to the lender

Annual percentage rate   If a mortgage loan is made at 7 percent but also requires three points in prepaid interest or other service fees, the loan really costs more than 7 percent. The exact rate depends on the length of the proposed mortgage and requires some complicated calculations. The rate, which would total slightly more than 7 percent, is known as the **annual percentage rate (APR)**. Regulation Z of the Truth in Lending Act requires that the borrower be advised of the APR in advertisements and in writing when a loan is placed. It is intended to help borrowers compare widely differing mortgage plans but often simply adds to their confusion. Regulation Z is discussed further in Chapter 11.

Buydowns   With some mortgage plans, lending institutions are willing to lower the interest rate in return for payment of extra points. The arrangement is known as a **buydown**. Many buydowns lower the rate for a period of time, for example, by 3 percent the first year of the loan, 2 percent the second year, and 1 percent the third year (3-2-1-buydown). Other buydowns last for the whole term of the loan.

■ TAX-DEDUCTIBLE INTEREST PAYMENTS

Taxpayers may deduct from their income tax returns the amount of interest paid on mortgage loans up to a total of $1 million if borrowed to acquire and/or improve both a first and a second (vacation) residence. Interest on additional borrowing (second mortgages, home equity loans) of up to $100,000 also qualifies for income tax deduction, no matter what the money is used for. When any borrowing or refinancing results in an amount that exceeds the previous amount outstanding, that excess portion of the loan is called equity. As per the aforementioned, any equity amount in excess of $100,000 may not be deducted. Homeowners also may deduct all property taxes, prepaid interest points (whether paid by buyer or seller) and any mortgage prepayment penalties. Somewhat different income tax regulations apply to mortgage loans on investment property and to refinance mortgages.

Prepayment

Some mortgage notes charge a **prepayment premium (penalty)** if the loan is paid off before its full term. The clause within a mortgage that covers this subject and indicates whether the loan can be prepaid is called the *prepayment penalty clause*. If the loan cannot be prepaid, the clause will outline the penalty the borrower suffers if the loan is prepaid before it matures.

In commercial loans, lenders may require lock-ins or yield maintenance. A lock-in provides an initial period whereby the loan may not be prepaid. With yield maintenance, the lender requires that interest be paid as if the loan had gone to full-term maturity.

Any prepayment will bear a penalty consisting of the unpaid interest for the remaining term of the loan from the date of prepayment.

For a one- to six-family dwelling used as a principal residence, the maximum prepayment premium a lender may charge in New York is 90 days' interest on the unpaid balance if the loan is paid in full during the first year. No penalty may be charged after the loan is a year old. No prepayment penalties may be charged on FHA or VA loans.

Tax and Insurance Reserves

Many lenders require that borrowers provide a reserve, or escrow, fund to meet future real estate taxes and insurance premiums. Payments for these items are impounded by the lender from the borrower. When the mortgage loan is made, the borrower starts the reserve by depositing funds (the impounding) to cover partial payment of the following year's tax bill. The insurance premium reserve is started with the deposit of one-twelfth of the annual tax and insurance premium liability. After that the monthly payments will include principal, interest, and escrow for tax and insurance reserves (**PITI**).

To be certain that these important bills are being paid, the lender accumulates the borrower's money in the escrow account. Property tax bills and insurance premium bills are sent directly to the lending institution, which pays them and renders an accounting to the borrower. The homeowner is entitled to 2 percent interest on the money thus held. When the mortgage loan is eventually paid off, any money remaining in the escrow account is returned to the borrower.

RESPA, the Federal Real Estate Settlement Procedures Act, limits the amount of tax and insurance reserves a lender may require.

■ SUMMARY

Mortgage loans involve a borrower, called a *mortgagor*, and a lender, known as a *mortgagee*. New York is a lien theory state and regards a mortgage as simply a financial claim on the real estate.

The borrower signs a note, a personal promise to repay the loan, and also a mortgage that pledges the real estate as security for the loan. The documents are entered into the public record. Like all liens, mortgages take priority in the order in which they are recorded. When the debt is fully repaid, a certificate of satisfaction is recorded to remove the lien.

Failure to live up to the provisions of the loan results in default, at which point the lender can use the mortgage's acceleration clause to declare the entire debt immediately payable. If that payment is not made, the lender can foreclose the loan and force a public auction of the property. If the sale does not yield enough to satisfy the debt, the lender can seek a deficiency judgment against the borrower.

When property is sold subject to an existing mortgage, the buyer has agreed to take it with the lien against it. When the buyer assumes the mortgage, the buyer also becomes personally responsible for the debt. A reduction certificate or estoppel certificate from the lender states the current amount of the remaining debt.

Mortgage loans are available from institutional lenders, such as banks and savings associations; credit unions; insurance companies (mainly large commercial loans); mortgage bankers; some government agencies; and private individuals (often the seller).

Most mortgage loans are *amortized*, or gradually paid off, through monthly payments that include interest and an additional amount toward reducing the debt. Interest rates may remain the same (fixed-rate) or be adjusted periodically as rates rise or fall (adjustable-rate, or ARM). *Usury* is the legal term for interest rates higher than those allowed by law. Sellers taking back mortgages are exempt from usury limits. Lenders are required to quote an annual percentage rate (APR) that takes into account closing costs and fees.

To ensure that property taxes are paid on time and hazard insurance premiums are kept current, many mortgage plans include escrow accounts, which is extra money collected monthly by the lender and used to pay those bills as they come due.

When points are charged as a loan is made, each point represents 1 percent of the loan. A buydown allows payment of more points in return for a lower interest rate.

Taxpayers may take as income tax deductions the interest on up to $1 million used to buy or improve a first or second home. Interest on additional borrowing of up to $100,000 is also deductible. All property taxes are income tax deductible.

CHAPTER 10 QUIZ

1. A new home cost $150,000, and the new owners borrowed $135,000 on a mortgage loan, paying $15,000 in cash as a down payment. That $15,000 now represents their
   a. loan-to-value ratio.
   b. equity.
   c. qualifying ratio.
   d. underwriting.

2. A mortgage broker generally
   a. brings borrower and lender together.
   b. makes mortgage loans using investors' funds.
   c. forecloses defaulted mortgages.
   d. places packages of loans in the secondary market.

3. A borrower obtains a 30-year mortgage loan for $176,000 at 7½ percent interest. If monthly payments of $1,230.62 are credited first to interest and then to principal, what will be the principal balance after the first payment is made?
   a. $174,990.00
   b. $175,110.00
   c. $175,123.62
   d. $175,869.38

4. When a young man buys his house, the seller allows affordable monthly mortgage payments of interest only over a ten-year basis so that the new homeowner can handle the payments. At the end of the tenth year, however, the seller wants the whole remaining debt paid off in a
   a. graduated payment.
   b. shared-equity payment.
   c. balloon payment.
   d. blanket payment.

5. With some exceptions, a homeowner may take as an income tax deduction any cost for
   a. a title insurance premium.
   b. interest on a mortgage.
   c. a homeowners' insurance premium.
   d. mortgage application fees.

6. New York's usury limits do NOT apply to interest on mortgage loans made by
   a. sellers.
   b. employer to employee.
   c. private community members.
   d. the Rural Economic and Community Development Administration.

7. A seller sold a home for $200,000 and agreed to pay three points to the buyer's lending institution. The buyer is putting 20 percent down on the property. How much will the points cost the seller?
   a. $900
   b. $1,600
   c. $4,800
   d. $6,000

8. A lending institution may require that the buyer send in an extra monthly payment to cover future bills for
   a. property taxes and insurance premiums.
   b. major repairs.
   c. possible default in monthly payments.
   d. water and municipal utilities.

9. The buyer of a $96,000 property is offered a mortgage with 10 percent down and a loan origination fee of 1½ percent. Disregarding other possible closing costs, how much cash must the buyer produce to complete the transaction?
   a. $1,290
   b. $1,440
   c. $9,600
   d. $10,896

10. The primary mortgage loan market includes institutions that
    a. make loans to borrowers.
    b. insure loans made to homeowners.
    c. buy and sell mortgage loans.
    d. sell interests in mortgage loan polls to investors.

11. Which is *NOT* a characteristic of mortgage bankers?

a. Make real estate loans
b. Offer checking accounts
c. Are regulated by the state
d. Sell mortgage loans to investors

12. First-time homebuyers who participate in Sonny Mae (SONYMA) loans receive loans made through

a. SONYMA directly.
b. the Federal Housing Administration.
c. the state treasurer's office.
d. local lending institutions.

13. A buyer is using a $150,000 inheritance to purchase a home valued at $600,000, borrowing the remaining funds from a local thrift. What is the loan-to-value ratio on the buyer's loan?

a. 20 percent
b. 25 percent
c. 50 percent
d. 75 percent

14. Borrowers allow mortgage loan lenders to place liens against their property without giving up ownership or possession in a process called

a. amortization.
b. alienation.
c. foreclosure.
d. hypothecation.

15. When property is mortgaged, the property owner must sign both a mortgage and a(n)

a. affidavit.
b. release.
c. note.
d. disclosure.

16. Failure to meet obligations of a mortgage results in

a. deficiency.
b. bankruptcy.
c. delinquency.
d. default.

17. A homeowner failed to make payments on his mortgage, and the borrower asked the court to hold a public sale. If the homeowner wants to retain the property, how long does he have to redeem it by paying all the moneys that are due?

a. 30 days after his last outstanding payment was due
b. 30 days after the lender begins foreclosure proceedings
c. Until the sale is scheduled
d. Until the moment of the sale

18. What does *friendly foreclosure* mean?

a. The lender accepts a deed from the borrower.
b. The lender returns mortgage payments made before the foreclosure sale.
c. The borrower is allowed to remain in the property as a renter.
d. The borrower continues to make mortgage payments after the foreclosure sale.

19. An owner of a New York home for two years just came into a windfall and wants to prepay her mortgage. Will she have to pay a prepayment penalty?

a. Yes, but only if her mortgage note contains notice of the prepayment penalty
b. Yes, because the mortgage loan is less than five years old
c. No, because no penalty may be charged if the loan is older than one year
d. No, because prepayment penalties on residential mortgages are forbidden in New York

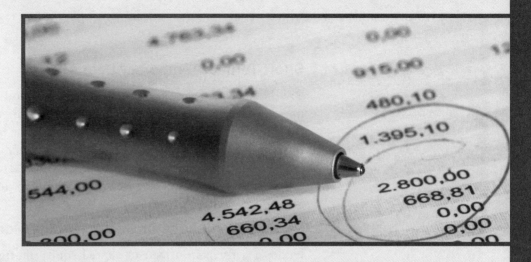

CHAPTER

11

Real Estate Finance

■ KEY TERMS

blanket mortgage
bridge loan
cap
ceiling
construction loans
conventional loans
convertibility
Equal Credit Opportunity
  Act (ECOA)
Fannie Mae (FNMA)
FHA loan
Freddie Mac (FHLMC)
Ginnie Mae (GNMA)

graduated-payment
  mortgage
home equity loan
imputed interest
index
interest-only mortgages
interim financing
jumbo loans
margin/spread
mortgage insurance
  premium (MIP)
negative amortization
nonconforming mortgage

open-end mortgage
package loan
partial release clause
Regulation Z
reverse annuity mortgage
sale-and-leaseback
secondary mortgage
  market
shared-equity mortgage
swing loan
underwriting
VA loans
wraparound mortgages

■ TYPES OF LOANS

Most loans described in this chapter are long-term mortgages intended for the purchase, improvement, or refinance of real estate. Before discussing those, however, we can examine other common types of borrowing.

Short-Term or Temporary Loans

The homeowner who is selling one residence and buying another may find it necessary to buy the new home before the closing date on the present one. In that situation, a temporary loan, variously called a **bridge loan**, a **swing loan**, or **interim financing**, may be arranged. This is generally viewed as a personal loan. Even though the borrower will probably be required to post some type of collateral to secure repayment, it is not viewed as a mortgage loan.

Participation Loans or Shared-Equity Mortgages

Under a participation loan or **shared-equity mortgage**, the purchaser receives help with the down payment, a low interest rate, or assistance with monthly payments from a partner. The "partner" may be a lending institution, the seller, or a relative.

Typically the partner receives

- a share of the profit when the property is sold,
- a share of any refinancing proceeds, or
- a share of profits derived from the income stream on an income-producing property.

Normally with a participation loan or shared-equity mortgage, the lender receives any proceeds in the form of deferred interest.

Package Loans

A **package loan** includes not only the real estate but also personal property such as appliances and furniture on the premises. In recent years, this kind of loan has been used to finance furnished condominium units.

Open-End Mortgages

Open-end mortgages are used by borrowers to obtain additional funds to improve property. The borrower "opens" the mortgage to increase the debt after the debt has been reduced by payments over time. Open-end mortgages are not to be confused with open mortgages; an *open mortgage* is one that may be repaid in full at any time without any prepayment penalty by the lender.

Credit cards make use of the same type of arrangement. The borrower/card holder may use the proceeds up to a prescribed limit. So long as the balance is paid down, the borrower/cardholder need not reapply for additional funds up to the prescribed limit.

Blanket Mortgages

Blanket mortgages cover more than one parcel or lot and are often used to finance subdivision developments. When one parcel or lot is sold, the borrower makes a partial payment to release it from the overall mortgage.

The **partial release clause** is an essential element and requirement for the subdivider. Without it, the subdivider may be successful in subdividing a larger parcel into many lots; however, without the release of the lien held by the lender, the subdivider will be unable to sell any of the lots. This clause should be included within the blanket mortgage at acquisition of the land parcel, prior to subdividing.

Wraparound Mortgages

Wraparound mortgages frequently are used to refinance or finance a purchase when an existing mortgage is to be retained. A wraparound mortgage is always a second mortgage. The buyer gives a large mortgage to the seller (the second recorded position), who will collect payments on the new loan, usually at a higher interest rate, and continue to make payments on the old loan (the first recorded position). Wraparound mortgages, like all unusual arrangements, require careful study by attorneys. The broker who negotiates a sale when an existing mortgage is to be retained should exercise special care not to give legal advice.

Graduated-Payment Mortgage

A **graduated-payment mortgage** (also known as a pledge account mortgage) is a mortgage in which the monthly payment for principal and interest graduates by a certain percentage each year for a specific number of years and then levels off for the remaining term of the mortgage. There are five different versions of the plan available in the FHA-245 program. The most popular is Plan III, in which payments increase at the rate of 7½ percent per year for five years.

The FHA-245 program is especially attractive to persons who may be just starting their careers and anticipate increases in their incomes and who want to obtain a home mortgage with a lower initial monthly installment obligation than would be available under a level payment plan. This plan helps borrowers qualify for loans by basing repayment schedules on salary expectations and anticipated home price appreciation. Because FHA underwriting guidelines are based on the first year's monthly requirement for principal and interest amortization, persons using FHA-245 can qualify for larger loan amounts than would ordinarily be available under other forms of financing.

Three features unique to the graduated payment mortgage are the following:

- The size of the individual payments is less than it would be under a fixed-payment loan.
- Negative amortization occurs during the initial years.
- The face amount of the note is greater than the funds disbursed at closing.

Reverse Annuity Mortgages

A **reverse annuity mortgage** (or reverse mortgage) allows senior citizens on fixed incomes to tap the equity buildup in their homes without having to sell. When savings, pensions, and Social Security are not enough income for the homeowner to live on, this type of mortgage can be useful. The homeowner receives a monthly check, a lump sum, a line of credit against which to draw, or a combination of these. No payments are due as long as the homeowner remains in the property, and a gradual debt, including interest, builds up against the real estate. The American Association of Retired Persons (AARP) has an excellent booklet titled *Home*

Made Money available to those who write to Equity Information, AARP, 601 E. St., NW, Washington, DC 20049. The Web site *www.reversemortgage.org* offers useful information.

Among the better reverse mortgage plans is that backed by the Department of Housing and Urban Development (HUD), which requires counseling so that the borrower understands exactly what is involved. HUD's is called a *home equity conversion mortgage*.

Purchase-Money Mortgages

Strictly speaking, a *purchase-money mortgage* is any loan that enables the purchase of real estate, as opposed to a second mortgage for further borrowing or a refinance mortgage that is used to pay off the original one.

The term is often used, however, for the situation in which a seller lends the buyer money to complete the purchase. The seller "takes back financing" and acts as the lender. A purchase-money mortgage may cover a portion of the purchase price or may be a first mortgage to finance the entire price.

Imputed interest   A purchase-money mortgage held by the seller is exempt from usury limitations on interest rate. If seller financing is at an artificially low interest rate, however, the Internal Revenue Service assumes a higher rate (**imputed interest**). The seller must charge at least 9 percent or a rate equal to the applicable federal rate (AFR), whichever is lower. The AFR is set monthly by the federal government and is usually somewhat below current national average rates. A seller who charges less will be taxed as though income were received at the required rate. An exception is made for certain transfers of vacant land within a family.

When a third party—perhaps an employer, relative, or individual investor—makes a private mortgage loan, it is important to follow the rules on the applicable federal rate.

Construction Loans

Also called building loan agreements, **construction loans** are made to finance the construction of improvements on real estate. These are always short-term loans. Depending on the type of project, terms range from 12 to 24 months. A construction loan can be difficult to secure unless the applicant works through a recognized builder or contractor. Payments are made on a scheduled basis to the general contractor or owner for work that has been completed since the previous payment. The lender usually inspects the work before each payment. This kind of mortgage loan generally bears a higher interest rate because of risks assumed by the lender. The borrower arranges for a permanent mortgage loan (also known as an end, or *takeout, loan*) when the work is completed.

Land Contracts

As discussed in Chapter 8, real estate can be purchased under a *land contract*. Real estate is often sold on contract when mortgage financing is not available or is too expensive or when the purchaser does not have a sufficient down payment. It should be noted that banks do not extend loans in the form of mortgages on unimproved land.

Sale-and-Leaseback Arrangements

Sale-and-leaseback agreements are sometimes used as a means of financing large commercial or industrial plants. The land and building used by the seller are sold to an investor, such as an insurance company. The investor then leases back the real estate to the seller, who continues to conduct business on the property as a tenant. This enables a business firm that has money invested in a plant to free that money for working capital.

The selling party also receives a tax deduction against profits derived from the sale, in the year of the sale, and through the payment of rent.

The buyer benefits from an assured long-term tenant. Real estate brokers should consult legal and tax experts when involved in this type of complex transaction.

Home Equity Loans

A form of second mortgage, the **home equity loan**, has grown in popularity in recent years. Homeowners whose property has appreciated in value may borrow up to new loan-to-value (LTV) ratios or, in one popular version, establish a line of credit that is based on the equity position in their home, borrowing against it as they choose. Some sellers do not realize that their home equity line of credit is really a second mortgage and must be paid off when they sell, as any other nonassumable mortgage must be.

In order to calculate the equity portion eligible for loan, one would follow these steps:

1. Derive the appraised value of the property at time of loan.
2. Multiply the figure from step one by the loan-to-value ratio at which a lender agrees to provide funds.
3. Subtract any outstanding existing mortgage balance(s).

In formula form, it would appear as follows:

(Appraised property value × Loan-to-value ratio) − Any existing mortgages
= Equity amount

Interest-Only and Optional-Payment Mortgages

In high-cost areas where the average buyer cannot afford normal monthly payments, some lenders offer **interest-only mortgages**, with monthly payments covering only the interest due and no debt reduction. Some even offer choose-your-own-payment-this-month mortgages. With these, payments might not even cover interest, with any shortfall added to the debt (negative amortization). These loans, which build no equity, are almost the equivalent of renting the property. If values in a particular area stop climbing or even remain level, borrowers can face serious problems.

■ METHODS OF FINANCE

Mortgage loans fall into several classifications:

- *Conventional loans* are those arranged entirely between borrower and lending institution.
- *Nonconventional or government-backed loans* include those insured by the Federal Housing Administration (FHA) or guaranteed by the Department of Veterans Affairs (VA). With both types, the actual loan comes from a local lending institution.
- *Loans directly from the government* include State of New York Mortgage Agency (SONYMA) mortgages and Rural Economic and Community Development Administration (formerly Farmer's Home Administration) (FmHA) loans.
- *Private loans* are those made by individuals, often the seller of the property or a relative of the buyer.

Conventional Loans

In making **conventional loans**, lending institutions set their own standards, governed always by banking regulations. As a result, a variety of mortgage plans is often offered, and some flexibility is occasionally available. A conventional loan may be useful where a short processing time is needed or where an unusual house or unusual buyer is involved. Conventional loans are also popular when interest rates for mortgage loans are low. Conventional mortgages may be fixed rate, adjustable rate, or a combination of plans.

Most fixed-rate conventional mortgages (with some exceptions) are not assumable by a subsequent buyer of the property; some adjustable-rate mortgages are assumable, but only when the buyer can prove financial qualification.

Private mortgage insurance   In general, conventional loans call for higher down payments (lower LTV ratio) than government-backed mortgages. Banking theory holds that it risks depositors' money to lend more than 80 percent of the value of real estate. With any down payment below 20 percent, therefore, a conventional loan in New York State must be accompanied by *private mortgage insurance (PMI)*. The borrower pays a yearly premium—or, optionally, a lump sum at closing—for insurance that protects the lender in case of loss after a foreclosure. (PMI should not be confused with life insurance.)

Increasingly in recent years, a borrower with a high credit score can qualify for more flexible arrangements. Qualifying ratios can be raised to allow higher monthly payments. Occasionally, a mortgage plan will accept only 10 percent down payment without requiring PMI coverage. With some other mortgage plans, borrowers are allowed to take out a short second (piggyback) mortgage for part or all of the required 20 percent down payment on the first mortgage. That arrangement requires them to pay, for several years, on two loans, but they avoid the expense of private mortgage insurance.

New York State law requires that the lender discontinue collecting PMI premiums when the loan has been paid down to 75 percent of the value of the property as appraised at the time of purchase.

For conventional mortgage loans placed after July 29, 1999, the federal government requires that lenders drop PMI coverage at the borrower's request when equity reaches 20 percent and that coverage be dropped automatically when it reaches 22 percent. Equity is calculated from current value or original appraisal, whichever is lower.

Adjustable-rate mortgages   An adjustable-rate mortgage, particularly popular when interest rates are high, offers the borrower a chance at lower interest rates if national interest levels drop. When rates across the country rise, however, the borrower may find the rate being raised.

The vocabulary of ARMs includes the following:

- *Adjustment period.* The anniversary on which interest rate and monthly payment adjustments may be made. Most borrowers elect one-year adjustments, but they might be made more frequently or only after three or five years.
- *Index.* The interest rate on the loan changes following an increase or decrease in a national indicator, or **index**, of current rates. The most commonly chosen index is the rate paid on one-year U.S. Treasury bills.
- *Margin.* The borrower pays a specific percentage above the index. That percentage is known as the **margin** or the **spread**; the margin or the spread represents the lender's profit when loaning to a borrower. If Treasury bills were selling at 6 percent interest, for example, the borrower with a 2 percent margin over Treasury bills would be charged 8 percent.
- *Cap.* The loan agreement may set a **cap** of, for example, 2 percent on any upward adjustment. If interest rates (as reflected by the index) went up 3 percent by the time of adjustment, the interest rate could be raised only 2 percent. Depending on the particular mortgage, the extra 1 percent might be treated one of three ways:
  1. It could be saved by the lender to be added at the next adjustment period.
  2. It could be absorbed by the lender with no future consequences to the borrower.
  3. It could be added to the amount borrowed so that the principal would increase instead of decreasing (negative amortization).
- *Ceiling.* A **ceiling** (sometimes called a lifetime cap) is a maximum allowable interest rate. Typically a mortgage may offer a five-point ceiling. If the interest rate started at 8 percent, it could never go beyond 13 percent, no matter what happened to national rates.
- *Negative amortization.* **Negative amortization** could result from an artificially low initial interest rate. It also could follow a hike in rates larger than a cap allows the lender to impose. Not all mortgage plans include the possibility of negative amortization. Sometimes, the lender agrees to absorb any shortfalls. The possibility must always be explored, however, when an ARM is being evaluated. The debt would be increasing, rather than being paid down.
- *Convertibility.* Some ARMs include **convertibility**; that is, the borrower may choose to change to a fixed-rate mortgage at then-current interest levels.

With some plans, any favorable moment may be chosen. More commonly, the option is available on the third, fourth, or fifth anniversary of the loan. The borrower may be charged a slightly higher interest rate in return for this option.

■ *Initial interest rate.* With many loan plans, the rate during the first year, or the first adjustment period, is set artificially low (discounted) to induce the borrower to enter into the agreement (teaser rate). Buyers who plan to be in a home for only a few years may be delighted with such arrangements. Other borrowers, however, may end up with negative amortization and payment shock.

■ *Assumability.* Many ARMs are assumable by a financially qualified next owner of the property, with the lender's approval and the payment of service fees.

To help consumers compare different ARMs, lenders must give anyone considering a specific ARM a uniform disclosure statement that lists and explains indexes, history of past interest rate changes, and other information. A method for calculating the highest possible payment is included. The disclosures must be furnished before the loan applicant has paid any nonrefundable application fee.

Current rates can be checked at *www.bankrate.com.*

FHA-Insured Loans

The FHA, which operates under HUD, does not lend money itself. Rather, it *insures mortgage loans made by approved lending institutions.* It does not insure the property, but it does insure the lender against loss. The common term **FHA loan,** then, refers to a loan that is not made by the agency but insured by it. Because the federal government insures the lending institution against loss, borrowers can place FHA mortgages with very low down payments. Information is available at *http://portal.hud.gov/hudportal/HUD?src=/federal_housing_administration.*

FHA 203(b) The most widely used FHA mortgage is known as 203(b) and may be placed on one- to four-family residences. The following are among the requirements set up by the FHA before it will insure a loan.

Owner/occupants The loan is available only to an owner/occupant, someone who intends to live in the property as a primary residence. (Investors may sometimes buy HUD foreclosures with 25 percent down.)

Mortgage insurance premium In addition to paying interest, the borrower is charged a lump sum of 1.5 percent of the loan as a **mortgage insurance premium (MIP).** This amount is payable in cash at the closing or may be financed for the term of the loan. If the loan is subsequently paid off within the early years of the loan, some refund of unused premium is due the borrower from HUD.

On FHA loans made since July 1991, borrowers are charged the initial lump-sum premium at closing and also 0.05 percent MIP (mortgage insurance premium) per month as interest for a number of years, depending on the size of the down payment. First-time homebuyers who complete a course in financial counseling are entitled to a small reduction in the size of their initial MIP.

For an FHA loan placed after 2000, the FHA will drop MIP payments when the principal balance has been reduced to 78 percent of original purchase price, but only after the first five years.

Estimate of value   The real estate must be evaluated by an FHA-approved appraiser. The maximum loan will be a percentage of the appraised value. If the purchase price is higher than the FHA appraisal, the buyer must pay the difference in a higher cash down payment or may decide not to purchase. On Section 203(b) loans, minimum down payment requirements are less than 3 percent. For really inexpensive houses (appraised at less than $50,000), the required down payment is 1.25 percent. This allows a loan-to-value ratio of 98.75 percent. On a house appraised at $40,000, the minimum down payment would be $500.

For houses appraised between $50,000 and $125,000, the LTV ratio is 97.75 percent. For houses valued at more than $125,000, it is 97.15 percent, and slightly higher in what are considered high-closing-cost areas.

FHA borrowers are allowed to finance a portion of their closing costs. The amount is added to the base loan amount. Sometimes the total amount borrowed may actually exceed the purchase price of the property.

The FHA sets top limits on its loans, which vary within the state. The highest levels in New York are set for areas in and around New York City, in parts of Long Island, and in Tioga County. The FHA raises its limits from time to time. For example, in 2006, the limits for single dwellings were at $200,160 in low-cost areas and more than $362,700 in high-cost counties. Since 2006, the FHA has temporarily increased their loan limits. The standard FHA single-family loan limit in 2010 for low-cost areas was at $271,050 with the high-cost area loan limit at $729,750. These limits became effective January 1, 2010 and were due to expire December 31, 2010. But FHA is maintaining these standards through September 30, 2011. Therefore, the standard FHA single-family loan limit is $271,050 for low-cost areas, and a loan limit of $729,750.00 for high-cost areas is in effect through the third quarter of 2011.

Repairs   The FHA requires its borrowers to be notified, before a purchase contract becomes binding, that its appraisers estimate value rather than condition in detail and that use of a home inspector is recommended. The FHA may, however, stipulate repair requirements that must be completed before it will issue mortgage insurance on a specific property. Certain energy-saving improvements may be financed along with an FHA mortgage.

Assumability   Older FHA loans may be assumed by the next owner of the property with no change in interest rate, no credit check on the buyer, and only a small charge for paperwork. The assumer could be a nonoccupant/investor. The original borrower is not released from liability, however, unless the new borrower is willing to go through a formal assumption, which involves the lender's approval of credit and income.

For FHA loans made after December 15, 1989, the buyer wishing to assume the mortgage must be a prospective owner/occupant and prove financial qualification; the original borrower is then relieved of liability. Optionally, the new borrower may pass a simple credit check and the property, a new appraisal, with the original borrower sharing joint liability for five years after the assumption.

Refinancing   The FHA offers a "streamline" refinancing for its loans, with minimal closing costs.

Other FHA programs   Among other FHA programs, which may or may not be handled by a particular local lender at any given time, are ARMs and special plans intended for veterans, for rehabilitation of housing being purchased, and for no-down-payment purchase of modest homes. Other FHA programs are sometimes available to finance mobile homes, manufactured housing, and condominiums. For first-time purchasers, the FHA offers special discounts for teachers, firefighters, and police officers buying HUD-foreclosed houses in "revitalization zones," and for first-time buyers who complete a course in financial management.

The program known as FHA 203(k) allows money to be borrowed to cover both the purchase and the rehabilitation of a house in need of substantial repair.

VA-Guaranteed Loans

The Department of Veterans Affairs (VA), formerly the Veterans Administration, can guarantee lending institutions against loss on mortgage loans to eligible veterans. Because the VA guarantees part of the loan, no down payment is required (though individual lenders may sometimes ask for a small down payment). The primary difference between FHA and VA programs is that the VA can loan an eligible borrower 100 percent financing. Even an FHA loan requires the borrower to make an initial investment/down payment. The VA has raised its maximum guarantee from time to time. It sets no limit on the amount borrowed, but in 2002, the guarantee was for up to $75,175. Currently, it is $104,250. It is used to guarantee the top 25 percent of the loan, so in practice, that amount could cover a loan of up to $417,000.

VA loans are intended only for owner-occupied property that is owned by veterans, or veterans and their spouses, and may be placed on one- to four-family residences. While the guarantee comes from the federal government, the loan is made by a local lending institution. The veteran pays a funding fee directly to the VA at closing. The amount of the funding fee depends on the size of the down payment:

- Nothing down or less than 5 percent: 2 percent
- Down payment between 5 and 10 percent: 1.5 percent
- Down payment of 10 percent or more: 1.25 percent
- Assumptions of VA loans: 0.5 percent

Those eligible through national guard/reservist service pay an extra 0.75 percent in funding fee.

Eligibility   The right to a VA guarantee does not expire. To qualify, a veteran must have a discharge that is "other than dishonorable" and the required length of service:

- For those in the national guard or the reserves, six years' service
- For those who enlisted before September 7, 1980, at least 90 days' continuous active service since September 16, 1940 (or 90 days' service during a war)
- For those who first enlisted after September 7, 1980, two years' active duty
- Reservists called up for at least 90 days during the Persian Gulf War, whether or not they went overseas

Veterans who apply for a VA loan must furnish a certificate of eligibility, which can be obtained by writing to

VA Regional Office   VA Regional Office
Federal Building   252 Seventh Avenue
111 West Huron Street or New York, NY 10001
Buffalo, NY 14202   800-827-8954
800-827-0619

Information is available at *www.benefits.va.gov/homeloans/*.

Veterans who have used some or all of their eligibility to guarantee one loan sometimes can place another VA mortgage. Eligibility may still be available if

- the first loan used only part of the guarantee,
- the original VA loan has been paid off and the home sold,
- the original VA loan was formally assumed by another veteran, or
- the applicant is the widow or widower of a veteran who died of a service-connected disability and has not remarried.

Qualified veterans' home loan entitlement will be restored one time only if the veteran has repaid the prior VA loan in full but has not disposed of the property securing that loan. If veterans wish to use their VA entitlement again, they must dispose of all property previously financed with a VA loan, including the property not disposed of under the "one time only" provision.

Assumability   Any VA mortgage loan made before March 1, 1988, may be assumed by the next owner of the property, who need not be a veteran and need not prove qualification to the lender or the VA. For loans made after March 1, 1988, the assumer (who need not be a veteran) must prove creditworthiness, and the original borrower is free of future liability.

Refinancing   VA loans may be refinanced with a streamline process for a fee of 0.5 percent.

Government Backing via the Secondary Market

Lenders in the primary mortgage market originate loans directly to borrowers. Some keep the loans in their own portfolios. Other primary lenders may sell packages of loans to large investors in what is known as the **secondary mortgage market**. This is how money continues to circulate through the system, thereby making borrowed funds available to qualified borrowers. A lender may wish to sell a number of loans when it needs more money to meet the mortgage demands in its area. The federal government is active in the secondary mortgage market.

A major source of secondary mortgage market activity is warehousing agencies, which purchase mortgage loans and assemble them into large packages of loans for resale to investors such as insurance companies and pension funds. The major warehousing agencies are Fannie Mae (formerly the Federal National Mortgage Association [FNMA]); Ginnie Mae (formerly the Government National Mortgage Association [GNMA]); and Freddie Mac (formerly the Federal Home Loan Mortgage Corporation [FHLMC]).

Fannie Mae Fannie Mae (FNMA) is (despite its name) a privately owned corporation. It raises funds to purchase loans by selling government-guaranteed FNMA bonds. Originally, FNMA started out as a governmental agency. When it became private, Ginnie Mae (GNMA) was created to fill its shoes. GNMA will be discussed next.

Mortgage bankers are actively involved with FNMA, originating loans and selling them to FNMA while retaining the servicing functions. FNMA is the nation's largest purchaser of mortgages.

When Fannie Mae talks, lenders listen. Because FNMA eventually purchases one mortgage out of every ten, it has great influence on lending policies. When Fannie Mae announces that it will buy a certain type of loan, local lending institutions often change their own regulations to meet the requirements. When lenders are experimenting with new types of loans, a Fannie Mae announcement can standardize the innovative mortgage plans and bring order out of chaos.

Ginnie Mae Ginnie Mae (GNMA) was formerly called the Government National Mortgage Association. The Ginnie Mae pass-through certificate lets small investors buy a share in a pool of mortgages that provides for a monthly "pass-through" of principal and interest payments directly to the certificate holder.

Freddie Mac Freddie Mac (FHLMC) also provides a secondary market for mortgage loans. Freddie Mac buys mortgages, pools them, and sells bonds with the mortgages as security.

Most lenders use a standardized mortgage application and other forms that are accepted by Freddie Mac and Fannie Mae.

Nonconforming loans When Fannie Mae and Freddie Mac announce that they will buy loans only up to a certain size ($417,000 for one-family homes), many local lenders set that as their own limit. Loans higher than Fannie Mae's or Freddie Mac's maximum loan limit are known as *nonconforming loans* or **jumbo loans**. The borrower who wants to place one would search for a local lending institution that either sells jumbo mortgages to private investors or makes portfolio loans, lending its own money and taking mortgages it intends to keep and collect. A jumbo loan usually carries a slightly higher rate of interest.

Nonconforming mortgages (portfolio loans) do not have to meet uniform under-writing standards and can be flexible in their guidelines. The borrower with an unusual credit situation or a unique house may need a nonconforming loan. A lending institution may want such loans at one time but not at other times. Following the rapidly changing mortgage market is often the greatest part of a real estate broker's work.

FINANCING LEGISLATION

The federal government regulates the lending practices of mortgage lenders through the Truth in Lending Act, Equal Credit Opportunity Act (ECOA), and Real Estate Settlement Procedures Act (RESPA).

Regulation Z

The Truth in Lending Act, enforced through Regulation Z (that is, the Truth in Lending Act as it applies to the advertisement of credit terms), requires that credit institutions inform the borrower of the true cost of obtaining credit so the borrower can compare the costs of various lenders and avoid the uninformed use of credit. All real estate transactions made for personal or agricultural purposes are covered. The regulation does not apply to business or commercial loans.

Regulation Z requires that the customer be fully informed of all finance charges, as well as the true annual interest rate, before a transaction is consummated. In the case of a mortgage loan made to finance the purchase of a dwelling, the lender must compute and disclose the annual percentage rate (APR) in a written truth-in-lending statement provided to the mortgagor.

Three-day right of rescission   In the case of most consumer credit transactions covered by Regulation Z, the borrower has three days in which to rescind (cancel) the transaction merely by notifying the lender. This right of rescission does not apply to residential purchase-money first mortgage loans but does apply to refinances. Lenders sometimes close on the loan but withhold the actual check until they are sure the borrower will not rescind. In situations where the money is needed immediately, borrowers may avoid the three-day wait by waiving their right to rescind.

Advertising   Regulation Z provides strict regulation of real estate advertisements that include mortgage financing terms. General phrases like "liberal terms available" may be used, but if specifics are given, they must comply with this act. The APR, which includes all charges rather than the interest rate alone, must be stated.

Specific credit terms, known as *triggering terms*—such as the down payment, monthly payment, dollar amount of the finance charge, or term of the loan—may not be advertised unless the following information is set forth as well: cash price; required down payment; number, amounts, and due dates of all payments; and APR. The total of all payments to be made over the term of the mortgage must also be specified unless the advertised credit refers to a first mortgage to finance acquisition of a dwelling. The expression "low down payment" would not be a triggering term.

Penalties   Regulation Z provides substantial penalties for noncompliance, ranging from a fine of $5,000 to $10,000 for each day the misleading advertising continues to a year's imprisonment. Licensees are cautioned and advised not to violate any of the provisions of Regulation Z.

Federal Equal Credit Opportunity Act

The federal **Equal Credit Opportunity Act (ECOA)** prohibits lenders and others who grant or arrange credit to consumers from discriminating against credit applicants on the basis of race, color, religion, national origin, sex, marital status, age (provided the applicant is of legal age), or dependence on public assistance. Lenders must inform all rejected credit applicants in writing of the principal reasons why credit was denied or terminated.

The National Affordable Housing Act requires that borrowers be presented with a statement of their rights if their loan servicing (the process by which a mortgage bank or subservicing firm collects the installment payment of interest and principal due from the borrower) is transferred. The borrower must be notified at least 15 days before the date of transfer and provided with a toll-free or collect-call phone number of the new servicer. Servicers are also required to acknowledge borrowers' inquiries within 20 days and act on them within 60 days.

■ LENDER'S CRITERIA FOR GRANTING A LOAN

Lender's Criteria for Granting a Loan
- Evaluating the property
- Evaluating the borrower
- Qualifying ratio

All mortgage lenders require that prospective borrowers file an application for credit that provides the lender with basic information. A prospective borrower must submit personal information including age, family status, employment, earnings, assets, and financial obligations. Details of the real estate that will be the security for the loan also must be provided, including legal description, improvements, and taxes. For loans on income property or those made to corporations, additional information is required, such as financial and operating statements, schedules of leases and tenants, and balance sheets. Self-employed applicants will be asked to show two years' income tax returns. Anyone employed by a family member will be asked to show a current pay stub and the most recent tax return.

Evaluating the Property

The value of the property is an important element of the lender's underwriting process. The amount of the loan is based on the sales price of the property or appraised value, whichever is less. The lender then applies its LTV ratio to this figure. For example, suppose the property's sales price is $150,000, its appraised value is $152,000, and the buyer is applying for a 90 percent loan (which means making a 10 percent down payment). To determine the maximum loan amount, the lender would multiply $150,000 (the lesser of the sales price and appraised value) by 90 percent. The maximum loan amount would be $135,000. (The borrower would have to make a $15,000 down payment.)

To determine the appraised value of the property, the lender will order that an appraisal be performed. When valuing the property, the appraiser will take into consideration such elements as the property's location, its size and square footage, the number of bedrooms and bathrooms, the size of the lot, and the condition of the property. If the property is a condominium or cooperative unit, the appraiser also will look at the project as a whole and examine the condominium declarations and bylaws filed with the attorney general or the cooperative's proprietary lease and bylaws. Appraisal is discussed in Chapter 16.

The lender is concerned about the value of the property because if the borrower defaults on the loan, the lender will have the property sold through a foreclosure process and use the proceeds of the sale to pay off the mortgage debt.

Evaluating the Potential Borrower

Because a credit report will be part of the application process, homebuyers are well advised to check their own reports early in the homebuying process to allow time for clearing up any errors. The three main reporting agencies are

- Equifax: 800-685-1111, *www.equifax.com;*
- Experian (formerly TRW): 800-682-7654, *www.experian.com;* and
- TransUnion: 800-916-8800, *www.transunion.com.*

Each of the three major reporting agencies is required to furnish one free credit report a year to anyone requesting it. With careful spacing, credit can be checked every four months. The report can be ordered on the Web site *www.annualcreditreport.com* or by phone at 888-322-8228. Some personal credit information will be requested for identification purposes, so it is important to contact only the exact site and not similar ones that have sprung up to take advantage of unwary borrowers.

Of course, a lender would much rather have its borrowers pay off their mortgage loans as agreed. If the applicant does not appear financially able to handle the mortgage payments comfortably or if the applicant's continued employment is doubtful, the loan application may be rejected. In recent years, however, some lenders offer special programs, perhaps at higher interest rates, to applicants with less-than-perfect credit scores. The Fannie Mae Foundation (800-605-5200; in Spanish, 800-916-8000) offers free pamphlets on understanding, evaluating, and repairing credit history.

Lenders like to see a reasonably stable income history, with at least two years' continuous employment or employment in the same line of work. Bonuses, commissions, and seasonal and part-time income are considered with certain time limits and employer verifications. Dividend and interest income, Social Security income, and pension income are included in qualifying the borrower. Projected rental income is accepted in varying amounts (for example, 50 percent on VA applications, 95 percent toward FHA qualification, 75 percent of actual cash flow with conventional loans). Unrelated co-borrowers may pool their incomes to qualify, just as a married couple might.

If the borrowers' income is marginal, the lender may look at their education and training to determine whether the borrowers' skills are in demand in the employment marketplace and whether their income is likely to increase in the future.

In judging whether a borrower qualifies to carry the requested loan, lenders analyze the present debts, including any with more than six months (VA and FHA) or ten months (conventional) to run. Lenders sometimes consider potential, as well as actual, balances on credit cards.

Borrowers usually must show that they have liquid assets amounting to the cash that will be required at closing without further borrowing. Some mortgage programs, however, allow a willing seller to pay part of the buyer's closing costs (*seller concessions*). A credit report also will be ordered on the applicant. An applicant who has gone through a bankruptcy may have to wait between one and five years after discharge, depending on the type of loan desired, and show good credit history since the bankruptcy.

Through the process known as **underwriting**, the lender analyzes the application information. Verification forms are sent to the applicant's employers, financial institutions, and lenders. These forms are returned to the lender and examined to make sure the information on the loan application is correct. The lender also studies the credit reports and the appraisal of the property before deciding whether to grant the loan.

Today, when computers analyze borrowers' qualifications, one numeric score summarizing credit history is useful. The widely used FICO score ranges from 300 to 850, with most people scoring in the 600s and 700s. A score of 750 might bring the offer of a low interest rate; below 620, it could be difficult to mortgage property at all.

FICO analyzes the subject's payment (on-time) record for 35 percent of the score. Current borrowing and credit limits account for 30 percent. Length of credit history (longer is better) makes up 15 percent, and the rest evaluates types of credit used, number of recent accounts, credit cards, installment loans, and the like.

Most mortgage lenders will ignore a bankruptcy when four years have passed since the discharge (not the filing).

The lender's acceptance is written in the form of a loan commitment, which creates a contract to make a loan and sets forth the details. This loan commitment must be signed by the borrower and returned to the lender within a specific time period.

Preapproval   Borrowers can go through the mortgage application process before they start house-hunting. Application and credit report fees are due, but the result can be a lender's statement that the applicant is qualified to borrow up to a certain maximum amount (subject, of course, to the adequate appraised value of the house that will eventually be offered as security). The buyer with mortgage preapproval is particularly welcome to sellers and may be in a stronger bargaining position.

Predatory lending   A few lenders have been known to make mortgage loans to unqualified borrowers regardless of repayment ability. Such loans often end with the property lost in foreclosure.

Predatory loans are usually at high rates of interest and carry large closing costs. Predatory lenders often urge borrowers to refinance again and again (flipping) to clear past debt, each time increasing the financial burden.

New York State has enacted laws against predatory lending, defined as loans at an interest rate eight or more percentage points over the yield on comparable Treasury notes. Predatory closing costs are defined as anything over 5 percent of the amount being borrowed. The law also addresses the problems of unreasonable balloon payment arrangements.

Subprime loans   Lending practices over recent years have led to a financial credit market crisis. This crisis has been termed by government and the media as the "subprime" loan crisis. In 2007, news began to surface about lending practices targeted to less-than-qualified borrowers because of an unprecedented rise in non-performing loans and foreclosures. Some of this practice involved adjustable-rate mortgages (discussed earlier in this chapter) that were due for rate adjustments. Other loans consisted of hidden fees, high interest rates, and closing costs. In many cases (currently under investigation by federal authorities), loans were originated with "money back at closing" to a buyer (also known as seller concessions). At closing, the buyer paid substantial portions of the money received to vendors involved in the transaction. Payment was made in the form of fees. These practices have led to federal investigations concerning potential banking fraud.

Qualifying Ratios

Housing expense ratio and total monthly obligations ratio   With each mortgage plan offered, the lender has certain qualifying ratios that will be applied to each borrower. A typical ratio for a conventional loan if the buyer has only moderately good credit is 28/36; the borrower will be allowed to spend up to 28 percent of gross monthly income for housing expenses (PITI—principal, interest, taxes, and insurance) and up to 36 percent of income for both housing expenses and other payments on long-term debts. The applicant must qualify under both ratios before the loan will be approved.

For example, suppose a prospective buyer earns $3,000 a month. She pays $350 a month on long-term debts, including a car loan and credit card balances. If a lender applies the qualifying ratios to her income, the results will be as follows:

- 28 percent of $3,000 is $840. This is the maximum monthly payment for the loan amount she will qualify for under the housing expense-to-income ratio.
- 36 percent of $3,000 is $1,080; $1,080 minus $350 (monthly long-term payments) equals $730. This is the maximum monthly payment for the loan amount she will qualify for under the total expenses-to-income ratio.

Because a borrower must qualify under both ratios, the highest monthly loan payment this borrower would qualify for is $730.

Other loan programs can have different ratios. For example, to qualify for an FHA loan, applicants can spend no more than 31 percent of their gross monthly income on housing expenses and no more than 43 percent of their gross monthly income on both housing expenses and payments on long-term debts. Before relaxing these qualifying ratios, FHA had prescribed a 29 percent housing expense ratio and a 41 percent total monthly obligations ratio.

To qualify for a VA loan, applicants must spend no more than 41 percent of their gross income on both housing expenses and long-term debt payments and must also meet the VA's cash flow guidelines (called residual income requirements). Ratio requirements can be changed from time to time.

■ SUMMARY

Mortgage loans include conventional loans, those insured by the FHA or an independent mortgage insurance company, those guaranteed by the VA, and loans from private lenders. Lenders may charge discount points; each point is 1 percent of the new mortgage. FHA and VA mortgages are generally assumable, with some exceptions and regulations.

Other types of real estate financing include purchase-money mortgages, buydowns, graduated-payment loans, shared-equity loans, reverse-annuity mortgages, blanket mortgages, package mortgages, open-end mortgages, wraparound mortgages, construction loans, sale-and-leaseback agreements, and land contracts.

Adjustable-rate mortgages are those under which the interest rate is changed each adjustment period to a stipulated margin above a national index of current mortgage rates. A cap may limit the size of possible adjustments, and a ceiling may limit the adjustment over the life of the loan. In instances where monthly payments do not cover the interest due, negative amortization is possible, with the total debt increasing instead of decreasing.

The federal government affects real estate financing by participating in the secondary mortgage market. The secondary market is composed of investors who purchase and hold the loans as investments. Fannie Mae (Federal National Mortgage Association), Ginnie Mae (Government National Mortgage Association), and Freddie Mac (Federal Home Loan Mortgage Corporation) take an active role in creating a secondary market by regularly purchasing mortgage loans from originators and retaining, or warehousing, them until investment purchasers are available.

Regulation Z, the federal Truth in Lending Act, requires that institutional lenders inform borrowers of all finance charges involved. Severe penalties are imposed for noncompliance. The federal Equal Credit Opportunity Act prohibits creditors from discriminating against credit applicants on the basis of race, color, religion, national origin, sex, marital status, age, or dependence on public assistance. The Real Estate Settlement Procedures Act (RESPA) requires that lenders inform both buyers and sellers in advance of all fees for the settlement of a residential mortgage loan.

When evaluating the borrowers' income, lenders typically use two ratios: the borrowers may not spend more than a certain amount (for example, 28 percent) of their gross monthly income on housing expenses or more than a certain amount (for example, 36 percent) of their gross monthly income on both housing expenses and other long-term debt payments.

CHAPTER 11 QUIZ

1. Private mortgage insurance (PMI) is usually required whenever the
   a. loan is to be placed with the FHA.
   b. property covers more than 2.5 acres.
   c. loan exceeds $67,500.
   d. conventional LTV ratio exceeds 80 percent.

2. The Department of Housing and Urban Development insures mortgage loans made through
   a. the FHA.
   b. the VA.
   c. Fannie Mae.
   d. Freddie Mac.

3. A couple wants to buy a home together. A mortgage application is likely to be denied, though, if they
   a. are not married.
   b. are self-employed.
   c. have low credit scores because of late credit card payments.
   d. have less than a 10 percent down payment.

4. The terms *index*, *margin*, and *cap* are used in evaluating what type of mortgage?
   a. Package
   b. Blanket
   c. Conventional
   d. Adjustable-rate

5. Negative amortization refers to a situation in which the
   a. debt is gradually reduced through monthly payments.
   b. debt grows larger instead of smaller each month.
   c. regular adjustments reduce the interest rate.
   d. interest rate may rise or fall according to an index.

6. A couple is purchasing a lakefront summer home in a new resort development. The house is completely equipped and furnished, and they have obtained a loan that covers all the personal as well as the real property. This kind of financing is called a(n)
   a. wraparound mortgage.
   b. package mortgage.
   c. blanket mortgage.
   d. unconventional loan.

7. A developer obtains one mortgage for a whole subdivision. As he sells each lot, he obtains a release of one parcel from the
   a. package mortgage.
   b. reverse mortgage.
   c. balloon mortgage.
   d. blanket mortgage.

8. A company has sold a local factory but intends to remain and rent it from the new owner. The new owner has put together a
   a. participation transaction.
   b. sale-and-leaseback.
   c. secondary market.
   d. reserve for escrow.

9. A savings and loan institution offers a mortgage plan with an 80 percent LTV ratio. On the purchase of a property appraised at $150,000, how much down payment will be required?
   a. $12,000
   b. $20,000
   c. $30,000
   d. $120,000

10. Fannie Mae's purpose is to
    a. insure loans.
    b. buy loans.
    c. make loans.
    d. service loans.

11. Regulation Z protects the consumer from
    a. misleading advertising of credit terms.
    b. fraudulent mortgage plans.
    c. discrimination in lending.
    d. substandard housing.

12. Fannie Mae is
    a. the leading purchaser of mortgages on the secondary market.
    b. a lender for homes in rural areas.
    c. a government agency that regulates interest rates.
    d. a government agency that regulates commercial banks.

13. Borrowers often use open-end mortgages to
    a. purchase vacant property.
    b. avoid upward rate adjustments.
    c. finance home improvements.
    d. temporarily pay for two homes.

14. Why is a wraparound mortgage ALWAYS in the second-lien position?
    a. Funds from a wraparound can only be used for home improvement.
    b. Wraparounds are always personal loans.
    c. The loan amount on wraparounds is capped at $50,000.
    d. The first mortgage is retained.

15. In what way does the IRS become involved in purchase-money mortgages?
    a. The IRS limits purchase-money mortgage amounts to $100,000.
    b. Buyers using seller financing receive favorable tax write-offs.
    c. Sellers offering purchase-money mortgages receive special tax exemptions.
    d. The IRS monitors the interest rate charged by the seller.

16. With which mortgage would negative amortization MOST likely occur?
    a. FHA-insured
    b. Interest-only
    c. Purchase-money
    d. Adjustable-rate

17. Unlike nonconventional loans, conventional loans are
    a. either insured or guaranteed by a government agency.
    b. arranged entirely between the borrower and lending institution.
    c. fixed-rate loans.
    d. open-end loans.

18. Unlike FHA loans, VA loans
    a. can provide 100 percent financing.
    b. require no interest for the first year.
    c. can be made on investment property.
    d. are made directly by the government.

19. Analysis of a mortgage loan application occurs in a process called
    a. loan servicing.
    b. documentation.
    c. underwriting.
    d. commitment.

20. The mathematical formula that lenders use to consider an applicant's potential monthly payment compared to the applicant's income is called a(n)
    a. index.
    b. qualifying ratio.
    c. margin.
    d. credit score.

CHAPTER 12

Mortgage Brokerage

■ KEY TERMS

fee agreement	mortgage commitment	preapproval loan
lender's rebate	nonconforming loan	prequalification
mortgage banker	preapplication	rate lock
mortgage broker	preapproval	underwriting

■ WHAT IS A MORTGAGE BROKER?

In residential and commercial real estate brokerage, a transactional broker deals primarily with arranging terms of a purchase or lease transaction. A **mortgage broker**, on the other hand, is an individual or entity that is registered by the New York State Banking Department with the ability to place, negotiate, solicit, and process residential or commercial mortgage loans. These services are performed for a fee. The fee may be paid by the borrower or the lender.

The mortgage broker will assist borrowers in obtaining financing necessary to conclude their transactions. Mortgage brokers will arrange financing in the following types of real property transactions:

- Acquisition
- Gut renovation
- Conversion
- Construction/development
- Refinancing of an existing mortgage on owned property

Loan financing will fall into two primary categories of debt: debt financing and equity financing.

■ MORTGAGE BROKER VERSUS MORTGAGE BANKER

A *mortgage broker* is an individual or entity that is registered by the New York State Banking Department with the ability to place, negotiate, solicit, and process residential mortgage loans. Mortgage brokers charge fees based on **fee agreements**, usually consisting of a percentage of the borrowed amount or a flat fee. In a lending transaction, a *fee agreement* is a compensation agreement that a borrower will enter into with a mortgage broker. In exchange, the mortgage broker assists the borrower in the placement and origination of funds with a lender. The fee agreement normally occurs simultaneously to that of the **preapplication** process (preapproval of the borrower). They introduce and arrange financing (for qualified borrowers seeking financing) with willing lenders and also handle the necessary loan application process.

A **mortgage banker** is an individual or entity that is licensed by the New York State Banking Department with the ability to originate a loan to a qualified borrower or borrowers.

Mortgage bankers utilize their own funds, generally comprised of borrowed funds, to originate loans. Financing may be in the form of either short-term or long-term loans. Once the loans are originated, mortgage bankers will immediately look to sell them to investors.

In order to qualify for mortgage banker licensing, an individual or entity must have

- a net worth of not less than $250,000;
- an open line of credit of not less than $1,000,000 provided by an insurance company or institutional bank;
- posting of a surety bond in an amount no less than $50,000;
- five previous years' experience in the business of originating residential loans;
- an honest and trustworthy character; and
- a current fingerprint card on file with the banking department in order to conduct a background check.

The license is issued with a one-year term for a fee of $1,000 per term.

When financing is funded on a long-term basis, these loans are subsequently sold to investors (in many cases, insurance companies) that purchase these types of loans.

FIGURE 12.1

Mortgage Broker Versus Mortgage Banker

Mortgage broker

- Is registered by the New York State Banking Department with the ability to place, negotiate, solicit, and process residential or commercial mortgage loan
- Assists borrowers in obtaining financing necessary to conclude their transactions

Mortgage banker

- Is licensed by the New York State Banking Department with the ability to *originate* a loan to a qualified borrower or borrowers
- Utilizes own funding, generally comprised of borrowed funds, to originate loans

■ TYPES OF FINANCING

Debt Financing

Debt financing is the most common form of borrowed funds. The debt placed on the property is combined with the borrower's down payment (or initial investment, as it is sometimes called) to equal the purchase price required by the sale. The loan would comprise two components: *borrowed* funds (loan amount) and *borrower* funds (down payment).

Types of Financing

■ Debt financing
■ Equity (or mezzanine) financing

In traditional residential transactions (the sale or rental of a property containing four or fewer units intended for dwelling purposes), the maximum debt financing ratios would break down as follows: 80 percent on borrowed funds and a 20 percent borrower-funded down payment.

There are programs that provide for greater than 80 percent debt financing. However, in these transactions, the borrower is required to purchase private mortgage insurance (PMI).

Equity Financing (Mezzanine Financing)

When borrowing occurs on real property, the lender will originate the loan amount as either the purchase price or the appraised value, whichever is less.

On large commercial development or acquisition transactions, there are times when the borrower may have insufficient funds to fulfill down-payment requirements. In these situations, the borrower may seek equity financing to narrow the gap.

Equity financing, or mezzanine financing, is the use of borrowed funds to help the borrower fulfill down-payment requirements.

The need to borrow funds to satisfy the down-payment requirement most often occurs as a result of one of two circumstances: (1) outright shortage of funds required to meet down-payment requirements or (2) a property's appraised value at the time financing is sought falls short of the borrower's anticipated value amount or purchase price. (This usually occurs when premiums are paid on purchase prices that are not supported by either income or comparable sales.)

Let's look at an example of how the second scenario may occur: A buyer is in contract to purchase an office building for $10,000,000. The lender is prepared to offer debt financing using the following loan-to-value ratio: 70 percent borrowed funds to 30 percent borrower funds, so at the time of loan application, the borrower has expectations that the loaned amount will equal $7,000,000 and the down payment will equal $3,000,000.

The property is subsequently appraised by the lender for $9,000,000. Using the above loan ratios, this means that the lender will originate a maximum debt financing loan amount of $6,300,000 ($9,000,000 × 0.70 = $6,300,000).

As a result, the borrower is now expected to fund the difference of $3,700,000 ($10,000,000 − $6,300,000 = $3,700,000). If the borrower does not have the additional $700,000, the borrower would have to raise that money through other sources. Many commercial lenders traditionally restrict borrowers from placing second mortgages on property on which they hold a first lien, so the borrower would be forced to seek equity or mezzanine financing to solve this dilemma.

Note: The aforementioned does not apply to the financing of a residential transaction (a transaction involving a property containing four or fewer units intended for dwelling purposes). Residential loan programs provide for higher loan-to-value ratios than commercial transactions.

■ THE ROLE OF A MORTGAGE BROKER IN A REAL ESTATE TRANSACTION

The purpose and role of the mortgage broker is to obtain a **mortgage commitment** by which a lender issues a loan commitment letter to the borrower to demonstrate willingness to fund the loan.

Generally, these loans tend to be **nonconforming loans**. As you learned in the previous chapter, a *nonconforming loan* is any loan that does not conform to or meet the requirements for purchase on the secondary market by either Fannie Mae or Freddie Mac. In addition, the role of the mortgage broker includes the following activities:

■ Analyzing the financial capability of the borrower for the purpose of determining **preapproval** or preapproved status (which allows the mortgage broker to determine the creditworthiness and ability to repay on the part of the borrower and the likelihood of the borrower's ability to originate a loan with a lender). A **preapproval loan** is a pending loan in which all of the underlying documents are on file and there is a strong probability that there are no credit or income issues stopping the loan from closing. It does not necessarily mean that the file has been underwritten by the lender that will commit to provide the funds for closing. **Prequalification** refers to a pending loan in which a mortgage broker believes that, based on a preliminary interview and a credit report, the borrowers will probably (subject to verification) be able to meet the loan requirements of a lender—assuming the borrowers are telling the truth about their financial situation and income status.

■ Preparation, handling, and submission of the *preapplication* loan papers (which aids the mortgage broker in arriving at a determination of preapproved status). The fee agreement normally occurs simultaneously to that of the preapplication process (preapproval of the borrower).

■ Shopping the borrower to all interested lenders

■ Filling out and submitting all loan applications

■ Assisting the borrower in accumulating the necessary paperwork (see below) for the lender to *underwrite* the loan (**Underwriting** is the evaluation process of insuring and verifying all borrower information necessary for the lender to issue a commitment)

■ Obtaining, analyzing, and communicating to the borrowers the terms associated with offers to lend from the various lenders under consideration, including any lender rebate. A **lender's rebate** (usually the amount a mortgage broker is compensated) is a partial refund following a purchase that involves a loan.

■ Carefully and accurately explaining the differences between loans and their associated payment options, such as a fixed-rate loan versus a variable-rate loan, an amortized loan versus an interest-only loan, and a short-term versus a long-term loan, including but not limited to any rate locks. A **rate lock** is a promise on the part of a lender that the mortgage loan will carry a specific interest rate, regardless of the prevailing rates when the loan is closed.

■ Bringing the entire matter to conclusion if all goes well

The paperwork lenders require to underwrite a loan includes at least two years of previous tax returns of the individual or entity borrowing the money and a personal financial statement indicating the borrower's net worth and listing assets and liabilities. If it is rental income-producing property, a reconstructed operating statement outlining income and expenses and all leases supporting the income must be shown to the lender. (In order for the borrower to certify the rent roll/income to the property, the lender may require estoppel certificates from the tenants.)

■ REQUIREMENTS AND RESPONSIBILITIES OF A MORTGAGE BROKER

Unlike mortgage bankers that originate and service loans as their business, mortgage brokers introduce lenders and borrowers to each other for a fee.

In order to become licensed as a mortgage broker, the individual or entity must

■ register with the New York State Banking Department;
■ have no less than two years' previous experience in the analysis of credit;
■ have underwriting education or experience (Licensed real estate brokers and attorneys need not show experience or education; however, licensed salespersons must have two years' prior experience in the business of residential mortgages.);
■ supply credit reports; and
■ supply fingerprints for background checks.

The license is for one year and is renewable; the fee for the license is $500.

■ DUAL AGENCY DISCLOSURE UNDER THE BANKING LAW

When a mortgage broker is also a real estate licensee, the potential for dual agency exists as well.

For example, a buyer asks the listing agent, who represents the seller in a transaction, if the agent could arrange financing for the purchase of that property. By accepting this role, the listing agent would be entering into a dual agent relationship.

We have already learned that prior to the creation of any dual agency two elements must exist: (1) the agent must give full disclosure to all interested parties to the transaction prior to the creation of the dual agency, and (2) the agent must subsequently receive the informed consent of all interested parties to the transaction.

■ SUMMARY

Mortgage brokers play a very key role in the active housing and commercial real estate markets. Not every buyer of real property or borrower of money has the time, knowledge, or patience to pursue this on their own. Mortgage bankers provide funding as options to conventional and unconventional lending practices. Both are regulated by the New York State Banking Department and, as such, are under close scrutiny. The business of mortgage brokering can be extremely lucrative. Regardless of whether a licensee engages in this practice, it is imperative to understand the role and importance of mortgage brokers.

CHAPTER 12 QUIZ

1. A registered mortgage broker in New York is able to place, negotiate, solicit, and
   a. foreclose mortgage loans.
   b. close mortgage loans.
   c. originate mortgage loans.
   d. process mortgage loans.

2. What are the two categories of mortgage loan financing?
   a. Debt financing and secondary financing
   b. Debt financing and equity financing
   c. Equity financing and mezzanine financing
   d. Equity financing and conventional financing

3. In traditional residential mortgage lending, what percent of the purchase price must be provided as a down payment?
   a. 10 percent
   b. 15 percent
   c. 20 percent
   d. 25 percent

4. Equity financing is the use of borrowed funds to help the borrower
   a. carry two mortgage loans before a home sale closes.
   b. finance home improvement projects.
   c. meet rising payments due to interest adjustments.
   d. fulfill down payment requirements.

5. Unlike a mortgage *broker*, a mortgage *banker*
   a. originates loans.
   b. negotiates loans.
   c. guarantees loans.
   d. insures loans.

6. Which is a qualification for mortgage banker licensing?
   a. Five years' residency in New York
   b. Five years' experience as a real estate salesperson
   c. Net worth of not less than $250,000
   d. Master's degree in banking or finance

7. A lender's willingness to fund a loan is known as a
   a. preapproval.
   b. promise to close.
   c. loan guarantee.
   d. mortgage commitment.

8. How many years of previous tax returns do lenders require of loan applicants when underwriting loans?
   a. One
   b. Two
   c. Three
   d. Four

9. Which property would MOST likely involve mezzanine financing?
   a. Regional shopping center
   b. A couple's vacation home
   c. Six-unit apartment building for senior citizens
   d. Residential home for disabled students

10. A mortgage broker determines a prospective borrower's creditworthiness and ability to repay a loan in a process called
    a. processing.
    b. underwriting.
    c. preapproval.
    d. certification.

CHAPTER 13

Land-Use Regulations

■ KEY TERMS

abutting	demography	police power
accessory (apartment) uses	development rights	restrictive covenant
ad valorem taxes	direct public ownership	SARA
assessed value	eminent domain	setbacks
building codes	escheat	special assessments
building permits	family units	special-use permit
census tract	group home	spot zoning
CERCLA	home occupations	subdivision regulations
certificate of occupancy (C of O)	infrastructure	taking
cluster zoning	laches	taxation
condemnation	lead agency	temporary certificate of occupancy (TCO)
cul-de-sac	master plan	variance
deed restriction	moratorium	zoning boards of appeal
	nonconforming use	zoning ordinances
	OPRHP	

■ PLANNING FOR THE FUTURE

While private property owners generally own the complete bundle of rights—that is, the rights to use, sell, lease, and improve their property—governments on all levels also have an interest in private property. It is in the government's interest to make sure that property owners do not use their property in such as way as to harm the public at large. For instance, property owners may not use their property to unduly pollute the air or water; to create a nuisance for neighbors; or to substantially decrease the value of a neighbor's property (such as by operating a factory within a residential neighborhood). The government protects its interest in the use of private property through broad land-use regulations, which range from zoning to environmental protection laws.

PRIVATE LAND-USE CONTROLS

The government is not the only entity that can regulate land use. Individual property owners and subdivision developers can restrict the uses to which land can be put. An individual seller or donor can set **deed restrictions**—for example, giving property to a grandchild with the restriction that no intoxicating liquors ever be served on the premises. The restriction would be binding on future owners as well. The restriction is set by including a restrictive covenant in the deed. In the past, deed restrictions might have forbidden any future sale of the property to a member of a particular religious or ethnic group. Today such restrictions are in violation of human rights laws and are not enforceable. Neither are restrictions that forbid owners from selling or mortgaging in the future.

A subdivider may establish restrictions on the right to use land through a **restrictive covenant** in a deed or by a separate recorded declaration. These restrictions are usually considered valid if they are reasonable and for the benefit of neighboring owners. They are binding on all future buyers in that subdivision.

Such restrictions usually relate to

- type of building;
- use to which the land may be put; and
- type of construction, to include height, setbacks, square footage, and cost.

"No dwelling of less than 2,000 square feet ever to be constructed in this subdivision" is an example. For example, some restrictions have a *time limitation*, "effective for a period of 25 years from this date."

Where a deed restriction and a zoning provision cover the same subject, *the more restrictive restriction will prevail.* (Zoning ordinances set forth and create restrictions as to permitted uses within the various classifications of zoning.) If deed restrictions say lots in a subdivision must measure at least two acres but the town allows half-acre lots, the two-acre restriction can be enforced by neighbors.

Enforcement of Deed Restrictions

Each lot owner has the right to apply to the court for an injunction to prevent a neighboring owner from violating the recorded restrictions. If granted, the court *injunction* will direct the violator to stop the violation or be in contempt of court. If neighbors stand idly by while a violation is being committed, they can lose the right through the doctrine governing **laches**; that is, loss of a right through undue delay or failure to assert it in time. In New York, neighboring owners have a two-year statute of limitations from the completion of the alteration or construction for objecting to violations of the general plan (type of building, height, setbacks).

■ GOVERNMENT POWERS

Government powers include the following:

- ■ *Taxation.* **Taxation** is a charge on real estate to raise funds to pay for government services.
- ■ *Police power.* **Police power** is the government's power to preserve order, protect the public health and safety, and promote the general welfare. It involves more than simply police protection. In the field of real estate, the use and enjoyment of property is subject to restrictions, including environmental protection laws, and zoning and building ordinances regulating the use, occupancy, size, location, construction, and rental of real estate.
- ■ *Eminent domain.* Through a **condemnation** suit a government may exercise **eminent domain** to acquire privately owned real estate for public use. *Eminent domain* is the right of government to take the property of a private individual, while *condemnation* is the process by which the taking is accomplished by the municipality.

For this to occur, three primary conditions must be met:

1. The proposed use must be declared by the court to be a public use.
2. Just compensation must be paid to the owner.
3. The rights of the owner must be protected by due process of law.

Condemnation proceedings are instituted only when the owner's consent cannot be obtained. Otherwise, public agencies acquire real property through negotiation and purchase from the owner.

When the courts find that a landowner's right to develop the land is restricted by government controls so that the land becomes essentially useless, courts have sometimes found that an illegal **taking** has occurred and that the landowner is entitled to compensation. In this situation, the landowner petitions the courts to require the remainder of the property to be condemned with just compensation awarded to the landowner.

Eminent domain comes into play only when the landowners involved have refused to sell and it forces them to do so. In 2005, the U.S. Supreme Court confirmed, in a controversial landmark decision, the right of the city of New London, Connecticut, to condemn homes owned by private individuals so the land could be used by a private developer. The city claimed the taking was justified because the proposed development would contribute to the economic well-being of the city. A similar situation is underway in Brooklyn, New York, where a new sports arena is the subject of the taking.

- ■ *Escheat.* State laws provide for ownership of real estate to revert, or **escheat**, to the state when an owner dies leaving no natural heirs and no will disposing of real property.

> **Government powers over land include the following:**
> - ■ Taxation
> - ■ Police power
> - ■ Eminent domain
> - ■ Escheat

Taxation

Ad valorem taxes are charged against each parcel according to the **assessed value** placed on land and improvements by a public official known as an assessor. Property is separated to account for values attributable to the land and building. Tax rates are set to raise whatever sum is needed for the public budget. A rate might be quoted as, for example, $26 per $1,000 of assessed valuation. The same rate, in a different community, might be expressed as $2.60 per $100, or 26 mills (a mill being one-tenth of a cent) per $1 of assessed value. At that rate, a house assessed at $100,000 would have a property tax bill of $2,600. Municipalities frequently assess real property at less than 100 percent of its full value. New York City assesses property at 100 percent of market value.

Special assessments are additional taxes that run for a few years to enable certain neighborhoods to pay for particular improvements. For example, property on one street might be subject to special assessment property taxes to install sidewalks or streetlights on that particular street. In New York City, special assessments are instituted in a business improvement district (BID). Areas are designated as BIDs to encourage the economic growth of the area. Properties within these districts benefit from added services such as added uniformed security and guides, common street corner trash removal, street sweeping, and economic programs. Properties within these BID areas benefit from added services and are subject to pay a special assessment charge to fund these improvements.

Protesting assessments   Taxpayers who feel their assessment is unfair can research tax records to see how their valuation compares with that of their neighbors. Obtaining solid data on comparative parcels is of prime importance in protesting an assessment. Recent nearby sales are particularly relevant.

Some assessors will visit the property and discuss the matter. If no agreement results, the next step is to present a grievance to the local assessment board of review. The taxpayer who wants to take matters beyond that point may go to court or take advantage of New York State's simple small claims procedure intended for review of grievances on residential property. When other actions have failed, a property owner may bring a *certiorari proceeding* asking for judicial review by a higher court, board, or tribunal. A certiorari proceeding falls under the category of an *Article 78 proceeding*; this is the appeal process available to a private landowner when a governmental body renders a negative determination on that landowner. This subject is covered in Chapter 1.

In New York, partial reduction of some property taxes may be available to qualified veterans, religious organizations, homeowners who claim a school tax relief or STaR reduction, and homeowners aged 65 or older who have limited income.

Property taxes have first priority as liens   Foreclosure of a tax lien is often *in rem*, against the property and not against the delinquent taxpayer personally. Some municipalities (such as New York City) conduct real estate tax lien sales in lieu of *in rem* proceedings.

■ PUBLIC LAND-USE CONTROLS

The government controls and regulates land use through (1) public land-use controls and (2) public ownership of land, including parks, schools, and expressways, by the federal, state, and local governments.

The increasing demands placed on our limited natural resources have made it necessary for cities, towns, and villages to increase their limitations on the private use of real estate. We now have controls over noise, air, and water pollution, as well as population density. Regulations governing use of privately owned real estate include planning; zoning; subdivision regulations; codes that regulate building construction, safety, and public health; and environmental protection legislation. (See Figure 13.1.)

The Master Plan

A local government recognizes development goals through a comprehensive **master plan**, also referred to as a general plan. The federal government's statistical gathering of information for small **census tracts** aids in the process. Cities and counties develop master plans to ensure that social and economic needs are balanced against environmental and aesthetic concerns. Plans take into account the **demography**, or makeup of the population in terms of age, social, and economic status. Physical surveys are also essential in preparing a master plan. Countywide plans must coordinate numerous civic plans to ensure orderly growth, including provision of **infrastructure**—roads, public utilities, schools, and the like. Occasionally, a municipality may put a temporary halt to further construction by declaring a **moratorium**. Plans are put into effect by zoning ordinances.

Zoning

Zoning ordinances are laws of local government authorities that control the use of land and structures within designated districts.

Zoning regulates such things as the following:

- *Use of the land.* Zoning may include categories of *use groups*, which indicate allowed uses within a given zone.
- *Lot sizes.* Zoning may require a minimum lot size to be considered a buildable lot.
- *Types of structures permitted.* This is determined by the zones the structures are in.
- *Building heights*
- *Transfer of air rights*
- **Setbacks.** Setbacks are the minimum distance from streets, neighboring properties, or sidewalks that structures may be built.
- *Density.* Density refers to the number of units that can be built in an area. Often the purpose of zoning is to implement a local master plan.

F I G U R E   13.1

Environmental Protection Legislation

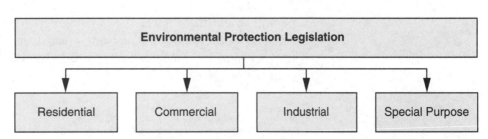

In New York, the power to regulate zoning is given to municipal governments; there are no statewide zoning ordinances. These local authorities enact zoning ordinances, grant any zoning variations, hold planning meetings, and listen to zoning appeals. As with other governmental agencies and departments, zoning meetings must be open to the public *(Sunshine Law)*.

Zoning ordinances generally divide land use into residential, commercial, industrial, vacant, agricultural, open space, institutional, and recreational classifications. Now, many communities include **cluster zoning**, which allows **abutting** housing closely grouped, usually in return for community open space, and *multiple-use zoning*, which permits unusual planned unit developments.

Zoning classifications found in a typical New York community might include R-1, one-family residential; R-2, multifamily residential; C-1, commercial-retail; C-2, heavy commercial; and I-1, Industrial or M-1 Manufacturing. Residential areas may be subdivided to provide for detached single-family dwellings, semidetached structures containing not more than four dwelling units, walkup apartments, high-rise apartments, and so forth. Variations exist among municipalities, and some may have as many as 15 classifications. In some cases, the use of land located *within one to three miles* of an incorporated area must receive approval and consent even though the property is not next to the village, town, or city.

With the growth of unconventional **family units**, including **group homes**, New York has set definitions for what constitutes the allowable occupation of a single-family home as persons related by blood, marriage, or adoption, or a group of up to three people who are not related, living together as a household unit. Court challenges to the definition of a family for residential purposes often arise, particularly in the case of group homes.

Tests commonly applied to determine if zoning violates the rights of individuals require that the

■ power be exercised in a reasonable manner;
■ provisions be clear and specific;
■ ordinance be free from discrimination;
■ ordinance promote public health, safety, and general welfare under the police power concept; and
■ ordinance apply to all property in a similar manner.

Zoning laws are enforced through local requirements that **building permits** be obtained before property owners build on their land. A permit will not be issued unless a proposed structure conforms to the permitted zoning, among other requirements.

Building permits also act as property information to the taxing authorities. Each permit, when issued, gives the building department of that municipality a fair estimate of the improvement being created, renovated, or demolished, so any improvement will probably lead to a reassessment of the subject property by the tax assessor's office.

Accessory building/use   An accessory building is one used for a purpose other than that of the principal building on the same lot. For example, a detached garage, pool house, or a storage shed would be considered an *accessory building*.

An **accessory (apartment) use** is a use other than that normally allowed. An example of an accessory use would be an apartment allowed by special permit and under prescribed conditions in a single-family residence (a mother-in-law apartment).

Home occupations are sometimes allowed in residential zones if they are not the main use of the building. Home occupations are subject to local ordinances.

Nonconforming use   A frequent issue is an existing building used in a particular way, which then does not conform to the zoning use upon enactment of the zoning law. Such a **nonconforming use** is allowed to continue. If the building is destroyed or torn down, however, any new structure must comply with the current zoning ordinance. Local laws may say that the right to a nonconforming use is lost if it is discontinued for a certain period, usually one or two years.

A city, village, town, or other municipality may from time to time perform *upzoning* within an area. For example, under the previous zoning, a half-acre lot contained building rights. Under the new zoning resolution, a buildable lot requires a full acre to comply. In this situation, the half-acre lot would be a legally nonconforming unit and would be grandfathered in under the former zoning resolution.

Zoning boards of appeal have been established in most communities to hear complaints about the effects of zoning ordinances on specific parcels of property. Petitions may be presented to the appeal board for exceptions to the zoning law. The board's determinations can be challenged in state courts through an Article 78 proceeding.

Zoning variations   Each time a plan is created or a zoning ordinance enacted, some owners are inconvenienced to the point of hardship. To alleviate some of the problems caused by zoning ordinances, two zoning variations are provided.

A **special-use permit** may be granted to allow a use of property that is in the public interest. For example, a restaurant may be built in an industrially zoned area if it is necessary to provide meal services for area workers, or a church might be allowed in a residential area.

Also, a property owner who has suffered hardship as a result of a zoning ordinance may seek a **variance**. For example, if an owner's lot is level next to a road but slopes steeply 50 feet back from the road, the zoning board may be willing to allow a variance so the owner can build closer to the road than normally would be allowed.

A *use variance* requires "unnecessary hardship." Property owners must show that

- they are deprived of all economic use or benefit;
- the hardship is unique, not universal to the area or neighborhood;

- the variance will not change the essential character of the neighborhood; and
- the alleged hardship is not self-created.

An *area variance* requires "practical difficulty," affecting the health, safety, or welfare of the community. Property owners must show that

- the variance will not cause an undesirable change or detriment to neighboring properties;
- the benefit sought by the party seeking the variance could not be achieved through other means;
- the variance would not have an adverse effect on environmental or physical conditions in the neighborhood or district;
- the difficulty suffered by the property owners was not self-created (does not preclude granting); and
- the requested variance is not substantial.

Spot zoning A special-use permit that is not in harmony with the neighborhood (a chemical plant in a residential area, for example) is considered **spot zoning**. When it benefits only the user and not the neighborhood, spot zoning is illegal in the state of New York.

Building Codes

Most cities and towns have enacted ordinances to specify *construction standards* that must be met during building construction or repair. These are called **building codes**, and they set minimum requirements for kinds of materials, sanitary equipment, electrical wiring, fire prevention standards, and the like. New York has a *statewide building code* that applies where no local code exists or where local codes are less restrictive.

Most communities require the issuance of a building permit by a building department or another authority before anyone can build a structure or alter an existing building. Officials can verify compliance with building codes and zoning ordinances by examining the plans and inspecting the work. After the new construction is found satisfactory, the inspector issues a **certificate of occupancy (C of O)** or, for an altered building, a *certificate of compliance*. On any new construction, a **temporary certificate of occupancy (TCO)** can be issued. The certificate of occupancy is also required for some transfers of existing buildings. If the construction violated a private deed restriction (discussed previously), a building permit still might be issued. A *building permit is merely evidence of the applicant's compliance with municipal regulations*. It does not, however, give the landowner the right to ignore private deed restrictions that may apply.

Subdivision Regulations

Article 9-A of the Real Property Law (9a RPL) governs subdivided lands. Among the requirements before land can be subdivided or built on are those set by the Interstate Land Sales Full Disclosure Act, and the environmental impact statement mandated by the state Environmental Quality Review Act (SEQRA). Where several agencies may be involved, the one that makes final decisions is known as the **lead agency**. Subdivision requirements are discussed in detail in Chapter 18.

Most communities have adopted **subdivision regulations**, often as part of a master plan. Subdivision regulations usually provide for

- location, grading, alignment, surfacing, and widths of streets, highways, and other rights-of-way;
- installation of sewers and water mains;
- minimum dimensions of lots;
- building and setback lines;
- areas to be reserved for public use, such as parks or schools; and
- easements for public utilities.

Suburban subdivisions normally will contain a cul-de-sac. A **cul-de-sac** is a street that is open at one end only and usually has a circular turnaround at the other end (a blind alley). The use of cul-de-sacs has become popular in residential subdivisions in place of the traditional grid pattern with numerous intersections.

Development Rights

In areas where the right to build commercial buildings is limited in height or square footage, particularly in New York City, the owners of small parcels that do not intend to use their rights (a church or small landmark building, for example) may sell their unused **development rights**, which can be transferred and used to construct a building on another lot, higher or larger than would otherwise be allowed. These unused development rights are called *air rights*. The use and market of air rights are more prevalent where highrise construction exists. In New York City and with some exceptions (such as landmark or historic properties), air rights are transferable with conditions. First, the transferor and the transferee must be within the same zone. Second, the properties must be contiguous to each other.

In some suburban areas, communities have bought development rights from the owners of agricultural properties. The owners are permitted to continue farming, thus preserving the rural atmosphere and avoiding additional residential subdivisions.

Environmental Protection Legislation

Federal and state legislators have passed a number of environmental protection laws in an attempt to respond to public concern over preservation of America's natural resources. Of particular importance are the New York Environmental Conservation Law and the federal Comprehensive and Environmental Response, Cleanup, and Liability Act of 1980 (**CERCLA**), discussed at greater length in Chapter 18. CERCLA places responsibility for cleanup of environmental disasters on the original offenders and also on current and future owners of the property, including lending institutions that might acquire the property through foreclosure.

In 1986, the Superfund Amendments and Reauthorization Act (**SARA**) further defined responsibility for cleanup caused by past activities. The amendment identifies "potentially responsible parties" (PRPs) responsible for the cost of cleanup.

Purchasers of contaminated property may be eligible to institute the "innocent landowners defense." This is available to purchasers of contaminated land when, under certain circumstances, they have a defense against liability for previous owners' actions, provided that there is proper diligent investigation of possible contamination before their purchase and that when contamination was discovered, the new property owners acted responsibly. Proof of an environmental audit before purchase would be a good defense.

Where several agencies are involved in an environmental audit, the work is coordinated by a *lead agency*.

The New York State Navigation Law, originally intended to cover liability for oil spills, includes an Environmental Lien Amendment under which the state can hold any property owner accountable for environmental cleanup.

Many of these laws were triggered by the 1978 Love Canal disaster, in which a toxic waste dump started leaking and contaminated a residential area and school, which had to be abandoned (although the government later claimed that the dangerous conditions were overstated).

Even when the federal and state officials declared part of the neighborhood cleaned up and safe, banks were unwilling to offer would-be buyers mortgage loans on the boarded-up houses, fearing liability if future problems arose. Lawsuits to determine who was liable for the cleanup involved Hooker Chemical and Plastics Corporation, which originally buried the chemicals; Occidental Chemical Corporation, which bought the Hooker company in 1968; and the school board and city of Niagara Falls, which built a grade school and roads on the site.

Wetlands   New York has legislated requirements to protect designated wetlands, those areas listed by the state as having groundwater on or near the surface of the land or meeting other definitions. Improvements may be constructed only with a state permit; most agricultural uses are exempt from the law. The federal government's Clean Waters Act also requires a permit from the Army Corps of Engineers and EPA approval for building on designated wetlands. Cities and counties also frequently pass environmental legislation of their own.

Real estate practitioners must be alert to possible environmental problems so that sellers and prospective buyers will be fully informed about potential liabilities. The subject is discussed more fully in Chapter 18.

Landmark Preservation

In New York State, local governments may enact regulations intended to preserve individual buildings and areas of historic or architectural significance. Regulations setting up local historic areas or landmark preservation districts may restrict owners' rights to alter the exteriors of certain old buildings. Interior remodeling is typically free from regulation; in most cases, however, a property owner located within a landmark district or historic district may not alter but only repair and maintain the existing façade. Individual buildings located outside an historic area also may be designated as landmarks. Applications for listing on the National Historic Register are made to New York's Office of Parks, Recreation and Historic Preservation (OPRHP), which passes them on to the federal government. If a building is listed on the national register, it is automatically listed also on the state's register.

■ DIRECT PUBLIC OWNERSHIP

A certain amount of land is owned by the government for such uses as municipal buildings, state legislature houses, schools, and military stations. **Direct public ownership** is a means of land control.

Publicly owned streets and highways serve a necessary function for the entire population. In addition, public land is often used for such recreational purposes as parks. National and state parks and forest preserves create areas for public use and recreation and at the same time help to conserve our natural resources. At present, the federal government owns approximately 775 million acres of land, much of which is in Alaska.

■ SUMMARY

Private land use controls are exercised by owners, often subdividers, who control use of subdivision lots through deed restrictions that apply to all lot owners. The usual recorded restrictions may be enforced by neighboring lot owners' obtaining a court injunction to stop a violator.

Government powers limiting private rights in land include taxation, eminent domain, police power, and escheat. The control of land use is exercised through public controls, private (or nongovernment) controls, and public ownership.

Public controls are ordinances based on the state's police power to protect the public health, safety, and welfare. Cities and municipalities enact master plans and zoning ordinances.

Zoning ordinances segregate residential areas from business and industrial zones and control not only land use but also height and bulk of buildings and density of population. Zoning boards of appeal can grant special-use permits and variances and recognize nonconforming uses. Subdivision regulations maintain control of development.

Building codes control construction by specifying standards for plumbing, sewers, electrical wiring, and equipment. A building inspector may issue a certificate of occupancy when a completed building meets standards.

In addition to land-use control on the local level, the state and federal governments have intervened to preserve natural resources through environmental legislation. Important are CERCLA and SARA, which placed responsibility on landowners for environmental cleanups, and wetlands legislation that limits building on designated lands.

Public ownership provides land for such public purposes as parks, highways, schools, and municipal buildings.

CHAPTER 13 QUIZ

1. In New York State, the MOST effective way to protest a high property tax assessment is to
   a. show that neighboring similar property is assessed at lower figures.
   b. produce proof of the cost basis of the property, purchase price plus improvements.
   c. place the property on the market and see how much is offered for it.
   d. offer to sell to the assessor for the assessed value.

2. A homeowner who is dissatisfied with assessed valuation can take a complaint to
   a. the assessor personally.
   b. a board of review.
   c. a small claims hearing.
   d. Any of the above

3. When the Thruway was constructed, the route ran through the Adams's farm. Adams refused to sell the necessary land. The state then used its right of eminent domain through a court proceeding known as
   a. escheat.
   b. variance.
   c. condemnation.
   d. downzoning.

4. The right of escheat allows New York State to acquire land
   a. through a developer's dedication of property.
   b. when someone dies without leaving a will or natural heirs.
   c. through a gift from a donor.
   d. when property taxes are not paid as due.

5. A house contains eight studio apartments, which is four more than zoning laws allow on that street. To receive a permit for a nonconforming use, the owner must prove that the
   a. present use is in the public interest because the neighborhood is short of rental units.
   b. house has been used that way every year since before the zoning ordinance was adopted.
   c. deed he received specifically lists eight apartments in the building.
   d. zoning ordinance is unreasonably restrictive.

6. A doctor goes before her local zoning board asking for permission to open an office in her residential neighborhood because the area has no medical facilities. She is asking for a
   a. variance.
   b. nonconforming use.
   c. special-use permit.
   d. restriction.

7. A homeowner asks the zoning board to allow him to build a fence to keep his children safe on a busy corner, though he does not have room for the required ten-foot setback. He is asking for a
   a. condemnation.
   b. nonconforming use.
   c. use variance.
   d. restriction.

8. Private land-use controls include
   a. subdivision regulations.
   b. deed restrictions.
   c. environmental protection laws.
   d. master plan specifications.

9. The building inspector who is satisfied that construction is satisfactory may issue a
   a. certificate of occupancy.
   b. subdivision regulation.
   c. restrictive covenant.
   d. conditional-use permit.

10. The purpose of a building permit is to
    a. override a deed restriction.
    b. maintain municipal control over the volume of building.
    c. provide evidence of compliance with municipal regulations.
    d. regulate area and bulk of buildings.

11. The New York State Navigation Law is concerned with
    a. riparian rights.
    b. environmental cleanups.
    c. the Barge Canal system.
    d. Niagara Falls.

12. CERCLA and SARA are federal laws establishing
    a. restrictions on wetlands development.
    b. national building code standards.
    c. liability for past environmental contamination.
    d. regulations for environmental safety in the workplace.

13. A Greek Revival home is located in a historic preservation district. The owner of the home probably may NOT change
    a. the number of bathrooms in the building.
    b. the exterior of the building.
    c. the interior of the building.
    d. either the exterior or the interior.

14. The term *laches* refers to
    a. loss of a right if it isn't exercised in time.
    b. responsibility for environmental cleanup.
    c. land set aside for recreational use in a master plan.
    d. the process of downzoning.

15. The grantor of real estate may place effective deed restrictions forbidding
    a. any future sale of the property.
    b. rental of the property to a member of a particular ethnic group.
    c. division of the parcel into small building lots.
    d. mortgaging of the property.

16. A deed restriction requires 250 feet of road frontage per lot. The town building code requires only 100 feet, and a builder constructs two houses on his 250-foot lot. The neighbors may
    a. ask the court to order one house torn down.
    b. act only before the builder has obtained certificates of occupancy.
    c. do nothing because the builder complied with all town regulations.
    d. enforce their rights by calling the police.

17. Which item is NOT one of the primary conditions that must be met for the government to exercise eminent domain?
    a. The proposed use must be approved by referendum of local voters.
    b. The proposed use must be declared by the court to be a public use.
    c. Just compensation must be paid to the owner.
    d. The rights of the owner must be protected by due process of law.

18. A community needs to build a new fire station to protect one neighborhood. To raise adequate funds, it is going to raise funds though taxation referred to as a(n)
    a. ad valorem tax.
    b. restrictive covenant.
    c. taking.
    d. special assessment.

19. In New York, zoning powers are given to
    a. voluntary community boards.
    b. municipal governments.
    c. county governments.
    d. state government.

20. The issuance of a building permit is likely to trigger
    a. an environmental survey.
    b. a zoning review.
    c. reassessment of the subject property.
    d. an immediate tax increase.

CHAPTER 14

Municipal Agencies

■ KEY TERMS

architectural review board
assessment rolls
buildings department
Conservation Advisory
   Council
county health department

infrastructure
Landmarks Preservation
   Commission
planned unit development
   (PUD)
planning boards

receiver of taxes
tax assessor
village board of trustees
wetlands
zoning boards of appeal

■ CITY/TOWN COUNCIL

With economic growth comes expansion. The need for quality control is addressed by state and local government officials who monitor and regulate growth in New York through various governmental agencies. These agencies perform specific functions to uphold federal, state, and local laws.

In New York City, the city council is the law-making body of government. The council is composed of 51 elected members from 51 council districts throughout the five boroughs. (See Figure 14.1.) The council's purpose is to

- provide a balance of power,
- monitor the performance of city agencies,
- make land-use decisions,
- approve the city's budget, and
- legislate over various other issues that arise.

FIGURE 14.1

New York City Council

New York City Council

- Fifty-one elected members (including *ex officio* members: speaker, majority leader, and minority leader), each of whom sits on at least three select or subcommittees
- Term limit of two consecutive terms
- New York public advocate presides at council meetings and is a member of all committees

A 1993 referendum placed term limits on council members. Elected members are limited to two consecutive terms in office. The head of the city council is commonly referred to as the speaker. The New York public advocate, who presides at city council meetings, is a member of all council committees. The public advocate is also given the power to introduce legislation.

The council sets up a variety of committees and has the sole purpose to act as a watchdog over a variety of city government functions. Each member of the council sits on at least three select or subcommittees.

Select committees include but are not limited to the following:

- Civil rights
- Community development
- Economic development
- Education
- Environmental protection
- Parks and recreation
- Public safety
- State and federal legislation
- Transportation and infrastructure issues

Subcommittees include but are not limited to the following:

- Landmarks
- Planning
- Public (affordable) housing
- Senior citizen centers
- Zoning

Each standing committee meets a minimum of once per month. The speaker, the majority leader, and the minority leader serve as *ex officio* members of every committee. The council is housed within New York City Hall.

The Syracuse council consists of nine members and the council president. In the city of Syracuse, no law can be passed without council approval. The council is also responsible for adoption of the city's annual budget. As in New York City, council members are elected officials. In Syracuse, council terms consist of four years for the president and the four members who are elected at-large or citywide and two years for the five other council members who are district councilors from each of the five Syracuse common council districts. The term limit for council members is eight years. (See Figure 14.2.)

F I G U R E   14.2

Syracuse City Council

Syracuse City Council

- Nine elected members plus the council president
- Term limit of eight years; terms range from two to four years for members and four years for the president

Council meetings are open to the general public. All council records are maintained by the city clerk and are available to be viewed and inspected by the general public during normal business hours.

Enactment of law is achieved through the following process:

1. An ordinance is introduced through the councilor as a new law, an amendment to an existing law, or a repeal of an existing law.
2. After a sponsorship decision is made regarding a law, it is submitted to the city clerk for creation of formal language.
3. The law is then calendared as an agenda item for the next council meeting.
4. Consideration is given to the agenda item by the entire council on the appointed day.
5. Any additional needs or concerns are expressed in a scheduled follow-up meeting.
6. During the follow-up meeting, the new legislation sponsor presents the need for the passing of law and defends it.
7. Subsequently (generally during the next scheduled council meeting), the council will vote to pass or defeat the proposed legislation.
8. If the law is passed and adopted by the council, the following usually will occur:
   - The law is presented to the council president for signature.
   - The law is subsequently sent to the city clerk's office.
   - It is then presented to the mayor's office via the city clerk.
   - If the mayor accepts the ordinance, it becomes law.
   - If the mayor disapproves, 30 days is given for the council to reconsider the ordinance.
   - During the reconsideration period, if two-thirds of the council members vote for approval of the ordinance, it is then considered to take effect.
9. The ordinance or local law (as the case may be) is entered in the official archives of the city clerk and becomes a recorded part of the official book.

■ VILLAGE BOARD OF TRUSTEES

As in city and town councils, members of a **village board of trustees** are elected officials.

For example, in the village of Croton-on-Hudson (Westchester County), the village is run via a council-manager form of government. The village board of trustees is composed of five elected members. The board's sole responsibility is the creation of functions and policies on behalf of its constituents.

The acting member and presiding officer of the board is the mayor (the mayor's position is not a full-time position). A full-time village manager is appointed and hired by the board of trustees. The village manager reports directly to the village board; the manager's duties consist of day-to-day village operational functions. In some villages, live trustee meetings can be viewed on public access television or webcasts.

City and town councils and village boards of trustees are granted the power to adopt new laws and ordinances to protect the health, safety, and general welfare of their constituents. Adaptation of zoning ordinances is one of the most important powers available to councils and village boards. Zoning ordinances are designed to ensure appropriate urban/suburban planning. They control and dictate all development within those municipalities.

ADOPTION OF BUDGET AND TAX RATE

The process of arriving at a real estate tax rate begins with the *adoption of a budget* by each county, city, school board, or other taxing district. The budget covers financial requirements for the coming fiscal year, which may be the January through December calendar year or some other 12-month period. The budget must include an estimate of all expenditures for the year and indicate the amount of income expected from all fees, revenue sharing, and other sources. The net amount remaining to be raised from real estate taxes is then determined from these figures.

Separate tax rates may be established for homestead and nonhomestead real estate. Homestead property in New York includes dwellings with no more than four units, mobile homes if owner-occupied and separately assessed, residential condominiums, farms, and some vacant land suitable for homestead-qualified buildings. Nonhomestead property includes industrial and commercial property and most vacant land.

Tax shares are sometimes negotiated between different taxing authorities, as with two towns that support one school district or when villages share the expense for a county sheriff's department.

SUBDIVISION

A subdivision refers to the process of dividing a single tract of land into smaller parcels. Land in large tracts must receive special attention before it can be converted into sites for homes, stores, or other uses. A subdivider buys undeveloped acreage and divides it into smaller lots for sale to individuals or developers or for the subdivider's own use. A developer (who also may be a subdivider) builds homes or other buildings on the lots and sells them. Developing is generally a much more extensive activity than subdividing. A developer may have a sales staff or may use the services of local real estate brokerage firms.

FIGURE 14.3

Municipal Agencies and Officials

Municipal Agencies and Officials

- **Planning board**—establishes criteria for community development, including dedication of land and compliance with zoning ordinances, and advises other boards on land-use matters
- **Zoning board of appeal**—hears complaints about the effects of zoning ordinances on specific parcels of property
- **Architectural review board**—approves new construction and remodeling
- **Buildings department**—ensures the safe and lawful use of properties and buildings via enforcement of the municipality's building code, electrical code, zoning resolution, New York State Labor Law, and New York State Multiple Dwelling Law
- **Planning department**—generally responsible for the municipality's physical and socioeconomic planning
- **Tax assessors**—responsible for making assessments in New York
- **Receivers of taxes/treasurers**—collect real property taxes on all properties contained within the assessment roll
- **Engineer**—works closely with the buildings department, public works department, and water department to ensure that construction projects are performed properly and the municipal infrastructure is in good working order

No uniform city planning and land development legislation affects the entire country. Most laws governing subdividing and land planning are controlled by state and local governmental bodies. New York State sets standards for villages, cities, and towns. Local governments may adopt more restrictive policies. *Article 9-A of New York's Real Property Law governs subdivision.*

A subdivision development plan must comply with any overall local master plan adopted by the county, city, village, or town. The developer must consider zoning laws and land-use restrictions adopted for health and safety purposes. Basic city plan and zoning requirements are not inflexible, but long, expensive, and frequently complicated hearings are usually required before alterations can be authorized.

A subdivider may not offer lots within a subdivision for sale unless the following has occurred:

- The developer files a plat map of subdivision (a rendering of what the subdivision will look like) with the municipality.
- All necessary regulatory approvals have been obtained.
- The plat map of subdivision has been recorded.

It should be noted that if a housing lot within a subdivision will use FHA financing, all FHA rules and guidelines (such as minimum building standards) must be met and adhered to by the developer.

A plat map of subdivision will ultimately dictate

- the permitted density (amount of improved structures or occupants allowed per acre) and
- street/traffic patterns within the subdivision (i.e., dead-end streets or cul-de-sacs).

Planned Unit Development

A **planned unit development** (PUD) is a planned combination of diverse land uses, such as housing, recreation, and shopping. These uses are contained in one development or subdivision.

■ PLANNING BOARD

Most villages, cities, and other areas incorporated under state laws have **planning boards** and/or *planning commissioners*. Planning boards are appointed positions. Communities establish strict criteria before approving new subdivisions. Frequently required are the dedication of land for streets, schools, and parks; the assurance by bonding that sewer and street costs will be paid; and compliance with zoning ordinances governing use and lot size and with fire and safety ordinances. Planning boards also advise all other boards on matters concerning land use.

■ THE MASTER PLAN

A local government recognizes development goals through a comprehensive *master plan*, also referred to as a *general plan*. The federal government's statistical gathering of information for small census tracts aids in the process. Cities and counties develop master plans to ensure that social and economic needs are balanced against environmental and aesthetic concerns. A **Conservation Advisory Council** is created by the local legislature to advise in the development, management, and protection of the community's natural resources and to prepare an inventory and map of open spaces. Plans take into account the demography, or makeup of the population in terms of age and social and economic status. Physical surveys are also essential in preparing a master plan. Countywide plans must coordinate numerous civic plans to ensure orderly growth, including provision of **infrastructure**—roads, public utilities, schools, and the like. Occasionally, a municipality may put a temporary halt to further construction by declaring a *moratorium*. Plans are put into effect by zoning ordinances.

■ ZONING BOARDS OF APPEAL

Zoning boards of appeal have been established in most communities to hear complaints about the effects of zoning ordinances on specific parcels of property. Petitions may be presented to the appeal board for exceptions to the zoning law. The board's determinations can be challenged in state courts through an Article 78 proceeding. An Article 78 proceeding is used as the legal appeal process and procedure instituted by a private individual or entity when petitioning the New York Supreme Court for reversal or relief from adverse decisions or conditions made by a public body of government against that party.

Zoning Variances

Each time a plan is created or a zoning ordinance enacted, some owners are inconvenienced to the point of hardship. To alleviate some of the problems caused by zoning ordinances, two zoning variations are provided:

1. A *special-use permit* may be granted to allow a use of the property that is in the public interest. For example, a restaurant may be built in an industrially zoned area if it is necessary to provide meal services for area workers, or a church might be allowed in a residential area.
2. A property owner who has suffered hardship as a result of a zoning ordinance may seek a *variance*. For example, if an owner's lot is level next to a road but slopes steeply 50 feet back from the road, the zoning board may be willing to allow a variance so the owner can build closer to the road than normally would be allowed.

A use variance requires "unnecessary hardship." Property owners must show that

■ they are deprived of all economic use or benefit;
■ the hardship is unique, not universal to the area or neighborhood;
■ the variance will not change the essential character of the neighborhood; and
■ the alleged hardship is not self-created.

An area variance requires "practical difficulty," affecting the health, safety, or welfare of the community. Property owners must show that

■ the variance will not cause an undesirable change or detriment to neighboring properties;
■ the benefit sought by the party seeking the variance could not be achieved through other means;
■ the variance would not have an adverse effect on environmental or physical conditions in the neighborhood or district;
■ the difficulty suffered by the property owners was not self-created (does not preclude granting); and
■ the requested variance is not substantial.

■ ARCHITECTURAL REVIEW BOARDS

Architectural review boards take on many approval functions. Their primary goal and purpose involves the approval (pertinent to individualized municipal ordinances) of new construction and remodeling.

Architectural review boards will review all applications for signage and façades on nonresidential property, all new construction and renovations (nonresidential), and any changes (paint color, additions, etc.).

The architectural review board also provides regulation and guidance for maintaining the quality of the exterior appearance of buildings and signs, either for new buildings/signs or modifications of existing buildings/signs.

■ WETLANDS COMMISSION

New York has legislated requirements to protect designated **wetlands**, those areas listed by the state as having groundwater on or near the surface of the land or meeting other definitions. Improvements may be constructed only with a state permit; most agricultural uses are exempt from the law. The federal government's Clean Water Act also requires a permit from the Army Corps of Engineers and EPA approval for building on designated wetlands. Cities and counties also frequently pass environmental legislation of their own.

Real estate practitioners must be alert to possible environmental problems so that sellers and prospective buyers will be fully informed about potential liabilities. The subject is discussed more fully in Chapter 18.

■ LANDMARKS PRESERVATION

In New York, local governments may enact regulations intended to preserve individual buildings and areas of historic or architectural significance. Regulations setting up local *historic areas* or *landmark preservation districts* may restrict owners' rights to alter the exteriors of certain old buildings. Interior remodeling is typically free from regulation; however, a property owner located within a landmark district or historic district may (under most cases) not alter but only repair and maintain the existing façade. Individual buildings located outside an historic area also may be designated as landmarks. Applications for listing on the National Register of Historic Places are made to New York's Office of Parks, Recreation and Historic Preservation (OPRHP), which passes them on to the federal government. If a building is listed on the national register, it is automatically listed also on the state register.

■ BUILDINGS DEPARTMENT

In all municipalities, the **buildings department's** activities are always primarily focused on the safety, health, and welfare of the general public. A municipality's building department is entrusted with the job of ensuring the safe and lawful use of properties and buildings via enforcement of the municipality's building code, electrical code, zoning resolution, New York State Labor Law, and New York State Multiple Dwelling Law.

Some of the main activities of a city, town, or village's building department would include issuing construction permits after careful plan review and examination, issuing demolition permits, inspecting properties, licensing trades, issuing certificates of occupancy (C of Os), and issuing public assembly permits.

Any person or entity that elects to demolish, alter, build an addition to, or erect a new structure must obtain a building permit from the Department of Buildings (DOB) to ensure that the resulting improvement or structure complies with all applicable laws.

Permit fees are generally based on the size of the structure for new buildings or for alteration or demolition work; the fee is usually based on the estimated cost of the project. Permits are granted when the following procedures are followed:

1. Plans for constructing a building or making an alteration are prepared by a New York state-licensed professional engineer or registered architect (typically retained by the owner).
2. The professional engineer or registered architect submits the plans to the department on behalf of the owner.
3. Any legal objections to the application or plans by the DOB examiner are presented to the project professional engineer or registered architect for resolution.
4. Once the DOB's objections have been satisfied, the application and plans are approved.

If the subject property is located within a landmark preservation district or historic district, then, in addition to the DOB's approval, additional approvals and permits will be needed, and permission from the **Landmarks Preservation Commission** must be obtained prior to the alteration or construction's inception.

In addition, many construction projects also routinely require permits from other municipal agencies before construction can begin. For example, in New York City under Express Service, some of these approvals (for sewer connections, drainage, septic, and builders' pavement plans) can now be obtained at the DOB. Formerly, these approvals were issued by the Department of Environmental Protection and Department of Transportation.

Applications for permits to construct on waterfront property are processed by the staff of the Department of Small Business Services (DSBS, formerly known as the Department of Ports and Trades) located at the DOB.

When construction results in a change of use, egress, or occupancy, a new (or amended) C of O is necessary. This is a document issued by the DOB indicating that the property conforms to all local laws, building codes, and regulations.

Most cities and towns have enacted ordinances to specify construction standards that must be met during building construction or repair. These are called building codes, and they set minimum requirements for kinds of materials, sanitary equipment, electrical wiring, fire prevention standards, and the like. New York has a statewide building code that applies where no local code exists or where local codes are less restrictive.

Most communities also require the issuance of a building permit by a buildings department or another authority before anyone can build a structure or alter an existing building. Officials can verify compliance with building codes and zoning ordinances by examining the plans and inspecting the work. After the new construction is found satisfactory, the inspector issues a C of O or, for an altered building, a certificate of compliance. On any new construction, a temporary certificate of occupancy (TCO) can be issued. The C of O is also required for some transfers of existing buildings.

PLANNING DEPARTMENT

A city, town, or village planning department is generally responsible for the municipality's physical and socioeconomic planning. This includes land use, environmental review, preparation of plans and policies, and providing technical assistance and planning information to public officials and government agencies.

In matters associated with development and improvement of the city, village, or town, the responsibilities of the director of planning (who in New York City also serves as chair of the City Planning Commission) include advising and assisting others in the preparation of strategic plans that have long-term implications for the municipality.

The planning department is further responsible for any land use requiring an analysis in support of the commission's review of proposals for the following:

- Zoning amendments
- Special permits under the zoning resolution
- Changes in the city, village, or town map
- Acquisition and disposition of public-owned property
- Acquisition of office space for municipality use
- Any site selection process used for determination of public facilities
- Any urban renewal plans and amendments
- Landmark and historic district designations

TAX ASSESSOR

Assessments in New York are made by municipal officials known as **tax assessors**. Assessments are made by towns, villages, cities, and, in a few cases, counties. The **assessment roll**, open to public inspection, contains assessments for all lands and buildings within the area.

In 1788, New York law mandated *full-value assessment*. The requirement was largely ignored, with most municipalities assessing at less than full value. In 1975, the court of appeals ordered the state either to enforce the law or to change it. More than 400 communities then went to full-value assessment voluntarily or under court order. In 1982, the legislature repealed the 200-year-old requirement. Under the regulations that went into force at that time, upstate communities were simply required to assess all property at a "uniform percentage of value," while New York City and Long Island were allowed to divide real property into four different classes for tax purposes. The question of full-value assessment remains controversial and hotly debated, with court challenges occurring frequently.

RECEIVER OF TAXES/TREASURER

Each municipality has a party or entity (in New York City, it is the Department of Finance) that acts as the **receiver of taxes** for the city, town, or village. The receiver is charged with collection of real property taxes on all properties contained within the assessment roll. An exception would be any tax-exempt property.

■ CITY/TOWN/VILLAGE ENGINEER

A city, town, or village's engineer will always work closely with the buildings department, public works department, and water department to ensure that construction projects are performed properly and the village's infrastructure (streets, sidewalks, parks, sewers, water mains, etc.) are in good working order.

Septic Systems

Household wastewater is made up of water from toilets, washing machines, dishwashers, sinks, bathtubs, and showers. The average family of four produces about 300 gallons of wastewater every day. A *septic system* is an individual treatment and disposal system that is usually built underground. A septic system consists of a large storage tank (septic tank), in which the wastewater is partially broken down by bacteria, and an absorption (leach) field, which receives and filters the wastewater. Solid material settles out of the wastewater, remains at the bottom of the septic tank, and must be pumped out periodically (at least once every three to five years).

Before a septic tank can be installed, the property owner must have the soil tested to determine how much wastewater the soil can process (percolation test). The septic tank also must be the correct size for the number of occupants; the proper size is determined by the number of bedrooms in the house. A professional engineer or registered architect must submit "as built" plans of the system to the **county health department** for approval.

When the septic tank is properly installed and maintained, a septic system is generally adequate for wastewater disposal and treatment. However, if the system is not working properly, there may be serious consequences, including contamination of ground water and wells; contamination of nearby streams, rivers, and lakes; and the pooling of wastewater above the surface.

There are various signs that a septic system is malfunctioning, including wastewater odors inside or outside the home, lush grass and spongy soil over the absorption field, pooled "gray" water over the absorption field, and sluggish or backed-up drains.

If the septic system has failed, pumping the septic tank may solve the problem. More serious malfunctions may require the installation of a new septic system, new fields, new pumps or distribution boxes, or the installation of a sewer system.

■ SUMMARY

In development, anyone with a clear understanding of the correct processes for obtaining approvals to new or existing projects will save both time and money. Cities, towns, and villages elect and appoint officials responsible for disposing of the day-to-day duties in the running of local government. Municipal agencies are set up primarily to protect the public while upholding local laws and ordinances. Budgets are adopted annually to meet the needs of running local government. As a result, tax rates are established to balance the budget. Planning boards, zoning boards, and planning commissions are empowered to regulate economic expansion and improvements resulting from them. County health departments oversee the approval process for installation of septic systems and other sewer approvals. Licensees are advised to familiarize themselves with the appropriate municipal agencies necessary to perform their job functions.

CHAPTER 14 QUIZ

1. City council members in both New York City and Syracuse are
   a. elected for life.
   b. unpaid volunteers.
   c. appointed by the mayor.
   d. subject to term limits.

2. The responsibility for adopting new laws to protect the health, safety, and general welfare of constituents in New York's villages is held by village
   a. mayors.
   b. boards of trustees.
   c. ombudsmen.
   d. zoning departments.

3. Which property would be taxed at a nonhomestead rate in New York?
   a. A foreign-auto repair garage
   b. A condominium in Albany
   c. A bungalow in Lake Carmel
   d. A mobile home in Retirement Acres

4. All of the following are responsibilities and functions that fall under the Planning Department of a city in New York *EXCEPT*
   a. zoning amendments.
   b. collection of property taxes.
   c. acquisition or disposition of publicly owned property.
   d. site selection of public facilities.

5. Which of the following *BEST* describes the Architectural Review Board's function(s)?
   a. The board reviews requests for variance.
   b. The board is involved with the approval of new construction and remodeling.
   c. The board deals with wetlands issues.
   d. The board issues mixed-use permits.

6. Which municipal agency is responsible for approving applications for signage and facades on nonresidential property?
   a. Buildings department
   b. Zoning board of appeal
   c. Architectural review board
   d. Planning board

7. Historic areas and landmarks preservation districts primarily restrict owners' rights to alter a building's
   a. exterior.
   b. interior.
   c. zoning.
   d. occupancy limits.

8. A homeowner is building an addition on his house to accommodate his elderly parents. The architect's plans require the external wall to be built one foot closer to the public sidewalk than allowed in zoning rules. In order to build according to these plans, the homeowner must obtain a
   a. special-use permit.
   b. variance.
   c. homestead exemption.
   d. setback license.

9. Before demolishing an engineer's equipment shed on its property, Acme Manufacturing must obtain a demolition permit from the local
   a. architectural review board.
   b. zoning board.
   c. buildings department.
   d. planning department.

10. A real estate salesperson who wanted to know the tax assessment for a specific property in a town would consult the town's
    a. assessment roll.
    b. tax log.
    c. exemption records.
    d. budget.

CHAPTER

15

Introduction to Construction

■ KEY TERMS

basement	framing	post-and-beam
beam	frieze board	construction
bearing walls	fuse box	R-value
blueprints	girder	septic system
British thermal units	header	sheathing
(BTUs)	heat pumps	siding
casement windows	insulation	sill plate
circuit breaker box	jalousie window	slab-on-grade
concrete slab foundation	joist and rafter roof	construction
crawlspace	Lally™ column	soffit
double-hung window	110-volt circuit	solar energy
eaves	percolation rate	sole plates
envelope	pier-and-beam foundation	specifications
fascia	pitch	studs
flashing	plasterboard/wallboard	truss roof
floating slab foundations	platform framing	220-volt circuit
foundation	construction	

■ SITE PREPARATION

In real estate practice, the term *site* is used to refer to a parcel of land that has been prepared for construction. Site preparation involves clearing the land and grading it to provide drainage and a building location. Large trees may be marked for retention as the land is cleared.

When site preparation occurs, landscaping considerations may be included for a variety of reasons. Some of the considerations may include the following:

- Soil erosion prevention
- Aesthetic appearance
- Area separation considerations
- Privacy

The use of landscaping can also provide shading to certain areas of a subject property, such as a yard or front lawn. In addition, most building codes require distinct walkways from the front housing entrance to driveways, streets, and other common areas within a development or community. The type of materials that may be used for these areas are dictated by the municipality where the property is situated.

Siting of the building may take into account which rooms will receive morning and evening sunlight and which side of the house will receive the prevailing winds. Access and utilities also must be provided for. In locations that are not served by public utilities, an on-site well and/or sanitary waste (septic) system may need to be installed. On-site wells and septic systems must meet standards established by the state Department of Health and enforced by the county departments of health. Other systems, including heating, ventilating, and cooling (HVAC), hot water, and electrical systems must meet standards set by the New York State Energy Code.

Zoning regulations must be reviewed to ensure that the site of the actual structure is in compliance—for example, ensuring that the structure complies with setback requirements and is an adequate distance from neighboring property lines and roads.

The New York State Energy Code also regulates building envelopes. The components that make up the **envelope** of the building (also known as the *building envelope*)—roof, walls, and windows—protect occupants from intruders, noises, and the elements; they can and should be made as energy efficient as possible.

REGULATION OF RESIDENTIAL AND COMMERCIAL CONSTRUCTION

Building construction begins with the construction documents: the plans and specifications. Plans and **blueprints** are scale drawings or renderings of the building and its various components, including floor plans, elevations, sections, and construction details. Separate plans are often drawn to show the locations and features of electrical, plumbing, HVAC, and sewage-disposal systems. **Specifications** are written text or narratives; they tell the builder what materials to use and may suggest what construction techniques to follow, which have a great impact on construction costs.

With construction documents in hand, the builder's or owner's next step is to obtain a building permit from the local permitting agency. This process involves the submission of plans and specifications and payment of a permit fee. The agency charged with this process will review the plans to ensure that the building meets the requirements of the building codes in effect in the locality. Separate permits may be required from agencies regulating construction, electrical systems, plumbing systems, and other aspects of the construction. Approval from environmental protection agencies may be required as well.

As construction progresses, the permitting agency or agencies will perform random and scheduled inspections of the building. If construction has progressed in accordance with the approved plans and specifications, the inspector(s) will issue approvals. The final approval results in a certificate of occupancy, which means the building is in total compliance with local building code requirements and is fit for human habitation.

New York State has a minimum standards building code, but local municipalities may *add* to it or *impose tighter restrictions*. Following are examples of local codes in various New York communities: requiring sprinkler systems, underground wiring, or sump pumps in all new residential construction; banning the use of polyvinyl chloride for plumbing; and requiring that plumbers, electricians, or builders be licensed and that they carry liability and workers' compensation insurance. New York's Board of Fire Underwriters must approve all electrical installations, independent of local approval.

■ WOOD-FRAME CONSTRUCTION

Most houses in New York are built with underlying wood-frame construction covered with an exterior of brick, stone, wood, vinyl, or aluminum siding. Wood-frame houses are preferred because they are less expensive than other kinds of construction, they can be built rapidly, they are easy to insulate, and they allow flexibility of design.

Architectural Styles

Although details of construction are rigidly specified by building codes, architectural styles may vary greatly. Some popular styles include colonial, Georgian, ranch, Cape Cod, contemporary, split-level, Dutch colonial, French provincial, and Spanish. Examples of several typical architectural styles are shown in Figure 15.1. Throughout this chapter, certain terms are followed by a bold number in brackets that refers to the numbered terms in the house diagram in Figure 15.2.

Foundations

The **foundation** includes footings, foundation walls, columns, pilasters, slab, and all other parts that provide support for the house. Foundations are constructed of cut stone, stone and brick, concrete block, poured concrete, and even specially treated wood. Poured concrete and concrete block are the most common because of their strength and resistance to moisture. In recent years, polystyrene foam has been used to insulate foundation walls. The two major types of foundations are concrete slab and pier and beam.

FIGURE 15.1

Architectural Styles

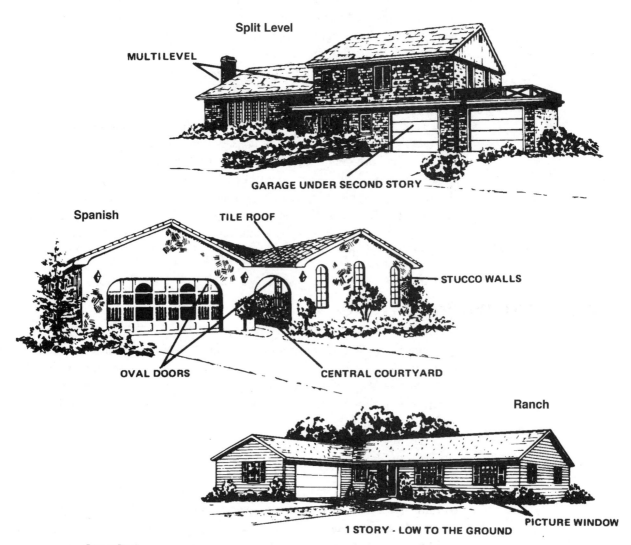

Split Level

MULTILEVEL

GARAGE UNDER SECOND STORY

Spanish

TILE ROOF

STUCCO WALLS

OVAL DOORS

CENTRAL COURTYARD

Ranch

1 STORY - LOW TO THE GROUND

PICTURE WINDOW

Cape Cod

1½ STORIES

SHINGLES

CENTRAL ENTRANCE

F I G U R E   15.1

Architectural Styles (continued)

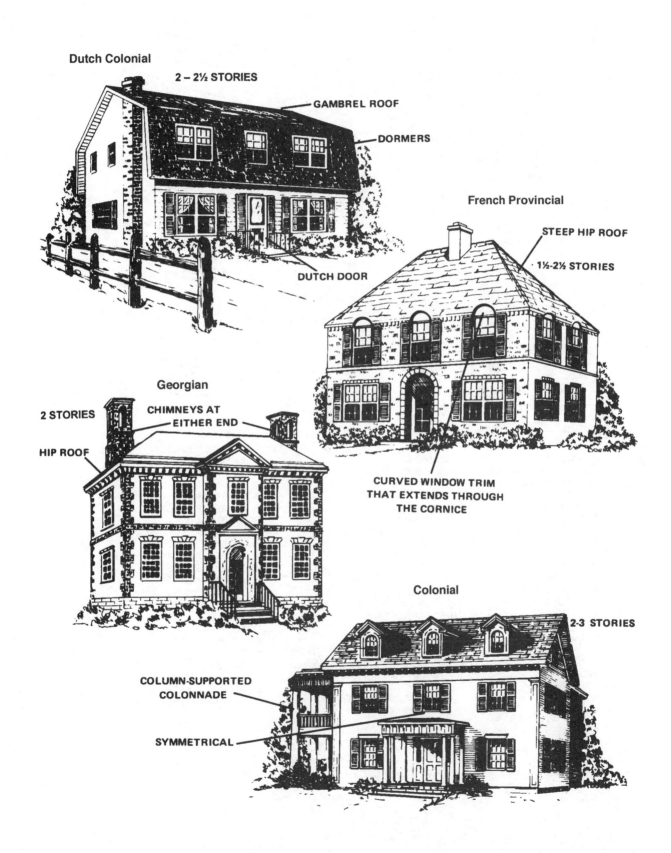

Dutch Colonial

2 – 2½ STORIES

GAMBREL ROOF

DORMERS

DUTCH DOOR

French Provincial

STEEP HIP ROOF

1½-2½ STORIES

CURVED WINDOW TRIM
THAT EXTENDS THROUGH
THE CORNICE

Georgian

2 STORIES

CHIMNEYS AT
EITHER END

HIP ROOF

Colonial

2-3 STORIES

COLUMN-SUPPORTED
COLONNADE

SYMMETRICAL

FIGURE 15.2

House Diagram

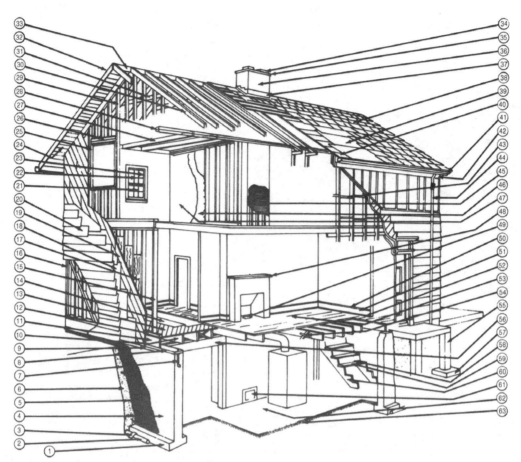

1. FOOTING
2. FOUNDATION DRAIN TILE
3. CRUSHED WASHED STONE
4. FOUNDATION WALL
5. DAMPPROOFING OR WEATHERPROOFING
6. BACKFILL
7. ANCHOR BOLT
8. SILL PLATE
9. TERMITE SHIELD
10. FLOOR JOIST
11. BAND OR BOX BEAM
12. SOLE PLATE
13. SUBFLOORING
14. BUILDING PAPER
15. WALL STUD
16. CORNER STUDS
17. INSULATION
18. HOUSE WRAP
19. WALL SHEATHING
20. SIDING
21. MULLION

22. MUNTIN
23. WINDOW SASH
24. EAVE (ROOF PROJECTION)
25. WINDOW JAMB TRIM
26. WINDOW HEADER
27. CEILING JOIST
28. TOP AND TIE PLATES
29. GABLE STUD
30. RAFTERS
31. COLLAR TIES
32. GABLE END OF ROOF
33. RIDGE BEAM
34. CHIMNEY FLUES
35. CHIMNEY CAP
36. CHIMNEY
37. CHIMNEY FLASHING
38. ROOFING SHINGLES
39. ROOFING FELT/ICE AND WATER MEMBRANE
40. ROOF SHEATHING
41. EAVE TROUGH OR GUTTER
42. FRIEZE BOARD

43. FIRESTOP
44. DOWNSPOUT
45. LATHS
46. PLASTERBOARD
47. PLASTER FINISH
48. MANTEL
49. ASH DUMP
50. BASE TOP MOULDING
51. BASEBOARD
52. SHOE MOULDING
53. FINISH MOULDING
54. CROSS BRIDGING
55. PIER
56. GIRDER
57. FOOTING
58. RISER
59. TREAD
60. STRINGER
61. CLEANOUT DOOR
62. CONCRETE BASEMENT FLOOR
63. CRUSHED WASHED STONE

Concrete slab   A **concrete slab foundation** is supported around the perimeter and in the center by concrete footings dug into the earth. It is made of poured concrete reinforced with steel rods. It rests directly on the earth, with usually a minimum of dampproofing between the concrete and the ground. Foundations formed by a single pouring of concrete are called *monolithic*, whereas those in which the footings and the slab are poured separately are referred to as **floating slab foundations**.

In addition, another form of slab construction is slab-on-grade construction. A **slab-on-grade construction** is a permanent foundation built on footings or a floating foundation made of concrete slabs reinforced with steel. The foundation is laid on a layer of sand or gravel and consists of a layer of insulation and reinforcing mesh covered by poured concrete.

Pier and beam   In a **pier-and-beam foundation**, shown in Figure 15.3, the foundation slab rests on concrete footing. The house framing is connected to the foundation by a treated wood **sill plate** bolted down with *anchor bolts*. The *floor joists* that provide the major support for the flooring rest on top of the treated *sills* (floor girders). The slab or concrete floor rests on top of the projecting parts of the footings. The space between the slab and the foundation is called the **crawlspace** or **basement**. The piers support the main **girder** or **beam** and are attached by lag bolts through the **Lally™ column** top plate.

Termite protection   In some areas of the state of New York, the earth is infested with termites, active antlike insects that are destructive to wood. After constructing the slab for the foundation, the ground may be chemically treated to poison termites and prevent them from coming through or around the foundation and into the wooden structure. Chemical or pressure treatment of lumber is used for sills and beams that are close to ground level. The installation of metal *termite shields* [9] also will provide protection.

F I G U R E   15.3

Pier-and-Beam Foundation

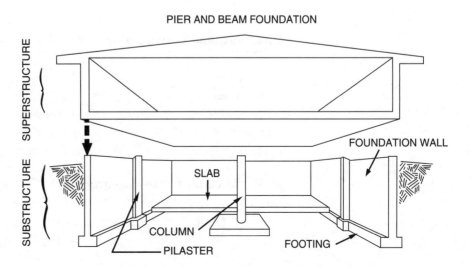

PIER AND BEAM FOUNDATION

■ EXTERIOR CONSTRUCTION

Walls and Framing

When the foundation is in place, the first floor deck is built and then the interior and exterior walls are framed. The exterior and some interior walls are known as **bearing walls**, because they support the floors, ceilings, and roof. (Some interior partitions, installed later, may be nonbearing.) The skeleton members of a building are called its **framing**. The walls of a frame are formed by vertical members called **studs** [15], spaced at even intervals, and attached to the sill. Many building codes require that for a one-story house the stud spacing not exceed 24 inches on centers. For a two-story house, the spacing may not exceed 16 inches. Studs rest on **sole plates** [12], which are secured to and rest on the *foundation wall* [4] in balloon framing. In constructing walls and floors, if the wall height is more than eight feet, the framer may install *firestops* [43], blocks nailed between studs or joists to stop drafts and retard the spread of fire.

Where there is an opening in a wall frame, such as for a door or window, a horizontal **header** is used to support the weight of the structure over the opening. Wider openings require larger headers for structural support. In masonry walls, the weight over a door or window opening may be supported by an arch or by a lintel. A *lintel* is a piece of stone, steel, or wood that is used to span the opening and support the wall above.

In framing, many builders are moving away from the traditional 2×4s placed 16 inches on center, using 2×6s instead. This allows a deeper wall for more extensive insulation.

Three basic types of wood-frame construction—platform, balloon, and post and beam—are shown in Figure 15.4.

Platform frame construction   The most common type of wall framing for both one-story and two-story residential structures is **platform framing construction**, also known as *western frame construction*. Only one floor is built at a time, and each floor serves as a platform for the next story. Wall studs are attached to the upper and lower plates, and the entire assemblage is then raised into place and anchored to the sill.

Balloon frame construction   This type of construction differs from the platform method in that the studs extend continuously from the foundation sill plate to the ceiling of the second floor. The second-floor joists rest on *ledger boards* or *ribbon boards* set into the interior edge of the studs. The balloon method gives a smooth, unbroken wall surface on each floor level, thus alleviating the unevenness that sometimes results from settling when the platform method is used. The balloon method has not been used much since about 1930.

Post-and-beam frame construction   With **post-and-beam construction**, the ceiling planks are supported on beams that rest on posts placed at intervals throughout the exterior of the house. Because the posts provide some of the ceiling support, rooms can be built with larger spans of space between the supporting side walls.

F I G U R E   15.4

Frame Construction

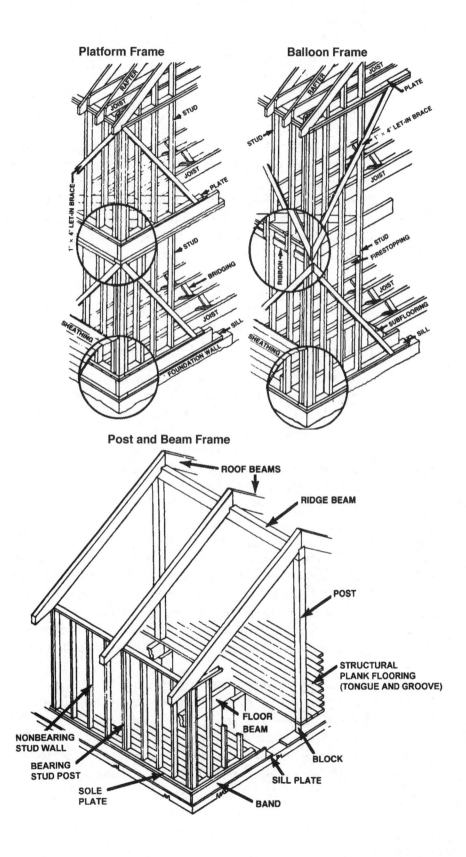

Platform Frame

Balloon Frame

Post and Beam Frame

In some houses, the beams are left exposed and the posts and beams are stained to serve as part of the decor.

Lumber   Lumber used in residential construction is graded according to moisture content and structural quality as established by the 1970 National Grade Rule. Grading rules require that lumber classified as dry have a moisture content of 19 percent or less. Lumber that has a higher moisture content is classified as green. All species and grades are assigned stress ratings to indicate their strength when used in spanning distances between two supports. Actual dimensions of lumber differ from nominal measurements. A 2×4 actually measures 1½" × 3½".

Exterior walls   After the skeleton is constructed, the exterior wall surface must be built and **sheathing** [19] and **siding** [20] applied. Sheathing is nailed directly to the *wall studs* [15] to form the base for siding and add rigidity to the wall system. Sheathing is generally hardboard, insulated board, or chipboard. If the house is to have a masonry veneer, the sheathing may be moisture-resistant gypsum board. Fabricated sheathings are available in both strip and sheet material. Sheathing is wrapped in tar paper or, more recently, in house wrap.

The final exterior layer, called *siding*, may be vinyl, wood, aluminum, stone, stucco, brick, or other material.

Insulation

To ensure adequate protection, **insulation** [17] should be placed in exterior walls and upper-floor ceilings. *Band insulation* of fiberglass is placed above the foundation walls. A sill sealer is placed between the foundation and the treated sill plate to reduce the infiltration of air and insects. The New York code requires varying amounts of insulation in different regions of the state, as well as storm windows and doors. For conversion of existing oil-fired units to gas or electric heat, *cap insulation* (under the attic floor) is required and storm windows or insulated glass where single-glazing had been used.

Insulation is rated according to its **R-value**, which indicates its resistance to heat transfer. The higher the R-value, the better the insulation. The most commonly used insulation material is fiberglass, which comes in either paper (i.e., Kraft) or foil-faced batts that can be placed between the studs. Other materials used are rigid polystyrene foam (i.e., Styrofoam), cellulose fiber (usually blown into existing structures), rock wool, or sprayed-in-place foam. Proper insulation will contribute to the efficiency of both heating and air-conditioning systems.

Each set of building plans must be certified by a licensed architect or engineer, who puts the appropriate energy code on the plan. Different styles and designs and different regions have varying code requirements. For example, the manufacturer of a log house may certify that no insulation is necessary (because the logs do the job and the windows are small), whereas a contemporary-style home with vast areas of glass could require a great deal of insulation.

Window and Door Units

After the exterior walls are framed, the next step is installation of exterior window and door units. Windows may be either side-hinged or vertically hinged (**casement windows**) or may slide up and down (*sash*). Basic window styles include the following:

- *Single-hung window*. A sash window with only one movable sash, usually the bottom one.
- *Double-hung window*. A sash window with two vertically sliding sashes; both single-hung and **double-hung window** sashes are controlled and held in place by springs or weights.
- *Slider window*. A sash window that opens by moving horizontally.
- *Casement/awning window*. A window hinged like a door that opens or closes by the action of a gear handle.
- *Jalousie window*. A **jalousie window** is formed by horizontal slats of glass that open or close vertically by the action of a gear.

Many modern windows can be removed from the inside for easy cleaning. Window frames are most commonly vinyl, wood, steel, or aluminum. The quality of a window depends on its construction, additional security, and insulating factors. State code requires either double-glazing (two panes of sealed glass with insulating airspace between) or storm windows.

The thickness of an interior door is usually 1⅜ inches; an exterior door is usually 1¾ inches. Most are made of mahogany, birch, walnut, or oak. Glass doors, screen doors with aluminum or steel frames, and insulated metal doors are primarily exterior doors used for patios, porches, or garden areas. Energy considerations dictate *triple-glazing* for many windows in recent years.

Roof Framing and Coverings

The construction of the skeleton framing for the roofing material is the next step in building. Residential roofs are made in several styles, including gabled, shed, salt box, and flat. Roof construction includes the *rafters* or *collar ties* [31], *sheathing* [40], and *exterior trimming* [42]. Skeleton framings are classified as either conventional (site built) or trusses. (See Figures 15.5 and 15.6.)

The slant of the roof is referred to as its **pitch**; shallow roofs sometimes give more trouble than steep ones that shed rain and snow more readily. Pitch is expressed as a ratio. If the total roof rise is 6 feet and the total span is 24 feet, the pitch would be 1/4. *Slope* is the term more commonly used to designate the incline. If the roof rises at a rate of 6" for every 12" of run (half the total span), the roof is said to have a *6 in 12 slope*. The triangular symbol above the roof in a set of architectural plans is where the numbers may be found.

Joist and rafter roof framing   A **joist and rafter roof** consists of *rafters* [30], *collar beams* [31], *ceiling joists* [27], and *ridge beam* [33]. Rafters are the sloping timbers that support the weight of the roof and establish the roof's pitch, or slant. Collar beams give rigidity to the rafters, and the ridge board aligns and receives the rafters.

FIGURE 15.5

Roof Construction

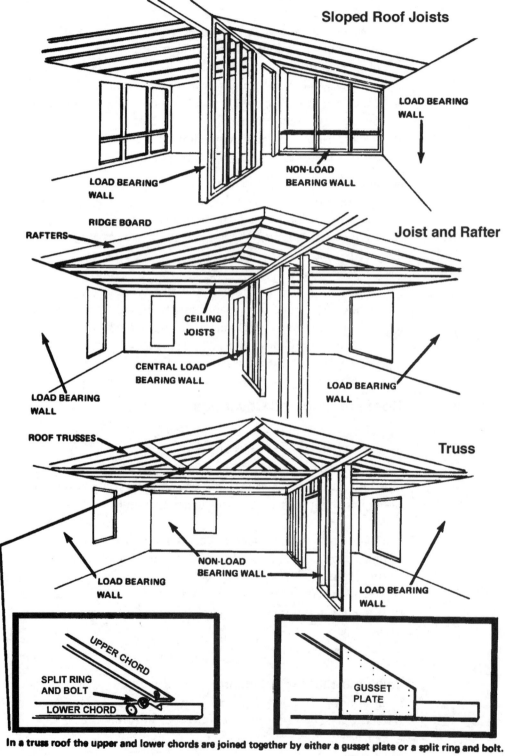

In a truss roof the upper and lower chords are joined together by either a gusset plate or a split ring and bolt.

FIGURE   15.6

Roof Styles

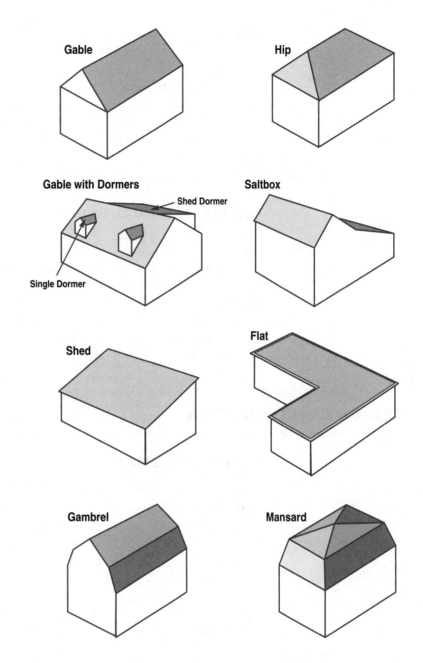

Truss roof framing   A truss roof has four parts. It has *lower chords*, *upper chords*, *"W" diagonals*, and *gusset plates*. The lower chords are similar to ceiling joists, and the upper chords are the equivalent of rafters in a joist and rafter roof. The "W" diagonals are the equivalent of the collar ties. Gusset plates are solid pieces of metal or wood that add rigidity to the roof. All integral parts are assembled and held in place by gusset plates, bolt connections, or nails. A truss roof is generally prefabricated at a mill and set in place in sections by a crane, while a joist and rafter roof is assembled piece by piece on the site.

Exposed rafter and roof framing   *Exposed*, or *sloping*, *rafter roofs* are often used with post-and-beam frame construction. The rafters are supported by central support posts at the exterior walls. There may be no ceiling joists or lower chords to provide additional support. The rafters in this type of roof are often left exposed for decorative purposes.

Exterior trim   The overhang of a pitched roof that extends beyond the exterior walls of the house is called the **eaves [24]**, or *cornice*. The cornice is composed of the **soffit**, *frieze board, fascia board, and extended rafters* and recently includes *soffit vents*. The **frieze board [42]** is the exterior wood trim board used to finish the exterior wall between the top of the siding and eaves, or overhang, of the roof framing. The **fascia** board is exterior trim used along the line of the butt end of the rafters where the roof overhangs the structural walls. The overhang of the cornice provides a decorative touch to the exterior of a house as well as some protection from sun and rain. (See Figure 15.7.)

Roof sheathing and roofing   With the skeleton roof in place, the rafters are covered with sheathing. The type and thickness of sheathing to be used depends on the choice of outside roofing material and rafter spacing. Shingles are commonly made of *fiberglass* or *asphalt* and are laid over plywood covered with tar paper. In recent years, the first three to six feet of a roof (depending on location and slope) are covered with an "ice and water" type membrane, which adheres to the sheathing and rip edge. If wood shingles are used, spaced sheathing of 1×4 boards may be used to provide airspace to allow the shingles to dry after rain. Metal **flashing** protects joists between the roof and the chimney or in roof valleys.

■ INTERIOR CONSTRUCTION

Walls and Finishing

Interior walls are usually covered with drywall (also called **plasterboard** or **wallboard**) [46], although lath [45] and plaster [47] may be used. Drywall is finished by a process known as taping and floating. Taping covers the joints between the sheets of drywall. Floating is the smoothing out of the walls over the joints and the rough edges where nails attach drywall to the studs. Texturing may be applied with a roller prior to painting.

Final features added include (1) *floor covering*, (2) *trim*, (3) *cabinet work*, and (4) *wall finishings* of paint, wallpaper, or paneling. Floor coverings of vinyl, asphalt tile,

FIGURE   15.7

Eave or Cornice

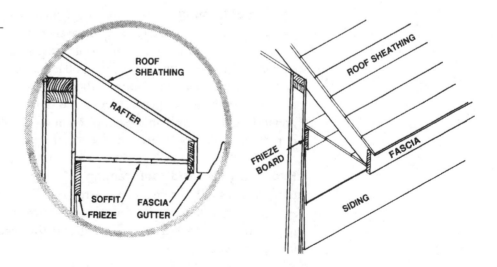

wood (either in strips or blocks), carpet, brick, stone, or ceramic tile are applied over the wood or concrete subflooring. Trim masks the joints between the walls and ceiling and gives a finished touch to the room. Cabinet work in the home may be either built in on the job or prefabricated in the mill.

Plumbing

If the house is supplied by a well, the state Department of Health sets various requirements for its location, for example, 25 feet from a cast iron sewer pipe and as much as 150 feet from the seepage pit of a **septic system**. It is also generally required that a well produce at least five gallons of water per minute of water supply.

Septic systems also are regulated as to their distance from a house or a well. **Percolation rate** tests must be performed to determine whether the soil will absorb effluent neither too quickly nor too slowly.

Plumbing must be installed subject to strict inspections and in accordance with local building codes that dictate materials and the method of installation. Sewer pipes are of cast iron, concrete, or plastic, whereas water pipes are of copper, plastic, or (in older homes) galvanized iron. Recently, plastic has been used more frequently for waste lines because it eliminates piping joints in the foundation slab and may be less expensive.

All drain pipes must be connected to vents leading out of the building to operate properly. Water supply pipes must be sized adequately to provide sufficient flow of water to faucets or fixtures. The main water lines in a home are usually 1-inch or ¾-inch diameter, while the branch lines running to individual outlets are ½-inch diameter.

Domestic hot water may be supplied directly from a coil in the heating system or by a separate hot-water heater. If a separate unit is used, the water is heated by electricity, gas, or oil. Well-water supplies may require water softeners.

Lead-tin solder, used widely for copper plumbing, has been under scrutiny by the Environmental Protection Agency, which limits lead content to 8 percent and recommends the use of tin-antimony solder instead.

Bathtubs, toilets, and sinks are made of cast iron or pressed steel coated with enamel, plastic, artificial marble, or, increasingly in recent years, fiberglass.

Heating and Air-Conditioning

Warm-air heating systems and hot-water baseboards are the most common heating systems in use today. Steam heat is found in some older homes. In recent years, some areas of northern New York have seen increasing dependence on wood as a fuel. A forced-warm-air system consists of a furnace, air handlers, warm-air distributing ducts, and ducts for the return air. Combination heating-cooling systems are common in new homes; the most common is the conventional warm-air heating system with a cooling unit attached.

Heating systems can be powered by electricity, oil, or natural gas. Oil-fired systems use oil from a storage tank located on the property, either above ground (AST) or buried underground (UST). (Note that should USTs leak, costly cleanup procedures will be required.) Natural gas may be supplied through a utility pipeline or from a separate pressurized gas tank on the property.

Each furnace has a capacity rated in **British thermal units (BTUs)**. The number of BTUs given represents the furnace's heat output from gas, oil, or electric firing. A heating and cooling engineer can determine the cubic area of the building as well as its construction, insulation, and window and door sizes and from these data can compute the furnace capacity required in the coldest possible weather and the cooling capacity needed for air-conditioning. Air-conditioning units are rated either in BTUs or in tons. Twelve thousand BTUs are equivalent to a one-ton capacity.

Most gas pipes for heating and cooking are made of black iron. A flexible plastic tubing is coming into use, although not all jurisdictions allow it yet. It requires fewer joints and is easier to install. Gas pipes are installed in the walls or run overhead in the attic, where adequate ventilation is possible. They are never placed in the slab.

Solar heating   One of the most promising sources of heat for residential buildings is **solar energy**. Most solar heating units suitable for residential use operate by gathering the heat from the sun's rays with one or more solar collectors. Water or air is forced through a series of pipes in the solar collector to be heated by the sun's rays. The hot air or water then is stored in a heavily insulated storage tank until it is needed to heat the house or for use as a hot-water heater.

More immediately practical in the New York state area is *passive solar heating*. Without any additional special equipment, a house may be built or remodeled to take advantage of the sun's rays. Large areas of glass on a southern exposure and few windows on the north side of a building are typical of passive solar arrangements. Substantial savings in fuel may be obtained.

Heat pumps, which utilize heat from outside air in a form of reverse air-conditioning, are often used in conjunction with backup heating units of more conventional design. Where electricity is expensive, use of a heat pump may bring down costs. The heat pump also serves in summer for air-conditioning. Geothermal systems utilize the constant temperature underground to aid in heating and cooling. At depths of four to six feet and greater, the earth maintains about the same temperature year-round, approximately 51°F to 56°F in New York state.

Ventilation   Ventilation in a home is important for several reasons: to provide fresh air for the occupants to breathe, to prevent the accumulation of moisture that could damage the structure, and to eliminate harmful or offensive gases and odors.

With today's emphasis on insulation and close-fitting windows and doors, proper ventilation can sometimes be overlooked. Enclosed unheated spaces such as attics and crawlspaces must be ventilated by screened openings in the structure. An attic may have vents through the roof, or (more sightly from the street) a ridge beam [32] that contains hidden vents. Bathrooms and kitchens are normally ventilated by means of fans that connect to ducts leading out of the building. Exhaust fumes from oil or gas-fired equipment also must be vented to the outside through ducts.

Electrical Services

Electrical power lines can be run underground or strung from power poles. Electrical services are brought into the home through a transformer and meter into a distribution panel (circuit breaker box or fuse box). The utility company owns and maintains the parts of the system up to and including the meter. The rest of the system, including the distribution panel and interior circuits, is the responsibility of the homeowner.

Electricity is measured in terms of volts, amperes (amps), and watts. Voltage indicates the strength of the electrical charge. Amperage indicates the amount of current that is flowing in response to the voltage. Wattage measures the amount of electric power that is being delivered and used.

Most residential circuits operate at approximately 110 volts and are rated to carry 15 or 20 amps of current. Larger appliances require 220-volt circuits and may draw 30 to 60 amps. The amount of amperage a circuit can carry is limited by the size (rating) of the fuse or circuit breaker that controls the circuit and the size (gauge) of the wire; **110-volt circuits** have two wires, one hot and one neutral, and they may also have a separate ground wire; **220-volt circuits** have two hot wires and one neutral wire and may have a separate ground wire as well.

Electrical wiring is rated by its gauge or thickness. A lower gauge indicates a larger diameter of wire. The gauge determines how much current (amperage) the wire can safely carry. For example, 15-amp circuits require 14-gauge wire, while 20-amp circuits call for 12-gauge wire. Most residential wiring is made of copper, although aluminum wiring is sometimes used. Aluminum wiring requires the use of specially designed receptacles that are approved for use with this type of wire.

Modern construction uses cable known as *Romex*, which has two or three insulated wires and a bare ground wire covered with a plastic sheathing. Exposed cable or wiring must be run through metal conduit to provide protection from physical damage. Conduit can be either rigid metal or plastic tubes or flexible metal tubing. Flexible conduit is sometimes called *Greenfield*.

The **fuse box** or **circuit breaker box** is the distribution panel for the many electrical circuits in the house. (See Figure 15.8.) In case of a power overload, the heat generated by the additional flow of electricity will cause the circuit to open, thus reducing the possibility of electrical fires. All electrical installations are inspected by the New York Board of Fire Underwriters. New York State standards require at least 100-ampere service and, for new home construction, a 110-volt smoke detector and a ground fault interrupter on each water hazard circuit (kitchen, baths, and exterior outlets). The ground fault interrupter is a supersensitive form of circuit breaker.

FIGURE 15.8

**Main Distribution Panel
Interior**

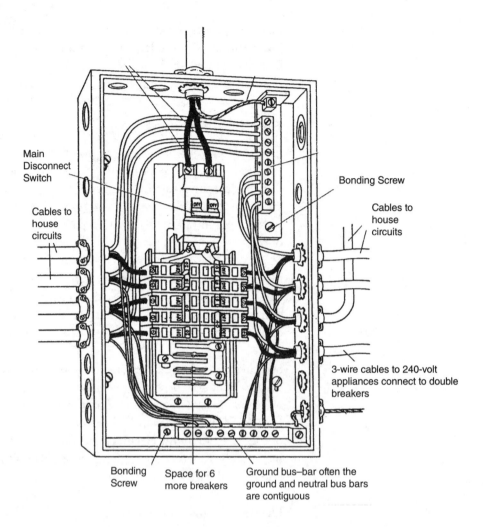

Main
Disconnect
Switch

Cables to
house
circuits

Bonding Screw

Cables to
house
circuits

3-wire cables to 240-volt
appliances connect to double
breakers

Bonding
Screw

Space for 6
more breakers

Ground bus–bar often the
ground and neutral bus bars
are contiguous

Residential wiring circuits are rated by the voltage they are designed to carry. In the past, most residences were wired only for 110-volt capacity. Today, because of the many built-in appliances in use, 220-volt service is standard.

A functioning carbon monoxide detector and smoke detector must be installed in every one- or two-family house, co-op, or condo constructed in New York state.

National Electric Code

The National Fire Protection Association is responsible for authoring the National Electric Code. The code has become a national standard for the service and installation of electricity. Its purpose is to protect the general public and respective property from hazards associated with the installation and use of electrical drawing equipment. The code is reviewed and/or renewed every three years.

■ NEW YORK LAWS

Home Improvement Law

New York State requires that the sale of home improvement goods and services costing more than $500 to homeowners, co-op owners, or tenants conform to certain regulations.

A copy of a written plain-English contract must be given to the customer before any work is done. It must contain the contractor's name, address, and telephone number; approximate start and completion dates; specifics of the work and materials (brands, model number, price); and a notice that the customer has an unconditional right to cancel the contract in writing within three days after it is signed.

Contractors are required to put into a trust (escrow) account in a New York bank any contract payments by a customer, to be withdrawn only under a reasonable payment schedule agreed to by contractor and customer or on substantial completion of the job. If the customer violates the contract, funds may be withdrawn only to the amount of the contractor's reasonable costs. As an alternative to the escrow account, the contractor may deliver to the customer, within ten days of receiving the funds, a bond guaranteeing that the customer's money will be properly used or returned.

Where the contractor fails to adequately secure customers' deposits, to provide a written contract, or otherwise violates the law, penalties include fines of up to 10 percent of the contract price, with a maximum of $1,000 for a first offense, $2,500 for a second one, and $5,000 for a third or succeeding violation.

New Home Warranty

With a few exceptions, New York requires that the buyer of a new home receive the following warranties: one year's protection against faulty workmanship and defective materials; two years' protection against defective installation of plumbing, electrical, heating, cooling, and ventilation systems; and six years' protection against major structural defects (a foundation that settles, a roof that sags, a wall that bows). Some builders carry warranty insurance at a cost of several hundred dollars per house.

Warranty law allows builders a reasonable time to make repairs and does not cover construction done by the buyer that is beyond the builder's control.

Notice of problems must be given to the builder within 30 days after expiration of the warranty. Lawsuits must be filed within four years for the one- and two-year warranties and within seven years for the six-year warranty. If the home is sold within the warranty period, the new owner is covered as the original owner was.

■ SUMMARY

State and local building codes set standards for health and safety in construction. Working drawings and written specifications establish the quality of materials and workmanship needed.

Foundations include footings, foundation walls, and slabs. The two major types of foundations are concrete slab and pier-and-beam.

Wood-frame construction is the type most frequently used in building single-family houses in New York State. The three basic types of exterior wall framing are platform, balloon, and post-and-beam. Multilevel balloon construction differs from the platform method in that the studs extend continuously to the ceiling of the second floor, whereas with the platform method only one floor is built at a time. Post-and-beam construction uses interior posts to support the roof.

Windows may be sash windows, which are single-hung, double-hung, or sliders; casement windows, side-hinged or vertically hinged; or jalousie windows, which are formed of horizontal slats of glass. Door styles include panel, slab, and hollow or solid core.

Skeleton roof framing may be joist and rafter, exposed rafter, or truss. The skeleton roof rafters or upper chords are covered with sheathing, generally plywood, and then covered with fiberglass, wood, slate, composite, ceramic, concrete type, or asphalt shingles.

Interior walls are generally covered with drywall and finished with paint or wallpaper. Final interior features include wall finishings, trim, floor covering, and cabinet work. Plumbing, heating, air-conditioning, and electrical wiring require careful installation to adhere to building codes.

New York State requires that the sale of home improvement goods and services costing more than $500 to homeowners, co-op owners, or tenants conform to certain regulations. New York requires that the buyer of a new home receive certain warranties.

CHAPTER 15 QUIZ

1. Written directions that tell the builder what materials to use or what construction technique to follow are known as
   a. specifications.
   b. directives.
   c. memoranda.
   d. blueprints.

2. Which is described as a 1½ story house?
   a. Split-level
   b. Ranch
   c. Colonial
   d. Cape Cod

3. Many building codes require that center spacing for studs on a one-story house not exceed
   a. 12 inches.
   b. 18 inches.
   c. 24 inches.
   d. 30 inches.

4. Which is a type of foundation?
   a. Balloon
   b. Pier-and-beam
   c. Lally column
   d. Chord

5. A piece of stone, steel, or wood used to span a door opening and support the wall above is called the
   a. footings.
   b. sill or beam.
   c. anchor bolts.
   d. lintel.

6. An R-value refers to
   a. stress and strength.
   b. resistance to heat transfer.
   c. heat output.
   d. moisture content.

7. The vertical parts of a house frame are called
   a. trusses.
   b. firestops.
   c. bolts.
   d. studs.

8. In a frame or wooden skeleton, studs rest on
   a. sole plates.
   b. balloons.
   c. joists.
   d. ridges.

9. Which characteristic is considered when grading lumber?
   a. Age
   b. Color
   c. Fragrance
   d. Moisture content

10. Sheathing is found on the outside
    a. walls.
    b. windows.
    c. foundation.
    d. doors.

11. Cap insulation, which has the greatest payback in lowered fuel bills, is found
    a. under the attic floor.
    b. on the basement ceiling.
    c. in sidewalls.
    d. just under the roof.

12. Sloping roof supports are called
    a. trusses.
    b. rafters.
    c. joists.
    d. studs.

13. Drywall is also known as
    a. plasterboard.
    b. siding.
    c. sheathing.
    d. paneling.

14. Heat from outside air is utilized through a
    a. reverse conditioner.
    b. passive solar system.
    c. heat pump.
    d. cold air return.

15. A contractor must give the customer a written contract in advance of any work when home improvement goods and services will cost more than
    a. $100.
    b. $250.
    c. $500.
    d. $750.

16. A new-home buyer receives a warranty of six years' protection against
    a. defective materials.
    b. structural defects.
    c. defective installation of heating systems.
    d. all of these.

CHAPTER 16

Valuation Process

■ KEY TERMS

appraisal
Appraisal Institute
arm's-length transaction
assemblage
comparable properties
comparative market
  analysis (CMA)
cost approach
demand
depreciation
direct costs
economic obsolescence
effective gross income
  (EGI)
evaluation
external obsolescence
FIRREA

federally related
  transaction
fee appraiser
functional obsolescence
gross income multiplier
  (GIM)
gross rent multiplier
  (GRM)
highest and best use
income capitalization
  approach
indirect costs
insured value
locational obsolescence
mortgage value
net operating income
  (NOI)

overall capitalization rate
  (OAR)
physical deterioration
plottage
potential gross income
  (PGI)
reconciliation
replacement cost
reproduction cost
sales comparison
  approach
staff appraiser
subject property
substitution
supply
valuation

■ CHARACTERISTICS OF REAL ESTATE

Unlike other commodities, real estate has unique characteristics that affect its value. These fall into two categories: (1) economic characteristics and (2) physical characteristics.

Economic Characteristics

There are four basic *economic characteristics* of land that will influence its value:

1. Relative scarcity
2. Improvements
3. Permanence of investment
4. Area preference

Relative scarcity   The total supply of land is fixed—*they aren't making any more!* Scarcity applies to the principle of value known as *supply and demand.* In total, there are seven basic principles of value. They will be covered later in this chapter, but let's briefly discuss how the principle of supply and demand relates to scarcity.

The availability of property for sale or for rent at various pricing levels creates the marketplace. When product availability exceeds the demand for that product, this economic force drives market pricing down. Of course, in the reverse, when the demand for a product exceeds the available inventory stock, this economic force drives prices up. It is, therefore, safe to conclude that the pricing of a parcel of property reflects the current scarcity of that parcel at that moment in time.

Improvements   The building of an improvement on one parcel of land has an effect on the value of neighboring parcels or on whole communities. For example, the construction of a shopping mall or the selection of a site for a landfill can influence values in a large area.

Basic Economic Characteristics Influencing Value

- Relative scarcity
- Improvements
- Permanence of investment
- Area preference

Although all land ownership comes with the *right* to improve, the nature of improvements is greatly restricted by local zoning. Improvements must always be

- legal uses,
- in compliance with zoning ordinances, and
- built in compliance with local building codes.

Permanence of investment   As the characteristic of scarcity suggests, land cannot be made or destroyed. Within this category of economic characteristics, permanence becomes the sole factor behind purchasers' willingness to invest large amounts of capital to improve property. The result of improvement generally leads to the supply side. Although improvements generally apply to new construction, existing structures may also be gutted and renovated. Even if older buildings are torn down, improvements such as drainage, electricity, water, and sewerage remain; so, generally speaking, prior improvements may be salvageable when the previous *infrastructure* remains.

Area preference   This economic characteristic, often called *situs*, refers to people's choices and preferences for a given area. It is what makes one house sell for twice as much as an almost identical one on the other side of town. As the old expression goes, the three most important factors in determining the value of real estate are location, location, and location. For example, an older property located in an area alongside newer properties will enjoy price appreciation merely as a result of its being near these newer properties.

Physical Characteristics

There are three basic *physical characteristics* of land:

1. Immobility (land is nonmovable)
2. Indestructibility (land is permanent)
3. Nonhomogeneity (each parcel of land is unique)

While the physical characteristics of any parcel of land will apply only to that land itself, the economic characteristics discussed previously are used to compare the value of one parcel of land in relation to another.

Immobility   Land is immobile. Even if soil is removed, that part of the earth's surface always remains. The geographic location can never be changed. Because land is immobile, *real estate laws and markets tend to be local in character.*

Indestructibility   Just as land is immobile, it is *durable and indestructible.* Land may diminish as a result of erosion or increase as a result of accretion; however, land cannot be made or destroyed.

Nonhomogeneity   No two parcels of land are ever exactly the same. Although there may be substantial similarity, *all parcels differ geographically* because each has its own location.

■ REAL ESTATE—THE BUSINESS OF VALUE

Value is not the same as price, nor is it the same as cost. *Value* can be defined as *the amount of goods or services that will be offered in the marketplace in exchange for any given product.* It also has been described as the *present worth of future benefits attributable to a property.*

In real estate, the concept of *cost (the price or purchase or production)* generally relates to the past, while *price (the amount of consideration, usually currency, that a buyer agrees to pay for an item and a seller agrees to sell that item for)* relates to the present, and *value (the worth of an item to one party or another)* relates to the future.

The following seven basic principles constitute value:

1. The principle of *supply and demand* emphasizes pricing's direct relationship to the availability and demand for a product.
2. **Substitution** refers to the reality that any informed investor would not pay more for a property than it would cost to purchase a substitute property of equal utility. For example, let's say you are shopping for a suit at Armani. The suit sells for $1,000. Later, you find the same suit at Bloomingdale's for $800. The principle of substitution suggests that in all likelihood, you will purchase the suit at Bloomingdale's rather than at Armani.

   The principle of substitution is the primary foundation for all three approaches to appraisal valuation:
   - ■ The *sales comparison approach,* which uses comparable sales, that is, the cost of acquiring a substitute property, to indicate how much an informed investor/buyer will pay for a particular property.

- The *cost approach* is based on single use/purpose property for which sales of comparable properties are few or nonexistent. These properties are valued by establishing the cost to reproduce or replace the property—combining land value with the cost of constructing the improvement (new) and then taking into account the accrued depreciation of existing improvements to the property. The final result will determine for the investor whether the subject property or a substitute is feasible.

- The *income capitalization approach* regards the property's value as being directly related to the income attributable from that property once a capitalization rate is applied. The principle of substitution applies in that the subject property is always measured against substitute investment alternatives bearing equal cash flow returns and risks.

3. *Anticipation* refers to the expectation that today's purchase will increase in value tomorrow.

4. **Highest and best use** is defined as the use that is most likely, legal, and desirable when measured against alternative likely, legal, and desirable uses and that conveys to its owner the greatest income and subsequent value attributable to the land. The highest and best use approach values sites in two ways:

- Highest and best use as vacant. This approach answers the question, Which use or improvement would most likely result in the greatest value attributable to the land if the land is (or were) vacant? Someone viewing a property as a development site is likely to disregard improvements made to the property. Given this example, one would view this site analysis "as vacant."

- Highest and best use as improved. This approach is identical to the "as vacant" method, with one exception: it requires including in the analysis the costs of demolition of the existing improvement. These demolition costs would not appear had the site already been vacant, and they are in addition to the costs of constructing the new improvement.

Normally, the current use of a property tends to be the highest and best use of that site; however, that is not always the case. For example, changes in zoning might allow for a project of greater *bulk* (the total legal and buildable square footage of a project) to be built in place of the existing structure. Once the zoning increase takes effect, the existing use of the property ceases to be the highest and best use of that site since it conforms to a lower standard. See Chapter 21 for more on zoning.

5. *External property influences* refer to the features outside of the property line that affect value.

- *Economies* are a direct result of the addition of area amenities by a municipality. Some of these amenities may include new highways, transportation systems, and water and sewer facilities.

- *Diseconomies*—the reverse of economies—are usually (but not always) the result of nonlocal reasons or events. Examples might include crime and pollution.

6. *Conformity* exists where there is uniformed use and a consistent construction style of properties in a given subdivision. Property values tend to remain stable or increase where conformity exists. A subdivision in which housing is all Tudor-style and the houses are similar in size would be an example of conformity.

7. *Increasing and decreasing returns.* Increasing returns occur when improvement(s) made to a property that cause the overall value of that property to increase as a result of that improvement's overall utility. This can also be referred to as an *underimprovement.* Decreasing returns occur when a property owner improves a property beyond the point of capital recapture (the return of the original principal investment) on a sale; in such an instance, the property is said to be *overimproved.* Usually, the result is that neighboring property owners experience increased property values, while the subject property remains limited in its value potential. From a resale point of view, it is not always wise to be the biggest or best house on the street.

■ SUPPLY AND DEMAND

The forces of *supply and demand* continually interact in the market to establish price levels. Usually when **supply** goes up, prices drop; when **demand** increases, prices rise. (See Figure 16.1.)

Supply and Demand in the Real Estate Market

Because real estate is fixed (immobile), the real estate market is relatively slow to adjust to changes in the factors that influence supply and demand. (See Figure 16.2.) The product cannot be removed from the market or transferred elsewhere, so an oversupply usually results in lower price levels. But because development of and construction on real estate take considerable time, increases in demand may not be met immediately. Thus, when demand is high, prices rise.

Factors Affecting Supply

Some of the factors affecting supply include:

■ *Product availability.* Inventory or lack thereof; vacancy and/or absorption rates
■ *Potential for new inventory.* New construction; renovations or conversions of existing product (for example, conversion from an antiquated office building to a new residential building)
■ *Labor supply and construction costs*
   — Increase or decrease in availability of raw materials or construction materials
   — Abundance or shortage of labor in the skilled building trades
   — Increase in the cost of building materials
   — High interest rates or scarce loans

FIGURE   16.1

Supply and Demand

Supply Exceeds Demand
"Buyer's Market"

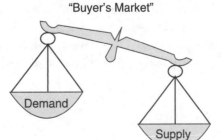

Demand Exceeds Supply
"Seller's Market"

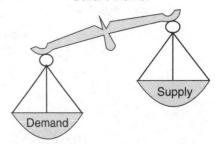

FIGURE 16.2

Factors Affecting Supply and Demand

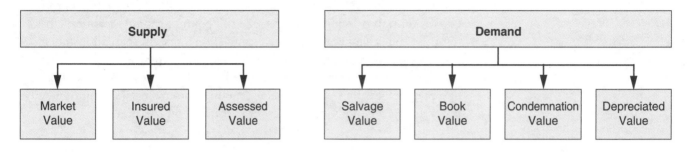

■ *Governmental controls and financial policies*
 — Local property taxation
 — Zoning ordinances
 — National interest rates

The government can greatly influence the amount of money available for real estate investment through its monetary policies.

At the local level, policies on taxation of real estate can have either positive or negative effects. Community *amenities* such as churches, schools, parks, and efficient governmental policies all affect the real estate market.

Factors Affecting Demand

Population   The basic human need for shelter grows or declines as the population changes. At any given time, some areas are gaining population while others are losing. In recent years, New York state's population has dropped. The makeup of the population, or *demographics*, also must be taken into account. For example, an increasing number of homes have been bought by single persons, one-parent families, and retirees.

Employment and wage levels   Employment levels in the community (the opening or closing of a large company, for example) have a major effect on the real estate market. Generally speaking, bullish real estate markets occur when unemployment rates are low. Income levels coupled by employment can spark the bull market. In these times, the working, income-earning consumer feels better about the prospect of taking on long-term debt. Often, the driving force behind this debt assumption is the desire to become a first-time homeowner or to upgrade or improve one's home.

These are factors that constitute demand in any market. However, future planning becomes critical since nothing lasts forever. The good times may become lean times. Economies are cyclical and as a result, leaner times, when they come, can ultimately punish the same party they rewarded when times were good.

Vacancy levels   Vacancy levels in a community provide a good indication of the demand for housing:

- A growing shortage of housing (a decrease in vacancies) will result in increasing rents.
- An overabundance of housing (an increase in vacancies) will force rents down.

Generally speaking, when rentals in housing are soft, sales markets are strong; and when sales markets are soft, rental markets are strong. However, if the demand within the sales markets exceeds the amount of available supply, the rental market can be strong. At the present time, this is the case in New York City where the supply is limited.

Interest rates   When mortgage interest rates fall, more buyers come into the market, which tends to drive prices up.

Interest rates and sales prices work in opposite directions:

- *Lower interest rates lead to increases in a property's pricing.* Sellers are aware of the liquidity in the market and, as a result, strive to achieve higher sales prices.
- *High interest rates lead to a decrease in a property's pricing.* Buyers are aware of the illiquidity in the market and as a result strive to achieve lower purchase prices.

■ APPRAISAL

An **appraisal** is a supported and defended estimate or opinion of value, while an **evaluation** is an analysis of a property and its attributes in which a value estimate is not required. The study may consider any aspect of the property, including the nature, quality, and utility of an interest in the real estate. **Valuation** is the process of estimating value for a specific set of interests as of a specific point in time for a real estate property. In the real estate business, the highest level of appraisal activity is conducted by professional real estate appraisers who are recognized for their knowledge, training, skill, and integrity in this field and who are licensed or certified by New York State. Within the appraisal industry, appraisers are governed by the *Uniform Standards of Professional Appraisal Practice (USPAP)*. The Financial Institutions Reform Recovery and Enforcement Act of 1989 **(FIRREA)** requires that any appraisal to be conducted involving a **federally related transaction** must use either a licensed certified or general appraiser. A *federally related transaction* is defined as any transaction in which a loan is originated by any financial institution or lender regulated by the federal government. This would include institutions or lenders regulated by the Federal Deposit Insurance Corporation (FDIC), Office of the Comptroller of Currency (OCC), National Credit Union Administration (NCUA), and Office of Thrift Supervision (OTS).

Formal appraisal reports are relied on in important decisions made by mortgage lenders, investors, public utilities, government agencies, businesses, and individuals.

Not all estimates of value are made by professional appraisers. Often, the real estate licensee must help sellers arrive at a market value for their property without the aid of a formal appraisal report. Such assistance is known as an *opinion of value* or a **comparative market analysis (CMA)**.

License law prohibits calling any opinion of value or CMA an "appraisal" unless it is prepared by a licensed, certified, or general appraiser. The usual penalty for doing so is the revocation of your real estate license.

A salesperson may sometimes be approached, however, to furnish a simple paid appraisal to help in division of property during divorce proceedings or to settle an estate. Such a determination of current value does not require any special license, but it should be performed under the supervision of the managing broker. This provides guidance and education in the process, and only the broker, of course, may charge the public for services.

Appraisals may be required in the following situations, among others:

- *Estate purposes*, to establish taxable value or facilitate fair division among heirs
- *Divorce proceedings*, where real estate forms part of property to be shared
- *Financing*, when the amount to be lent depends on the value of the property
- *Taxation*, to furnish documentation for a taxpayer's protest of assessment figures
- *Relocation*, establishing the amount to be guaranteed to a transferred employee
- *Condemnation*, arriving at fair compensation for property taken by government
- *Insurance*, estimating possible replacement expense in cases of loss
- *Damage loss*, used to support income tax deductions
- *Feasibility*, to study possible consequences of a particular use for property
- *Fair market value determinations*, often occurring in commercial lease transactions when the subject of rental value pertains to options to extend lease terms

A **fee appraiser** works as an independent contractor, offering services to a number of different clients. A **staff appraiser** is an in-house employee of an organization such as the FHA, a lending institution, or a large corporation. A fee appraiser's fees are generally based on time and expenses; fees are never based on a percentage of the appraised value.

■ TYPES OF VALUE

An appraiser may be asked to estimate one of several different types of value. (See Figure 16.3.) Some of the different types of value are as follows:

- *Market value* is the most common subject of the valuation process.
- *Assessed value* applies specifically to the process of real property taxation. It should be noted that assessed valuation may or may not resemble the property's actual market value.

- *Liquidation value* is usually obtained via a forced or hurried transaction. It can also be referred to as *book value*. This is the value that lenders will most often look to when providing financing to a business entity.
- *Insurable value* is used for insurance purposes. The **insured value** is used to determine the amount of insurance carried on the property. As insurance only covers improvements that are made to the land, segregating the land value from the improvement value is essential in the determination of the improvement's insurable value. For tax purposes, the IRS always values the land at 20 percent of the overall value of the property as improved. It should also be noted that insurable value uses the cost approach to valuation.
- *Investment value* is the value to an investor when some of the following items are taken into consideration: risk of investment and capital loss; rate of return on invested capital; return of invested capital; and management involvement.
- *Salvage value* is what components of property or a business may be sold for (at the end of their useful life).
- *Value in use* is the value derived from a property when its current use is not the property's highest and best use. An example might be land that is a potential development site but that the current owner utilizes as a farm. The land is valued based on its use (as a farm) and not on its highest and best use (as a development site).
- **Mortgage value** is normally established by appraisal. It represents the amount or value that the lender is willing to commit to the loan. It is also the difference between the buyer's initial equity investment (down payment) and the purchase price or appraised value of the property, whichever is less.

The most frequently sought type is market value.

Market Value

Market value is an important concept defined as the *probable price a property will bring in a competitive and open market, offered by an informed seller, and allowing a reasonable time to find a purchaser who buys the property with knowledge of all the uses to which it is adapted, neither buyer nor seller being under duress.*

Market value also presupposes an **arm's-length transaction**. This is defined as a transaction between relative strangers, individually trying to do the best for themselves. In essence, the parties are unrelated and are dealing from equal positions

FIGURE 16.3

Kinds of Value

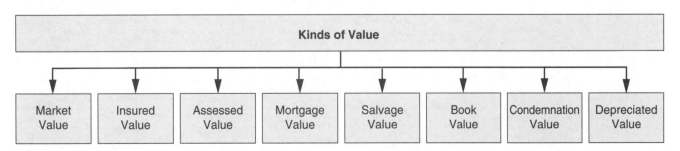

of bargaining. A sale between mother and son, for example, is not likely to be an arm's-length transaction and may not yield full market value for the property.

Included in the definition of market value are the following key points:

- Market value is the most *probable price* a property will bring.
- Payment must be made in *cash* or its equivalent.
- Both buyer and seller must act *without undue pressure*.
- A *reasonable length of time* must be allowed for the property to be exposed in the open market.
- Both buyer and seller must be *well informed* about the property's assets, defects, and potential.
- Market value presupposes an *arm's-length transaction*.

Market value versus market price   *Market value* is an estimate based on an analysis of comparable sales and other pertinent market data. *Market price*, on the other hand, is what a property *actually* sells for—its *selling price*. Theoretically, the ideal market price would be the same as the market value.

There are circumstances under which a property may be sold below market value, such as a seller who is forced to sell quickly or a sale arranged between relatives.

Market value versus cost   One of the most common errors made in valuing property is to assume that cost to build represents market value.

Cost and market value are most often equal when a newly constructed house is being appraised. Once the last house in the new subdivision has been sold, however, market value may go up because those who want to live in that particular neighborhood have to compete for whatever houses become available. On the other hand, construction of an expressway nearby may make the houses less desirable, and market value might drop. *Cost hasn't changed; value has*.

It is important to note that cost consists of two components:

1. Hard costs or direct costs that include
   - cost of land,
   - cost of brick and mortar, and
   - cost of labor to produce the improvement.
2. Soft costs or indirect costs that consist of
   - architectural and engineering fees,
   - professional fees (appraiser),
   - financing costs,
   - marketing costs,
   - lease-up costs (commissions),
   - administration, and
   - filing fees.

■ APPROACHES TO APPRAISAL

Real estate is usually appraised in one of three ways:

1. *Sales comparison approach*
2. *Cost approach*
3. *Income capitalization approach*

Each approach is appropriate for solving different valuation problems. All appraisals study the **subject property** (the parcel being evaluated) through all three methods while weighting the approaches appropriately and *reconciling* the results for a final estimate of value.

Sales Comparison Approach

The **sales comparison** (market data) **approach** evaluates property through careful study of similar parcels recently sold. (See Table 16.1.) These recently sold properties are referred to as **comparable properties**, or *comps*. Adjustments are made upward or downward to the comparables' sales price figures depending on whether their various components exist in the property being appraised. There are three categories of adjustments that an appraiser will study:

1. *Transactional differences*—financing at the time of the comparable's sale, conditions at the time of sale, and market conditions adjustment from the date of sale to present
2. *Locational differences*
3. *Physical characteristics*

When making adjustments, the appraiser identifies the differences between the comparable properties and the subject property:

■ When the comparable property is *superior* to the subject property in an area of comparison, the appraiser *subtracts* that amount from the sales price of the comparable.
■ When the comparable property is *inferior* to the subject property in an area of comparison, the appraiser *adds* that amount to the sales price of the comparable.

Appraisers *never* adjust the subject property. They will only adjust the sales price of the comparables to reflect and arrive at a *range of value*. Appraisals will always fall into a range of value since they are opinions of value. The appraised value can be any value that falls within the actual range of value determined through this process.

The sales comparison approach is based on research and study of the data gathered. It is most appropriate for valuation of residential one- to four-family residences.

Cost Approach

The **cost approach** estimates the amount needed to reproduce or replace the property being studied. This approach is most appropriate for non-income-producing buildings that cannot easily be compared with others such as hospitals, schools, libraries, houses of worship, and fire stations. It also is the primary and only approach used for insurance purposes.

TABLE 16.1

Sales Comparison Approach to Value

	Subject property	Comparable A	Comparable B	Comparable C	Comparable D	Comparable E
		$118,000	112,000	$121,000	$116,000	$110,000
Location	Good	Same	Poorer +4,500	Same	Same	Same
Age	6 years	Same	Same	Same	Same	Same
Size of lot	60' × 135'	Same	Same	Larger −5,000	Same	Larger −5,000
Landscaping	Good	Same	Same	Same	Same	Same
Construction	Brick	Same	Same	Same	Same	Same
Style	Ranch	Same	Same	Same	Same	Same
No. of rooms	6	Same	Same	Same	Same	Same
No. of bedrooms	3	Same	Same	Same	Same	Same
No. of baths	1½	Same	Same	Same	Same	Same
Sq. ft. of living space	1,500	Same	Same	Same	Same	Same
Other space (basement)	Full Basement	Same	Same	Same	Same	Same
Condition—exterior	Average	Better −1,500	Poorer +1,000	Better −1,500	Same	Poorer +2,000
Condition—interior	Good	Same	Same	better −500	Same	Same
Garage	2-car attached	Same	Same	Same	Same	Poorer +5,000
Other improvements						
Financing Date of sale		Current	1 yr. ago +3,500	Current	Current	Current
Net adjustments		−1,500	+9,000	−7,000	-0-	+2,000
Adjusted value		$116,500	$121,000	$114,000	$116,000	$112,000

Note: Because the value range of the properties in the comparison chart (excluding comparable B) is close, and comparable D required no adjustment, an appraiser would conclude that the indicated market value of the subject is $116,000.

The cost approach to appraisal is used when

- the subject of an appraisal is a single-purpose property and
- where comparable sales are nonexistent.

The cost approach considers not only the cost of reconstructing improvements but also the amount of **depreciation** that already has subtracted value from the property.

Depreciation falls into three categories:

1. **Physical deterioration**

2. **Functional obsolescence** (undesirable or outmoded features)
3. **External obsolescence** (**economic obsolescence** or **locational obsolescence**), defined as undesirable factors located beyond the property lines

Because physical deterioration exists within the property line, it is considered a curable event by the property owner. Functional obsolescence also occurs within the property line and can also be either a curable or noncurable event. An item is said to be curable when the cost to repair or replace it is equal to or less than the overall value that it will add to the property. An item is said to be noncurable when the cost to remediate it is greater than the overall value that the remediated item will add to the property.

Unlike physical deterioration and functional obsolescence (which are events that occur within the property line and can be curable or noncurable events), external obsolescence occurs from forces outside the property line that are not in the control of the property owner. As a result, external obsolescence is considered to be a noncurable event.

Reproduction cost is defined as the cost to create an exact replica of the subject property, while **replacement cost** is defined as the amount of capital necessary to construct the improvement using modern-day materials when a reproduction of the improvement is unachievable. This will not result in an exact replica of the improvement.

When calculating reproduction or replacement cost (new), direct and indirect costs must be taken into consideration. **Direct costs** are the expenditures necessary for the labor and materials used in the construction of a new improvement, including contractor's overhead and profit, while **indirect costs** are construction expenses for items other than labor and materials (e.g., financing costs, taxes, administrative costs, contractor's overhead and profit, legal fees, interest payments, insurance costs during construction, and lease-up costs).

The process of reproduction or replacement (particularly in the absence of an active sales market for similar properties) ultimately creates a comparable property exactly like the subject. The difference is that the replacement is looked at as *new*, while the subject suffers from depreciation (a loss of value attributable to any one or a combination of three events—physical deterioration, functional obsolescence, and external obsolescence) of its aged components.

Using the cost approach, the following are the three steps used for calculating the appraised value:

Step 1   Determine the reproduction/replacement cost (new). This is accomplished by using one of three cost estimating methods:

1. The *quantity survey method* entails a detailed costing process of all construction materials, cost of labor to construct the improvement, builders' return on the invested capital, and soft costs associated with the completion of the finished product such as architectural and engineering costs. The items of consideration are multiplied by the cost per item.

2. With the *unit-in-place method*, each component required to construct the improvement is studied. The appraiser then calculates the costs related to each of the components of the improvement to derive an amount. Components consist of items such as foundations, walls, floors, roofing, and paving.

3. The *comparative-unit method* (also known as the square-foot or cubic-foot method) multiplies the cost per square or per cubic foot to construct an improvement by the square feet of living area contained in the subject property. This method is more widely used than the quantity survey method and the unit-in-place method.

Step 2   Determine the amount of accrued depreciation (total loss in value due to physical deterioration, functional obsolescence, and external obsolescence) attributable to the subject property and subtract that from the figure calculated in step 1. This new figure, representing accrued depreciation, can be determined by utilizing any of the three methods for determining accrued depreciation:

1. The *breakdown method* is used to appraise older single-family homes and income-producing properties. In each case, depreciation categories are analyzed separately.

2. The *market extraction method* includes the study of comparable properties that have experienced the same or similar degrees of depreciation.

3. The *lump-sum age-life method* is the most popular method for appraisers using the cost approach to appraise residential property. The basis of this method is a measure or ratio of the property's economic or useful life as it relates to the property's effective age. Effective age is defined as the age of a property as a result of the condition of the improvement and the utility of the improvement.

The formula for calculating accrued depreciation using the lump-sum age-life method is as follows:

(Effective age ÷ Economic life) × Reproduction/replacement cost new = Accrued depreciation

Step 3   Determine the site value (land value) and add it to the figure calculated in step 2. Site values can always be derived through studying comparable sales. Each property that sells, regardless of property type, has underlying land as one of its components. Land comps are identified by separating land and improvement values.

The cost approach in formula form is as follows:

Reproduction/replacement cost (new) − Accrued depreciation + Site value = Appraised value

Income Capitalization Approach

The **income capitalization approach** to appraisal estimates value by analyzing the income generated by the property being considered. It is most appropriate and effective for the valuation of rental property. The income approach uses three types of ratios:

1. Gross income multiplier (GIM), a measure of annual income

TABLE 16.2

Cost Approach to Value

Subject property: 155 Potter Drive

Land valuation: Size 60' × 135' @ $450 per front foot =	$27,000
Plus site improvements: driveway, walks, landscaping, etc. =	8,000
Total	$35,000

Building valuation: Replacement cost
1,500 sq ft @ $85 per sq ft = $127,500

Less depreciation:		
Physical depreciation		
Curable		
(items of deferred maintenance)		
exterior painting	$4,000	
Incurable (structural deterioration)	9,750	
Functional obsolescence	2,000	
External depreciation	-0-	
Total depreciation	$15,750	
Depreciated value of building		111,750
Indicated value by cost approach		$146,750

2. Gross rent multiplier (GRM), a measure of monthly income
3. Overall capitalization rate (OAR), a measure of income and value as it relates to an investor's return on invested capital

The **gross income multiplier (GIM)** is the ratio of the property's sales price to the annual gross income of the property.

For example, a property sells for $1,200,000 and has an annual gross income of $100,000. This will produce a GIM of 12 ($1,200,000 ÷ $100,000 = 12). In simple terms, this property sold for 12 times the gross income attributable to the property. While this method offers a quick calculation of property value, it is unreliable because the property has expenses attributable to operations. This method views the *income only*, without considering the property's expenses.

The **gross rent multiplier (GRM)** is the ratio of the property's sales price to the monthly rental income. (GRM = Sales price ÷ Monthly rental income) Table 16.3 shows some examples of GRM comparisons.

Valuation using the **overall capitalization rate (OAR)** estimates value by comparing capitalization rates to the income attributable to the property.

This is not a simple process, as it is truly up to the investor to determine the actual **net operating income (NOI)** of the subject property. In order to understand this method, we must examine the three events in real property ownership:

1. As part of the *acquisition*, the investor analyzes the income and expenses of the subject purchase to calculate the net operating income.
2. During the *holding* period, the property owner analyzes income and expenses of the subject purchase to calculate the net operating income. Next, the property owner will use this information to create a *discounted cash flow analysis*, which indicates when to sell, when to refinance, and whether to continue to hold the property.
3. The *reversion* process is merely the sale of the property, when the investors revert to their original investment of cash.

TABLE 16.3	Comparable no.	Sales price	Monthly rent	GRM
Gross Rent Multiplier	1	$93,000	$650	144
	2	78,500	450	174
	3	95,500	675	141
	4	82,000	565	145
	Subject	?	625	?

Based on an analysis of these comparisons, a GRM of 145 seems reasonable for homes in this area. In the opinion of an appraiser, then, the estimated value of the subject property would be $625 × 145, or $90,625.

Only a holder of the property (see 2 in Table 16.3) can provide an accurate picture of the property's operating expense history. Therefore, any investor or appraiser appraising a property for acquisition purposes should be knowledgeable enough to estimate the expenses accurately in order to ensure a more accurate calculation of the NOI. The importance of generating an accurate figure is primarily due to the relationship between the NOI of a property and the property's value to another.

The following are steps in estimating value using the income capitalization approach.

Step 1 (income analysis)   This step begins with an examination of the **potential gross income (PGI)**. This figure represents the gross rent roll or gross receipts attributable through rental activities *if the property were 100 percent leased*. Determination of this figure is as a direct result of adding *contract rents and projected rents*. Contract rent is income derived from current rent-paying tenants (better known as *actual income*), while *projected rent* is predicated on market conditions. It is extremely rare that any building is ever truly 100 percent rented. Step 2 addresses this reality.

Step 2 (income analysis)   This step calculates the *vacancy and collection loss* (V&C) by examining the leasing and vacancy history. On existing property, you must determine average vacancy rates; on new construction, this figure is determined by analyzing market condition studies in conjunction with neighboring property vacancy rates. This step also involves an examination of the property tenants, which will determine the quality of tenancy as well as the ability of the occupants to pay the rent.

The anticipated sum of the V&C is deducted from the PGI.

This rate is always calculated as a percentage figure. Because it represents a percentage of loss attributable to vacancy/collections, it is subtracted from the PGI figure.

Next, establish whether any *other income* (OI) is attributable to the property. Other income can be defined as income that is not derived from the main activity of the property. For example, a highrise apartment building may contain commercial spaces such as a garage, retail space, and/or commercial space. Income derived through these activities is deemed other income.

Any other income is then added to the difference between the PGI and the V&C. This will give the appraiser or investor a figure that represents the **effective gross income (EGI)**. In essence, effective gross income is the income attributable to a property, after deducting vacancy and collection losses, while adding in any other income derived from that property.

Summary of steps 1 and 2 (income analysis):

Potential gross income (PGI) – Vacancy and collection loss (V&C) + Other income (OI) = Effective gross income (EGI)

Step 3 examines the expense side of a property.

Step 3 (expense analysis)   There are operating expenses associated with running all income-producing properties. These expenses can be broken down into three categories:

1. Fixed expenses
2. Variable expenses
3. Reserves for replacements

Fixed expenses are expenses that do not vary as a result of a property's occupancy rate. Regardless of the property's leasing activities, these expenses remain constant for the year of analysis. Fixed expenses consist of only two items: *property taxes* and *property insurance*.

Variable expenses are expenses that will fluctuate up or down with the property's leasing activities. Variable expenses consist of the following:

■ Maintenance
■ Repairs
■ Payroll
■ Utilities
■ Trash removal
■ Management fees

Reserves for replacements is available cash on hand meant to pay for any anticipated or unanticipated major capital improvement to the property. Examples might include a new roof, new mechanical equipment, or façade restoration.

Once the appraiser identifies the three categories of property expenses, the three are added together. This amount is subtracted from the EGI to calculate the property's NOI.

The NOI represents the cash flow attributable to the property *after* deducting all property-related expenses but *before* deducting any debt service (mortgage payments) or federal income taxes, which would include items such as mortgage interest, depreciation allowances, and carryover and suspended losses brought forward from previous years.

Generally, an appraiser obtains the information for income and expenses from a *reconstructed income and expense (operating) statement*. A simplified version of the income approach is illustrated in Table 16.4.

Step 3 (expense analysis) at a glance is as follows:

Effective gross income (EGI) – Operating expense (OE) = Net operating income (NOI)

STEPS IN THE APPRAISAL PROCESS

Real Estate is Appraised Using One of These Three Different Approaches:

1. Sales comparison approach
2. Cost approach
3. Income capitalization approach

Appraisers derive value through the systematic observation of appropriate market data selection and the application of a variety of value methods, which allow them to make a conclusion regarding the property's value.

There are seven steps in the appraisal process:

1. Definition of the assignment
2. Preliminary analysis
3. Analysis of highest and best use
4. Estimation of land value
5. Application of the three approaches to appraisal
6. Reconciliation of the values toward a final estimate of value
7. Appraisal report

Defining the assignment This requires that the appraiser understand the legal description of the property being appraised, know what property rights are being valued, and determine the appropriate "effective date" or "as of date" to be used. Remember, *appraisals are only good for one day—the date of preparation.* The reason for this is that conditions inside and outside the property line can change at any time and any such change can directly affect the property value.

Preliminary analysis This step includes the selection and collection of appropriate data necessary for the observation of market and environment conditions.

TABLE 16.4

Income Capitalization Approach to Value

Gross annual rental income estimate		$60,000
Less vacancy and collection losses (estimated) @ 6%		– 3,600
Income from other sources		$56,400
Effective gross income		+ 600
Expenses:		$57,000
Real estate taxes	$9,000	
Insurance	1,000	
Heat	2,800	
Maintenance	6,400	
Utilities, electricity, water, gas	800	
Repairs	1,200	
Decorating	1,400	
Replacements of equipment	800	
Legal and accounting	600	
Management	3,000	
Total expenses		$27,000
Annual net operating income		$30,000
Capitalization rate = 10%		
Capitalization of annual net income:		30,000

Indicated value by income approach = $300,000

Analysis of highest and best use   This analysis involves the comparison of alternative legal and financially viable uses that may exist on the property. As previously discussed in this chapter, the purpose is to make a determination as to which legally permissible use would contribute to securing the highest value for the land.

Estimation of land value   The site is valued through a careful review and comparison of other comparable land sales. Any property that sells has land underneath it; therefore, comps are always available for valuing land.

Application of the three approaches to appraisal   These three approaches are the sales comparison approach, the cost approach, and the income capitalization approach discussed previously.

Reconciliation of the values toward a final estimate of value   This process requires the appraiser to determine through careful weighting which of the value indications derived from the three appraisal methods best solves the appraisal problem. Although an appraisal report will contain value indications derived from all three approaches, the appraiser ultimately selects the one value indication that will best represent the solution to the assignment. If more than one approach to value is used, different indications of value may result. Reconciliation is the art of analyzing and weighing the findings from the approaches used.

Whenever possible, all three approaches should be used as a check on the final estimate of value. The process of reconciliation is more complicated than simply averaging the estimates. With certain kinds of properties, one approach will be more valid and reliable than the others.

For example, the income approach is rarely used when appraising a single-family residence, and the cost approach is of limited value unless the home is relatively new; therefore, appraisers generally give the greatest weight to the direct sales comparison approach. In appraising income or investment property, the income capitalization approach is normally given the greatest weight. The cost approach is usually assigned the greatest weight in appraising churches, libraries, museums, schools, and other special-use properties where there is little or no income or sales revenue. From this analysis, or reconciliation, a single estimate of market value is produced.

Appraisal report   Appraisers commonly deal with various types of reports. They include *oral reports, form reports, and narrative reports*.

Oral reports are delivered to the client or appropriate party orally. Appraisers (as required by *USPAP*) must support and defend their estimate of value. At the least within this type of report, the appraiser is required to include at minimum a property description, details on any assumptions made and any conditions affecting valuation conclusion, and the value conclusion and reasoning behind that conclusion.

Form reports are typically used in appraisals involving financing through financial institutional lending. They generally consist of three to five pages. In order for secondary market players such as Fannie Mae, Ginnie Mae, and Freddie Mac to purchase these loans, it is necessary that the indication of value be in this report format.

Narrative reports apply to large commercial projects. There are three types of narrative reports that are recognized in this category of reporting by *USPAP: summary reports, self-contained reports, and restricted reports.*

Summary reports include some but not all of the information necessary to support and defend the estimate of value. Regardless of information submitted and/or reported, appraisers are always required to maintain within their files all information used in deriving the estimate of value.

Self-contained reports are very in-depth and detailed appraisal reports. They generally consist of all supporting information contained within the appraiser's files. This would include supporting data, data description, appraiser's reasoning, and valuation analysis.

Restricted reports are reports that are intended only for the client.

■ COMPARATIVE MARKET ANALYSIS

"Real estate properly priced is half sold." The *seller* determines the listing price for the property. Because the average seller usually does not have the background to make an informed decision about a fair market price, the real estate agent should be prepared to offer knowledge, information, and expertise in this area.

A broker or salesperson can help the seller by furnishing a comparative market analysis (CMA). This study compares the prices of recently sold homes that are similar in location, style, and condition to the home being put on the market (the *subject property*). Among the Internet sites offering data on recent sales in any given neighborhood are *www.Domania.com and www.realestate.yahoo.com.*

A CMA differs from a direct sales comparison appraisal in several ways. It is usually offered as a free service by a salesperson or broker and is used merely as a market tool to establish a listing for sales price, whereas the paid appraisal rendered by a fee appraiser focuses on value. Both studies analyze recent sales of similar properties, but the CMA does so differently. It includes material not usually considered in regular appraisals, such as information on nearby properties that failed to sell, for example, and a list of competing properties currently on the market. It also includes significant DOM (days on the market before the sale) information. Broker license law and ethics dictate that unless one is a licensed state-certified or general appraiser, a CMA may never be called or referred to as an appraisal.

Once brokers have information on the subject property, they must select properties with the same general characteristics from the neighborhood (or a similar neighborhood) that have sold recently, that are listed, and that have recently failed to sell. The brokers then use the information about these comparable properties ("comps") to arrive at an informal estimate of value of the subject property.

Brokers generally uses a comparative market analysis form, similar to the one illustrated in Figure 16.4, to prepare a written CMA to present to the property owner. A well-researched and well-prepared CMA will help brokers explain that the eventual selling price is set by the buying public through the operation of supply and demand in the open market. The CMA gives sellers an effective way to judge the market and choose a reasonable listing price.

Buyer Appeal

Buyer appeal applies to the initial impression that any buyer feels or has about a particular property that is under consideration. This usually relates to the appearance of the property as viewed from the curb—also referred to as curb appeal.

Market Position

Market positioning compares the amount of similar properties that are available to that of the subject property. The purpose of this analysis is to determine how the subject property can be differentiated from competing properties that are simultaneously up for sale, while providing potential solutions to successful marketing procedures.

Assets and Drawbacks

Depending on the property in question, most properties can be compared to other availabilities through a close investigation as to the property's assets and drawbacks. When completing a CMA, this process of determining a property's assets or drawbacks may include but not be limited to items of comparison, such as

- community location,
- accessibility to alternate means of public transportation,
- traffic patterns,
- buyer appeal, and
- neighborhood amenities.

Area Market Conditions

Area market conditions will vary from time to time due to the cyclical nature of the real estate market. Issues such as supply and demand, availability of credit, and competing properties will dictate any area market conditions. When conditions are good, properties tend to sell relatively quickly. When conditions are poor, the opposite occurs. Careful consideration should be given to the market conditions when preparing a CMA. This will avoid overpricing or underpricing a property. When conducting a CMA, a licensee is charged with the duty of giving a fair estimate or opinion of the property's value. Failure to do so will result in disciplinary action by the DOS.

Recommended Terms

It is no secret that a sales transaction offering favorable terms of sale will sell faster than one with unfavorable terms. For example, seller financing is viewed as a favorable condition. The buyer saves money on closing costs for which he or she would normally pay more in any institutional financing transaction. Immediate

FIGURE 16.4

Comparative Market Analysis

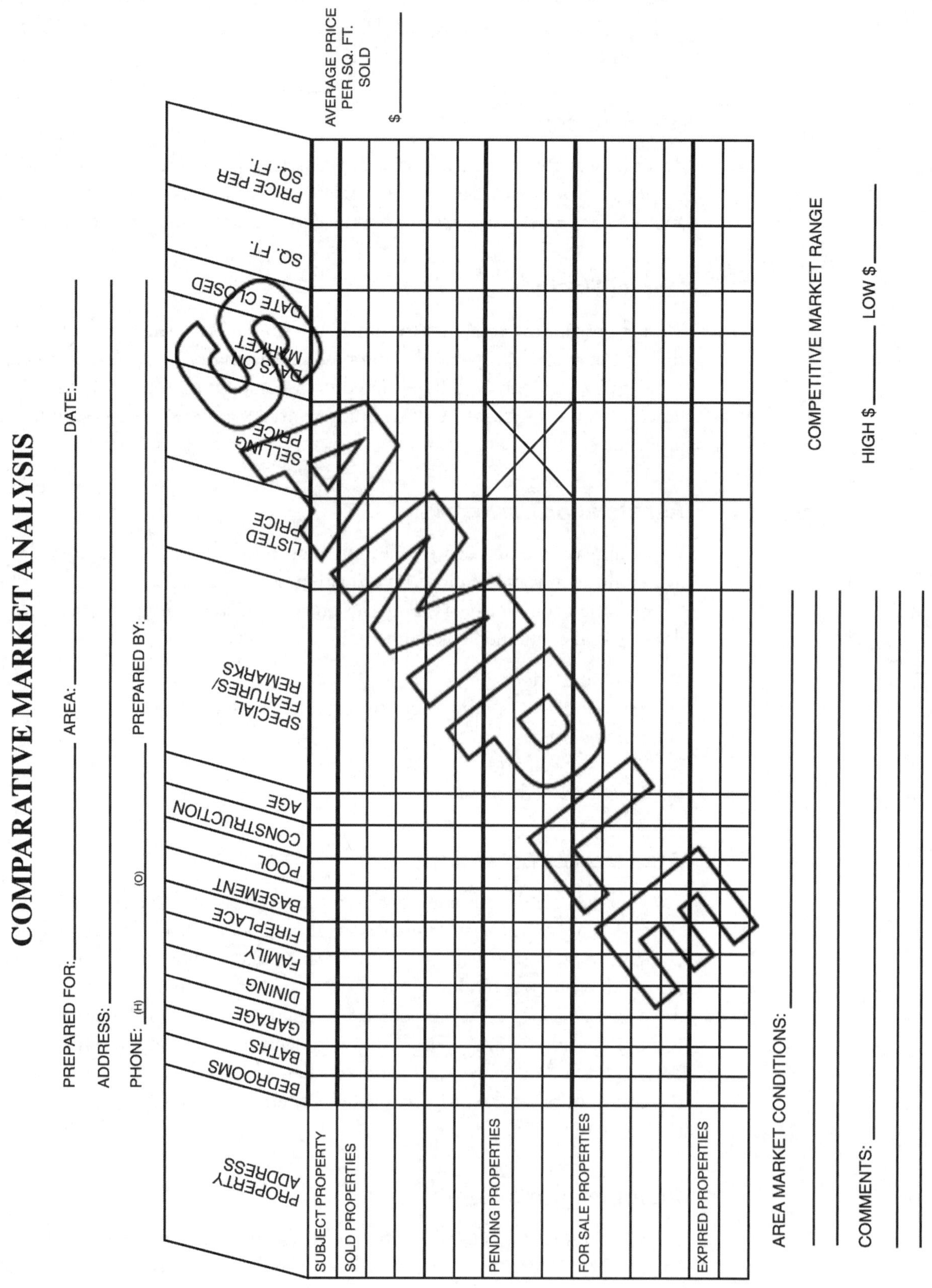

COMPARATIVE MARKET ANALYSIS

PREPARED FOR: ______ AREA: ______ DATE: ______

ADDRESS: ______

PHONE: (H) ______ (O) ______ PREPARED BY: ______

PROPERTY ADDRESS	BEDROOMS	BATHS	GARAGE	DINING	FAMILY	FIREPLACE	BASEMENT	POOL	CONSTRUCTION	AGE		SPECIAL FEATURES/ REMARKS	LISTED PRICE	SELLING PRICE	DAYS ON MARKET	DATE CLOSED	SQ. FT.	PRICE PER SQ. FT.
SUBJECT PROPERTY																		
SOLD PROPERTIES																		
PENDING PROPERTIES														X				
														X				
														X				
FOR SALE PROPERTIES																		
EXPIRED PROPERTIES																		

AVERAGE PRICE PER SQ. FT. SOLD $______

COMPETITIVE MARKET RANGE

HIGH $______ LOW $______

AREA MARKET CONDITIONS: ______

COMMENTS: ______

occupancy creates another favorable condition that will aid in the favorable and quick disposition of the property. When obtaining a listing, a licensee should always inquire as to the potential for obtaining favorable terms from the seller. This will always assist the licensee in bringing about a successful sale.

Market Value Range

A market value range is always achieved when comparing similar sold properties. This is referred to as the range of value. For example, after comparing three to six comparable sold properties, a licensee discovers that the comparable sales indicate the range of value to be $250,000 to $265,000 for the subject property. At this point, depending on the condition of the property and the desire on the part of the seller to effectuate a quick sale, the licensee may recommend the middle range as the target price. Of course, the final decision concerning offering price will always be that of the property owner; the licensee's role is to present all the facts to the principal.

■ THE REAL ESTATE AGENT'S ROLE

In valuing property and presenting the owner with a CMA, the real estate agent must be careful to act competently and with due diligence. The agent should keep a copy of the CMA presented to the owner and also copies of any documentation used to complete the CMA. Agents should make sure that owners understand the estimates of value, how those estimates were determined, and what they mean to the owner.

Basic Principles of Value

A number of economic principles affect the value of real estate. The most important are defined in the following paragraphs.

Plottage   The principle of **plottage** holds that the merging of adjacent lots into one larger parcel may produce a higher total value than the sum of the two sites valued separately. For example, if two adjacent lots are valued at $35,000 each, their total value if consolidated into one larger lot might be $90,000. The process of merging the two lots under one owner is known as **assemblage**.

Contribution   The value of any component of a property is what its addition contributes to the value of the whole. For example, the cost of installing an air-conditioning system and remodeling an older office building must be analyzed to see if it would be worth doing for the anticipated increase it would bring in rental income.

Competition   This principle states that excess profits tend to attract competition. For example, the outstanding success of one fast-food outlet may attract investors to open others in the area. This could mean less profit for all. That would be taken into consideration in the type of appraisal known as a *feasibility study*.

Change   No physical or economic condition remains constant. Real estate is subject to natural phenomena such as tornadoes, fires, and routine wear and tear of the elements. Also, like any business, the real estate business is subject to the demands of its market. An appraiser takes into account the past and possible future effects of natural phenomena and the behavior of the marketplace.

Figure 16.5 outlines the seven steps an appraiser takes in carrying out an assignment.

■ THE PROFESSION OF APPRAISING

Until the early 1990s, when the federal government directed each state to license and certify appraisers, professional designation was made through membership in appraisal societies. Different designations require varying levels of education, specific courses in appraisal, examinations, demonstration appraisals, experience, and continuing education. The **Appraisal Institute**, the largest private society, offers the prestigious designations MAI (Member, Appraisal Institute) and SRA (Senior Residential Appraiser).

Some professional appraisers belong to more than one society. Those along the Niagara frontier, for example, may join an international society, FIABCI. Where expert testimony is provided for court proceedings or before a public body such as

FIGURE 16.5

The Appraisal Process

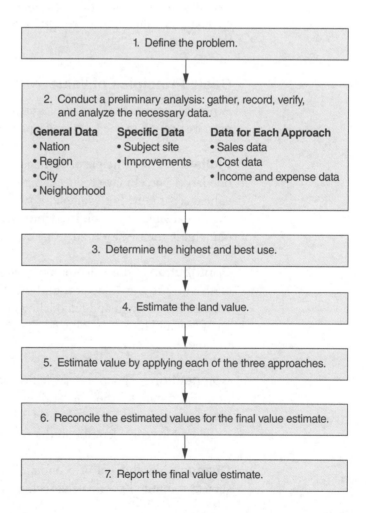

1. Define the problem.

2. Conduct a preliminary analysis: gather, record, verify, and analyze the necessary data.

General Data	Specific Data	Data for Each Approach
• Nation	• Subject site	• Sales data
• Region	• Improvements	• Cost data
• City		• Income and expense data
• Neighborhood		

3. Determine the highest and best use.

4. Estimate the land value.

5. Estimate value by applying each of the three approaches.

6. Reconcile the estimated values for the final value estimate.

7. Report the final value estimate.

a zoning board, specific credentials (MAI, SRA, or state licensing or certification) may be required.

Licensing and Certification

Federal and state governments suggest licensing or certification for all appraisals, but they *require* it only for federally related appraisal assignments with a transaction value of at least $250,000. (An appraisal is federally related if there is a federal government tie-in, such as if the appraisal is used for lending purposes and the lender is a federally chartered bank or savings and loan.)

New York's appraisal licensing and certification process provides for four types of appraiser licenses or certifications:

1. *Appraiser assistant license*. An appraiser assistant must work under the supervision of a state licensed or certified appraiser, who must cosign all the appraisal reports. An appraiser assistant license is good for two years and may be renewed once.
2. *Licensed residential appraiser*. A licensed real estate appraiser may appraise noncomplex one- to four-unit residential real property with a transaction value of less than $1,000,000, and complex ones up to $250,000.
3. *Certified residential appraiser*. A certified residential appraiser may appraise any residential property up to four units.
4. *Certified general appraiser*. A certified general appraiser may appraise any real property.

Education requirements Various appraisal courses must be completed, depending on the type of license or certification the applicant is seeking. The following is a brief overview of the education requirements that became effective January 1, 2008:

Licensed appraiser assistant
- 150 classroom hours of approved courses
- No previous experience necessary
- No exam required, but the applicant is only eligible to take the state exam for the category of education that has been completed

Licensed residential appraiser
- 150 classroom hours of approved qualifying courses
- 2,000 hours accumulated experience in no less than 24 months
- Sit for and pass a new state exam based on the 2008 qualifying courses

Certified residential appraiser
- 200 classroom hours of approved qualifying courses
- Associate degree (or higher) or 21 college semester hours in specific courses
- 2,500 hours accumulated experience in no less than 24 months
- Sit for and pass a new state exam based on the 2008 qualifying courses

Certified general appraiser
- 300 classroom hours of approved qualifying courses
- Bachelor's degree (or higher) or 30 college semester hours in specific courses

■ 3,000 hours accumulated experience in no less than 30 months
■ Sit for and pass a new state exam based on the 2008 qualifying courses

Note: The criteria does not affect appraisers licensed prior to January 2008; however, appraisers seeking an upgrade from current standing will be required to conform and meet with the requirements of these standards.

The law also prescribes the following: "No state certified real estate appraiser or state licensed real estate appraiser shall supervise more than three (3) licensed real estate appraiser assistants."

The three components for licensure/certification are as follows:

1. Education
2. Experience
3. Exam

In conjunction with the aforementioned, the New York State Real Estate Appraisal Board has adopted the "segmented approach" toward the implementation of the requirements that took effect January 1, 2008. This means that any aspect or component requirement of education, experience, or exam that has been completed prior to January 1, 2008, will have served to satisfy that one component.

For example, if an applicant for a license as a certified general appraiser has completed the required 180 hours of education and fulfilled the experience requirement as was prescribed under the laws prior to January 1, 2008 but not passed the New York State exam, the DOS will accept the previous education and experience toward fulfillment of current requirements, but the applicant will still be required to complete and pass the new New York State exam.

Examination and experience   Licensed assistants are qualified to work at entry-level assignments, assisting under supervision. All other applicants must have at least two years' full-time appraisal experience and pass state examinations of increasing difficulty for various types of license or certification. In addition, they must present evidence of varying numbers of required hours appraising different types of property.

Application   License and certification applications and information are available on the Division of Licensing Services Web site at *www.dos.state.ny.us/licensing/*.

As applicable fees do change from time to time, the applicant is always advised to check as to the appropriate fee at the time of application. However, at the present time a $300 nonrefundable fee must accompany completed applications. If the application is in order, the applicant will receive an admission card to a scheduled walk-in examination (there is a $50 exam fee). The applicant must score 75 percent or higher on the exam. Renewals require 28 hours of continuing education and a 7-hour *USPAP* update course.

F I G U R E   16.6

Uniform Residential Appraisal Report

Uniform Residential Appraisal Report   File

The purpose of this summary appraisal report is to provide the lender/client with an accurate, and adequately supported, opinion of the market value of the subject property.

SUBJECT

Property Address		City		State	Zip Code
Borrower	Owner of Public Record			County	

Legal Description

Assessor's Parcel #	Tax Year	R.E. Taxes $
Neighborhood Name	Map Reference	Census Tract

Occupant ☐ Owner ☐ Tenant ☐ Vacant   Special Assessments $ ☐ PUD   HOA $ ☐ per year ☐ per month
Property Rights Appraised ☐ Fee Simple ☐ Leasehold ☐ Other (describe)
Assignment Type ☐ Purchase Transaction ☐ Refinance Transaction ☐ Other (describe)

Lender/Client	Address

Is the subject property currently offered for sale or has it been offered for sale in the twelve months prior to the effective date of this appraisal? ☐ Yes ☐ No
Report data source(s) used, offering price(s), and date(s).

CONTRACT

I ☐ did ☐ did not analyze the contract for sale for the subject purchase transaction. Explain the results of the analysis of the contract for sale or why the analysis was not performed.

Contract Price $ Date of Contract   Is the property seller the owner of public record? ☐ Yes ☐ No Data Source(s)
Is there any financial assistance (loan charges, sale concessions, gift or downpayment assistance, etc.) to be paid by any party on behalf of the borrower? ☐ Yes ☐ No
If Yes, report the total dollar amount and describe the items to be paid.

NEIGHBORHOOD

Note: Race and the racial composition of the neighborhood are not appraisal factors.

Neighborhood Characteristics	One-Unit Housing Trends	One-Unit Housing	Present Land Use %
Location ☐ Urban ☐ Suburban ☐ Rural	Property Values ☐ Increasing ☐ Stable ☐ Declining	PRICE AGE	One-Unit %
Built-Up ☐ Over 75% ☐ 25–75% ☐ Under 25%	Demand/Supply ☐ Shortage ☐ In Balance ☐ Over Supply	$ (000) (yrs)	2-4 Unit %
Growth ☐ Rapid ☐ Stable ☐ Slow	Marketing Time ☐ Under 3 mths ☐ 3–6 mths ☐ Over 6 mths	Low	Multi-Family %
Neighborhood Boundaries		High	Commercial %
		Pred.	Other %

Neighborhood Description

Market Conditions (including support for the above conclusions)

SITE

Dimensions	Area	Shape	View

Specific Zoning Classification   Zoning Description
Zoning Compliance ☐ Legal ☐ Legal Nonconforming (Grandfathered Use) ☐ No Zoning ☐ Illegal (describe)
Is the highest and best use of the subject property as improved (or as proposed per plans and specifications) the present use? ☐ Yes ☐ No If No, describe

Utilities Public Other (describe)	Public Other (describe)	Off-site Improvements—Type Public Private
Electricity ☐ ☐	Water ☐ ☐	Street ☐ ☐
Gas ☐ ☐	Sanitary Sewer ☐ ☐	Alley ☐ ☐

FEMA Special Flood Hazard Area ☐ Yes ☐ No FEMA Flood Zone   FEMA Map #   FEMA Map Date
Are the utilities and off-site improvements typical for the market area? ☐ Yes ☐ No If No, describe
Are there any adverse site conditions or external factors (easements, encroachments, environmental conditions, land uses, etc.)? ☐ Yes ☐ No If Yes, describe

IMPROVEMENTS

General Description	Foundation	Exterior Description materials/condition	Interior materials/condition
Units ☐ One ☐ One with Accessory Unit	☐ Concrete Slab ☐ Crawl Space	Foundation Walls	Floors
# of Stories	☐ Full Basement ☐ Partial Basement	Exterior Walls	Walls
Type ☐ Det. ☐ Att. ☐ S-Det./End Unit	Basement Area sq. ft.	Roof Surface	Trim/Finish
☐ Existing ☐ Proposed ☐ Under Const.	Basement Finish %	Gutters & Downspouts	Bath Floor
Design (Style)	☐ Outside Entry/Exit ☐ Sump Pump	Window Type	Bath Wainscot
Year Built	Evidence of ☐ Infestation	Storm Sash/Insulated	Car Storage ☐ None
Effective Age (Yrs)	☐ Dampness ☐ Settlement	Screens	☐ Driveway # of Cars
Attic ☐ None	Heating ☐ FWA ☐ HWBB ☐ Radiant	Amenities ☐ Woodstove(s) #	Driveway Surface
☐ Drop Stair ☐ Stairs	☐ Other Fuel	☐ Fireplace(s) # ☐ Fence	☐ Garage # of Cars
☐ Floor ☐ Scuttle	Cooling ☐ Central Air Conditioning	☐ Patio/Deck ☐ Porch	☐ Carport # of Cars
☐ Finished ☐ Heated	☐ Individual ☐ Other	☐ Pool ☐ Other	☐ Att. ☐ Det. ☐ Built-in

Appliances ☐ Refrigerator ☐ Range/Oven ☐ Dishwasher ☐ Disposal ☐ Microwave ☐ Washer/Dryer ☐ Other (describe)
Finished area **above** grade contains: Rooms   Bedrooms   Bath(s)   Square Feet of Gross Living Area Above Grade
Additional features (special energy efficient items, etc.)

Describe the condition of the property (including needed repairs, deterioration, renovations, remodeling, etc.).

Are there any physical deficiencies or adverse conditions that affect the livability, soundness, or structural integrity of the property? ☐ Yes ☐ No If Yes, describe

Does the property generally conform to the neighborhood (functional utility, style, condition, use, construction, etc.)? ☐ Yes ☐ No If No, describe

FIGURE 16.6

Uniform Residential Appraisal Report (continued)

Uniform Residential Appraisal Report

File #

There are _____ comparable properties currently offered for sale in the subject neighborhood ranging in price from $ _____ to $ _____ .

There are _____ comparable sales in the subject neighborhood within the past twelve months ranging in sale price from $ _____ to $ _____ .

FEATURE	SUBJECT	COMPARABLE SALE # 1		COMPARABLE SALE # 2		COMPARABLE SALE # 3	
Address							
Proximity to Subject							
Sale Price	$		$		$		$
Sale Price/Gross Liv. Area	$ sq. ft.	$ sq. ft.		$ sq. ft.		$ sq. ft.	
Data Source(s)							
Verification Source(s)							
VALUE ADJUSTMENTS	DESCRIPTION	DESCRIPTION	+(-) $ Adjustment	DESCRIPTION	+(-) $ Adjustment	DESCRIPTION	+(-) $ Adjustment
Sale or Financing Concessions							
Date of Sale/Time							
Location							
Leasehold/Fee Simple							
Site							
View							
Design (Style)							
Quality of Construction							
Actual Age							
Condition							
Above Grade	Total	Bdrms.	Baths	Total	Bdrms.	Baths	Total	Bdrms.	Baths	Total	Bdrms.	Baths
Room Count							
Gross Living Area	sq. ft.	sq. ft.		sq. ft.		sq. ft.	
Basement & Finished Rooms Below Grade							
Functional Utility							
Heating/Cooling							
Energy Efficient Items							
Garage/Carport							
Porch/Patio/Deck							
Net Adjustment (Total)		☐ + ☐ -	$	☐ + ☐ -	$	☐ + ☐ -	$
Adjusted Sale Price of Comparables		Net Adj. % Gross Adj. %	$	Net Adj. % Gross Adj. %	$	Net Adj. % Gross Adj. %	$

I ☐ did ☐ did not research the sale or transfer history of the subject property and comparable sales. If not, explain

My research ☐ did ☐ did not reveal any prior sales or transfers of the subject property for the three years prior to the effective date of this appraisal.

Data source(s)

My research ☐ did ☐ did not reveal any prior sales or transfers of the comparable sales for the year prior to the date of sale of the comparable sale.

Data source(s)

Report the results of the research and analysis of the prior sale or transfer history of the subject property and comparable sales (report additional prior sales on page 3).

ITEM	SUBJECT	COMPARABLE SALE #1	COMPARABLE SALE # 2	COMPARABLE SALE # 3
Date of Prior Sale/Transfer				
Price of Prior Sale/Transfer				
Data Source(s)				
Effective Date of Data Source(s)				

Analysis of prior sale or transfer history of the subject property and comparable sales

Summary of Sales Comparison Approach

Indicated Value by Sales Comparison Approach $

Indicated Value by: Sales Comparison Approach $ _____   Cost Approach (if developed) $ _____   Income Approach (if developed) $ _____

This appraisal is made ☐ "as is", ☐ subject to completion per plans and specifications on the basis of a hypothetical condition that the improvements have been completed, ☐ subject to the following repairs or alterations on the basis of a hypothetical condition that the repairs or alterations have been completed, or ☐ subject to the following required inspection based on the extraordinary assumption that the condition or deficiency does not require alteration or repair:

Based on a complete visual inspection of the interior and exterior areas of the subject property, defined scope of work, statement of assumptions and limiting conditions, and appraiser's certification, my (our) opinion of the market value, as defined, of the real property that is the subject of this report is

$ _____ , as of _____ , which is the date of inspection and the effective date of this appraisal.

Freddie Mac Form 70 March 2005   Page 2 of 6   Fannie Mae Form 1004 March 2005

FIGURE 16.6

Uniform Residential Appraisal Report (continued)

Uniform Residential Appraisal Report

File #

ADDITIONAL COMMENTS

COST APPROACH

COST APPROACH TO VALUE (not required by Fannie Mae)	
Provide adequate information for the lender/client to replicate the below cost figures and calculations.	
Support for the opinion of site value (summary of comparable land sales or other methods for estimating site value)	
ESTIMATED ☐ REPRODUCTION OR ☐ REPLACEMENT COST NEW	OPINION OF SITE VALUE = $
Source of cost data	Dwelling Sq. Ft. @ $ =$
Quality rating from cost service Effective date of cost data	Sq. Ft. @ $ =$
Comments on Cost Approach (gross living area calculations, depreciation, etc.)	
	Garage/Carport Sq. Ft. @ $ =$
	Total Estimate of Cost-New = $
	Less Physical | Functional | External
	Depreciation =$( )
	Depreciated Cost of Improvements =$
	"As-is" Value of Site Improvements =$
Estimated Remaining Economic Life (HUD and VA only) Years	Indicated Value By Cost Approach =$

INCOME

INCOME APPROACH TO VALUE (not required by Fannie Mae)
Estimated Monthly Market Rent $ X Gross Rent Multiplier = $ Indicated Value by Income Approach
Summary of Income Approach (including support for market rent and GRM)

PUD INFORMATION

PROJECT INFORMATION FOR PUDs (if applicable)
Is the developer/builder in control of the Homeowners' Association (HOA)? ☐ Yes ☐ No Unit type(s) ☐ Detached ☐ Attached
Provide the following information for PUDs ONLY if the developer/builder is in control of the HOA and the subject property is an attached dwelling unit.
Legal name of project
Total number of phases Total number of units Total number of units sold
Total number of units rented Total number of units for sale Data source(s)
Was the project created by the conversion of an existing building(s) into a PUD? ☐ Yes ☐ No If Yes, date of conversion
Does the project contain any multi-dwelling units? ☐ Yes ☐ No Data source(s)
Are the units, common elements, and recreation facilities complete? ☐ Yes ☐ No If No, describe the status of completion.
Are the common elements leased to or by the Homeowners' Association? ☐ Yes ☐ No If Yes, describe the rental terms and options.
Describe common elements and recreational facilities

Freddie Mac Form 70 March 2005 Page 3 of 6 Fannie Mae Form 1004 March 2005

FIGURE 16.6

Uniform Residential Appraisal Report (continued)

Uniform Residential Appraisal Report   File #

This report form is designed to report an appraisal of a one-unit property or a one-unit property with an accessory unit; including a unit in a planned unit development (PUD). This report form is not designed to report an appraisal of a manufactured home or a unit in a condominium or cooperative project.

This appraisal report is subject to the following scope of work, intended use, intended user, definition of market value, statement of assumptions and limiting conditions, and certifications. Modifications, additions, or deletions to the intended use, intended user, definition of market value, or assumptions and limiting conditions are not permitted. The appraiser may expand the scope of work to include any additional research or analysis necessary based on the complexity of this appraisal assignment. Modifications or deletions to the certifications are also not permitted. However, additional certifications that do not constitute material alterations to this appraisal report, such as those required by law or those related to the appraiser's continuing education or membership in an appraisal organization, are permitted.

SCOPE OF WORK: The scope of work for this appraisal is defined by the complexity of this appraisal assignment and the reporting requirements of this appraisal report form, including the following definition of market value, statement of assumptions and limiting conditions, and certifications. The appraiser must, at a minimum: (1) perform a complete visual inspection of the interior and exterior areas of the subject property, (2) inspect the neighborhood, (3) inspect each of the comparable sales from at least the street, (4) research, verify, and analyze data from reliable public and/or private sources, and (5) report his or her analysis, opinions, and conclusions in this appraisal report.

INTENDED USE: The intended use of this appraisal report is for the lender/client to evaluate the property that is the subject of this appraisal for a mortgage finance transaction.

INTENDED USER: The intended user of this appraisal report is the lender/client.

DEFINITION OF MARKET VALUE: The most probable price which a property should bring in a competitive and open market under all conditions requisite to a fair sale, the buyer and seller, each acting prudently, knowledgeably and assuming the price is not affected by undue stimulus. Implicit in this definition is the consummation of a sale as of a specified date and the passing of title from seller to buyer under conditions whereby: (1) buyer and seller are typically motivated; (2) both parties are well informed or well advised, and each acting in what he or she considers his or her own best interest; (3) a reasonable time is allowed for exposure in the open market; (4) payment is made in terms of cash in U. S. dollars or in terms of financial arrangements comparable thereto; and (5) the price represents the normal consideration for the property sold unaffected by special or creative financing or sales concessions* granted by anyone associated with the sale.

*Adjustments to the comparables must be made for special or creative financing or sales concessions. No adjustments are necessary for those costs which are normally paid by sellers as a result of tradition or law in a market area; these costs are readily identifiable since the seller pays these costs in virtually all sales transactions. Special or creative financing adjustments can be made to the comparable property by comparisons to financing terms offered by a third party institutional lender that is not already involved in the property or transaction. Any adjustment should not be calculated on a mechanical dollar for dollar cost of the financing or concession but the dollar amount of any adjustment should approximate the market's reaction to the financing or concessions based on the appraiser's judgment.

STATEMENT OF ASSUMPTIONS AND LIMITING CONDITIONS: The appraiser's certification in this report is subject to the following assumptions and limiting conditions:

1. The appraiser will not be responsible for matters of a legal nature that affect either the property being appraised or the title to it, except for information that he or she became aware of during the research involved in performing this appraisal. The appraiser assumes that the title is good and marketable and will not render any opinions about the title.

2. The appraiser has provided a sketch in this appraisal report to show the approximate dimensions of the improvements. The sketch is included only to assist the reader in visualizing the property and understanding the appraiser's determination of its size.

3. The appraiser has examined the available flood maps that are provided by the Federal Emergency Management Agency (or other data sources) and has noted in this appraisal report whether any portion of the subject site is located in an identified Special Flood Hazard Area. Because the appraiser is not a surveyor, he or she makes no guarantees, express or implied, regarding this determination.

4. The appraiser will not give testimony or appear in court because he or she made an appraisal of the property in question, unless specific arrangements to do so have been made beforehand, or as otherwise required by law.

5. The appraiser has noted in this appraisal report any adverse conditions (such as needed repairs, deterioration, the presence of hazardous wastes, toxic substances, etc.) observed during the inspection of the subject property or that he or she became aware of during the research involved in performing this appraisal. Unless otherwise stated in this appraisal report, the appraiser has no knowledge of any hidden or unapparent physical deficiencies or adverse conditions of the property (such as, but not limited to, needed repairs, deterioration, the presence of hazardous wastes, toxic substances, adverse environmental conditions, etc.) that would make the property less valuable, and has assumed that there are no such conditions and makes no guarantees or warranties, express or implied. The appraiser will not be responsible for any such conditions that do exist or for any engineering or testing that might be required to discover whether such conditions exist. Because the appraiser is not an expert in the field of environmental hazards, this appraisal report must not be considered as an environmental assessment of the property.

6. The appraiser has based his or her appraisal report and valuation conclusion for an appraisal that is subject to satisfactory completion, repairs, or alterations on the assumption that the completion, repairs, or alterations of the subject property will be performed in a professional manner.

Freddie Mac Form 70   March 2005   Page 4 of 6   Fannie Mae Form 1004   March 2005

F I G U R E   16.6

Uniform Residential Appraisal Report (continued)

Uniform Residential Appraisal Report   File

APPRAISER'S CERTIFICATION: The Appraiser certifies and agrees that:

1. I have, at a minimum, developed and reported this appraisal in accordance with the scope of work requirements stated in this appraisal report.

2. I performed a complete visual inspection of the interior and exterior areas of the subject property. I reported the condition of the improvements in factual, specific terms. I identified and reported the physical deficiencies that could affect the livability, soundness, or structural integrity of the property.

3. I performed this appraisal in accordance with the requirements of the Uniform Standards of Professional Appraisal Practice that were adopted and promulgated by the Appraisal Standards Board of The Appraisal Foundation and that were in place at the time this appraisal report was prepared.

4. I developed my opinion of the market value of the real property that is the subject of this report based on the sales comparison approach to value. I have adequate comparable market data to develop a reliable sales comparison approach for this appraisal assignment. I further certify that I considered the cost and income approaches to value but did not develop them, unless otherwise indicated in this report.

5. I researched, verified, analyzed, and reported on any current agreement for sale for the subject property, any offering for sale of the subject property in the twelve months prior to the effective date of this appraisal, and the prior sales of the subject property for a minimum of three years prior to the effective date of this appraisal, unless otherwise indicated in this report.

6. I researched, verified, analyzed, and reported on the prior sales of the comparable sales for a minimum of one year prior to the date of sale of the comparable sale, unless otherwise indicated in this report.

7. I selected and used comparable sales that are locationally, physically, and functionally the most similar to the subject property.

8. I have not used comparable sales that were the result of combining a land sale with the contract purchase price of a home that has been built or will be built on the land.

9. I have reported adjustments to the comparable sales that reflect the market's reaction to the differences between the subject property and the comparable sales.

10. I verified, from a disinterested source, all information in this report that was provided by parties who have a financial interest in the sale or financing of the subject property.

11. I have knowledge and experience in appraising this type of property in this market area.

12. I am aware of, and have access to, the necessary and appropriate public and private data sources, such as multiple listing services, tax assessment records, public land records and other such data sources for the area in which the property is located.

13. I obtained the information, estimates, and opinions furnished by other parties and expressed in this appraisal report from reliable sources that I believe to be true and correct.

14. I have taken into consideration the factors that have an impact on value with respect to the subject neighborhood, subject property, and the proximity of the subject property to adverse influences in the development of my opinion of market value. I have noted in this appraisal report any adverse conditions (such as, but not limited to, needed repairs, deterioration, the presence of hazardous wastes, toxic substances, adverse environmental conditions, etc.) observed during the inspection of the subject property or that I became aware of during the research involved in performing this appraisal. I have considered these adverse conditions in my analysis of the property value, and have reported on the effect of the conditions on the value and marketability of the subject property.

15. I have not knowingly withheld any significant information from this appraisal report and, to the best of my knowledge, all statements and information in this appraisal report are true and correct.

16. I stated in this appraisal report my own personal, unbiased, and professional analysis, opinions, and conclusions, which are subject only to the assumptions and limiting conditions in this appraisal report.

17. I have no present or prospective interest in the property that is the subject of this report, and I have no present or prospective personal interest or bias with respect to the participants in the transaction. I did not base, either partially or completely, my analysis and/or opinion of market value in this appraisal report on the race, color, religion, sex, age, marital status, handicap, familial status, or national origin of either the prospective owners or occupants of the subject property or of the present owners or occupants of the properties in the vicinity of the subject property or on any other basis prohibited by law.

18. My employment and/or compensation for performing this appraisal or any future or anticipated appraisals was not conditioned on any agreement or understanding, written or otherwise, that I would report (or present analysis supporting) a predetermined specific value, a predetermined minimum value, a range or direction in value, a value that favors the cause of any party, or the attainment of a specific result or occurrence of a specific subsequent event (such as approval of a pending mortgage loan application).

19. I personally prepared all conclusions and opinions about the real estate that were set forth in this appraisal report. If I relied on significant real property appraisal assistance from any individual or individuals in the performance of this appraisal or the preparation of this appraisal report, I have named such individual(s) and disclosed the specific tasks performed in this appraisal report. I certify that any individual so named is qualified to perform the tasks. I have not authorized anyone to make a change to any item in this appraisal report; therefore, any change made to this appraisal is unauthorized and I will take no responsibility for it.

20. I identified the lender/client in this appraisal report who is the individual, organization, or agent for the organization that ordered and will receive this appraisal report.

Freddie Mac Form 70   March 2005   Page 5 of 6   Fannie Mae Form 1004   March 2005

F I G U R E   16.6

Uniform Residential Appraisal Report (continued)

Uniform Residential Appraisal Report   File

21. The lender/client may disclose or distribute this appraisal report to: the borrower; another lender at the request of the borrower; the mortgagee or its successors and assigns; mortgage insurers; government sponsored enterprises; other secondary market participants; data collection or reporting services; professional appraisal organizations; any department, agency, or instrumentality of the United States; and any state, the District of Columbia, or other jurisdictions; without having to obtain the appraiser's or supervisory appraiser's (if applicable) consent. Such consent must be obtained before this appraisal report may be disclosed or distributed to any other party (including, but not limited to, the public through advertising, public relations, news, sales, or other media).

22. I am aware that any disclosure or distribution of this appraisal report by me or the lender/client may be subject to certain laws and regulations. Further, I am also subject to the provisions of the Uniform Standards of Professional Appraisal Practice that pertain to disclosure or distribution by me.

23. The borrower, another lender at the request of the borrower, the mortgagee or its successors and assigns, mortgage insurers, government sponsored enterprises, and other secondary market participants may rely on this appraisal report as part of any mortgage finance transaction that involves any one or more of these parties.

24. If this appraisal report was transmitted as an "electronic record" containing my "electronic signature," as those terms are defined in applicable federal and/or state laws (excluding audio and video recordings), or a facsimile transmission of this appraisal report containing a copy or representation of my signature, the appraisal report shall be as effective, enforceable and valid as if a paper version of this appraisal report were delivered containing my original hand written signature.

25. Any intentional or negligent misrepresentation(s) contained in this appraisal report may result in civil liability and/or criminal penalties including, but not limited to, fine or imprisonment or both under the provisions of Title 18, United States Code, Section 1001, et seq., or similar state laws.

SUPERVISORY APPRAISER'S CERTIFICATION: The Supervisory Appraiser certifies and agrees that:

1. I directly supervised the appraiser for this appraisal assignment, have read the appraisal report, and agree with the appraiser's analysis, opinions, statements, conclusions, and the appraiser's certification.

2. I accept full responsibility for the contents of this appraisal report including, but not limited to, the appraiser's analysis, opinions, statements, conclusions, and the appraiser's certification.

3. The appraiser identified in this appraisal report is either a sub-contractor or an employee of the supervisory appraiser (or the appraisal firm), is qualified to perform this appraisal, and is acceptable to perform this appraisal under the applicable state law.

4. This appraisal report complies with the Uniform Standards of Professional Appraisal Practice that were adopted and promulgated by the Appraisal Standards Board of The Appraisal Foundation and that were in place at the time this appraisal report was prepared.

5. If this appraisal report was transmitted as an "electronic record" containing my "electronic signature," as those terms are defined in applicable federal and/or state laws (excluding audio and video recordings), or a facsimile transmission of this appraisal report containing a copy or representation of my signature, the appraisal report shall be as effective, enforceable and valid as if a paper version of this appraisal report were delivered containing my original hand written signature.

APPRAISER

Signature_____
Name _____
Company Name _____
Company Address_____

_____
Telephone Number _____
Email Address_____
Date of Signature and Report _____
Effective Date of Appraisal _____
State Certification # _____
or State License # _____
or Other (describe) _____ State # _____
State _____
Expiration Date of Certification or License _____

ADDRESS OF PROPERTY APPRAISED

_____
_____

APPRAISED VALUE OF SUBJECT PROPERTY $ _____

LENDER/CLIENT
Name _____
Company Name _____
Company Address_____
_____
Email Address _____

SUPERVISORY APPRAISER (ONLY IF REQUIRED)

Signature_____
Name _____
Company Name _____
Company Address_____

_____
Telephone Number _____
Email Address_____
Date of Signature _____
State Certification # _____
or State License # _____
State _____
Expiration Date of Certification or License _____

SUBJECT PROPERTY

☐ Did not inspect subject property
☐ Did inspect exterior of subject property from street
　　Date of Inspection _____
☐ Did inspect interior and exterior of subject property
　　Date of Inspection _____

COMPARABLE SALES

☐ Did not inspect exterior of comparable sales from street
☐ Did inspect exterior of comparable sales from street
　　Date of Inspection _____

Freddie Mac Form 70   March 2005   Page 6 of 6   Fannie Mae Form 1004   March 2005

■ SUMMARY

The economic characteristics of land include scarcity, improvements, permanence of investment, and area preferences (situs). The physical characteristics are immobility, nonhomogeneity, and indestructibility.

A property's value is the present worth of its future benefits. Value is not the same as price; price is determined in the marketplace.

Because of its unique characteristics, real estate is relatively slow to adjust to the forces of supply and demand. Supply is the amount of goods available. Demand is the number of people willing to accept those goods at a given price.

To appraise real estate is to estimate its value. Although there are many types of value, the most common objective of an appraisal is to estimate market value—the most probable sales price of the subject property.

Value is an estimate of future benefits, cost represents a measure of past expenditures, and price is the actual amount of money paid for a property. Basic to appraising are certain underlying economic principles, such as highest and best use, substitution, supply and demand, conformity, anticipation, increasing and diminishing returns, progression, regression, plottage, contribution, competition, and change. A professional appraiser analyzes property through three approaches to value. In the sales comparison approach, the subject property is compared with similar nearby properties that have sold recently. Adjustments are made to account for any differences. With the cost approach, an appraiser calculates the cost of building a similar structure on a similar site. Then the appraiser subtracts depreciation (losses in value), which reflects the differences between new property of this type and the present condition of the subject property. The income capitalization approach is based on the relationship between the rate of return an investor requires and the net income the property produces.

A special version of the income approach called the gross rent multiplier is computed by dividing the sales price of a property by its gross monthly rent.

The application of the three approaches normally results in three different estimates of value. In the process of reconciliation, the validity and reliability of each approach are weighed objectively to arrive at the single best and most supportable conclusion of value.

New York State's appraisal licensing and certification process provides for licensure or certification in four categories, requiring various courses and experience. These four categories are licensed appraiser assistant, licensed real estate appraiser, certified residential appraiser, and certified general appraiser.

CHAPTER 16 QUIZ

1. A couple will not drop the asking price on their house because "it's already priced below market value." Their agent needs to explain that
   a. if nobody comes forward to offer that sum, by definition it can't be market value.
   b. market value is an ideal figure seldom actually reached in today's real estate climate.
   c. they can expect to get market value only if they find a buyer who is under pressure.
   d. if they wanted to get market value, they should not have put their house into a widespread multiple-listing system.

2. The single MOST important factor in estimating the value of real property is its
   a. quality of construction.
   b. size.
   c. location.
   d. original cost.

3. Any two parcels of real estate
   a. can never be the same.
   b. can be the same only with identical tract houses.
   c. are considered the same if they have identical sales prices.
   d. are identical because of situs.

4. Real estate markets tend to be
   a. similar across the country.
   b. statewide in their characteristics.
   c. stable despite economic changes.
   d. local in character.

5. An appraiser is asked to estimate the market value of a church. He will give MOST emphasis to which appraisal approach?
   a. Cost
   b. Income
   c. Competitive analysis
   d. Sales comparison

6. The income approach to appraisal is MOST appropriate for a(n)
   a. tract ranch house.
   b. library.
   c. apartment house.
   d. vacant lot.

7. The sales comparison approach to appraisal utilizes
   a. asking prices for property on the market.
   b. building costs in the area.
   c. analysis of functional obsolescence.
   d. recent sales prices of similar parcels.

8. An example of external obsolescence might be a
   a. faulty heating system.
   b. poor floor plan.
   c. tenant who will not pay rent.
   d. used-car lot next door.

9. The MOST likely price that would be paid by an informed buyer when property is widely exposed on the market is known as the
   a. cost.
   b. listing price.
   c. sales price.
   d. market value.

10. In the final analysis, selling price for real estate is set by the
    a. seller.
    b. broker.
    c. comparative market analysis.
    d. buying public.

11. As a fully qualified appraiser, he would
    a. discover value.
    b. ensure value.
    c. estimate value.
    d. establish value.

12. The appraiser who works for a number of different clients is known as a(n)
    a. fee appraiser.
    b. freelance appraiser.
    c. staff appraiser.
    d. in-house appraiser.

13. The expression *arm's-length transaction* is defined as a transaction between
    a. relative strangers.
    b. competent adults.
    c. competitive individuals.
    d. family members.

14. Market value is *BEST* defined as the
    a. gross rental income of the property.
    b. cash flow after debt service.
    c. most likely price obtainable on the open market.
    d. highest and best use of the subject property.

15. An example of an arm's-length transaction is one between
    a. father and daughter.
    b. employer and employee.
    c. broker and salesperson.
    d. two strangers.

16. Market value and cost are often equal when property
    a. remains in the family a long time.
    b. was recently constructed.
    c. is sold in an arm's-length transaction.
    d. receives a weighted appraisal.

17. Highest and best use of real estate is defined as the use that produces the MOST value to
    a. benefit the community.
    b. conformity.
    c. progression.
    d. the land.

18. "Why should I pay more when I can buy almost the same house new for less?" is an example of the principle of
    a. substitution.
    b. conformity.
    c. anticipation.
    d. change.

19. The principle of value that states that two adjacent parcels of land combined into one larger parcel may have a greater value than the two parcels' value separately is called
    a. substitution.
    b. plottage.
    c. highest and best use.
    d. contribution.

20. You are appraising a subject property that is the house at 23 Oak. A comparable house recently sold at 54 Oak is similar to the subject property; however, it has a fireplace, and the subject property does not. What use do you make of the value of the fireplace?
    a. Subtract the value from the comparable
    b. Add the value to the comparable
    c. Ignore it
    d. Reconcile it

21. From the reproduction or replacement cost of the building, an appraiser deducts depreciation, which represents
    a. the remaining useful economic life of the building.
    b. remodeling costs to increase rentals.
    c. loss of value due to any cause.
    d. costs to modernize the building.

22. The term *external obsolescence* refers to
    a. poor landscaping.
    b. a faulty floor plan.
    c. wear and tear.
    d. a loss of value attributable to issues resulting from factors beyond the property line.

23. If a property's annual net income is $37,500 and it is valued at $300,000, what is its capitalization rate?
    a. 12.5 percent
    b. 10.5 percent
    c. 15 percent
    d. 18 percent

24. The term *reconciliation* refers to which of the following?
    a. Loss of value owing to any cause
    b. Separating the value of the land from the total value of the property to compute depreciation
    c. Analyzing the results obtained by the three approaches to value to determine a final estimate of value
    d. The process by which an appraiser determines the highest and best use for a parcel of land

25. A salesperson is asked by a friend's family to provide an opinion of value for a single home. The estimate of value will be used for estate tax purposes. The salesperson has never prepared a paid opinion of value and has no special training beyond her license-qualifying courses and several years' sales experience. Her *BEST* course of action is to

    a. refuse the work and explain that she is not certified.
    b. offer a free appraisal.
    c. accept the assignment and charge a normal fee.
    d. prepare the opinion of value under her broker's guidance.

Human Rights and Fair Housing

■ KEY TERMS

Americans with
  Disabilities Act (ADA)
blockbusting
cease and desist orders
Civil Rights Act of 1866
Code for Equal
  Opportunity
Department of
  Housing and Urban
  Development (HUD)

Executive Law
federal Fair Housing Act
  of 1968
filtering down
New York Human Rights
  Law
New York State Division of
  Human Rights
nonsolicitation order
protected classes

Real Property Law
redlining
reverse discrimination
steering
testers

■ EQUAL OPPORTUNITY IN HOUSING

Federal, state, and local laws about human rights and fair housing affect rentals, sales, and every phase of the real estate sales process from listing to closing.

The goal of these equal opportunity laws and regulations is to create a single, unbiased housing market, one in which all homeseekers have the opportunity to buy any home in the area they choose and can afford. The student of real estate must be aware of undesirable and illegal housing practices so as to avoid them. Failure to comply with fair housing practices is not only grounds for loss of license but also an unlawful act.

■ FEDERAL FAIR HOUSING LAWS

The efforts of the federal government to guarantee equal housing opportunities to all U.S. citizens began soon after the Civil War with the **Civil Rights Act of 1866**. This law, an outgrowth of the Civil War, prohibits any type of discrimination based on *race* or *color*. "All citizens of the United States shall have the same right in every state and territory as is enjoyed by white citizens thereof to inherit, purchase, lease, sell, hold, and convey real and personal property." The act provides no exceptions. It is enforceable by a suit in federal court.

A summary of fair housing laws appears in Table 17.1.

Federal Fair Housing Act of 1968

In 1968, the first significant event that greatly encouraged the progress of fair housing occurred: the passage of the **federal Fair Housing Act of 1968**, which is contained in *Title VIII of the Civil Rights Act of 1968*. This law originally provided that it is unlawful to discriminate on the basis of *race*, *religion*, or *national origin* when selling or leasing residential property.

In 1974, an amendment added *sex* (gender) as another of the **protected classes**, and in 1988 two new classes were added: those with *handicaps* and *familial status* (presence of children in the family). Protection of the handicapped extends to those with hearing, mobility, and visual impairments; recovering alcoholics; AIDS; and mental retardation. Anyone currently using illegal drugs is not protected as handicapped, nor are those who pose a threat to the health or safety of others.

TABLE 17.1

Fair Housing Laws Summary

Law	Protected Classes
New York City	Citizenship, lawful occupation, sexual orientation
Civil Rights Act of 1866	Prohibits discrimination in housing based on race or color (without exception)
Title VIII of the Civil Rights Act of 1968 (Federal Fair Housing Act)	Prohibits discrimination in housing based on race, color, religion, or national origin (with certain exceptions)
Housing and Community Development Act of 1974	Extends prohibitions to discrimination in housing based on sex (gender)
Fair Housing Amendments Act of 1988	Extends protection to cover handicaps and families with children (with exceptions)
New York Executive Law	Covers race, creed, color, national origin, sex, disability, age, sexual orientation, and marital and military status (some exceptions)
New York Real Property Law	Prohibits discrimination based on presence of children in a family or pregnancy
Americans with Disabilities Act	Prohibits discrimination based on disabilities

Disabled   Landlords must make *reasonable accommodations for the disabled*—for example, allowing a guide dog in a no-pets building or setting aside easy-access parking for a handicapped tenant. Tenants who need to make reasonable modifications to an apartment must be allowed to do so if they agree to restore the property to its original condition when the rental is over. Newly constructed multifamily buildings with four or more units must provide wheelchair access to all ground-floor units and to all upper-floor units in buildings with elevators.

Senior   Housing developments intended for *older persons* may exclude children if such developments are occupied solely by persons 62 and older, or if 80 percent of the units are occupied by at least one person 55 or older and there are policies and procedures published and adhered to demonstrating an intent to provide housing for persons 55 or older.

Prohibited acts   The federal Fair Housing Act specifically prohibits the following acts, where they are based on prospective tenants' or buyers' membership in a protected group:

- *Refusing to sell, rent, or negotiate* with any person, or otherwise making a dwelling unavailable to any person

- **FOR EXAMPLE**   Broker Bill is negotiating a listing with Seller Sue. Sue informs Bill that she will not sell her property to anyone who is not a "God-fearing Christian." Because refusing to sell on the basis of religion is a forbidden practice, Bill should refuse to accept the listing.

- *Changing terms, conditions, or services* for different individuals as a means of discrimination

- **FOR EXAMPLE**   The Sky Towers Apartments has a policy of collecting a $500 security deposit from its tenants. However, in the case of families with children, Sky Towers requires a security deposit of $1,000. This variation in the terms of the apartment leases on the basis of familial status is a violation of fair housing laws.

- *Practicing discrimination* through any statement or advertisement that restricts the sale or rental of residential property

- **FOR EXAMPLE**   Jones Realty advertises its listings in the classified section of the local newspaper. The ads include the slogan "Jones Realty—specializing in homes for Asian immigrants." The ad's implication that certain housing is more suitable to persons of a particular race, color, or national origin is a clear violation of fair housing requirements. (This is known as **steering**.)

- *Representing to any person*, as a means of discrimination, that a dwelling is not available for sale or rental

- **FOR EXAMPLE**   When George applies to rent an apartment, the manager takes his application but informs him that there are no units currently available. While it is true that all the units are currently occupied, one of the tenants is due to move out in three days. The manager simply prefers to rent the unit to a woman because she believes they make better tenants. This is a case of unlawful housing discrimination on the basis of sex.

■ *Making a profit by inducing owners* of housing to sell or rent because of the prospective entry into the neighborhood of persons of a particular race, color, religion, national origin, handicap, or familial status

■ **FOR EXAMPLE** Acme Real Estate Company is running a direct mail campaign attempting to solicit listings from the predominantly white Alderbrook neighborhood. Included in the direct mail package are the results of a demographic study that projects that the population of Alderbrook will become increasingly nonwhite in the next few years. Use of such "scare tactics" to generate profit through increased listings puts Acme in violation of fair housing laws. (This is known as **blockbusting**.)

■ *Altering the terms or conditions for a home loan* to any person who wishes to purchase or repair a dwelling or otherwise denying such a loan as a means of discrimination

■ **FOR EXAMPLE** Citywide Mortgage Company has a policy of refusing to make loans for properties located in the Valley View neighborhood, claiming that borrowers from Valley View have historically been at higher risk of default. Because this policy does not consider the creditworthiness of individual borrowers from Valley View, it is more than likely intended to discriminate against such borrowers on the basis of some other characteristic, such as race or national origin. (This is known as **redlining**.)

■ *Denying people membership* or limiting their participation in any multiple listing service, real estate brokers' organization, or other facility related to the sale or rental of dwellings as a means of discrimination

■ **FOR EXAMPLE** A multiple listing service cannot lawfully exclude brokers from participation on the basis of their race, color, sex, religion, age, national origin, familial status, or handicap.

Exceptions The following exemptions to the federal Fair Housing Act are provided:

■ The sale or rental of a single-family home is exempted when the home is owned by an individual who does not own more than three such homes at one time and when the following conditions exist: (a) *a broker, salesperson, or agent is not used*; and (b) *advertising is not used*. Only one such sale by such an individual is exempt from the law within any 24-month period.
■ The rental of units is exempted in an *owner-occupied one- to four-family dwelling* (but again, discriminatory advertising may not be used).
■ Dwelling units owned by *religious organizations* may be restricted to people of the same religion, if membership in the organization is not restricted on the basis of race, color, national origin, handicap, or familial status.
■ A *private club* that is not in fact open to the public may restrict the rental or occupancy of lodgings that it owns to its members, as long as the lodgings are not operated commercially.

HUD Advertising Guidelines

In New York, real estate advertising is often monitored by state and federal government agencies to detect evidence of discriminatory practices. There has been much confusion about what types of property descriptions are and are not appropriate

TABLE 17.2

HUD's Advertising Guidelines

Category	Rule	Permitted	Not Permitted
Race Color National origin	No discriminatory limitation/ preference may be expressed	"master bedroom" "good neighborhood"	"white neighborhood" "no French"
Religion	No religious preference/ limitation	"chapel on premises" "kosher meals available" "Merry Christmas"	"no Muslims" "nice Christian family" "near great Catholic school"
Sex	No explicit preference based on sex	"mother-in-law suite" "master bedroom" "female roommate sought"	"great house for a man" "wife's dream kitchen"
Disability	No exclusions or limitations based on disability	"wheelchair ramp" "walk to shopping"	"no wheelchairs" "able-bodied tenants only"
Familial status	No preference or limitation based on family size or nature	"two-bedroom" "family room" "quiet neighborhood"	"married couple only" "no more than two children" "retiree's dream house"
Photographs or illustrations of people	People should be clearly representative and nonexclusive	Illustrations showing ethnic races, family groups, singles, etc.	Illustrations showing only singles, African-American families, elderly white adults, etc.

or legal to use in an ad. In an effort to clarify federal regulations regarding real estate advertising, HUD issued the following policy guidelines in January 1995 (see Table 17.2):

Race, color, national origin

Real estate advertisements should state no discriminatory preference or limitation on account of race, color, or national origin. Use of words describing the housing, the current or potential residents, or the neighbors or neighborhood in racial or ethnic terms (e.g., white family home, no Irish) will create liability under this section.

However, advertisements that are racially neutral will not create liability. Thus, complaints over use of phrases such as master bedroom, rare find, or desirable neighborhood should not be filed.

Religion

Advertisements should not contain an explicit preference, limitation, or discrimination on account of religion (e.g., no Jews, Christian home). Advertisements that use the legal name of an entity that contains a religious reference (for example, Roselawn Catholic Home) or those that contain a religious symbol (such as a cross) standing alone may indicate a religious preference. However, if such an advertisement includes a disclaimer (such as the statement, "This home does not discriminate on the basis of race, color, religion, national origin, sex, handicap, or familial status"), it will not violate the act. Advertisements containing descriptions of properties (apartment complex with chapel) or services (kosher meals available) do not on their face state a preference for persons likely to make use of those facilities and are not violations of the act.

The use of secularized terms or symbols relating to holidays, such as Santa Claus or the Easter Bunny, or St. Valentine's Day images, or phrases such as "Merry Christmas," "Happy Easter," or the like, does not constitute a violation of the act.

Sex

Advertisements for single-family dwellings or separate units in a multifamily dwelling should contain no explicit preference, limitation, or discrimination based on sex. Use of the term master bedroom does not constitute a violation of either the sex discrimination provisions or the race discrimination provisions. Terms such as mother-in-law suite and bachelor apartment are commonly used as physical descriptions of housing units and do not violate the act.

Disability

Real estate advertisements should not contain explicit exclusions, limitations, or other indications of discrimination based on disability (e.g., no wheelchairs). Advertisements containing descriptions of properties (great view, fourth-floor walkup, walk-in closets), services or facilities (jogging trails), or neighborhoods (walk to bus stop) do not violate the act. Advertisements describing the conduct required of residents ("nonsmoking," "sober") do not violate the act. Advertisements containing descriptions of accessibility features are lawful (wheelchair ramp).

Familial status

Advertisements may not state an explicit preference, limitation, or discrimination based on familial status. Advertisements may not contain limitations on the number or ages of children or state a preference for adults, couples, or singles. Advertisements describing the properties (two-bedroom, cozy, family room), services and facilities (no bicycles allowed), or neighborhoods (quiet streets) are not racially discriminatory and do not violate the act.

Jones v. Mayer

The second significant fair housing development of 1968 was the Supreme Court decision in the case of *Jones v. Alfred H. Mayer Company.* In its ruling, the court held that the Civil Rights Act of 1866 "prohibits all racial discrimination, private or public, in the sale and rental of property."

This decision is important because although the 1968 federal law exempts individual homeowners and certain groups, the 1866 law *prohibits all racial discrimination without exception.* So despite any exemptions in the 1968 law, an offended person may seek a remedy for racial discrimination under the 1866 law against any homeowner, regardless of whether the owner employed a real estate broker and/or advertised the property. *Where race or color is involved, no exceptions apply.* (In 1987, U.S. Supreme Court decisions implied that the 1866 law, to which there are no exceptions, extended to ethnic and/or religious groups as well.)

Brown v. Board of Education

In 1954, under this case, the U.S. Supreme Court reversed a previous ruling on *Plessy v. Ferguson* (1896). Separate facilities (previously decided as legally acceptable) were ruled to be unequal.

Equal Housing Poster

An equal housing opportunity poster (illustrated in Figure 17.1) can be obtained from HUD. Displayed in a broker's office, it informs the public about fair housing laws and shows the firm's intention to comply. Displaying the poster is not a legal requirement, but when HUD investigates a broker for discriminatory practices, it considers failure to display it as evidence of discrimination. The poster should be prominently displayed in any location where the broker conducts business, including model homes.

FIGURE   17.1

Equal Housing Opportunity Poster

U.S. Department of Housing and Urban Development

EQUAL HOUSING
OPPORTUNITY

We Do Business in Accordance With the Federal Fair Housing Law

(The Fair Housing Amendments Act of 1988)

It is Illegal to Discriminate Against Any Person Because of Race, Color, Religion, Sex, Handicap, Familial Status, or National Origin

- ■ In the sale or rental of housing or residential lots
- ■ In advertising the sale or rental of housing
- ■ In the financing of housing

- ■ In the provision of real estate brokerage services
- ■ In the appraisal of housing

- ■ Blockbusting is also illegal

Anyone who feels he or she has been discriminated against may file a complaint of housing discrimination:
    1-800-669-9777 (Toll Free)
    1-800-927-9275 (TDD)

**U.S. Department of Housing and Urban Development
Assistant Secretary for Fair Housing and Equal Opportunity
Washington, D.C. 20410**

Previous editions are obsolete   form HUD-928.1A (2/2003)

Blockbusting and Steering

Blockbusting and steering are undesirable housing practices frequently discussed in connection with fair housing. They are prohibited by federal and New York state law.

Blockbusting means *inducing homeowners to sell by using scare tactics about the entry of a certain group into the neighborhood.* The blockbuster frightens homeowners into selling and makes a profit through sales commissions or by buying the homes cheaply, then selling them at considerably higher prices to minority persons. In some cases where a defined area or neighborhood is the subject of excessive solicitation by brokerage firms, a nonsolicitation order may be issued by the secretary of state. A **nonsolicitation order** is a directive to all real estate brokers and real estate salespersons. The nonsolicitation order directs that all brokers and salespersons must refrain from soliciting listings for the sale of residential property within a designated geographic area. A nonsolicitation order prohibits any and all types of solicitation directed at or toward homeowners in the designated geographic area. The types of solicitation that are prohibited include but are not limited to letters, postcards, telephone calls, door-to-door calls, handbills, and postings in public areas. In addition, a nonsolicitation order may contain such other terms or conditions as the secretary of state may determine are, on balance, in the best interest of the public, which would include but not be limited to the affected owners and licensees. Failure to comply results in disciplinary action by the New York Department of State.

Steering is the channeling of home seekers to particular areas on the basis of race, religion, country of origin, or other protected class. Steering is often difficult to detect, because the steering tactics can be so subtle that home seekers are unaware that their choices have been limited. Steering may be done unintentionally by agents who are not aware of their own unconscious assumptions. Even if unconscious or unintentional, discrimination is still illegal. An increasingly common means of detecting steering is the use of testers, discussed later in this chapter.

Redlining

Denying applications for mortgage loans or insurance policies in specific areas without regard to the economic qualifications of the applicant is known as *redlining.* This practice, which often contributes to the deterioration of older, transitional neighborhoods, is frequently based on race rather than on any supportable objections to the applicant. As a result of redlining practices, a filtering down effect can occur. **Filtering down** is the process by which housing units formerly occupied by middle- and upper-income families decline in quality and value and become available to lower-income occupants.

Enforcement

A person who believes illegal discrimination has occurred has up to one year after the alleged act to file a charge with the **Department of Housing and Urban Development (HUD)** or may bring a federal suit within two years.

For those who think their rights may have been violated, HUD maintains toll-free hot lines: 800-669-9777 (voice) and 800-927-9275 (TTD). Complaints may also be made by mail to the following address:

> Fair Housing and Equal Opportunity
> HUD Regional Office
> 26 Federal Plaza, Suite 3541
> New York, NY 10278-0068
> *http://portal.hud.gov/hudportal/HUD?src=/program_offices/*
> *fair_housing_equal_opp*

HUD will investigate, and if the department believes a discriminatory act has occurred or is about to occur, it may issue a charge. Any party involved (or HUD) may choose to have the charge heard in a federal district court. If no one requests the court procedure, the charge will be heard by an administrative law judge within HUD itself.

The administrative judge has the authority to issue an *injunction* (court order). This would order the offender to do something (rent to the complaining party, for example) or to refrain from doing something. In addition, penalties can be imposed, ranging from $10,000 for a first violation to $25,000 for a second violation within five years to $50,000 for further violations within seven years. If the case is heard in federal court, an injunction and actual and punitive damages are possible, with no dollar limit. The Department of Justice may also on its own sue anyone who seems to show a *pattern of illegal discrimination*. Dollar limits on penalties in such cases start at $50,000, with a possible $100,000 penalty for repeat violations.

The guilty party may be required to pay the other side's legal fees and court costs, which can add up to substantial amounts.

Complaints brought under the Civil Rights Act of 1866 must be taken directly to a federal court. The only time limit for action is three years, which is New York's statute of limitations for *torts*, that is, *injuries done by one individual to another*. There is no dollar limit on damages.

Threats or Acts of Violence

The federal Fair Housing Act of 1968 contains provisions protecting the rights of those who seek the benefits of the open housing law as well as the rights of owners, brokers, or salespersons who assist them. Threats and intimidation should be reported immediately to the local police and to the nearest office of the Federal Bureau of Investigation (FBI).

Americans with Disabilities Act of 1992

The **Americans with Disabilities Act (ADA)** of 1992, a federal antidiscrimination law, was enacted primarily to protect disabled persons from discrimination in public accommodations and commercial facilities. It also provides protection from discrimination and mandates easy access in new multifamily housing with four or more units.

Tenants who wish to make alterations at their own expense to make an existing dwelling unit more accessible may do so. The landlord may require that such tenants restore the premises, as necessary, to their original state when vacating.

NEW YORK HUMAN RIGHTS LAW

Protected classes under the New York Executive Law for Fair Housing cover race, creed, color, national origin, sex, disability, age, sexual orientation, military status, and marital status (some exceptions).

Blockbusting, forbidden under federal statutes, is specifically mentioned in the **New York Human Rights Law** (Article 15, Executive Law) and also is prohibited by a New York Department of State (DOS) regulation. The DOS has, in the past, responded to complaints by the public by issuing **cease and desist orders** that prohibit canvassing for listings to certain homeowners.

A person charging discrimination may initiate a private lawsuit (with no dollar limit mentioned under state law) and also may lodge a complaint with the DOS if the offender is licensed. A complaint also may be filed with the **New York State Division of Human Rights** *within a one-year period.*

Under sections of the **Executive Law**, New York statutes broaden the nondiscrimination rules to cover commercial real estate. They also add several other categories in which discrimination is prohibited, including age, sexual orientation, military status, and marital status. The age provisions apply only to those 18 and older.

The **Real Property Law** forbids denial of rental housing because of children or an eviction because of a tenant's pregnancy or new child. The rules extend to mobile homes.

Various exceptions are made to the New York State rules, but these exceptions will not apply where the discrimination is racially based because the federal Civil Rights Act of 1866, which covers race, permits no exceptions. With that in mind, New York State excepts

- public housing that may be aimed at one specific age group,
- restriction of all rooms rented to members of the same sex,
- rental of a room in one's own home, and
- restriction of rentals to persons 55 years of age or older.

Although an owner sometimes may discriminate under these exemptions, *a licensee may not participate in the transaction*, either through ownership or employment. In general, the New York statutes cover renting, selling, leasing, and advertising. Public accommodations also are included. The law further forbids any real estate board to discriminate in its membership because of any of the listed categories, which in this case includes age. New York regulations are generally more restrictive than federal laws. Table 17.3 summarizes the categories covered by the various federal and New York State laws.

TABLE   17.3

Category Summary of Fair Housing Laws

	Civil Rights Act of 1866	Fair Housing Act of 1968	New York Law	New York City
Citizenship				Yes
Race	Yes	Yes	Yes	Yes
Color	Yes	Yes	Yes	Yes
Religion		Yes	Yes ("creed")	Yes
National origin		Yes	Yes	Yes
Lawful occupation				Yes
Sex		Yes (1974)	Yes	Yes
Age			Yes (older than 18)	Yes
Disability		Yes (1988)	Yes	Yes
Sexual orientation			Yes	Yes
Marital status			Yes	Yes
Children in family (Familial status)		Yes (1988)	Yes	Yes
Military status			Yes	
Exceptions	No	Yes	Yes	Yes

Cease-and-Desist Lists and Nonsolicitation Orders

Cease-and-desist lists apply to areas that have been subjected to excessive and repetitive solicitation by real estate licensees. Upon determination of an event, the secretary of state has the power to create a neighborhood zone requiring that all licensees "cease and desist" from soliciting within that zone. A licensee's failure to comply with this order will subject him or her to DOS disciplinary action.

A nonsolicitation order is also issued by the secretary of state. This nonsolicitation order is intended to prevent solicitation with the intent to create blockbusting (previously discussed).

Local Regulations

Local governments may add other groups to the list of protected categories. The New York City Human Rights Commission has adopted the standard of *domestic partner* (an unmarried adult person who can prove emotional and financial commitment and interdependence) for gay or lesbian couples who deal with co-op boards. The definition also has been used in disputes over rights to rent-controlled and rent-stabilized apartments. The city also prohibits discrimination on the basis of *lawful occupation or citizenship* and allows no exceptions to fair housing laws for the rental of an owner-occupied multiple dwelling.

■ CODE FOR EQUAL OPPORTUNITY

The National Association of REALTORS® has adopted a **Code for Equal Opportunity**. The code sets forth suggested standards of conduct for REALTORS® so that they may comply with fair housing laws. The REALTORS® Code, while it does not have the force of law, asks equal treatment for those classes protected by state and federal law and also for one more class, *sexual preference*.

Voluntary

The National Association of REALTORS® has a voluntary cooperative agreement with HUD. This agreement, called the *Fair Housing Partnership Agreement*, stipulates that HUD and the National Association of REALTORS® will work together to identify fair housing issues, concerns, and solutions.

■ IMPLICATIONS FOR BROKERS AND SALESPERSONS

To a large extent, the laws place the burden of responsibility for effecting and maintaining fair housing on real estate licensees, brokers, and salespeople. *A complainant does not have to prove specific intent, but only the fact that discrimination occurred. In addition, brokers are liable for the discriminatory behavior of their salespeople and employees, even if they have nondiscrimination policies in effect and are not aware of the illegal activities.*

A broker can take the following steps to ensure compliance with fair housing laws:

■ Include the fair housing logo and/or slogan in all display ads and all classified ads of six column inches or more
■ Prominently display the fair housing logo and/or slogan in all brochures, circulars, billboards, signs, and direct mail advertising, as well as any other forms of marketing
■ When using human models in an advertisement, select the models in such a way as to indicate that the housing is available to all persons without regard to race, color, religion, sex, national origin, familial status, or handicap
■ Prominently display the fair housing poster at all real estate offices, model homes, or other locations where properties are offered for sale or rent
■ Make fair housing information readily available to salespeople and employees, and encourage them to become familiar with it and to attend fair housing education programs
■ Directly inform salespeople and employees of their responsibilities under the fair housing laws through in-house or other training
■ Establish and monitor office procedures to ensure compliance with fair housing regulations and objectives. At a minimum, such procedures should ensure that prospective buyers and renters are made aware of all available properties within their price range and areas of interest and are provided with complete and accurate information.

- Use the "Equal Employment Opportunity" slogan in all employment advertising and take appropriate steps to ensure a broad range of potential recruits
- Require that salespeople educate sellers regarding their fair housing obligations by providing them with fair housing brochures and other information, and refuse to accept listings from sellers who do not agree to abide by fair housing requirements

In addition, the National Association of REALTORS® suggests posting a sign stating that it is against company policy as well as state and federal laws to offer any information on the *racial, ethnic, or religious composition of a neighborhood* or to place restrictions on listing, showing, or providing information on the availability of homes for any of these reasons.

If a prospect still expresses a locational preference for housing based on race, the association's guidelines suggest the following response: "I cannot give you that kind of advice. I will show you several homes that meet your specifications. You will have to decide which one you want."

The responsibility of brokers for the discriminatory behavior of their salespeople presents unique problems. Although brokers may wish to limit their control of salespeople to protect the salesperson's independent contractor status, effective control of behavior in the area of fair housing is essential to protect brokers from liability under civil rights laws. Brokers should have formal office policies regarding discriminatory behavior, and they should require that salespeople acknowledge in writing that they understand those policies and that they have received adequate training to be aware of the requirements of the fair housing laws.

In addition, brokers must have some system for monitoring the activities of salespeople in regard to fair housing compliance. One way to do this is through a record-keeping system that requires that salespeople keep a record of all prospects, including the prospects' qualifying information, the properties that were identified for the prospects, and the prospects' reactions to each individual property. Periodic review of such records by the broker will help identify any instances where a salesperson may be in violation of fair housing standards.

Discrimination involves a sensitive area—human emotions. The broker or salesperson who complies with the law still has to deal with a general public whose attitudes cannot be altered by legislation alone. Therefore, a licensee who wishes to comply with the fair housing laws and also succeed in the real estate business must work to educate the public.

In recent years, brokers sometimes have been caught in the middle when local governments enacted well-meaning **reverse discrimination** regulations. Intended to preserve racial balance in given areas, local laws sometimes run counter to federal and state rules, posing a real problem for the conscientious licensee.

From time to time, real estate offices are visited by **testers** or *checkers*, undercover investigators who want to see whether all customers and clients are being treated with the same cordiality and are being offered the same free choice within a given price range. For example, two testers—one black and one white—with similar qualifications and interests may separately visit a real estate office to inquire about properties. If the two testers are treated differently by the office or are shown a different range of properties, it may be an indication of unlawful discriminatory behavior by the office. Courts have held that the practice of using testers is permissible as the only way to test compliance with the fair housing laws that are of such importance to American society.

When a broker is charged with discrimination, it is *no defense* that the offense was unintentional or the broker did not know the law. Citing past service to members of the same minority group is of little value. The agent's best course is to study fair housing law, develop sensitivity, and follow routine practices to reduce the danger of unintentionally hurting any member of the public.

These practices include careful record keeping for each customer: financial analysis, properties suggested, houses shown, and check-back phone calls. Using a standard form for all qualifying interviews is essential. Special care should be taken to be on time for appointments and to follow through on returning all phone calls. Besides helping to avoid human rights violations, these practices are simply good business practices and should result in increased sales.

■ SUMMARY

Federal regulations regarding equal opportunity in housing are principally contained in two laws. The Civil Rights Act of 1866 prohibits all racial discrimination, and the federal Fair Housing Act (Title VIII of the Civil Rights Act of 1968) prohibits discrimination on the basis of race, color, religion, sex, national origin, handicap, or familial status (the presence of children in a family) in the sale or rental of residential property. Discriminatory actions include refusing to deal with an individual or a specific group, changing any terms of a real estate or loan transaction, changing the services offered for any individual or group, making statements or advertisements that indicate discriminatory restrictions, or otherwise attempting to make a dwelling unavailable to any person or group because of membership in a protected class. Some exceptions apply to owners but none to brokers and none when the discriminatory act is based on race. Complaints under the federal Fair Housing Act may be reported to and investigated by the Department of Housing and Urban Development and may be taken to a U.S. district court. Complaints under the Civil Rights Act of 1866 must be taken to a federal court.

New York's Executive Law (Human Rights Law) adds age, sexual orientation, military status, and marital status to the grounds on which discrimination is forbidden.

The National Association of REALTORS® Code for Equal Opportunity suggests a set of standards for all licensees to follow, including equal service regardless of a customer's or client's sexual preferences.

CHAPTER 17 QUIZ

1. The owner of a duplex is *advertising* for a tenant for the other half of her home. Which of these ads would violate human rights law?
   a. No pets
   b. Nonsmoker preferred
   c. No children
   d. No Republicans need apply

2. A salesperson was listing a house. The seller informed the salesperson that he would not sell to a member of a particular religious sect. The salesperson should
   a. accept the listing, resolving not to discriminate himself.
   b. explain to the seller why he should change his mind.
   c. refuse the listing and discuss the situation with his broker.
   d. refer the seller to another real estate company.

3. Which act is permitted under the federal Fair Housing Act?
   a. Advertising property for sale only to a special group
   b. Altering the terms of a loan for a member of a minority group
   c. Refusing to make a mortgage loan to an individual with a poor credit history
   d. Telling nervous owners in a changing neighborhood to sell before their homes lose value

4. The Civil Rights Act of 1866 prohibits discrimination on the basis of
   a. race or color.
   b. gender.
   c. previous enslaved status.
   d. age or national origin.

5. "I hear they're moving in; there goes the neighborhood. Better sell to me today!" is an example of
   a. steering.
   b. blockbusting.
   c. redlining.
   d. testing.

6. The broker who suggests only predominantly white areas to a white couple when there are others in their price range is guilty of
   a. blockbusting.
   b. redlining.
   c. steering.
   d. nothing; this is permitted under the Fair Housing Act of 1968.

7. Which would *NOT* be permitted under the federal Fair Housing Act?
   a. The Harvard Club in New York will rent rooms only to graduates of Harvard who belong to the club.
   b. A no-pets policy, evenly applied, refuses rental to the owner of a guide dog.
   c. A convent refuses to furnish housing for a Jewish man.
   d. All of these are forbidden under the act.

8. Under federal law, families with children may be refused rental or purchase in any building where occupancy is reserved exclusively for those who are at *LEAST* age
   a. 55.
   b. 60.
   c. 62.
   d. 65.

9. A lending institution may *NOT* refuse to make a residential real estate loan simply because of the
   a. questionable financial situation of the applicant.
   b. location of the property.
   c. appraisal below purchase price.
   d. deteriorated condition of the building.

10. Under federal law, no exceptions apply when rental discrimination is based on
    a. race.
    b. gender.
    c. handicap.
    d. country of origin.

11. A Utica landlord refused to rent to anyone on public assistance and thereby violated

   a. no law.
   b. the New York Executive Law.
   c. the Fair Housing Act of 1968.
   d. the Civil Rights Act of 1866.

12. The Ithaca housewife who refuses to rent rooms to any students is in violation of

   a. no law.
   b. the New York Executive Law.
   c. the Fair Housing Act of 1968.
   d. the Civil Rights Act of 1866.

13. Refusing an apartment to a couple because they are unmarried violates

   a. no law.
   b. the New York Executive Law.
   c. the Fair Housing Act of 1968.
   d. the Civil Rights Act of 1866.

14. The Fly-by-Night Mortgage Company makes it a practice not to lend money on any inner-city property. This illegal practice is known as

   a. redlining.
   b. blockbusting.
   c. steering.
   d. qualifying.

15. A court found a landlord guilty of illegal discrimination and ordered her to rent her next available apartment to the person who was unfairly hurt. The court order is an example of

   a. punitive damages.
   b. actual damages.
   c. an injunction.
   d. a monetary penalty.

16. The seller who requests prohibited discrimination in the showing of a home should be told,

   a. "As your agent I have a duty to warn you that such discrimination could land you in real trouble."
   b. "I am not allowed to obey such instructions."
   c. "If you persist, I'll have to refuse to list your property."
   d. All of these.

17. A good precaution against even unconscious discrimination is

   a. detailed record keeping on each customer.
   b. use of a standard financial interview form.
   c. routine follow-up phone calls.
   d. all of these

18. The federal Fair Housing Amendments of 1988 added which of the following as new protected classes?

   a. Handicap and familial status
   b. Occupation and source of income
   c. Political affiliation and country of origin
   d. Prison record and marital status

19. The fine for a first violation of the federal Fair Housing Act could be as much as

   a. $500.
   b. $1,000.
   c. $5,000.
   d. $10,000.

20. The only defense against an accusation of illegal discrimination is proof that it

   a. was unintentional.
   b. didn't cause financial loss to anyone.
   c. arose because the agent was ignorant of the law.
   d. didn't occur.

21. Undercover investigations to see whether fair housing practices are being followed are sometimes made by

   a. testers.
   b. evaluators.
   c. operatives.
   d. conciliators.

18

Environmental Issues

■ KEY TERMS

asbestos

asbestosis

building-related illness
(BRI)

chlordane

chlorofluorocarbons
(CFCs)

Clean Air Act

Comprehensive
Environmental
Response,
Compensation, and
Liability Act (CERCLA)

due diligence

electromagnetic fields

environmental impact
statement

Environmental Protection
Agency (EPA)

Freon

friable

groundwater

hazardous substances

landfill

lead poisoning

Leaking Underground
Storage Tanks (LUST)

mold

percolation test

pollution

polychlorinated biphenyls
(PCBs)

potentially responsible
parties

radioactive waste

radon gas

Safe Drinking Water Act

septic system

sick building syndrome
(SBS)

State Environmental
Quality Review Act
(SEQRA)

Superfund Amendments
and Reauthorization Act
(SARA)

termites

underground storage
tanks

urea-formaldehyde foam
insulation (UFFI)

■ POLLUTION AND ENVIRONMENTAL RISKS IN REAL ESTATE TRANSACTIONS

Environmental concerns have come to the forefront of contemporary issues. Both actual and perceived pollution problems have the ability to stir anger, fear, and other feelings. Indeed, perhaps no other modern issue has a greater ability to elicit strong emotions.

The actual dollar value of real property can be affected significantly by both real and imagined pollution. The desirability and salability of land and buildings may change drastically. Also, the cost of cleaning up and removing pollution may be much greater than the dollar value of the property.

In some areas of the United States, mortgage and title insurance approvals in many cases depend on inspection of the property for **hazardous substances** and proof of their absence.

For all these reasons, real estate professionals should be alert to the possibility of pollution and hazardous substances on property being sold. Knowledgeable real estate professionals should ask property owners about the possibility of hazardous substances. In addition, licensees can expect increasing numbers of questions from concerned customers.

Pollution is an impurity in the environment that was not there originally. The simple act of throwing a piece of paper on the ground creates an unsightly, minor form of pollution. Major pollution problems can result from hazardous substances associated with industrial and other activities, such as farming. Real estate licensees often do not have the technical expertise required to determine whether a hazardous material is present on or near the property. Government agencies and private consulting firms may be contacted for information, guidance, and detailed study.

■ LONG-STANDING ISSUES

Water

Water contamination exists in every state in the United States; what varies is the degree of contamination. Contaminants that can endanger health include *bacteria, viruses, protozoa, nitrates, metals such as lead or mercury, fertilizers, pesticides, and radon.* Sources that can also affect the taste and odor of water include industrial discharges, runoff from urban areas (such as landfills), septic systems that are improperly located and maintained, and pesticides and fertilizers from agricultural areas.

Contaminated water can cause a variety of physical symptoms, from mild stomachaches and intestinal cramping to severe nausea and diarrhea, kidney and liver damage, and death. Some adverse effects, even if nonfatal, may last for one or two weeks, others may last for months or years. Recent evidence indicates that water contaminants (particularly nitrates and radon) cause cancer.

The quality of drinking water can be tested by a local health authority or water supplier. Federal regulations (the **Safe Drinking Water Act**) require that public water suppliers periodically test the drinking water for contamination. Well water can be tested by health authorities or private laboratories. Some experts advise testing private water supplies at least once a year. If water contamination is suspected, alternate sources of water should be used until the water is deemed safe.

The term **groundwater** includes not only the runoff at ground level but also the underground water systems used for wells, both private and public. Underground streams are formed in the rocks, crevices, and caves under the ground and flow just as dramatically as do rivers aboveground. This underground water table can be as shallow as two or three feet below the surface or extend all the way down to several hundred feet.

Contamination of this water supply is a serious health threat. Water can be contaminated from a number of sources, including waste disposal sites and underground storage tanks. Heavy regulation in these areas is about the only protection the general public has against water contamination. Once contamination has been identified, its source can be eliminated, but such a process is often time-consuming and extremely expensive. Many times, freshwater wells must be relocated.

Effective November 19, 2007, Westchester County adopted the Private Well Water Testing Law. The purpose of this law was to protect purchasers of real property containing wells from unknowingly purchasing properties (in Westchester County) that might have substandard water supplies. The burden of this law falls primarily on a seller of real property when that property is served by a well or on the landlord of that property when the transaction involves a lease of property that is or will be serviced by a well. Compliance would include but not be limited to the following:

- Water testing for any new wells
- Water testing requirements for leased property served by an existing well
- Water testing requirements for any property for sale served by an existing well

When a property is sold in Westchester County, the seller is required to arrange for the water to be tested and to report the results to the interested party(s) purchasing the property. Aside from both buyer and seller certifying in writing that they have conducted the test and reviewed the results, a copy of the test and its results must be sent to the County Health Department. The test results are sent to the County Health Department directly from the certified lab that conducted the test.

Waste Disposal Sites

The United States has become increasingly a *throwaway* society. Landfill operations have been the main receptacle for this type of garbage. A **landfill** is a site excavated and lined with either a clay or synthetic liner to prevent leakage of waste material into the local water system. Garbage is then laid at the bottom of the excavation and a layer of topsoil is compacted onto it. The procedure is used again and again until the excavation has been filled. It is then *capped* with two to four feet of topsoil on the very top and then planted with some type of vegetation. Completed landfills have been used for such purposes as parks and golf courses.

The construction and maintenance of a landfill operation is heavily regulated by state and federal authorities. Well-run landfill operations do not have to be a source of pollution. However, landfills at improper locations and improperly managed sites have been a source of major problems. Landfills constructed on the wrong type of soil will leak waste into nearby wells, causing major damage. Federal, state, and local authorities and private industry have set up test wells around such landfill operations to monitor the water in the local areas constantly.

Radioactive waste is material that has accumulated as waste from nuclear energy power plants and from various uses of radioactive material in medicine and scientific research. Emissions from such waste can be extremely harmful, sometimes causing cancer or even death.

Radioactive material can have a life expectancy of thousands of years. Much is still to be learned about disposal techniques, and in most cases the only alternative is to put the material in some type of containment facility. The container is then either buried or dropped in the sea. The obvious problem is that sometimes these containers can leak or be damaged in transit.

Although waste disposal is heavily regulated, no one is interested in living next to a hazardous waste dump. Real estate professionals must be aware of such facilities in their areas and take the appropriate action when dealing with potential buyers or sellers.

Septic Systems

Household wastewater is made up of water from toilets, washing machines, dishwashers, sinks, bathtubs, and showers. The average family of four produces about 300 gallons of wastewater every day. A **septic system** is an individual treatment and disposal system that is usually built underground. A septic system consists of a large storage tank (septic tank), in which the wastewater is partially broken down by bacteria, and an absorption (leach) field, which receives and filters the wastewater. Solid material settles out of the wastewater, remains at the bottom of the septic tank, and must be pumped out periodically (at least once every three to five years).

Before a septic tank can be installed, the property owner must have the soil tested to determine how much wastewater the soil can process (**percolation test**). The septic tank also must be the correct size for the number of occupants, and the proper size is determined by the number of bedrooms in the house. A professional engineer or registered architect must submit "as built" plans of the system to the department of health for approval.

When the septic tank is properly installed and maintained, a septic system is generally adequate for wastewater disposal and treatment. However, if the system is not working properly, there may be serious consequences, including contamination of groundwater and wells; contamination of nearby streams, rivers, and lakes; and the pooling of wastewater above the surface.

There are various signs that a septic system is malfunctioning, including wastewater odors inside or outside the home, lush grass and spongy soil over the absorption field, pooled "gray" water over the absorption field, and sluggish or backed-up drains.

If the septic system has failed, pumping the septic tank may solve the problem. More serious malfunctions may require the installation of a new septic system, new fields, new pumps or distribution boxes, or the installation of a sewer system.

Termites

Termites are antlike insects that live in the earth. In some New York regions, termites are a common problem for homeowners because these insects are so destructive to wood. In other parts of the state, termites are seldom encountered. In some areas, purchasers may make a contract contingent on a satisfactory termite inspection before closing, or lenders may require it.

It is vital that when a structure is built, no untreated wood touches the soil. The ground often is treated before laying the foundation, to keep termites from coming up through the foundation. Metal termite shields also may be used.

Termite damage, which typically occurs in homes that are more than five or ten years old, is often hard to detect. Termite inspectors must probe the foundation and base wood structure of a house with a tool similar to an ice pick. If the pick sinks down into the wood, it has probably been eaten away inside (although rot also may be the culprit). Termites may also leave tunnel-like trails as evidence of their presence.

When termite damage or infestation is present, a thorough extermination is required, and the termite damage must be repaired. This must be done only by someone specifically licensed by the New York State Department of Environmental Conservation (DEC). A common method is to drill holes around the property and fill them with a solution that kills the insects.

Asbestos

Asbestos is a mineral found in rocks that has been used for many years as insulation on plumbing pipes and heat ducts and as general insulation because it is a poor conductor of heat. It also has been used in floor tile and in roofing material.

Because of its heat-containing property and the fact that it is relatively inexpensive, asbestos has been used in the insulation of almost all types of buildings, especially public buildings such as libraries, schools, and government buildings. Although it remains relatively harmless if not disturbed, it can become life-threatening when removed because of the accompanying dust.

Contemporary environmental concerns affecting real estate include asbestos, lead, radon gas, mold, indoor air quality, and PCBs.

Exposure to the dust can come in several ways. One is when the asbestos material gets old and starts to disintegrate. Remodeling projects that include the removal of asbestos shingles, roof tile, or insulation can cause the dust to form in the air and expose people in the area to the health hazard. Medical problems include **asbestosis,** a chronic lung disease that involves difficult breathing and sometimes death;

lung cancer; and mesothelioma, a cancer of the chest and abdominal membranes. They can show up many years after the patient was exposed to asbestos dust.

Testing and, if necessary, removal should be done only by contractors who have been specially trained and are approved by either the federal **Environmental Protection Agency (EPA)** or New York State. Special clothing and respirators are used. Testing is done through bulk sampling of the materials, monitoring of the air, or a technique known as *wipe sampling*.

Once a building has been determined to have asbestos, the owner can take several approaches. One is to leave well enough alone. Asbestos roofing, floor tile, and insulation, if undisturbed and not **friable** (fraying or crumbling), do not pose a health problem. An alternative is to remove the material, with the work done, again, only by approved professionals.

The third approach is to encapsulate the material; in other words, if the exposure comes because of the dust in the air, it is possible to contain the dust by enclosing the insulation with a plastic or paint that does not allow the dust to reach the air. Again, such procedures should be carried out by professionals.

Lead Poisoning

Lead has been used for centuries because of its pliability and its ability to block water flow. It has been used as an ingredient in paint and also in the installation of water pipes. Soil around a building may become contaminated as exterior lead-based paint deteriorates.

Lead becomes a health hazard when ingested. Once in the body, it can impair physical and mental development in young children and aggravate high blood pressure in adults.

Lead poisoning comes from two main sources. The first is peeling or flaking paint that small children sometimes put into their mouths or that contributes to contaminated dust in the air. The second is the plumbing system. Sometimes lead in connecting water pipes or in insulation for hot-water heaters contaminates the water that flows through them. Concentrated amounts of lead can lead to serious health effects.

Lead was used in many oil-based paints until 1978. Once various health problems were linked to lead poisoning, lead was immediately banned as an ingredient of any paint material. Other limitations have been imposed on all materials that contain lead to keep the lead away from all materials that may be ingested. However, one can still be exposed to lead in many older homes.

Paint is tested for lead by sending a sample to a laboratory. If it is found, it may be left undisturbed if it is not flaking, or it is sometimes covered with drywall, paneling, or wallpaper. Actual removal is a complicated procedure that must not be undertaken by amateurs. Dust released into the air can be highly dangerous and difficult to eliminate.

Lead in the water system also is tested by sending a sample to a qualified laboratory. The water should be drawn directly from the faucet, because lead leaches into water as it stands in the pipes. After a minute or so, a sample may no longer contain enough lead to show up in testing. Remediation includes replacement of old lead plumbing or pipes joined by lead solder.

Both sellers and landlords must disclose information regarding lead-based paint to buyers and renters of pre-1978 residential properties. Sellers and landlords must disclose the location of any lead-based paint that they are aware of, provide a copy of any report concerning lead-based paint in the property to buyers or tenants, give buyers or tenants a copy of a pamphlet on lead-based paint prepared by the government, and offer buyers or tenants a ten-day period in which to have the home tested for lead-based paint. Licensees are also required to disclose any knowledge they have of the existence of lead-based paint. (See Figures 18.1, 18.2, 18.3, 18.4.)

Although sellers and landlords must make these disclosures, this law does not actually require them to test for lead-based paint or make any repairs. The prospective buyer or tenant could, however, cancel the purchase contract or the lease.

Various localities may have laws requiring testing or treatment for lead, particularly with rental housing. In New York City, if children under seven years of age reside in rented property, landlords are required to test for lead dust and to remedy chipping paint.

The state's Web site is *www.health.state.ny.us/environmental*.

Radon Gas

Radon gas is an odorless, radioactive gas produced by the decay of other radioactive materials in rocks under the surface of the earth. As radon is released from the rocks, it finds its way to the surface and is usually released into the general atmosphere. In some cases, it is trapped in buildings and increases in concentration. Radon enters a house through cracks in the foundation or through floor drains. It can become concentrated in crawl spaces or in basements. Long-term exposure to radon gas is said to cause lung cancer.

Radon was identified as being a hazardous problem in homes in 1984. Since that time, the EPA has established levels of radon gas believed to be unsafe. Testing techniques also have been developed that allow homeowners to determine the exact quantity of radon gas in their homes. The level of radon that necessitates remediation is 4 picocuries (pCi). Its effects are particularly hazardous to a smoker.

Radon testing kits are widely available in hardware stores. The homeowner should follow directions and then send a canister to a laboratory for analysis.

Generally, the elimination of radon gas from a home is a relatively simple matter. It can be removed from drinking water by a special filtration system. Gas is removed from the indoor air by ventilation systems or exhaust fans.

Disclosure of Lead-Based Paint and Lead-Based Hazards

LEAD-BASED PAINT OR LEAD-BASED PAINT HAZARD ADDENDUM

It is a condition of this contract that, until midnight of _____ , Buyer shall have the right to obtain a risk assessment or inspection of the Property for the presence of lead-based paint and/or lead-based paint hazards* at Buyer's expense. This contingency will terminate at that time unless Buyer or Buyer's agent delivers to the Seller or Seller's agent a written inspection and/or risk assessment report listing the specific existing deficiencies and corrections needed, if any. If any corrections are necessary, Seller shall have the option of (i) completing them, (ii) providing for their completion, or (iii) refusing to complete them. If Seller elects not to complete or provide for completion of the corrections, then Buyer shall have the option of (iv) accepting the Property in its present condition, or (v) terminating this contract, in which case all earnest monies shall be refunded to Buyer. Buyer may waive the right to obtain a risk assessment or inspection of the Property for the presence of lead-based paint and/or lead based paint hazards at any time without cause.

*Intact lead-based paint that is in good condition is not necessarily a hazard. See EPA pamphlet "Protect Your Family From Lead in Your Home" for more information.

Disclosure of Information on Lead-Based Paint and Lead-Based Paint Hazards

Lead Warning Statement

Every Buyer of any interest in residential real property on which a residential dwelling was built prior to 1978 is notified that such property may present exposure to lead from lead-based paint that may place young children at risk of developing lead poisoning. Lead poisoning in young children may produce permanent neurological damage, including learning disabilities, reduced intelligence quotient, behavioral problems, and impaired memory. Lead poisoning also poses a particular risk to pregnant women. The Seller of any interest in residential real property is required to provide the Buyer with any information on lead-based paint hazards from risk assessments or inspections in the Seller's possession and notify the Buyer of any known lead-based paint hazards. A risk assessment or inspection for possible lead-based paint hazards is recommended prior to purchase.

Seller's Disclosure (initial)

_____ (a) Presence of lead-based paint and/or lead-based paint hazards (check one below):

❏ Known lead-based paint and/or lead-based paint hazards are present in the housing (explain).

_____

_____

❏ Seller has no knowledge of lead-based paint and/or lead-based paint hazards in the housing.

_____ (b) Records and reports available to the Seller (check one below):

❏ Seller has provided the Buyer with all available records and reports pertaining to lead-based paint and/or lead-based paint hazards in the housing (list documents below).

_____

_____

❏ Seller has no reports or records pertaining to lead-based paint and/or lead-based paint hazards in the housing.

Buyer's Acknowledgment (initial)

_____ (c) Buyer has received copies of all information listed above.

_____ (d) Buyer has received the pamphlet *Protect Your Family from Lead in Your Home*.

_____ (e) Buyer has (check one below):

❏ Received a 10-day opportunity (or mutually agreed upon period) to conduct a risk assessment or inspection for the presence of lead-based paint and/or lead-based paint hazards; or

❏ Waived the opportunity to conduct a risk assessment or inspection for the presence of lead-based paint and/or lead-based paint hazards.

Agent's Acknowledgment (initial)

_____ (f) Agent has informed the Seller of the Seller's obligations under 42 U.S.C. 4582(d) and is aware of his/her responsibility to ensure compliance.

Certification of Accuracy

The following parties have reviewed the information above and certify, to the best of their knowledge, that the information provided by the signatory is true and accurate.

Buyer: _____ (SEAL) Date _____

Buyer: _____ (SEAL) Date _____

Agent: _____ Date _____

Seller: _____ (SEAL) Date _____

Seller: _____ (SEAL) Date _____

Agent: _____ Date _____

Disclosure of Information on Lead-Based Paint and/or Lead-Based Paint Hazards (Leasing)

Disclosure of Information on Lead-Based Paint and/or Lead-Based Paint Hazards

Lead Warning Statement

Housing built before 1978 may contain lead-based paint. Lead from paint, paint chips, and dust can pose health hazards if not managed properly. Lead exposure is especially harmful to young children and pregnant women. Before renting pre-1978 housing, lessors must disclose the presence of known lead-based paint and/or lead-based paint hazards in the dwelling. Lessees must also receive a federally approved pamphlet on lead poisoning prevention.

Lessor's Disclosure.

(a) Presence of lead-based paint and/or lead-based paint hazards (Check (i) or (ii) below):

(i) _____ Known lead-based paint and/or lead-based paint hazards are present in the housing (explain).

_____

(ii) _____ Lessor has no knowledge of lead-based paint and/or lead-based paint hazards in the housing.

(b) Records and reports available to lessor (Check (i) or (ii) below):

(i) _____ Lessor has provided the Lessee with all available records and reports pertaining to lead-based paint and/or lead-based paint hazards in the housing (list documents below).

_____

(ii) _____ Lessor has no reports or records pertaining to lead-based paint and/or lead-based paint hazards in the housing.

Lessee's Acknowledgment (initial)

(c) _____ Lessee has received copies of all information listed above.

(d) _____ Lessee has received the pamphlet *Protect Your Family from Lead In Your Home.*

Agent's Acknowledgment (initial)

(e) _____ Agent has informed the lessor of the lessor's obligations under 42 U.S.C. 4852d and is aware of his/her responsibility to ensure compliance.

Certification of Accuracy

The following parties have reviewed the information above and certify, to the best of their knowledge, that the information they have provided is true and accurate.

_____	_____	_____	_____
Lessor	Date	Lessor	Date
_____	_____	_____	_____
Lessee	Date	Lessee	Date
_____	_____	_____	_____
Agent	Date	Agent	Date

FIGURE 18.3

New York City Lead Paint Notice

(03/07)

NEW YORK CITY LEAD PAINT NOTICE
[To be Attached to the Lease of the Apartment]
LEASE/COMMENCEMENT OF OCCUPANCY NOTICE FOR PREVENTION OF LEAD-BASED PAINT HAZARDS—INQUIRY REGARDING CHILD

You are required by law to inform the owner if a child under six years of age resides or will reside in the dwelling unit (apartment) for which you are signing this lease/commencing occupancy. If such a child resides or will reside in the unit, the owner of the building is required to perform an annual visual inspection of the unit to determine the presence of lead-based paint hazards. **IT IS IMPORTANT THAT YOU RETURN THIS FORM TO THE OWNER OR MANAGING AGENT OF YOUR BUILDING TO PROTECT THE HEALTH OF YOUR CHILD.** If you do not respond to this notice, the owner is required to attempt to inspect your apartment to determine if a child under six years of age resides there.

If a child under six years of age does not reside in the unit now, but does come to live in it at any time during the year, you must inform the owner in writing immediately. If a child under six years of age resides in the unit, you should also inform the owner immediately at the address below if you notice any peeling paint or deteriorated subsurfaces in the unit during the year.

Please complete this form and return one copy to the owner or his or her agent or representative when you sign the lease/commence occupancy of the unit. Keep one copy of this form for your records. You should also receive a copy of a pamphlet developed by the New York City Department of Health and Mental Hygiene explaining about lead-based paint hazards when you sign your lease/commence occupancy.

CHECK ONE: ☒ A child under six years of age resides in the unit

☐ A child under six years of age does not reside in the unit.

_____(Occupant signature)

Print occupant's name, address and apartment number_____

_____

(NOT APPLICABLE TO RENEWAL LEASE) Certification by owner: I certify that I have complied with the provisions of §27-2056.8 of Article 14 of the Housing Maintenance Code and the rules promulgated thereunder relating to duties to be performed in vacant units, and that I have provided a copy of the New York City Department of Health and Mental Hygiene pamphlet concerning lead-based paint hazards to the occupant.

_____(Owner signature)

RETURN THIS FORM TO_____

_____

OCCUPANT: KEEP ONE COPY FOR YOUR RECORDS
OWNER COPY/OCCUPANT COPY

F I G U R E   18.4

Annual Notice to Tenant or Occupant in Buildings with Three or More Apartments

To: Tenant   From: Landlord

Date:

ANNUAL NOTICE

PROTECT YOUR CHILD FROM LEAD POISONING AND WINDOW FALLS

New York City law requires that tenants living in buildings with 3 or more apartments complete this form and return it to their landlord before February 15, each year. If you do not return this form, your landlord is required to visit your apartment to determine if children live in your apartment.

Peeling Lead Paint	Window Guards
By law, your landlord is required to inspect your apartment for peeling paint and other lead paint hazards at least once a year if a child under 6 years of age (5 years or younger) lives with you.	By law, your landlord is required to install window guards in all your windows if a child under 11 years of age (10 years or younger) lives with you, OR if you request them (even if no children live with you).
▪ You must notify your landlord in writing if a child under 6 comes to live with you during the year.	▪ ONLY windows that open to fire escapes, and one window in each first floor apartment when there is a fire escape on the outside of the building, are legally exempt from this requirement.
▪ If a child under 6 lives with you, your landlord must inspect your apartment and provide you with the results of these paint inspections.	▪ It is against the law for you to interfere with installation, or remove window guards where they are required. Air conditioners in windows must be permanently installed.
▪ *Always report peeling paint to your landlord. Call 311 if your landlord does not respond.*	▪ Window guards must be installed so there is no space greater than 4½ inches above or below the guard, on the side of the guard, or between the bars.
▪ Your landlord must use safe work practices to repair all peeling paint and other lead paint hazards.	
These requirements apply to buildings with 3 or more apartments built before 1960. They also apply to buildings built between 1960 and 1978 if the landlord knows that lead paint is present.	These requirements apply to all buildings with 3 or more apartments, regardless of when they were built.

Fill out and detach the bottom part of this form and return it to your landlord.

✂ -

Please check all boxes that apply:

☐ A child under 6 years of age (5 years or younger) lives in my apartment.

☐ A child under **11** years of age (10 years or younger) lives in my apartment and:
  ☐ Window guards are installed in all windows as required.
  ☐ Window guards need repair.
  ☐ Window guards are NOT installed in all windows as required.

☐ No child under **11** years of age (10 years or younger) live in my apartment:
  ☐ I want window guards installed anyway.
  ☐ I have window guards, but they need repair.

Last Name	*First Name*		*Middle Initial*	
Street Address	*Apt.#*	*City*	*State*	*Zip Code*
Signature		*Date*	*Telephone Number*	

Deadline for return: February 15

Return form to: Name and address of landlord or managing agent. Call **311** for more information on preventing window falls and lead poisoning.

DOHMH-approved: October 01, 2006

For new construction, the federal EPA has guidelines to help builders avoid radon hazards. New York's radon information line is 800-458-1158.

Indoor Air Quality

Indoor air quality has become increasingly significant as two results of poor air quality have become more readily diagnosed. These are *sick building syndrome* and *building-related illness*.

Sick building syndrome (SBS) is the name for a wide range of symptoms suffered by building occupants. These symptoms are present only when the occupants are in the building and subside when the occupants leave the building. They include headaches, dizziness, drowsiness, memory loss, coughing, asthma, hoarseness, stinging skin, runny noses, and watery eyes.

Building-related illness (BRI), caused by toxic substances or pathogens, continues to affect the building occupant even after he or she has left the building. BRI symptoms include hypersensitivity, pneumonitis, asthma, and certain allergic reactions.

The major sources of interior air contamination include *volatile inorganic compounds* (chemical emissions from products such as paints, adhesives, cleaners, pesticides, fixtures, and furnishings), *microorganisms* (fungi, bacteria, viruses, pollen, and mites), and *particulates* (dust and dander). **Urea-formaldehyde foam insulation (UFFI)**, used in the past as an insulating material, is no longer a concern.

Mold   In recent years, homeowners have become increasingly alert to the presence of **mold** in buildings. Mold grows in moist environments. Some varieties are toxic, others are harmless. Treatment includes remediation of leaks and damp areas. Brokers can alert sellers and buyers to roof leaks, as evidenced by ceiling stains, and to evidence of dampness in basements.

Polychlorinated Biphenyls

Polychlorinated biphenyls (PCBs) are found mostly in electrical equipment. For example, transformers found in electrical vaults within basements of buildings may contain PCBs. Although this type of electrical equipment is slowly being replaced by other equipment, transformers and other electrical equipment should be inspected by the local electric utility experts and replaced if they are found to contain PCBs.

The EPA or New York's DEC can test groundwater and soil around buildings where contamination by leaking PCBs is suspected. The problem is handled by removal and replacement of the soil.

Chlordane

Chlordane is a manufactured chemical that was used as a pesticide in the United States from 1948 to 1988. The EPA has found potential long-term and short-term health effects for humans. Use of this chemical has been banned.

■ FUTURE CONCERNS

Underground Storage Tanks

Underground storage tanks have been used in both residential and commercial settings for many years. One estimate is that three million to five million underground storage tanks in the United States contain hazardous substances, including gasoline. The risk comes when such containers become old, rusted, and start to leak. The toxic material then can enter the groundwater to contaminate wells and pollute the soil.

The most obvious source of such pollution is the millions of gas stations scattered around the United States. Older stations sometimes have steel tanks that have developed leaks through oxidation (rusting). Another major source is the underground containers that were used to hold fuel oil for older homes. Many times the homeowner has converted the heating system to natural gas and has abandoned the use of the old oil tank. This, again, raises the risk of leakage and pollution of the general area.

Recent federal legislation has called for the removal of leaking tanks and all the polluted soil around them. The tank and the soil are then disposed of in a hazardous waste facility. Such a program is extremely expensive, sometimes costing hundreds of thousands of dollars to revamp a gas station, for instance. Legislation regarding underground storage tanks is discussed in more detail later in this chapter.

Electromagnetic Fields

Electromagnetic fields are generated by the presence and movement of electrical charges, that is, electric current. Electromagnetic fields are generally associated with the use of electric power. Common sources of electromagnetic fields (aside from those generated by the earth's magnetic field) include high tension (or high voltage) transmission lines; primary and secondary distribution lines; and electric appliances inside homes, such as televisions, computers, microwave ovens, conventional electric ovens, electric blankets, and electric clocks.

Currently, there is controversy over exactly what, if any, damage is caused by electromagnetic fields. Some evidence suggests that exposure to electromagnetic fields may cause cancer, hormonal changes, and changes in behavior. Other studies have found no damage.

Reducing exposure to electromagnetic fields ranges from the simple to the impossible. For example, if a home is built near primary or secondary transmission lines, occupants can do little to reduce their exposure except move. On the other hand, exposure to electromagnetic fields generated by electrical appliances can be reduced by sitting or standing farther away from them—it is generally assumed that standing a distance of two to three feet away from low-voltage electrical appliances is safe.

Figure 18.5 illustrates various potential problems in residential construction.

FIGURE 18.5

Environmental Hazards

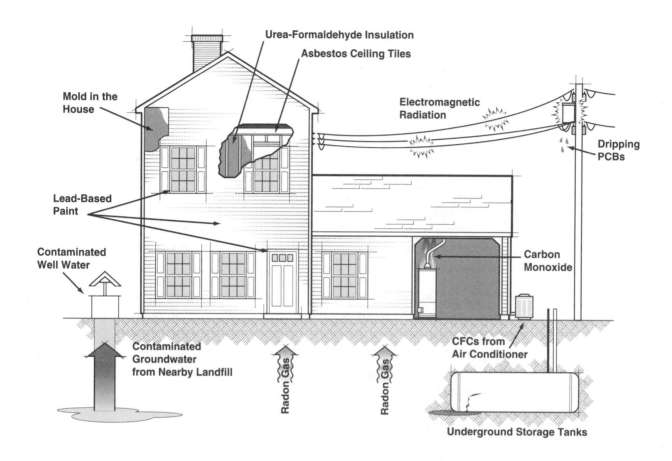

Chlorofluorocarbons

Chlorofluorocarbons (CFCs) are considered to be a significant cause of the depletion of the ozone layer around the earth, a condition that contributes to the development of cataracts and skin cancer. CFCs are gases produced by the propellants used in older aerosol containers and by a refrigerant called **Freon**. (When used in its liquid form, Freon removes, or absorbs, heat; when released, it becomes a gas.) The **Clean Air Act** mandates that CFCs are no longer legal in aerosol cans, and the use of Freon is no longer allowed. However, old-model refrigerators, automobile air conditioners, residential air conditioners, freezers, and heat pumps may present potential leakage problems. The removal of Freon from older appliances is required by law and must be done in a manner that protects the air from contamination.

■ ENVIRONMENTAL ASSESSMENTS

New York's **State Environmental Quality Review Act (SEQRA)** requires the submission of an **environmental impact statement** for any activity where environmental concerns may be present. In such cases, a *Phase I Environmental Assessment* (or *audit*) should be performed. A Phase I Environmental Assessment is an investigation conducted by an environmental professional to determine whether hazardous substances are present on or being released from the property. It is commonly performed before commercial or industrial property is purchased.

A Phase I assessment consists of reviewing the previous ownership and uses of the property by examining all deeds, easements, leases, restrictions, and covenants for a period of 50 years; aerial photographs; any recorded environmental cleanup liens; federal, state, and local government records of sites or facilities where there has been a release of hazardous substances; and a visual site inspection of the property and all its improvements.

If the Phase I assessment discloses the presence or release of hazardous substances on the property, further action may be necessary to confirm the contamination. If confirmation is necessary, a *Phase II Environmental Assessment* will be performed, which consists of sample testing and evaluation. The Phase II assessment must be conducted by a qualified environmental engineer.

Phase III includes remedying the contamination, if any is confirmed, and *Phase IV* includes management of the environmental hazards.

■ LEGAL CONSIDERATIONS

Most legislation dealing with environmental problems has been enacted within the past two decades. Although the EPA was created at the federal level to oversee such problems, several other federal and state agencies are similarly involved.

Federal environmental law is administered by agencies such as the U.S. Department of Transportation under the Hazardous Material Transportation Act; the Occupational Safety and Health Administration (OSHA) and the U.S. Department of Labor, which administer the standards for all employees working in the manufacturing sector; and the EPA, which administers such laws as the Toxic Substance Control Act, the federal Clean Water Act, and the Resource Conservation and Recovery Act.

The need for federal legislation was recognized after the Love Canal situation developed in New York. A hazardous-waste leak created untold problems from both a physical health and a property standpoint.

An *environmental assessment* consists of investigating, testing and confirming, remedying, and managing the contamination.

The **Comprehensive Environmental Response, Compensation, and Liability Act (CERCLA)** was created in 1980. It established a fund of $9 billion, called the *Superfund*, to clean up uncontrolled hazardous waste dumps and to respond to spills. It created a process for identifying **potentially responsible parties** and ordering them to take responsibility for the cleanup action. A landowner may become liable under this act when there has been a release or there is a threat of release of a hazardous substance. Regardless of whether the contamination is the result of the landowner's actions or those of others, the owner might be held responsible for cleaning up any resulting contamination. The liability includes the cleanup of the landowner's property and any neighboring property that has been contaminated.

On the EPA Web site, *www.epa.gov,* you can search by zip code for known or potentially contaminated sites.

Superfund Amendments and Reauthorization Act (SARA)

In 1986, the United States Congress passed the **Superfund Amendments and Reauthorization Act (SARA)**, reauthorizing the Superfund. The amended statute contains stronger cleanup standards for contaminated sites and provides five times the funding of the original Superfund, which expired in September 1985.

The amendments created a concept called *innocent landowner immunity.* Lawmakers recognized that, in certain cases, a landowner in the chain of ownership might have been completely innocent of all wrongdoing and therefore should not be held liable. To establish that an owner is innocent, the damage must have been caused by a previous owner. The innocent landowner must not have had either actual or constructive knowledge of the damage. Most important, the innocent owner must show that *due care* was taken when the land was purchased (the landowner made a reasonable search—preferably an environmental audit—to determine that the property was free of damage).

Underground Storage Tanks

Underground chemical or petroleum storage tanks have been regulated under a 1984 amendment to the Resource Conservation and Recovery Act. A program called **Leaking Underground Storage Tanks (LUST)** was established to govern *installation, maintenance, monitoring, and failure of underground storage tanks.*

The basic provisions of the program require that owners of commercial underground storage tanks and pipes register current tanks, meet standards for installation, make the tanks leak proof for their entire lives, install leak-detection systems, keep the required records, and install no bare steel tanks in soils that will cause rust (otherwise the tanks must be corrosion-proof). Owners also must correct leaks and have funds available to cover potential damage from leaks.

Federal law generally *exempts* farm and residential tanks holding fewer than 1,100 gallons of motor fuel that is used for noncommercial purposes, tanks storing heating oil at the premises where it is consumed, and septic tanks. An important legal point is that LUST places the financial responsibility on the tank owner.

Currently, fuel storage tanks with a capacity of 1,100 gallons or more also are regulated under New York's Underground Storage Tank Act. However, owners of small residential tanks are also liable for cleanup costs under the state's Environmental Response Act if there is a leak or spill from their tanks. Because of this liability, it is sometimes difficult to sell property that has an underground tank. Old abandoned gas stations pose a particular problem.

Contamination problems are caused by rusting tanks, leaky piping, and spills or overfills during fuel delivery. A recommended practice is that homeowners replace tanks every 15 years, routinely inspect tank fittings, and monitor fuel levels with a dipstick during summer months to detect any unwarranted fuel losses. Homeowners should use aboveground tanks, if possible, and purchase quality equipment to minimize the risk of any significant contamination problem.

■ IMPLICATIONS OF ENVIRONMENTAL LAW

The real estate professional must be aware of the exposure of all parties involved. As mentioned earlier, sellers often carry the most of the liability. Innocent landowners may be held responsible even though they did not know that the property had been exposed to environmental pollution.

It also is necessary to advise the buyer of the potential for risk posed by neighboring properties. If the broker represents a seller whose property abuts a gas station, the broker must be aware of the possibility of a leak and make the appropriate disclosures. All possible risk should be disclosed to the buyer in any situation in which there might be an environmental problem.

The days of caveat emptor (let the buyer beware) are dwindling. Both the statutes and the courts are taking steps to protect the innocent buyer whenever possible. The real estate professional must help protect the buyer in all situations.

Liability of Real Estate Professionals

Additional liability is created for other parties to the transaction. For instance, the real estate appraiser must mention and make the proper adjustments in the estimate of market value. Most of the environmental problems associated with residential units can be cleaned up, and the adjustment to market value typically reflects the cost of that work.

The mortgage lender is protected under certain conditions through the 1986 amendments to the Superfund Act. But in any event, the lender must be notified of any potential problems existing with the property.

The insurance carrier might also be affected. Mortgage insurance companies will protect the lender's investment in the mortgage and may be required to carry part of the ultimate responsibility in case of a loss. More important, the hazard insurance carrier may be deemed directly responsible for damages if environmental concerns were included in the policy.

All parties to the real estate transaction should be certain to ascertain that **due diligence** has been conducted on the property by having an *environmental screening* done before the purchase of the property. The environmental screening may take the form of a report or become a thorough environmental audit with complete engineering and scientific tests being conducted.

■ BUILDING GREEN

Heightened environmental awareness combined with increasing energy costs has recently led toward a movement of building "green." The purpose behind green building is to

- ■ minimize waste while maximizing efficiency,
- ■ utilize alternative, renewable energy sources,
- ■ improve air and water quality, and
- ■ use land and natural resources responsibly.

Many newly constructed green buildings feature higher energy efficiency while minimizing negative environmental impact. For example, green buildings will use less potable water (low-flow fixtures), and many have "green roofs" on which plants can grow, resulting in less stormwater runoff. Green building also focuses on ways to provide energy that can be naturally replenished, such as solar power, as a means to reduce our country's dependence on fossil fuels. Reduction in this arena will certainly provide future benefits to the environment.

Properties are now being built to qualify for green building certifications and designations, such as the Leadership in Energy and Environmental Design (LEED) certification. "LEED certified" refers to a set of voluntary standards developed by the private nonprofit U.S. Green Building Council (USGBC). As of 2008, approximately 500 LEED-certified green buildings are located throughout the United States.

While neither the Environmental Protection Agency (EPA) nor the Department of Energy (DOE) has yet developed mandated standards for green building, Energy Star, a joint program of the EPA and the DOE, provides a set of voluntary standards for which energy-efficient products and practices are evaluated. Increasingly, some jurisdictions are requiring energy conservation and other green features for government-funded buildings, such as New York City's PlaNYC 2030 for Sustainability.

■ SUMMARY

In today's marketplace, environmental concerns have significant effects on real estate values. The desirability of property is affected by the presence of pollution, and the cost of cleaning up and removing the sources of pollution may be greater than the value of the land itself.

Several long-standing concerns include water pollution (including groundwater pollution), waste disposal sites, contamination caused by septic systems, and damage caused by termites. Some of the more contemporary issues include asbestos, lead poisoning, radon gas, indoor air quality, and PCBs. Some environmental issues that are becoming more important include underground storage tanks, electromagnetic fields, and CFCs.

There are four phases of environmental assessments: Phase I, an investigation to determine where hazardous substances may be present; Phase II, an investigation to confirm the presence of contaminants; Phase III, which includes remedying the contamination; and Phase IV, which includes managing environmental hazards on an ongoing basis.

One of the most important environmental laws that directly affects property owners is the Comprehensive Environmental Response, Compensation, and Liability Act (CERCLA), which established a Superfund to clean up uncontrolled hazardous waste and to respond to spills. It also imposes liability on past, current, and future owners for the costs of cleaning up contaminants. An amendment (SARA) allows some immunity for the subsequent innocent owner who exercised due diligence before buying.

Large underground storage tanks are regulated by both federal and state law: the Resource Conservation and Recovery Act and the New York Leaking Underground Storage Tank Act.

CHAPTER 18 QUIZ

1. Which is a potential polluter of drinking water?
   a. Asbestos
   b. Freon
   c. Termites
   d. Pesticides

2. Owners of older homes *MUST* advise prospective buyers or tenants about possible hazards of
   a. iron deposits.
   b. lead paint.
   c. electric transmission wires.
   d. urea-formaldehyde foam insulation.

3. Asbestos has been widely used for
   a. solder.
   b. encapsulation.
   c. insulation.
   d. paint.

4. Which is a hazardous gas?
   a. Radon
   b. Lead
   c. Asbestos
   d. Radioactive waste

5. Eliminating radon from a house is generally
   a. a fairly simple matter.
   b. done by an EPA-trained specialist.
   c. an impossibility.
   d. hazardous.

6. Sick building syndrome (SBS)
   a. requires treatment with insecticides.
   b. subsides when the occupant leaves the building.
   c. is covered by CERCLA.
   d. is associated with contaminated drinking water.

7. A percolation test
   a. is used before a septic tank is installed.
   b. reveals the presence of lead in paint.
   c. can detect the presence of radon.
   d. is proof of due diligence.

8. Asbestos should be removed by a
   a. seller.
   b. buyer.
   c. handyman.
   d. certified professional.

9. The federal government regulates farm and residential fuel storage tanks when capacity reaches
   a. 550 gallons.
   b. 1,750 gallons.
   c. 1,100 gallons.
   d. 2,000 gallons.

10. A Phase I environmental assessment is common before purchasing a
    a. ranch.
    b. commercial property.
    c. condominium.
    d. residential lot.

11. Documents indicating past uses of the subject property are examined in which phase of an environmental audit?
    a. Phase I
    b. Phase II
    c. Phase III
    d. Phase IV

12. CERCLA established the
    a. EPA.
    b. Landfill Act.
    c. Superfund.
    d. OSHA.

13. Which precaution is aimed at preventing termites?
    a. Keep landscaping at least five feet from the foundation
    b. Use flexible plastic water pipes to avoid leaks
    c. Paint all wood with latex paint
    d. Keep untreated wood from touching soil

14. Mold grows in environments that are

a. moist.
b. dry.
c. bright.
d. hot.

15. In order for a property owner to qualify for *innocent landowner immunity*, the owner must *NOT* have had either actual or constructive knowledge of the damage and, at the time of purchasing the property, must have

a. requested an environmental survey from the mortgage lender.
b. obtained a Phase I assessment of the property.
c. shown due care to determine that the property was not damaged.
d. owned the property for one year or less.

19

Independent Contractor/Employee

■ KEY TERMS

employee

errors and omissions
insurance

independent contractors
Social Security taxes

■ SALESPERSON EMPLOYMENT STATUS

All licensed salespersons and associate brokers are required by law to work under the supervision of a sponsoring broker in their real estate activities. In doing so, the salesperson may either be hired as an employee or associated with a broker as an independent contractor.

The distinction between an *employee* and an *independent contractor* is an important one, with significant tax consequences as well as important effects on the ability of brokers to control the activities of their salespeople. Regardless of what status one falls under according to the tax laws, part 175.21 of the Real Property Law requires that sponsoring brokers supervise their licensees at all times.

Employee Status

The employer-employee relationship allows a broker to exercise certain controls over salespeople. The broker can require that an **employee** adhere to regulations affecting working hours, mandatory sales meetings, office routine, and dress standards.

As an employer, a broker is required by the federal government to withhold **Social Security tax** and income tax from the compensation paid to employees. The tax laws require every taxpayer to pay annually 15.3 percent Social Security tax. Under this relationship 7.65 percent withholding tax is withheld from the employee's paycheck. The employer is then required to match that amount on behalf of the employee. An employee is covered by unemployment insurance and workers' compensation. A broker may provide employees with fringe benefits such as health insurance, pension plans, sick leave, and paid vacations. Such benefits are variously estimated to add 25 percent to 50 percent to the cost of an employee's base salary. A broker who chooses to regard salespersons as employees must take such costs into consideration when working out commission schedules and salaries. Because the broker provides all office services and benefits, employees are only entitled to certain tax deductions, none of which are related to their employment. They are not eligible for the self-employment deductions that are available to independent contractors.

Common Law Employee, Case Law, and New York State

The subject of whether a licensee is categorized as an independent contractor or as an employee is a direct derivative of Internal Revenue Service (IRS) determinations. New York law follows IRS guidelines for classification of a worker for federal tax purposes. As such, federal laws dictate four categories of worker classifications:

1. **Common law employee.** Under tax laws, a common law employee is a category of worker that for federal tax purposes is defined as any person that by that persons' associated profession is deemed to have employee status.
2. **Statutory nonemployee.** Under tax laws, this worker is deemed to be an independent contractor and not an employee.
3. **Statutory employee.** Under tax laws, this worker is classified as an employee.
4. **Independent contractor.** Under tax laws, this worker is not classified as an employee because of the lack of control over the individual by the employing party. The use of the term *employing party* should not be confused or interpreted as an employer/employee relationship.

Independent Contractor Status

IRS Tax Code, Section 3508 (a and b), covers the specifics of independent contractor status. Most salespersons act as **independent contractors.** A survey by the National Association of REALTORS® found that nine out of ten real estate firms treated their sales associates as independent contractors. Brokers traditionally have maintained this relationship to avoid the bookkeeping problems of withholding taxes, Social Security payments, unemployment insurance, and other such items that become complex when based not on a regular salary but on unpredictable commissions.

Of course, it is up to the broker and the salesperson to choose what the relationship will be. If the parties choose the independent contractor relationship, under the tax laws, it is imperative that three basic tests of employment exist.

Tests of Employment

The broker who chooses independent contractor status for associates should keep on file agreements signed by the associates, with wording that has been reviewed by the broker's attorney. *Safe-harbor guidelines* provide that the IRS will not challenge independent contractor status where the associate

- is licensed as a real estate broker or salesperson;
- has income based solely on sales output that is not tied in any way to hourly wages; and
- performs services pursuant to an executed written contract (see Figure 19.1 requirement No. 2) specifying
  — independent contractor 3 status and
  — that the licensee will be responsible for payment of the licensee's own income taxes.

Failure to meet these basic tests of employment renders (by default) the working relationship as that of an employer and employee.

In 1986, New York State adopted similar guidelines on independent contractor status for real estate licensees, whose situation had been unclear with regard to state programs such as unemployment insurance and workers' compensation insurance. The New York Department of Labor, in evaluating associates' status with regard to unemployment insurance, also stresses the importance of a current, written contract between broker and salesperson. A sample contract that meets the Department of Labor requirements suggested by the New York State Association of REALTORS® is shown in Figure 19.1.

The requirements for independent contractor status under New York State law are as follows:

- Substantially all the licensee's compensation (whether or not paid in cash) for services performed on behalf of the broker must be directly related to sales or other output, rather than to the number of hours worked.
- There must be a written contract for services between the broker and the licensee, *executed within the past 15 months*, that indicates that the licensee is engaged as an independent contractor.
- The written contract between the broker and licensee must not have been executed under duress (i.e., the broker may not force the licensee to sign the agreement, although the broker may choose not to maintain the licensee's license if the licensee refuses to sign).
- The written contract must contain the following provisions:
  — The licensee will be treated for all purposes by the broker as an independent contractor.
  — The licensee will be paid a commission directly related to gross sales or other output without deduction for taxes.
  — The licensee will not receive any compensation related to the number of hours worked.
  — The licensee will not be treated as an employee for federal or state tax purposes.
  — The licensee may work any hours the licensee chooses.
  — The licensee may work out of the licensee's home as well as out of the broker's office.
  — The licensee is free to engage in outside employment.

FIGURE 19.1

Sample Independent Contractor Agreement

INDEPENDENT CONTRACTOR RELATIONSHIP AGREEMENT

AGREEMENT, this day of ___, by and between _____ residing at _____ (hereinafter referred to as the "Sales Associate") and _____ having a principal place of business at _____ (hereinafter referred to as the "Broker").

WITNESSETH:

WHEREAS, Sales Associate and Broker are each respectively duly licensed pursuant to Article 12-A of the Real Property Law of the State of New York, and WHEREAS, the parties hereto have freely and voluntarily entered into this Agreement, without duress.

NOW, THEREFORE, in consideration of the mutual promises herein contained, it is hereby agreed as follows:

Sales Associate is engaged as an independent contractor associated with the Broker pursuant to Article 12-A of the Real Property Law and shall be treated as such for all purposes, including but not limited to Federal and State Income taxation, withholding tax regulations, Unemployment Insurance, and Workers' Compensation coverages.

Sales Associate (a) shall be paid a commission on Sales Associate's gross sales, if any, without deduction for taxes, which commission shall be directly related to sales or other output; (b) shall not be entitled to draw against commissions; (c) shall not receive any remuneration related to the number of hours worked; and (d) shall not be treated as an employee with respect to such services for Federal and State Income tax purposes.

Sales Associate shall be permitted to work such hours as Sales Associates may elect to work.

Sales Associate shall be permitted to work out of Sales Associate's residence or the offices of Broker or any other location in the sole discretion of Sales Associate.

Sales Associate shall be free to engage in outside employment.

Broker may provide office facilities and supplies for the use of Sales Associate. All other expenses, including but not limited to automobile, travel, and entertainment expenses, shall be borne by Sales Associate.

Broker may offer initial training and hold periodic sales meetings. The attendance by Sales Associate shall be at the option of Sales Associate.

Broker may offer a group insurance plan and if Sales Associate wishes to participate therein, all premiums shall be paid by Sales Associate.

Broker may elect, but shall be under no obligation, to assign leads to Sales Associates on a rotating basis. Sales Associate shall be responsible for procuring Sales Associate's own leads.

Broker and Sales Associate shall comply with the requirements of Article 12-A of the Real Property Law and the regulations pertaining thereto. Such compliance shall not affect Sales Associate's status as an independent contractor nor shall compliance be construed as an indication that Sales Associate is an employee of Broker for any purpose whatsoever.

This contract and the association created thereby may be terminated by either party hereto at any time upon notice give by one party to the other.

For purposes of this Agreement, the term "Broker" shall include individual real estate brokers, real estate brokerage companies, real estate brokerage corporations, and any other entity acting as a principal broker. The term "Sales Associate" shall include real estate sales associates and real estate brokers, who, as real estate licensees, associate with and place their real estate license with a principal broker.

Sales Associate hereby agrees to and hereby assigns to Broker irrevocably and without the necessity of any additional consideration, all of Sales Associate's right, title, and interest in any copyright rights or other intellectual property rights in any property listing posted by Sales Associate in the MLS system or otherwise provided to the MLS. Such right, title, and interest shall be deemed assigned as of the moment of creation without any further action of the part of either party, During and after the term of this Agreement, Sales Associate shall confirm such assignment by executing and delivering such assignments or other instruments and take any action necessary to enable Broker to secure, protect, enforce, and defend its copyrights in such data and/or content.

This Agreement shall be governed and construed in accordance with the laws of the State of New York.

No waiver of any of the provisions of this Agreement or any of the rights or remedies of the parties hereto shall be valid unless such waiver is in writing, signed by the party to be charged therewith.

Whenever in this Agreement any notices are required to be given, such notices shall be in writing and shall be sent by registered mail or certified mail, return receipt requested, to the party entitled to receive the same.

This Agreement and all of it's terms, covenants, and provisions insofar as applicable, shall be binding upon and inure to the benefit of the parties hereto, their respective heirs, executors, administrators, successors, and assigns.

IN WITNESS WHEREOF, the individual parties hereto have hereunder set their hands and seals, and any corporate party has caused this instrument to be signed by a corporate officer and caused its corporate seal to be hereunto affixed, all as of the day and the year first above written.

_____

Sales Associate

(SEAL) _____

Broker

— The broker may provide office facilities and supplies for use by the licensee, but the licensee will otherwise bear the licensee's own expenses, including automobile, travel, and entertainment expenses.

— The licensee and broker will act in accordance with the terms of the Real Property Law and Department of State real estate regulations.

— Either the licensee or the broker may terminate the agreement at any time on notice to the other.

The existence of a written agreement is clearly an important aspect of maintaining an independent contractor relationship between the broker and the salesperson. However, the written agreement will not prevent employee status from being implied as a result of the conduct of the broker and salesperson. For example, if the broker requires that the salesperson attend staff meetings or includes the salesperson in a company pension plan, this may be seen as evidence that the relationship between them is actually that of employer and employee. The consequences of such a determination can be drastic for both the broker and the salesperson. It is important to note that in the event the broker engages employees as well as independent contractors, and where organization manuals of conduct exist, the broker should maintain a manual that relates *only* to employees and a separate manual that relates *only* to independent contractors.

Remember, the broker may not appear to the taxing authorities to be exercising any sort of control over the activities of an independent contractor. The word *independent* speaks for itself. Regardless, license law does not excuse brokers from the responsibility of supervision (part 175.21) over their sales staff at *all* times.

The contract between the broker and the salesperson or associate broker should be renewed each year. The contract should include provisions for the termination of association.

For the broker, the determination that a salesperson is actually an employee will result in liability for state and federal unemployment insurance premiums; workers' compensation and disability insurance coverages; and federal and state withholding taxes, including the employer's share of Social Security taxes. For the salesperson, the result will be the inability to claim self-employment expense deductions on IRS Form 1040 Schedule C, as well as the fact that the salesperson's commission payments will be subjected to withholding for all applicable state and federal taxes.

The dilemma for brokers who want to maintain independent contractor status for their associates is that this limits the ability of the brokers to control the activity of their salespeople. Too much control often leads to the conclusion that the salesperson is an employee. On the other hand, brokers are legally liable for the actions of their salespeople and have an obligation under the Real Property Law and Department of State regulations to supervise their salespeople's activities. New York State law regarding independent contractor status for real estate licensees recognizes part of this dilemma and specifically states that compliance with the Real Property Law and Department of State real estate regulations will not be construed as an indication of employee status. (See Figure 19.2.)

F I G U R E 19.2

Unemployment Insurance Notice for Real Estate Salesperson

NEW YORK STATE,
DEPARTMENT OF LABOR,
UNEMPLOYMENT INSURANCE DIVISION
NOTICE TO EMPLOYERS

Persons Engaged in Real Estate Sales

Effective October 1, 1986, services performed by a licensed real estate broker or sales associate are excluded from coverage if it can be proven that all of the following conditions are met:

(A) substantially all of the remuneration (whether or not paid in cash) for the services performed by such broker or sales associate is directly related to sales or other output (including the performance of services) rather than to the number of hours worked;

and

(B) the services performed by the broker or sales associate are performed pursuant to a written contract executed between such broker or sales associate and the person for whom the services are performed within the past twelve to fifteen months;

and

(C) such contract was not executed under duress and contains the following provisions:

1. that the broker or sales associate is engaged as an independent contractor associated with the person for whom services are performed pursuant to Article 12-A of the Real Property Law and shall be treated as such for all purposes;

2. that they (a) shall be paid a commission directly related to their gross sales or other output without deduction for taxes; (b) shall not receive any remuneration related to the number of hours worked; and (c) shall not be treated as employees with respect to such services for federal and state tax purposes;

3. that they shall be permitted to work any hours they choose;

4. that they shall be permitted to work out of their own homes or the office of the person for whom services are performed;

5. that they shall be free to engage in outside employment;

6. that the person for whom the services are performed may provide office facilities and supplies for the use of the broker or sales associate, but that they shall otherwise bear their own expenses, including but not limited to automobile, travel, and entertainment expenses;

7. that the person for whom the services are performed and the broker or sales associate shall comply with the requirements of Article 12-A of the Real Property Law and the regulations pertaining thereto, but such compliance shall not affect their status as independent contractors nor should it be construed as an indication that they are employees of such person for any purpose whatsoever;

8. that the contract and the association may be terminated by either party at any time upon notice to the other.

Errors and omissions insurance A broker may carry **errors and omissions insurance** on all salespeople, regardless of their status as employees or independent contractors. The cost may be borne by the broker or by the salesperson. In these increasingly litigious times, it has become common for more companies to turn to errors and omissions insurance. It is not uncommon for a broker to require his or her licensees to contribute their proportionate shares of the broker's annual premium for this insurance coverage. Errors and omissions insurance will normally not cover the following acts:

- Fraud
- Antitrust
- Fair housing violations

Broker Employee/Independent Contractor Income-Reporting Requirements

Regardless of what status a licensee takes on through employment, the employing broker bears income-reporting responsibilities.

With regard to employees, the broker's responsibilities consist of

- for reporting purposes, obtaining an accurate Social Security number from the employee;
- requiring the employee to fill out a W-4 form (completion of this form will determine the level of federal withholding taxes assessed from each pay period; unless amended, this form remains the basis of federal withholding taxes); and
- at year's end, preparing the W-2 and W-3 forms and distributing them to the employee for tax preparation purposes and to the Social Security Administration for the reporting of income and tax individually withheld.

With regard to independent contractors, the broker's responsibilities consist of

- for reporting purposes, obtaining an accurate Social Security number from the independent contractor;
- requiring the independent contractor to fill out a W-9 form; and
- at year's end, preparing the 1096 and 1099 forms and distributing the 1099 to the independent contractor for tax preparation purposes and both the 1096 and 1099 forms to the IRS for the reporting of income.

■ SUMMARY

Whether a salesperson is employed as an employee or an independent contractor has serious implications for both the salesperson and the broker. Employees are subject to tax withholding and may not file Schedule C to deduct business expenses for federal income tax purposes. Brokers must withhold income and Social Security taxes from employees but not from independent contractors. Employees are covered by programs such as unemployment insurance and workers' compensation, and the employer is responsible for the premiums and taxes associated with these programs.

The classification of a licensee as an employee or an independent contractor depends on the conduct of the licensee and the broker. A written agreement is important under federal and state law to show independent contractor status, but other factors are of equal or greater significance. The compensation of an independent contractor must be related to performance and not to hours worked, and the broker is limited in the degree of control that may be exerted over an independent contractor's behavior. Participation in benefits such as pension plans or sick pay may indicate that the licensee is an employee.

CHAPTER 19 QUIZ

1. Unlike salespersons who are employees, independent contractors
   a. collect workers' compensation.
   b. qualify for paid vacations.
   c. take self-employment income tax deductions.
   d. file for unemployment compensation.

2. A broker may require a salesperson who is an independent contractor to
   a. work established hours.
   b. comply with Article 12-A of Real Property Law.
   c. accept a regular salary.
   d. have an oral contract.

3. A salesperson who is an independent contractor is entitled to
   a. unemployment insurance.
   b. workers' compensation.
   c. federal and state withholding.
   d. supervision and guidance.

4. A broker was excited to hear that a super salesperson is moving to town. In attempting to recruit the new salesperson to work for him as an independent contractor, what can the broker legally say?
   a. "If you give me April, May, and June, I will pay you for a July vacation."
   b. "If you cover the office on Saturdays and Sundays, I'll give you Monday to Wednesday off."
   c. "My salespeople have earned above market for six months."
   d. "I can promise you $3,000 a week for the first 12 weeks."

5. An independent contractor is generally
   a. paid a regular salary, with commissions as a bonus.
   b. reimbursed for all business expenses.
   c. paid commissions on sales.
   d. given two weeks of paid vacation each year.

6. How often should the contract between the broker and the independent contractor salesperson be renewed?
   a. Every quarter
   b. Every six months
   c. Every 15 months
   d. Only when the agreement changes

7. An employee is legally required to receive
   a. an employer-sponsored retirement plan.
   b. unemployment insurance.
   c. health insurance.
   d. commissions on sales.

8. Whether a licensee is an independent contractor or an employee, the broker must
   a. pay the individual for hours spent in the office.
   b. pay for the individual's automobile expenses.
   c. require the individual to fill out a W-4 form.
   d. obtain the individual's Social Security number.

9. Salespeople who join a real estate company as independent contractors will probably have to pay for their own
   a. office space.
   b. errors and omissions insurance.
   c. contract forms and For Sale signs.
   d. hospitalization insurance.

10. The broker whose associates are independent contractors may still insist that they
    a. keep regular office hours.
    b. sign a written contract for services.
    c. attend sales meetings.
    d. be paid by the hour.

CHAPTER 20

Income Tax Issues in Real Estate Transactions

■ KEY TERMS

active income
adjusted basis
appreciation
boot
capital gains
cost recovery

depreciation/depreciable
basis
installment sale
like-kind exchange
long-term gains
passive income

portfolio income
primary residence
qualified intermediary
short-term gains
taxable income

■ TAXPAYER RELIEF ACT OF 1997

The Taxpayer Relief Act of 1997 had a significant impact on the financial realities of real property ownership. The act provided taxpayers with substantial tax savings and modified how gains on real property would be taxed.

Prior to passage of the act, a gain on the sale of a **primary** or *principal* **residence** was taxed at a rate of 28 percent. The new act lowered the rate on capital gains to 20 percent; this rate was further reduced to the current rate of 15 percent on long-term gains.

A *primary or principal residence* is defined as the location where a taxpayer has resided for at least two out of the previous five years prior to the sale of the property; in addition, the residence must be used as the primary place of residence (when the taxpayer files his or her income tax return). To qualify, the two-year period can consist of either 730 days of ownership or 24 months of ownership.

If taxpayers have previously sold their property and have otherwise taken the tax exclusion called for under the act, they do not qualify for the exclusion unless the current sale is at least two years after the time the taxpayers benefited from the previous exclusion.

Recognizing that certain unforeseen circumstances do arise in life, the IRS has provided exceptions to this two-year ruling. The following are some of the categories of exceptions: sales resulting from health-related issues; sales resulting from changes in employment that require the taxpayer to relocate; sales resulting from eminent domain/condemnation proceedings, divorce, legal separation, or death; and residence damaged through natural disasters, terrorism, or acts of war.

In the late 1990s, the act motivated owners to sell their properties because they could expect to pay less in taxes and keep more of the profit from the sales. This sparked the beginning of a bull market in residential sales nationwide. Housing values throughout the country began to rise. Some markets like New York City experienced geometric price growth. States such as Florida experienced population growth that led to increased development and property values. Resale markets appeared in areas such as Miami and Boca Raton; previously, due to the abundance of available land in those areas, resale markets were almost nonexistent. The cost of new construction kept resale values at below what purchasers had paid at the time of their acquisition. As available land diminished, property values increased and resale markets gained greater visibility.

■ USING IRA FUNDS TOWARD DOWN PAYMENTS

In any given tax year, taxpayers who deposit qualified amounts in individual retirement accounts (IRAs) may deduct these amounts from their **taxable income** (income subject to taxation). This results in a tax savings to the individual taxpayer.

Deposits and earnings on deposits in an IRA account are tax-deferred funds that may be withdrawn at age 59½ without penalty (although withdrawn funds are subject to income taxes at the ordinary tax rate of the individual taxpayer).

Early withdrawals (prior to age 59½) are penalized by an additional 10 percent over and above the taxpayer's ordinary tax rate.

First-time home purchasers may withdraw up to $10,000 toward a down payment without experiencing the additional 10 percent early withdrawal penalty.

■ DEDUCTIONS ON A PRIMARY/PRINCIPAL RESIDENCE

Two categories of tax deductions are available to homeowners. These deductions are available for property owners who use their property as a principal residence. These deductions consist of real property taxes and mortgage interest.

Property Taxes

The amount of real property taxes paid on a home in any given tax year are deductible from a property owner's overall tax bill in the year that the property tax is paid. This includes any special assessments over and above the local ad valorem property tax.

For example, a property owner pays a property tax of $10,000. In addition to the tax, the property is located in an area designated a *business improvement district* (BID). That district benefits from extra neighborhood services such as added security, trash removal, and street cleaning.

The amount assessed to the property owners who benefit from the BID program is over and above the normal property tax paid by other property owners who do not benefit from the BID program. This additional assessment becomes an added tax deduction for that property owner.

Mortgage Interest

Mortgage interest paid by any property owner in any given tax year is deductible up to certain limits. They may deduct the interest in the following instances (under specific conditions): home acquisition financing, refinanced loans, and home equity loans.

On home acquisition financing used to purchase, improve, or build, property owners may deduct interest on up to $1,000,000 in debt if the homeowners file income taxes as married filing jointly; or they may deduct interest on up to $500,000 in debt if filing as married filing separate.

> **Mortgage interest is deductible in**
> - home acquisition financing,
> - refinanced loans, and
> - home equity loans (under specific conditions).

Property owners may deduct mortgage interest on *refinanced loans* when replacing the previous loan with a new loan for an amount equal to or less than the previous loan.

Mortgage interest may be deducted on *home equity loans* when property owners borrow funds against the equity in their property. However, borrower may only deduct interest on up to $100,000 of home equity debt. When refinanced loans include borrowed funds that are over and above the original loan amount, that portion over and above the previous loan amount is deemed equity and bears the same limitations as above.

Mortgage interest also can include any origination fees that were paid when obtaining the mortgage. These fees are commonly called discount points.

Mortgage interest also includes any up-front charges a borrower is required to pay, and they are deductible in the year they are paid. However, that does not apply to refinanced loans. The borrower would be required by the IRS to recover those amounts over the life of the loan. The recovery of these amounts is commonly referred to as *amortizing* the costs over the remaining life of the loan.

■ POINTS AND CLOSING COSTS

Points

When making loans, lenders often receive origination fees in the form of points or discount points. Points represent prepaid interest to the lender. One point is equal to 1 percent of the borrowed amount.

Points are deductible in the year that they are paid under certain circumstances: if the loan is secured by real property that acts as a residence; if the settlement statement indicates that the amount paid is categorized as either loan discount points or loan origination fee; if the points are paid at closing to a lender of money; and when payment of origination fees/points is a common practice in a particular area. *This applies to acquisition financing and not to refinanced loans.*

Closing Costs

Real property transactions usually require a team of professionals who assist in concluding a transaction. As a result, additional costs in closing a real property transaction arise. Some of the parties that may be used at any point in a transaction include brokers, attorneys, appraisers, surveyors, and title companies.

There are fees associated with the services provided by each of the participating parties that assist a buyer in concluding a real property transaction. These costs are called closing costs. When added to the purchase price, these costs represent the purchaser's total acquisition costs.

On owner-occupant property, these expenses are *not* deductible in the year of acquisition. On income-producing property, these costs are included and are recovered or depreciated as part of the **depreciable basis. Cost recovery** is another term for depreciation; depreciable basis is the beginning dollar amount (representing the improvement's value) that constitutes the annual depreciation deduction allowed under the Taxpayer Relief Act.

While owners of income-producing properties are permitted to depreciate the improvement portion of the property, owners of primary/principal residences and vacation homes are not permitted to apply depreciation deductions.

■ SECOND HOMES

Anyone owning a second home may deduct property taxes and interest up to certain limits. (This includes vacation homes that are second homes.)

Owners of vacation homes may lease their property in any given tax year for a period of less than 15 days without income reporting requirements; however, when an owner of a vacation home leases the property for a period greater than 14 days, the vacation home is viewed as income-producing property and taxed accordingly.

In the event that homeowners and their family use the home for a period greater than 14 days, or the equivalent of 10 percent of the period that the property was leased, the home is then treated as a residence and not as an income-producing property.

■ CAPITAL GAINS

Under the federal taxation system, **capital gains** (or losses as the case may be) fall into two categories: **short-term gains**, which are defined as any gains that result from a sale where the property was held for one year or less, and **long-term gains**, which are defined as any gains that result from a sale where the property was held for one year or more. Capital gains usually occur as a direct result of **appreciation**. Appreciation is an increase in the worth or value of a property due to economic or related causes, which may prove to be either temporary or permanent; it is the opposite of depreciation.

Under the act, short-term gains are normally taxed at ordinary income rates. Long-term gains are taxed at a maximum rate of 15 percent; however, when a taxpayer falls into a 15 percent tax bracket, long-term gains are only taxed at a rate of 5 percent.

On income-producing property, capital gains are calculated using the property's adjusted basis. The **adjusted basis** is the financial interest that the Internal Revenue Service attributes to an owner of an investment property for the purpose of determining annual depreciation and gain or loss on the sale of the asset. If a property was acquired by purchase, the owner's basis is the cost of the property plus the value of any capital expenditures for improvements to the property, minus any depreciation allowable or actually taken. This new basis is called the adjusted basis. In addition, any depreciation taken in previous tax years must be recaptured at the time of sale. The recapture tax rate on previously taken depreciation is 25 percent. An owner of a primary/principal residence may not benefit from depreciation deduction allowances.

■ SALE OF A PRIMARY/PRINCIPAL RESIDENCE

At the beginning of this chapter, we briefly highlighted the tax savings resulting from the Taxpayer Relief Act. Now let's see how the tax savings apply to the sale of your primary home.

Under the act, when a primary/principal residence is sold, a taxpayer filing a tax return as a single filer may exclude up to $250,000 from the total gain realized at sale. A taxpayer filing a tax return as married filing jointly may exclude up to $500,000 from the total gain realized at sale of a principal/primary residence. This is commonly called the $250,000/$500,000 rule.

To qualify as a primary/principal residence, the property must be the location where a taxpayer has resided for at least two out of the previous five years prior to the sale of the property; and the two-year period must consist of either 730 days of ownership or 24 months of ownership.

In December 2007, the Mortgage Forgiveness Debt Relief Act of 2007 took effect. This important amendment to the tax laws governing capital gains tax treatment concerns *surviving spouses* in the sale of a primary residence. The amendment reads as follows:

> *Section 7 – Application of Joint Return Limitation for Capital Gains Exclusion to Certain Post-Marriage Sales of Principal Residences by Surviving Spouses.*
>
> *a)*
>
> *Sale within 2 years of spouse's death – Section 121 (b) of the Internal Revenue Code of 1986 (relating to limitations) is amended by adding at the end the following new paragraph:*
>
> > *(4) Special Rule for Certain Sales by Surviving Spouses – In the case of a sale or exchange of property by an unmarried individual whose spouse is deceased on the date of such sale, paragraph (1) shall be applied by substituting $500,000 for $250,000 if such sale occurs not later than 2 years after the date of death of such spouse and the requirements of paragraph (2) (A) were met immediately before such date of death.*

The effective date applies to sales or exchanges after December 31, 2007.

■ THE SALE OF INVESTMENT PROPERTY

The Taxpayer Relief Act classifies income in three separate categories: *active income*, *passive income*, and *portfolio income*.

The Three Categories of Income
■ Active
■ Passive
■ Portfolio

Active income is any income attributable to a direct activity of employment. This includes income derived from salaries, commissions, consulting fees, gratuities, or any other form of employment income.

Passive income is any income attributable to passive activities whereby the individual taxpayer is not directly involved in the day-to-day activities of the income-producing vehicle. This includes income derived from income-producing real estate and stocks and bonds. All rental income from investments falls under this category as well.

The act provides that the taxpayer, unless treated as an *active participant*, may only deduct passive losses of up to $3,000 against active taxable income. An investor who is an active participant may deduct up to $25,000 from active taxable income; however, in order to receive the $25,000 deduction, the participant must not have an adjusted gross income of greater than $100,000.

Portfolio income can be defined as any income derived from items such as dividends received through ownership stock, interest received from any source, and royalties received on intellectual property.

■ CALCULATING TAXABLE INCOME

When calculating the income taxes attributable to income-producing activities, the following formula is used:

$$
\begin{array}{rl}
& \text{Net operating income} \\
+ & \text{Reserves for replacements} \\
- & \text{Mortgage interest} \\
- & \text{Annual depreciation} \\
- & \text{Carryover/suspended losses (if any)} \\
= & \text{Taxable income}
\end{array}
$$

For example, assume that a property's net operating income amounts to $177,550. The reserve for replacements is $10,000. The mortgage interest paid in that year is $50,000. The annual depreciation allowance is $10,000. The investor is passive and has a carryover/suspended loss of $5,000 (carried forward). The calculation of the investor's taxable income would look like this:

$$
\begin{array}{rl}
& \$177,550 \text{ (NOI)} \\
+ & \$\,10,000 \text{ (Reserves for replacements)} \\
- & \$50,000 \text{ (Mortgage interest)} \\
- & \$\,10,000 \text{ (Annual depreciation)} \\
- & \$\,3,000 \text{ (Allowed passive carryover/suspended loss)} \\
= & \$124,550 \text{ (Taxable income)}
\end{array}
$$

■ CALCULATING THE GAIN OR LOSS

Income Taxes on Sale of Property

When a property is sold, any profits realized are called gains, or capital gains. Under the Taxpayer Relief Act, capital gains are subject to taxation. To calculate the gain or loss for an owner-occupant residential property, one must take into account the purchase price paid at acquisition, inclusive of closing expenses (basis), the cost of any capital improvements made to the property during the holding period (which forms the adjusted basis), and the sales price (minus costs of sale).

The gain or loss is the difference between *the purchase price plus capital improvements* and *the sales price* (minus costs of sale). These capital improvements could include kitchen and bathroom renovations, the addition of a swimming pool, or a new deck, for example. The costs of sale deducted from the sales price might include any closing costs or points paid by the seller, attorney's fees, real estate commissions, and survey costs.

FIGURE 20.1

Taxable income × Marginal rate = Income tax

Formula for Calculating Income Taxes on Investment Property

When calculating the gain or loss realized from the sale of owner-occupant residential property, you would use the following formula:

Realized amount from sale – Adjusted basis = Capital gain

In the case of owner-occupant residential property, only the costs that consist of prepaid interest are deductible in the year of purchase. All other costs of closing are not deductible within the year of sale and are added to the purchase price.

When calculating the gain or loss for a property held for business or investment purposes, a different formula is used to calculate realized gain or loss. (See Figure 20.2.) The difference is the deduction of depreciation on investment property. The depreciation taken in previous years affects the depreciable basis of the property. Each year, the depreciable basis is reduced by the amount of that year's depreciation allowance.

For example, a property owner is eligible for an annual depreciation deduction in the amount of $10,000 per year. The owner has held the property for ten years and, as a result, has realized $100,000 of total depreciation deductions on the property. If the original depreciable basis consisted of $400,000 at the time of sale, the book value (value for tax purposes) of that property would then be $300,000.

■ DEPRECIATION

We have previously examined various deductions that are available to owners of real property. Now let's examine an important deduction that is available only to owners of income-producing properties.

Depreciation, or *cost recovery*, is defined as a decrease or loss in the value of real property attributable to any of three events: physical deterioration, functional obsolescence, and external obsolescence.

Physical deterioration   *Physical deterioration* can be defined as a loss in value of the improvement resulting from use, lack of maintenance, or element exposure.

It is a loss that occurs gradually over time. It is not an event that is due to a sudden destruction of the improvement. A roof that leaks as a result of its age, a damaged compressor in an air-conditioning unit, and the cracking exterior building masonry are all examples of physical deterioration.

Physical deterioration is usually a *curable* (rather than a noncurable) event. A *curable event* is defined as one for which the cost of remediation results in equal or greater property value through its utility and addition to the property.

FIGURE   20.2

Formula for Calculating Gains or Losses on Investment Property

Purchase price
+ Closing costs
+ Capital improvements made during holding period
– Accrued depreciation
= **Adjusted basis**

Noncurable physical deterioration exists when the cost of remediation is greater than the added value of the correction, particularly as it relates to its utility and addition to the property.

Functional obsolescence The existence of key inadequacies and obsolete features is termed *functional obsolescence*. Examples include outdated interior design features, insufficient bathrooms in relation to the size of the home, column spacing versus an absence of columns, outdated lighting fixtures, and inadequate design and layout.

As is the case with physical deterioration, these inadequacies or obsolete features may be curable or noncurable. A property that has been overimproved or suffers from too many columned spaces is considered to be suffering from noncurable functional obsolescence.

External obsolescence *External obsolescence* can be defined as a loss of value attributable to external forces outside of the property line and, therefore, outside the control of the property owner.

Because the loss is a result of forces outside of the owner's property line and control, this form of obsolescence is always viewed as a noncurable event. Examples include adverse changes in zoning, condemnation for new roadways, and neighborhood deterioration.

Depreciation is a term that applies in what we'll call the tax world rather than the cash world. The tax world establishes the tax consequences resulting from a property's income operations, which means it establishes a property's book value. The cash world is where properties are bought and sold and a property's market value is determined. (See Table 20.1.)

As a result of age and wear and tear, a property's improvement loses its value. This loss does not reflect the actual value of the property as it relates to the cash world; however, it does establish the value of the property for tax purposes. This becomes even more important at the time of sale.

There are three primary events in investment property ownership: (1) acquisition (when the property is purchased), (2) holding period (when the property is held in ownership), and (3) reversion (the point at which the investor sells the property and reverts back to their original investment—cash).

Depreciation is a deduction available to the property owner during the holding period. However, upon reversion (sale), it must be recaptured; that is, taxes must be paid on it. Currently under the Taxpayer Relief Act, recaptured depreciation taken during the holding period is taxed at 25 percent.

Think of it as a save-now/pay-later plan. Tax savings are realized during the holding period tax savings (save now), but tax must be paid on the recaptured depreciation at reversion (pay later).

	Cash World		**Tax World**
TABLE 20.1	Potential gross income		Net operating income
	− Vacancy and collection loss	+	Reserves for replacements
Cash World and Tax	+ Other property income	=	**Adjusted net operating income**
World at a Glance	= **Effective gross income**	−	Mortgage interest
	− Operating expenses	−	Annual depreciation
	= **Net operating income**	−	Carryover/Suspended loss
	− Annual debt service	=	**Taxable income**
	= **Before-tax cash flow**	×	Marginal rate
	− Income tax	=	**Income tax**
	= After-tax cash flow		

Straight-Line Depreciation Method

Depreciation is a form of cost recovery. The terms have the same meaning and can be interchanged in dialogue. Under the Taxpayer Relief Act, there are prescribed rules as to how you can apply depreciation toward the taxation process.

Recovery periods   Before the Taxpayer Relief Act, depreciation schedules were to a great extent at the option of the property owner (depreciation is taken over a schedule of cost recovery). The property owner was able to use accelerated cost recovery periods.

Currently, the act provides for only two straight-line cost recovery periods. The two cost recovery periods (as they apply to the property type) are 27½ years and 39 years.

The 27½-year cost recovery period applies to all residential income-producing property for which 80 percent of the income attributable to the property is derived from the improvement.

The 39-year cost recovery period applies for commercial investment property, which includes but is not limited to office buildings, shopping centers, industrial parks, and professional buildings such as medical office complexes.

Let's look at an example of how this works. In order to do that, we first need to learn how to calculate the depreciable basis.

Calculating the Depreciable Basis

Depreciable basis can be defined as the total acquisition cost of an interest in real property minus the value of the land. (Remember, land is never depreciable.)

It should be noted that acquisition costs include and are not limited to legal fees, broker commissions, appraisals, surveys, and title insurance.

When these amounts are totaled over and above the purchase price, the resulting figure represents the property's depreciable basis. It is the dollar amount used to

FIGURE   20.3

Calculating the Depreciable Basis

Herman buys a residential income-producing property. At closing, he pays the following acquisition costs:

Property purchase price	$325,750
Legal fees	+ 1,000
Broker commission	+ 10,000
Appraisal	+ 2,000
Survey	+ 2,000
Title insurance	+ 3,000
Adjusted total acquisition cost	= $343,750
Improvement ratio	× 0.80
Depreciable basis	= $275,000

calculate the annual deduction allowance. (An example of how depreciable basis is calculated is shown in Figure 20.3.)

Now we can use the depreciable basis of $275,000 to calculate the annual depreciation attributable to this property. As we have previously learned, residential income-producing property would use the cost recovery schedule of 27½ years.

See Figure 20.4 for the calculation of depreciation on Herman's residential income-producing property.

■ LIKE-KIND EXCHANGES (IRS SECTION 1031 EXCHANGES)

Unlike the tax treatment for primary/principal residence property, the sale of investment property does not allow the owner-seller the $250,000/$500,000 tax exclusion from capital gains. Therefore, income-producing investments fall under the section of the IRS code titled 1031. This section of the tax law applies to *tax-deferred* exchanges of like-kind property. The term *tax-deferred* refers to the freedom from present-day taxation resulting from a gain (or loss), such that the taxes associated with that gain (or loss) are postponed to a future time and subsequent event. A tax-deferred or **like-kind exchange** (also referred to as a 1031 exchange) is an exchange of property for property as opposed to property for money. Relinquished property is held for investment in any commercial activity, such as a trade or business, and is exchanged for a replacement property that is used in the same manner.

Terms commonly used to refer to *relinquished* property include *sale*, *downleg*, *exchange*, and *phase I property*. Terms commonly used for *replacement* property include *purchase*, *upleg*, *target*, and *phase II property*.

In these transactions, taxable gains can be deferred when a property is exchanged for other like-kind property. The following types of property can qualify for an exchange: commercial property, industrial property, income-producing residential

FIGURE   20.4

Calculating the Annual Depreciation Allowance

Depreciable basis ÷ Recovery period (in years) = Depreciation allowance

Depreciable basis	$275,000
Recovery period in years	÷ 27.5
Depreciation allowance	**$10,000 per year**

property, any vacant property held for investment purposes (dealers excluded), hotels, motels, and leaseholds that bear lease terms greater than 30 years.

The following parties would *not* qualify for a 1031 exchange: dealers, owners of personal residences, related parties, and properties located outside of the United States. Also, if either party to an exchange were to sell the exchanged property less than two years after the time of the exchange, that party would not qualify.

Gains are deferred when the exchange involves the owner of a property trading up in value. However, there are times when one party to an exchange either trades down in value or receives unlike-kind property in the form of personal property, cash, or mortgage relief. In these circumstances, the portion deemed *unlike-kind property* (or *realized gain*) is termed **boot**. In a 1031 exchange, this portion (boot) is taxable to the extent that a gain exists.

In order for an exchange to qualify, the replacement property or properties must be identified within 45 calendar days from the date of closing on the relinquished property (the identification period). (See Figure 20.5.)

Identification rules include the three-property rule, the 200 percent rule, and the 95 percent rule:

- *Three-property rule.* The exchanging party may identify up to three replacement properties. In this scenario, there is no regard to the fair market value of the identified properties.
- *200 percent rule.* The exchanging party may identify multiple properties; however, the aggregate fair market value of the identified replacement properties may not exceed 200 percent of the value of the relinquished property.
- *95 percent rule.* The exchanging party may identify numerous properties with no regard to the fair market value of the identified replacement properties, only if the exchanging party receives at least 95 percent of the aggregate value of all the identified replacement properties. This must occur prior to the 180-day period.

The exchange must occur no later than *the earlier of either* (1) 180 days from the sale of the original property or (2) the tax-return due date (including extension). (See Figure 20.6)

FIGURE   20.5

Section 1031 (Like-Kind) Exchange

Section 1031 (Like-Kind) Exchange
- Exchange must include like-kind property.
- Any exchanging party must utilize a *qualified intermediary.*
- Any realized gain or unlike-kind property received is called *boot* and is subject to tax.
- Seller must identify replacement property or properties within 45 calendar days of closing on the relinquished property.
- Replacement property or properties must follow identification rules.
- Seller must close on replacement property or properties at the earlier of
  - 180 days from the sale of the original property or
  - before the tax return due date (including extension).
- A *reverse exchange* occurs when the exchanging party purchases a replacement property or properties before selling the subject of the exchange.

FIGURE 20.6

Identification and Exchange Period Timeline

← 45 days ←	180 days*
Identification Period	Total Time for Exchange

Exchange with a
Qualified Intermediary

* The exchange must occur no later than:
180 days from the sale of the relinquished property; or
the tax-return due date (including extension),
whichever date is earlier.

The exchange must be handled by a **qualified intermediary**. A *qualified intermediary* is the hired entity that facilitates the exchange on behalf of the property owner/taxpayer. The qualified intermediary must be a party unrelated to the party exchanging. The intermediary may not include parties such as accountants, attorneys, investment bankers or brokers, or employees of the party to the exchange.

The qualified intermediary facilitates the exchange for a fee and receives the relinquished property from the exchanging party with the intent to sell the property to the buyer. The qualified intermediary purchases the replacement property from the seller (with the intent of transferring same to the exchanging party) and handles all funds during the exchange in order for the taxpayer to avoid realized taxable gain. (See Figure 20.7.)

In a 1031 tax-deferred sale, the taxpayer may not have possession or access to any of the funds realized from the sale, hence the need for the qualified intermediary. The taxpayer handles all funds, documents, and title issues for the exchanging party.

Another form of exchange is a *reverse exchange* in which the exchanging party purchases a replacement property or properties *before* selling the subject of the exchange. In essence, the exchange process is reversed. This is a complicated and more expensive transaction. In order to qualify, all of the same time elements apply as with a standard like-kind exchange.

■ INSTALLMENT SALES

In a transaction involving a property that is transferred by an **installment sale** contract, the seller receives the purchase price in installment payments rather

FIGURE 20.7

Like-Kind Exchange

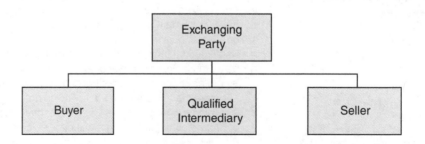

than in full at closing. This occurs over the agreed-on term of the installment contract.

During the installment periods, the seller retains title to the property and transfers title via deed only after all installments have been paid under the contract. The seller defers payment of taxes on installment amounts not received and only pays taxes on installments actually received in the year they are received.

This type of transaction resembles that of a layaway plan at any merchant. The merchant holds title to the item until such time as all installments are made.

LOW-INCOME HOUSING TAX INCENTIVES

In an effort to promote the development of affordable housing, the federal government provides developers with tax credits as an encouragement to build such housing. A tax credit can be defined as a dollar-for-dollar credit against one's tax liability.

For example, an owner of affordable housing has received a tax credit in the amount of $10,000. His tax liability in the current year is $25,000. When applying the tax credit, the taxpayer would owe $15,000 ($25,000 – $10,000).

Incentive programs include the following:

- A 4 percent credit per year is given if a property that has not previously been used for low-income housing is converted to low-income housing.
- A 4 percent credit per year is offered when construction entails federal subsidies.
- The federal government offers a credit of 9 percent of the cost to construct or rehabilitate low-income housing per annum for ten years. The cost must be greater than $2,000 per unit.

These tax credits are applicable and can be used to reduce both active and passive income tax consequences.

SUMMARY

When a property is sold, any profits realized are called gains or capital gains. Under the Taxpayer Relief Act of 1997, capital gains are subject to taxation. To calculate the gain or loss for an owner-occupant residential property, you must take into account the purchase price paid at acquisition, inclusive of closing expenses (basis), the cost of any capital improvements made to the property during the holding period (which forms the adjusted basis), and the sales price (minus costs of sale).

Profits derived from the sale of residential owner-occupant transactions are treated differently than income-producing property held for investment purposes. Under certain conditions, owner-occupant transactions allow for the seller to retain profits of either $250,000 or $500,000 ($250,000/500,000 rule) without paying capital gains taxes on these profits. Under certain conditions applicable to tax laws, the $250,000/500,000 rule can be repeated every two years.

For investment property, the vehicle used to defer capital gains tax is called a 1031 tax-deferred exchange. In a 1031 exchange, property may be "traded up" with no tax consequence at the time of exchange. Any unlike property is referred to as boot and is taxed at the appropriate tax rate. The sold property is referred to as the relinquished property, and the new property is called the replacement property. Within 45 days from the closing of the relinquished property, the seller must identify the replacement property or properties. That person must then close on any identified property at the earlier of 180 days from the closing of the relinquished property or the tax return due date with all extensions. Failure to do so will result in capital gains taxes due.

CHAPTER 20 QUIZ

1. A primary residence is the location where, prior to the sale, the taxpayer has resided for at *LEAST*
   a. one of the previous three years.
   b. two of the previous three years.
   c. two of the previous five years.
   d. three of the previous five years.

2. A seller sold his old home earlier this year and took his tax exclusion. How long does he have to wait before the sale of his current home would qualify for an exclusion?
   a. One year
   b. Two years
   c. Three years
   d. Four years

3. A buyer would like to purchase a condo, but she does not have the down payment. How much money can she withdraw from her IRA without incurring the additional 10 percent early withdrawal penalty?
   a. $3,000
   b. $5,000
   c. $10,000
   d. $12,000

4. A buyer purchased a condo for $250,000. Which items will she be able to deduct when preparing her income tax for the year in which she purchased the condo?
   a. Interest paid during the year
   b. Points paid during the year
   c. Interest and points paid during the year
   d. Interest, points, and closing costs paid during the year

5. A property owner has a vacation home on a lake. How many days can the owner lease this home to friends before the IRS views it as income-producing property?
   a. 7 days
   b. 14 days
   c. 21 days
   d. 30 days

6. The amount of money that the Taxpayer Relief Act allows taxpayers to exclude from the gain realized on the sale of a primary residence is based on whether the taxpayer files as single or as married filing jointly. This rule is commonly referred to as the
   a. $50,000/$100,000 rule.
   b. $100,000/$150,000 rule.
   c. $150,000/$250,000 rule.
   d. $250,000/$500,000 rule.

7. Which form of income on an investment property is considered passive income?
   a. Rents paid by commercial tenants
   b. Salary paid to the managing partner
   c. Commission paid to the rental agent
   d. Fees paid to the landscaping consultant

8. Which cost to a property owner is considered a capital improvement?
   a. Advertising fees for property sale
   b. Replacement of floor tiles
   c. Maintenance of historical facade
   d. Addition of an attached garage

9. Which feature of a property is an example of functional obsolescence?
   a. Inadequate electrical current to run an air conditioner
   b. Newly opened fast-food restaurant on adjacent property
   c. Kitchen cabinets that need resurfacing
   d. Two abandoned homes on the same block

10. The three primary events in investment property ownership are acquisition, holding period, and
    a. carryover.
    b. cost recovery.
    c. reversion.
    d. depreciation.

11. What is the cost recovery period for commercial investment property?

    a. 27.5 years

    b. 29 years

    c. 39 years

    d. 39.5 years

12. Which phrase is used when describing the property that is exchanged in a 1031 exchange?

    a. Like-kind

    b. Owner-occupied

    c. Installment sales

    d. Tax-exempt

13. A family is paying 3 points on a $350,000 mortgage loan. What is their dollar cost for this charge?

    a. $350

    b. $3,500

    c. $9,500

    d. $10,500

14. Long-term gains are gains that result from a sale in which the property was held for

    a. one year or more.

    b. three years or more.

    c. five years or more.

    d. ten years or more.

15. With regard to income-producing property, *cost recovery* is another term for

    a. gains.

    b. debt service.

    c. depreciation.

    d. capital gains.

CHAPTER

21

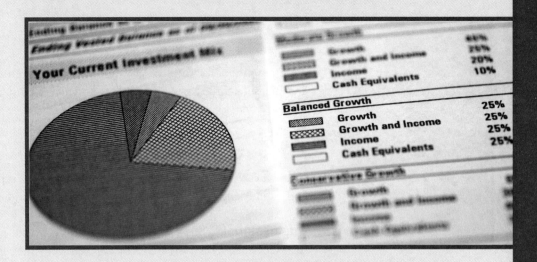

Commercial and Investment Properties

■ KEY TERMS

after-tax cash flow (ATCF)

anchor tenant

before-tax cash flow (BTCF)

capitalization rate

cash-on-cash return

cash flow

debt service

discounted cash flow analysis

effective gross income (EGI)

equity dividend rate

fixed expenses

gross income

lease escalation clause

leverage

liquidity

net operating income (NOI)

other income (OI)

potential gross income (PGI)

pro forma statement

rate of return

rentable area

reserves for replacements

tax shelter

time value of money

usable area

variable expenses

■ CHARACTERISTICS OF REAL PROPERTY INVESTMENTS

When purchasing income-producing real property, the investor's goal is not simply to purchase bricks and mortar but ultimately to purchase income. It is the income that equates to the returns on their invested capital. Aside from the fact that real property serves as another vehicle that houses income for the investor, investors are also seeking real property ownership as a form of tax shelter. A **tax shelter** is often used to describe some of the tax advantages of real estate or other investments, such as noncash deductions for cost recovery (depreciation), interest, taxes, and postponement or even elimination of certain taxes. Prior to parking large amounts of capital in any investment property, the investor will examine and measure three basic elements: *risk, liquidity,* and *leverage.*

Risk

Before committing money to an investment, the investor measures the various types of risk associated with the investment. The types of risk that any investor will examine include business risk, capital risk, and financial risk.

Business risk *Business risk* refers to the risk that an investment will not yield the necessary return on investor capital. This may occur as a result of changes in the potential gross income attributable to leasing activities, contract rents, or operating expenses.

This type of risk is analyzed in order to determine events that could undermine the investor's pro forma statement. The pro forma statement is an estimation and projection of how much **net operating income (NOI)** will be available through the property's income and expense activities in any future periods. In some cases, it may be based on contract rents and historical property activities, while in other cases, it may simply be an educated guess and projection. *Net operating income* is defined as the income realized after making deductions for property operational expenses. (See the discussion later in this chapter.)

> **Three Types of Risk for Investors**
> - Business risk
> - Capital risk
> - Financial risk

There are two basic types of business risk: *dynamic risk* and *static risk. Dynamic risk* is uninsurable risk associated with changes in the economy, income taxes, and supply versus demand issues. *Static risk* is insurable risk associated with events such as accident liability, fire, theft, and vandalism.

Due to the insurable nature of static risk, investors are able to underwrite these events by purchasing insurance. However, because dynamic risk is uninsurable, investors will seek higher returns on invested capital to compensate for this risk. Risk is a major factor in determining a rate of return on investments. As the expression goes, "The greater the risk, the greater the reward."

Capital risk *Capital risk* is associated with the investor's ability to secure borrowed funds at affordable rates.

Financial risk *Financial risk* measures the **leverage** (the use of borrowed funds) that may be comfortably placed on property. This is measured in relationship to investor equity funds. For example, when borrowed funds are used with low equity down payments, any change in the property's income or expenses can greatly increase the financial risk of loss to the investor.

Liquidity

An important part of any investment is **liquidity**. Sale transactions do not develop overnight. They require time. *Liquidity* is the ability to convert an asset into cash quickly.

However, liquidity does take on another meaning. Investors are faced with the question of whether at the time of sale, they will profit from the sale.

For example, the financial crisis of the new millennium caused many property owners to experience up-side-down equity. This simply meant that when purchased by another, the debt balances on these properties exceeded the total value of the property. These types of transactions (if and when consummated) were commonly labeled "short sales."

Examples of other liquid assets include investment vehicles such as stocks, bonds, cash, and savings accounts.

Leverage

Leveraging refers to the use of borrowed funds, which depends on the availability of funds within the debt credit markets. The ratio of debt to investor equity must be studied carefully. For example, high borrowing ratios with low down payments can create greater degrees of risk associated with the borrower's loss of invested capital. Any change in the income downward or change in expenses upward will spell disaster in this leverage situation. Therefore, important decisions are required by the investor.

■ TYPES OF INVESTMENT PROPERTY

Various property types become more or less appealing to different types of investors, depending on their goals and resources. Some investors are attracted to vacant unimproved land that they intend to develop in the future, while others prefer improved properties as their investment vehicles. Property types that might act as investment vehicles include the following:

- Unimproved land
- Commercial properties, such as offices, retail stores, shopping centers and malls, and hotels and motels
- Residential properties (single-family and multifamily)
- Mixed-use properties
- Manufacturing properties, such as industrial, light manufacturing, and loft properties
- Fee simple ownership rather than leasehold property

Unimproved Land

Ownership of unimproved land is the simplest form of real property ownership that there is. Another name for the land is *fee*. Given these two facts (the simplicity of this ownership and the definition of the word *fee*), this type of ownership is also called *fee simple ownership*. (For more on this subject, see Chapter 4.)

In the past, most investments in real property were made on the warehousing of unimproved land, but the country's population growth gave investors sound economic reasoning for development of the land as it generated a demand for improved real property.

Today, there are a variety of investor types. Some prefer ownership of unimproved land, while others prefer investing in improved property. In either case, the financial appetites of different investors will dictate their unique approaches to real property acquisition and ownership.

Although investment in unimproved land has traditionally been considered *dead money* during the investor holding period because it is non-income-producing, those fortunate enough to have warehoused ownership in land are presently benefiting from geometric value appreciation. For example, in the business districts of Manhattan, vacant, unimproved, and commercially zoned land is almost nonexistent, causing land values and development costs to soar. As a result, investors have been forced to seek affordable real property investment in the surrounding areas. This is the primary consideration behind the creation of submarkets.

Office Space

Investment in commercial office properties is extremely popular. Large urban projects attract investors such as real estate investment trusts (REITs), pension funds, insurance companies, and large syndicates of investors that pool their money.

Commercial office properties, which are occupied by businesses, can be single-tenant or multitenant properties. Depending on location, office buildings come in various sizes. They can be *lowrise* buildings consisting of 1 to 3 stories above grade, *midrise* buildings consisting of 4 to 10 stories above grade, or *highrise* buildings consisting of 11 stories and higher.

The location and zoning of a parcel of real estate dictates that property's size and building height. Larger-size projects generally occupy urban business districts, while suburban locations generally yield smaller projects.

For example, and with very few exceptions, Nassau County (Long Island) has height restrictions that generally do not allow for a building height greater than three stories above grade. This limits the amount of buildable square footage that may be constructed.

Because new commercial development is by design, owner/developers build any given project with the intent of appealing to the demand created by the space needs of the end user.

For example, a suburban developer is building a speculative property. Location, zoning, and lot size will only allow for the construction of an improvement containing small floor sizes. As a result, the owner-developer's property will appeal to the small space user as opposed to the larger space user.

Don't be fooled by the simplicity of the example above. Development of real property requires tremendous amounts of planning, risk, time, and money. In addition, the right timing, location, project size, and construction are essential to any property's success.

Retail Stores

Retail property takes a variety of sizes and forms. The size of the project will dictate what category of retail the property falls into. For example, urban retail can be one neighborhood store on a residential block, while suburban retail consists of a variety of different retail options.

Retail space is broken down into different classes: strip centers, neighborhood centers, shopping malls, regional shopping centers, and outlet malls. Normally, the size of the facility determines the category or class of the center.

The size and success of a project are always dependent on and measured according to the needs of the surrounding community. The success of a retail project can also be measured by the available supply in relationship to the market demand for that type of space.

The type of retail facility that would be appropriate for a retail site is dependent on a variety of issues. Some issues that might affect a project's overall success are the need for added retail services, the need for the type of product line to be sold, or the market share to be captured within the geographic covered area.

When considering the shoppers who may frequent a particular retail site, developers must also consider the availability of public transportation to the retail site, parking, traffic, and/or pedestrian patterns, and the availability of other product line functions in relation to the subject site.

A variety of product lines will attract consumers. Retail product lines can be broken down into two categories of functions: *generative* and *suscipient*.

Generative retail sites and product lines are those that consumers have in mind as distinct destinations when beginning their shopping journeys (for example, car dealerships, department stores, and national brand retailers). Suscipient retailers are not generative in nature, but attract and service passing customers (newsstands, electronics stores, and fast–food restaurants).

Shopping Centers and Malls

Regional shopping centers   Regional shopping centers are among the largest type of retail centers. These centers vary in size, ranging from hundreds of thousands of square feet to as much as a few million square feet. They are enclosed and usually service a large radius of the local area with a variety of services and product lines. Most of the time, they contain one or more large **anchor tenants**. An *anchor tenant* is defined as a large space user whose presence will attract other tenants with the same or different product lines. As it relates to the financing of new construction projects, anchor tenants are also essential to the investor. Any development without an anchor tenant is labeled speculative. Lenders are generally reluctant to lend money in speculative transactions.

Anchor tenants are destinational retailers (generative) and, as such, create a draw for other retail uses (suscipient). These different uses generate other types of services or amenities, such as large multiscreen cinemas, bowling alleys, restaurants, banks and ATMs, and other ancillary retail uses.

A consumer seeking an item is very focused on where that item can be found. Many retailers benefit from a close proximity to the generative services provided by anchor tenants like department stores, because those tenants bring shoppers whose initial destination is the generative retailer but who then may turn their attention to other stores. Those shoppers may locate their needs within the initial destination, visit neighboring center stores to achieve their goals, or simply purchase other goods and services provided by supporting retailers.

Millions of consumer dollars are spent annually in nondestinational locations within regional centers. The retailers benefit from the draw created by the anchor tenants and realize greater sales figures. The existence of the anchor tenant is primarily why a smaller retailer is attracted to that facility. Although retailers look to benefit from the overflow of the anchor tenant, the attraction and draw of their own product line should not be overlooked.

Shopping malls   Shopping malls are usually midsize complexes. Like regional centers, they are enclosed or contain pedestrian cover to allow the shopper and the retailer immunity from inclement weather. This provides uninterrupted year-round shopping. Also like regional centers, shopping malls have anchor tenants. The anchor can be a small department store, movie theater, or other consumer attracting use.

Strip centers   Strip centers (also called *strip malls*) are usually small in nature. They generally contain 6 to 15 stores that range in services. A strip center will not serve a large radius of residents; rather, it will generally only be known by the immediate residents of that area or neighborhood.

Neighborhood shopping centers   The neighborhood shopping center includes the neighborhood convenience store. Sharing the center's location and population draw will be other service-oriented retailers such as dry cleaners, hardware stores, fast-food chains, restaurants, and others.

Factory outlet malls and centers   Factory outlet malls and centers, which gained popularity in the late 1980s and early 1990s, are where retailers ship their close-out and unsold goods. These goods originate from the retailers' prime locations. Factory outlet malls and centers become the final destination for all unsold articles, which are sold at a fraction of the original cost.

Due to the nature of the goods being sold, inexpensive locations are preferred. Lower rental costs allow the retailer to concentrate their efforts on the sale and disposition of these items. Locating within these types of malls eliminates the financial burdens associated with mainstream locations that command higher rents. It is difficult to remain profitable in mainstream locations while selling marked-down inventory. The country's bargain hunters have certainly contributed to the overall popularity and success of these types of developments.

Hotels and Motels

Hotel and motel properties generally cater to persons seeking interim stays. Despite the fact that people "take up residence" in hotels and motels, these properties are in fact zoned commercial rather than residential.

In large cities, it is not uncommon to find hotel or motel properties that cater to short-term and long-term stays. For example, a hotel highrise property that consists of 400 rooms could be split into two sections, with the lower portion consisting of traditional short-term hotel accommodations and the upper portion of permanent long-term housing, such as a cooperative or condominium formation with hotel services.

An example of this can be seen in the redevelopment of the world-renowned Plaza Hotel in New York City.

Single-Family and Multifamily Residential Properties

Because housing is a necessity for everyone, it is in greater demand than other types of investment real property. The single-family housing market is the most active of all real estate markets.

Investors look to multifamily housing to generate income (cash returns on the invested capital) through rental activities. Multifamily housing can be found in the following categories of property construction: *lowrise* (usually 2 to 6 family dwellings), *midrise* (generally up to 50 units), and *highrise* (larger developments consisting of 50 units or more).

Mixed-Use Properties

In the mid 1980s, mixed-use property became very popular. In some cases, the driving force was municipal tax benefits that were available on these types of properties. Often, tax benefits arise out of the need for additional housing or other uses.

In other cases, zoning permitting, developers created mixed-use properties to maximize income generation from the properties' rental activities. An example of this would be a midrise or highrise property with commercial use in the lower portion and residential use in the upper portion of the building.

Manufacturing Properties

Manufacturing property is broken down into three primary types: heavy industrial, light manufacturing, and loft or warehouse buildings.

Heavy industrial properties are the places where raw materials are converted into useful objects through manufacturing processes. The assembly and distribution of product lines occurs in light manufacturing facilities. Loft or warehouse buildings provide the space for finished products to be stored prior to being shipped to their final destinations.

These types of properties have experienced a renaissance of late. Many loft buildings have been converted into residential loft-style living units, which is certainly evident in the New York City market.

Fee Simple Ownership Versus Leasehold Property

Throughout New York State, land owners arrange long-term ground leases with others. Whereas fee simple ownership (ownership in the land) is always preferred, it is not always possible for the land to be purchased. In this event, individuals and legal business entities enter into long-term ground leases. The purpose behind the long-term lease is to arrange for financing for the construction of an improvement. When the improvement is fully constructed, the leaseholder benefits through rental income activity. Although the improvement ultimately reverts back to the original landowner at termination of the ground lease, it is still a very popular form of investment.

■ PROPERTY FINANCIAL ANALYSIS AND TERMINOLOGY

Three Phases of Financial Analysis and Property Ownership

Previously in this course, you learned that investment property undergoes three primary events and phases of financial analysis: acquisition, holding, and reversion.

To review, the process of *acquisition* involves conducting financial analysis to determine the feasibility of an investment project and the impact of acquisition. During the *holding* period, financial analysis is conducted to determine whether the property owner should sell the asset, hold the asset, or refinance the loan covering the asset. The aforementioned property owner's questions during the holding period are generally answered by creating a pro forma statement. A **pro forma statement** is the projection of future income and expenses or other results. It is frequently found in a prospectus for an offering of a real estate security, such as a limited partnership to own income property. A pro forma statement should be clearly labeled as a projection and distinguished from operating figures, which are based on actual past performance. A **discounted cash flow analysis** is used in a similar manner to that of a pro forma statement; however, the discounted cash flow analysis reflects an analysis of actual versus projected income activities. The discounted cash flow analysis also takes into account the time value of money. The **time value of money** deals with and is based on the purchasing power of the dollar when received. *Reversion* (or sale) involves financial analysis to determine the investment returns achieved through the proceeds of a sale of the property when the investor reverts to his or her original investment of cash.

Cash World Versus Tax World

In order to make sound financial decisions concerning property investment, the investor must analyze the income and expense activities of the property in question. In Chapter 20, you learned that every investor deals with two worlds: the cash world and the tax world.

In the cash world, properties are bought and sold, which establishes their market value. The tax world involves the tax consequences resulting from a property's income operations, which establish a property's book value.

Reconstructed Income and Expense Statement

Deriving the net operating income   Income-producing property involves a relationship between a landlord and tenants. Lease agreements outline the scope of each party's responsibilities and also represent the contract rent payments that are made to a landlord over the term of the lease. These contract rents provide the income activity to the property. These rents are referred to as the property's gross income. **Gross income** is the total income derived from a business, wages, or from income-producing property before adjustments or deductions for expenses, depreciation, taxes, and similar allowances—that is, all income, or "the top line."

Reconstructed income/expense statements are created annually to reflect upward or downward changes in the income stream of a property, as well as the expenses attributable to the running of the property. They are also used to formulate a property's annual budget.

The purpose of examining a reconstructed income and expense statement is to identify or derive the property's net operating income (NOI). Accomplishing this requires careful inspection of income and expense activity.

NOI can be defined as the **cash flow** attributable to the property *after* deducting all operational property-related expenses *but before* deducting any debt service (mortgage payments) or federal income taxes, which would include items such as mortgage interest, depreciation allowances, and carryover and suspended losses brought forward from previous years.

The following explains how a reconstructed income and expense statement is created.

Step 1: Income analysis   The first step in the income analysis process is the examination of the **potential gross income (PGI)**. *Potential gross income* is the gross rent roll or gross receipts attributable to the rental activities of a property if that property were 100 percent leased.

As you learned in Chapter 16, this figure is a direct result of contract rents from leased spaces/units and projected rents from currently vacant spaces/units. The sum of the contract rents and the projected rents represents the PGI of the property in any given year.

With few exceptions, income-producing property will experience vacancies from time to time. In addition, financial and/or business climates may change for tenants within the investment property, resulting in collection losses that arise as tenants are unable to meet their rent obligations. This usually requires the property owner to engage appropriate legal assistance to evict the nonpaying party.

The vacancy and collection loss (V&C), which is always expressed as a percentage figure, represents a percentage of loss attributable to vacancy and collections; this figure is subtracted from the PGI. For example, an investor applies a 5 percent vacancy and collection loss against the PGI of a property. By doing so, the investor during the holding period is suggesting that she expects the property to be at

95 percent occupancy levels. Therefore, because it is over and above what was anticipated, any leasing income over the expected 95 percent occupancy equates to added profit for the investor. In essence, the owner/investor looks at 95 percent occupancy as their 100 percent level.

Furthermore, by application of an appropriate capitalization rate to the income, value is derived. It would be prudent that the maximum price this investor would want to pay be based on the 95 percent occupancy income calculation.

The next step in evaluating property income is a review of any **other income (OI)** sources attributable to the property. *Other income* can be defined as income that is not derived from the main activity of the property.

For example, a highrise apartment building may contain commercial spaces or may generate additional income through retail space, garage rent (if leased to a private operator), parking income (if operated by ownership), rental income from rooftop satellite dishes, or redistributing wholesale energy to tenants at retail energy rates (submetered electric, discussed later in this chapter).

Income derived through these and other indirect rental activities is deemed other income. Any other income is then *added* to the difference between the PGI and the V&C. The resulting amount is a figure that represents the property's **effective gross income (EGI)**. The effective gross income is the income attributable to a property after deductions have been made for vacancy and collection losses and after adding any other income derived from that property. (See Figure 21.1.)

Step 2: Operating expense analysis   Every property experiences expenses associated with the running of that property. Operating expenses are broken down into three basic categories of expenses: *fixed expenses*, *variable expenses*, and *reserves for replacements*.

Fixed expenses can be defined as expenses that do not vary as a result of a property's occupancy rate. Regardless of the property's leasing activities, these expenses remain constant for the year of analysis. Fixed expenses consist of *only* property taxes and property insurance.

Variable expenses are those expenses that will fluctuate upward or downward with the property's leasing activities. Variable expenses consist of property maintenance, repairs, payroll, utilities, trash removal, and management fees.

Reserves for replacements can be defined as available cash on hand to effectuate any anticipated or unanticipated major capital improvement to the property, for example a new roof, new mechanical equipment, or façade restoration.

FIGURE 21.1	**Potential gross income (PGI)**
	− Vacancy and collection loss (V&C)
Formula for Calculating	+ Other income (OI)
Effective Gross Income	= **Effective gross income (EGI)**

FIGURE   21.2

**Formula for Calculating
Net Operating Income**

> **Effective gross income (EGI)**
> – Operating expenses (OE)
> = **Net operating income (NOI)**

After calculating the EGI, the expense amount representative of each category of property expense must be added together to derive the total operating expenses for that property. The total amount is then subtracted from the EGI to derive the property's NOI (see Figure 21.2).

NOI represents the cash flow attributable to the property *after* deducting all property-related expenses *but before* deducting any debt service (mortgage payments) or federal income taxes (which would include items such as mortgage interest, depreciation allowances, and carryover and suspended losses brought forward from previous years).

Leveraging and Capitalization

The reconstructed income and expense statement only examines the income and expenses attributable to the property; it does not examine or include any issues relating to *leveraging* of the property. In real property transactions, leveraging is the use of borrowed funds. Borrowed funds are added to the borrower's own available funds and when combined, these funds are used to complete the acquisition of property.

The only purpose of the reconstructed income and expense statement is to derive the property's NOI. By deriving the NOI, the investor is able to calculate his or her overall return on investment through a process called *capitalization*.

Capitalization is the present value of the income stream that a property produces. **Capitalization rates** are normally market driven and are subjectively arrived at by the needs of the investor. Remember, the investor is not purchasing bricks and mortar but income/cash flow activities. That income can be reported as a **rate of return** (ROI) on the overall investment. ROI is defined as annual profit (based on a prescribed interest rate) sought by the investor on the overall cost of acquisition. It is based on the purchase price.

In the process of capitalization, the investor asks, "What is the most I am willing to pay (based on my desired rate of return) to own the NOI being generated by the property?" In this case, the investor is solely looking at the income as it relates to the maximum price the investor will pay to own that income.

IRV is a helpful formula used in capitalization calculations. IRV stands for *income, rate,* and *value.* (See Figure 21.3.)

The following example explains how the IRV formula calculations work. An income-producing property yields an NOI of $177,550. The investor is using a 10 percent discount rate of return of sales price to income or a 10 percent capitalization rate on income to sales price for their investment. The calculation would work as follows:

FIGURE 21.3

IRV Formula

IRV

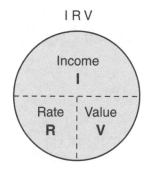

Income = Rate   × Value
Rate = Income ÷ Value
Value = Income ÷ Rate

To achieve value (sales price) when income (NOI) and return rate are provided:

$ 177,550
÷   0.10
$1,775,550

To achieve income (NOI) when value (sales price) and return rate are provided:

$1,775,500
×   0.10
$ 177,550

To achieve a return rate when income (NOI) and value (sales price) are provided:

$177,550
÷1,775,550
        0.10

IRV also guides the user as to which arithmetic function need be applied. Notice the horizontal line creating two hemispheres within the circle in Figure 21.3:

■ When the income and rate amounts are known, we divide to obtain the value.
■ When the income and value amounts are known, we divide to obtain the rate.
■ When the rate and value are known, we multiply to obtain the income.

Investors who are performing a financial analysis for the purpose of acquiring property are also concerned about their return on equity. This may or may not include the use of borrowed funds in completing the acquisition. Using borrowed funds creates an added expense to the investor called **debt service**. *Debt service* is defined as the incremental cost of periodic (usually monthly) principal and interest payments required to pay back the borrowed funds. The next step is for the investor to calculate the **before-tax cash flow (BTCF)** attributable to the property. *Before-tax cash flow* is defined as the cash flow attributable to a property after deducting the annual cost of debt service.

FIGURE   21.4

Formula for Calculating Before-Tax Cash Flow

> **Net operating income (NOI)**
> − Annual debt service (ADS)
> = **Before-tax cash flow (BTCF)**

Deriving the Before-Tax Cash Flow

Once we derive the NOI, the next step is to reduce the NOI by the amount required to service any debt placed on the property. The annual cost of financing is subtracted from the NOI. The difference produces the before-tax cash flow (BTCF) amount. (See Figure 21.4.)

Once the BTCF is established, the investor is interested in calculating his or her equity dividend rate. The *equity dividend rate* is defined as the percentage of profit that the investor receives only on the cash he or she invested in the property (commonly referred to as **cash-on-cash return**). This excludes any financing. This also aids the investor in determining the amount of down payment necessary to achieve the desired equity dividend rate. The formula for calculating the equity dividend rate is as follows:

Before-tax cash flow ÷ Equity = Equity dividend rate

The formula for determining the down payment required to achieve the desired equity dividend rate is as follows:

Before-tax cash flow ÷ Equity dividend rate = Required down payment

The final step in the cash world financial analysis is to determine the property's **after-tax cash flow (ATCF)**. *After-tax cash flow* is the amount of remaining cash flow after deductions are made from the before-tax cash flow for income taxes resulting from the property's income activities. (See Figure 21.5.)

However, in order to calculate the income taxes attributable to income activity and to derive the after-tax cash flow, we must visit the tax world. Figure 21.6 shows the formula used to calculate income taxes.

Using this formula, assume the following property information:

> Net operating income = $177,550
> Reserves for replacements = $10,000
> Mortgage interest = $50,000
> Annual depreciation = $15,000
> Carryover/suspended loss = $3,000
> Marginal rate = 28%

FIGURE   21.5

Formula for Calculating After-Tax Cash Flow

> **Before-tax cash flow (BTCF)**
> − Income taxes (IT)
> = **After-tax cash flow (ATCF)**

Based on the previous assumptions, the taxes would be calculated in the following manner:

Step 1: Calculate the adjusted net operating income.

$177,550 (NOI)
+ 10,000 (R&R)
$187,550 (ANOI)

Note: In the cash world, reserves for replacements is deducted as an operating expense to arrive at the NOI. However, because reserves for replacements consist of cash on hand, if this money is not spent, it is carried over as an asset into the following year's ledger. It is for this reason that reserves are added back in within the tax world. A deduction cannot be taken on unspent funds.

Step 2: Calculate the taxable income.

$187,550 (ANOI)
– 50,000 (MI)
– 15,000 (AD)
– 3,000 (CSL)
$119,550 (TI)

Step 3: Calculate the income tax.

$119,550 (TI)
×   0.28 (MR)
$33,474 (IT)

Based on the above assumptions, the income tax attributable to the income activities on this property is $33,474.

At this point, we go back to the cash world to complete our analysis. The formula for calculating the after-tax cash flow is as follows:

    Before-tax cash flow (BTCF)
– Income taxes (IT)
= After-tax cash flow (ATCF)

The before-tax cash flow is calculated by subtracting the annual debt service from the net operating income.

FIGURE 21.6

**Formula for Calculating
Income Taxes on
Investment Property**

   Net operating income (NOI)
+ Reserves for replacements (RR)
– Mortgage interest (MI)
– Annual depreciation (AD)
– Carryover/suspended losses, if any (CSL)
= **Taxable income (TI)**
× Marginal rate (MR)
= **Income tax (IT)**

Assume that the annual debt service (the principal and interest payments) is $75,000. If the net operating income is $177,550 and the income taxes are $33,474, the calculation to derive the after-tax cash flow would be as follows:

NOI	=	$177,550
ADS	=	− 75,000
BTCF	=	$102,550
IT	=	− 33,474
ATCF	=	$ 69,076

The following are formulas for the cash world and tax world in complete form:

CASH WORLD	TAX WORLD
Potential gross income	**Net operating income**
− Vacancy and collection loss	+ Reserves for replacements
+ Other property income	= **Adjusted net operating income**
= **Effective gross income**	− Mortgage interest
− Operating expenses	− Annual depreciation
= **Net operating income**	− Carryover/Suspended loss

CASH WORLD	TAX WORLD
− Annual debt service	= **Taxable income**
= **Before-tax cash flow**	× Marginal rate
− Income tax	= **Income tax**
= **After-tax cash flow**	

COMMERCIAL PROPERTY SPACE MEASUREMENT

Rentable Area

In New York, commercial property rents are calculated on an annual basis per square foot of space rented. In deriving the annual base rent amount, the property owner calculates the space's **rentable area**. *Rentable area* is the total area or square footage of a floor or unit of space in an office building (as determined by the property owner) to be used for the purposes of calculating the annual rent. This is the square footage that a tenant pays rent on. This square-foot figure is based on a full-floor tenancy.

The formula for calculating the rentable area on any given space will vary depending on the method of measurement used. For example, New York City uses both the Real Estate Board of New York (REBNY) guidelines for measurement as well as those of the Building Owners and Managers Association (BOMA), which are different.

To calculate the annual base rent that will be charged, the rentable area is multiplied by the dollars charged per square foot. In New York, it is customary for the dollar-per-square-foot figure to be expressed as an annual dollar-per-square-foot amount. By contrast, in Los Angeles, the price per square foot is quoted on a monthly basis.

No regulation or law governs rentable-area calculations in New York. Outside of guidelines provided to their members by local boards such as the REBNY or associations such as BOMA, it is an arbitrary calculation made by the property owner. This calculation often becomes the subject of controversy in negotiations with tenants. The rentable area of any space within an office building usually includes a proportionate share of non-income-producing spaces such as the entrance lobby, building common areas, and mechanical floors or spaces. Therefore, in actuality, the tenant pays rent based on square footage that is greater than the interior square footage that the tenant actually uses.

A rentable measurement guideline might be the following: area measured to the inside finished surface of the outer building walls, to exclude vertical penetrations (i.e., stairs, elevator shafts, etc.) of the floor.

Loss Factor

In square-footage terms, the difference between the rentable area and the actual interior space measurement is called the *loss factor*. The *loss factor*, which is commonly expressed as a percentage, is defined as the difference between the *usable area* (discussed next) and *rentable area*. In almost every city in the country, a loss factor is prevalent in commercial property space measurement. Loss factors are calculated by using the following formula:

Loss factor = (Rentable area – Usable area) ÷ Rentable area

The quotient can be expressed in either as a square-footage measurement or in percentage terms.

For example, assume that the rentable area of an office space is 10,000 square feet. The usable area consists of 8,000 square feet. Calculation of the loss factor is as follows:

(10,000 rentable sq ft – 8,000 usable sq ft) ÷ 10,000 rentable sq ft = 0.20

Thus, the loss factor expressed as a percentage is 20 percent. The loss factor expressed in square footage is represented by the quotient: 2,000 square feet (10,000 – 8,000).

Usable Area

Usable area is the area obtained by subtracting the loss factor from the rentable area. The concept is applied to account for the space taken up by office items such as furniture, office equipment (e.g., copy machines), and personnel. Usable measurement can be calculated from the inside tenant wall (separating the common areas from the office) to the window line, but methods for establishing this figure vary.

Guidelines for measuring usable area might read: "Area measured to the inside finished surface of the permanent outer walls to the finished surface of the office side of the common areas and to the center of any partitions that separate the office from adjacent areas. No deductions are made for convectors, columns, or other space obstructions."

This space measurement variable is extremely important when evaluating space layout and is commonly used in the space planning process. The space planner bypasses the rentable area measurement in the layout process and will determine the usable area first. This helps the planner verify space use and efficiency. Usable space measurement is more important to the tenant than it is to the owner. Because of the different approaches to space measurement that exist, owners are often reluctant to represent usable area to tenants.

Carpetable Area

Carpetable area is not a term used by property owners, but it can be defined as the usable space measurement minus columns, convectors, walls, and floor obstructions of all types within a given space. It is the area that you could lay carpet down or walk on. It is an essential measurement for interior furniture planning.

Take, for example, a 1980s construction highrise office building with a perimeter heating, ventilating, and air-conditioning (HVAC) system that is housed in a convector that measures a depth of two feet from the window. Anyone planning an office layout would want to use the carpetable-square-foot method rather than the usable-square-foot method to determine what furniture will fit in the space. A 20-foot-by-20-foot usable-square-foot office with a 2-foot convector would yield an 18-foot-by-18-foot carpetable office.

A tenant comparing one space over another would probably find carpetable area to be the truest form of space measurement, so it is a reasonable measure for conducting a financial analysis to determine the better of the spaces under consideration. Table 21.1 is an example of a carpetable-square-foot space analysis.

In Table 21.1, the rentable area and loss factor of building 1 suggest a better efficiency of space over that of buildings 2 and 3. However, when the square footage of the three buildings under comparison is reduced to carpetable square feet, the differences in all three spaces are shown to be much less dramatic.

T A B L E 21.1	Comparative information	Building 1	Building 2	Building 3
	Spaces compared	Space #1	Space #2	Space #3
Carpetable Square Foot Space Analysis	Rentable square feet (RSF)	10,000	10,000	10,000
	Rent per rentable square foot	$30.00	$28.00	$27.50
	Annual rent	$300,000.00	$280,000.00	$275,000.00
	Rentable to usable			
	Loss factor rentable-usable	20%	25%	30%
	Usable square feet	8,000	7,500	7,000
	Rent per usable square foot	$37.50	$37.33	$39.29
	Usable to carpetable			
	Loss factor usable-carpetable	15%	10%	5%
	Carpetable square feet	6,800	6,750	6,650
	Rent per carpetable square foot	$44.12	$41.48	$41.35

Add-on Factors

When calculating loss factors, the purpose is to derive the usable square footage. When calculating the rentable square footage from the usable square footage, an *add-on factor* is applied. The add-on factor is the difference between the usable and rentable square footage when added to the usable square feet. It is normally expressed in percentage terms and is the reciprocal of the loss factor.

For example, assume a full floor in an office building measures 8,000 usable square feet. The loss factor is assumed to be 20 percent, or 2,000 square feet. The add-on factor is derived using the following formula:

Add-on factor = Loss factor (in square feet) ÷ Usable area

Let's apply the formula using the assumptions from the example above:

Loss factor (in square feet): 2,000
Usable area: 8,000
Add-on factor = 2,000 ÷ 8,000 = 0.25

Thus, the add-on factor is 25 percent that we now multiply in addition to the usable square footage. This is demonstrated as follows:

Add-on factor = 25%
Usable square footage = 8,000
Calculation = 8,000 × 1.25 = 10,000

Add-on factors are also used in another way. In parts of New York, commercial office property owners quote rent in terms of usable square feet; in these cases, the property owner has not provided in the rent for capital investment and expenses associated with non-income-producing spaces within the property but will include an add-on factor to compensate for common area maintenance (CAM) charges. The add-on factor represents each tenant's proportionate share of the CAM charges.

■ LEASE TYPES

A variety of lease types are used in commercial real estate; which lease is used depends on the type of property transaction. The four types of leases commonly used in a commercial office and retail property are as follows:
- Gross lease
- Net lease
- Percentage lease
- Loft lease

Gross Lease

In a gross lease, the lessee (tenant) pays the lessor (landlord) basic rent. The base rent is inclusive of all property charges at that time. In essence, the lessor bears financial responsibility for furnishing all services associated with the tenancy. Generally, lease provisions also provide for rent escalation clauses (covered later in this chapter). These clauses are included to protect the lessor against increased costs of property taxes and operations by establishing that these same increases will later be passed on to the tenant. Gross leases without rent escalation clauses are used in residential transactions.

Net Lease

In a net lease, the lessee (tenant) pays the lessor (landlord) a *net rent*. It is termed *net rent* because the amount does not include any consideration for the property operational costs and taxes. It represents the NOI to the property owner or, in other terms, the owner's profit. In a net lease, the lessee is required to pay for some or all of the property taxes and operational costs. This differs from the gross lease in which the financial burden for these expenses is the landlord's.

In a net lease covering a single-tenant property, the tenant pays the landlord the net rent and is also responsible for all expenses associated with the property.

In net leases covering a multitenant property, tenants pay the landlord the net rent and are also responsible for their proportionate share of all expenses associated with operating and maintaining the property.

For example, assume that a tenant occupies 10,000 rentable square feet in a 100,000 rentable-square-foot office building. The tenant's proportionate share is determined using the following formula:

Tenant's share = Space footage ÷ Building footage
Tenant's share = 10,000 ÷ 100,000 = 0.10

Thus, in this example, the tenant's proportionate share is 10 percent.

Percentage Lease

Percentage leases can be gross or net leases. They are commonly used in retail lease transactions. In a percentage lease, the lessee (tenant) pays the lessor (landlord) a minimum base rent plus a percentage of the merchant's sales over a *natural breakeven*. The break-even point is the amount in sales that a retailer must reach before a percentage of sales must be paid to the landlord as additional rent. Any amounts derived from percentage of sales over the natural breakeven results as additional rent to the retail tenant. The formula for calculating the natural breakeven follows:

Natural breakeven = Annual rent ÷ Percentage of sales

For example, assume the following information:

Base monthly rent: $5,000
Percentage of sales: 5%
(over natural breakeven)
Calculation:

Step 1: Derive the annual rent by multiplying the monthly rent by 12.

$5,000 × 12 = $60,000

Four Types of Commercial Leases

- Gross lease
- Net lease
- Percentage lease
- Loft lease

Step 2: Obtain the natural breakeven of $1,200,000 by dividing the annual rent ($60,000) by the percentage of sales of 5 percent.

Natural breakeven = $60,000 ÷ 0.05

When the minimum base rent is high, the landlord receives a lower percentage of sales because the natural break-even point that must be reached is higher than it would be for a lower rent amount. When the minimum base rent is below market, the usual consideration is to pay the landlord a higher percentage of annual sales. This type of lease would not be used in a nonretail transaction.

Loft Lease

Loft properties are used for storage and warehousing. Due to the nature of this type of use, property owners have no need to offer services that would normally be required in an office building. This includes services such as space cleaning, janitorial services, air-conditioning, and 24/7 building elevator service. Loft leases are generally used when the property owner need not include any of these types of building services.

■ LEASE CLAUSES

A lease is a contract. Contracts are agreements between competent parties to do or to refrain from doing a legal act or acts for consideration between the contracting parties. As commercial leases tend to be long term in nature, it is vital that there be a clear understanding between the landlord and the tenant as to their responsibilities under the lease. Lease clauses are complex, and the way the clause is written can affect the tenancy in any number of ways.

Use Clause

The use clause describes the tenant business use permitted within the demised premises. Depending on the language contained within this clause, the use clause provides either a broad or narrow scope of use attributable to the subject space. This clause is important to both landlord and tenant. A landlord's concern is that a tenant use the space in accordance with a lawful business use (for example, no gambling within the demised space) and that the tenant's use will not violate the property's certificate of occupancy issued by the municipality (for example, a residential use in a commercial property).

Today, in almost every case, a landlord's consent is required prior to commencement of any assignment or subletting of the existing obligation. Situations arise in which the use clause is the deciding factor behind a landlord's willingness to grant his or her consent to an assignment or sublease of the demised space to a new party. This might be due to any number of things.

For example, assume the use clause were to read as follows: "Tenant shall use and occupy the demised premises for a Sales Office of a Stock Brokerage and for no other purpose."

Due to the restrictive nature of the above use clause example, this language could inhibit efforts on the part of the tenant/lessee to assign or sublease the space to anyone other than someone in the stock brokerage business.

As you can see from the above example, this clause requires careful thought, planning, and negotiating on the part of both the landlord/lessor and the tenant/lessee. Careful consideration in preparation of this clause can help prevent costly legal problems.

Attornment

Attornment is the section within a lease that describes the party to whom the tenant is required to pay rent as well as the only party from which the landlord will accept the rent. These details may also come in the form of a letter (letter of attornment) rather than as a clause within the lease. This would occur when the property is sold to another party. In this situation, the selling party directs that future rent payments be made to the new owner of the property.

A landlord will not accept payment of rent from any individual or entity other than the individual or entity that is a party to the lease. If, for example, a landlord in a residential rent-regulated unit were to accept rent from any individual or entity other than the party to the lease, that acceptance of rent from the uninterested party to the transaction might create unintended rights of occupancy and possession for that party. For this reason, landlords will not accept payment of rent from any party other than the interested party to the transaction.

Estoppel Clause

An estoppel certificate is a legal form that states that the unpaid balance due on a lease, loan, or other agreement to receive monies as of a specified date is in full force and existence. It prevents any purchaser of the lease, loan, or other agreement to receive monies from claiming that the payor owes more than the stated amount. Tenants within income-producing properties may from time to time be asked to execute one or more estoppel certificates during their tenancy.

Estoppel certificates are used in two frequent types of transactions: In the sale of a property, an estoppel certificate is used by the selling party to certify the rental income that was provided to the buying party. In a refinancing of a mortgage or other property loan, the certificate is used to certify the income attributable to the property through income activities and contract rents.

Sublease/Assignment Clause

During the term of a lease, tenants may need to relocate. In order to avoid paying rent in two places, they may dispose of the initial lease obligation through assignment or subletting of their interest to another.

Although on the surface this may seem simple, the process requires careful consideration. Some areas of consideration include the landlord's rights and options triggered by a request for consent to an assignment or sublease.

These rights and options might be landlord's recapture rights (the landlord's right to terminate the lease as opposed to consenting to the assignment or subletting); landlord's right to have the space assigned or subleased to them at the same financial terms achieved from a third party (likely to occur when the sublease rent is below market for the building); retention of any profits derived through an assignment or sublease; attornment (property owner's willingness to accept rent directly from the assignee or sublessee rather than from the prime tenant); the timing, manner, and conditions of how the landlord's consent is achieved; and the financial responsibility of the primary tenant after the assignment or subletting occurs.

It is important to point out that corporate mergers and acquisitions can often provide the mechanism to trigger assignment/subleasing rights for the landlord; they may also change the intended use of the premises by the tenant. This clause is usually covered in great detail in separate lease riders.

In addition, commercial leases do not provide inherent rights to the tenant regarding the landlord's consent to an assignment or sublease. It must be arranged within the lease negotiation.

Subordination Clause/Nondisturbance Clause

The subordination clause in a lease deals with the leaseholder's rights in relation to other lien positions or encumbrances within that property and sets forth the priority that a lease takes in relationship to the rights of a ground (land) owner or a lender of money.

This clause requires that the rights of the leaseholder are junior or secondary to the rights of others. This requirement takes on significant meaning when the subject involves a foreclosure by a lender since the subordination clause places the leaseholder in a precarious position.

The clause is intended to take current and future property financing into consideration. Lenders, as a practice, will not take a second or junior position when lending money to a property owner; they will always have priority as senior lienholder to any other holder of rights in the real property. As you already know, a lease acts as an encumbrance on and to real property. Therefore, the need for setting the priority of rights concerning these issues arises.

For example, if a lender were to foreclose on a property owner, as a direct result of that foreclosure proceeding, any lease that did not include a subordination nondisturbance agreement would be subject to cancellation. This agreement would represent an acknowledgment by the lender of the terms of the lease entered into between the landlord and tenant. In buildings occupied by large anchor tenants, these tenants will have invested sizable amounts of money in the form of tenant improvement work. As a result, they will seek protection of their investment. This is achieved by requesting that the property owner obtain this letter from their lender.

■ ELECTRIC SERVICE IN NEW YORK

In New York, there are three types of electric delivery systems serving consumers and businesses: direct-meter electric service, submetered electric service, and rent-inclusion electric service.

Direct-Metered Electric Service

This type of electric service is commonly found in residential households. With direct-metered electric service, each unit is hooked up to and serviced by the utility company responsible for that area. The energy consumer receives direct billing from the utility company and is responsible for paying for only the actual consumption measured by a meter reading. The utility company bills to each unit or household, and each bill represents the actual electrical consumption for that unit. Charges are predicated on kilowatt hours of consumption. The rate charged to the occupant is a retail rate per kilowatt hour of consumption.

Submetered Electric Service

Submetering occurs when a property owner purchases electricity in bulk for the entire building. The property owner is responsible for paying one master bill for service to the entire property (common areas as well as offices and/or resident units). The utility company or other energy provider sells the electric service to the property owner at wholesale rates. The property owner then redistributes this service through the existing feeders and risers to the property and invoices the end user at retail energy rates. This setup is appealing to property owners because it creates a new profit center. The difference between the wholesale rate that the property owner pays to the utility company and the retail rate that the property owner charges tenants becomes added profit to ownership. For the utility company, this translates to tremendous cost savings in manpower and expense relating to meter-reading, billing, and collection issues.

As a result of this arrangement, service is unchanged and uninterrupted to the end energy consumer; however, meter-reading and billing functions become the responsibility of the property owner. As a result of the added cost of meter reading and billing, a commercial office property owner charges the tenant an administrative surcharge over and above actual meter consumption. Administrative charges range from as low as 3 percent to as high as 25 percent. The average administrative charge on submetered electricity usually ranges from 5 percent to 15 percent. Let's look at an example of how this would work.

Assume the utility section of a tenant's lease contains a charge of 110 percent (100 percent is consumption and 10 percent is administrative charge). The first meter reading indicates the tenant has consumed $1,000 worth of electricity for the month. The calculation of the charges to the tenant is as follows:

$1,000 \times 1.10 = $1,100

In this example, the tenant pays an additional 10 percent administrative charge in the amount of $100. This amount will fluctuate as the consumption increases or decreases.

Rent-Inclusion Electric Service

This type of electric service is typical of 1960s and 1970s construction. In this type of electric service, one master meter is used to measure the entire building's consumption. This version of energy delivery has created a tremendous profit center for owners of large commercial properties. The term *rent-inclusion* does not mean that the electric service is included in the quoted rent figure. Instead, it is added to the rent figure. The formula for calculating the annual base electric charge is as follows:

Annual base electric charge = Property annual cost of electric service ÷ Rentable area of property

Let's look at an example to see how this works. Assume the following property transaction information: The annual electric bill for an office property is $3,000,000. The building measures one million rentable square feet, and electric service is charged on a rent-inclusion basis. The base rent for space is $50.00 per rentable square foot.

The base electric charge attributable to each tenant would be calculated as follows:

$3,000,000 (electric charges) ÷ 1,000,000 square feet (building size) = $3.00 per square foot

We divided the annual electric bill by the total rentable square footage attributable to the property. This calculation yielded a $3 per square foot base electric charge. This is the minimum charge for each and every tenant in that property. Regardless of individual consumption, each party pays the minimum base charge of $3 per square foot of rented space.

If the base rent for space is $50 per rentable square foot and the base electric charge is $3 per rentable square foot, the total annual rent inclusive of electric would be $53 per rentable square foot.

The language contained in a lease for this type of electric service allows the property owner to survey individual electric consumption from time to time. This will determine whether any tenant is consuming more than the base rate charged. Should the survey reveal that an occupant consumes a greater amount of energy, the lease would provide for the property owner to adjust the base rate to a higher amount.

Please note that electrical lease clauses will normally provide for any increases relating to electric rate increases and increased consumption.

Any tenant whose actual consumption is less than the amount covered by the $3-per-square-foot base charge is essentially subsidizing larger energy users in this type of property. This version of energy delivery would be the least favorable method of energy service to a tenant who underutilizes consumption as it relates to the minimum base amount charged. Very few buildings of a residential nature use this category of electric service.

■ LEASE ESCALATION CLAUSES

History and Purpose

During the 1950s and most of the 1960s, inflation was not a factor that affected a property's net operating income; however, the economy of the mid-1960s demonstrated what the ravaging and spiraling effects of inflation could do to a property's bottom line. Commercial property owners were not prepared for this cycle of inflation. Lease provisions did not include full protective clauses providing for inflationary property expense pass-through. At that time, rents were fixed and only included provisions for a small portion of any property tax increase to be passed through to the tenant in the form of additional rent. There were no lease provisions covering passing on the increased cost of operational property expenses to tenants.

This state of affairs gave rise to the lease escalation clause, which was used to protect the commercial property owner against the increased cost in operations that arises from inflation.

As the years progressed, these lease escalation clauses developed into highly sophisticated and complex provisions that took on a variety of shapes and forms. Hybrid formulas and lease clauses also developed.

Because of their financial impact, these clauses required strong consideration and scrutiny on the part of tenants. In the early stages of escalation clause evolution, landlords initially looked to pass-through clause coverage for all (in net leases) or some of the property taxes (in gross leases) and all (in net leases) or some of the operating expenses (in gross leases).

However, landlords soon discovered that these clauses afforded them other property-ownership benefits. These benefits included recapture of future increased operation costs, recapture of future increased property tax costs, and more important, creation of a new property profit center.

Landlords discovered that the incorporation of complex and sophisticated language in lease escalation clauses yielded greater amounts of money than that simply necessary to cover intended operational costs.

The concept of lease escalation had never been introduced in the real estate arena before this period, and most tenants were clueless as to the economic impact of these clauses. It took five to ten years of rent increase experience (resulting from these clauses) before these same tenants became aware of the impact of lease escalation. Tenants found that the financial impact of these clauses was greater than the base rents they initially bargained for.

Tenants who signed leases for $5 per square foot may have found themselves paying $10 or more per square foot at lease termination because of these rent escalation clauses—an unanticipated doubling of occupancy costs. This reality gave birth to a more sophisticated tenant who, as the expression goes, was "once bitten and twice shy." Landlords who had become accustomed to this newfound profit center had to adjust to the now wiser tenant. This led to the evolution of a variety of rent escalation clauses that are used today. Let's examine each of these clauses next.

Proportionate Share/Occupancy

Proportionate share is a term used in leases to indicate the tenant responsibility with respect to increased costs in property operations. Proportionate share refers to tenant space as a percentage of the gross rentable area of the building. The formula for determining the proportionate share is as follows:

Proportionate share = Tenant rentable area ÷ Building gross rentable area

Imagine a tenant who occupies 10,000 rentable square feet in a building with a total gross rentable area of 100,000 square feet. Applying the above formula results in the following:

Proportionate share = 10,000 ÷ 100,000 = 0.10 (10%)

The tenant's proportionate share is 10 percent. That figure will be used in future calculations related to increases in the property taxes and operating expenses of the building.

For example, assume that a property's taxes increase the year after initial tenant occupancy. In the year of initial tenant occupancy, property taxes amount to $50,000 for the entire building; the subsequent year, the tax increases to $75,000 for the entire property. The tenant's tax escalation clause suggests that the tenant pay an additional rent amount to compensate the landlord for this property tax increase. To determine the tenant's additional payment, the tenant's proportionate share of the increase is calculated. This two-step process is shown as follows:

Step 1: Determine the building-wide increase over the base amount

New tax amount:	$75,000
Base tax amount:	− $50,000
Building tax increase:	$25,000

Step 2: Calculate the tenant share of the increase

Building tax increase:	$25,000
Tenant proportionate share:	× 0.10
Tenant rent increase:	$ 2,500

There are flaws in the application of the proportionate share, however. For instance, if the total area of the building includes retail spaces, calculating the proportionate share becomes more complicated. If the share being calculated is exclusive of these spaces, this will yield a higher share per tenant than if these spaces were included. The effect is shown as follows:

Assume the following:		
Building gross rentable area	=	100,000 square feet
Total rentable area of property office portion	=	75,000 square feet
Total rentable area of property retail portion	=	25,000 square feet
Total rentable area of tenant space	=	50,000 square feet

Based on the above building information, the tenant's proportionate share can be determined. If the retail space from the total building area is excluded, the calculation would be as follows:

Proportionate share = 50,000 ÷ 75,000 = 0.6667

The proportionate share is 0.6667, or 67 percent, of the building. If all of the building spaces were included, the proportionate share of expenses to the tenant would be calculated this way:

Proportionate share = 50,000 ÷ 100,000 = 0.50

When including all building spaces, the proportionate share is 0.50, or 50 percent, of the building.

As shown in these examples, depending on the method of calculating proportionate shares, outcomes can vary widely. Remember, all increases in building operating expenses are applied to the proportionate share, and any increase in expenses becomes the financial responsibility of the tenant. Certainly, the tenant would prefer a proportionate share commensurate with the second illustration (50 percent), while the landlord would likely opt for the first illustration (67 percent). As a result, negotiating this issue can be quite controversial.

It important to note that because vacancies arise at various times during property ownership, each tenant may be subject to a different base amount. This base amount is always established by a base-year period.

Base Year

Base years are used in leases for the purpose of passing through increased costs in property operations. A *base year* is the beginning point at which a tenant bears financial responsibility for property operational increases and tax costs.

In an existing building with previous operating history, the base year is generally the same year as the year of occupancy. However, when the subject property is new construction, careful consideration must be given to establishing the appropriate base year operating and tax amounts. New construction would not have any previous operating history to compare to, so on these projects developers estimate operating budgets. An understated base year amount will result in immediate and additional rent increases.

The base year establishes that year's expense amount for property taxes and operational costs. Leases provide clauses indicating that increases over the base year amount will be passed through to the tenant in the form of additional rent payments. The calculation always applies the proportionate share of occupancy to the difference between the base year and the current year's amount. This was previously demonstrated in the discussion of proportionate share.

Improperly negotiated base years present many financial dangers to both the landlord and tenant. Depending on the role of the licensee, there are various approaches to this negotiation. These approaches might include establishing the base year only when the property reaches a certain occupancy level, establishing the base year when the property is completed and/or ready for occupancy by the tenant, or the landlord and tenant reaching an agreed-on estimated amount (in dollars per square foot) to act as the base amount. This last scenario, commonly referred to as an operating stop, will be discussed next.

Operating/Real Estate Tax Stop

An *operating stop* is the prescribed dollar-per-square-foot amount in annual property operating expenses that it is a landlord's responsibility to cover. Any overage incurred to operate the property is borne by the tenant and paid as additional rent to the landlord.

Consider a new construction project with no operating history. The property owner and prospective tenant negotiate an operating stop amount of $8.00 per square foot. The tenant signs the lease and subsequently moves into the property. Within a short period, the building owner establishes that the true operating cost is $9.50 per square foot. The tenant would then be subject to an immediate increase in rent of $1.50 per square foot.

Real Property Tax Clause

Property taxes are assessed to all properties, unless tax-exempt. Landlords will negotiate leases with tax escalation clauses, which provide for the passing through of all increases in property taxes to the tenants. The landlord and tenant negotiate the base year as a beginning point for future increases to be passed through to the tenant and also negotiate and establish the proportionate share of tenant space relative to the total area of the building. This share is the percentage that is applied to any property tax increase.

Direct Operating Escalation Clause

The direct operating escalation clause allows a commercial property owner to pass through any increased cost of property operations to a tenant. *Direct operating escalation* is defined as the property's annual dollar increase over the base year amount, which translates to a rent increase to each tenant according to the tenant's proportionate share. This pass-through comes in the form of an annual operating statement. The statement reflects the costs associated with all aspects of running the property. The new amount is compared with the previous year's amount, and the difference represents the increased cost of operations for the property that year. To derive the tenant's increase in rent, the increase over the previous year is multiplied against the tenant's proportionate share.

For example, assume the following information:

Base year operating amount $50,000
Subsequent year operating amount $75,000
Tenant's proportionate share 10%
Step 1: Establish the increase over the base
$75,000
− 50,000
$25,000

Step 2: Apply the tenant's proportionate share to derive the rent increase

$25,000
×   0.10
$ 2,500

Porter's Wage Escalation Formula

Porter's wage is another form of commercial lease escalation that approaches direct operating expenses in a different way and eliminates arguments over the inclusion and exclusion of certain items in the definition of operating expense.

The porter's wage escalation formula concerns laborers in the commercial property, including the concierge, elevator starter, porters, superintendent, and building engineer. *Porter's wage* is defined as the minimum hourly wage rate paid to a commercial property worker based on a 40-hour workweek. This wage compensation is based on a collective bargaining agreement, which historically is negotiated every three years and is of public record. The contract is negotiated between the union representing the paid workers and a representative of commercial property owners. In New York City, the union is Local 32B/J, and the owner representative is the Realty Advisory Board (RAB).

In the early days of operating escalation pass-throughs, tenants would often dispute that certain property charges were excessive and/or unnecessary to the operation of the property. During this period, porter's wage was instituted to avoid auditing of the owner's books. Porter's wage is a formula, so it was impossible to argue with the calculation and its application, and as a result, owners were not required to open their books to tenants for auditing. The institution of porter's wage escalation closed the books on operating disputes.

This escalation is most prevalent in the northeast region of the country than anywhere else. The formula ties increases in the minimum hourly wage rate to per-square-foot charges. This approach takes on a variety of forms. Let's examine an example of the most common form: penny-for-penny.

Under the penny-for-penny formula, every penny that workers receive as an increase in their minimum hourly wage rate equates to a penny-per-square-foot increase in rent for the tenant.

Assume a tenant signs a lease for 10,000 square feet at a rental rate of $50.00 per square foot. The lease contains a porter's wage escalation clause. The base wage rate for the year of occupancy is $17.50 per hour. The following year, the wage rate increases by $0.50 per hour to $18.00. The formula for calculating the rent increase is as follows:

Rent increase = Rentable area of tenant space × Wage rate increase over the base rate
10,000 sq ft × $0.50 = $5,000 annual rent increase to tenant

There are many variations of this formula, and each is modified to conform to the market conditions at the time of negotiations.

Fringe benefits   Market conditions may necessitate including fringe benefits as a consideration within this formula. Fringe benefits include paid vacations, sick days, and health insurance, for example.

Including fringe benefits within the formula will always result in a greater hourly wage rate. The wage rate is a base amount that the property owner pays the laborer per hour; benefits are then added on to the wage rate, which may increase the hourly wage rate by 25 percent or even as much as 100 percent.

Fixed Percentage Increases

A fixed-percentage increase is another approach to rent escalation. During lease negotiations, landlord and tenant agree on a fixed percentage that is applied annually to the fixed rent. The formula is as follows:

> Annual fixed rent increase = Fixed annual rent × Annual percentage increase

For example, assume a fixed annual rent of $10,000 and that the landlord and tenant agree on an annual percentage increase of 3 percent:

> Annual fixed rent increase = $10,000 × 0.03 = $300

The increase is $300 for the year, so the new rent is $10,300. This represents a cumulative or compounded increase.

Consumer Price Index (CPI)

The *consumer price index* (CPI) is an index that acts as a measure of the purchasing power of the U.S. dollar as it relates to the purchase of a basket of goods, services, and products. It is also used to measure the rise or fall in the rate of inflation. The CPI is published monthly by the Bureau of Labor Statistics. There are many versions of the CPI, for example, All Urban Consumers, Urban Wage Earners/Clerical Workers, and All Cities.

All Urban Consumers covers consumer issues, whereas Urban Wage Earners/Clerical Workers includes salaried workers, self-employed/independent contractors, and other categories. The All Cities index takes into account national trends for approximately 30 major cities. There are other indexes, but these three are the most common.

CPI was originally introduced into lease escalation for the purpose of dollar value preservation. Because of inflation, we can assume that today's dollar is always worth more than tomorrow's dollar. In order to preserve the investment's bottom line against the ravages of inflation, owners felt that it made sense to apply the CPI as a step toward income preservation. They were comfortable that periodic increases in rent would act as a hedge against increasing costs of operating expenses. They anticipated that, as long as inflation remained controlled, the cost of operating expenses would follow suit. Should inflation rise at a faster pace, the property owner was hedged against the financial exposure through the CPI rent pass-through.

FIGURE 21.7

Formula for Consumer Price Index Rent Adjustments

Step 1: Determine the percentage change in the CPI over the base month or year
Percentage change in CPI = (CPI adjustment – Base period) ÷ Base month or year
Step 2: Determine the corresponding rent increase
Rent increase = Annual rent × Percentage change in CPI

Also through the use of this index to rent escalation, owners were able to avoid opening their books to tenants and avoid disputes over annual expenses for their properties.

The CPI is calculated by examining current monthly index figures as they relate to the previous monthly index figures. Periods used in commercial leases range from monthly, quarterly, semiannually, or annual adjustments. When calculating the CPI, one would derive the increased percentage change by examining the previous month's figures. Unlike direct operating that utilizes a base year for the calculation, CPI is published monthly. Therefore, the ownership's bookkeeping practices will dictate whether to apply a monthly, quarterly, semiannual, or annual adjustment. (See Figure 21.7.)

■ SUMMARY

Like stocks and bonds, real property is a vehicle used to house cash flow. Cash flow equates to investor returns. Rates of return are measured by a variety of risk factors that the investor is exposed to; the higher the risk, the greater the reward sought by that investor.

When acquiring income-producing property, the investor must understand the importance of the various formulas used to analyze cash flow. Determining the net operating income of a property enables the investor to capitalize the income to derive an appropriate purchase price. After acquisition, the investor is faced with other property decisions, specifically, whether to hold the property, sell the property, or refinance the debt.

During the holding period, the commercial property owner negotiates and enters into leases with commercial tenants. Both landlord and tenant come to the negotiating table with one thought in mind: achieving the very best deal they can make. Tenants should have an understanding of the various rent escalation clauses used in these types of transactions. The licensee is challenged with learning the intricacies of all types of rent escalations and their effects on a given transaction. The mere understanding of the definition of each clause is not enough. It is critical to also understand the accounting process and each clause's impact on the overall transaction.

CHAPTER 21 QUIZ

1. An estimation and projection of how much net operating income will be available through a property's income and expenses activities in any future periods is the investor's
   a. operating report.
   b. capitalization report.
   c. cash flow statement.
   d. pro forma statement.

2. Which event demonstrates capital risk in the ownership of an apartment building?
   a. A fire in the laundry room causes smoke damage to two apartments.
   b. The owner is not able to sell the building quickly enough to take advantage of another investment opportunity.
   c. Overbuilding in the community causes a drop in demand for rental units.
   d. Rising interest rates make it impossible for an owner to secure an affordable loan.

3. Long-term ground leases are used when the land for a project
   a. contains environmental hazards.
   b. cannot be purchased.
   c. is owned by the government.
   d. has not been zoned for the planned use.

4. The tax world for investment property establishes the tax consequences resulting from a property's income operations, which establish a property's
   a. book value.
   b. cash flow.
   c. leverage.
   d. rate of return.

5. Net operating income can be defined as the cash flow attributable to the property after deducting all operational property-related expenses but before deducting any federal income taxes or
   a. maintenance expenses.
   b. management fees.
   c. debt service.
   d. utilities.

6. Income attributable to a property after deductions have been made for vacancy and collection losses and after adding in other income derived from the property is called the property's
   a. potential gross income.
   b. effective gross income.
   c. net operating income.
   d. taxable income.

7. Operating expenses associated with income property include fixed expenses, variable expenses, and
   a. losses.
   b. unanticipated expenses.
   c. taxes.
   d. reserves for replacements.

8. Fixed expenses are expenses that do NOT vary as a result of a property's
   a. tax status.
   b. location.
   c. occupancy rate.
   d. leverage.

9. For a real estate investor, the use of borrowed funds is called
   a. depreciation.
   b. debt service.
   c. liquidity.
   d. leverage.

10. Which item is subtracted from net operating income when calculating income taxes on investment property?
    a. Annual depreciation
    b. Other income
    c. Unspent reserves
    d. Management fees

11. In New York, the dollar-per-square-foot base rent charged on a property is expressed as a(n)
    a. weekly basis.
    b. monthly basis.
    c. semiannual basis.
    d. annual basis.

12. The difference between the usable area and the rentable area of commercial property is called the

   a. loss factor.
   b. depreciation.
   c. passive space.
   d. dead area.

13. An add-on factor is sometimes used to represent each tenant's proportionate share of

   a. vacancy loss.
   b. utility or water/sewer surcharges.
   c. common area maintenance charges.
   d. annual lease-rate increase.

14. A natural break/break-even point is likely to be included in a

   a. percentage lease.
   b. gross lease.
   c. net lease.
   d. loft lease.

15. A landlord will only accept a rent payment from the party that is named in the lease section called

   a. assignment.
   b. attornment.
   c. negotiability.
   d. assumption.

16. Porter's wage is a form of

   a. reserve.
   b. labor contract.
   c. tax shelter.
   d. lease escalation.

CHAPTER 22

Property Management

■ KEY TERMS

anchor stores
boiler and machinery insurance
business interruption insurance
capital expenses
casualty insurance
Certified Property Manager (CPM)
contents and personal property insurance
corrective maintenance
Division of Housing and Community Renewal (DHCR)
fiduciary
fire and hazard insurance
general agent
household income
industrial property

lessee
lessor
liability insurance
management agreement
management proposal
market analysis
maximum base rent (MBR)
multiperil policies
neighborhood analysis
office property
operating budget
planned unit development
preventive maintenance
primary residence
property analysis
property maintenance
property management reports

property manager
regional analysis
rent control
rent roll
rent stabilization
replacement cost
residential property
retail property
risk management
Section 8
security deposit
stabilized budget
surety bonds
tenancy for years
variable expense
workers' compensation acts

■ PROPERTY MANAGEMENT

In recent years, the increased size of buildings; the technical complexities of construction, maintenance, and repair; and the trend toward absentee ownership by individual investors and investment groups have led to the expanded use of professional property managers for both residential and commercial properties. The Department of Housing and Urban Development (HUD) maintains a useful Web site at *http://portal.hud.gov/hudportal/HUD?src=/groups/landlords*.

Property management has become so important that some brokerage firms maintain separate management departments. Many corporations that own real estate have also established property management departments. Many real estate investors manage their own property, however, and must acquire the knowledge and skills of a property manager.

Although the license law allows an exception for those salaried employees who work for one employer alone, in other instances property managers must hold real estate licenses. Any person or entity that performs property management services on behalf of another must be licensed as a real estate broker. In Chapter 1, we learned that *collection of rents* is an activity that requires a broker's license. Any salaried employee within the employ of a broker need not hold a real estate license to assist in the disposition of the broker's responsibilities to a property owner.

Property managers may look to corporate owners, apartment and condominium associations, homeowners' associations, investment syndicates, trusts, and absentee owners as possible sources of management business.

If you are a real estate management company, you may or may not need a real estate broker's license, depending on the services you provide. If you collect rent or place tenants in vacant spaces on behalf of your landlord client, you need a broker's license because you are acting as a fiduciary (handling other people's money). If your services are strictly maintenance, you do not need a real estate broker's license.

■ THE PROPERTY MANAGER

A **property manager** does more than just find tenants and collect rents. A property manager's job is to maximize income while maintaining the value of the property.

Thus, the property manager is closely involved in a variety of activities related to generating income, including budgeting, market analysis, advertising, and negotiating leases.

Because it is important that the value of the property be maintained or enhanced as well, the manager is also involved in property maintenance, security supervision, and insurance evaluation.

A property manager may be an individual, a part of a property management firm, or a member of a real estate firm. The property manager also may be in charge of managing corporate-owned property or work for a trust.

In addition, the working relationship between a property manager/firm (as the case may be) and the property owner falls into the category of a *general agent*. A **general agent** is one who is authorized by a principal to represent the principal in a specific range of matters. As a general agent, the property manager/firm is also called a *fiduciary*. A **fiduciary** is one in whom the highest form of trust and confidence is placed, such as a reference to a broker employed under the terms of a listing contract or buyer agency agreement. (See Chapter 2.)

■ TYPES OF PROPERTY THAT ARE MANAGED

Property can be divided into five major categories for management purposes:

1. Residential property (including condominiums, cooperatives, and subsidized housing)
2. Office property
3. Retail property
4. Industrial property
5. Planned unit development

Residential Property

Residential property includes any type of property that is used for dwelling space. Both single-family homes and multifamily residences can be managed by a professional property manager, although the management of multifamily properties is more common. Multifamily residences include garden apartments, walkup buildings, highrise complexes, cooperatives, and condominiums. Multifamily residences may have a live-in *resident manager*.

Office Property

Office property includes lowrise buildings, highrise complexes, and office or business parks. The ownership and occupancy of office property varies widely, from one owner-occupant to a multitude of individual tenants with a single, nonoccupant owner. Some office properties attract certain types of tenants, such as medical professionals, financial consultants, and so forth. Office properties can be found in both urban areas and suburban areas.

Retail Property

Retail property comes in a wide range, from freestanding buildings to traditional shopping centers. Shopping centers come in many different sizes, including strip centers, neighborhood centers, community centers, regional shopping centers, and super-regional malls. Discount and factory outlet shopping centers also are becoming increasingly common.

Industrial Property

Industrial property is defined as all land and facilities used for manufacturing and the storage and shipment of goods. Industrial property may be a large, individually owned and occupied property or a large industrial park with several tenants.

Planned Unit Development

A **planned unit development** is a planned combination of diverse land uses, such as housing, recreation, and shopping, in one contained development or subdivision.

◼ THE MANAGEMENT AGREEMENT

The first step in taking over the management of any property is to enter into a management agreement with the owner. A **management agreement** is a contract or working agreement between the owner of income property and a management firm or individual property manager that outlines the scope of the manager's authority. This agreement creates an agency relationship between the owner and the property manager. A property manager usually is considered a *general agent*, whereas a real estate broker under a listing agreement usually is considered a *special agent*. As agent, the property manager is charged with the usual fiduciary duties.

The management agreement should be in writing and should cover the following points:

> **A management plan includes the following:**
>
> 1. Market analysis
> 2. Operating budget
> 3. Financing proposals
> 4. Recommendations for managing a property

- *Identification of the parties.* The name of the owner of the property should appear in the agreement just as it does on the deed to the property. If the owner is a partnership, each partner should sign the contract. If the owner is a corporation, a duly authorized officer of the corporation must sign the contract.
- *Description of the property.* Typically, the street address of the property is sufficient, but it is always wise to use a legal description in real estate documents. It is important that the contract be clear on the extent of the property to be managed. For instance, if an office building is the subject of the management agreement but the building contains a coffee shop that is to be managed separately, that exclusion should be carefully noted.
- *Time period the agreement will be in force.* The length of the term is purely a matter of negotiation between the parties. Property owners generally want a shorter time, to allow them to seek other management if they are not satisfied with the current arrangements. On the other hand, property managers usually insist on a contract term that is long enough to make all the extra work required during the initial start-up period worthwhile. One year is usually the minimum time. It is also a good idea to include provisions for canceling or renewing the agreement on proper notice.
- *Definition of management's responsibilities.* All duties should be stated, and exceptions should be noted. The manager's responsibilities include preparing monthly earnings statements (itemizing income and expenses) and making the necessary disbursements to keep the property operating smoothly. It is important to detail what will happen if the property's account does not contain enough funds to cover the required disbursements.

- *Extent of manager's authority as an agent.* This provision should state what authority the manager is to have in such matters as hiring, firing, and supervising employees; fixing rental rates for space; making expenditures; and authorizing repairs within certain limits.
- *Owner's responsibilities.* The owner's responsibilities need to be as clearly defined as the manager's. For instance, is the owner responsible for maintaining proper insurance? The owner also should be responsible for providing the manager with a list of monthly payments, including debt service, taxes, and special assessments.
- *Reporting.* Frequent detailed **property management reports** allow the owner to monitor the manager's work and serve as a basis for planning policy.
- *Management fee.* The fee can be based on a percentage of gross or net income, a commission on new rentals, a fixed fee, or a combination of these. A fixed fee is often to the manager's disadvantage, because a new fee must be negotiated with the owner before the fee is increased, no matter how much work the manager is completing. A percentage fee will increase if the manager is effective in generating income from the property and decrease if the property's income decreases. A minimum guaranteed fee plus a percentage guarantees the manager at least a certain amount per unit to reimburse the manager for spending time on jobs that do not necessarily increase revenues immediately.
- *Allocation of costs.* The agreement should state which of the property management expenses, such as custodial and other help, advertising, supplies, and repairs, are to be paid by the owner.

■ FUNCTIONS OF THE PROPERTY MANAGER

Property management can be broken down into two necessary functions: operations and financial reporting.

Operations

Operations entails the day-to-day running of the property. These responsibilities consist of interior and exterior maintenance. Interior maintenance includes maintenance of mechanical equipment such as elevators and heating, ventilating, and air-conditioning (HVAC) systems. In addition to maintenance of the mechanicals, interior maintenance includes common-area maintenance (CAM) and janitorial services in office buildings.

Exterior maintenance includes items such as exterior façade maintenance and restoration, preventative maintenance, repairs, and procedural inspections as required by local laws. For example, in New York City, buildings that exceed 75 feet in height are required to comply with local law 10/11 (façade maintenance and restoration). Also included in exterior maintenance are sidewalk maintenance and repair, landscaping, and repaving and restripping of parking facilities.

A property manager preserves the value of an investment property while generating income as an agent for the owners. A property manager is expected to merchandise the property and control operating expenses to maximize income. A manager should maintain and modernize the property to preserve and enhance the owner's capital investment. The manager carries out these objectives by securing suitable tenants, collecting rents, caring for the premises, and hiring and supervising employees.

Rent Roll

Rental income-producing property   In the sale of multifamily dwellings and other income-producing properties, the seller should be ready to present a reconstructed statement of income and expenses, preferably prepared by an accountant. A **rent roll** should show the name of each tenant, amount of rent, expiration date of each lease, and amount of security deposits. (See Figure 22.1.)

Financial Reporting

Financial reporting involves budgeting and controlling operating expenses, which are expenses that are considered a part of daily operations; keeping

F I G U R E   22.1

Rent Roll

Project Address				
Name of tenant	Unit number	Amount of rent	Expiration date of lease	Security deposit

proper accounts; reporting income and expense activity; and conducting income analysis.

The income and expense activity reported (usually according to schedules outlined in the management agreement) generally includes these items: amounts collected in rents and additional rents, delinquent rents, monthly expenses of the property, cash reserve positions (funds used to perform unanticipated major capital improvements), and upcoming vacancies.

The income analysis generally includes a discounted cash flow analysis to determine returns on invested capital, refinance opportunities and timing, and whether to continue holding the property or sell; cash-on-cash returns (equity dividend rate); and internal rate of return analysis.

■ PLANNING AND BUDGETING

Based on the needs of ownership, one of the first things a property manager does when a property management agreement is signed (and sometimes even before a property management agreement is signed) is to develop a **management proposal**. A management proposal includes, at the minimum, a market analysis, an operating budget, financing proposals, and recommendations as to how the property should be managed. (See Figure 22.2.)

Market Analysis

The **market analysis** includes a regional analysis, a neighborhood analysis, and a property analysis.

The purpose of the market analysis is to give the manager information about the local economic conditions, the supply of and demand for similar properties in the neighborhood, and the competitiveness of other properties that are similar to the property to be managed.

F I G U R E   22.2

Management Proposal

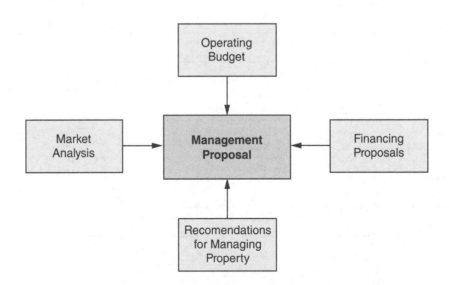

Regional analysis   A **regional analysis** includes economic and demographic information about the regional or metropolitan area in which the property is located.

For example, the regional analysis may include figures on local wage levels, employment levels, major employers, population trends, and the availability of transportation and government services. All of these separate pieces of information are used to derive a clear picture of the local economy. Essentially, the property manager is seeking the answer to the question, Is there a healthy demand for this type of property in this regional or metropolitan area?

Neighborhood analysis   A **neighborhood analysis** is similar to the regional analysis in its focus on economic factors, government services, demographics, and transportation.

However, a neighborhood analysis focuses on the local rather than the regional level. Generally speaking, property management activities take place on a local, or neighborhood, level, so it is important to be familiar with neighborhood trends. A neighborhood usually is defined as an area with limits defined by some natural or artificial boundaries, such as major arterial thoroughfares, a body of water, or a type of land use.

Sometimes, a neighborhood is only a few square blocks; sometimes, it is a few square miles.

The health of a neighborhood's economy can be measured by several factors: the number and types of businesses in the area, growth trends, wage levels, the property tax base, and current rental and occupancy rates.

Obviously, areas that contain well-diversified businesses, have low vacancy rates and high rents, and are experiencing growth are more economically healthy than neighborhoods that are experiencing the opposite trends. A property manager generally will have an easier time finding and keeping tenants in economically prosperous neighborhoods.

The presence of government and utility services is important. Adequate fire and police protection, well-maintained roads, and the easy availability of electricity, gas, water, and a sewage disposal system are all necessary to attract both residential and office tenants. Transportation also is important. A neighborhood served by good arterial roads, highways, or freeways; bus or train travel; or other means of transportation tends to be valued more highly by tenants. Good transportation makes commuting to and from work and places of entertainment easier for residential tenants, makes the transportation of goods and services easier for industrial and office tenants, and makes shopping access easier for retail tenants.

Especially for residential tenants, extra amenities that can be found in the neighborhood also are important. For example, convenient access to parks, schools, restaurants, playgrounds, theaters, and places of worship are all important to potential tenants.

Special attention should be paid to vacancy rates for similar properties in the neighborhood. Not only do vacancy (or occupancy) rates indicate the economic climate in the neighborhood, they also reflect the supply of and demand for similar properties in the neighborhood. Supply and demand has a tremendous impact on the rental levels that can be charged for the subject property. For example, an oversupply of rental space means a high vacancy rate and probably a demand for lower rates. On the other hand, an undersupply of rental space usually translates into low vacancy rates and rent increases.

Property analysis   Examining the region and the neighborhood gives property managers a good idea of the economic climate and the supply of and demand for similar types of properties. From the information gathered, property managers also should be able to tell what the optimum rental rates are for competitive space in the neighborhood. This information is usually derived by conducting a neighborhood analysis (as it relates to the subject property).

At this point, property managers need to turn their attention to the subject property itself. Property managers must determine how the subject property compares with competitive properties. Is the subject property in a stronger or a weaker position than competing properties to attract tenants?

In the **property analysis**, property managers examine the terms of each tenant's existing lease, the quantity and quality of the rentable space, and the physical condition of the property itself.

As property managers study existing leases, they are gauging the amount and durability of the rental income. Managers also examine lease renewal rates for the building (tenant turnover), vacancy rate, and bad debt rate.

These elements help determine whether tenant relations are managed wisely and whether the rental rate is right for the current market.

Curb appeal—the building's overall appearance—is one of the more important elements the manager studies. Curb appeal includes the building's age, design, and condition.

Managers also check the interior space, including measuring the total amount of rentable space in commercial property or the number of units in residential property; the layout; and the hardware and fixtures (such as carpeting and plumbing).

The physical condition of all aspects of the property is inspected in light of housekeeping and maintenance requirements.

Part of the property analysis includes studying the features of comparable properties in the neighborhood to determine how the subject property measures up. If the subject property has less curb appeal and higher tenant turnover than competing properties, this may mean that maintenance has been ignored in the past, that current rental rates are too high, or that tenant services are lacking.

Owner objectives   After property managers have analyzed a region, neighborhood, and subject property, they will probably analyze the *goals of the owner*. Those goals may vary from maximizing income or cash flow to increasing the value of the property. It is the manager's job to put the owner's goals into concrete terms so that the management plan can reflect those goals (and the manager can more easily achieve them).

Budgeting

An important part of the planning stage includes preparing a *detailed operating budget*. A property manager should develop an **operating budget** based on anticipated revenues and expenses and reflecting the long-term goals of the owner. (See Figure 22.3.) The goal and purpose is to ultimately achieve a stabilized budget. While a budget relates to a project's operational expenses, a **stabilized budget** is when the budgeted/allocated funds used to cover operating expenses remain constant for a period of time.

The manager begins by allocating money for continuous fixed expenses such as real property taxes and insurance premiums. Next, the manager establishes a *capital reserve budget* for such variable expenses as employees' salaries, repairs, decorating, and supplies. A **variable expense** is the property expenses that vary according to the occupancy level, such as supplies, water, and any management fees that are tied to the amount of rent collected.

The amount allocated for the reserve fund can be computed from the previous yearly costs of variable expenses.

If an owner and a property manager decide that modernization or renovation of the property will enhance its value, the manager should budget money to cover the costs of remodeling, which are called **capital expenses**. The manager should be thoroughly familiar with the principle of contribution (an improvement is only worth the additional value it adds to the property, not its cost) or seek expert

FIGURE   22.3

Operating Budget

Income			
	3 studio @ $2,000/month	× 12 months	$72,000
	6 one-bedroom @ $3,500/month	× 12 months	$252,000
	3 two-bedroom @ $5,000/month	× 12 months	$180,000
	Total anticipated income		$504,000
Expenses	Real estate taxes		$59,500
	Salaries		$15,000
	Insurance		$6,000
	Utilities		$5,000
	Administrative		$1,200
	Repairs		$1,000
	Supplies		$800
			$88,500
Capital expenses (remodeling, upgrading property)			+ $5,000
Total expenses			$93,500
Income			$504,000
Expenses			− $93,500
Cash flow			$410,500

advice when estimating any increase in value expected from an improvement. In the case of large-scale construction, the expenses charged against the property's income should be spread over several years. Although budgets should be as accurate an estimate of cost as possible, adjustments may sometimes be necessary, especially in the case of new properties.

■ MARKETING

One of the first steps a property manager must take when beginning to manage a new property is to develop a marketing proposal. Unless a property is effectively marketed, well-qualified tenants will be difficult to find and existing tenants will fail to renew their leases.

Marketing plans vary widely, depending on the type of property that is being managed. Obviously, a property manager will develop an entirely different marketing plan for residential property than for industrial property. However, some marketing principles apply to any type of property. First, property managers must be thoroughly acquainted with the property they are trying to market. The property's features, as well as the property's layout, should be known and noted. Managers must be familiar with the property's strengths as well as its weaknesses. And managers should make sure the property is "prepared" for the marketing effort—that is, that the space is clean and in good condition.

Another marketing principle that property managers should be aware of is that satisfied tenants are the best, most cost-effective way to market the property. Happy tenants give good referrals and can often supply names of other prospective tenants.

Marketing Activities

A successful marketing plan includes both advertising/promotional efforts and person-to-person selling. Property managers must be able to engage effectively in all three types of activities. (See Figure 22.4.)

Advertising The way in which a property manager advertises property depends a great deal on the type of property. Residential, commercial, and industrial properties draw tenants from different sectors of the public. Furthermore, new properties are often advertised in a different manner from established concerns. For example, a newly completed large apartment complex needs to find hundreds of new tenants at the same time, whereas an existing apartment complex needs to find only replacement tenants on an ongoing basis.

Several media vehicles can be effectively used to market rental space, including the Internet, signs, newspaper advertising, periodicals, radio and television, and direct mail. Most advertising plans combine one or more of these media. This does not mean that a manager should solely depend on media vehicles in the lease-up of the property. Direct canvassing by phone or visiting prospective tenants located in other neighboring properties can also be extremely effective. Promotional parties to preview office spaces or open houses on new listings are effective as well.

FIGURE   22.4

Marketing Plan

Marketing Plan (Residential)

Business Name:

Address:

I. Features of the Property
A. List unique features of the property (for example):
Skylights
Loft
Multistory elevator building
Furnished unit
B. Layout of the property:
Square footage _____
C. Property's strengths and weaknesses:

Strengths	Weaknesses
1. _____	1. _____
2. _____	2. _____
3. _____	3. _____
4. _____	4. _____

II. Marketing Activities (Select the most relevant methods for this property)
A. Advertising:
Internet
Signage (curb appeal)
Newspaper advertising
Periodicals
Radio
Television
Direct mail
B. Promotions:
Press release
Prepare presentations for special interest groups
Volunteer/share professional expertise
C. Selecting tenants:
Qualify prospective tenants
Tenant's space needs
Price range
Required improvements
Create interest and desire for tenants
Tour exterior and interior of the space
Be able to describe property's special features and benefits
Be prepared to address any potential questions or objections

Signs that identify the management firm for the building and the contact person should be placed outside residential, office, and retail properties. When space is currently available, For Rent signs describing the type of space can be posted outside the building or in vacant store windows. Billboards are sometimes used for large industrial or commercial properties.

Newspaper advertising is perhaps the most commonly used medium. Classified advertisements are used for residential properties, and the larger display ads are used for large residential complexes and sometimes retail or office space. Regional periodicals and other publications are used to advertise large residential and retail properties. Many newspapers also post their classified ads on the Internet.

Radio advertising sometimes is used for large residential, commercial, and industrial properties. Its major disadvantage is that radio audiences cannot be targeted very effectively; there are likely to be few potential tenants among the listeners. The same is true for television, with the added disadvantage that television advertising is costly.

Direct mail can be used effectively for some industrial and commercial properties. Well-tailored mailing lists often can be obtained for likely prospects, so direct marketing can be targeted to an appreciative audience. Of course, the direct mail pieces must look professional. Brochures often are developed for large residential, commercial, and industrial properties and are given to prospects who actually inquire about available space. Distributing flyers to the brokers in one's area can provide immediate awareness of upcoming vacancies or sales as well.

Promotions *Promotional efforts* include any activities that serve to improve the reputation of the building and increase its desirability to tenants. For example, the property manager may speak in front of various interest groups, offer to share professional expertise, prepare press releases and send them to various local publications, and send news releases to real estate sections of newspapers or real estate journals. Promotional activities generally translate into free advertising, which is why they can be so valuable to a property manager.

Selecting tenants This aspect of marketing involves the responses of the property manager or management staff to a prospective tenant. The manager or employee needs expert selling skills to deal effectively with qualifying the prospect, creating interest, dealing with objections, and negotiating and closing the agreement.

Qualifying the prospect includes determining the prospective tenant's space needs, price range, parking needs, and required improvements. In selecting commercial or industrial tenants, a manager should be sure that each tenant will "fit the space." The manager should be certain that the size of the space meets the tenant's requirements; the tenant will have the ability to pay for the space for which it contracts; the tenant's business will be compatible with the building and the other tenants; and if the tenant is likely to expand in the future, expansion space will be available.

If the tenant's needs coincide with the available space, the manager can move to the next step, creating interest and desire on the tenant's part. Note that it is a waste of time and money to try to interest a tenant in available space when it will not suit that tenant's needs. The tenant either will reject the space or will sign a lease but vacate the premises before the end of the lease term.

In selecting tenants, the property manager must comply with all federal and local fair housing laws. Tenants with handicaps must be allowed to make appropriate modifications at their own expense if they agree to return the property to its original state when they leave.

Creating interest and desire is largely a matter of describing the property's special features and benefits while showing the prospect the building. Taking a tour of both the exterior and interior of the building and of both the rentable space and the common areas is advisable. Any questions the prospect may have about the space should be answered promptly, and objections should be dealt with persuasively. Once all answers have been given and objections resolved, the manager then moves to the negotiation and closing stage of marketing. Getting the tenant to sign on the dotted line is, naturally, the prime objective of marketing. After a prospect becomes a tenant, the manager must be sure that the tenant remains satisfied.

■ MANAGING LEASES AND TENANT RELATIONS

The manager who has moved through the marketing stages and found rental prospects then must attend to managing leases and tenant relations.

Renting the Property

The role of the manager in managing a property should not be confused with that of a broker acting as a leasing agent and solely concerned with renting space. If the property management company does not engage in leasing activities, the property manager may enlist the services of a leasing agent, but that agent does not undertake the full responsibility of maintaining and managing the property.

For low-income or moderate-income residential rentals, managers and owners may want to consider participating in the FHA's **Section 8** program. Qualified tenants pay no more than 30 percent of their income in rent, with HUD carrying the rest. The property must meet certain standards.

Setting rental rates   A basic concern in establishing rental rates is that income from the rentable space must cover the fixed charges and operating expenses and also provide a fair return on the investment. Consideration also must be given to prevailing rates in comparable buildings and the current level of vacancy in the property to be rented—supply and demand. Following a detailed survey of the competitive space available in the neighborhood, prices should be adjusted for differences between neighboring properties and the property being managed. Annual rent adjustments are often warranted.

As discussed in Chapter 7, rent can be calculated in at least four different ways:

1. With a *net lease*, the tenant pays not only rent but also some or all of the property charges.
2. With a *triple-net lease*, the tenant pays everything (taxes, repairs, insurance, and everything except any mortgage charges).
3. The tenant on a *percentage lease* pays a fixed rent plus a certain share of the tenant's income (for example, store sale's receipts) over a *natural break* figure.
4. With residential property, most rents are on a *gross lease* basis, with the landlord bearing all property charges except, in some cases, utilities.

Office and commercial space rentals are usually quoted according to the annual rate per square foot of space leased. The lease/leases that are entered into by the landlord and tenant most probably will fall under the category of a tenancy for years. A **tenancy for years** refers to a less-than-freehold estate (or tenancy) in which the property is leased for a definite, fixed period, whether 60 days, any fraction of a year, a year, or ten years. In most states, such a tenancy can be created only by express agreement, which should be written if the tenancy is longer than one year. The tenancy for years must have a definite term, beginning and ending on dates specified in the lease. In the absence of a statute or agreement, the tenancy is considered personal property and passes to the tenant's heirs on his or her death. The tenancy ends on the last day of the term of the lease with no need for the parties to give notice of termination. If the tenant continues in possession, he or she is a *holdover tenant* or a *tenant at sufferance*. Most ground leases and commercial leases are tenancies for years.

If a high level of vacancy exists, an immediate effort should be made to determine why. *A high level of vacancy does not necessarily indicate that rents are too high.* The trouble may be inept management or defects in the property. Conversely, *a high percentage of occupancy might indicate an effective rental program, but it could also mean that rental rates are too low.* With an apartment house or office building, whenever the occupancy level exceeds 90 to 95 percent, serious consideration should be given to raising rents.

Negotiating Leases

A lease is a contract, and like any other contract, it must satisfy certain requirements to be valid. These requirements include competent parties, consideration, offer and acceptance, and a lawful purpose. Many leases also must be in writing, according to the provisions of the statute of frauds.

Leases also must contain a description of the property, the amount of rent and additional rent (i.e., utility charges), when it is due, the term of the lease, the use of the premises, and the rights and obligations of each party.

Typically, the tenant's main obligation is the prompt payment of rent. The lease usually provides for a late penalty if the rental payment is paid after a certain date and termination of the lease if the rent remains unpaid after proper notice by the landlord.

In addition, under a lease agreement, the tenant is referred to as the lessee. A **lessee** is the person/tenant to whom property is rented or leased. The landlord is referred to as the lessor. A **lessor** is the person/landlord who rents or leases property to another.

Security deposits usually are required. Security deposits protect the landlord from tenant default. They are available to the landlord should the tenant fail to pay accrued rent or should the tenant damage the property (beyond normal wear and tear). Security deposits should be held in a separate account, and if the deposit is required to be held in an interest-bearing account, the tenant is entitled to all but 1 percent of the interest earned on the deposit. The 1 percent may be retained by the owner as an *administrative charge* to act toward compensation for managing the account. It should be noted that a security deposit can be posted by a tenant via personal guarantee, cash deposit, or letter of credit (LC).

In commercial office lease transactions, landlords prefer instruments such as letters of credit (a letter of credit is issued by the tenant's bank for a credit amount representing the cash value of the security deposit) over cash deposits. This is due to federal laws that govern bankruptcy. By law, in a bankruptcy, unexpired leases are considered executory contracts (not fully executed or performed). As a result, cash deposits held by a landlord can be attached by creditors of the bankrupt party or entity. A letter of credit, on the other hand, is originated by a chartered federal institution.

Tenants usually are also required to

- comply with local laws and regulations (such as land-use laws and health and safety codes),
- seek permission before altering or improving the property, and
- remove personal property on vacating the premises.

Landlords generally are required to maintain the common areas and guarantee the tenant's "quiet enjoyment" of the premises. Quiet enjoyment becomes a confused issue. It does not mean peace and quiet; it is a title issue that suggests that as long as the tenant complies with the financial and legal terms contained within the lease, the tenancy will not be disturbed. That is, the tenant has exclusive possession of the premises, and the landlord may gain entrance only for certain purposes with the proper notice or in emergency situations.

Other lease provisions may address items such as the following:

- Possession of the premises
- Rental rate adjustments
- Tax and insurance requirements
- Subordination requirements
- Condemnation
- Assignment and subletting
- Fire and casualty damage

One of the most important elements involved with managing leases is negotiating tenant alterations and tenant concessions. The property manager must maintain a proper balance between flexibility and practicality. While managers want to offer tenants the proper incentives to enter into a lease, they also must keep the "bottom line" in mind and not enter into a transaction that is not in the ultimate best interests of the property owner. Some concessions commonly made to tenants are tenant improvement construction allowances, free rent, and reimbursement of moving expenses. Additional considerations might include expansion options (guaranteeing the tenant the option to lease additional space), rights of first refusal, or renewal options.

Collecting Rents

Once the tenant has signed the lease and moved onto the premises, a major responsibility of the manager becomes lease administration and rent collection. The best way to minimize problems with rent collection is to make a *careful selection* of tenants in the first place. A desire for a high level of occupancy should not override good judgment. A property manager should investigate annual reports for public companies, financial references of individuals, local credit bureaus, and, when possible, the prospective tenant's former landlord.

The terms of rental payment should be spelled out in detail in the lease agreement. A *firm and consistent collection plan* with a sufficient system of notices and records should be established. In cases of delinquency, every attempt must be made to make collections without resorting to legal action. When it is required, a property manager must be prepared to initiate and follow through with legal counsel.

Tenants' Rights

New York's Multiple Dwelling Law, in effect in New York City and Buffalo, sets the following requirements for buildings with three or more living units: automatic self-closing and self-locking doors, two-way voice buzzers (for buildings with *eight or more* units), mirrors in each self-service elevator, and peepholes and chain door-guards on the entrance door of each apartment.

Tenants may install their own additional locks but must provide the landlord with a duplicate key on request. Heat must be provided from October 1 to May 31. Additional regulations apply in various communities.

Postal regulations require that landlords of buildings with three or more units provide secure mailboxes. *Smoke and carbon monoxide detectors* always are required. In New York City, tenants with children younger than 11 must receive *window guards* on request. Protective guards also must be installed on all public hall windows. In addition, as of September 2010, New York City has passed a new law concerning bedbug disclosure (discussed in Chapter 3).

Throughout the state, landlords of buildings with three or more apartments are specifically required to keep apartments and public areas in good repair and keep electrical, plumbing, sanitary, heating, and ventilation systems in good working order. Landlords also must maintain appliances that are furnished to tenants. Landlords have a legal duty to keep buildings free of vermin, dirt, and garbage. Under the federal lead-paint disclosure law, landlords as well as real estate licensees also have the duty to inform their tenants of hazards posed by lead-based paint. For landlords, failure to do so can result in fines. A licensee's failure to do so will subject the licensee to disciplinary action with DOS as well as civil fines.

A landlord may enter the tenant's apartment only with reasonable prior notice, to provide repairs or service in accordance with the lease or to show the apartment to prospective tenants or purchasers. The landlord may enter without prior permission only in an *emergency*.

Tenants who are disabled have the right to make alterations to improve accessibility at their own expense. Landlord may not charge such tenants more rent or a larger security deposit but may require that the tenants post a bond to ensure that the property is restored as much as is necessary on vacating.

Mobile home park tenants must be offered at least a one-year written lease. If they do not have leases, they are entitled to 90 days' written notice before rent increases. Rules must not be changed without 30 days' written notice. Rules must be posted conspicuously or a copy given to each tenant who moves in. Late rent payment charges are limited to 5 percent after a ten-day grace period.

Mobile home park tenants, whether they own or rent the home itself, are governed by the same rules as any other tenants with regard to security deposits, subleasing, sharing space, eviction, and related matters. (In New York, a mobile home is not considered real property unless it is permanently affixed to the land on a foundation.)

Owners may not discriminate against mobile home tenants with children and may not charge extra for children. Owners have the right to sell their homes within the park with the consent of the park owner, which consent may not be unreasonably withheld. Park owners may not require any fee or commission in connection with the sale of a mobile home unless they act as sales agents pursuant to a written contract. Owners may not foster park monopolies.

Owners of mobile home parks with more than two units must register with the New York Division of Housing and Community Renewal (DHCR), which enforces the rights of mobile home tenants in the state.

■ MAINTAINING THE PROPERTY

One of the most important functions of a property manager is the supervision of **property maintenance**. A manager must learn to balance services and costs to satisfy the tenants' needs while minimizing operating expenses. *Maintenance* covers several types of activities. First, the manager must *protect the physical integrity* of the property to ensure that the building and grounds stay in good condition over the long term. Repainting the exterior or replacing the heating system will help keep the building functional and decrease routine maintenance costs.

Preventive maintenance is performed to head off future trouble, as contrasted with **corrective maintenance**, which repairs damage already incurred.

A property manager also must *supervise routine cleaning and repairs* of the building, including cleaning of common areas, minor carpentry and plumbing, and regularly scheduled upkeep of heating, air-conditioning, and landscaping.

In addition, especially when dealing with commercial or industrial space, a property manager will be called on to make tenant improvement alterations to the interior of the building to meet the functional demands of the tenant. These alterations can range from repainting to completely gutting the interior and redesigning the space. Tenant improvements are especially important when renting new buildings because the interior is usually left incomplete so that it can be adapted to the needs of individual tenants (make-ready).

Supervising the modernization or renovation of buildings that have become functionally obsolete and thus unsuited to today's building needs is also important. The renovation of a building often increases the building's marketability and thus its possible income. This was particularly the case in many parts of lower Manhattan after the tragic events of September 11, 2001. Antiquated office buildings that lay vacant were purchased by investors that intended to convert the properties to residential units. The emergence of a residential neighborhood resulted from the conversion and renovation of these properties. Before September 11, 2001, residential living was relatively sparse in that section of Manhattan.

Hiring Employees Versus Contracting for Services

One of the major decisions a property manager faces is whether to contract for maintenance services from an outside firm or hire on-site employees to perform such tasks. This decision should be based on a number of factors, including size of the building, complexity of tenants' requirements, and availability of suitable labor.

■ OWNER RELATIONS, REPORTS, AND INSURANCE

A property manager is an agent of the property owner, and thus must act in a fiduciary capacity. The manager must act in the best interests of the owner and owes the owner the duties of loyalty and good faith.

Owner Relations

When first taking over managing a property, a property manager should begin building a good foundation for effective owner/manager relations immediately. In the planning process, the manager should have learned the owner's goals and developed the management plan accordingly. The manager should have obtained all the necessary vital information about the owner, including the owner's name, address, telephone number, Social Security number, state employment number, and information on the owner's accountant, attorney, and insurance broker. Information about the owner's property financing is also vital. If the property is already operational, current tenant security deposits must be accounted for and long-term accounting procedures established. It also may be necessary for the manager to have the owner set up a working capital fund for operating expenses.

Once the relationship has been established, the manager should go about setting up a procedure for *regular owner contact*. Typically, the major form of communication between the manager and owner is a *monthly earnings report*. This report includes information on receipts, expenses, and cash flow. The report should be accompanied by a personal letter from the manager, enumerating any special concerns or other information that the manager feels the owner should know.

The property manager should quickly get to know how involved each owner wishes to be in the management of his or her property. Some owners want to be very involved and expect frequent communication from the manager.

Insurance Coverage

One of the most important responsibilities of a property manager is to protect the property owner against all major insurable risks. **Risk management** is the evaluation and selection of appropriate property and other insurance. In some cases, a property manager or a member of the management firm may be a licensed insurance broker. To avoid charges of *self-dealing*, the owner should be made aware of the situation and consent to it.

In any case, a competent, reliable insurance agent who is well versed in all areas of insurance pertaining to property should be selected to survey the property and make recommendations. Final decisions, however, must be made by the property owner. *An insurance broker must have passed a state examination to secure a special license to sell insurance.*

Many kinds of insurance coverage are available to income property owners and managers. Some of the more common types include the following:

- *Fire and hazard.* **Fire and hazard insurance** policies provide coverage against direct loss or damage to property from a fire on the premises. Standard fire coverage can be extended to cover hazards such as windstorm, hail, smoke damage, or civil insurrection. Most popular today is the all-risks or special form.
- *Business interruption.* Most hazard policies insure against the actual loss of property but do not cover loss of revenues from income property. **Business interruption insurance** covers the loss of income that occurs if the property cannot be used to produce income.
- *Contents and personal property.* Inland marine insurance, or **contents and personal property insurance**, covers building contents and personal property during periods when they are not actually located on the business premises.
- *Liability.* Public **liability insurance** covers the risks an owner assumes when the public enters the building. Medical expenses are paid for a person injured in the building as a result of landlord negligence. Another liability risk is that of medical or hospital payments for injuries sustained by building employees in the course of their employment. These claims are covered by state laws known as **workers' compensation acts**. These laws require that a building owner who is an employer obtain a workers' compensation policy from a private insurance company.
- *Casualty.* **Casualty insurance** policies include coverage against theft, burglary, vandalism, and machinery damage as well as health and accident. Casualty policies usually are written on specific risks, such as theft, rather than being all-inclusive.
- *Surety bonds.* **Surety bonds** cover an owner against financial losses that result from an employee's criminal acts or negligence while carrying out his or her duties. A blanket crime policy is most often chosen.
- *Boiler and machinery coverage.* **Boiler and machinery insurance** covers repair and replacement of heating plants, central air-conditioning units, and other major equipment.

Lower premiums may be offered on property that qualifies as a *highly protected risk (HPR)*, based on the quality of water supply, sprinklers, alarms, security personnel, and loss control programs. Many insurance companies offer **multiperil policies** for apartment and business buildings. These include standard types of commercial coverage: fire, hazard, public liability, and casualty.

Claims　When a claim is made under a policy insuring a building or other physical object, either of two methods can determine the amount of the claim. One is the depreciated, or actual, cash value of the damaged property; the other is replacement cost. If a 30-year-old building is damaged, the timbers and materials are 30 years old and, therefore, do not have the same value as new material. Thus, in determining the amount of the loss under what is called *actual cash value*, the cost of new material would be reduced by the estimated depreciation, based on the time the item had been in the building.

The alternate method is to cover **replacement cost**. This represents the actual amount a builder would charge to replace the damaged property at the time of the loss, including materials. When purchasing insurance, a manager must assess whether the property should be insured at full replacement cost or at a depreciated cost. As with homeowners' policies, commercial policies usually carry *coinsurance* clauses that require coverage up to 80 percent of the building's replacement value.

Many property managers, faced with filing an insurance claim, call on professional *private adjusters*, who are skilled in representing owners in negotiations with insurers.

■ SKILLS REQUIRED OF A PROPERTY MANAGER

As is evident from the detailed description of a property manager's *functions*, a wide variety of skills are required of a property manager. During their career, property managers will "wear many hats" and be called on to display expertise in a number of areas.

Property managers need to be a *human relations experts* because they handle owner-tenant relations as well as union negotiations on occasion. *Research and planning skills* are required to prepare a marketing plan and perform market analyses. Managers need excellent *accounting skills* to prepare budgets and monthly reports and to help ensure that the owner's income goals are reached. *Marketing skills*, such as advertising, promotional activities, and person-to-person selling skills, are a must to maintain a high occupancy rate. *Negotiating skills* are required for entering into lease agreements. And, of course, the property must be *well maintained*, so managers must know enough about physical operations to see to it that both the exterior and the interior of a building are kept in good condition. Property managers should also have a general knowledge of construction and ecology issues.

In addition, property managers must have skills that include the following:

- An understanding of building systems, such as
    - heating, ventilating, and air-conditioning (HVAC);
    - structural engineering;
    - waterproofing;
    - plumbing;
    - electrical;
    - gas, oil, water, and chiller water;
    - security;
    - maintenance; and
    - elevators
- A working knowledge of local laws
- An understanding of local, state, and national codes and regulations

- Knowledge and/or experience in other areas, such as
  - union negotiations,
  - real estate appraisal,
  - finance and money markets,
  - depreciation techniques, and
  - local market conditions

Finally, property managers should have a working knowledge of local, state, and national codes and regulations. Property managers must ensure that their activity does not include the unauthorized practice of law (*Duncan and Hill* decision). This can easily occur when the drafting of legal documents is involved.

■ THE MANAGEMENT FIELD

Office building management requires attention to local economic conditions and planning for the specific type of tenants who are likely to suit the space best. For example, dentists and doctors are likely to remain as tenants because they hesitate to change addresses.

Managing retail space such as shopping malls involves the careful selection for the right blend of tenants. Large **anchor stores**, especially with nationally known names (e.g., Sears, Macy's), will set the tone for a mall and make it easier to attract other tenants. One goal is to find the right balance; for example, too many shoe stores may make for ruinous competition, but it takes a certain number of shoe stores to attract shoe buyers to that location.

Managers of residential property handle every sort of dwelling from single houses to mobile homes. Their main concern, besides maintenance of the property, is the selection and servicing of tenants.

Professional management is usually hired by the homeowners' association of a condominium or the corporation that owns a cooperative. While management is not involved with selection of tenants, maintaining harmonious relationships while enforcing the organization's rules and regulations can be a major challenge. Security, repairs, and maintenance form a large part of the manager's duties.

For those interested in pursuing a career in property management, most large cities have local associations of building and property owners and managers that are affiliates of regional and national associations. The Institute of Real Estate Management is associated with the National Association of REALTORS®. Members may earn the designation **Certified Property Manager®** (CPM). Information can be found at *www.irem.com*. The Building Owners and Managers Association International (BOMA International) is a federation of local associations of owners and managers, primarily of office buildings. Visit *www.boma.org/Pages/default. aspx* for more information about BOMA International. Participation in groups like these allows property managers to gain valuable professional knowledge and to discuss their problems with other managers facing similar issues. Management designation also is offered by the National Association of Home Builders, the New York Association of Building Owners, and the International Council of Shopping Centers.

A growing field is management of cooperatives and condominiums. The manager hired by a homeowners' organization must develop different techniques because owners and tenants are one and the same. The Community Associations Institute (CAI) is a nonprofit organization founded in 1974 to research and distribute information on association living and offers training and designation for specialized management.

■ RENT REGULATIONS

Aside from the disclosures necessary to be made to all tenants (see Chapter 3), rent regulation in New York State is administered by the Office of Rent Administration of the New York State Division of Housing and Community Renewal (DHCR). It includes two programs: *rent control* and *rent stabilization*. Visit *www.dhcr.state.ny.us/index.htm* for more information.

Rent Control

Rent control dates back to the housing shortage that followed World War II and generally covers property containing three or more units constructed before February 1947 and located in one of the 64 municipalities where the system is in effect. These include New York City, Albany, Buffalo, and parts of Albany, Erie, Nassau, Rensselaer, Schenectady, and Westchester counties. Also covered are tenants who have been in continuous residence since May 1, 1953, in one- or two-family dwellings in the participating communities.

For buildings with three or more units, the regulations apply to an apartment continuously occupied by the present tenant since July 1, 1971 (with some exceptions in Nassau County). When such an apartment is vacated, it moves to rent stabilization status or is removed from regulation, depending on the municipality.

Rents in controlled apartments initially were based on rentals in effect when rent control was first imposed in 1943. Outside New York City, the DHCR determines maximum allowable rates of rent increases, which are available to landlords every two years. Within New York City, a **maximum base rent (MBR)** is established for each apartment and is adjusted every two years. Tenants may challenge proposed increases if the building has been cited for violations or the owner's expenses do not warrant an increase.

Under rent control, rent may be increased if the landlord increases services, if the landlord installs a major capital improvement, in cases of hardship, and to cover high labor and fuel costs. Rents will be reduced if the landlord fails to correct violations or reduces essential services.

The law prohibits harassment of rent-controlled tenants or retaliatory eviction of tenants who exercise their right to complain to a government agency about violations of health or safety laws.

Rent Stabilization

In New York City, **rent stabilization** applies to apartments in buildings of six or more units constructed between February 1, 1947, and January 1, 1974. Buildings with three or more units that have been constructed or extensively renovated since 1974 with special tax benefits are also subject to rent stabilization while the tax benefits continue.

Outside New York City, rent stabilization applies in those communities that have adopted the Emergency Tenant Protection Act (ETPA). Each community sets a limit on the size of buildings to be covered; in no case is the program applied to property with fewer than six living units.

Where rent stabilization applies, maximum allowable rent increases are set annually by local rent stabilization boards. Tenants may choose one- or two-year renewal leases.

The DHCR has set up a special unit to assist the owners of buildings with fewer than 50 rental units in filling out registration forms and with record keeping and bookkeeping. The department's main office is located at 25 Beaver St., New York, NY 10004; 212-480-6700; *www.dhcr.state.ny.us/index.htm.*

Luxury Decontrol

Under current rent stabilization laws, when stabilized units reach a legal registered (with the DHCR) monthly rent of $2,000 or more, the landlord is permitted to petition the NYC Department of Finance to receive determination as to the occupant's household income. **Household income** is defined as the income earned by any lawful occupant housed within the stabilized unit.

This includes income from any legal occupant living in the unit and is included on your tax return. If the owner receives confirmation from the Department of Finance that the occupant has exceeded $175,000 taxable income for two consecutive years prior to the legal rent reaching $2,000 or more, the owner may move to decontrol the unit.

A landlord may move to decontrol a stabilized unit if the legal registered rent with the DHCR is $2,000 or more per month when the unit is vacant, or if the legal registered rent with the DHCR is $2,000 or more per month and the occupant earns taxable income in excess of $175,000 (as reported on the federal tax return) for two consecutive years prior to the rent reaching or exceeding $2,000 per month.

If it is discovered that the occupant does not maintain the residence as his or her **primary residence** (defined as the location that the taxpayer files as the address of his or her primary living quarters), the landlord may move to decontrol the unit.

■ SUMMARY

Property management is a specialized service to owners of income-producing properties in which a manager, as agent of the owner, becomes administrator of the property.

A management agreement must be prepared carefully to define and authorize the manager's duties and responsibilities.

The manager draws up a budget of estimated variable and fixed expenses. The budget also should allow for any proposed expenditures for major renovations or modernizations. These projected expenses, combined with the manager's analysis of the condition of the building and the rent patterns in the neighborhood, will form the basis on which rental rates for property are determined.

The property manager is responsible for soliciting tenants whose needs are suited to the space and who are capable of meeting the proposed rents. The manager usually collects rents, maintains the building, hires employees, pays taxes for the building, and deals with tenant problems.

One of the manager's primary responsibilities is supervising maintenance, which includes safeguarding the physical integrity of the property and performing routine cleaning and repairs as well as adapting interior space and design to suit tenants' needs.

In addition, the manager is expected to secure adequate insurance coverage for the premises. The basic types of coverage applicable to commercial structures include fire and hazard insurance on the property and fixtures; business interruption insurance to protect the owner against income losses; and casualty insurance to provide coverage against such losses as theft, vandalism, and destruction of machinery. The manager also should secure public liability insurance to insure the owner against claims made by people injured on the premises and workers' compensation policies to cover the claims of employees injured on the job. The Multiple Dwelling Law in New York City and Buffalo sets health and safety standards for apartment buildings. As it pertains to a working assignment, a property manager or a licensee is advised to become familiar with rent control and rent stabilization laws and how they apply in various parts of the state. Local communities have additional regulations. The state also regulates mobile home parks.

The Institute of Real Estate Management, a branch of the National Association of REALTORS®, awards the most widely recognized designation in the field, the CPM, Certified Property Manager®.

CHAPTER 22 QUIZ

1. Must a manager allow modifications of the premises to accommodate a handicapped tenant who offers to pay for the work?
   a. Yes, and the landlord must pay for the adaptations
   b. No, if more suitable accommodations are for rent within a reasonable distance
   c. No, unless the apartment is located in a rent-controlled building
   d. Yes, but the tenant must return the premises to its original condition on leaving

2. What is the maximum percentage of their income that participants in the FHA's Section 8 program may pay in rent?
   a. 10 percent
   b. 20 percent
   c. 30 percent
   d. 40 percent

3. In the absence of rent regulations, the amount of rent charged is determined by the
   a. management agreement.
   b. market conditions.
   c. operating budget.
   d. local apartment owners' association.

4. Office rentals usually are figured by the
   a. front foot.
   b. amount of desk space.
   c. number of rooms.
   d. square foot.

5. From a management point of view, when apartment building occupancy reaches 98 percent, what would this indicate?
   a. The building is poorly managed.
   b. The building is run-down.
   c. The building is a desirable place to live.
   d. Rents should be raised.

6. Which should NOT be a consideration in selecting a tenant?
   a. The size of the space versus the tenant's requirements
   b. The tenant's ability to pay
   c. The racial and ethnic backgrounds of the tenant
   d. The compatibility of the tenant's business with other tenants' businesses

7. A property manager fee is normally paid as
   a. a percentage of income derived from rentals.
   b. rebates from suppliers.
   c. key money.
   d. a rebate from fees paid outside workers.

8. What is the minimum lease term that must be offered to tenants in mobile home parks?
   a. 30 days
   b. 90 days
   c. 180 days
   d. One year

9. While her tenants are at work, Laura Landlady may enter their apartment
   a. to leave them a note.
   b. to check on their housekeeping.
   c. in case of fire.
   d. for any purpose.

10. Which insurance policy insures the property owner against the claims of employees injured on the job?
    a. Business interruption
    b. Workers' compensation
    c. Casualty
    d. Surety bond

11. A delivery person slips on a defective stair in an apartment building and is hospitalized. A claim against the building owner for medical expenses will be made under which of the following policies held by the owner?

    a. Workers' compensation
    b. Casualty
    c. Liability
    d. Fire and hazard

12. A property manager hires a full-time janitor for one of the buildings she manages. While repairing a faucet in one of the apartments, the janitor steals a television. The property manager could have protected the owner against liability for this type of loss by purchasing

    a. liability insurance.
    b. workers' compensation insurance.
    c. a surety bond.
    d. casualty insurance.

13. The initials CPM stand for

    a. chargeback percentage mortgage.
    b. contract priority maintenance.
    c. Certified Property Manager®.
    d. cardiopulmonary manipulation.

14. Rent regulations in New York are administered by the

    a. New York City Housing Bureau.
    b. Department of State (DOS).
    c. Department of Housing and Urban Development (HUD).
    d. New York Department of Housing and Community Renewal (DHCR).

15. When the original tenant dies or moves out, a rent-controlled apartment with a rent of $850 per month may become eligible for

    a. rent control.
    b. rent stabilization.
    c. comparative hardship.
    d. freeze.

16. The rent-stabilization program is known outside New York City as

    a. ETPA.
    b. DHCR.
    c. CPR.
    d. HPR.

17. The DHCR's special unit for helping owners with registration, bookkeeping, and record keeping is aimed at apartment buildings with fewer than

    a. 3 units.
    b. 8 units.
    c. 50 units.
    d. 100 units.

CHAPTER

23

Taxes and Assessments

■ KEY TERMS

ad valorem taxes	grievance	taxable status date
aged exemption	homestead	tax certiorari
appropriation	in rem	tax foreclosure
assessment roll	levy	tax liens
assessments	mill	tax sale
equalization factor	nonhomestead	true tax
full-value assessment	real property tax rates	

■ TAX LIENS

State and local governments impose *taxes* on real estate to support government services. Because the location of real estate is permanently fixed and ownership cannot be hidden, the government can levy taxes with a high degree of certainty that they will be collected. Liens (claim or charge against the property of another) for property taxes, which usually have priority over other previously recorded liens, may be enforced by the court-ordered sale of the real estate.

Real estate taxes are of two types: *general real estate tax*, or *ad valorem tax*, and *special assessment tax*, or *improvement tax*. Both are levied against specific parcels of property and automatically become liens on those properties.

General Tax (Ad Valorem Tax)

The general real estate tax is made up of taxes levied by the state, cities, towns, villages, and counties. Other taxing bodies are school districts, park districts, lighting districts, drainage districts, water districts, and sanitary districts. Municipal authorities operating recreational preserves such as forest preserves and parks also may be authorized by the legislature to levy real estate taxes.

General real estate taxes are known as **ad valorem** (to the value) **taxes** because the amount of the tax is determined by the value of the property being taxed.

Special assessments are levied only on the parcels of real estate that will benefit from improvements in a limited area. They may be levied, for example, to pay for sidewalks, curbs, or streetlights in a particular neighborhood.

Special Assessments (Improvement Taxes)

Property owners may request the improvements, or the local government may propose them. Hearings are held and notices given to owners of the property affected. An *ordinance* may be adopted that sets out the nature of the improvement, its cost, and a description of the area to be assessed. The assessment is then spread over the various parcels of real estate that will benefit. The assessment often varies from parcel to parcel because not all will benefit equally from the improvement.

■ THE TAXATION PROCESS

Assessment

Assessments in New York are made by municipal officials known as *assessors*. Assessments are made by towns, villages, cities, and, in a few cases, counties. The **assessment roll**, open to public inspection, contains assessments for all taxable lands and buildings within the area.

In 1788, New York law mandated **full-value assessment**. The requirement was largely ignored, with most municipalities assessing at less than full value. In 1975, the court of appeals ordered the state either to enforce the law or to change it. More than 400 communities then went to full-value assessment voluntarily or under court order. In 1982, the legislature repealed the 200-year-old requirement. Under the regulations that went into force at that time, most of New York State was simply required to assess all property at a "*uniform* percentage of value," while New York City and Long Island were allowed to divide real property into four different classes for tax purposes. The question of full-value assessment remains controversial and hotly debated, with court challenges occurring frequently.

Differences in assessments　Upon inspection of the public records, it would not be uncommon to find that assessments differ from municipality to municipality as well as from one property to another. In most cases, lower assessments suggest older construction, lower land values, or a combination of both events. New construction experiences the opposite effect.

Undeclared improvements   Undeclared improvements (when discovered by the taxing authorities) are dealt with severely. Payment of back taxes is usually the penalty. Undeclared improvements are those made to a property without obtaining a building permit. The building permit process gives the taxing authority two benefits: (1) the improvement will be made in compliance with all local laws and building codes (a primary function of government is to protect the health, safety, and welfare of the general public), and (2) the ability to reassess the property by at least the value of the improvement as it relates to the property's value.

Reassessment and the sale of property   When property is sold throughout the state, the sale triggers a reassessment. In deriving the subject property's new assessment, the assessment for the year of the sale is measured against the "target" assessment resulting from the sale. The target is the new assessment determination. For example, in New York City, a sale requires careful examination of three items: (1) the tax base in the year of sale, (2) the transitional tax (the difference between the tax in the year of sale and the target tax), and (3) the target assessment. For example:

Target assessment resulting from the sale	$500,000
Tax assessment in the year of the sale	− 300,000
Transitional assessment	$200,000

In New York City, an assessment may not exceed 20 percent in any tax year (with certain exceptions). Therefore, the transitional tax of $200,000 above must be phased in over a five-year period. This requires a two-step process:

Step 1: Determine the annual transitional assessment
$200,000 ÷ 5 years = $40,000 annual increased assessment

Step 2: Arriving at the target assessed value

Assessment in year of sale	$300,000
Assessment year 1 following the sale	$340,000
Assessment year 2 following the sale	$380,000
Assessment year 3 following the sale	$420,000
Assessment year 4 following the sale	$460,000
Assessment year 5 following the sale	$500,000

Licensees are cautioned to disclose to a buyer that the sale will trigger a reassessment of the property. The buyer should not rely on the tax in the year of sale remaining the same.

Equalization   Uniformity among districts that may assess at different rates is achieved through use of an **equalization factor.** The New York State Board of Equalization and Assessment receives reports on sales prices and calculates an equalization rate for each municipality. This factor is intended to equalize the assessments in every taxing jurisdiction across the state. No equalization factor applies where full-value assessment is used.

The assessed value of each property is multiplied by the equalization factor, and the tax rate then is applied to the equalized assessment. For example, the assessments in one district are determined to be 20 percent lower than average assessments throughout the rest of the state. This underassessment can be corrected by applying an equalization factor of 125 percent to each assessment in that district.

Thus, a parcel of land assessed for tax purposes at $98,000 would be taxed on an equalized value of $122,500 ($98,000 × 1.25 = $122,500).

Tax rates   The process of arriving at a real estate tax rate begins with the *adoption of a budget* by each county, city, school board, or other taxing district. The budget covers financial requirements for the coming fiscal year, which may be the January through December calendar year or some other 12-month period. The budget must include an estimate of all expenditures for the year and indicate the amount of income expected from all fees, revenue sharing, and other sources. The net amount remaining to be raised from real estate taxes is then determined from these figures.

Separate tax rates may be established for **homestead** and **nonhomestead** real estate. Homestead property in New York includes dwellings with no more than four units, mobile homes if owner-occupied and separately assessed, residential condominiums, farms, and some vacant land suitable for homestead-qualified buildings. Nonhomestead property includes industrial and commercial property and most vacant land.

Tax shares are sometimes negotiated between different taxing authorities, as when two towns support one school district or villages share the expense for a county sheriff's department.

Appropriation

The next step is **appropriation**, the action that authorizes the expenditure of funds and provides for the sources of the money. Appropriation involves the adoption of an ordinance or the passage of a law setting forth the specifics of the proposed taxation.

The amount to be raised from the general real estate tax then is imposed on property owners through a tax **levy**, the formal action taken to impose the tax.

The tax rate for each individual taxing body is computed separately. To arrive at a tax rate, the total monies needed for the coming fiscal year are divided by the total assessments of all real estate located within the jurisdiction of the taxing body. **Real property tax rates** represent the ratio of tax dollars charged in either per hundred or per thousand dollars of assessed valuation. Tax rates are also called mill rates. For example, a taxing district's budget indicates that $300,000 must be raised from real estate tax revenues, and the assessment roll (assessor's record) of all taxable real estate within this district equals $10 million. The tax rate is computed thus:

$300,000 ÷ $10,000,000 = 0.03 or 3%

The tax rate may be stated in a number of different ways. In many areas, it is expressed in mills. A **mill** is *¹⁄₁₀ of a cent or $0.001*. The tax rate may be expressed as a mill ratio, in dollars per hundred or in dollars per thousand. The tax rate computed in the foregoing example could be expressed as

30 mills (per $1 of assessed value) or $3 per $100 of assessed value
or $30 per $1,000 of assessed value

Tax bills   A property owner's tax bill is computed by applying the tax rate to the assessed valuation of the property. For example, on property assessed for tax purposes at $90,000, at a tax rate of 3 percent, or 30 mills, the tax will be $2,700 ($90,000 × 0.030 = $2,700). If an *equalization factor* is used, the computation on a property with an assessed value of $120,000 and a tax rate of 4 percent with an equalization factor of 120 percent would be as follows:

$120,000 × 1.20 = $144,000

$144,000 × 0.04 = $5,760 tax

Penalties in the form of monthly interest charges are added to all taxes that are not paid when due. The due date also is called the *penalty date*. (Where a lending institution maintains an escrow account to meet a mortgagor's taxes, tax bills may be sent directly to the lender. After the taxes are paid, the receipted bills are forwarded to the property owner.)

New York cities, towns, villages, and school districts generally send out their own tax bills, which may include the county tax levy. Improvement district charges are usually included in the town tax bill; benefit charges are often billed separately. State, town, and county taxes run from January to December and are payable in advance. Villages may begin their tax year either in March or, more commonly, in June. School taxes are levied from July 1 through June 30, but the tax may not be payable until September or October in some areas and may be payable in installments. School taxes, therefore, are paid in arrears for several months. City taxes frequently are payable in two or four installments during the year.

Exemptions

Most property owned by cities, various municipal organizations (schools, parks, and playgrounds), the state and federal governments, religious organizations/ corporations, hospitals, or educational institutions are tax-exempt. The property must be used for tax-exempt purposes; if not, it is subject to tax.

New York also allows special exemptions to reduce real estate tax bills for certain property owners or land uses. Veterans may be eligible for reductions in some property taxes. Real estate tax reductions are sometimes granted to attract industries or to encourage construction of low-income or multifamily housing. In specific agricultural districts, New York may offer reductions for agricultural land to encourage the continuation of agricultural uses. Farmers may claim exemption from school taxes for some or all of their acreage. New York State allows local taxing authorities to grant partial exemptions to homeowners who construct in-law apartments, to the disabled, and to Gold Star parents, who have lost a child in combat. Every homeowner is entitled to school tax relief (STaR), as described below.

Elderly exemption   The state allows local governments (towns, counties, and school districts) to offer partial exemption from property taxes on a primary residence to certain homeowners aged 65 or older with modest incomes, at levels that change from year to year. Exemptions can range from 10 to 50 percent, depending on income levels, including Social Security payments. Application is made through the local village, town, or city hall assessor's office and must be renewed each year.

Applicants who do not understand how early in the year tax rolls are closed (**taxable status date**) are often disappointed to find that they must wait up to two years before receiving any benefit. This special tax treatment is known officially by the inelegant title **aged exemption**, and is only an option that the towns, counties, and school districts may adopt. Those who receive it also will receive the STaR abatement described below. New York's tax status date, before which applications should be made, is March 1.

Veterans exemption   Qualified veterans who served during a conflict may receive partial property tax exemption of 15 percent of the value of a primary residence (co-op apartments are not eligible). Those who served in combat are eligible for an additional 10 percent. The exemption, which may not total more than $5,000, is calculated differently for older veterans discharged before newer regulations took effect. The tax abatement is partial, applying to general municipal taxes but not to school tax. It renews automatically each year. In addition, spouses, widows, and widowers of eligible veterans also receive benefits. The amount of benefit depends on whether the veteran served in a combat area and/or was disabled.

STaR program   In the late 1990s, the state instituted a School Tax Relief program (STaR), giving every homeowner who applied a permanent reduction in school taxes on a main residence.

Elderly homeowners with income of less than $79,050 in 2011 (adjusted periodically) may apply for enhanced (higher) STaR reductions, but must reapply yearly. Any senior receiving the age exemption described above automatically receives an enhanced STaR reduction as well.

Cooperative/Condominium Abatement (NYC)   The New York City Real Property Tax Classification System breaks down taxable real property into four tax classes. Approximately 82 percent of housing in New York City is comprised of cooperative and condominium units. The New York City Department of Finance provides a property tax abatement program that is only available to class 2 properties. Whereby class 1 property includes all residential one to three family homes, class 2 property includes all other residential properties that are not categorized in class 1. This would include the following:

- Rental buildings and all other residential
- Cooperatives
- Condominiums

Class 2 would not include the following:

- Hotels
- Motels
- Other similar properties

Depending on the average assessed value of the unit, cooperative and condominium housing is currently eligible for an abatement of 17.5 percent or 25 percent of the unit owner's property tax. Average tax savings would resemble the following:

- If the abatement is 17.5 percent, savings might consist of approximately $900.
- If the abatement is 25 percent, savings might consist of approximately $1,325.

Disabled crime victim and Good Samaritan exemption New York City provides a property tax abatement for

- disabled crime victims, and
- Good Samaritan exemption.

This program provides tax relief to disabled crime victims whose disability is derived directly from a crime or a Good Samaritan who suffered a disability while trying to prevent a crime.

Eligibility requires individuals to modify their homes to accommodate their respective disability. If eligible, homeowners are compensated for the direct cost of the renovations or improvements to the home that are necessary to accommodate their disability.

True tax The real estate broker taking the listing of a parcel of real estate should be alert to the possibility of exemptions and exercise diligence in ascertaining the **true tax** figure, before any special exemptions held by the present owner are subtracted.

A great deal of tax information is available on the Internet. New York City's Department of Finance can be accessed at *www.nyc.gov/html/dof/html/home/home. shtml*.

Protesting assessments Property owners who claim that errors were made in determining the assessed value of their property may present their objections and request adjustments from the appropriate municipality grievance board. There are three basic grievances: (1) overassessment, (2) disagreement on full value, and (3) unequal assessment ratios. Those who investigate records in the assessor's office may be able to show that the description on file for their property lists more lot size, floor space, or amenities than they actually have. Also persuasive are comparisons with neighboring parcels that indicate the protester's assessment is unreasonably high. Documentation to back up the claims can be compiled from the public records.

Problems should be discussed first with the local assessor; it is not necessary to wait for an official *grievance day*. The next step is to apply for a hearing, filing a document known as a **grievance** with the county clerk or local tax appeals board. At the next level, a simple and inexpensive small claims procedure is available in New York State for owner-occupied one to four-family dwellings if the property has an equalized value of less than $150,000 or if the reduction being sought is less than 25 percent. At this point, it is the petitioning property owner's burden to provide evidence for the grievance. Evidence would consist of sales information (neighboring comparable sales), assessment information, and assessment ratios (partial value vs. full value). Hearing decisions could result in (1) a full grievance assessment reduction, (2) a partial grievance assessment reduction, or (3) no reduction. Protests also can be taken to the regular court system in a **tax certiorari** proceeding.

Enforcement of Tax Liens

To be enforceable, real estate taxes must be *valid*, which means they must be levied properly, used for a legal purpose, and applied equitably to all affected property. Real estate taxes that have remained delinquent for the period of time specified by state law can be collected through either **tax foreclosure** (similar to mortgage foreclosure) or **tax sale**. Many cities and villages enforce their own **tax liens** through tax sales; in most cases, towns do not. Some foreclosures are **in rem**, against the property on which taxes are delinquent, without proceeding against the individual owner. When a lienholder, often a municipality, decides to go to court for an in rem foreclosure and subsequently takes title to the property, the lienholder becomes the owner, and the owner and the former owner lose any right or claim to the property. The lienholder (new owner) may then keep the property or dispose of it by sale.

Tax sales are held after a published notice and often are conducted by the tax collector as an annual public sale. The purchaser of the lien must pay at least the amount of delinquent tax and penalty owing. The delinquent taxpayer may redeem the property at any time before the tax sale by paying the delinquent taxes plus interest and charges (any court costs or attorney's fees); this is known as an *equitable right of redemption*.

Once property has been sold at a tax sale, the property owner is usually free of any personal liability for the unpaid taxes.

■ SUMMARY

Real estate taxes are levied by local authorities. Tax liens generally are given priority over other liens. Payments are required before stated dates, after which penalties accrue. Special assessments are levied to spread the cost of improvements such as new sidewalks, curbs, or paving over the particular parcels of real estate that benefit from them.

Partial exemption from property taxes is granted to certain senior citizens on modest incomes (aged exemption), to some veterans, and to others for various reasons.

The appraisal process begins with assessment of the taxable value of each parcel. New York mandates either equitable or full-value assessment with variations from one jurisdiction to another adjusted through the use of equalization rates. The money to be raised through taxation is then divided by the total assessment roll to arrive at the tax rate. The tax bill for each parcel is determined by multiplying the tax rate by assessed valuation.

Various taxing authorities send tax bills at different times of the year. Unpaid taxes become a lien against property, usually taking precedence over other liens, and may be enforced through tax foreclosure or sale.

An owner may lose title to property for nonpayment of taxes if the real estate is sold at a tax sale.

CHAPTER 23 QUIZ

1. The amount of an ad valorem tax is
   a. determined by the property's value.
   b. the same amount for all properties.
   c. based on the owner's use of the property.
   d. based on the owner's ability to pay.

2. Sidewalk repairs in one area of the town of Brighton will MOST likely be paid for through a(n)
   a. mechanic's lien.
   b. special assessment.
   c. ad valorem tax.
   d. utility lien.

3. When real estate is assessed for tax purposes,
   a. the homeowner may appeal to a local board of review.
   b. a protest must take the form of a personal suit against the assessor.
   c. the appeal process must start in state court.
   d. no appeal is possible.

4. New York does NOT allow special tax exemptions to
   a. veterans.
   b. farmers.
   c. recipients of public aid.
   d. the elderly.

5. A specific parcel of real estate has a market value of $180,000 and is assessed for tax purposes at 25 percent of market value. The tax rate for the county in which the property is located is 30 mills. The tax will be
   a. $180.
   b. $450.
   c. $1,350.
   d. $5,400.

6. What is the annual school tax on a property valued at $135,000 and assessed for tax purposes at $47,250 with an equalization factor of 125 percent when the tax rate is 25 mills?
   a. $1,417.50
   b. $1,476.56
   c. $4,050.00
   d. $4,218.00

7. The *true tax* on a property is the
   a. tax actually collected on a property.
   b. tax applied after a property reassessment.
   c. combination of property tax and owner's income tax.
   d. tax before exemptions are subtracted.

8. An in rem foreclosure proceeds against the
   a. property.
   b. owner of the property.
   c. property tenant.
   d. property and the owner.

9. During the statutory period of redemption, New York property sold for delinquent taxes may be redeemed by
   a. paying back taxes, penalties, and interest.
   b. paying back taxes, penalties, interest, and one year future taxes.
   c. successful protest of the initial tax lien.
   d. obtaining an appropriate tax exemption in arrears.

10. In New York districts where assessments are used at full value, the state
    a. offers broader tax exemptions.
    b. imposes a lower tax rate.
    c. uses no equalization factor.
    d. does not permit special assessments.

11. The elderly homeowner who wants a large STaR property tax reduction must
    a. be qualified to receive welfare.
    b. reapply every year.
    c. have no school children living in the home.
    d. consent to a lien being placed on the property.

12. What are transitional tax assessments used for?
    a. To close the gap between a tax assessment in the year of sale and the target assessment
    b. To ease the increase for a homebuyer who is not eligible for exemptions held by the seller
    c. To decrease the tax liability of property owners who are facing foreclosures
    d. To encourage construction of multifamily property or in-law apartments

CHAPTER

24

Condominiums and Cooperatives

■ KEY TERMS

alteration agreement
black book
board package
bylaws
common elements
condominium
condop
cooperative/co-op
cooperative association
co-op loan

covenants, conditions,
  and restrictions
  (CC&Rs)
declaration
flipping
flip tax
holder of unsold shares
house rules
letter of intent
maintenance

offering statement/plan
proprietary lease
red herring
recognition agreement
reserves
share loan
sponsor
underlying mortgage

■ COOPERATIVE OWNERSHIP

A **cooperative, cooperative association**, or **co-op** is defined as

- a structure that contains two or more units,
- in which occupancy and possession of the units vests with ownership of stock in a corporation that owns fee simple interest or has a leasehold interest in the structure and
- in which the shareholder receives an occupancy agreement known as the **proprietary lease**.

The purchaser of a cooperative is an owner of shares of stock (personal property) in a co-op corporation and directly resembles a tenant in leased property (a leasehold estate). The proprietary lease is the agreement that gives the shareholder the right to occupy a particular unit. It is the interest held as a direct result of ownership of stock in the cooperative corporation that owns the property. The ownership of the shares and proprietary lease will run and continue for the earlier of

- life of the cooperative corporation or
- until the unit occupant transfers his/her interest in same.

The shareholder pays monthly maintenance to the co-op corporation rather than rent. Included in the maintenance paid by the unit shareholder is the proportionate share of real property taxes due for that unit. This is measured in a cost-per-share charge to each unit within the cooperative.

For example, assume the building is charged $100,000 for annual property tax and there are 100,000 shares of outstanding stock that have been issued to all unit shareholders of the cooperative.

Step 1: Calculating the per share cost

By dividing the tax cost by the outstanding number of shares, a $1 per share charge is attributable to each share issued for each applicable unit (as shown in Step 2):

$100,000 (annual tax) ÷ 100,000 (number of outstanding shares issued) = 1.00/share

Step 2: Calculating each unit shareholder's property tax liability

If a unit were to have 2,000 shares, the monthly maintenance would reflect this liability in either one lump sum payment or a 1/12 payment each month to pay that unit's proportionate share of the property tax liability.

2,000 (shares) × $1.00 (per share charge for tax) = $2,000 annual unit tax

The necessity for this calculation extends further. Payments such as property taxes and underlying cooperative mortgages provide each shareholder with an annual income tax deduction. Calculating the allowance per shareholder will be solely reliant on

- the amount per share that each deduction represents, and
- the number of shares attributable to the unit in question.

Cooperative ownership is common in the New York City metropolitan area and in some resort areas. Under the usual cooperative arrangement, a corporation (generally organized as a not-for-profit entity) holds title to the land and the building.

Purchaser of an apartment in the building receives stock in the corporation and a proprietary lease for their individual apartment.

Unlike in single-family housing and condominiums where individual owners and tenants receive individual unit tax bills, the cooperative property receives only one tax bill. Real estate taxes are paid on the whole building by the corporation.

A single mortgage, known as the **underlying mortgage**, covers the entire building. Property taxes, mortgage interest and principal on the underlying mortgage, and operating/maintenance expenses on the property are shared by the tenants/shareholders as monthly **maintenance** charges.

Proprietary leaseholders may individually finance their apartments with a cooperative loan. When a co-op loan is placed on an individual unit by the tenant/shareholder, the lender will always request the board of directors to execute a recognition agreement to the favor of the lender. The recognition agreement provides the lender with the ability to step in and cure

- any default in payment of monthly maintenance, or
- any other issue that might affect their lien with the shareholder on the shares of stock attributable to the unit.

Most proprietary leases provide that they may not be assigned, transferred, or sublet without the advance written consent of the board of directors.

Although cooperative tenants/owners do not actually own an interest in real estate (they own stock, which is *personal property*), they do control the property through their *board of directors*.

Board memberships are elected positions. The only exception to this occurs when cooperative bylaws provide for board positions to be established by appointment rather than election. This is usually the case when shares in the corporation are held as sponsor-held shares or in the case of qualified holders of unsold shares. (These subjects will be discussed later in this chapter.)

One disadvantage of cooperative ownership became particularly evident during the Great Depression and still must be considered. If enough owner-occupants become unable to promptly pay their monthly assessments, the corporation may be forced to allow underlying mortgage and property tax payments to go unpaid. Should this unfortunate situation occur, the entire property could be sold by court order in a foreclosure suit. Such a sale would destroy the interests of all occupants/shareholders, even those who paid their assessments. The cooperative would be dissolved, and the property would probably revert back to a rental property. Shareholders with outstanding unit co-op loan balances will still have to pay off their loan.

Accumulation of a substantial reserve fund offers some protection to the cooperative as a whole. Most lenders regard as suitable a cooperative reserve fund consisting of an amount equal to but not less than three months' annual operating budget. For example, assume a cooperative annual budget of $1,200,000.

This budget would imply a building operating cost of $100,000 per month, so the cooperative reserve fund should contain a balance of at least $300,000.

Furthermore, cooperatives and condominiums are organized as non-for-profit organizations. As a result, they cannot have unlimited amounts laying around in a reserve fund. Every dollar must be slated toward some future event. This information can usually be found within the financial statements of the property. In addition, coops and condos cannot return any monies to their shareholders or owners (as the case may be). Any amount received from the cooperative corporation by a shareholder is treated as a dividend. In order for a dividend to be paid to a shareholder, the corporation had to be profitable. These entities are organized as not-for-profit organizations.

The tenant/shareholder does not own the actual real estate and may not place a regular mortgage against the unit. Instead, shares are pledged as security for a personal loan. The loan is commonly called a co-op loan. Boards of directors, sensitive to the financial dependence of one tenant on the others, sometimes set down payment requirements that are more stringent than those asked by lending institutions. In some cases, boards may even refuse prospective tenants unless the purchase is to be made for all cash.

The Internal Revenue Service (IRS), however, offers the owner of a cooperative unit the same income tax treatment as the owner of a condominium or a single home. Before January 2008, that portion of maintenance charges that covers property taxes and mortgage interest may be taken as a deduction as long as the property's other income sources did not violate the 80/20 rule that was in place *before the current change in law* that occurred in December 2007 (Mortgage Forgiveness Debt Relief Act of 2007). Before January 2008, this earlier 80/20 rule stated that no more than 20 percent of the cooperative's income was to be derived from non-shareholder sources and activities, such as rental of commercial space and vending or washing machine concessions, also referred to as passive income activity. (See Chapter 20.) Because of the risks associated with loss of the not-for-profit status that cooperatives are formed under, this greatly restricted the cooperative from charging and receiving market rents. In addition, interest paid on each individual co-op owner's own loan is treated as mortgage interest and would be deductible.

As of December 2007 and as part of the Mortgage Forgiveness Debt Relief Act of 2007, section 216(b)(1)(D) of the Internal Revenue Code of 1986 (which defines cooperative housing corporations) provided relief to cooperative housing. The change in law allows housing cooperatives to determine commercial rents *without* sacrificing tax benefits to shareholders of the cooperative.

To fall under the amendment, cooperative housing must meet one or more of the following requirements for the taxable year in which the taxes and interest (as described in subsection [a]) are paid or incurred:

- Eighty percent or more of the corporation's gross income for that taxable year is derived from tenant-shareholders.
- During the taxable year, 80 percent or more of the total square footage of the corporation's property is used or is available for use by the

tenant-shareholders for residential purposes or purposes that are ancillary to that of residential use.

■ Ninety percent or more of the expenditures of the corporation paid or incurred during such taxable year are paid or incurred for the acquisition, construction, management, maintenance, or care of the corporation's property for the benefit of the tenant-shareholders. (See Figure 24.1.)

The effective date of the amendment applies to sales or exchanges after December 2007. While the old law restricted cooperatives from charging market rents for commercial spaces, under the new law that limit has been eliminated.

Due Diligence Issues

Performing due diligence means doing your homework; in a cooperative, this pertains primarily to the review of financial statements and board minutes. As in any property acquisition, a study of the subject is required. In a cooperative transaction, the due diligence process begins with an accepted offer. The purchaser will engage an appropriate team of professionals to aid in the review and ultimate conclusion of the transaction. This team may include (but is not be limited to) a broker, an attorney, an accountant/CPA, an architect/engineer, and contractors.

The items to be studied include the cooperative's financial statements and the board meeting minutes; a lien search, which is similar to a title search, is also conducted.

The purchaser will normally require a review of the previous two years' financial statements. In underwriting a co-op unit loan, the purchaser's lender will require submission of this information. The financial statement will contain explanations concerning the cooperative's underlying mortgage financing, including the outstanding principal balance as of the date of the report, interest rate, and date of maturity of the loan; maintenance history; assessment history and proposed charges; and reserve fund balance.

The review of the board minutes usually covers the minutes from the two years before the sale. This review uncovers the co-op's prior operating history. The minutes will also provide some indication of the cooperative's future plans concerning items such as major capital improvements (e.g., window replacement, roof replacement, elevator replacement, lobby renovation, façade restoration, and schedule of

F I G U R E   24.1

Mortgage Forgiveness Debt Relief Act Requirements

Cooperative housing must meet one or more of the following requirements for the taxable year in which the taxes and interest are paid or incurred:

1. Eighty percent or more of gross income is derived from tenant-shareholders.
2. Eighty percent or more of total square footage is utilized for or is available for residential purposes or purposes that are ancillary to residential use.
3. Ninety percent or more of the expenditures of the corporation are paid or incurred for the acquisition, construction, management, maintenance, or care of the corporation's property for the benefit of the tenant-shareholders.

The effective date of the amendment applies to sales or exchanges after December 2007.

local law compliance); maintenance increases or decreases; and current or future assessments. In addition, the due diligence process will also uncover whether or not a flip tax is required on transfer of the unit shares at closing. A **flip tax** is a tax imposed by the cooperative on the sale of a unit within said building. This fee can be based on a percentage of the gross sale, net sale, gain, or the number of shares held by the shareholder or a fixed number determined by the cooperative board. The flip tax can be paid by the purchaser, seller, or shared by both parties; however, custom usually dictates that the seller pay the flip tax. These fees are income/revenue-generating devises and are utilized by a cooperative for the purpose of increasing its reserve fund.

A lien search is performed during a due diligence review to determine whether a loan against the shares exists and whether there are any judgments against the seller of the shares.

Fee Simple and Leasehold Cooperatives

One extremely important consideration is the determination of what type of estate is being granted. Co-ops can be organized as either fee simple estates or leasehold estates:

- *Fee simple estates.* Organization of a cooperative as a fee simple estate provides for ownership of unlimited duration by the cooperative corporation.
- *Leasehold estates.* Organization of a cooperative as a leasehold estate provides for ownership with a limited duration determined by the lease term between the cooperative corporation and the underlying landowner. Ownership in this form extends for as long as the cooperative land lease is in effect. Upon termination of the land lease, the property reverts back to the original landowner, and cooperative ownership is dissolved.

Purchase and Sale Documents

A variety of documents are required in the purchase and sale of cooperatives. These include:

- *Proprietary lease.* A proprietary lease is the occupancy agreement given to a shareholder at closing of a cooperative sale.
- *Stock certificates.* These are documents that indicate the number of shares designated to each subject unit and, at closing, are issued by the cooperative corporation to the shareholder.
- *Offering plan.* A disclosure statement concerning the subject property is termed an **offering plan**. The disclosure statement is provided by the sponsor of a primary sale and the unit shareholder-owner on a resale. An **offering statement/plan** is a document created and issued by a sponsor that is either in the process of converting a building or developing a new building. Its purpose is to provide an interested party with full disclosure of all facts pertinent to the project. In real property transactions, an approved offering plan is called the black book.
- *House rules.* The cooperative's habitation rules that govern all shareholders are known as **house rules**. The house rules of a cooperative can be of particular importance to the agent. With regard to sensitive issues of the purchaser, knowledge of house rules can save the agent countless hours of

work. For example, a prospective buyer may be seeking a property that has a no-pets provision; knowing this, the licensee should seek property with a house rule to that effect. In multifamily unit cooperatives, it would not be uncommon for house rules to include provisions for carpeting a certain percentage of the unit's flooring.

■ *Alteration agreement.* An **alteration agreement** is an agreement between the shareholder and the co-op. With rare exceptions, the majority of proprietary leases require an approval process for shareholder improvements. A shareholder will be required to obtain the prior written consent of the cooperative board of directors before any work can be performed. The co-op will require this agreement be executed prior to the commencement of shareholder unit improvements.

When simple decorative work functions are performed, most co-ops accept informal sketches and a written description of work for their consideration. When the shareholder alterations appear to be substantial, the preparation and submission of plans (blueprints) and specifications (written narrative) outlining the scope of work are usually required. The shareholder will be required to obtain all necessary permits and approvals from the appropriate governing bodies and to post necessary insurance coverage naming the cooperative and other interested parties as additionally insured. In addition, the shareholder is also normally required to indemnify and hold the cooperative harmless from and against any issues that arise out of the alteration.

Other submissions to the board might also include, but not be limited to, the following:

■ *Credit report authorization form*—submitted to the cooperative for the purpose of conducting a background check. This search is conducted by the co-op or the managing agent. The authorization form will also contain information such as applicant name; current address and monthly payment information (rent or mortgage); Social Security number; driver's license number as well as make, year, and model of car; a list of all occupants who will reside or occupy the unit; names of nearest relatives; names of personal references; employment information; all sources of income; banking information; and credit references.

■ *Board package*—documentation that contains personal and financial information of the prospective shareholder. The **board package** is submitted to the board of directors for consideration and potential acceptance or rejection of the proposed shareholder. So long as no discriminatory acts have occurred, it is solely up to the board of directors whether to accept or decline an applicant. Should the board decide to decline the applicant, the board is not required to provide that party with reasoning for the denial.

Board packages include, but are not limited to, the submission of the following items: a purchase application, which will contain all pertinent applicant information; contract of sale; landlord reference letter; personal financial statement listing assets and liabilities; bank balance confirmation letter; employer reference letter; income tax returns from the previous two to three years; and personal reference letters.

The pertinent applicant information supplied includes applicant name; attorney firm name, address, and phone number; proposed closing date and time; current principal place of residency; citizenship information; a list of occupants who will be housed within the cooperative unit; schools and colleges attended by occupants; names of all current cooperative residents known to the applicant; and whether applicant will house pets.

> **Additional Information Needed When Purchase Includes Financing**
>
> ■ Bank commitment letter
> ■ Recognition agreements

The contract of sale will outline the transaction between seller and purchaser. It will also include the appropriate New York State required disclosure forms, such as the lead–based paint disclosure and the window guard form.

Bank balance confirmation letters state the types of accounts held and the balance in U.S. dollars. The employer reference letter states the current job position, current salary, and length of employment. If the applicant is self-employed, an accountant's letter stating all current assets and liabilities and a projection of the following year's income will be included.

It is important to note that there is no statutorily prescribed form of board package. Board packages are not regulated, so each cooperative creates its own version of document submission requirements.

Loans originated in cooperatives are not mortgages. They are called *share loans* or *co-op loans*. A **share loan** or **co-op loan** is an agreement entered into by a borrower and a lender to finance the borrower's acquisition of the borrower's cooperative interest. When the purchase of a co-op includes financing, the following additional information is required:

■ *Signed bank commitment letter.* This letter is issued by the lender as evidence of the lender's willingness to extend the co-op loan to the borrower.
■ *Aztech form recognition agreement.* A **recognition agreement** is a document signed by the borrower, lender, and co-op board. The signature by the co-op acknowledges the lending party's lien interest in the shares covered by the unit. These agreements normally call for the cooperative to notify the lender of any default by the shareholder/borrower (such as the nonpayment of maintenance fees).

If an applicant does not receive the approval of the co-op board of directors, the cooperative is not required by law to issue a reason for refusal.

Interview Preparation

When preparing for a board interview, timing can always be a factor. This is certainly the case when bank financing plays a role in the co-op transaction. Normally, a lender sets the interest rate upon receipt of a signed commitment letter. The lender then holds that rate in place for a certain period (e.g., 30 days) following receipt of the executed commitment letter. In the event the interview and acceptance of the proposed shareholder occurs after the 30-day rate lock-in period, the borrower will be asked by the lender to pay additional fees to hold the interest rate in place. This can become an expensive proposition for the buyer-borrower, so timing and scheduling of board interviews are critical.

Most boards are required to meet once a month according to a schedule normally prescribed within the cooperative's bylaws (for example, the second Tuesday of every calendar month). A licensee should always be familiar with the board's practices concerning monthly meetings. This knowledge will aid the licensee in preparing and submitting the board package in time for the next scheduled monthly meeting.

After the board reviews the submitted package, questions may arise concerning the contents of the package. The agent should move toward helping to answer any questions posed by the board or their representative.

If all goes well, the purchaser will be granted an interview with the board. Prior to the interview, the agent should conduct a dry run meeting with the buyer. In this meeting, the buyer should be made completely aware of all matters included in his or her package. During the board interview, the buyer should always provide full disclosure.

Primary Residency and Subletting Issues

Primary residence living was the key reason behind the creation of cooperatives. Investment units in a cooperative are not well regarded by lenders. A lender that believes a property is comprised of a substantial amount of investor units will be less likely to originate loans for that property. Owners of primary residences are less likely to default on loans than investors. In defaulting, the investor loses money, but the primary resident would lose the residence. When the cooperative represents a person's primary residence, that person is less likely to default on the loan.

In order to better understand this, let's examine the following types of shares held in a cooperative: sponsor shares, unsold shares, and sold shares.

When formation of property is held in cooperative form, the organizing party of a co-op is referred to as the **sponsor**. Any shares held by the original sponsor of the co-op are called *sponsor shares*. Consent of the board of directors of the co-op is not required to sell sponsor shares; the board does not have the power to accept or deny the selection of a shareholder.

FIGURE 24.3

Types of Cooperative Shares

Types of Cooperative Shares

- **Sponsor shares**—any shares held by the original sponsor of the co-op
- **Unsold shares**—shares held by any person or legal entity; holder and family may not reside in unit
- **Sold shares**—shares purchased by parties with the intent of residing within the unit

<table>
<tr><td>

Types of Cooperative Shares

- Sponsor shares
- Unsold shares
- Sold shares

</td></tr>
</table>

A **holder of unsold shares** is any person or legal entity designated by the original sponsor to be a holder of these shares. A holder of unsold shares receives benefits similar to those of the sponsor; these include the ability to sell the shares to anyone without the board's consent and the unlimited ability to sublease the unit to any individual without the board's consent.

In order for one to be considered a holder of unsold shares, the holder and/or any member of the holder's family may not reside in the unit. Any residency by holders or their family renders their shares *sold shares*.

Sold shares are those purchased by parties with the intent of residing within the unit. When purchased from a sponsor or a holder of unsold shares, upon occupancy of the unit, the shares are deemed sold. Unlike sponsor shares or unsold shares, sold shares fall under the auspices of the board of directors of the co-op (e.g., the right to approve or disapprove of a sublet or sale).

Typical Closing Costs/Fees

In New York City, approximately 82 percent of housing is held in cooperative ownership. The following information is intended to provide an overview of what sellers and buyers of cooperatives can expect to pay or experience in closing costs and other related items. Some of the seller costs include the following:

- State transfer tax on the deed ($2 per $500 of purchase price or fraction thereof)
- For residential transactions that occur in New York City, New York City transfer tax of either
  - 1 percent of the purchase price (up to $500,000 or less),
  - 1.425 percent of the purchase price for sales over $500,000
- New York State estimated capital gains withholding tax of 7.7 percent of any gain; exceptions include, but may not be limited to the following:
  - If the property represented the sellers primary residence for at least two years out of the last five years
  - If at the time of sale, the selling party was a legal resident of New York State
  - The sale was a qualified 1031 exchange
- Unless otherwise exempt by law, a federal withholding tax of 10 percent retained by the buyer. This will usually apply to a seller of property who is not a legal permanent resident of the U.S. Most transactions are exempt from this requirement as the parties are legal permanent residents of the United States.
- Legal fees
- Brokerage commissions
- Move-out elevator fees
- Flip tax (generally about 2 percent of the purchase price, however, it varies from co-op to co-op)
- Transferring agent fee (varies from property to property)
- Mortgage payoff fees

In most cases, with the possible exception of flip taxes, most of these seller fees would be applicable to condominium transactions as well.

■ CONDOMINIUMS

The buyer of a **condominium** receives a deed conveying fee simple ownership of the unit and an undivided interest in the **common elements**. (See Figure 24.4.) The unit itself usually consists of little more than airspace bounded by the innermost layers of construction, often interior drywall.

Chief among the common elements are the land and the exteriors of the buildings. Also common property are foyers; hallways; main walls; basements; elevators; stairwells; heating, plumbing, and electrical systems; and in suburban locations, driveways, private roads, sidewalks, lawns, landscaping, and recreational facilities. In addition, the condominium typically does not have an underlying loan on the land and common elements. However, on occasion, an underlying loan may be placed to finance certain capital improvements. It is subsequently repaid through assessments to the unit owners. These assessments are over and above the normal monthly common charges.

In most respects, the law regards a residential condominium owner as it would the owner of a single detached house. The unit receives an individual tax account number and tax bill and may be mortgaged as a house would be. Unlike in cooperative ownership in which a master insurance policy is held for the cooperative by the corporation, the condominium owner places a separate insurance policy on the living space. Income tax advantages are identical to those for single homes. Owners are free to sell the property, lease it, give it away, or leave it to heirs. Each unit is financially independent, and if an adjoining unit is foreclosed, no obligation is incurred by the other owners.

Owners are, however, bound by the **bylaws** of an owners' association to which all belong. The bylaws are the rules and regulations that govern the activity of the condominium. Monthly fees are levied for the maintenance, insurance, and management of common elements. If unpaid, these common charges become a lien against the individual unit and even may be enforced by foreclosure. The bylaws also set up **covenants, conditions, and restrictions (CC&Rs)**; for example, they may prohibit the display of For Sale signs or painting the front door bright red. Owners even may adopt bylaws that restrict leasing of the units.

F I G U R E   24.4

Condominium Ownership

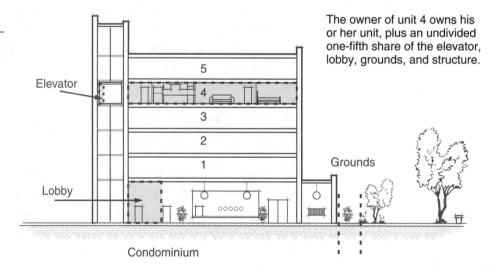

The owner of unit 4 owns his or her unit, plus an undivided one-fifth share of the elevator, lobby, grounds, and structure.

Selling Condominiums

A condominium is usually managed by an elected *board of managers*. When there are more than 25 units, a board often hires professional management. The broker who deals in such properties must be concerned with some items that do not apply to the marketing of single homes. The buyer of a condominium must receive detailed statements about the property, should read the CC&Rs, and must be alerted to any unpaid common charges against the unit. Prospective buyers should also examine the **reserves**, funds set aside to accumulate for large expenses resulting from major capital improvements like new roofs or heating units. The sale of a condominium is arranged on a special form of contract. In most cases, the owners' association retains a first right of refusal. This means that if the association disapproves of the incoming occupant, the owners' association must purchase that same unit from the selling party at the same terms as the prospective buyer.

Although it is most widely used for residential property, condominium ownership is growing for professional buildings, office buildings, and shopping malls.

■ CONDOMINIUM/COOPERATIVE CONSTRUCTION AND CONVERSION

Many condominium and cooperative projects, particularly in the New York City area, are *conversions* from rental properties. The sale of any form of shared housing is considered a *public offering* and falls under the jurisdiction of the New York State attorney general's office. If the proposal is for a condominium, a *declaration*, along with floor plans for each unit, must be filed with the county clerk. The **declaration** contains a complete description of the land, building, and individual units; describes common elements; and states the percentage of ownership for each unit. Bylaws are also included.

Whether for new construction or a conversion, the developer or sponsor must file a *disclosure statement* (or *offering plan*) with the attorney general's office. The statement includes an architect's or engineer's report of the physical condition of the building, a statement of past and projected expenses, prices for each unit and expected amount of tax deductions, management arrangements, a description of the corporation (if a cooperative), and a sample unit deed (for a condominium).

The declaration is included in the disclosure statement. If the offering is for a cooperative, the disclosure statement includes the form of the proprietary lease.

After it has been reviewed by the attorney general's office, the *preliminary prospectus* for a conversion, or **red herring**, is available for inspection by present tenants. At this point, it is subject to modification. When a plan is accepted for filing by the attorney general's office (usually within four to six months in the case of a conversion and 30 days in the case of new construction), it is issued as a **black book** (also known as the offering plan) to potential buyers. It is usually at this point that *flipping* of contracts may occur. **Flipping** is a transaction in which one party contracts to buy a property with the intention of quickly transferring (or flipping) the property over to the ultimate buyer.

Conversion Restrictions

If the property is occupied, special regulations safeguarding the rights of tenants are in effect in New York City and in parts of Westchester, Nassau, and Rockland counties. Under a *noneviction plan* in Westchester, Nassau, and Rockland counties, unless at least 15 percent of present tenants agree to purchase their units, the property may not be converted to condominium or cooperative ownership. In New York City, the property may be converted under a noneviction plan if purchase agreements are signed for 15 percent of the apartments (whether by tenants or nontenants).

If the sponsor intends to evict present tenants at the expiration of their leases (referred to as an *eviction plan*), at least 51 percent of the tenants must state their intention to purchase. Other communities across the state are eligible to adopt the regulations if they choose. Disabled persons and those older than 62 are exempt from eviction. To encourage tenant participation, the sponsor may offer discounts that frequently average out to 20 percent to one-third off the list price.

Nonpurchasers may have three-year protection from eviction under an eviction plan, and tenants in occupancy have a 90-day exclusive right to purchase and other benefits. If the sponsor elects to pursue the noneviction (15 percent) route, all those tenants who do not wish to purchase may remain as tenants under whatever rent regulations may be in effect. The sponsor's inside sales staff, working as employees, are not required to hold any real estate license.

Condo Issues

The sponsor's role is primarily in the creation and ultimate sale of the condominium. As we previously learned, condominiums are created by conversion of rental property or as new construction. The sponsor creates the initial offering plan. When the offering plan is approved by the attorney general's office, the sponsor is then permitted to commence with the sale of the condominiums to others.

At a certain point in the sell-off of the units, the sponsor appoints board members and a managing agent to facilitate the management of the property for the unit owners. Going forward, the purpose behind the board and management appointments is to limit the sponsor's further involvement in the property. This does not alleviate the sponsor from financial responsibility that survives the sellout of the units. In addition, as sales continue, the sponsor is required to relinquish any control of the board to the owner-purchasers (also known as turnover or sponsor turnover).

New Development

Purchasers of a condominium new development are required to do their homework, or due diligence. This entails the reading of the initial offering plan, a function usually performed by the purchaser's attorney. The buyer or buyer's attorney will look for issues in the offering plan that may involve the buyer's exposure to special risks. As we have previously learned in this chapter, the offering plan must be furnished to the buyer, and its purpose is to provide the buyer with the property information and disclosures necessary to verify and validate property tax issues, square footage and floor plan, any hidden fees, and closing date(s).

Letters of intent A letter of intent usually comes in the form of an offer. Written offers are generally nonbinding. The letter of intent is used as a vehicle to reserve a specific unit or units. It also sets forth an understanding of the terms of the transaction between the sponsor and prospective purchaser. This process usually occurs in the early stages of construction.

Legal ramifications of a letter of intent The mere submission of an offer to purchase is nonbinding on the parties. Neither party is bound by the offer unless the offer has been accepted by the seller and both parties have entered into a formal written contract of purchase and sale. However, a letter of intent can be used to indicate the interest of the parties to enter into a more formalized arrangement at some point in the future. Although letters of intent are not legally binding and do not create any obligation on the part of either party, they do have their advantages. For the buyer, a letter of intent shows the seller the buyer's willingness to pursue the transaction. It may even include a price lock-in at project inception pricing levels. For the developer, the letter of intent can serve a different purpose. It can be shown to a lender to induce that lender to fund the developer's project. By showing a lender that numerous parties have indicated interest in a project, the development takes on a different appearance: it is not viewed by the lender as speculative. This can be a major advantage when seeking construction or permanent financing.

Price changes As construction and sales progress, the sponsor creates offering plan amendments. These amendments address the price changes that occur over time and register this information with the attorney general's office. Early sales generally reflect aggressive pricing by the sponsor meant to ensure immediate sales. Depending on market conditions at the time of development and as the units are sold, gradual price increases occur. This is common practice on new developments. Amendments to the offering plan are also filed to disclose other changes to the project.

Certificate of occupancy A certificate of occupancy (C of O) is issued by the department of buildings of the municipality where the property is located. When issued, the C of O indicates that the property conforms to all local building codes and is ready for habitation. Prior to the issuance of a permanent C of O, the building may receive a temporary C of O, or TCO. This is particularly important to transactions involving financing. In order to extend financing to a qualified borrower, lenders require either a TCO or a permanent C of O.

Title insurance Title insurance is not a requirement under law, but it is purchased to protect the buyer against any current or future defects discovered in the title that was transferred. In addition, whenever the financing of a condominium is involved, as a condition of the borrowing, lenders will require the borrower to purchase a title insurance policy.

Closing costs Closing costs on condominiums directly resemble the costs associated with other types of fee simple purchase closings.

The sponsor-seller pays for the preparation of the deed used to transfer the title and transfer taxes associated with the sale.

The buyer will pay for prorated charges due the sponsor-seller, mansion taxes resulting from the purchase of a unit over $1,000,000, recording of the deed, title insurance policies, mortgage recording taxes, and any other item unique to that transaction.

Condominium board packages do not differ from cooperative board packages. The purpose of the package for the condo board is to establish the buyer's financial qualification. All of the same financial information contained in a cooperative board package can also be found in a condominium package. This includes income information and verification (to include details regarding salary, commission, bonus, interest, dividend, capital gains from the sale of investments, and business equity); details on assets and related topics (to include available cash on hand, stocks, bonds, mutual funds, T-bills, and retirement pension plan information and balances); and financing information (to include loan-to-value ratio, loan amount, and down payment).

■ CONDOPS

As indicated previously, cooperatives are generally organized as not-for-profit entities. In order to preserve this status under the tax laws, the IRS places restrictions on cooperatives regarding the co-op's passive income activities. (Passive income activities include rents for commercial spaces, satellite dishes, vending machines, or other income-producing activity outside of maintenance payments.)

In the case of cooperatives, the main income activity to the property comes in the form of monthly maintenance payments received from the co-op's shareholders. Until the restriction was repealed in 2007, the 80/20 rule restricted the co-op from achieving passive income activity in excess of an amount representing 20 percent of its operating budget in any given year.

Due to the old 80/20 rule, a hybrid of condominiums and cooperatives, called a condop, emerged. Formation was usually in new construction or created when the condop was situated in leasehold property. A condop was a condominium in which the developer had solved the 80/20 issue through ownership retention in the project's income-producing sources listed above. It was always the intent of the sponsor to sell off the residential units to individuals while retaining an interest in the commercial spaces within the development for future income-producing purposes. The income benefited the developer while it directly solved the 80/20 issue for the property.

The end result of the condop structure is condominium ownership in the land by the residential units and condominium ownership in the land by the developer for the commercial spaces. The residential portion of the property is operated as a cooperative. As a result of this setup, units are subject to condominium bylaws. The cooperative shareholder receives condominium flexibility in matters concerning sales and subletting.

Regardless of how the living units will be operated, the condominium bylaws always state how the property must be run. Unlike cooperatives that possess the right to decline an applicant for purchase and sale of shares associated with a living unit, condominium's only have the right of first refusal. In order to be exclusionary, the board of managers must exercise this right. In doing so, the board would have to match the sales price of the proposed sale with the new applicant and close on the transaction. This event is not very common.

From an income tax point of view, a cooperative's organizational structure offers higher tax benefits than those of a condominium. The extra benefit consists of a unit per share deduction of the interest attributable to the underlying mortgage on the cooperative. This deduction is not available in condominium ownership. Tax deductibility creates an additional marketing tool for the developer for the sale of residential units.

■ SUMMARY

New construction of rental housing has decreased due primarily to the rising cost of land and development costs. With the dwindling inventory of available land comes rising land costs. These rising land costs have given way to two popular types of housing: cooperatives and condominiums. In co-ops, the purchaser receives ownership in shares of stock within the corporation that owns the property. These shares constitute personal property, not real property. Condominium purchasers receive a deed to their unit; their ownership consists of two elements: ownership in their unit and ownership in common areas. In addition, a hybrid of these housing vehicles has emerged known as condops.

Whether a property is new construction or existing construction, careful attention is required when reading offering plans. The offering plans are designed to inform the reader as to disclosures concerning the property and its features.

One of the most important features to a condo or co-op transaction is the preparation of the board package. The board package is designed to be a full submission of all financial and personal information concerning the prospective purchaser. Preparation is usually accomplished with the assistance of the licensee. Board package preparation is truly a talent, and the package itself acts as a personal introduction and presentation of the prospective purchaser.

CHAPTER 24 QUIZ

1. In a cooperative, each apartment purchaser receives
   a. fee simple ownership of the apartment.
   b. undivided ownership in the cooperative.
   c. tenancy-in-common ownership of the entire building.
   d. stock in a corporation.

2. The habitation rules that govern all shareholders in a cooperative are called
   a. house rules.
   b. articles of the corporation.
   c. recognition agreements.
   d. covenants, conditions, and restrictions (CC&Rs).

3. The income tax treatment for an owner of a cooperative apartment
   a. does not allow the deduction of interest paid on the co-op loan.
   b. is about the same as for the owner of a single home.
   c. only allows the co-op owner to deduct the interest paid on the cooperative's underlying mortgage.
   d. differs completely from that for homeowners because the individual unit is not really owned.

4. When an individual wants to purchase a unit in a cooperative, personal and financial information about the individual is submitted to the board of directors in what is called the
   a. prospective portfolio.
   b. board package.
   c. offering plan.
   d. recognition agreement.

5. The organizing party in the formation of a cooperative is called the
   a. director.
   b. proprietor.
   c. sponsor.
   d. founder.

6. Which act is NOT allowed for the holder of unsold shares of a cooperative?
   a. Selling the shares without consent of the board
   b. Subleasing the unit without the consent of the board
   c. Establishing the selling price of a unit
   d. Residing in the unit

7. Unlike a cooperative, a condominium typically does NOT
   a. have a board of directors.
   b. provide homeowner tax benefits to unit owners.
   c. have an underlying loan on the land and common elements.
   d. allow investors to purchase units.

8. When a building is being converted to a condominium for public offering, the sponsor must file a proposal called a
   a. declaration.
   b. proclamation.
   c. conversation statement.
   d. letter of intent.

9. Residents of a building who learn that the building they live in might be converted to condominiums have the opportunity to read about the conversion in the
   a. offering plan.
   b. bylaws.
   c. red herring.
   d. letter of intent.

10. What government unit is responsible for approving public offerings of condominiums in New York?
    a. Commissioner of New York State Law
    b. County Real Property Director
    c. Commissioner of Human Rights
    d. Attorney General

11. What is the major objective of condominium conversion restrictions?

    a. Safeguarding the rights of tenants
    b. Protecting the sponsor's investment
    c. Achieving diversity among residents
    d. Stabilizing the price of housing

12. An interested buyer heard that a developer is creating a condominium project in which he would like to live. The buyer can express interest and make an offer for purchasing a unit in the project by using a(n)

    a. unsolicited bid.
    b. declaration of interest.
    c. offering plan.
    d. letter of intent.

13. When the buyer purchased her cooperative apartment, she received financing from ABC bank, which required the co-op board to sign a form acknowledging the bank's lien interest in the buyer's interest in the co-op shares. This form is called the

    a. alteration agreement.
    b. declaration of interest.
    c. recognition agreement.
    d. offering plan.

14. In a condop, the residential portion of the property is structured as

    a. a condominium.
    b. a co-op.
    c. single homes.
    d. rental units.

15. The 80/20 rule that applies to co-ops restricts the level of

    a. maintenance fee increases.
    b. sublets.
    c. passive income.
    d. application rejections.

CHAPTER 25

Property Insurance

■ **KEY TERMS**

actual cash value

boiler and machinery
   insurance

business interruption
   insurance

casualty insurance

certificate of insurance

coinsurance clause

contents and personal
   property insurance

deductible

fire and hazard insurance

homeowners' insurance
   policy

liability insurance

monoline policy

multiperil policy

package policy

property insurance

replacement cost

surety bonds

umbrella policy

workers' compensation
   acts

■ **INSURANCE COVERAGE**

Purpose of Property Insurance

One of the most important responsibilities of property ownership is to protect the integrity of the property from and against all major insurable risks. Chapter 21 covers various types of risk, including two types of business risk: *dynamic* and *static*.

Dynamic risk is defined as the *uninsurable* risk associated with changes in the economy, income taxes, and supply versus demand issues. *Static risk* is defined as *insurable* risk associated with events such as accident liability, fire, theft, and vandalism.

Due to the insurable nature of static risk events, the investor and/or homeowner is able to underwrite these events through the purchase of **property insurance**.

In cases where absentee ownership exists, a management firm may be hired to act in a custodial capacity. The firm is charged with the responsibility of overseeing the property (see Chapter 22).

Either the owner or the property management company will arrange for insurance coverage on a subject property. In some cases, a property manager or a member of the management firm may even be a licensed insurance broker. To avoid future charges of *self-dealing* in this arena, the owner should be made aware of the situation by disclosure from the appropriate party and consent to it in advance of services being rendered in this area. In other cases, the purchase of insurance can be accomplished through the use of independent agents, insurance companies, or insurance brokers.

Insurance companies prefer dealing with independent agents or insurance brokers for placement of commercial policies. For residential policies, some insurance companies offer direct policy placement to members of the general public. In either case, a competent, reliable insurance agent who is well versed in all areas of insurance pertaining to property should be selected to survey the property and make recommendations. Final decisions, however, must be made by the property owner. *An insurance broker must have passed a state examination to secure a special license to sell insurance.*

Types of Coverage

Many kinds of insurance coverage are available to income-producing property owners and managers. Some of the more common types include the following:

- *Fire and hazard*. **Fire and hazard insurance** policies provide coverage against direct loss or damage to property from a fire on the premises. Standard fire coverage can be extended to cover hazards such as windstorm, hail, smoke damage, or civil insurrection. Most popular today is the all-risks or special form.
- *Business interruption*. Most hazard policies insure against the actual loss of property but do not cover loss of revenues from income property. **Business interruption insurance** covers the loss of income that occurs if the property cannot be used to produce income.
- *Contents and personal property*. Inland marine insurance, or **contents and personal property insurance**, covers building contents and personal property (which includes any property that is movable, such as a briefcase) during periods when they are not actually located on the business premises.
- *Liability*. Public **liability insurance** covers the risks an owner assumes when the public enters the building. Medical expenses are paid for a person injured in the building as a result of owner/landlord negligence. Another liability risk is that of medical or hospital payments for injuries sustained by building employees in the course of their employment. These claims are covered by state laws known as **workers' compensation acts**. These laws require that a building owner who is an employer obtain a workers' compensation policy from a private insurance company.

■ *Casualty.* **Casualty insurance** policies include coverage against theft, burglary, vandalism, and machinery damage as well as health and accident. Casualty policies usually are written on specific risks such as theft, rather than being all-inclusive.

■ *Surety bonds.* **Surety bonds** cover an owner against financial losses that result from an employee's criminal acts or negligence while carrying out his or her duties. A blanket crime policy is most often chosen.

■ *Boiler and machinery coverage.* **Boiler and machinery insurance** covers repair and replacement of heating plants, central air-conditioning units, and other major equipment.

■ *Umbrella coverage.* An **umbrella policy** is a type of excess liability coverage with two basic forms: *personal* and *commercial.* Personal umbrella policies are designed to provide coverage for those areas and items that would fall between the cracks with other policies. Personal umbrella policies do not cover the individual in business activities, but commercial coverage is available to underwrite these events. Commercial coverage operates in a similar manner as personal umbrella coverage but does not provide personal umbrella protection.

Types of Insurance Coverage

■ Fire and hazard
■ Business interruption
■ Contents and personal property
■ Liability
■ Casualty
■ Surety bonds
■ Boiler and machinery coverage
■ Umbrella coverage

Homeowners can purchase any of these policies that do not apply to operation of income-producing property or commercial activities.

Lower premiums may be offered on property that qualifies as a *highly protected risk (HPR),* based on the quality of water supply, sprinklers, alarms, security personnel, and loss control programs. Many insurance companies offer **multiperil policies** for apartment and business buildings. These include standard types of commercial coverage: fire, hazard, public liability, and casualty.

Monoline policy   A **monoline** policy bears greater relevancy to insurers than to the insured. This type of policy provides only one line or area of coverage. In addition, many states restrict the insurance provider from further offering any line or type of coverage other than the line being offered.

For example, state insurance laws include provisions that any insurer who provides financial guaranty insurance (a policy that provides for protection against loss of income that falls short of a minimum prescribed threshold amount) would be restricted to offering only that line or type of insurance.

Package policy   A **package** policy is one policy that provides for a variety of different coverage types.

Certificates of insurance   Whenever real estate transactions include financing (acquisition financing or refinancing of a loan), lenders require advance proof of coverage. This is usually accomplished by submitting an *insurance certificate* or a **certificate of insurance.** Issuing certificates of insurance has been the accepted means of proving appropriate insurance coverage for many years in both commercial and residential real property closings.

As a result of the ever-changing climate in the insurance industry, many insurers are adding a variety of disclaimers (exclusions) to standard certificates of insurance. In the eyes of many lenders, these disclaimers can at times render the issued certificate worthless. A careful review of the insurance certificate or policy will reveal critical areas of coverage and will include considerations to other areas of concern, such as damage and destruction (to include rent abatement issues and business interruption), waivers of subrogation, requirements of insurance, force majeure, indemnity sections, and cancellation notices.

The minimum coverage required by lending parties will usually consist of an amount equal to or greater than the amount borrowed.

Commercial Claims

Insurance policies utilize the cost approach to valuation, which involves the same techniques used by an appraiser for either single-use/purpose property or new construction. Therefore, when a claim is made under a policy insuring a building or other physical object, either of two methods can determine the amount of the claim. One is the depreciated, or actual, cash value of the damaged property. The other is replacement cost. If a 30-year-old building is damaged, the timbers and materials are 30 years old and, therefore, do not have the same value as new material. Thus, in determining the amount of the loss under what is called **actual cash value**, the cost of new material would be reduced by the estimated depreciation, based on the time the item had been in the building.

The alternate method is to cover **replacement cost**. This represents the actual amount a builder would charge to replace the damaged property at the time of the loss, including materials. When purchasing insurance, a manager must assess whether the property should be insured at full replacement cost or at a depreciated cost. As with homeowners' policies, commercial policies usually carry *coinsurance* clauses that require coverage up to 80 percent of the building's replacement value. The figure of 80 percent is derived from the federal tax laws that state that land (which is never depreciable or insurable) always represents 20 percent of the overall property's value. For example, assume that a property is valued at $500,000. To determine the value of the improvement, the value of the land must be subtracted from the overall value:

> Insurable value of the improvement = Total value of land and improvement
> × Percentage representing the insurable improvement
> Insurable value of the improvement = $500,000 × 0.80 = $400,000

Many property managers, faced with filing an insurance claim, call on professional private adjusters, who are skilled in representing owners in negotiations with insurers.

Residential Claims

Homeowners' insurance policies also contain a **coinsurance clause**; this provision typically requires that the insured maintain fire insurance on the property equal to at least 80 percent of the *replacement cost* of the dwelling. (As noted above, this 80 percent figure is meant to account for the fact that the land represents 20 percent of the property's value.) Replacement cost is generally calculated by taking the replacement cost (new) of the item(s) minus any accrued depreciation. With such a policy, the owner may make a claim for the cost of the repair or replacement of the damaged property without deduction.

In any event, the total settlement may not exceed the face value of the policy. Because of coinsurance clauses, it is important that homeowners review their policies regularly to be certain that the coverage provided is equal to at least 80 percent of the current replacement cost of their homes. Some policies carry automatic increases in coverage to adjust for inflation.

Homeowners' Insurance

As you learned in Chapter 9, homeowners' insurance policies are an important part of the closing of a property transaction. Where mortgage financing is involved, the buyer must bring to the closing proof of insurance on the property and, occasionally, proof of flood insurance. The insurance policy or binder usually names the lender as lienholder, additionally insured and copayee in case of loss under the policy. In almost every case, a deductible will exist. The **deductible** (as it relates to insurance policies) represents the monetary portion of the damages the property owner will bear if and when a covered loss occurs.

Although it is possible for a homeowner to obtain individual policies for each type of risk, most residential property owners take out insurance in the form of a packaged **homeowners' insurance policy**. These standardized policies insure holders against the destruction of their property by fire or windstorm, injury to others that occurs on the property, and theft of any personal property on the premises that is owned by the insured or members of his or her family.

The homeowners' policy also includes *liability insurance* for personal injuries to others resulting from the insured's acts or negligence, voluntary medical payments and funeral expenses for accidents sustained by guests or resident employees on the property of the owner, and physical damage to the property of others caused by the insured.

Characteristics of homeowners' packages   There are four major forms of homeowners' policies. The *basic* form, known as *HO-1*, provides property coverage against fire or lightning; glass breakage; windstorm or hail; explosion; riot or civil commotion; damage by aircraft; damage from vehicles; damage from smoke; vandalism and malicious mischief; theft; and loss of property removed from the premises when endangered by fire or other perils.

Increased coverage is provided under a *broad* form, known as *HO-2*, that also covers falling objects; weight of ice, snow, or sleet; collapse of the building or any part of it; bursting, cracking, burning, or bulging of a steam or hot water heating system or of appliances used to heat water; accidental discharge, leakage, or overflow of water or steam from within a plumbing, heating, or air-conditioning system; freezing of plumbing, heating, and air-conditioning systems, and domestic appliances; and injury to electrical appliances, devices, fixtures, and wiring from short circuits or other accidentally generated currents.

Further coverage is provided by *comprehensive* forms, *HO-3*, the most popular form, and *HO-5*. These policies cover all possible perils except flood, earthquake, war, and nuclear attack.

Other policies include *HO-4*, a form designed specifically for apartment renters (renters policy), and *HO-6*, a broad-form policy for condominium owners. Apartment and condominium policies generally provide fire and windstorm, theft, and public liability coverage for injuries or losses sustained within the unit but usually do not extend to cover losses or damages to the structure. The structure is insured by either the landlord or the condominium owners' association.

The HO-8, or *market value policy*, is a modified version of the HO-1 basic policy. It provides for actual cash value coverage in place of replacement cost coverage for a building. Under this coverage, the insurance company's settlement figure will not exceed the amount required to repair or replace the dwelling. This policy form is generally used when the replacement value of the property exceeds its market value. Such is usually the case for older homes.

It is important to note that homeowner policies will not cover any loss resulting from a change in building codes. This change may require the property owner to replace the improvement with building materials that are not covered under the policy. However, one may purchase additional coverage in the form of a rider to the homeowners' policy covering these events and additional costs. At present time, most insurance companies will not issue coverage in excess of 125 percent of replacement cost. (See Figure 25.1.)

It should be noted that cooperative shareholder insurance policies resemble that of a renters' policy. Due to the fact that the cooperative corporation owns the land and improvements attached thereto, they are responsible for obtaining the necessary insurance coverage for building. In most cooperatives, the cooperative corporation is responsible to effectuate repairs to any condition that forms a part of the real property. This generally covers anything inside the walls, floors, and ceilings of the shareholder unit. For this reason, individual shareholders will only need to insure their personal property (contents) and, in some cases, obtain some form of liability insurance coverage.

FIGURE   25.1

Replacement Value Coverage

Assume the following information:

1. A fire occurs and the improvement is destroyed.
2. Policy replacement cost limits are $400 per square foot.
3. A change in building codes no longer allows the use of the same building materials used in the previous improvement.
4. Costs for replacements in compliance with the building codes are now estimated at $475 per square foot.
5. The insured has purchased a rider providing for replacement value coverage up to 125 percent.

Maximum replacement coverage would be calculated as follows:

Maximum replacement coverage = Existing policy replacement cost limit × Extended coverage under a separate rider

Maximum replacement coverage = $400 per square foot × 1.25 = $500 per square foot

In this scenario, maximum extended coverage would be up to $500 per square foot. The insurance policy would cover the total replacement of the improvement.

Condominiums operate in the same manner as other fee simple transactions. The property owner purchases a homeowners' policy.

Federal Flood Insurance Program

Property owners in certain areas must obtain flood damage insurance before they can obtain federally related mortgages. Federally related loans include those made by banks, savings and loan associations, or other lenders whose deposits are insured by federal agencies (FDIC or FSLIC); those insured by the FHA or guaranteed by the VA; mortgages administered by the U.S. Department of Housing and Urban Development; and loans intended to be sold by the lender to Fannie Mae, Ginnie Mae, or Freddie Mac. An owner may be able to avoid purchasing flood insurance by furnishing a survey showing that the lowest part of the building is above the 100-year flood mark. Information on national flood insurance can be obtained by calling 800-358-9616, by visiting *www.fema.gov*, or by writing to the Federal Emergency Management Agency at Box 1038, Jessup, MD 20794.

Tax Reserves/Impounds and Insurance Reserves (Escrows)

A *reserve or impound* is a sum of money set aside to be used later for a particular purpose. This reserve or impound will usually occur when financing is arranged on the acquisition of property. The mortgage lender generally requires that the borrower establish and maintain a reserve so that there will be sufficient funds to pay property taxes and renew hazard insurance when these items become due. To set up the reserve, the borrower makes a lump-sum payment or equal monthly installment payments to the lender when the mortgage money is paid out (usually at the time of closing) or after closing. After that, the borrower pays into the escrow account an amount equal to one month's portion of the *estimated* general tax and insurance premium as part of the monthly PITI (principal, interest, taxes, and insurance) payment to the mortgage company.

Cancellation and Nonrenewals of a Policy

Generally, insurance policies covering real property are for a term of one year. This is not to imply that longer-term policies are unavailable; however, when a policy is purchased, it has a commencement and expiration date. Notices are sent out to the insured advising that the policy is due to expire on the policy expiration date. The notice will also include declaration pages indicating the cost of the premium to renew the policy. The policyholder decides whether to extend the policy. If the term of the policy lapses, insurance coverage ceases to exist on the subject property unless the policy is renewed for an additional term.

On some occasions, insurance providers will refuse coverage. This may occur as a result of a review of the subject's loss run schedule. The *loss run schedule* is the insurance term for a schedule showing previous claim history. Prior to extending a policy for coverage, the insurer performs this process as part of the insurer's underwriting program.

Problems in Obtaining Insurance

Generally speaking, insurance policies are not difficult to arrange. However, certain types of coverage are harder to achieve than others. An example would be flood insurance and, in some cases, terrorism insurance. The difficulty is not the origination of the policy as much as the expensive premiums associated with it. When originating insurance coverage, it is always advisable to leave as much time as possible to shop for appropriate coverage and inexpensive premiums.

New York Property Insurance Underwriting Association

The New York Property Insurance Underwriting Association is a joint underwriting association. It was created in 1968 under the laws of the state of New York. Its purpose was to meet the basic insurance needs of the public. Since its inception, the association has been responsive to the varied needs of the insuring public and provides a variety of property insurance coverage, such as the following:

- Vandalism
- Fire
- Loss of rent
- Business interruption

Coastal Residents Assistance

Federal and state legislators are constantly focused on coastal and natural catastrophe concerns. This includes hurricanes and other weather-related acts. Programs such as FEMA provide financial assistance to those affected by these events. Other flood perils are generally covered by federal flood insurance (previously discussed).

Insurance Policy Deductibles

Property insurance policies contain policy deductible amounts. These amounts are deducted from the initial insurance recovery amount. The deductible is borne by the policyholder. For example, a policy contains a $1,000 deductible from any covered loss. If the recovered amount under the policy totals $10,000, the net payment to the insured would be $9,000. In almost every case, low deductible amounts result in higher premiums for that policy.

New York disclosure requirements regarding deductibles   Chapter 44 of the Laws of 1998 enacted a new Section 3445 of the Insurance Law. This law required the superintendent of insurance to establish by regulation disclosure requirements concerning the existence of any deductible in a homeowners' insurance policy. Under Section 3445, the form of notice that was to be provided by an insurer to an insured was intended to explain in clear and plain language the amount of the deductible as well as how the deductible would apply to the issued policy.

Real Estate Agent's Role

Most real property transactions involve some form of mortgage financing. When such is the case, a lender will always require proof of property insurance coverage.

The licensee is advised to bring this awareness to the buyer's attention early in the transaction. Failure to address this issue can cause a delay in closing the sale or, in some cases, the deal will not be consummated. The licensee is encouraged to

- suggest that the buyer arrange for insurance coverage in advance,
- contact an insurance broker to arrange for same,
- explain the purpose and costs for having property insurance,
- explain the lender's interest in property insurance,
- explain the escrow of property insurance along with property taxes, and
- explain when to obtain property insurance if there is a cash sale.

■ SUMMARY

Insurance serves the purpose of protecting property owners against perils that are normally beyond their control. Individual policies guard against a variety of events, while commercial policies are used in business and commerce. A residential property acquisition in which financing is involved requires the purchaser/borrower to provide proof of property coverage. This is normally accomplished through certificates of insurance. The purpose behind insuring the property is to protect the owner against a variety of risks while simultaneously protecting the lender's secured interest on the property.

Commercial policies can range from actual value policies to replacement value coverage. When calculating replacement value, the cost approach is utilized to determine the value of the improvement. This approach takes into consideration the cost of the new improvement less accrued depreciation within the existing improvement prior to the peril. The accrued depreciation is deducted to account for the age of the existing improvement.

Some insurance providers offer monoline policies (only one line or area of coverage), while others provide package policies (policies that provide for a variety of different coverage types). In certain areas and transactions, flood insurance may be necessary. As the need may arise, a licensee should be familiar with the various types of insurance policies available.

CHAPTER 25 QUIZ

1. Which event is an example of static risk?
   a. Market value of a home drops after a major employer leaves the community.
   b. A vandal causes extensive damage by breaking windows and spraying graffiti.
   c. The IRS changes deductibility of interest paid on mortgages.
   d. Market value of a home rises as interest rates drop and demand rises.

2. Fire and hazard insurance policies can be extended to cover
   a. employees' criminal acts.
   b. personal property when it is not located in the property.
   c. medical expenses for visitors injured on the property.
   d. damage from windstorms.

3. Business interruption insurance covers
   a. the loss of income.
   b. damage to the premises.
   c. injuries of people working on the property.
   d. loss of value due to market trends.

4. Excess liability coverage that provides coverage for those areas that would "fall between the cracks" with other policies is referred to as
   a. surety bonds.
   b. multiperil insurance.
   c. umbrella coverage.
   d. monoline policies.

5. Casualty insurance policies are usually written
   a. on specific risks.
   b. for broad, inclusive coverage.
   c. to cover employee negligence.
   d. as multiperil policies.

6. An insurance policy that provides only one area of coverage is known as a(n)
   a. limited policy.
   b. umbrella policy.
   c. monoline policy.
   d. package policy.

7. Proof to a lender that a property is covered by insurance is provided through a(n)
   a. insurance certificate.
   b. insurance reserve.
   c. affidavit of coverage.
   d. claim escrow.

8. What would typically be the minimum insurance coverage required on an apartment building loan of $600,000?
   a. $600,000 or greater
   b. $540,000
   c. $420,000
   d. $300,000

9. The two methods used to determine the amount of a commercial claim are depreciated cash value of the damaged property and
   a. actual value.
   b. replacement cost.
   c. land value.
   d. estimated value.

10. The MOST comprehensive homeowners' insurance package is
   a. HO-1.
   b. HO-2.
   c. HO-3.
   d. HO-4.

11. An insurance reserve is usually required on an acquired property when
   a. the construction is less than five years old.
   b. the property is located in a high-risk area.
   c. the purchaser is a first-time owner.
   d. financing is arranged.

12. A loss run schedule shows the history of a subject's
   a. previous claims.
   b. premium payments.
   c. property ownership.
   d. credit activity.

CHAPTER

26

Real Estate Mathematics

■ KEY TERMS

acre	hectare	real property tax rate
front foot	IRV formula	

■ PERCENTAGES

Many real estate computations are based on the calculation of percentages. A percentage expresses a portion of a whole. For example, 50 percent means 50 parts of the possible 100 parts. Percentages greater than 100 percent contain more than one whole unit. Thus 163 percent is one whole and 63 parts of another whole. A whole is always expressed as 100 percent.

Unless a calculator with a percent key is being used, the *percentage must be converted either to a decimal or to a fraction*. To convert a percentage to a decimal, move the decimal two places to the left and drop the percent sign. Thus,

$$60\% = 0.6 \qquad\qquad 7\% = 0.07 \qquad\qquad 175\% = 1.75$$

Think of $1.00 in coins. Just as there are 100 pennies in a dollar, percentages are the 100 smaller units that together equal a whole number of 1. In decimal form, 60 cents ($0.60) would be written the same way as 60 percent (0.60).

To change a percentage to a fraction, place the percentage over 100. For example,

$$50\% = \frac{50}{100}$$

$$115\% = \frac{115}{100}$$

These fractions then may be *reduced* to make it easier to work the problem. To reduce a fraction, determine the largest number by which both numerator and denominator can be divided evenly. For example,

$$\frac{25}{100} = \frac{1}{4} \text{ (both numbers divided by 25)}$$

$$\frac{49}{63} = \frac{7}{9} \text{ (both numbers divided by 7)}$$

Percentage problems contain three elements: *percentage*, *total*, and *part*. To determine a specific percentage of a whole, multiply the percentage by the whole:

Percentage × Whole = Part
5% × 200 = 10

For example, a broker is to receive a 7 percent commission on the sale of a $150,000 house. What will the broker's commission be?

0.07 × $150,000 = $10,500 broker's commission

This formula is used in calculating mortgage loan interest, brokers' commissions, loan origination fees, discount points, amount of earnest money deposits, and income on capital investments.

A variation, or inversion, of the percentage formula is used to find the total amount when the part and percentage are known:

$$\textbf{Whole} = \frac{\textbf{Part}}{\textbf{Percentage}}$$

For example, the Masterson Realty Company received a $9,600 commission for the sale of a house. The broker's commission was 6 percent of the total sales price. What was the total sales price of this house?

$$\frac{\$9,600}{0.06} = \$160,000 \text{ total sales price}$$

This formula is used in computing the total mortgage loan principal still due if the monthly payment and interest rate are known. It is also used to calculate the total sales price when the amount and percentage of commission are known, and the market value of a property when the assessed value and the ratio (percentage) of assessed value to market value are known.

The formula may be used by a real estate salesperson: A buyer has $29,500 available for a down payment, and she must make a 25 percent down payment.

How expensive a home can she purchase? The question is $29,500 is 25 percent of what figure?

$$\frac{\$29,500}{0.25} = \$118,000$$

Such a problem also may be solved by the use of ratios. Thus, $29,500 is to what number as 25 percent is to 100 percent?

$$\frac{\$29,500}{?} = \frac{25}{100}$$

One type of percentage problem may take several forms. For example, a man sold property for $90,000. This represents a 20 percent loss from his original cost. What was his cost?

In this problem the student must resist the impulse to multiply everything in sight. Taking 20 percent of $90,000 yields nothing significant. The $90,000 figure represents 80 percent of the original cost, and the question resolves itself into $90,000 is 80 percent of what figure?

$$\frac{\$90,000}{0.80} = \$112,500$$

Again, a woman clears $88,200 from the sale of her property after paying a 10 percent commission. How much did the property sell for? Taking 10 percent of $88,200 is an incorrect approach to the problem because the commission was based not on the seller's net but on the full, unknown sales figure; $88,200 represents 90 percent of the sales price.

$$\frac{\$88,200}{0.90} = \$98,000$$

To determine the percentage when the amounts of the part and the whole are known:

$$\text{Percent} = \frac{\text{Part}}{\text{Whole}}$$

This formula may be used to find the tax rate when taxes and assessed value are known or the commission rate when sales price and commission amount are known.

The **IRV formula**, which should be memorized, is basic to investment capitalization problems. It works as follows:

Income = Rate × Value
Rate = Income ÷ Value
Value = Income ÷ Rate

FIGURE 26.1

IRV Formula

I R V

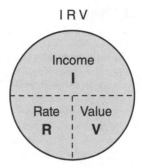

Note the horizontal line within the circle. This line represents a division process when the income and rate figures are provided to calculate the value. In order to calculate the rate, the same process is used when the income and value figures are given.

IRV stands for the following:

- Income, which is the net operating income
- Rate, a percentage figure written in decimal form
- Value, generally the value of a property when a prescribed rate of capitalization is applied

■ RATES

Property taxes, transfer taxes, and insurance premiums are usually expressed as rates. **Real property tax rates** represent the ratio of tax dollars charged in either per hundred or per thousand dollars of assessed valuation. Tax rates are also called mill rates. A rate is the cost expressed as the amount of cost per unit. For example, tax might be computed at the rate of $5 per $100 assessed value in a certain county. The formula for computing rates is as follows:

$$\frac{\textbf{Value}}{\textbf{Unit}} \times \textbf{Rate per unit} = \textbf{Total}$$

For example, a house has been assessed at $90,000 and is taxed at an annual rate of $25 per $1,000 assessed valuation. What is the yearly tax?

$$\frac{\$90,000}{1,000} \times \$25 = \text{Total annual tax}$$

$90,000 ÷ $1,000 = 90 (increments of $100)
90 × $25 = $2,250 total annual tax

■ AREAS AND VOLUMES

To compute the area of a square or rectangular parcel, use the following formula:

Area = Width × Depth

The area of a rectangular lot that measures 100 feet wide by 200 feet deep would be

100' × 200' = 20,000 sq ft

The first figure given always represents front feet; a lot described as "80' × 150'" is 80 feet across and 150 feet deep. Where front footage represents a large part of the value (lakefront, for example), real estate is occasionally priced per **front foot**, with the amount that extends back from the lake left out of the calculation of value. Area is always expressed in square units.

To compute the amount of surface in a triangular area, use the following formula:

Area = ½ (Base × Height)

The base of a triangle is the bottom, on which the triangle rests. The height is an imaginary straight line extending from the point of the uppermost angle straight down to the base. (See Figure 26.2.)

For example, a triangle's base is 50 feet, and its height is 30 feet. What is its area?

½ (50' × 30') = Area in sq ft
½ (1,500) = 750 sq ft

To compute the area of an irregular room or parcel of land, divide the shape into regular rectangles, squares, or triangles. Next, compute the area of each regular figure and add the areas together to obtain the total area.

Example: Compute the area of the hallway shown in Figure 26.3.

FIGURE 26.2

Computing Area of Triangle

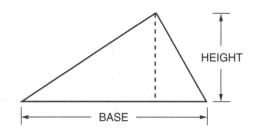

FIGURE 26.3

Measurements of Irregular Shape for Computing Area

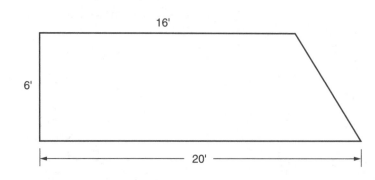

FIGURE   26.4

**Computing Area of
Irregular Shape**

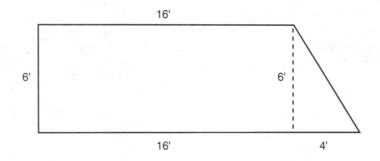

Make a rectangle and a triangle by drawing a single line through the figure. (See Figure 26.4.)

Compute the area of the rectangle:

> Area = Length × Width
> 16' × 6' = 96 sq ft

Compute the area of the triangle:

> Area = ½ (Base × Height)
> ½ (4' × 6') = ½ (24) = 12 sq ft

Total the two areas:

> 96' + 12' = 108 sq ft in total area

The cubic capacity of an enclosed space is expressed as volume, which is used to describe the amount of space in any three-dimensional area, such as the interior airspace of a room, measured to determine what capacity heating unit is required. The formula for computing cubic or rectangular volume is as follows:

> Volume = Length × Width × Height

Volume is always expressed in cubic units.

For example, the bedroom of a house is 12 feet long, 8 feet wide, 8 feet high to the ceiling. How many cubic feet does the room enclose? (See Figure 26.5.)

> 8' × 12' × 8' = 768 cu ft

FIGURE   26.5

**Computing Volume of
Three-Dimensional Area**

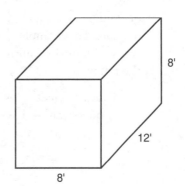

FIGURE 26.6

FIGURE   26.6

Measurements of a House for Computing Volume

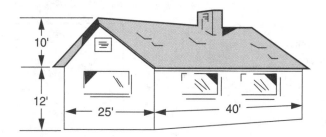

FIGURE   26.7

Computing Volume of a House

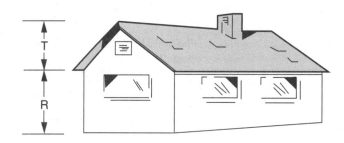

To compute the volume of a triangular space, such as the airspace in an A-frame house, use the following formula:

Volume = ½ (Length × Height × Width)

For example, what is the volume of airspace in the house shown in Figure 26.6?

First, divide the house into two shapes, rectangular and triangular, as shown in Figure 26.7:

Find the volume of *T*:

Volume = ½ (Length × Height × Width)
½ (25' × 10' × 40') = ½ (10,000) = 5,000 cu ft

Find the volume of *R*:

25' × 40' × 12' = 12,000 cu ft

Total volumes *T* and *R*:

5,000' + 12,000' = 17,000 cu ft of airspace in the house

Cubic measurements of volume are used to compute the construction costs per cubic foot of a building, the amount of airspace being sold in a condominium unit, or the heating and cooling requirements for a building. When either area or volume is computed, all dimensions used must be given in the same unit of measure. For example, one may not multiply two feet by six inches to get the area; two feet must be multiplied by one-half foot. Thus, it is important to remember the following:

1 yard = 3 feet
1 square yard = 3' × 3' = 9 square feet
1 cubic yard = 3' × 3' × 3' = 27 cubic feet

■ LAND UNITS AND MEASUREMENTS

Some commonly used land units and measurements follow:

■ A *rod* is 16½ feet.

■ A *chain* is 66 feet, or 100 links.

■ A *mile* is 5,280 feet.

■ An **acre** contains 43,560 square feet. Memorize this one.

■ A *section* of land is one square mile and contains 640 acres; a *quarter section* contains 160 acres; a *quarter of a quarter section* contains 40 acres.

■ A *circle* contains 360 degrees; a *half segment* of a circle contains 180 degrees; a *quarter segment* of a circle contains 90 degrees. *One degree* (1°) can be subdivided into 60 minutes (60'), each of which contains 60 seconds (60"). One-and-a-half degrees would be written 1°30'.

■ A *mill* is one-tenth of a cent, $0.001. When a property tax is quoted as 23 mills, that means $0.023 per $1 of assessed value, the same rate as $23 per $1,000.

Where the metric system is used, a **hectare** is equal to 10,000 square meters, or about 2.471 acres.

CHAPTER 26 QUIZ

1. A rectangular lot measures 60 feet wide and has an area of 1,200 square yards. What is the depth of the lot?
   a. 20 feet
   b. 180 feet
   c. 20 yards
   d. 90 yards

2. A buyer is applying for an FHA mortgage on a house priced at $108,000. The maximum loan-to-value ratio is 97.75. What is the minimum down payment?
   a. $1,054
   b. $1,080
   c. $2,108
   d. $2,430

3. Two brothers invested in a property equally. One brother claimed that he should be entitled to 80 percent of the profits when the property was sold because he was the older brother. How is 80 percent expressed as a reduced fraction?
   a. 80/100
   b. 8/10
   c. 2/5
   d. 4/5

4. A house is valued at $198,000. It is to be insured for 80 percent of its cost. Insurance will cost $6 per $1,000. What is the annual insurance premium?
   a. $95.40
   b. $119.80
   c. $950.40
   d. $1,198.00

5. A homeowner received a net amount of $74,000 from the sale of his house after paying $1,200 in legal and other fees and 6 percent sales commission. What was the selling price of the house?
   a. $80,000
   b. $78,440
   c. $79,640
   d. $79,000

6. A lending institution will allow its borrowers to spend 28 percent of their income for housing expense. What will be the maximum monthly payment allowed for a family with annual income of $57,000 and no other debts?
   a. $399
   b. $1,330
   c. $1,596
   d. None of these

7. A salesperson works on a 50/50 commission split with her broker. If she lists a house at $156,000 for 6 percent commission and sells it for $154,000, how much will the salesperson receive?
   a. $4,620
   b. $4,680
   c. $9,220
   d. $9,360

8. A homeowner's monthly mortgage payment for principal and interest is $628.12. His property taxes are $1,800 a year, and his annual insurance premium is $365. What is his total monthly payment for PITI (principal, interest, taxes, and insurance)?
   a. $808.54
   b. $1,921.24
   c. $778.12
   d. None of these

9. A lot measuring 120' × 200' is selling for $300 a front foot. What is its price?
   a. $720,000
   b. $60,000
   c. $36,000
   d. $800,000

10. A five-acre lot has front footage of 300 feet. How deep is it?
    a. 145.2 feet
    b. 726 feet
    c. 88 feet
    d. 160 feet

11. The broker of Happy Valley Realty recently sold a couple's home for $79,500. The broker charged the couple 6½ percent commission and will pay 30 percent of that amount to the listing salesperson and 25 percent to the selling salesperson. What amount of commission will the listing salesperson receive from the sale?

a. $5,167.50
b. $1,550.25
c. $3,617.25
d. $1,291.87

12. A buyer signed an agreement to purchase a condominium apartment. The contract stipulated that the previous apartment owners replace the damaged bedroom carpet. The carpet the buyer has chosen costs $16.95 per square yard plus $2.50 per square yard for installation. If the bedroom dimensions are as illustrated, how much will the previous apartment owners have to pay for the job?

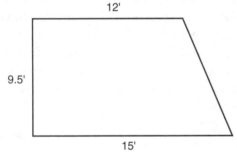

a. $241.54
b. $189.20
c. $277.16
d. $2,494.46

13. Four investors pooled their savings and purchased a vacation home for $125,000. If one of them invested $30,000 and two of them each contributed $35,000, what percentage of ownership was left for the fourth investor?

a. 20 percent
b. 24 percent
c. 28 percent
d. 30 percent

14. A parent is curious to know how much money his son and daughter-in-law still owe on their predatory mortgage loan. He knows that the interest portion of their last monthly payment was $391.42. If the young couple is paying interest at the rate of 11½ percent, what was the outstanding balance of their loan before that last payment was made?

a. $43,713.00
b. $40,843.83
c. $36,427.50
d. $34,284.70

15. A couple bought their home on Sabre Lane a year ago for $98,500. Property in their neighborhood is said to be increasing in value at a rate of 5 percent annually. If this is true, what is the current market value of the couple's real estate?

a. $103,425
b. $93,575
c. $104,410
d. None of these is within $50

16. A home on Dove Street is valued at $95,000. Property in this area is assessed at 60 percent of its value, and the local tax rate is $28.50 per thousand. What is the amount of the monthly taxes for this home?

a. $1,625.50
b. $570.00
c. $270.75
d. $135.38

17. A homeowner is planning to construct a patio in her backyard. An illustration of the surface area to be paved appears here. If the cement is to be poured as a six-inch slab, how many cubic feet of cement will be poured into this patio?

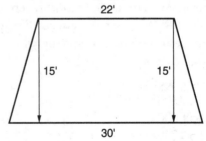

a. 660 cubic feet
b. 450 cubic feet
c. 330 cubic feet
d. 195 cubic feet

529

18. A salesperson receives a monthly salary of $500 plus 3 percent commission on all of his listings that sell and 2½ percent on all his sales. None of the listings that the salesperson took sold last month, but he received $3,675 in salary and commission. What was the value of the property the salesperson sold?

    a. $147,000
    b. $127,000
    c. $122,500
    d. $105,833

19. A residence has proved difficult to sell. A salesperson suggests it might sell faster if the homeowners enclose a portion of the backyard with a privacy fence. If the area to be enclosed is as illustrated, how much would the fence cost at $6.95 per linear foot?

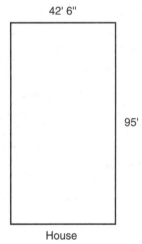

42' 6"

95'

House

    a. $1,911.25
    b. $1,654.10
    c. $1,615.88
    d. $955.63

20. A landlord leases the 12 apartments in the Overton Arms for a total monthly rental of $4,500. If this figure represents an 8 percent annual return on his investment, what was the original cost of the property?

    a. $675,000
    b. $450,000
    c. $54,000
    d. $56,250

21. A 100-acre farm is divided into house lots. The streets require one-eighth of the whole farm, and there are 140 lots. How many square feet are in each lot?

    a. 35,004
    b. 31,114
    c. 27,225
    d. 43,560

22. In a sale of residential property, real estate taxes for the current calendar year amounted to $975 and have already been paid by the seller. The sale is to close on October 26; what is the amount of real estate proration to be credited the seller?

    a. $173.33
    b. $162.50
    c. $798.96
    d. $83.96

23. The buyer is assuming the seller's mortgage. The unpaid balance after the most recent payment (the first of the month) was $61,550. Interest is paid in arrears each month at 13 percent per annum. The sale is to close on September 22; what is the amount of mortgage interest proration to be credited to the buyer at the closing?

    a. $666.97
    b. $488.97
    c. $177.82
    d. $689.01

24. A salesperson's commission on a sale was $14,100, which was 6 percent of the sales price. What was the sales price?

    a. $235,000.00
    b. $154,255.31
    c. $846,000.00
    d. $234,500.00

25. A 30-year fixed-rate amortized mortgage for $100,000 at 11 percent interest requires monthly payments of $952.34 for principal and interest. What is the total amount of interest paid on this loan during the life of the mortgage?

    a. $114,280.00
    b. $242,842.40
    c. $314,272.60
    d. $330,000.00

26. A couple is buying a house for $120,000 and seek a fixed-rate loan of $90,000 for 25 years. One lender offers them a 10 percent loan with no points, with monthly payments of $817.85. A second lender requires two points for a 9½ percent loan, with monthly payments of $786.35. If the couple decides to pay the points and take the lower-interest loan, how long will it take before the savings on their lower payments have made up for that extra cost at closing?

    a. Two years, eight months
    b. Three years, two months
    c. Four years, nine months
    d. Seven years, four months

27. A couple receives two offers for their property at the same time. One offer is for $95,000 in cash. The other offer of $100,000 is subject to obtaining a conventional mortgage loan with 20 percent down payment and they ask the sellers to pay three points to their lending institution. The sellers decide to accept the all-cash offer. If they had accepted the other offer instead, they would have received

    a. $2,000 more at closing.
    b. $2,400 less at closing.
    c. $2,600 more at closing.
    d. $3,000 less at closing.

28. A buyer purchases a new ranch house for $178,000 and borrows $150,000 on a mortgage loan. The state's mortgage tax is $0.50 per $100 for the first $10,000 borrowed on a one- or two-family residence, and $0.75 per $100 on the remainder. How much will the buyer owe in mortgage tax at closing?

    a. $1,050
    b. $1,100
    c. $1,400
    d. $1,500

29. New York State charges a transfer tax of $2 per $500 sales price or fraction thereof when real property is sold. A couple listed their home for $200,000 and accepted an offer for $198,600; the buyer obtained a mortgage loan for $160,000. How much did the sellers pay in transfer tax?

    a. $397.20
    b. $398.00
    c. $796.00
    d. $800.00

30. A buyer purchased a 1,300-square-foot cooperative apartment on the Upper West Side of Manhattan for $425,000, which was $15,000 less than the listed price. How much did the apartment cost per square foot?

    a. $306
    b. $315
    c. $327
    d. $338

Appendix

■ WEB LINKS

Chapter 1

Division of Licensing Services: *www.dos.state.ny.us/licensing/*
Division of Licensing Services (license application):
   www.dos.state.ny.us/licensing/eaccessny.html

Chapter 3
Department of Finance, Automated City Register Information Service:
   www.nyc.gov/html/dof/html/jump/acris.shtml
DHCR (Complaint form):   *www.dhcr.state.ny.us/Forms/*
Federal Emergency Management Agency: *www.fema.gov*

Chapter 9
Federal Emergency Management Agency: *www.fema.gov*

Chapter 10
Lending Tree: *www.lendingtree.com*
E-loan: *www.eloan.com*
New York State, Homes & Community Renewal: *www.nyhomes.org/index.htm*
New York State, Rural Development: *www.rurdev.usda.gov/ny*

Chapter 11
National Reverse Mortgage Lenders Association: *www.reversemortgage.org*
Bankrate (current rates):   *www.bankrate.com*
HUD Federal Housing Administration:
   http://portal.hud.gov/hudportal/HUD?src=/federal_housing_administration
VA Regional Office: *www.benefits.va.gov/homeloans/*
Equifax: *www.equifax.com*
Experian: *www.experian.com*
TransUnion: *www.transunion.com*
Annual Credit Report: *www.annualcreditreport.com*

Chapter 16

Domania: *www.Domania.com*
Yahoo! Real Estate: *www.realestate.yahoo.com*
Division of Licensing Services: *www.dos.state.ny.us/licensing/*

Chapter 17

Fair Housing and Equal Opportunity, HUD Regional Office:
    http://portal.hud.gov/hudportal/HUD?src=/program_offices/fair_housing_equal_opp

Chapter 18

New York State, Department of Health: *www.health.state.ny.us/environmental*
EPA: *www.epa.gov*

Chapter 22

Department of Housing and Urban Development (HUD):
    http://portal.hud.gov/hudportal/HUD?src=/groups/landlords
Institute of Real Estate Management: *www.irem.com*
BOMA International: *www.boma.org/Pages/default.aspx*
New York State Division of Housing and Community Renewal
    (DHCR): *www.dhcr.state.ny.us/index.htm*

Chapter 23

New York City's Department of Finance:
    www.nyc.gov/html/dof/html/home/home.shtml

Chapter 25

Federal Emergency Management Agency: *www.fema.gov*

Salesperson's Review Examination

1. Real estate salespersons may *NOT*

   a. assist a broker in leasing transactions.

   b. be under 21 years of age.

   c. accept commissions from their supervising broker.

   d. operate their own real estate business.

2. Who of the following requires a real estate license?

   a. A public officer performing official duties

   b. A cousin charging a fee for finding you an apartment to rent

   c. A resident manager employed by the owner to manage rentals

   d. A person acting under the order of a court (for example, an executrix)

3. A licensed salesperson need *NOT*

   a. be 19 or older.

   b. be a citizen or legal permanent resident of the United States.

   c. have completed a 75-hour prelicensing (qualifying) course.

   d. have passed the state's licensing examination.

4. Licensees who change their business address must

   a. place a public notice in the classified ads.

   b. correct the official record during the next renewal.

   c. have their broker notify the DOS and pay the appropriate fee.

   d. notify only the former employing broker.

5. The first step a municipality takes in determining its real estate tax rate is

   a. determining payment capacity of taxpayers.

   b. gathering rate information from other cities.

   c. assessing taxable properties.

   d. establishing a budget.

6. What type of financing is used for subdivisions to cover more than one parcel or lot?

   a. Jumbo loan

   b. Bridge loan

   c. Blanket mortgage

   d. Construction loan

7. A municipality's roads, public utilities, and schools are called

   a. equity.

   b. infrastructure.

   c. tax base.

   d. fixed assets.

8. When someone claims to be an agent but there is not an agreement, the principal may establish an agency by ratification, which is

   a. after-the-fact acceptance of the agreement.

   b. filing the agency agreement with the licensing authorities.

   c. substituting a new agent for an acting agent.

   d. negotiating comprehensive terms with the acting agent.

9. Which fact about the buyer would *NOT* have to be disclosed by a seller's broker to the seller?

   a. The buyer's unemployed status

   b. The racial mix of the buyer's family

   c. The appraised value of a comparable home in the vicinity

   d. Plans to split the commission with the cooperating broker

10. If an agent acts in a way that damages a principal by violating the agent's fiduciary duties, penalties for breach of fiduciary duties would *NOT* include

    a. loss of the commission.

    b. a negative judgment in a criminal suit.

    c. loss of license plus fines and penalties.

    d. rescission of the transaction by court order.

11. A couple asked their salesperson not to mention that they were being sued with the possibility of being assessed large monetary damages. They were anxious because the sellers might not wish to consider their offer to purchase if they were to lose the lawsuit. The salesperson should
    a. not mention it since she represents the couple.
    b. disclose it as a fact materially affecting the buyers' ability to purchase the property.
    c. ask the couple for personal financial statements to determine their qualifications.
    d. tell the seller that the couple is well-qualified to purchase the property.

12. A written agreement that creates an agency relationship between a broker and a seller is called a
    a. mutuality.
    b. bond.
    c. confidentiality.
    d. listing agreement.

13. In New York, a principal acting in good faith can cancel a listing
    a. up to three business days after signing.
    b. until the property has been advertised.
    c. anytime, although some fees may be due to the broker.
    d. anytime, but only if the broker consents to the termination.

14. The MOST common way of creating an agency relationship is through a(n)
    a. express agency.
    b. exclusive agency.
    c. implied agreement.
    d. coupled agreement.

15. An agency may be terminated at any time for all of the following reasons EXCEPT
    a. death or incompetence of either party.
    b. mutual agreement.
    c. bankruptcy of either party.
    d. criminal investigation of either party.

16. A notable study by the Federal Trade Commission found that the public was totally confused about the relationship between
    a. selling agents and buyers.
    b. buying agents and sellers.
    c. real estate salespersons and brokers.
    d. brokers and unlicensed assistants.

17. Which act BEST demonstrates a seller's agent's fiduciary duty of loyalty?
    a. Not revealing a seller's eagerness to sell
    b. Following the seller's exact instructions
    c. Reporting the status of earnest money being held
    d. Placing the seller's interest above the agent's own

18. The possibility of dual agency should be discussed
    a. only after the buyer makes an offer on a house listing.
    b. at the time the agency agreement is entered into.
    c. when one of the agency relationships is terminated.
    d. when negotiations are completed.

19. Regardless of who procures the buyer, a broker will earn a commission if the property is sold during the listing term under a(n)
    a. exclusive-right-to-sell listing.
    b. exclusive-agency listing.
    c. open listing.
    d. net listing.

20. The listing agent with an exclusive agency listing is NOT entitled to a commission when the listing is sold by
    a. another broker.
    b. the listing agent.
    c. the seller.
    d. the cooperating broker.

21. The IRS will not challenge the independent contractor status of a real estate salesperson as long as the salesperson
    a. does not work out of his or her home office.
    b. works according to a schedule planned by the broker.
    c. receives benefits from the supervising broker.
    d. has income based solely on sales output.

22. The *Duncan and Hill* decision recommended that New York State brokers and salespersons who prepare purchase and sales contracts protect themselves against
    a. breaching fiduciary duties.
    b. losing business to real estate attorneys.
    c. charges of unauthorized practice of law.
    d. accepting fraudulent documents.

23. On a fixed-rate, 30-year mortgage loan, the amount of interest included in each payment
    a. remains the same over the life of the loan.
    b. increases over the life of the loan.
    c. decreases over the life of the loan.
    d. may increase or decrease, depending on rate changes.

24. In New York, any conventional loan with a down payment below 20 percent must be accompanied by
    a. private mortgage insurance.
    b. interest rate caps.
    c. homeowner counseling.
    d. monthly payment ceilings.

25. Which term correctly reflects the amount of prepaid interest (required by a lender) at closing of a mortgage loan?
    a. Points
    b. Down payment
    c. Origination fees
    d. Commission

26. The bundle of legal rights includes
    a. enjoyment, possession, disposition, control, and exclusion.
    b. adverse possession, mortgage rights, and fixtures.
    c. fee simple ownership, reversionary interest, and undivided interest.
    d. air rights, emblements, grants, and life estates.

27. The term *land* includes
    a. all improvements.
    b. trees.
    c. buildings.
    d. roads.

28. Four people hold title to a small hotel as tenants in common. The owners
    a. may sell their individual interest without consent of the others.
    b. automatically inherit from the other owners.
    c. must own equal shares in the property.
    d. must continue the interest or the property must be sold.

29. The ability to turn an asset into cash is referred to as
    a. exchange.
    b. convertibility.
    c. liquidity.
    d. leverage.

30. A life estate
    a. is a part of the bundle of rights.
    b. was originally granted to royalty but has since been given to all property owners.
    c. provides that the tenant has the right to deed the property to his or her heirs.
    d. is limited to the life of a specific person.

31. A financial claim against real estate that provides security for a debt or obligation of the owner is called a(n)
    a. easement.
    b. lien.
    c. deed restriction.
    d. license.

32. A driveway that illegally extends beyond the land of the owner is called
   a. an easement.
   b. adverse possession.
   c. an encroachment.
   d. tacking.

33. The purpose of filing a lis pendens is to
   a. give notice that there is a cloud on the title.
   b. give notice that a foreclosure is pending.
   c. announce that a lease is in effect for 99 years.
   d. record the deed transfer.

34. Which would be considered a legal description of land?
   a. Street address filed with the tax assessor's office
   b. Description of a lot from a recorded subdivision plot
   c. Subdivision title and lot number
   d. Property tax account number

35. Which statement about grantors and grantees is TRUE?
   a. The grantor is always a competent adult giving good title to a grantee who is also a competent adult.
   b. The grantor accepts the deed and the grantee is the competent adult who gives the deed.
   c. The grantor has the legal capacity to execute the deed to an identifiable grantee.
   d. The grantee has legal rights to the property and may pass those rights to the grantor.

36. Something of value given in exchange for real property is called
   a. earnest money.
   b. consideration.
   c. boot.
   d. leverage.

37. Investors in investment properties give consideration to the tax world, which involves the tax consequences resulting from a property's
   a. resale value.
   b. community contribution.
   c. annual appreciation.
   d. income operations.

38. Net operating income for an investment property is defined as the cash flow attributable to the property after deducting all property-related operational expenses, which includes
   a. mortgage interest.
   b. federal income taxes.
   c. mortgage payments.
   d. property insurance.

39. The difference between a net lease and a gross lease is
   a. in a gross lease, the tenant pays for everything, and in a net lease, the landlord is responsible for property charges.
   b. in a net lease, the landlord charges a percentage of the tenant's profit, and the gross lease allows the tenant all of the profit.
   c. in a gross lease, the tenant pays a fixed rent while the landlord is responsible for property charges, and in a net lease, the tenant usually pays for some or all of the property charges as well.
   d. a landlord may give a net or gross lease to commercial tenants but may not give a gross lease to a residential tenant.

40. The potential receipts for a property's rental activities if that property were 100 percent leased are referred to as
   a. potential gross income.
   b. effective gross income.
   c. feasible operating income.
   d. cash flow.

41. The effective gross income is calculated after the property's potential gross income is reduced by its
   a. vacancy and collection losses.
   b. taxes and insurance.
   c. operating expenses.
   d. attorney and real estate fees.

42. Which is considered a fixed expense for a commercial property?
   a. Management fees
   b. Maintenance expenses
   c. Property taxes
   d. Utilities

43. The cash on hand to pay for anticipated or unanticipated capital improvements for a commercial building is referred to as
    a. reserve for replacements.
    b. liquidity.
    c. variable expense budget.
    d. debt service.

44. The cost required to pay back borrowed funds is called
    a. debt service.
    b. amortization.
    c. buydown.
    d. points.

45. For a commercial property, the difference between the usable area and rentable area is called the
    a. adjustment rate.
    b. depreciation.
    c. negative space.
    d. loss factor.

46. Mortgage loan closing information must be prepared on a special HUD form called the
    a. Fair Sales Report.
    b. Official Closing Statement.
    c. Homeowner's Bill of Rights.
    d. Uniform Settlement Statement.

47. A seller had paid all of his property tax for the year. If the annual taxes were $3,250, using the 360-day year or 12 months of 30 days each, how much should the seller expect to be returned at the closing on July 1?
    a. $1,345
    b. $1,625
    c. $3,250
    d. $500

48. The purpose of the closing statement is to
    a. account for each party's debits and credits.
    b. give title to the purchaser.
    c. record the exchange in the county clerk's office.
    d. report the seller's gain to the Internal Revenue Service.

49. The due-on-sale clause in a mortgage is also known as the
    a. demising clause.
    b. habendum clause.
    c. acceleration clause.
    d. alienation clause.

50. A gradual paying-off of a debt by periodic installments is
    a. accretion.
    b. acceleration.
    c. amortization.
    d. alienation.

51. The use of borrowed funds is referred to as
    a. acceleration.
    b. margin.
    c. liquidity.
    d. leverage.

52. An executory contract exists when
    a. both parties have fulfilled their promises.
    b. something remains to be done.
    c. one party makes a promise to be kept only if a second party does something.
    d. both parties promise to perform under and as required by the contract.

53. The State of New York Mortgage Agency (SONYMA) provides
    a. loans with low down payments.
    b. loans for first-time homebuyers.
    c. loans for specific purposes in specific locations.
    d. All of these

54. What minimum percentage of the replacement cost of a dwelling does the coinsurance clause in homeowners' insurance policies typically require that the insured maintain in fire insurance on the property?
    a. 60 percent
    b. 70 percent
    c. 80 percent
    d. 90 percent

55. The funds that mortgage lenders generally require borrowers to maintain so that sufficient funds will be available to pay property taxes and renew hazard insurance are called

    a. assessments.

    b. points.

    c. contingencies.

    d. reserves.

56. Which type of homeowners' insurance policy is specifically designed for condominium owners?

    a. HO-1

    b. HO-2

    c. HO-5

    d. HO-6

57. Interest paid by any property owner in a tax year may be deductible for home acquisition financing, home equity loans, and

    a. refinanced loans.

    b. closing costs.

    c. credit card loans.

    d. vehicle loans.

58. For how many of the previous five years must a property owner have resided in a property for it to be considered a primary residence at the time of sale?

    a. One

    b. Two

    c. Three

    d. Four

59. What is the maximum amount that first-time home purchasers may withdraw from their IRA accounts to use for a down payment without experiencing the additional 10 percent early withdrawal penalty?

    a. $10,000

    b. $15,000

    c. $20,000

    d. $25,000

60. Nonconforming use is a term used in reference to property that

    a. extends over lot lines.

    b. is in need of deferred maintenance.

    c. does not comply with zoning requirements.

    d. has not been recorded.

61. A light industrial plant has been operating in compliance with the zoning classifications. After a zoning change to single-family residential use, the owner of the industrial plant is permitted to

    a. convert the building to condominiums.

    b. continue the present use until buildings are destroyed or torn down.

    c. build an addition to the plant.

    d. rebuild the plant if it is destroyed by natural causes.

62. Zoning regulations are generally created in order to

    a. ensure increasing property values.

    b. guarantee that all property will be applied to its highest and best use.

    c. implement a local master plan.

    d. limit growth within the community.

63. The ordinances by which cities and towns specify minimum requirements for the construction or repair of buildings are referred to as

    a. eminent domain.

    b. master plans.

    c. home rule.

    d. building codes.

64. Why is wood-frame construction preferred when building MOST houses in New York State?

    a. It does not require insulation.

    b. It is usually built in a factory.

    c. It is less expensive than other kinds of construction.

    d. It offers little design flexibility.

65. What is the maximum amount of money a taxpayer filing a tax return as a single filer may exclude from the total gain realized at sale?

    a. $100,000

    b. $150,000

    c. $250,000

    d. $300,000

66. New York requires that the buyer of a new home receive a warranty that protects against faulty workmanship and defective materials for
   a. one year.
   b. two years.
   c. three years.
   d. four years.

67. The proper size for a proposed septic tank is determined by the
   a. number of bathrooms.
   b. number of bedrooms.
   c. overall square feet of living space.
   d. size of the building lot.

68. British thermal units (BTUs) rate the capacity of
   a. a furnace's heat output.
   b. insulation's resistance to heat transfer.
   c. double-glazed windows' thermal properties.
   d. the hot water tank.

69. A concrete slab foundation is reinforced with
   a. Styrofoam.
   b. gravel.
   c. crushed stone.
   d. steel rods.

70. The purchaser of a cooperative is
   a. regarded by law like the owner of a single detached home.
   b. joint owner in the common elements.
   c. a fee simple owner of a living unit.
   d. an owner of shares of stock in a co-op corporation.

71. Information needed to prepare a comparative market analysis should include the
   a. original cost.
   b. names of the former owners.
   c. equalization rate.
   d. construction and age of the building.

72. What is the name of the preliminary prospectus made available to present tenants of a rental property that is being converted to condominiums?
   a. Black book
   b. Red herring
   c. Board package
   d. Recognition agreement

73. What is the name of shares in a cooperative held by the original organizing party of the co-op?
   a. Sponsor shares
   b. Black book shares
   c. Director shares
   d. Developer shares

74. The probable price a property will bring in a competitive and open market is known as the
   a. market value.
   b. market price.
   c. competitive value.
   d. competitive price.

75. In real estate, the concept of price generally relates to
   a. the past.
   b. the present.
   c. the future.
   d. any of the above.

76. In an appraisal of an apartment building with bathroom fixtures that are outdated for today's renters and require replacement, the depreciation would be classified as
   a. physical deterioration, curable.
   b. physical deterioration, incurable.
   c. functional obsolescence, curable.
   d. functional obsolescence, incurable.

77. A broker only shows houses in one particular part of town to Asian buyers. This violation of fair housing law is called
   a. steering.
   b. blockbusting.
   c. redlining.
   d. misrepresentation.

78. Real estate advertising should NOT
   a. refer to the location of public schools.
   b. claim that a community is exclusive.
   c. include words relating to family relationships.
   d. state a preference for young adults.

79. A difference between a condominium and a condop is that in a condop, the
    a. tenants in occupancy have a 90-day exclusive right to purchase their units.
    b. owner retains an interest in the development for future income-producing purposes.
    c. purchasers of units must submit board packages for consideration by the board of directors.
    d. shareholder does not own the actual real estate and may not place a regular mortgage against the unit.

80. Although a property owner may be exempted sometimes from discrimination laws, a real estate licensee
    a. is exempt as an owner.
    b. can list the property for sale, noting the exemption.
    c. can advertise the noted exemption.
    d. may not participate in the transaction in any way.

81. When a lender refuses to make loans in a given neighborhood populated by racial minorities, it is an example of
    a. steering.
    b. blockbusting.
    c. credit deviation.
    d. redlining.

82. A permitted exemption to the federal Fair Housing Act is
    a. a church-owned apartment complex if language in the lease restricts tenancy members of a specific national origin.
    b. a commercial restaurant and lounge owned by a private club that refuses to admit individuals of a certain ethnic group.
    c. the absentee owner of a four-unit building who charges higher rent to members of certain religious groups.
    d. a rental in an owner-occupied four-unit building that is not advertised.

83. Why are lenders less likely to originate loans for cooperative properties in which a high number of units are investor owned rather than owner occupied?
    a. The federal government provides special support to lenders that make loans to owner-occupied properties.
    b. Owners of primary residences generally have higher incomes than residents who lease units in cooperatives.
    c. Owners of primary residences are less likely to default on loans than investors.
    d. Cooperatives with a high percentage of leased units are usually located in areas where housing demand is lower.

84. Unlike a mortgage broker, a mortgage banker
    a. processes loans.
    b. arranges loans for purchases.
    c. obtains mortgage commitments.
    d. originates loans.

85. The percentage of profit that the investor receives only on the cash he invested in the property is called
    a. cash-on-cash return.
    b. net profit.
    c. cash flow.
    d. gross income.

86. Asbestos was used in buildings for
    a. insulation.
    b. flooring.
    c. support.
    d. pest control.

87. Lead poisoning commonly comes from peeling paint and
    a. roofing.
    b. insulation.
    c. plumbing.
    d. decay.

88. Mitigation of which pollutant is relatively simple and inexpensive?
    a. Asbestos
    b. Lead paint
    c. Radon
    d. UFFI

89. The purpose of a mortgage broker is to help the borrower obtain a(n)

a. loan commitment.
b. interest-rate cap.
c. down payment.
d. escrow closing.

90. What is the relationship between a property manager and the property owner?

a. The property manager is a special agent.
b. The property manager is a general agent.
c. The property manager is a subagent.
d. The property manager is an employee, not an agent.

91. A property manager is expected to merchandise the property to maximize income and

a. control operating expenses.
b. achieve 100 percent occupancy.
c. minimize tax liabilities.
d. maximize capital gains.

92. If a seller paid a 6 percent commission that amounted to $15,040, what was the sales price?

a. $240,300
b. $250,667
c. $260,999
d. $275,249

93. A building is 110' × 75' and the seller is asking $120 per square foot. What is the asking price?

a. $610,000
b. $750,000
c. $880,000
d. $990,000

94. One of a property manager's responsibilities is to maintain the building's overall appearance, which is called

a. curb appeal.
b. salability.
c. physical plant.
d. frontage capital.

95. For taxing purposes in New York, nonhomestead real estate includes MOST

a. condominiums.
b. mobile homes.
c. vacant land.
d. single-family homes.

96. Municipalities reflect the tax assessments for all lands and buildings within their jurisdictions on

a. equalization tracts.
b. homestead archives.
c. tax journals.
d. assessment rolls.

97. What term refers to the freedom from present-day taxation resulting from a gain, such as a gain from the sale of an investment property?

a. Tax-exempt
b. Tax-deferred
c. Tax shelter
d. Tax-deductible

98. An IRS Section 1031 exchange involves the exchange of

a. money for tax benefits.
b. property for money.
c. property for property.
d. tax benefits for property.

99. A percentage lease is commonly used when the tenant is a

a. warehouse.
b. manufacturer.
c. public agency.
d. retail business.

100. What is the legal form that states that the unpaid balance due on a lease, loan, or other agreement to receive monies as of a specified date is in full force and existence?

a. Estoppel clause
b. Escalation clause
c. Meet-or-release clause
d. Habendum clause

Glossary

abstract of title The condensed history of the title to a particular parcel of real estate.

abstract of title with lawyer's opinion An abstract of title that a lawyer has examined and has certified to be, in the lawyer's opinion, an accurate statement of fact.

abutting Lying immediately next to, as with two parcels of real estate with a common lot line.

acceleration clause The clause in a note or mortgage that can be enforced to make the entire debt due immediately if the mortgagor defaults.

accession The acquisition of land by deposits from an adjoining stream; also the acquisition of fixtures or improvements built on one's land by another.

accessory (apartment) use An additional apartment, usually small, sometimes allowed in an area zoned for one-family homes, which might be used for elderly grandparents; an accessory use would be something in addition to occupation of a home, possibly a small home business.

accountability The agent's fiduciary duty to account to the principal, particularly for any money involved in the transaction.

acceptance The grantee's taking of a deed of transfer.

accretion The increase or addition of land by the deposit of sand or soil washed up naturally from a river, lake, or sea.

accrued items On a closing statement, items of expense that have been incurred but are not yet payable, such as interest on a mortgage loan.

acknowledgment A formal declaration made before a duly authorized officer, usually a notary public, by a person who has signed a document.

acre A measure of land equal to 43,560 square feet, 4,840 square yards, 4,047 square meters, 160 square rods, or 0.4047 hectare.

active income Any income attributable to a direct activity of employment.

act of waste *See* waste.

actual cash value When a claim is made under a policy insuring a building or other physical object, either of two methods can determine the amount of the claim. One is the depreciated, or actual, cash value of the damaged property. The other is replacement cost.

actual eviction Action whereby a defaulted tenant is physically ousted from rented property pursuant to a court order. *See also* eviction.

actual notice That which is known; actual knowledge.

adjacent Lying near to but not necessarily in actual contact with.

adjoining Contiguous; attaching, in actual contact with.

adjustable-rate mortgage (ARM) A mortgage loan in which the interest rate may increase or decrease at specific intervals, following an economic indicator.

adjusted basis The financial interest that the Internal Revenue Service attributes to an owner of an investment property for the purpose of determining annual depreciation and gain or loss on the sale of the asset.

adjustments Divisions of financial responsibility between a buyer and seller (also called *prorations*).

administrative discipline The Department of State's enforcement of license laws, rules, and regulations through the use of reprimands and denial, suspension, or revocation of licenses.

administrative law Laws concerned with the conduct of government agencies.

administrator A person appointed by the court to administer the estate of a deceased person who left no will, that is, who died intestate.

ad valorem tax A tax levied according to value; generally used to refer to real estate tax. Also called the *general tax*.

adverse possession The actual, visible, hostile, notorious, exclusive, and continuous possession of another's land under a claim of title. Possession for ten years may be a means of acquiring title.

affidavit A written statement sworn to before an officer who is authorized to administer an oath or affirmation.

affidavit of entitlement to commission A document claiming commission that may be entered in the public records but does not become a lien against the property.

affirmative marketing Program to inform all buyers in a minority community about housing opportunities available, without discrimination.

after-tax cash flow The amount of remaining cash flow after deductions are made from the before-tax cash flow for income taxes resulting from the property's income activities.

aged exemption New York state's partial exemption of school tax for low-income elderly homeowners.

agency That relationship wherein an agent is employed by a principal to do certain acts on the principal's behalf.

agency coupled with an interest An agency relationship in which the agent has an interest in the property.

agency disclosure form Describes the roles of sellers' agents, buyers' agents, listing brokers' agents, and dual agents; New York law requires that brokers and salespersons give prospective sellers and buyers (or landlords and tenants) this disclosure statement.

agent One who undertakes to transact some business or to manage some affair for another by authority of the latter.

agreement in writing and signed New York's statute of frauds requirement for a valid sales contract, or a lease for more than one year.

agricultural real estate Farms, timberland, pasture land, and orchards.

air rights The right to use the open space above a property, generally allowing the surface to be used for another purpose.

alienation The act of transferring property to another.

alienation clause The clause in a mortgage stating that the balance of the secured debt becomes immediately due and payable at the mortgagee's option if the property is sold.

alluvion Extra soil deposited on shore by the action of water.

alteration agreement An agreement between the shareholder and the cooperative.

amenities Elements of a property or its surroundings that contribute to its attractiveness to potential buyers and to owner satisfaction.

American Bar Association The American Bar Association (ABA) is the national representative of the legal profession. Its purpose is for serving the general public as well as the legal profession through the promotion of justice, professionalism, and, most of all, respect for the law.

Americans with Disabilities Act (ADA) Federal law requiring reasonable accommodations and accessibility to goods and services for persons with disabilities.

amortized loan A loan in which the principal as well as the interest is payable in monthly or other periodic installments over the term of the loan.

amperage Amount of electrical current, measured in amperes (amps).

anchor stores Large stores, often nationally known department stores, whose presence attracts other tenants to a shopping mall.

annual percentage rate (APR) Rate of interest charged on a loan, calculated to take into account up-front loan fees and points. Usually higher than the *contract interest rate*.

antitrust laws Laws designed to preserve the free enterprise of the open marketplace by making illegal certain private conspiracies and combinations formed to minimize competition.

apartment information vendor A person who, for a fee, brings landlords and tenants together.

apartment-sharing agent One who brings together roommates and housemates.

appeals Complaints made to a higher court requesting the correction of errors in law made by lower courts.

appellate division Courts of appeal.

apportionments Adjustment of the income, expenses, or carrying charges of real estate usually computed to the date of closing of title so that the seller pays all expenses to that date.

appraisal An estimate of a property's valuation by an appraiser who is usually presumed to be expert in this work.

Appraisal Institute Largest private organization for professional appraisers.

appraiser An independent person trained to provide an unbiased estimate of value.

appreciation An increase in the worth or value of a property due to economic or related causes; the opposite of depreciation.

appropriation The process of levying property taxes; also, the setting aside of part of a subdivision for public use. *See* dedication.

appurtenances Those rights, privileges, and improvements that belong to and pass with the transfer of real property but are not necessarily a part of the property, such as rights-of-way, easements, and property improvements.

APR *See* annual percentage rate.

arbitration A hearing before a person chosen by the parties or appointed to hear a dispute and render a determination.

architectural review board This board takes on many approval functions, primary of which involves the approval of new construction and remodeling.

ARM *See* adjustable-rate mortgage.

arm's-length transaction A transaction between relative strangers, all trying to do the best for themselves individually.

Army Corps of Engineers Federal body responsible for regulating waterways and drainage.

Article 9A The section of New York State's Real Property Law relating to subdivision.

Article 12A The section of New York State's Real Property Law relating to real estate licenses.

Article 78 procedure Legal process for contesting the action of a governmental body.

asbestos Commonly used insulating mineral that becomes toxic when it is exposed and fibers and dust are released into the air.

asbestosis Lung disease caused by exposure to asbestos.

"as is" Contract words indicating that the seller makes no guarantees or warranties about the property; not always effective if challenged in court.

assemblage The merging of two separate parcels under one owner.

assessed value A valuation placed on property by a public officer or a board as a basis for taxation.

assessment The imposition of a tax, charge, or levy, usually according to established rates.

assessment review board A local body empowered to hear protests by property-owning taxpayers, and to lower or raise assessments.

assessment roll Public record listing assessed value for all real property in a village, town, city, or county.

assignment The transfer in writing of interest in a bond, mortgage, lease, or other instrument.

associate broker A broker who chooses to work as a salesperson under the name and supervision of another broker.

assumption of mortgage Acquiring title to property on which there is an existing mortgage and agreeing to be personally liable for the terms and conditions of the mortgage, including payments.

attorney-in-fact A person who has been given a power of attorney on behalf of a grantor. The power must be recorded and ends on the death of the grantor.

attorney review clause Needed when the buyer and the seller choose to have an attorney study the contract. The attorney must complete the contract review within the agreed-on time. The contract will be legally binding at the end of this period unless an attorney for the buyer or seller disapproves it.

attorney's opinion of title Report in which a lawyer examines and evaluates an abstract of title.

avulsion The removal of land when a stream suddenly changes its channel.

balloon payment The final payment of a mortgage loan that is considerably larger than the required periodic payments because the loan amount was not fully amortized.

bankruptcy A federal court procedure to relieve an overburdened debtor of certain liabilities.

bargain and sale deed A deed that carries with it no warranties against liens or other encumbrances but that does imply that the grantor has the right to convey title.

bargain and sale deed with covenant A deed in which the grantor warrants or guarantees the title against defects arising during the period of the grantor's tenure and ownership of the property but not against defects existing before that time.

basement Space wholly or partly below grade, usually not used for living accommodations.

basis The cost that the Internal Revenue Service attributes to an owner of an investment property for the purpose of determining annual depreciation and gain or loss on the sale of the asset.

beam Structural member, usually horizontal, used for support.

bearing walls Walls that serve as more than simple partitions and that support ceiling, upper stories, or roof.

benchmark A permanent reference mark or point established for use by surveyors in measuring differences in elevation. *See* datum.

beneficiary The person who receives or is to receive benefits resulting from certain acts.

bequeath To give or hand down by will; to leave by will.

bequest That which is given by the terms of a will.

bilateral contract A contract in which both parties promise to do something; an exchange of promises.

bill of sale   A written instrument given to pass title of personal property from vendor to vendee.

binder   An agreement that may accompany an earnest money deposit for the purchase of real property as evidence of the purchaser's good faith and intent to complete the transaction.

biweekly mortgage   A loan that is paid in 26 half (biweekly) payments each year, resulting in an earlier payoff and lower interest costs over the life of the loan.

black book   Offering plan for a cooperative or condominium as accepted for filing by the attorney general and used for marketing.

blanket mortgage   A mortgage covering more than one parcel of real estate.

blanket unilateral offer of subagency   Traditionally, a seller's automatic consent to subagency by submitting a listing to a MLS.

blind ad   An advertisement that does not name the person placing the ad, or indicate that it was placed by a licensed real estate broker.

blockbusting   The illegal practice of inducing homeowners to sell their property by making representations regarding the entry or prospective entry of minority persons into the neighborhood.

blueprint   An architect's or engineer's plan for a building, including floor plan, dimensions, and specifications, to be followed by the builder.

blue-sky laws   Common name for those state and federal laws that regulate the registration and sale of investment securities.

board of directors   Elected managing body of a corporation, specifically of a cooperative apartment building.

Board of Fire Underwriters   New York State agency responsible for oversight of electrical systems and for enforcing its electrical code.

board of managers   Elected managing body of a condominium.

board package   These are documents that contain personal and financial information of the prospective shareholder. The board package is submitted to the board of directors for its consideration and potential acceptance of the proposed shareholder.

boiler and machinery insurance   Insurance policy covering repair and replacement of major equipment and systems such as central air conditioners and heating plants.

bond   The evidence of a personal debt that is secured by a mortgage or other lien on real estate.

boot   Money or property given to make up any difference in value or equity between two properties in an *exchange*.

branch office   A secondary place of business apart from the principal or main office from which real estate business is conducted.

breach of contract   Violation of any terms or conditions in a contract without legal excuse—for example, failure to make a payment when it is due.

bridge loan   A short-term loan designed to cover a gap between the sale of one property and the purchase of another (also called a *swing loan*, *temporary loan*, or *interim financing*).

British thermal unit (BTU)   A unit of measure of heat that is used to rate air-conditioning and heating equipment capacity. One BTU raises one pound of water one degree Fahrenheit.

broker   One who buys and sells for another for a fee. *See also* real estate broker.

brokerage   The business of buying and selling for another for a fee.

broker's agent   A broker who assists the listing broker in marketing a property under a formal agency agreement.

building codes   Regulations established by state and local governments fully stating the structural requirements for building.

building line   A line fixed at a certain distance from the front and/or sides of a lot, beyond which no building can project.

building loan agreement   An agreement whereby the lender advances money to an owner with partial payments at certain stages of construction.

building permit   Written permission from the local government to build or alter a structure.

building-related illness (BRI)   Symptoms such as hypersensitivity, asthma, and allergic reactions caused by toxic substances and pathogens in a building that remain with the affected individual even when he or she is away from the building. *See* sick building syndrome.

buildings department   The municipal department entrusted with the job of ensuring the safe and lawful use of properties and buildings via enforcement of applicable municipal codes and state laws.

bullet loan   A short- or intermediate-term (three to five years) interest-only loan with a balloon payment at the end of the term (also called an *intermediate loan* or *conduit financing*).

bundle of legal rights The concept of land ownership that includes ownership of all legal rights to the land—for example, possession, control within the law, and enjoyment.

Bureau of Land Management A governmental agency that is part of the U.S. Department of the Interior. Its purpose is to administer public lands owned by the federal government.

business interruption insurance Insurance policy coverage against a financial loss resulting from a property's inability to generate income.

buydown A financing technique used to reduce the monthly payments for the first few years of a loan. Funds in the form of points are given to the lender by the builder or seller to buy down or lower the effective interest rate paid by the buyer, thus reducing the monthly payments for a set time.

buyer agency An agency relationship in which the broker/agent represents the interests of the buyer.

buyer's broker A broker who has entered into an agreement to represent a buyer (the broker's principal and client) in finding a suitable property.

bylaws Rules and regulations adopted by an association.

cap With an adjustable-rate mortgage, a limit, usually in percentage points, on how much the interest rate or payment might be raised in each adjustment period. For *lifetime cap, see* ceiling.

capital expense Money spent on permanent improvements that add value to property.

capital gains Profits realized from the sale of assets such as real estate.

capitalization A mathematical process for estimating the value of a property using a proper rate of return on the investment and the annual net income expected to be produced by the property.

capitalization rate The rate of return a property will produce on the owner's investment.

capital reserve budget Money set aside to meet anticipated large expenditures for major improvements.

case law Law resulting from past court decisions.

casement window A window that opens on hinges.

cash flow The net spendable income from an investment.

cash-on-cash return This is another term for equity dividend rate.

casualty insurance Insurance policy coverage against theft, burglary, vandalism, physical damage to systems, and health and accident coverage on a specific-risk basis.

caveat emptor A Latin phrase meaning "Let the buyer beware."

CBS Memory aid for an appraiser's adjustments: Comparable Better, Subtract.

CC&Rs Covenants, conditions, and restrictions of a condominium or cooperative development.

cease and desist order A prohibition against brokers' canvassing for listings, either from certain individual homeowners or in certain areas.

ceiling With an adjustable-rate mortgage, a limit, usually in percentage points, beyond which the interest rates or monthly payment on a loan may never rise. Sometimes known as a *lifetime cap*.

census tract A small geographic area designated by the Bureau of the Census.

CERCLA The federal Comprehensive Environmental, Responsibility, Compensation, and Liability Act, which established procedures for remediation of contaminated areas.

certificate of compliance (C of C) Verification that a construction project meets certain standards, primarily safety-related.

certificate of incorporation A document filed with the New York Secretary of State, describing the purpose of an intended corporation and details about the organization.

certificate of insurance Whenever real estate transactions include financing (acquisition financing or refinancing of a loan), lenders require advance proof of coverage. This is usually accomplished by submitting an insurance certificate or a certificate of insurance.

certificate of occupancy (C of O) Document issued by a municipal authority stating that a building complies with building, health, and safety codes and may be occupied.

certificate of title A statement of opinion of title status on a parcel of real property based on an examination of specified public records.

Certified Property Manager (CPM) A real property manager who has completed specific educational requirements, demonstration reports, and qualified for the CPM designation, which is granted by the Institute of Real Estate Management of the National Association of REALTORS®.

certiorari proceeding A judicial proceeding seeking higher court review of a lower court's decision in a case or proceeding.

chain of title The conveyance of real property to one owner from another, reaching back to the original grantor.

change of association/change of broker Occurs only when a new sponsoring broker submits a change of association form to the DOS signed by the salesperson or associate broker (as the case may be) and the new sponsoring broker.

Chapter 7, Chapter 11, Chapter 13 Different forms of bankruptcy.

chattel Personal property such as household goods or fixtures.

chattel mortgage A mortgage on personal property.

checkers *See* testers.

chlordane An insecticide banned in the 1980s.

chlorofluorocarbons (CFCs) Gases produced by propellants once used in aerosol sprays and the common coolant Freon. CFCs are linked to depletion of the earth's ozone layer.

civil law The laws dealing with wrongs one person does another.

Civil Rights Act of 1866 Federal law that prohibits racial discrimination in the sale and rental of property.

Clean Air Act The law prohibiting the use of Freon in refrigerators and spray cans.

client The principal.

closing date The date on which the buyer takes title to the property.

closing statement A detailed cash accounting of a real estate transaction showing all cash received, all charges and credits made, and all cash paid out in the transaction.

cloud on the title An outstanding claim or encumbrance that, if valid, would affect or impair the owner's title.

clustering The grouping of home sites within a subdivision on smaller lots than normal with the remaining land used as common areas.

cluster zoning Zoning that allowed the grouping of buildings on small lots to allow for extra parcels of open space.

CMA *See* comparative market analysis.

Code for Equal Opportunity Professional standard of conduct for fair housing compliance, promulgated by the National Association of REALTORS® (NAR).

C of C *See* certificate of compliance.

C of O *See* certificate of occupancy.

coinsurance clause A clause in insurance policies covering real property that requires that the policyholder maintain fire insurance coverage generally equal to at least 80 percent of the property's actual replacement cost.

commercial law The division of law dealing with business and industry.

commercial paper Notes, checks, certificates of deposit, and other promises to pay money.

commercial real estate Business property, including offices, shopping malls, theaters, hotels, and parking facilities.

commercial transaction Any transaction involving the sale or rental of a building that contains five or more units intended for dwelling purposes or for commercial or industrial use.

commingling The illegal act of a real estate broker who mixes other people's money with his or her own.

commission Payment to a broker for services rendered, such as in the sale or purchase of real property; usually a percentage of the selling price.

common elements Parts of a property normally in common use by all of the condominium residents.

common law The body of law based on custom, usage, and court decisions.

community property A system of property ownership not in effect in New York.

company dollar A broker's net commission income after cooperating brokers and the firm's own salespersons have been paid.

comparable property In appraisal, a similar nearby property, recently sold, whose price can be analyzed in relation to the property being appraised.

comparables Properties listed in an appraisal report that are substantially equivalent to the subject property. Also called *comps*.

comparative market analysis (CMA) A study, intended to assist an owner in establishing listing price, of recent comparable sales, properties that failed to sell, and parcels presently on the market.

competent parties Those recognized by law as being able to contract with others; usually those of legal age and sound mind.

completion bond Bond furnished by a subdivider, guaranteeing completion of the undertaking.

Comprehensive Environmental Response, Compensation, and Liability Act (CERCLA) Enacted in 1980 and reauthorized by the Superfund Amendments and Reauthorization Act of 1986 (SARA), this federal law imposes liability on lenders, occupants, operators, and owners for correcting environmental problems discovered on a property.

concrete slab foundation Foundation made of poured concrete and steel rod reinforcement, resting on a waterproof sheet directly on the ground; supported by sunken concrete beams (footings).

condemnation A judicial or administrative proceeding to exercise the power of eminent domain through which a government agency takes private property for public use and compensates the owner.

condominium The absolute ownership of an apartment or a unit (generally in a multiunit building) plus an undivided interest in the ownership of the common elements, which are owned jointly with the other condominium unit owners.

condop A condop is a hybrid of condominiums and cooperatives in which the developer had solved the 80/20 issue through ownership retention in the project's income-producing sources. In a condop structure, there is condominium ownership in the land by the residential units and condominium ownership in the land by the developer for the commercial spaces. The residential portion of the property is operated as a cooperative.

confidentiality An agent's duty to keep the principal's information confidential.

consent decree Agreement by which an accused party promises not to do something illegal in the future, without admitting it was done in the past.

Conservation Advisory Council Created by the local legislature to advise in the development, management, and protection of the community's natural resources and to prepare an inventory and map of open spaces.

consideration (1) That received by the grantor in exchange for a deed. (2) Something of value that induces a person to enter into a contract. Consideration may be *valuable* (money) or *good* (love and affection).

constitutional law That law arising from the federal and state constitutions.

construction loan *See* interim financing.

constructive eviction Landlord actions that so materially disturb or impair the tenant's enjoyment of the leased premises that the tenant is effectively forced to move out and terminate the lease without liability for any further rent.

constructive notice Notice given to the world by recorded documents. Possession of property is also considered constructive notice.

contents and personal property insurance Coverage of personal property and other building contents when they are not on the insured premises.

contingency A provision in a contract that requires that a certain act be done or a certain event occur before the contract becomes binding.

continuing education The Department of State's requirement that licensees complete additional study before licenses can be renewed.

contract An agreement entered into by two or more legally competent parties by the terms of which one or more of the parties, for a consideration, undertakes to do or refrain from doing some legal act or acts.

contract for deed A contract for the sale of real estate wherein the purchase price is paid in periodic installments by the purchaser, who is in possession of the property even though title is retained by the seller until final payment. Also called an *installment contract* or *land contract*.

contract law That law dealing with contracts between parties.

conventional loan A loan not insured or guaranteed by a government.

conversions Process by which an existing residential property is changed into a cooperative or condominium.

convertibility An adjustable-rate mortgage in which the borrower may elect to change to a fixed-rate mortgage, either whenever current rates are favorable or at specific set conversion dates.

convey In real estate, to transfer interest or rights to another party.

conveyance The transfer of title of land from one to another. The means or medium by which title to real estate is transferred.

cooperating broker A broker other than the listing broker who is involved in a real estate transaction. In an MLS transaction, a subagent of the seller, unless a declared agent of the buyer.

cooperative A residential multiunit building whose title is held by a corporation owned by and operated for the benefit of persons living within the building, who are the stockholders of the corporation, each possessing a proprietary lease.

co-op loan An agreement entered into by a borrower and a lender to finance the borrower's acquisition of the borrower's cooperative interest.

co-ownership Ownership by two or more persons.

corporation An entity or organization created by operation of law whose rights of doing business are essentially the same as those of an individual.

corporation franchise tax Tax levied on corporations as a condition of allowing them to do business in New York State.

corporation law Those laws dealing with the creation, conduct, and dissolution of corporations.

corrective maintenance Repairs made on damage already incurred (contrasted with *preventive maintenance*).

cost approach The process of estimating the value of property by adding to the estimated land value the appraiser's estimate of the reproduction or replacement cost of the building, less depreciation.

cost basis *See* basis.

cost recovery Internal Revenue Service term for the accounting use of depreciation.

counteroffer A new offer made as a reply to an offer received.

county boards of health County-level boards with authority over public health issues, such as sanitary systems, water supplies, and food standards.

county planning boards Primarily advisory county agencies that promulgate reporting requirements and standards; county planning boards have greater authority in rural counties.

covenants Agreements written into deeds and other instruments promising performance or nonperformance of certain acts.

covenants, conditions, and restrictions (CC&Rs) Provision in condominium bylaws restricting the owners' usage of the property.

CPA Appraiser's memory aid in making adjustments: Comparable Poorer, Add.

CPM Certified Property Manager, a designation awarded by the Institute of Real Estate Management.

crawlspace Space too low for standing upright, usually in basement but occasionally in an attic.

credit On a closing statement, an amount entered in a person's favor.

criminal law That branch of law defining crimes and providing punishment.

cubic-foot method A technique for estimating building costs per cubic foot.

cul-de-sac A street that is open at one end only and usually has a circular turnaround at the other end (a blind alley).

current rent roll List of present tenants' rent.

curtesy/dower Legal rights each spouse has in the other's real property; no longer observed in New York State.

curvilinear system Street pattern system that integrates major arteries with smaller winding streets and cul-de-sacs.

customer A potential buyer of real estate; should not be confused with a property seller (i.e., listing broker's client).

damages The indemnity recoverable by a person who has sustained an injury, either to person, property, or rights, through the act or default of another.

datum Point from which elevations are measured. Mean sea level in New York harbor, or local datums.

DBA "Doing business as"; an assumed business name.

dealer An IRS classification for a person whose business is buying and selling real estate on his or her own account.

debit On a closing statement, a charge or amount a party owes and must pay at the closing.

debtors in possession In foreclosure, a borrower who retains possession but is still responsible for all junior liens to the property as well as liable to the IRS for tax on the debt that is forgiven. In this situation, a debtor in possession will seek a workout with a lender whenever possible.

debt service Mortgage payments, including principal and interest on an amortized loan.

DEC The New York Department of Environmental Conservation.

decedent A person who has died.

declaration A formal statement of intention to establish a condominium.

dedication The voluntary transfer of private property by its owner to the public for some public use such as for streets or schools.

deed A written instrument that, when executed and delivered, conveys title to or an interest in real estate.

dedication by deed The voluntary transfer of private property by its owner to the public for some public use such as for streets or schools. A quitclaim deed is often used for the process.

deductible As it relates to insurance policies, represents the monetary portion of the damages the property owner will bear if and when a covered loss occurs.

deed restriction An imposed restriction in a deed for the purpose of limiting the use of the land by future owners.

default The nonperformance of a duty, whether arising under a contract or otherwise; failure to meet an obligation when due.

deficiency judgment A personal judgment levied against the mortgagor when a foreclosure sale does not produce sufficient funds to pay the mortgage debt in full.

delinquent taxes Unpaid past-due taxes.

delivery and acceptance The transfer of the possession of a thing from one person to another.

demand The desire for economic goods people are willing and able to buy at a given price at a specific time.

demising clause A clause in a lease whereby the landlord (lessor) leases and the tenant (lessee) takes the property.

demography The statistical study of populations: births, deaths, ages, etc.

denial, suspension, or revocation of license Actions by which the Department of State enforces real estate laws, rules, and regulations.

density zoning Local ordinances that limit the number of housing units that may be built per acre within a subdivision.

Department of Environmental Conservation (DEC) Agency that issues permits for developments in or around a protected wetland or other environmentally sensitive area.

Department of Housing and Community Renewal The New York State department charged with administering rent regulations.

Department of Housing and Urban Development (HUD) Federal agency that administers the Fair Housing Act of 1968.

Department of State (DOS) The New York State agency that supervises real estate licensees, through its Division of Licensing Services.

Department of Transportation State agency with oversight of New York's highway system.

deposition Sworn testimony that may be used as evidence in a suit or trial.

depreciable basis The beginning dollar amount (representing the improvement's value) that constitutes the annual depreciation deduction allowed under the Taxpayer Relief Act.

depreciation In appraisal, a loss of value in property due to any cause, including physical deterioration, functional obsolescence, and external (locational) obsolescence.

descent Acquisition of an estate by inheritance in which an heir succeeds to the property by operation of law.

description In real estate, the portion of a document that defines the subject property in specific legal terms.

designation An indication of special training and expertise, awarded by various real estate organizations.

determinable fee estate A fee simple estate in which the property automatically reverts to the grantor on the occurrence of a specified event or condition.

developer One who improves land with buildings, usually on a large scale, and sells to homeowners and/or investors.

development rights The rights to develop and improve property, sometimes sold to another landowner to be used on a different parcel.

devise A gift of real property by will; the act of leaving real property by will.

devisee One who receives a bequest of real estate made by will.

devisor One who bequeaths real estate by will.

direct costs The expenditures necessary for the labor and materials used in the construction of a new improvement, including contractor's overhead and profit.

direct public ownership Land-use control method through which land is owned by the government for such public uses as municipal buildings, parks, schools, and roads.

direct sales comparison approach An appraisal method in which a subject property is evaluated in comparison with similar recently sold properties; most useful for single residential properties.

disclosure   A broker is responsible for keeping a principal fully informed of all facts that could affect a transaction. A broker who fails to disclose such information may be liable for any damages that result.

disclosure statement   Document that must be filed by the developer of a new or converted condominium or cooperative project, including an architect's or engineer's evaluation of the structure, an expense statement, prices per unit, and other financial and administrative information.

discounted cash-flow analysis   A discounted cash flow analysis is used in a similar manner to that of a pro forma statement; however, the discounted cash flow analysis reflects an analysis of actual versus projected income activities. The discounted cash flow analysis also takes into account the time value of money.

discounting   Method for mathematically calculating present value of money, based on time and the discount rate.

discount points   An added loan fee charged by a lender to make the yield on a lower-than-market-value loan competitive with higher-interest loans.

discount rate   Rate of return needed to compensate an investor for risk; the Federal Reserve's loan rate for eligible banks.

disintermediation   A tight-money real estate lending market (in which real estate loans are more difficult to obtain) that results when investors choose to invest in stocks, bonds, and mutual funds rather than savings accounts, limiting the funds available to lenders.

disposition   Investment strategy for reconciling anticipated gain or loss with the risk involved.

distance learning   These are classes completed online.

Division of Housing and Community Renewal (DHCR)   New York agency that administers rent control and stabilization programs.

documentary evidence   *See* alienation clause.

double-hung window   A sash window with two vertically sliding sashes; both single-hung and double-hung window sashes are controlled and held in place by springs or weights.

due diligence   The process of investigating the circumstances regarding a financial or business transaction thoroughly enough to satisfy the care of an unrelated, objective party.

due process   Legal procedures that protect the rights of the individual.

duress   Unlawful constraint or action exercised on a person who is forced to perform an act against his or her will.

earnest money deposit   Money deposited by a buyer under the terms of a contract, to be applied to the purchase price if the sale is closed.

easement   A right to use the land of another for a specific purpose, as for a right-of-way or utilities; an incorporeal interest in land. An easement appurtenant passes with the land when conveyed.

easement appurtenant   An easement involving adjacent parcels that runs with the land (is permanently attached), so that subsequent owners are bound by it, and it passes with the land when conveyed.

easement by condemnation   The government's right to use private property, for example, to build a sidewalk.

easement by grant   An easement given (usually by deed) by one landowner to another.

easement by implication   Arises when "reasonably necessary" and created by the actions of the parties involved.

easement by necessity   An easement allowed by law as necessary for the full enjoyment of a parcel of real estate; for example, a right of ingress and egress over a grantor's land.

easement by prescription   An easement acquired by continuous, open, uninterrupted, exclusive, and adverse use of the property for the period of time prescribed by state law.

easement for light and air   Abutting owners attempt to purchase rights to light and air over a neighbor's property. Such an easement should be granted in writing.   **easement in gross**   An easement that is not created for the benefit of any *land* owned by the owner of the easement but that attaches *personally to the easement owner*.

eave   Overhang or roof projection beyond the outside walls of a house.

economic obsolescence   A form of external obsolescence, a reduction of property value resulting from a change in the economics of the area in which the property is located.

effective gross income   Effective gross income is the income attributable to a property after deductions have been made for vacancy and collection losses and after adding any other income derived from that property. Effective gross income (EGI) = Potential gross income (PGI) − Vacancy and collection loss (V&C) + Other income (OI).

electromagnetic field (EMF) Invisible energy fields created by the movement of electrical currents in high tension wires and electrical appliances. EMFs may be responsible for occurrences of cancer, hormonal changes, and behavioral disorders.

emblements Growing crops, such as grapes and corn, that are produced annually through labor and industry; also called *fructus industriales*.

eminent domain The right of a government or quasi-public body to acquire property for public use through a court action called *condemnation*.

employee One who works under the supervision and control of another, as contrasted for income tax purposes with an independent contractor.

encroachment A building or some portion of it—a wall or fence, for instance—that extends beyond the land of the owner and illegally intrudes on some land of an adjoining owner or a street or alley.

encumbrance Any claim by another—such as a mortgage, a tax or judgment lien, an easement, an encroachment, or a deed restriction on the use of the land—that may diminish the value of a property.

endorsement An act of signing one's name on the back of a check or note with or without further qualifications.

envelope The components that make up the building (also known as the *building envelope*)—roof, walls, and windows—protect occupants from intruders, noises, and the elements; they can and should be made as energy efficient as possible.

environmental impact study Report detailing the effect of a proposed development on the existing environment, including possible alternative measures to remedy or repair environmental damage.

Environmental Protection Agency (EPA) A federal agency involved with the problems of air and water pollution, noise, pesticides, radiation, and solid-waste management. EPA sets standards, enforces environmental laws, conducts research, allocates funds for sewage-treatment facilities, and provides technical, financial and managerial assistance for municipal, regional, and state pollution control agencies.

Equal Credit Opportunity Act (ECOA) The federal law that prohibits discrimination in the extension of credit because of race, color, religion, national origin, sex, age, or marital status.

equalization The raising or lowering of assessed values for tax purposes in a particular county or taxing district to make them equal to assessments in other counties or districts.

equalization factor A multiplier that adjusts for different communities' tax assessment policies.

equitable title The interest held by a vendee under a land contract or an installment contract; the equitable right to obtain absolute ownership to property when legal title is held in another's name.

equity The interest or value that an owner has in property over and above any mortgage indebtedness and other liens.

equity dividend rate This is the percentage of profit that the investor receives only on the cash he or she invested in the property (commonly referred to as cash-on-cash return).

equity of redemption A right of the owner to reclaim property before it is sold through foreclosure by the payment of the debt, interest, and costs.

erosion The gradual wearing away of land by water, wind, and general weather conditions; the diminishing of property caused by the elements.

errors and omissions insurance A form of malpractice insurance for real estate brokers.

escape clause A provision in a contract that allows one party to unilaterally void the contract without penalty; for instance, a seller may be allowed to look for a more favorable offer, while the purchaser retains the right to drop all contingencies or void the contract if another offer is received.

escheat The reversion of property to the state or county, as provided by state law, in cases where a person dies intestate without heirs capable of inheriting or when the property is abandoned.

escrow The closing of a transaction through a third party called an *escrow agent*. Also can refer to earnest money deposits or to a mortgagee's trust account for insurance and tax payments.

estate The degree, quantity, nature, and extent of interest that a person has in real property.

estate at will The occupation of lands and tenements by a tenant for an indefinite period, terminable by one or both parties at will.

estate for years An interest for a certain, exact period of time in property leased for a specified consideration.

estate in land The degree, quantity, nature, and extent of interest a person has in real property.

estate tax Federal tax levied on property transferred on death.

estoppel   The situation in which a party is prevented by the party's own acts from taking a different position because it would cause detriment to another party.

estoppel certificate   A document in which a borrower certifies the amount he or she owes on a mortgage loan and the rate of interest. Often used for *reduction certificate*.

evaluation   An analysis of a property and its attributes in which a value estimate is not required. The study may consider any aspect of the property, including the nature, quality, and utility of an interest in the real estate.

eviction   A legal process to oust a person from possession of real estate.

eviction plan   Method of converting a rental property into a condominium or cooperative, in which existing tenants will be evicted when their leases expire.

evidence of title   Proof of ownership of property; commonly a certificate of title, a title insurance policy, an abstract of title with lawyer's opinion, or a Torrens registration certificate.

exchange   A transaction in which all or part of the consideration for the purchase of real property is the transfer of *like-kind* property (that is, real estate for real estate).

exclusive-agency listing   A listing contract under which the owner appoints a real estate broker as his or her exclusive agent. The owner reserves the right to sell without paying anyone a commission.

exclusive right to represent   The most common form of buyer agency agreement.

exclusive-right-to-sell listing   A listing contract under which the owner appoints a real estate broker as his or her exclusive agent and agrees to pay the broker a commission when the property is sold, whether by the broker, the owner, or another broker.

executed contract   A contract in which all parties have fulfilled their promises and thus performed the contract.

execution   The signing and delivery of an instrument. Also, a legal order directing an official to enforce a judgment against the property of a debtor.

Executive Law   New York State Human Rights Law.

executor   A male person, corporate entity, or any other type of organization designated in a will to carry out its provisions.

executor's deed   A document signed by the executor of an estate, transferring ownership of real property to a devisee or natural heir.

executory contract   A contract under which something remains to be done by one or more of the parties.

executrix   A woman appointed to perform the duties of an executor.

exemption   With an exemption, a licensee is excused from a given requirement that otherwise would apply.

express agency   An agency that is specifically stated, orally or in writing.

express contract   An oral or written contract in which the parties state the contract's terms and express their intentions in words.

external obsolescence   Reduction in a property's value caused by factors outside the subject property, such as social or environmental forces or objectionable neighboring property.

fair employment laws   Laws designed to prevent employers from making their hiring and firing decisions on factors unrelated to job performance.

Fair Housing Amendment Act of 1988   Effective March 12, 1989, this amendment to the federal Fair Housing Act added two more classes protected from discrimination: those physically and mentally handicapped, and those with children under age 18.

Fair Housing Partnership Agreement   Voluntary agreement between NAR and HUD to cooperate in identifying fair housing problems, issues, and solutions.

familial status   A protected class under fair housing laws, which refers to the presence of children in a family.

family units   For the purposes of defining single-family residence, New York State considers a family one or more persons related by blood, marriage, or adoption; or up to three persons not so related who live together.

Fannie Mae   A quasi-government agency established to purchase any kind of mortgage loans in the secondary mortgage market from the primary lenders.

fascia   Flat board on the outside of a soffit.

federal Fair Housing Act of 1968   The federal law that prohibits discrimination in housing based on race, color, religion, sex, handicap, familial status, or national origin. Amended in 1988 to include persons with physical and mental disabilities, and those with children under 18.

Federal Home Loan Mortgage Corporation (FHLMC)   *See* Freddie Mac.

federally related transaction   Any transaction in which a loan is originated by any financial institution or lender regulated by the federal government.

Federal National Mortgage Association (FNMA)   *See* Fannie Mae.

fee agreement   A compensation agreement that a borrower will enter into with a mortgage broker.

fee appraiser   An appraiser who works as an independent contractor, performing appraisal services for various clients.

fee simple estate   The maximum possible estate or right of ownership of real property, continuing forever. Sometimes called a *fee* or *fee simple absolute*.

FHA loan   A loan insured by the Federal Housing Administration and made by an approved lender in accordance with the FHA's regulations.

fiduciary   One in whom trust and confidence is placed; a reference to a broker employed under the terms of a listing contract or buyer agency agreement.

fiduciary duties   The specific legal duties an agent owes to the principal.

fiduciary relationship   A relationship of trust and confidence as between trustee and beneficiary, attorney and client, or principal and agent.

filtering down   The process by which housing units formerly occupied by middle- and upper-income families decline in quality and value and become available to lower-income occupants.

financing statement   *See* Uniform Commercial Code.

fire and hazard insurance   Policy providing coverage for direct loss of or damage to property resulting from fire, storms, hail, smoke, or riot.

FIRREA   The Financial Institutions Reform, Recovery, and Enforcement Act of 1989 regulates financial institutions and requires that either a licensed certified or general appraiser must be used to conduct any appraisal involving a federally related transaction.

first substantive contact   The point at which agents must disclose and obtain signed acknowledgments of their agency relationships.

fixed expenses   Expenses that do not vary as a result of a property's occupancy rate. Fixed expenses consist of only property taxes and property insurance.

fixture   An item of personal property that has been converted to real property by being permanently affixed to the realty.

flashing   Waterproofing material used to seal seams of roof, chimney, and walls.

flipping   A transaction in which one party contracts to buy a property with the intention of quickly transferring (or flipping) the property over to the ultimate buyer.

flip tax   A tax imposed by the cooperative on the sale of a unit within said building. This fee can be based on a percentage of the gross sale, net sale, gain, or the number of shares held by the shareholder or a fixed number determined by the cooperative board. The flip tax can be paid by the purchaser, seller, or shared by both parties; however, custom usually dictates that the seller pay the flip tax.

floating slab foundation   Type of concrete slab foundation in which the footings and slab are poured separately.

forbearance   A legally binding promise to refrain from doing some act.

foreclosure   A procedure whereby property pledged as security for a debt is sold to pay the debt in the event of default in payments or terms.

franchise   An organization that leases a standardized trade name, operating procedures, supplies, and referral service to member real estate brokerages.

fraud   Deception that causes a person to give up property or a lawful right.

Freddie Mac   A corporation established to purchase primarily conventional mortgage loans in the secondary mortgage market.

freehold estate   An estate in land in which ownership is for an indeterminate length of time, in contrast to a leasehold estate.

Freon   Chemical substance, formerly used in refrigerators and spray cans, now prohibited because it contributes to air pollution.

friable   Crumbly, breaking off (as in some asbestos insulation).

frieze board   A horizontal exterior band or molding located directly below the cornice.

front foot   A standard measurement, one foot wide, of the width of land, applied at the frontage on its street line.

full covenant and warranty deed   A deed that provides the greatest protection, in which the grantor makes five legal promises (covenants of seisin, quiet enjoyment, further assurances, warranty forever, against encumbrances) that the grantee's ownership will be unchallenged.

full-value assessment   Practice of assessing property at its full value, rather than by a percentage of full value.

fully amortized loan   A debt that is completely paid off at the end of a specific number of even payments, each containing interest and a portion toward reducing the principal.

functional obsolescence A loss of value to an improvement to real estate due to functional problems, often caused by age or poor design.

fuse box Area where electric service enters a building and is distributed to various circuits.

future interest A person's present right to an interest in real property that will not result in possession or enjoyment until some time in the future.

gains Any gains that result from a sale where the property was held for one year or less.

gap A defect in the chain of title of a particular parcel of real estate; a missing document or conveyance that raises doubt as to present ownership.

general agent One authorized to act for the principal in a specific range of matters.

general contractor A construction specialist who enters into a formal contract with a landowner or lessee to construct a building or project.

general lien The right of a creditor to have all of a debtor's property—both real and personal—sold to satisfy a debt.

general partnership *See* partnership.

general tax *See* ad valorem tax.

Ginnie Mae A government agency that plays an important role in the secondary mortgage market. It sells mortgage-backed securities that are backed by pools of FHA and VA loans.

girder The heavy beam, wood or steel, that furnishes the main support for the first floor.

Government National Mortgage Association (GNMA) *See* Ginnie Mae.

grace period Additional time allowed to perform an act or make a payment before a default occurs.

graduated lease A lease that provides for a graduated change at stated intervals in the amount of the rent to be paid; used largely in long-term leases.

graduated payment mortgage A mortgage in which the monthly payment for principal and interest graduates by a certain percentage each year for a specific number of years and then levels off for the remaining term of the mortgage.

grant A sale or gift of real property.

grantee A person who receives a conveyance of real property from the grantor.

granting clause Words in a deed of conveyance that state the grantor's intention to convey the property. This clause is generally worded as "convey and warrant," "grant," "grant, bargain and sell," or the like.

grantor The person transferring title to or an interest in real property to a grantee.

GRI (Graduate, REALTORS® Institute) A professional designation earned by any member of a state-affiliated Board of REALTORS® who completes specific courses approved by the board.

gridiron pattern Street pattern systems that evolved out of the government rectangular survey, featuring a regular grid of straight-line streets and alleys.

grievance A complaint, particularly that made by a taxpayer protesting property tax assessment figures.

gross income Total income from property before any expenses are deducted.

gross income multiplier The figure used as a multiplier of the gross annual income of a property to produce an estimate of the property's value.

gross lease A lease of property under which a landlord pays all property charges regularly incurred through ownership, such as repairs, taxes, and insurance.

gross operating income Rent actually collected on an income property.

gross rental income Total amount collected in rents, from which expenses must be paid.

gross rent multiplier (GRM) A figure used as a multiplier of the gross rental income of a property to produce an estimate of the property's value.

ground lease A lease of land only, on which the tenant usually owns a building or is required to build as specified in the lease. Such leases are usually long-term net leases; the tenant's rights and obligations continue until the lease expires or is terminated through default.

groundwater Surface runoff and underground water systems.

group boycott An agreement among members of a trade to exclude other members from fair participation in the activities of the trade.

group home A living unit housing more than three unrelated individuals.

habendum clause That part of a deed beginning with the words "to have and to hold" following the granting clause and defining the extent of ownership the grantor is conveying.

hazardous substances Materials such as chemicals, industrial and residential by-products, biological waste, and other pollutants that pose an actual or suspected threat to human health, quality of life, and the environment.

headers Horizontal supports above doors and windows.

heat pump Mechanism that uses heat from outside air to reduce heating and air-conditioning costs.

hectare Land measurement equivalent to 10,000 square meters, or approximately 2.471 acres.

heir One who might inherit or succeed to an interest in land under the state law of descent when the owner dies without leaving a valid will.

highest and best use That possible use of land that would produce the greatest net income and thereby develop the highest land value.

holder of unsold shares A holder of unsold shares is any person or legal entity designated by the original sponsor to be a holder of these shares. A holder of unsold shares receives benefits similar to those of the sponsor; these include the ability to sell the shares to anyone without the board's consent and the unlimited ability to sublease the unit to any individual without the board's consent.

holding period The time an investment or asset is possessed.

holdover tenancy A tenancy whereby a lessee retains possession of leased property after his or her lease has expired and the landlord, by continuing to accept rent, agrees to the tenant's continued occupancy.

holographic will A will that is written, dated, and signed in the testator's handwriting but is not witnessed.

home equity loan A loan (sometimes called a *line of credit*) under which property owners use their residence as collateral and can then draw funds up to a prearranged amount against the property.

home inspectors Licensed professionals who conduct a thorough visual survey of a property's structure, systems, and site conditions and prepare an analytical report that is valuable to both purchasers and homeowners.

home occupations Small business or creative activities, allowed to residents in an area otherwise zoned entirely residential.

homeowners' association A nonprofit group of homeowners in a condominium, cooperative, or planned unit development (PUD) that administers common elements and enforces covenants, conditions, and restrictions.

homeowners' insurance policy A standardized package insurance policy that covers a residential real estate owner against financial loss from fire, theft, public liability, and other commercial risks.

homestead Land that is owned and occupied as the family home. The right to protect a portion of the value of this land from unsecured judgments for debts.

household income Income earned by any lawful occupant housed within the stabilized unit.

house rules The cooperative's habitation rules that govern all shareholders are known as house rules.

HVAC Heating, ventilation, and air-conditioning systems.

hypothecation This occurs when the borrower pledges the property without giving up ownership or possession of the property.

illiquidity Refers to the difficulty in selling an asset for full value on short notice (lack of assets that can be quickly converted to cash).

impact fees Charges levied by a local government to help the community absorb the public costs involved in the development of a new subdivision.

implied agency An agency established not by words, but by the actions of the parties.

implied contract A contract under which the agreement of the parties is demonstrated by their acts and conduct.

implied creation of a subagency The unintended creation of a fiduciary relationship through an informal cooperation arrangement between brokers.

implied warranty of habitability A theory in landlord/tenant law in which the landlord renting residential property implies that the property is habitable and fit for its intended use.

improvement Any structure erected on a site to enhance the value of the property—buildings, fences, driveways, curbs, sidewalks, or sewers.

imputed interest An IRS concept that treats some concessionary low-interest loans as if they had been paid and collected at a statutory rate.

income capitalization approach The process of estimating the value of an income-producing property by capitalization of the annual net income expected to be produced by the property during its remaining useful life.

incompetent A person who is unable to manage his own affairs by reason of insanity, imbecility, or feeblemindedness.

independent contractor Someone retained to perform a certain act but subject to the control and direction of another only as to the end result and not as to the way in which he or she performs the act; contrasted with employee.

index With an adjustable-rate mortgage, a measure of current interest rates, used as a basis for calculating the new rate at the time of adjustment.

index lease A lease in which the rental figure is adjusted periodically according to the government's cost-of-living index.

indirect costs Construction expenses for items other than labor and materials (e.g., financing costs, taxes, administrative costs, contractor's overhead and profit, legal fees, interest payments, insurance costs during construction, and lease-up costs).

industrial real estate Warehouses, factories, land in industrial districts, and research facilities (sometimes referred to as *manufacturing property*).

inflation The gradual reduction of the purchasing power of the dollar, usually related directly to the increases in the money supply by the federal government.

informed consent Agreement to an act based on the full and fair disclosure of all the facts a reasonable person would need in order to make a rational decision.

infrastructure Basic public works such as utilities, roads, bridges, sewer and water systems, etc.

inheritance tax New York State tax levied on those who inherit property located in the state.

injunction An order issued by a court to restrain one party from doing an act deemed to be unjust to the rights of some other party.

in rem A proceeding against the realty directly as distinguished from a proceeding against a person.

installment contract *See* land contract.

installment sale A method of reporting income received from the sale of real estate when the sales price is paid in two or more installments over two or more years.

instrument A written legal document created to effect the rights of the parties.

insulation Material that protects a surface from cold or heat.

insured value Used to determine the amount of insurance carried on the property.

interest A charge made by a lender for the use of money. Also, a legal share of ownership in property, whether the entire ownership or partial.

interest-only mortgage Mortgage in which monthly payments cover only the interest due and offer no debt reduction.

interest rate The percentage of a sum of money charged for its use.

interim financing A short-term loan usually made during the construction phase of a building project (in this case often referred to as a *construction loan*).

internal rate of return (IRR) Discount rate that, when applied to both positive and negative cash flows, results in zero net present value.

Interstate Land Sales Full Disclosure Act A federal law that regulates the sale of certain real estate in interstate commerce.

intestate The condition of a property owner who dies without leaving a valid will.

involuntary alienation Transfer of real estate without the owner's initiative, as in foreclosure or condemnation.

involuntary bankruptcy A bankruptcy proceeding initiated by one or more of the debtor's creditors.

involuntary lien A lien imposed against property without consent of the owners (i.e., taxes, special assessments).

irrevocable consent An agreement filed by an out-of-state broker stating that suits and actions may be brought against the broker in the state where a license is sought.

IRV formula The relationship among interest, rate, and value.

jalousie window A window that is formed by horizontal slats of glass that open or close vertically by the action of a gear.

joint tenancy Ownership of real estate between two or more parties who have been named in one conveyance as joint tenants. On the death of a joint tenant, the deceased's interest passes to the surviving joint tenant or tenants.

joint venture The joining of two or more people to conduct a specific business enterprise.

joist and rafter roof Roofing system that relies on sloping timbers supported by a ridge board and made rigid by interconnecting joists.

judgment The formal decision of a court regarding the respective claims of the parties to an action.

jumbo loan A loan that exceeds FNMA and FHLMC maximum loan limits.

junior lien   An obligation such as a second mortgage that is subordinate in priority to an existing lien on the same realty.

kickbacks   The return of part of the commission as gifts or money to buyers or sellers.

laches   Loss of a legal right through undue delay in asserting it.

Lally™ columns   Upright columns that support the main beams of a building.

land   The earth's surface, extending downward to the center of the earth and upward infinitely into space.

land contract   *See* contract for deed.

landfill   A site for the burial, layering, and permanent storage of waste material, consisting of alternating layers of waste and topsoil.

landlord   One who rents property to another.

land patents   Document the transfer of land ownership from the federal government to individuals.

last will and testament   An instrument executed by an owner to convey the owner's property to specific persons after the owner's death.

latent defects   A hidden defect that is not discoverable by ordinary inspection.

law of agency   The law that governs the relationships and duties of agents, clients, and customers. *See also* agent.

lead agency   In an environmental survey, the one agency that coordinates the process.

lead poisoning   Illness, including the impairment of physical and mental development in children and aggravated blood pressure in adults, resulting from the ingestion of lead toxins, primarily in paint or plumbing.

Leaking Underground Storage Tanks (LUST)   Federal environmental protection program to protect the nation's groundwater by identifying underground tanks and preventing or correcting leakage of hazardous materials.

lease   A written or oral contract between a landlord (the lessor) and a tenant (the lessee) that transfers the right to exclusive possession and use of the landlord's real property to the lessee for a specified period of time and for a stated consideration (rent).

lease escalation clause   The lease escalation clause is used to protect the commercial property owner against the increased cost in operations that arises from inflation.

leasehold estate   A tenant's right to occupy real estate during the term of a lease; generally considered personal property.

legacy   A disposition of money or personal property by will.

legal description   A description of a specific parcel of real estate complete enough for an independent surveyor to locate and identify it.

legality of object   The requirement that a valid and enforceable contract may not involve an illegal purpose or one that is against public policy.

lender's rebate   A partial refund following a purchase that involves a loan.

lessee   Tenant.

lessor   Landlord.

letter of intent   A vehicle to reserve a specific unit or units and sets forth an understanding of the terms of the transaction between the sponsor and prospective purchaser.

leverage   The use of borrowed money to finance the bulk of an investment.

levy   The placing of tax liens against real property.

liability insurance   Standard package homeowners' insurance policy coverage for personal injuries to others resulting from the insured's acts or negligence; voluntary medical payments and funeral expenses for accidents sustained by guests or resident employees on the property and physical damage to other's property.

license   (1) A privilege or right granted to a person by a state to operate as a real estate broker or salesperson. (2) The revocable permission for a temporary use of land.

lien   A right given by law to certain creditors to have their debt paid out of the property of a defaulting debtor, usually by means of a court sale.

lien theory   Some states interpret a mortgage as being purely a lien on real property. The mortgagee thus has no right of possession but must foreclose the lien and sell the property if the mortgagor defaults.

life estate   An interest in real or personal property that is limited in duration to the lifetime of its owner or some other designated person.

life tenant   A person in possession of a life estate.

like-kind exchange   An exchange of property for property as opposed to property for money.

limited liability company (LLC)   A hybrid business entity that combines the managerial freedom of partnerships with the limited liability for owner and avoidance of income taxes offered by corporations.

limited partnership   *See* partnership.

liquidated damages   An amount of money, agreed to in advance, that will serve as the total compensation due to the injured party if the other does not comply with the contract's terms.

liquidity   The ability to sell an asset and convert it into cash at a price close to its true value in a short period of time.

lis pendens   A recorded legal document giving constructive notice that an action affecting a particular property has been filed in court.

listing agent   The broker with whom sellers enter into a valid listing agreement for the sale of their real estate.

listing agreement   A contract between a landowner (as principal) and a licensed real estate broker (as agent) by which the broker is employed as agent to sell real estate on the owner's terms within a given time, for which service the landowner agrees to pay a commission or fee.

listing broker   The agent hired by a property owner to assist in the marketing of real estate.

litigation   Lawsuits.

littoral rights   (1) A landowner's claim to use water in large navigable lakes and oceans adjacent to her property. (2) The ownership rights to land bordering these bodies of water up to the high-water mark.

LLP   A limited liability partnership.

loan servicing   The lender's duties in administering a loan, such as collecting payments, accounting and bookkeeping, maintaining records, and issuing loan status reports to the borrower.

loan-to-value (LTV) ratio   The relationship between the amount of the mortgage loan and the market value of the real estate being pledged as collateral.

locational obsolescence   A form of external obsolescence; a reduction of property value resulting from conditions outside the property.

long-term gains   Any gains that result from a sale where the property was held for one year or more.

loyalty   The fiduciary duty that requires an agent to put the principal's interest above all others, including the agent's.

maintenance   This is defined as the general upkeep of a property.

management agreement   Employment contract between property owner and manager, under which the manager assumes the responsibility for administering and maintaining the property as the owner's general agent.

management proposal   A property manager's report to the owner of a plan for supervising the property.

margin   With an adjustable-rate mortgage, the number of points over an *index* at which the interest rate is set.

marginal tax rate   Percentage at which the last dollar of income is taxed; top tax bracket.

marital status   A protected class under New York State law that does not allow sellers or landlords to base decisions on whether prospective occupants are married or not.

marketable title   Good or clear title reasonably free from the risk of litigation over possible defects.

market allocation   An agreement among members of a trade to refrain from competition in specific areas.

market analysis   Study undertaken by a property manager of the local and regional market, as well as the underlying property itself, to provide information about the economic conditions, supply, demand, and similar competing properties.

market data approach   *See* direct sales comparison approach.

market price   The actual selling price of a property.

market value   The probable price a ready, willing, able, and informed buyer would pay and a ready, willing, able, and informed seller would accept, neither being under any pressure to act.

master plan   A comprehensive plan to guide the long-term physical development of a particular area.

maximum base rent (MBR)   Under rent control, the maximum rent allowable for an individual unit.

mechanic's lien   A statutory lien created in favor of contractors, laborers, and material suppliers who have performed work or furnished materials in the erection or repair of a building.

mediation   Method for dealing with disputes; the person running the session does not make a determination, but rather brings the parties into agreement.

meeting of the minds   An essential component of a valid contract, a "meeting of the minds" occurs when all parties agree to the exact terms.

memorandum of sale   A nonbinding information sheet prepared by brokers in some New York localities that states the essential terms of the agreement; the final contract is later drawn up by an attorney.

metes-and-bounds description   A legal description of a parcel of land that begins at a well-marked point and follows the boundaries, using direction and distances around the tract, back to the place of beginning.

Metropolitan Transport Authority (MTA) Regional agency with taxing power and jurisdiction over certain air and land rights.

mill One-tenth of one cent. A tax rate of 52 mills would be $0.052 tax for each dollar of assessed valuation of a property.

minimum building standards Degree of quality and care mandated by the state; local codes and regulations may require adherence to a higher standard.

minor A person under 18 years of age.

MIP Mortgage insurance premium.

misdemeanor A crime less than a felony but greater than a violation.

misrepresentation A false statement or concealment of a material fact made with the intent of causing another party to act.

mold Natural organism, a fungus, that grows in damp area; sometimes toxic.

monoline policy This policy provides only one line or area of coverage. It bears greater relevancy to insurers than to the insured.

month-to-month tenancy A periodic tenancy; that is, the tenant rents for one period at a time. In the absence of a rental agreement (oral or written), a tenancy is generally considered to be month to month.

monument A fixed natural or artificial object used to establish real estate boundaries for a metes-and-bounds description.

moratorium A period of delay; in real estate usually refers to a community's temporary halt to development.

mortgage A conditional transfer or pledge of real estate as security for the payment of a debt. Also, the document creating a mortgage lien.

mortgage bankers Companies that are licensed to make real estate loans that are sold to investors.

mortgage broker An individual who acts as an intermediary between lenders and borrowers for a fee.

mortgage commitment The process in which a lender issues a loan commitment letter to the borrower to demonstrate willingness to fund the loan.

mortgage contingency clause A common provision that allows the buyer a certain period of time to obtain a commitment for financing at a specified interest rate for a certain amount of money. It usually lasts for 30 to 60 days, depending on the average time needed to obtain a loan commitment.

mortgage debt service Property owner's expense for payments (usually monthly) on mortgages.

mortgagee A lender in a mortgage loan transaction.

mortgage insurance premium (MIP) Lump sum premium for mortgage insurance coverage, payable either in cash at closing or financed over the mortgage term.

mortgage lien A lien or charge on the property of a mortgagor that secures the underlying debt obligations.

mortgage reduction certificate An instrument executed by the mortgagee setting forth the present status and the balance due on the mortgage as of the date of the execution of the instrument.

mortgage value Normally established by appraisal, it represents the amount or value that the lender is willing to commit to the loan. It is also the difference between the buyers initial equity investment (down-payment) and the purchase price or appraised value of the property, whichever is less.

mortgagor A borrower who conveys his or her property as security for a loan.

multiperil policies Insurance policies offering protection from a range of potential perils, such as fire, hazard, public liability, and casualty, in a single policy.

multiple listing service A marketing organization composed of member brokers who agree to share their listings with one another in the hope of procuring ready, willing, and able buyers more quickly and efficiently.

negative amortization Gradual building up of a large mortgage debt when payments are not sufficient to cover interest due and reduce the principal.

negative cash flow Negative figure resulting when expenditures on an investment exceed the income it produces.

negligence An unintentional tort caused by failure to exercise reasonable care.

negotiable instrument A signed promise to pay a sum of money.

neighborhood analysis A property manager's study of nearby rental availability and market rental figures.

net lease A lease requiring that the tenant pay not only rent but also some or all costs of maintaining the property, including taxes, insurance, utilities, and repairs.

net listing A listing based on the net price the seller will receive if the property is sold. Under a net listing, the broker is free to offer the property for sale at any price to increase the commission. Outlawed in New York.

net operating income (NOI) The income projected for an income-producing property after deducting losses for vacancy and collection and operating expenses.

net present value (NPV) Difference between the present value of all positive and negative cash flows.

New York City Department of Environmental Protection (DEP) Local agency with authority over the city's water supply (from its source to local reservoirs), and which ensures that construction projects do not interfere with the watershed.

New York General Obligations Law The state's version of the statute of frauds, which requires, among other provisions, that any agreements relating to the sale of real estate must be in writing.

New York Human Rights Law State law prohibiting discrimination in housing.

New York State Division of Human Rights Agency with which a complaint of housing discrimination may file a complaint within one year of the alleged act.

New York State Lawyers' Fund The New York State Lawyers' Fund was created in 1982. Its primary mission and purpose is the protection of legal consumers from the dishonest conduct in the practice of law.

nonconforming mortgage Flexible loan that does not meet standard uniform underwriting requirements, usually structured for borrowers who have unique credit situations or who wish to purchase an unusual property.

nonconforming use Use of land that is not allowed by the local zoning ordinance.

noneviction plan Method of converting a rental property into a condominium or cooperative.

nonhomestead Not used as the owner's primary residence: buildings with more than four dwelling units, industrial and commercial property, and most vacant land.

nonhomogeneity A lack of uniformity; dissimilarity. Because no two parcels of land are exactly alike, real estate is said to be nonhomogeneous.

nonsolicitation order A directive to all real estate brokers and real estate salespersons to refrain from soliciting listings for the sale of residential property within a designated geographic area. The types of solicitation that are prohibited include but are not limited to letters, postcards, telephone calls, door-to-door calls, handbills, and postings in public areas.

notary public A public officer who is authorized to take acknowledgments to certain classes of documents such as deeds, contracts, and mortgages and before whom affidavits may be sworn.

note An instrument of credit given to attest a debt.

notice Information available through the public records or through inspection of property. Also, notification by landlord or tenant of intention to terminate a rental.

notice of pending legal action *See* lis pendens.

novation Substituting a new obligation for an old one or substituting new parties to an existing obligation.

nuisance An act that disturbs another's peaceful enjoyment of property.

NYSAR New York State Association of Realtors®.

obedience The agent's fiduciary duty to obey all lawful instructions of the principal.

obsolescence *See* external obsolescence; functional obsolescence.

offer and acceptance Two essential components of a valid contract; a "meeting of the minds," when all parties agree to the exact terms.

offering statement/plan A document that is created and issued by a sponsor that is either in the process of converting a building or developing a new building. Its purpose is to provide an interested party with full disclosure of all facts pertinent to the project.

office property Any type of structure (lowrise, highrise, complex, or campus) used by nonmanufacturing, nonretail tenants such as medical, legal, and financial professionals.

open-end mortgage A mortgage loan that is expandable to a maximum dollar amount, the loan being secured by the same original mortgage.

open listing A listing contract under which the broker's commission is contingent on the broker's producing a ready, willing, and able buyer before the property is sold by the owner or another broker.

operating budget A property manager's detailed plan for expenses.

OPRHP New York State's Office of Parks, Recreation, and Historic Preservation.

option An agreement to keep open for a set period an offer to sell or purchase property.

option to renew Provision of a lease giving the tenant the right to extend the lease for an additional period of time on set terms.

other income (OI) Income that is not derived from the main activity of the property.

overall capitalization rate (OAR) A figure that estimates value by comparing capitalization rate to income.

package loan   A real estate loan used to finance the purchase of both real property and personal property, such as the purchase of a new home that includes carpeting, window coverings, and major appliances.

package mortgage   A method of financing in which the loan that finances the purchase of a home also finances the purchase of items of personal property such as appliances.

package policy   One policy that provides for a variety of different coverage types.

parcel   A specific piece of real estate.

parol evidence rule   A rule of evidence providing that a written agreement is the final expression of the agreement of the parties, not to be varied or contradicted by prior or contemporaneous oral or written negotiations.

participation financing   A mortgage in which the lender participates in the income of the mortgaged venture.

participation loan   A mortgage arrangement in which the lender receives a share of the venture's profits or the real estate's appreciation.

partition   The division of real property made between those who own it in undivided shares.

partnership   An association of two or more individuals who carry on a continuing business for profit as co-owners. A *general partnership* is a typical form of joint venture in which each general partner shares in the administration, profits, and losses of the operations. A *limited partnership* is administered by one or more general partners and funded by limited or silent partners who are by law responsible for losses only to the extent of their investments.

party wall   A wall that is located on or at a boundary line between two adjoining parcels of land and is used by the owners of both properties.

passive income   Income derived from an investment activity in which the investor does not take an active management or participatory role.

percentage lease   A lease commonly used for commercial property whose rental is based on the tenant's gross sales at the premises.

percolation   The soil's ability to process water.

percolation rate   A figure establishing how quickly liquid can drain through the ground.

percolation test   A test to see if a septic tank will work successfully in a specific location.

periodic estate   An interest in leased property that continues from period to period—week to week, month to month, or year to year.

periodic lease   A lease with has no specific ending date. Generally these leases are month-to-month. A periodic lease (also known as a periodic tenancy or period estate) is automatically renewed each time the tenant pays rent to the landlord.

personal property   Items, called *chattels*, that do not fit into the definition of real property; movable objects.

personal property law   That section of the law dealing with chattels.

personal representative   The administrator or executor appointed to handle the estate of a decedent.

physical deterioration   Loss of value due to wear and tear or action of the elements.

pier and beam foundation   Foundation style in which partly submerged columns (piers) support the foundation slab, with an air pocket (crawlspace) between the slab and the ground.

pitch   Slope of a roof expressed as a ratio of height to span.

PITI   Principal, interest, taxes, and insurance: components of a regular mortgage payment.

planned unit development (PUD)   A planned combination of diverse land uses such as housing, recreation, and shopping in one contained development or subdivision.

planning board   Municipal body overseeing orderly development of real estate.

plasterboard/wallboard   Prepared 4' by 8' boards often used as wall finish in place of plaster.

plat   A map of a town, section, or subdivision indicating the location and boundaries of individual properties.

platform framing construction   Common form of construction for one- and two-story residential buildings; one floor is built at a time, with the lower floor providing a platform on which the upper floor is built.

plat of subdivision   A map of a planned subdivision, entered in the public records.

plottage   The increase in value or utility resulting from the consolidation (assemblage) of two or more adjacent lots into one larger lot.

PMI   Private mortgage insurance.

POB   *See* point of beginning.

pocket card   Copy of a real estate license, issued by the Department of State, to be carried in the licensee's wallet.

point   A unit of measurement used for various loan charges; one point equals 1 percent of the amount of the loan. *See also* discount points.

point of beginning   In a metes-and-bounds legal description, the starting point of the survey, situated in one corner of the parcel. Also called *place of beginning*.

police power   The government's right to impose laws, statutes, and ordinances, including zoning ordinances and building codes, to protect the public health, safety, and welfare.

policy and procedures guide   A broker's compilation of guidelines for the conduct of the firm's business.

pollution   Artificially created environmental impurity.

polychlorinated biphenyls (PCBs)   Potentially hazardous chemical used in electrical equipment, principally transformers.

portfolio income   Any income derived from items such as dividends received through ownership stock, interest received from any source, and royalties received on intellectual property.

portfolio loan   Mortgage loan not intended for sale on the secondary market; nonconforming loan.

possessory/nonpossessory rights   Indicates and implies certain rights inherent to the occupant (possessory) or no rights to the property if person does not occupy the property. Easements fall into the category of nonpossessory rights or interests within land owned by another.

post-and-beam construction   An old framing method in which ceiling planks are placed on beams (often left exposed).

potential gross income (PGI)   The gross rent roll or gross receipts attributable through rental activities if a property is 100 percent leased.

potentially responsible parties (PRPs)   Under Superfund, the landowners suspected of contaminating a property.

power of attorney   A written instrument authorizing a person, the *attorney-in-fact*, to act as agent on behalf of another person.

preapplication   Process of preapproval of the borrower.

preapproval loan   A pending loan in which all of the underlying documents are in file and there is a strong probability that there are no credit or income issues stopping the loan from closing.

precedent   A court decision that serves as authority for later cases.

preliminary prospectus   Description of new or converted condominium or cooperative property, subject to change, available for inspection by present tenants after review by the attorney general (also referred to as a *red herring*).

premises   Lands and tenements; an estate; the subject matter of a conveyance.

prepaid item   A bill paid by the seller for something the buyer will benefit from: the coming year's property taxes, for example. Buyer will reimburse seller at closing for the unused portion.

prepayment clause   A clause in a mortgage that gives the mortgagor the privilege of paying the mortgage indebtedness before it becomes due.

prepayment premium (penalty)   A charge imposed on a borrower who pays off the loan principal early.

prequalification   Refers to a pending loan in which a mortgage broker believes that, based on a preliminary interview and a credit report, the borrower will probably (subject to verification) be able to meet the loan requirements of a lender—assuming the borrower is telling the truth about his or her financial situation and income status.

present value of money   Money's value changes over time. For example, the present value of $1 receivable in one year is $1 minus the lost potential interest on the dollar. If the interest rate is 7 percent, then the present value of $1 to be received in one year is 93 cents today.

preventive maintenance   Maintenance done to avoid possible future damage.

price-fixing   An agreement between members of a trade to artificially maintain prices at a set level.

primary mortgage market   Lenders who make loans directly to real estate borrowers.

primary residence   The location where a taxpayer has resided for at least two out of the previous five years prior to the sale of the property; in addition, the residence must be used as the primary place of residence (when the taxpayer files an income tax return).

principal   (1) A sum lent or employed as a fund or an investment as distinguished from its income or profits. (2) The original amount (as in a loan) of the total due and payable at a certain date. (3) A main party of a transaction; the person for whom the agent works.

principal broker   *See* supervising broker.

priority   The order of position or time.

private mortgage insurance (PMI)   Insurance that limits a lender's potential loss in a mortgage default, issued by a private company rather than by the FHA.

probate   To establish the will of a deceased person.

procuring cause of sale   The effort that brings about the desired result. Under an open listing the broker who is the procuring cause of the sale receives the commission.

professional home inspections   Examination of a property's structure and systems performed by a trained professional for either prospective buyers, lenders, or homeowners.

pro forma statement   Financial statement showing what is expected to occur, particularly with income property.

progression   Economic principle that a lower-quality property's worth will be enhanced by its proximity to higher-quality properties.

property analysis   A property manager's examination of leases and rental rates.

property maintenance   The care and work put into a building to keep it in operation and general repair. Contrasted with permanent improvements.

property management report   A property manager's regular report to the owner.

property manager   An individual who manages real estate for another person for compensation. A property manager's job is to maximize income while maintaining the value of the property. Thus, the property manager is closely involved in a variety of activities related to generating income, including budgeting, market analysis, advertising, and negotiating leases.

proprietary lease   A written lease in a cooperative apartment building, held by the tenant/shareholder, giving the right to occupy a particular unit.

prorations   Expenses, either prepaid or paid in arrears, that are divided or distributed between buyer and seller at the closing.

prospectus   A printed statement disclosing all material aspects of a real estate project.

protected classes   Groups of individuals who have been found to be in need of protection by federal, state, or local laws and regulations against discriminatory actions or conditions.

public grant   A transfer of land by a government body to a private individual.

public offering   A transaction falling under the jurisdiction of the New York attorney general's office, requiring certain specific transactional and financial disclosures. The sale of any form of shared housing in New York is a public offering.

public records   Each company's collection of documents affecting the title to real property; filed documents affecting real estate, maintained by county officials and open to inspection by anyone who is interested.

PUD   *See* planned unit development.

puffing   Exaggerated or superlative comments or opinions not made as representations of fact and thus not grounds for misrepresentation.

pur autre vie   For the life of another. A life estate pur autre vie is a life estate that is measured by the life of a person other than the grantee.

purchase-money mortgage (PMM)   A note secured by a mortgage or deed of trust given by a buyer, as borrower, to a seller, as lender, as part of the purchase price of the real estate.

pyramid   Investment strategy of refinancing existing properties and using the borrowed money.

qualified intermediary   The hired entity that facilitates a like-kind exchange on behalf of the property owner/taxpayer.

quiet enjoyment   The right of an owner or a person legally in possession to the use of property without interference of possession.

quiet title suit   *See* suit to quiet title.

quitclaim deed   A conveyance by which the grantor transfers whatever interest he or she has in the real estate, if any, without warranties or obligations.

radioactive waste   Hazardous by-product of uses of radioactive materials in energy production, medicine, and scientific research.

radon gas   Odorless, naturally occurring radioactive gas that becomes hazardous when trapped and accumulated in unventilated areas of buildings. Long-term exposure to radon is suspected of causing lung cancer.

rate lock   A promise on the part of a lender that the mortgage loan will carry a specific interest rate, regardless of the prevailing rates when the loan is closed.

rate of return   The ratio between earnings and the cost of the investment.

ratification   The situation in which a party is prevented by his own acts from taking a different position because it would cause detriment to another party.

ready, willing, and able buyer   One who is prepared to buy property on the seller's terms and is ready to take positive steps to consummate the transaction.

real estate   A portion of the earth's surface extending downward to the center of the earth and upward infinitely into space, including all things permanently attached thereto, whether by nature or by a person.

real estate broker   Any person, partnership, association, or corporation that sells (or offers to sell), buys (or offers to buy), or negotiates the purchase, sale, or exchange of real estate, or that leases (or offers to lease) or rents (or offers to rent) any real estate or the improvements thereon for others and for a compensation or valuable consideration.

real estate investment syndicate   Business organization in which individuals combine their resources to invest in, manage, or develop a particular property.

real estate investment trust (REIT)   Trust ownership of real estate by a group of individuals who purchase certificates of ownership in the trust.

real estate mortgage investment conduit (REMIC)   A tax vehicle created by the Tax Reform Act of 1986 that permits certain entities that deal in pools of mortgages to pass income through to investors.

real estate sales contract   A contract for the sale of real estate, in which the purchaser promises to pay the agreed purchase price and the seller agrees to deliver title to the property.

real estate salesperson   A person licensed by the state to assist a licensed broker in the field of real estate.

Real Estate Settlement Procedures Act (RESPA)   The federal law that requires certain disclosures to consumers about mortgage loan settlements. The law also prohibits the payment or receipt of kickbacks and certain kinds of referral fees.

real property   Real estate plus all the interests, benefits, and rights inherent in ownership. Often referred to as *real estate*.

Real Property Law   New York law governing the real estate profession, including prohibitions against discrimination in housing.

real property tax rates   Represent the ratio of tax dollars charged in either per hundred or per thousand dollars of assessed valuation. Tax rates are also called mill rates.

REALTORS®   A registered trademark term reserved for the sole use of active members of local REALTOR® boards affiliated with the National Association of REALTORS®.

reasonable care   A broker's duty to perform duties properly.

receiver of taxes   Party or entity charged with the collection of real property taxes on all properties contained within the assessment roll.

reciprocity   An arrangement by which states agree to honor each other's licenses, as with real estate salespersons or brokers.

recognition agreement   A document signed by the borrower, lender, and co-op board. The signature by the co-op acknowledges the lending party's lien interest in the shares covered by the unit. These agreements normally call for the cooperative to notify the lender of any default by the shareholder/borrower (such as the nonpayment of maintenance fees).

reconciliation   The final step in the appraisal process, in which the appraiser weighs the estimates of value received from the direct sales comparison, cost, and income approaches to arrive at a final estimate of value for the subject property.

recording   The act of entering or recording documents affecting or conveying interests in real estate in the recorder's office established in each county.

record of association   A broker's report to the state about sponsorship of a salesperson or associate broker.

rectangular survey system   A system established in 1785 by the federal government providing for surveying and describing land outside the 13 original colonies by reference to principal meridians and base lines.

redemption period   A period established by state law during which a property owner has the right to redeem his or her real estate from a tax sale by paying the sales price, interest, and costs.

red herring   Preliminary offering plan for a cooperative or condominium project submitted to the attorney general and to tenants and subject to modification.

redlining   The illegal practice of a lending institution denying loans or restricting their number for certain areas of a community.

reduction certificate   A statement from the lender detailing the amount remaining and currently due on a mortgage, usually sought when a mortgage is being assumed or prepaid (also referred to as an *estoppel certificate*).

referee's deed   A deed delivered when property is conveyed pursuant to court order.

reference to a plat   A form of legal description, which cites the book and page on which the subject property can be identified on a map.

regional analysis Study of the economic and demographic character of the larger regional or metropolitan area in which a property is located.

regression Economic principle that the worth of a higher-quality property will be diminished by its proximity to lower-quality properties.

Regulation Z Law requiring credit institutions and advertisers to inform borrowers of the true cost of obtaining credit; commonly called the Truth in Lending Act.

release The act or writing by which some claim or interest is surrendered to another.

release clause A mortgage clause that permits part of the mortgaged property to be released from the lien; often used with blanket mortgages.

remainder The remnant of an estate that has been conveyed to take effect and be enjoyed after the termination of a prior estate, as when an owner conveys a life estate to one party and the remainder to another.

remainder interest The remnant of an estate that has been conveyed to take effect and be enjoyed after the termination of a prior estate, such as when an owner conveys a life estate to one party and the remainder to another.

remainderman The person who is to receive the property after the death of a life tenant.

rent A fixed, periodic payment made by a tenant of a property to the owner for possession and use, usually by prior agreement of the parties.

rentable area The total area or square footage of a floor or unit of space in an office building (as determined by the property owner) to be used for the purposes of calculating the annual rent.

rent control State or local regulations restricting the amount of rent that may be charged for particular properties.

rent roll A rent roll shows the name of each tenant, amount of rent, expiration date of each lease, and amount of security deposits.

rent stabilization Local regulations that stem from the adoption of the Emergency Tenant Protection Act, and that limit maximum allowable rent increases.

replacement cost The construction cost at current prices of a property that is not necessarily an exact duplicate of the subject property but serves the same purpose or function as the original.

reproduction cost The construction cost at current prices of an exact duplicate of the subject property.

rescission The canceling of a contract.

reserves Money set aside to accumulate for future expenses.

reserves for replacements Available cash on hand to effectuate any anticipated or unanticipated major capital improvement to the property; for example, a new roof, new mechanical equipment, or façade restoration.

residential property Real estate used as a dwelling.

residential real estate All property used for housing, from acreage to small city lots, both single-family and multifamily, in urban, suburban, and rural areas.

residential transaction Any transaction involving the sale or rental of a building that contains four or fewer units intended for dwelling purposes.

resident manager A property manager who resides on the site.

restraint of trade The unreasonable restriction of business activities as the result of the cooperation or conspiracy of members of the trade.

restriction A limitation on the use of real property, generally originated by the owner or subdivider in a deed.

restrictive covenant Provisions placed in a deed by the grantor, restricting future uses for the property.

retail property Any type of property used for commercial retail purposes, including storefronts, shopping centers, and enclosed malls.

return The income from a real estate investment, calculated as a percentage of cash invested.

reverse mortgage A loan under which the homeowner receives monthly payments based on his or her accumulated equity rather than a lump sum. The loan must be repaid at a prearranged date or upon the death of the owner or the sale of the property.

reverse discrimination (benign discrimination) Housing discrimination, usually based on quotas, designed by a municipality to achieve a racial balance perceived as desirable.

reversion The remnant of an estate that the grantor holds after she has granted a life estate to another person, if the estate will return, or revert, to the grantor; also called a *reverter*.

reversionary interest The remnant of an estate that the grantor holds after he or she has granted a life estate to another person, if the estate will return, or revert, to the grantor; also called a *reverter*.

reversionary right The return of the rights of possession and quiet enjoyment to the lessor at the expiration of a lease.

revocation An act of recalling a power of authority conferred, such as the revocation of a power of attorney, a license, or an agency.

rider An amendment or attachment to a contract.

right of first refusal A provision that a condominium or cooperative association has the first right to purchase if a member wishes to sell his or her unit.

right of survivorship *See* joint tenancy.

right-of-way The right to pass over another's land more or less frequently according to the nature of the easement.

riparian rights An owner's rights in land that borders on or includes a stream, river, or lake. These rights include access to and use of the water.

risk management The evaluation and selection of appropriate property and other insurance.

R-value Numerical measurement of insulating material's resistance to heat transfer; a higher R-value indicates superior insulation.

Safe Drinking Water Act Federal law requiring local public water suppliers to periodically test the quality of drinking water.

sale-leaseback A transaction in which an owner sells improved property and, as part of the same transaction, signs a long-term lease to remain in possession of the premises.

sales comparison approach The process of estimating the value of a property by examining and comparing actual sales of comparable properties.

sales contract A contract containing the complete terms of the agreement between buyer and seller for the sale of a particular parcel of real estate.

salesperson A person who performs real estate activities while employed by or associated with a licensed real estate broker.

SARA The federal Superfund Amendments and Reauthorization Act, concerned with environmental cleanups.

satisfaction of mortgage *See* satisfaction piece.

satisfaction piece A document provided by the mortgagee, stating that the debt has been paid off. A document acknowledging the payment of a debt. Also called *satisfaction of mortgage*.

S corporation A form of corporation taxed as a partnership.

secondary mortgage market A market for the purchase and sale of existing mortgages, designed to provide greater liquidity of mortgages.

section A portion of a township under the rectangular survey (government survey) system. A section is a square with mile-long sides and an area of one square mile, or 640 acres.

Section 8 Federal housing assistance program administered by the FHA, in which low- and moderate-income tenants pay a fixed portion of their income in rent, with HUD paying the remainder.

Section 1031 property exchange A tax-deferred exchange of like-kind investment or commercial property.

security agreement A document pledging personal property as security for a debt.

security deposit A payment by a tenant, held by the landlord during the lease term and kept (wholly or partially) on default or destruction of the premises by the tenant.

seisin The possession of land by one who claims to own at least an estate for life therein.

self-dealing The act of a broker who lists property and then buys it and collects the agreed-on commission.

seller agency The practice of representing the seller in a real estate transaction.

seller's agent Broker or agent who advises seller on a fair listing price, gives hints how the seller can enhance the marketability of the house, and shows property to several buyers.

selling broker The broker who successfully finds a ready, willing, and able buyer for a property (may or may not be the listing broker).

sensitivity analysis Analysis of a projected investment, to discover which variable is most significant in anticipated cash flow.

septic system Wastewater treatment and disposal system used by individual households.

SEQRA New York's State Environmental Quality Review Act, requiring environmental impact statements before certain development projects.

servient estate Land on which an easement exists in favor of an adjacent property (called a *dominant estate*).

setback The amount of space local zoning regulations require between a lot line and a building line.

severalty Ownership of real property by one person only; also called *sole ownership*.

shared-appreciation mortgage A mortgage loan in which the lender, in exchange for a loan with a favorable interest rate, participates in the profits (if any) when the property is eventually sold.

shared-equity mortgage A loan in which the lender will receive part of any appreciation on the property.

share loan An agreement entered into by a borrower and a lender to finance the borrower's acquisition of the borrower's cooperative interest.

sheathing Material applied to framing members to form walls, often plywood, insulating material, or sheetrock.

Sherman (and Clayton) Antitrust Acts Federal legislation prohibiting business practices that limit competition.

sick building syndrome (SBS) Range of symptoms, such as asthma, coughing, and hoarseness, that are related to the individual's presence in the affected building, but that disappear when he or she is not exposed to the building's environment. *See* building-related illness.

siding Exterior wall finish of a building: commonly brick, shingles, or clapboard, wood or vinyl.

silent partner One who takes no part in managing the enterprise, and whose possible losses are usually limited to his or her investment.

sill plates Horizontal supports on top of the foundation.

single agency An agency relationship in which the agent represents a single party.

situs The location of a property.

slab-on-grade construction Concrete slab poured on prepared earth as a foundation.

small claims court A special local court for settling disputes without the need for attorneys or expensive court costs.

Social Security tax A tax of 15 percent required of every taxpayer; half of the tax is withheld from an employee's paycheck and half must be paid by the employer.

soffit Horizontal finish for the underside of a roof overhang.

solar energy Use of solar collectors to convert heat from the sun into usable heat and energy for a building.

sole proprietorship A business owned by one individual.

Sonny Mae (SONYMA) The State of New York Mortgage Agency.

special agent One authorized by a principal to perform a single act or transaction.

special assessment A tax or levy customarily imposed against only those specific parcels of real estate that will benefit from a proposed public improvement like a street or sewer.

special-purpose buildings Real estate not residential, commercial, industrial, or agricultural. Includes schools, hospitals, churches, and government-held property.

special-purpose real estate Religious institutions, schools, cemeteries, hospitals, and government-held land.

special-use permit Permission granted by a local government to allow a use of property that, although in conflict with zoning regulations, is nonetheless in the public interest (a house of worship in a residential neighborhood, for instance, or a restaurant in an industrial zone).

special warranty deed A deed in which the grantor warrants, or guarantees, the title only against defects arising during the period of his or her tenure and ownership of the property and not against defects existing before that time, generally using the language "by, through, or under the grantor but not otherwise."

specifications The architect's or engineer's detailed instructions for material used in construction.

specific lien A lien affecting or attaching only to a certain specific parcel of land or piece of property.

specific performance suit A legal action brought in a court of equity in special cases to compel a party to carry out the terms of a contract.

sponsor The developer or owner organizing and offering for sale a condominium or cooperative development.

sponsoring broker The principal broker in a real estate firm, who undertakes to train and supervise associated licensees.

spot zoning Special zoning actions that affect only a small area. Uses that are not in harmony with the surrounding uses are illegal in New York.

spread With an adjustable-rate mortgage, the percentage above an index at which the interest rate is set that represents the lender's profit when loaning to a borrower.

stabilized budget When the budgeted/allocated funds used to cover operating expenses remain constant for a period of time.

staff appraiser A professional appraiser employed in-house to perform appraisals solely for the employer.

State Environmental Quality Review Act (SEQRA) New York's State Environmental Quality Review Act, which requires environmental impact statements before certain development projects.

statute of frauds The part of state law requiring that certain instruments, such as deeds, real estate sales contracts, and certain leases, be in writing to be legally enforceable.

statute of limitations That law pertaining to the period of time within which certain actions must be brought to court; in New York, six years for contracts.

statutory law Law that is established by legislative bodies.

statutory lien A lien imposed on property by statute—a tax lien, for example—in contrast to a voluntary lien such as a mortgage lien that an owner places on his or her own real estate.

statutory redemption The right of a defaulted property owner to recover the property after its sale by paying the appropriate fees and charges.

statutory redemption period Period of time after a tax sale in which the delinquent taxpayer may regain the property by paying the back taxes, penalties, interest, and costs.

steering The illegal practice of channeling home seekers to particular areas for discriminatory ends.

straight-line depreciation An accounting "expense" against rental income, arrived at by dividing the cost of the building by the number of years allowed by the Internal Revenue Service.

straight-line method A method of calculating cost recovery for tax purposes, computed by dividing the adjusted basis of a property by the number of years chosen.

straight loan A loan in which only interest is paid during the term of the loan, with the entire principal amount due with the final interest payment.

studs Upright supports that form a part of the framing wall.

subagency An agency relationship in which the broker's sales associate, or a cooperating broker assumes a fiduciary duty to the principal who has designated the broker as an agent.

subagent A broker's sales associate in relation to the principal who has designated the broker as an agent.

subchapter S corporation *See* S corporation.

subcontractor *See* general contractor.

subdivide Partitioning a tract of land to sell it as individual lots.

subdivision A tract of land divided by the owner, known as the *subdivider*, into blocks, building lots, and streets according to a recorded subdivision plat.

subdivision regulations New York State requirements for subdivisions, which apply as soon as the fifth lot is sold off a larger parcel.

subject property The property being appraised.

subject to a mortgage When a property is taken "subject to" a mortgage, the purchaser is not personally liable to the mortgagee for satisfaction of the pre-existing debt (unless the purchaser agrees to be held liable).

sublease *See* subletting.

subletting The leasing of premises by a tenant to a third party for part of the tenant's remaining term. *See also* assignment.

subordination agreement These are voluntary written agreements between lienholders to change the priority of mortgage, judgment, and other liens under certain circumstances.

subrogation The substitution of one creditor for another with the substituted person succeeding to the legal rights and claims of the original claimant.

subscribing witness One who writes his name as witness to the execution of an instrument.

substitution An appraisal principle stating that the maximum value of a property tends to be set by the cost of purchasing an equally desirable and valuable substitute property.

subsurface rights Ownership rights in a parcel of real estate of any water, minerals, gas, oil, and so forth that lie beneath the surface of the property.

suit for possession A court suit initiated by a landlord to evict a tenant from leased premises after the tenant has breached one of the terms of the lease or has held possession of the property after the lease's expiration.

suit to quiet title A court action intended to establish or settle the title to a particular property, especially when there is a cloud on the title.

Superfund Amendments and Reauthorization Act (SARA) Federal law defining landowner responsibility for cleanup of environmental contamination resulting from past activities. Establishes innocent landowner defense against liability for contamination caused by prior owners.

supervising broker   The one broker registered with the Department of State as in charge of a real estate office, responsible for the actions of salespersons and associate brokers.

supply   The amount of goods available in the marketplace to be sold at a specific price.

surety bond   Bond covering an owner against financial losses resulting from the criminal acts or negligence of employees in the course of performing their job.

surface rights   Ownership rights in a parcel of real estate that are limited to the surface of the property and do not include the air above it (air rights) or the minerals below the surface (subsurface rights).

surrender   The cancellation of a lease by mutual consent of the lessor and the lessee.

surrogate's court (probate court)   A court having jurisdiction over the proof of wills, the settling of estates, and adoptions.

survey   The process by which a parcel of land is measured and its area ascertained; also, the map showing the measurements, boundaries, and area.

suspension or revocation   The action of punishing violations of the license law by recalling a license temporarily (*suspension*) or permanently (*revocation*).

swing loan   A short-term loan similar to a bridge loan that uses the strength of the borrowers' equity in the property they are selling to purchase a new property.

syndicate   A combination of people or firms formed to accomplish a joint venture of mutual interest.

tacking   Adding or combining successive periods of continuous occupation of real property by several different adverse possessors.

takeout loan   A loan commitment obtained prior to a lender extending a construction loan, under the terms of which the takeout lender will pay off the construction loan once the work is finished. Provides assurance for the construction lender that the initial short-term loan will be satisfied.

taking   Government restriction on use of property, to the extent that the owner must be compensated for loss of value.

taxable status date   The date, often in March, on which a community's tax assessment rolls are fixed for the coming year.

tax assessor   Municipal official who makes tax assessments for towns, villages, cities, and, in a few cases, counties.

taxation   The process by which a government or municipal quasi-public body raises monies to fund its operation.

tax basis   The original cost basis for property, reduced by depreciation and increased by the amount spent on capital improvements.

tax certiorari   Appeal in state court of a ruling by the local assessment board of review.

tax credit   A direct reduction in tax payable, as opposed to a deduction from income.

tax deed   An instrument, similar to a certificate of sale, given to a purchaser at a tax sale.

tax-deferred exchange   A means by which one investment property can be exchanged for a similar one of equal value, with no immediate or capital gain tax consequences.

tax depreciation   *See* straight-line depreciation.

tax foreclosure   Legal proceeding (comparable to a private mortgage foreclosure) brought by a taxing body against the property itself (*in rem*); former owner loses all rights and claims.

tax lien   A charge against property created by operation of law. Tax liens and assessments take priority over all other liens.

tax rate   The rate at which real property is taxed in a tax district or county. For example, real property may be taxed at a rate of 0.056 cents per dollar of assessed valuation (56 mills).

tax sale   A court-ordered sale of real property to raise money to cover delinquent taxes.

tax shelter   Property throwing off an income-tax loss that can offset other income.

temporary certificate of occupancy (TCO)   Document issued by a municipal authority stating that a building complies with building, health, and safety codes and may be occupied; expires six months from the date of issue, or earlier if specified on the certificate itself.

tenancy at sufferance   One who comes into possession of land by lawful title and keeps it afterward without any title at all.

tenancy at will   An estate that gives the lessee the right to possession until the estate is terminated by either party; the term of this estate is indefinite.

tenancy by the entirety   The joint ownership acquired by husband and wife during marriage. On the death of one spouse, the survivor becomes the owner of the property.

tenancy for years   Refers to a less-than-freehold estate (or tenancy) in which the property is leased for a definite, fixed period of time, whether 60 days, any fraction of a year, a year, or ten years. In most states, such a tenancy can be created only by express agreement, which should be written if the tenancy is longer than one year. Most ground leases and commercial leases are tenancies for years.

tenancy in common   A form of co-ownership by which each owner holds an undivided interest in real property as if he or she were sole owner. Each individual owner has the right to partition. Tenants in common have no right of survivorship.

tenant   One who holds or possesses lands or tenements by any kind of right or title.

term   The originally scheduled period of time over which a loan is to be paid.

termination of association notice   Notice sent to the Department of State by a principal broker, stating that a particular licensee is no longer under the broker's supervision.

termites   Wood-boring insects whose presence causes structural damage.

term loan   *See* straight loan.

testate   Having made and left a valid will.

testator   The (male) maker of a valid will.

testatrix   The (female) maker of a valid will.

testers   Members of civil rights and neighborhood organizations, often volunteers, who observe real estate offices to assess compliance with fair housing laws.

tie-in arrangement   An arrangement by which provision of certain products or services is made contingent on the purchase of other, unrelated products or services.

time is of the essence   A phrase in a contract that requires the performance of a certain act within a stated period of time.

time-sharing   Undivided ownership of real estate for only a portion of the year.

time value of money   Deals with and is based on the purchasing power of the dollar when received.

title   Evidence that the owner of land is in lawful possession thereof; evidence of ownership.

title insurance policy   A policy insuring the owner or mortgagee against loss by reason of defects in the title to a parcel of real estate, other than the encumbrances, defects, and matters specifically excluded by the policy.

title search   An examination of the public records to determine the ownership and encumbrances affecting real property.

title theory   Some states interpret a mortgage to mean that the lender is the owner of mortgaged land. Upon full payment of the mortgage debt, the borrower becomes the landowner.

Torrens system   A method of evidencing title by registration with the proper public authority, generally called the *registrar*.

tort   A civil wrong done by one person against another.

town house   A hybrid form of real estate ownership in which the owner has fee simple title to the living unit and land below it, plus a fractional interest in common elements.

township   The principal unit of the rectangular survey (government survey) system, a square with six-mile sides and an area of 36 square miles.

trade fixtures   Articles installed by a tenant under the terms of a lease and removable by the tenant before the lease expires.

transfer of development rights   Method by which one developer can buy unused rights belonging to a landowner.

transfer tax   Tax stamps required to be affixed to a deed by state and/or local law.

trespass   An unlawful intrusion on another's property.

triple-net lease   A lease under which the tenant pays everything (taxes, repairs, insurance, and everything except any mortgage charges).

true tax   Actual taxes payable for a property after all exemptions and reductions for which the property or its owner is qualified.

truss roof   Particularly strong roofing system composed of chords, diagonals, and gusset plates; preassembled at a mill.

trust   A fiduciary arrangement whereby property is conveyed to a person or an institution, called a *trustee*, to be held and administered on behalf of another person, called a *beneficiary*.

trust account   Escrow account for money belonging to another.

trust deed   An instrument used to create a mortgage lien by which the mortgagor conveys his or her title to a trustee, who holds it as security for the benefit of the note holder (the lender); also called a *deed of trust*.

trustee   *See* trust.

trustor The individual who establishes a trust.

220-volt circuit 220-volt circuits have two hot wires and one neutral wire and may have a separate ground wire as well.

UFFI Urea-formaldehyde foam insulation, considered carcinogenic, no longer used.

umbrella policy An insurance policy that covers additional risk beyond several underlying policies.

underground storage tanks Buried containers used for storage or disposal of chemicals, fuel, and gas that pose an actual or potential environmental hazard in the event of a leak.

underlying mortgage A single mortgage, known as the underlying mortgage, covers the entire building.

underwriting The process by which a lender evaluates a prospective borrower's application through verification of employment and financial information and analysis of credit and appraisal reports.

undisclosed dual agency Representation of both principal parties in the same transaction without full written disclosure to and approval of all parties.

undivided interest *See* tenancy in common.

undivided loyalty Fiduciary duty owed by the agent to the principal or client.

unenforceable contract A contract that seems on the surface to be valid, yet neither party can sue the other to force performance of it.

Uniform Commercial Code A codification of commercial law, adopted in most states, that attempts to make uniform all laws relating to commercial transactions, including chattel mortgages and bulk transfers.

Uniform Settlement Statement (HUD Form 1) A special form designed to detail all financial particulars of a transaction.

unilateral contract A one-sided contract wherein one party makes a promise so as to induce a second party to do something. The second party is not legally bound to perform; however, if the second party does comply, the first party is obligated to keep the promise.

unities The four unities traditionally needed to create a joint tenancy: unity of title, time, interest, and possession.

universal agent One empowered by a principal to represent him or her in all matters that can be delegated.

usable area Usable area is the area obtained by subtracting the loss factor from the rentable area.

usury Charging interest at a rate higher than the maximum established by law.

valid contract A contract that complies with all the essentials of a contract and is binding and enforceable on all parties to it.

VA loan A mortgage loan on approved property made to a qualified veteran by an authorized lender and guaranteed by the Department of Veterans Affairs to limit the lender's possible loss.

valuation Estimated worth or price. The act of valuing by appraisal.

value The power of a good or service to command other goods in exchange for the present worth of future rights to its income or amenities.

value-in-use Present worth of future benefits of ownership of a parcel of real estate.

variable expense The property expenses that vary according to the occupancy level, such as supplies, water, and any management fees that are tied to the amount of rent collected.

variance Permission obtained from zoning authorities to build a structure or conduct a use that is expressly prohibited by the current zoning laws; an exception from the zoning ordinances.

vendee A buyer under a land contract or contract of sale.

vendor A seller under a land contract or contract of sale.

vicarious liability Liability that is created not because of a person's actions but because of the relationship between the liable person and other parties.

violation An infraction of the law less serious than a misdemeanor.

voidable contract A contract that seems to be valid on the surface but that may be rejected or disaffirmed by one of the parties.

void contract A contract that has no legal force or effect because it does not meet the essential elements of a contract.

voltage Force of an electric current, measured in volts.

voluntary alienation Transfer of title by gift or sale according to the owner's wishes.

voluntary lien A lien created by the owner's voluntary action, such as a mortgage.

waiver The renunciation, abandonment, or surrender of some claim, right, or privilege.

warranty deed A deed in which the grantor fully warrants good clear title to the premises.

waste An improper use or an abuse of a property by a possessor who holds less than fee ownership, such as a tenant, life tenant, mortgagor, or vendee.

wetland survey An intensive examination of property, coordinated by the U.S. Army Corps of Engineers, to determine whether it should be classified and protected as a wetland.

will A written document, properly witnessed, providing for the transfer of title to property owned by the deceased, called the *testator*.

without recourse Words used in endorsing a note or bill to denote that the future holder is not to look to the endorser in case of nonpayment.

workers' compensation acts State insurance program, paid for by employers, to compensate those hurt on the job.

wraparound loan A method of refinancing in which the lender refinances a borrower by lending an amount over the existing first mortgage amount without disturbing the priority of the first mortgage.

wraparound mortgage An additional mortgage in which another lender refinances a borrower by lending an amount including the existing first mortgage amount without disturbing the existence of the first mortgage.

year-to-year tenancy A periodic tenancy in which rent is collected from year to year.

zone An area set off by the proper authorities for specific use subject to certain restrictions or restraints.

zoning boards of appeal Official local government bodies established to hear complaints about the impact of zoning ordinances on individual properties, and to consider variances and special-use permits.

zoning ordinances An exercise of police power by a municipality to regulate and control the character and use of property.

Answer Key

Following are the correct answers to the Chapter Quiz questions and the Salesperson's Review Examination. In parentheses following the correct answers are references to the pages where the question topics are discussed or explained. If you have answered a question incorrectly, be sure to go back to the page or pages noted and restudy the material until you understand the correct answer.

Chapter 1

License Law

1. c. (3)
2. d. (1)
3. c. (2)
4. c. (3)
5. c. (5)
6. d. (14)
7. c. (4)
8. c. (5)
9. d. (5)
10. c. (5)
11. b. (10)
12. d. (21)
13. a. (10)
14. b. (21)
15. a. (25)
16. a. (26)
17. b. (26)
18. c. (5)
19. b. (14)
20. b. (18)
21. a. (18)
22. b. (18)
23. d. (19)
24. c. (20)

Chapter 2

The Law of Agency

1. a. (34)
2. b. (41)
3. b. (44–45)
4. b. (51–52)
5. c. (46–47)
6. c. (40)
7. c. (51)
8. c. (39–40)

9. d. (45)
10. d. (49)
11. b. (50)
12. c. (50)
13. c. (51)
14. c. (51)
15. a. (49)
16. d. (53)
17. c. (47)
18. a. (54)
19. d. (45)
20. b. (41)

Chapter 3

Agency and Real Estate Brokerage

1. b. (59)
2. d. (74–75)
3. c. (59)
4. d. (75)
5. b. (71)
6. d. (73)
7. d. (68)
8. b. (68)
9. b. (73)
10. d. (74)
11. c. (60)
12. a. (69)
13. c. (69–70)

Chapter 4

Estates and Interests

1. b. (106)
2. d. (107)
3. b. (105)
4. b. (107)
5. c. (106)

6. c. (107)
7. a. (108)
8. c. (109–110)
9. d. (117)
10. c. (110)
11. a. (109)
12. b. (106)
13. d. (111)
14. b. (111)
15. a. (111)
16. c. (112)
17. b. (113)
18. a. (117)
19. b. (114)
20. b. (114)
21. b. (114)
22. b. (117)
23. d. (116–117)
24. b. (118)
25. a. (119)
26. d. (120)
27. a. (120)
28. c. (120)
29. c. (123)
30. c. (119)

Chapter 5

Liens and Easements

1. b. (133)
2. b. (130)
3. b. (130)
4. a. (133)
5. c. (133)
6. a. (135)
7. d. (134)
8. a. (134)
9. c. (134)
10. b. (131)

11. d. (136)
12. d. (139)
13. b. (137)
14. d. (136)
15. b. (136)
16. a. (138)
17. d. (136)
18. a. (131)
19. c. (130)
20. a. (136)
21. c. (137)

Chapter 6

Real Estate Instruments: Deeds

1. a. (154)
2. b. (144)
3. c. (156)
4. d. (156)
5. c. (144)
6. a. (151)
7. c. (152)
8. b. (150)
9. b. (151)
10. b. (151)
11. b. (152)
12. d. (159)
13. d. (159)
14. b. (154)
15. a. (154)
16. c. (155)
17. d. (155)
18. a. (150)

Chapter 7

Real Estate Instruments: Leases

1. b. (161)
2. a. (162)
3. c. (169)
4. d. (163)
5. d. (165)
6. b. (163)
7. d. (168)
8. d. (169)
9. c. (170)
10. b. (170)
11. d. (171)
12. c. (172)
13. d. (166)

14. a. (171)
15. b. (167)
16. a. (162)
17. a. (171)
18. b. (169)

Chapter 8

Real Estate Instruments:
Contracts

1. b. (177)
2. b. (177)
3. d. (177)
4. c. (177)
5. b. (178)
6. a. (178)
7. b. (189)
8. d. (189)
9. c. (179)
10. a. (194)
11. a. (182)
12. c. (179)
13. d. (192)
14. d. (181)
15. b. (194)
16. b. (194)
17. b. (189)
18. a. (190)
19. a. (193)
20. a. (193)
21. c. (180)
22. b. (195)
23. b. (180)
24. d. (196)
25. c. (197)

Chapter 9

Title and Closing Costs

1. a. (220)
2. a. (203)
3. c. (205)
4. a. (205)
5. d. (222)
6. d. (219)
7. b. (219)
8. c. (219)
9. c. (203)
10. a. (204)
11. d. (205, 208)

12. d. (212)
13. c. (216)
14. d. (210)
15. c. (211)
16. b. (211)
17. b. (211–212)
18. c. (212)
19. a. (217)
20. b. (224)
21. b. (224)
22. d. (224)
23. a. (224)
24. a. (224)
25. c. (224)
26. a. (210)
27. d. (212)
28. d. (220)
29. b. (217)
30. c. (216)

Chapter 10

Mortgages

1. b. (238)
2. a. (239)
3. d. (238)
4. c. (241)
5. b. (244)
6. a. (243)
7. c. (243)
8. a. (234)
9. d. (238)
10. a. (238)
11. b. (239)
12. d. (240)
13. d. (238)
14. d. (232)
15. c. (232)
16. d. (232)
17. d. (235)
18. a. (235)
19. c. (244)

Chapter 11

Real Estate Finance

1. d. (254)
2. a. (256)
3. c. (263)
4. d. (255)

5. b. (255)
6. b. (250)
7. d. (250)
8. b. (253)
9. c. (262)
10. b. (260)
11. a. (261)
12. a. (262)
13. c. (250)
14. d. (257)
15. d. (252)
16. d. (255)
17. b. (254)
18. a. (258)
19. c. (264)
20. b. (265)

Chapter 12
Mortgage Brokerage

1. d. (273)
2. b. (272)
3. c. (272)
4. d. (272)
5. a. (271)
6. c. (271)
7. d. (273)
8. b. (274)
9. a. (272–273)
10. c. (273)

Chapter 13
Land-Use Regulations

1. a. (280)
2. d. (280)
3. c. (279)
4. b. (279)
5. b. (283)
6. c. (283)
7. c. (283)
8. b. (278)
9. a. (284)
10. c. (284)
11. b. (286)
12. c. (285)
13. b. (286)
14. a. (278)
15. c. (278)
16. a. (278)

17. a. (280)
18. d. (279)
19. b. (282)
20. c. (282)

Chapter 14
Municipal Agencies

1. d. (291)
2. b. (292–293)
3. a. (293)
4. b. (299)
5. b. (296)
6. c. (296)
7. a. (298)
8. b. (296)
9. c. (297)
10. a. (299)

Chapter 15
Introduction to Construction

1. a. (304)
2. d. (305)
3. c. (310)
4. b. (309)
5. d. (310)
6. b. (312)
7. d. (310)
8. a. (310)
9. d. (312)
10. a. (316)
11. a. (312)
12. b. (315)
13. a. (316)
14. c. (318)
15. c. (321)
16. b. (321)

Chapter 16
Valuation Process

1. a. (334)
2. c. (327)
3. a. (327)
4. d. (327)
5. a. (335)
6. c. (338–339)
7. d. (335)
8. d. (337)

9. d. (334)
10. d. (345)
11. c. (331)
12. a. (332)
13. a. (333–334)
14. c. (334)
15. d. (333–334)
16. b. (334)
17. d. (343)
18. a. (327)
19. b. (347)
20. a. (335)
21. c. (336–337)
22. d. (337)
23. a. (339)
24. c. (343)
25. d. (332)

Chapter 17
Human Rights and Fair Housing

1. c. (365)
2. c. (373)
3. c. (365)
4. a. (370)
5. b. (368)
6. c. (368)
7. b. (363)
8. c. (363)
9. b. (368)
10. a. (370)
11. a. (370)
12. a. (370)
13. b. (370)
14. a. (368)
15. c. (369)
16. d. (363–364)
17. d. (374)
18. a. (362)
19. d. (369)
20. d. (374)
21. a. (373)

Chapter 18
Environmental Issues

1. d. (378)
2. b. (386–387)
3. c. (382)
4. a. (383)

5. a. (383)
6. b. (388)
7. a. (380)
8. d. (382)
9. c. (392)
10. b. (391)
11. a. (391)
12. c. (391)
13. d. (381)
14. a. (388)
15. c. (392)

Chapter 19

Independent Contractor/
Employee

1. c. (399)
2. b. (403)
3. d. (402)
4. c. (402)
5. c. (402)
6. c. (400)
7. b. (402)
8. d. (404)
9. d. (402)
10. b. (400)

Chapter 20

Income Tax Issues in Real Estate
Transactions

1. c. (410)
2. b. (407)
3. c. (407)
4. c. (408)
5. b. (409)
6. d. (410)
7. a. (411)
8. d. (412)
9. a. (414)
10. c. (414)
11. c. (415)
12. a. (416)
13. d. (409)
14. a. (410)
15. c. (415)

Chapter 21

Commercial and Investment
Properties

1. d. (430)
2. d. (424)
3. b. (430)
4. a. (430)
5. c. (437)
6. b. (432)
7. d. (432)
8. c. (425)
9. d. (425)
10. a. (437)
11. d. (437)
12. a. (438)
13. c. (440)
14. a. (441–442)
15. b. (443)
16. d. (451)

Chapter 22

Property Management

1. d. (468)
2. c. (469)
3. c. (479–480)
4. d. (469)
5. d. (470)
6. c. (468)
7. a. (481)
8. d. (473)
9. c. (472)
10. b. (475)
11. c. (475)
12. c. (475)
13. c. (480)
14. d. (478)
15. b. (478)
16. a. (478)
17. c. (478)

Chapter 23

Taxes and Assessments

1. a. (484)
2. b. (484)
3. a. (489)
4. c. (487–488)
5. c. (487)

6. b. (485)
7. d. (489)
8. a. (490)
9. a. (490)
10. c. (485)
11. b. (488)
12. a. (485)

Chapter 24

Condominiums and
Cooperatives

1. d. (493)
2. a. (497)
3. b. (495)
4. b. (498)
5. c. (500)
6. d. (501)
7. c. (502)
8. a. (503)
9. c. (503)
10. d. (503)
11. a. (504)
12. d. (505)
13. c. (499)
14. b. (506)
15. c. (506)

Chapter 25

Property Insurance

1. b. (510–511)
2. d. (511)
3. a. (511)
4. c. (512)
5. a. (512)
6. c. (512)
7. a. (512)
8. a. (517)
9. b. (513)
10. c. (514–515)
11. d. (516)
12. a. (516)

Chapter 26
Real Estate Mathematics

1. **b. 180 feet**

    1,200 sq yd × 9 = 10,800 sq ft

    Area = Length × Width

    10,800 = Length × 60

    10,800 ÷ 60 = 180 ft

2. **d. $2,430**

    $108,000 × 97.75% maximum loan amount

    $108,000 × 97.75% = $105,570

    $108,000 – $105,570 = $2,430 minimum down payment

3. **d. 4/5**

    80% = 80/100

    80/100, divide both numbers by 20 = 4/5

4. **c. $950.40**

    $198,000 × 80% = $198,000 × 0.80 = $158,400 insured value

    $158,400 ÷ 1,000 = 158.4 thousands

    158.4 × $6 per thousand = $950.40

5. **a. $80,000**

    $74,000 + $1,200 = $75,200 sales price less commission

    $75,200 = 94% of sales price

    $75,200 ÷ 0.94 = $80,000 sales price

6. **b. $1,330**

    $57,000 ÷ 12 = $4,750 monthly income

    $4,750 × 0.28 = $1,330 permissible mortgage payment

7. **a. $4,620**

    $154,000 × 0.06 = $9,240 total commission

    $9,240 × 0.50 = $4,620 salesperson's share

8. **a. $808.54**

    $1,800 ÷12 = $150 monthly property taxes

    $365 ÷ 12 = $30.42 monthly insurance premium

    $150 + $30.42 + $628.12 = $808.54 total monthly payment

9. **c. $36,000**

    120 front feet × $300 = $36,000 sales price

10. **b. 726 feet**

43,560 feet per acre × 5 = 217,800 sq ft

217,800 ÷ 300 = 726 feet deep

11. **b. $1,550.25**

$79,500 sales price × 6½ commission = $79,500 × 0.065 = $5,167.50 Happy Valley's commission

$5,167.50 × 30% or $5,167.50 × 0.30 = $1,550.25 listing salesperson's commission

12. **c. $277.16**

12' × 9.5' = 114 square feet, area of rectangle

½(3' × 9.5') = ½(28.5) = 14.25 square feet, area of triangle

114 + 14.25 = 128.25 sq ft

To convert square feet to square yards, divide by 9:

128.25 ÷ 9 = 14.25 sq yd

$16.95 carpet + $2.50 installation = $19.45 cost per square yard

$19.45 × 14.25 sq yd = $277.1625, rounded to $277.16

13. **a. 20%**

$30,000 (investor #1) + $35,000 (investor #2) + $35,000 (investor #3) = $100,000

$125,000 − $100,000 = $25,000

Investor #4's contribution

Part ÷ Whole = Percentage

$25,000 ÷ $125,000 = 0.20, or 20%

14. **b. $40,843.83**

391.42 × 12 = $4,697.04 annual interest

Part ÷ Whole = Percentage

$4,697.04 ÷ 11½% or $4,697.04 ÷ 0.115 = $40,843.826

15. **a. $103,425**

$98,500 × 5% = $98,500 × 0.05 = $4,925 annual increase in value

$98,500 + $4,925 = $103,425 current market value

16. **d. $135.38**

$95,000 × 60% or $95,000 × 0.60 = $57,000 assessed value

divided by 1,000 because tax rate is stated per thousand dollars

$57,000 ÷ 1,000 = 57

57 × $28.50 = $1,624.50 annual taxes

divide by 12 to get monthly taxes

$1,624.50 ÷ 12 = $135.375

17. **d. 195 cubic feet**

22' × 15' = 330 square feet, area of rectangle

½(4' × 15') = ½(60) = 30 square feet, area of each triangle

30 × 2 = 60 square feet, area of two triangles

330 + 60 = 390 square feet, surface area to be paved

6" deep = ½ ft

390 × ½ = 195 cubic feet, cement needed for patio

18. **b. $127,000**

$3,675 – $500 salary = $3,175 commission on sales

$3,175 ÷ 2.5% = $3,175 ÷ 0.025 = $127,000, value of property sold

19. **c. $1,615.88**

Two sides of 95' plus one side of 42'6"

95' × 2 = 190 ft

42'6" = 42.5 ft

190 + 42.5 = 232.5 linear feet

232.5 × $6.95 = $1,615.875

20. **a. $675,000**

$4,500 × 12 = $54,000 annual rental

$54,000 ÷ 8% or $54,000 ÷ 0.08 = $675,000, original cost of property

21. **c. 27,225 square feet**

100 acres × 43,560 square feet per acre = 4,356,000 total square feet

4,356,000 × 7/8, available for lots = 3,811,500 sq ft

3,811,500 ÷ 140 lots = 27,225 square feet per lot

22. **a. $173.33**

$975 ÷ 12 months = $81.25 property tax per month

$81.25 ÷ 30 days = $2.708 property tax per day

$81.25 × 2 months = $162.50

$2.708 × 4 days = $10.832

$162.50 + $10.832 = $173.332, rounded to $173.33, prepaid unused tax

23. **b. $488.97**

$61,550 × 13% = $61,550 × 0.13 = $8,001.50 annual interest

$8,001.50 ÷ 12 months = $666.792 interest per month

$666.792 ÷ 30 days = $22.226 interest per day

$22.226 × 22 days = $488.972, rounded to $488.97, unpaid back interest

24. **a. $235,000**

$14,100 commission ÷ 6% commission rate = $14,100 ÷ 0.06 = $235,000 sales price

25. b. $242,842.40

30 years × 12 months = 360 payments

360 payments × $952.34 = $342,842.40 total payments for principal and interest

$342,842.40 total payments − $100,000 principal repayment = $242,842.40 total interest paid

26. c. Four years, nine months

Two points on a $90,000 loan = $90,000 × 0.02 or 2 percent = $1,800 paid in points

$817.85 − $786.35 = $31.50 saved each month with lower payment

$1,800 ÷ $31.50 = 57.14 months to recoup the payment of points

57.14 months = 4 years, 9 months

27. c. $2,600 more at closing

$80,000 × 3% or 0.03 = $2,400 payment for points

$100,000 − $95,000 = $5,000 received with the higher offer

$5,000 − $2,400 payment for points = $2,600 realized with the higher offer after payment of points

28. b. $1,100

$10,000 ÷ $100 = 100

100 × 0.50 = $50 tax on first $10,000

$150,000 − $10,000 = $140,000

$140,000 ÷ $100 = $1,400

$1,400 × 0.75 = $1,050

$50 + $1,050 = $1,100 total mortgage tax

29. c. $796

$198,600 sales price ÷ $500 = 397.2 (rounded to 398)

398 × $2 = $796 transfer tax

30. c. $327

$425,000 purchase price ÷ 1,300 square feet = 326.92 or $327 per square foot

Salesperson's Review
Examination

1. **d.** (4)
2. **b.** (3)
3. **a.** (5)
4. **c.** (14)
5. **d.** (293)
6. **c.** (250)
7. **b.** (300)
8. **a.** (36)
9. **b.** (42, 43)
10. **b.** (46)
11. **b.** (44, 45)
12. **d.** (19)
13. **c.** (51)
14. **a.** (35)
15. **d.** (35)
16. **a.** (38)
17. **d.** (43)
18. **b.** (35, 36)
19. **a.** (73)
20. **c.** (73)
21. **d.** (400)
22. **c.** (182)
23. **c.** (241)
24. **a.** (240)
25. **a.** (220)
26. **a.** (105)
27. **b.** (105)
28. **a.** (114)
29. **c.** (105)
30. **d.** (112)
31. **b.** (129)
32. **c.** (138)
33. **a.** (135)
34. **b.** (146)
35. **c.** (149)
36. **b.** (150)
37. **d.** (430)
38. **d.** (432, 433)
39. **c.** (440, 441)
40. **a.** (431)
41. **a.** (432)
42. **c.** (432)
43. **a.** (432)
44. **a.** (341)
45. **d.** (438)
46. **d.** (212)
47. **b.** (223, 224)
48. **a.** (217)
49. **d.** (237)
50. **c.** (240)
51. **d.** (425)
52. **b.** (178)
53. **d.** (239)
54. **c.** (514)
55. **d.** (516)
56. **d.** (514, 515)
57. **a.** (409)
58. **b.** (410)
59. **a.** (407)
60. **c.** (283)
61. **b.** (283)
62. **c.** (304)
63. **d.** (284)
64. **c.** (305)
65. **c.** (410)
66. **a.** (321)
67. **b.** (380)
68. **a.** (318)
69. **d.** (309)
70. **d.** (493)
71. **d.** (344, 345)
72. **b.** (503)
73. **a.** (500)
74. **a.** (334)
75. **b.** (327)
76. **c.** (414)
77. **a.** (368)
78. **c.** (365)
79. **d.** (506–507)
80. **d.** (364)
81. **d.** (368)
82. **d.** (364)
83. **c.** (500)
84. **d.** (271)
85. **a.** (435)
86. **a.** (381, 382)
87. **c.** (383)
88. **c.** (383)
89. **a.** (274)
90. **b.** (459)
91. **a.** (460)
92. **b.** (521)
93. **d.** (524)
94. **a.** (464)
95. **c.** (486)
96. **d.** (484)
97. **b.** (416)
98. **c.** (416, 417)
99. **d.** (469)
100. **a.** (443)

Index

Notes

Notes